TREES, SHRUBS, AND VINES ON THE
UNIVERSITY OF NOTRE DAME CAMPUS

# Trees, Shrubs, and Vines on the University of Notre Dame Campus

Barbara J. Hellenthal
Thomas J. Schlereth
Robert P. McIntosh

A SESQUICENTENNIAL BOOK

University of Notre Dame Press
Notre Dame            London

Library of Congress Cataloging-in-Publication Data


Hellenthal, Barbara J., 1950-
    Trees, shrubs, and vines on the University of Notre Dame campus /
Barbara J. Hellenthal, Thomas J. Schlereth, Robert P. McIntosh.
        p.  cm.
    "A Notre Dame sesquicentennial book."
    Includes Indexes.
    ISBN 0-268-01878-2 (acid-free paper)
    1. Woody plants—Notre Dame.   2. University of Notre Dame.
I. Schlereth, Thomas J.   II. McIntosh, Robert P. (Robert Patrick)   III. Title.
QK159.H44  1993
582.1'5'0977289—dc20                                          93-24764
                                                              CIP

A Sesquicentennial Book

# Contents

v

# Foreword

I have lived virtually my entire adult life on the Notre Dame campus and in that time have welcomed thousands of campus visitors–beginning students and their parents, returning alumni, family, friends, new faculty, guest speakers, and a Who's Who of national and international dignitaries. These occasions almost never pass without mention of the striking beauty of our campus; in fact, that very often is the first topic of conversation. "Your campus is so beautiful." "What a marvelous environment this must be to work in." "How fortunate you are to live in such a setting."

How fortunate we are indeed, those of us who live and study and work here, to have the gift of this campus ourselves and to have the opportunity to share it with so many others. And how easy it is, as with all such gifts, to take these magnificent surroundings for granted, to accept the beauty of the campus as a mere given, without cause or history or credit.

The great value of this new book is that it reminds us–and in most entertaining fashion–that the Notre Dame campus did not just spring full-blown into its beauty, an Indiana Eden awaiting only the arrival of Father Sorin and his religious brothers. On the contrary, the many thousands of plantings on campus–their types and variety and placement–represent the deliberate efforts of a succession of men and women from the very founding of the University to our own day. As always with Notre Dame, my fellow religious of Holy Cross are prominent among these people, notably Brother Peter Fitzpatrick, C.S.C., who with Father Sorin created the grand design for Notre Dame Avenue and the Main Quad; Brother Philip Neri Kunze, C.S.C., who over fifty years made it his work to bring to Notre Dame as many varieties of North American trees, shrubs, and vines as would grow here; and Father Peter Hebert, C.S.C., who in a more recent half century both greatly expanded and catalogued Notre Dame's campus plantings.

Even Father Julius Nieuwland, C.S.C., Notre Dame's most renowned scientist, is part of this story, for he spent some seventeen years as a professor of botany before turning to the chemistry research that would bring him fame. Indeed, another value of this book is in demonstrating how the physical evolution of the Notre Dame campus has been allied to the University's academic development. Botany literally was the seed for the growth of the sciences at Notre Dame, and the intent of all those who have plotted and planted in the University's grounds has been to make this place a living botanical garden.

The fruit of this labor is the beauty we so enjoy today, even if we know nothing of its origins or details. But of course, the principal aim of this volume is precisely to help us identify the individual shrubs, trees, and vines of campus, and it does so wonderfully, not only with its detailed listings of campus flora, but also with its finely described walking tour.

As a city boy set down here in the garden that is Notre Dame, I extend my personal thanks to the authors for their most welcome history and guide. The proud roster of those whose work is tied to Notre Dame's beauty now rightly will include Barbara Hellenthal, Thomas Schlereth, and Robert McIntosh.

Rev. Edward A. Malloy, C.S.C.
President, August 1993

viii

# Acknowledgment

Many individuals have contributed to this book. Two people leading the Sesquicentennial celebration deserve special mention. James E. Murphy, Associate Vice President for University Relations (now emeritus), who was Executive Director of the Sesquicentennial Committee, and Roger Schmitz, Vice President and Associate Provost, who was Co-chair of the Sesquicentennial Committee, proposed the project and then provided continued encouragement and generous financial support.

Ronald Hellenthal, Professor of Biological Sciences, gave us his career's worth of computer expertise. He developed the computer databases used to document the campus flora, programmed the conversion of the data into useable form, devised the formatting operations for layout of the text, and, finally, produced the camera-ready final copy of the book.

Four undergraduate biology majors worked on the project. Alicia Biagi, Kristina Hannam, and Jennifer Slate did much of the field work, in all kinds of weather, that verified Father Hebert's old plant site records while Hong Nhi Ly prepared the 2,000 voucher specimens for permanent inclusion in the University's herbarium. William Thistlethwaite, Superintendent of Landscape Services, and Patrick McCauslin, Assistant Superintendent, willingly and at a moment's notice, provided information about recent campus plantings and commemorative trees as it was needed. Morton Fuchs, Chairman of the Department of Biological Sciences, provided facilities and staff support. Loretta Wasmuth, Victoria Harman, Joan Smith, and Kathy Troth, the department's secretarial staff, carried out numerous tasks with a high degree of professionalism. Richard Jensen, Professor of Biology at St. Mary's College, identified most of the oak specimens. The staff of the University of Notre Dame Press brought their considerable skills and enthusiasm to the project. Carole Roos, as editor, and Margaret Gloster, as designer, brought the many facets of the book together.

The University of Notre Dame Archives staff–Wendy Clauson Schlereth, Director and University Archivist; Charles Lamb, Assistant Director; Peter Lysy, Associate Archivist; and Jennifer Webber, Assistant Archivist–and Jacqueline Dougherty at the Province Archives Center were most helpful in various aspects of the authors' research. John DeLee, Director of Utilities at Notre Dame, James Pfeil, CAD Engineer, and Gene Giles, Supervisor of Data Systems, aided in the development of the walking tour map. Marten Schalm, Jr., provided the base for the campus map.

The book is a reflection of the priority that Notre Dame's Administration has placed on knowing and understanding our campus and its natural surroundings. This recognition of what is important for maintaining the historical integrity–both human and natural–of the campus becomes critical as the University's facilities continue to expand. Rev. Edward Malloy, C.S.C., President; Rev. William Beauchamp, C.S.C., Executive Vice President; Thomas Mason, Vice President for Business Affairs; and David Woods, Director of Support Services; should be acknowledged for their far-reaching outlook concerning preservation of the campus.

The C.S.C. community, from Father Sorin to the present, should be recognized for their vision and long-term commitment to the campus as a special place. Father Hebert spent his lifetime documenting the campus flora. Father Hesburgh, President Emeritus, encouraged him to compile his work into a catalogue that others could use. Finally, Father James J. McGrath, Associate Professor of Biological Sciences, oversaw the publication of that catalogue in 1967. This series of events has led to the present book, which probably would not have been undertaken without the impetus of Father Hebert's earlier work.

Another important group that needs to be acknowledged is the staff of the Department of Landscape Services: our grounds crew. Their diligent work, which must be daunting on the day after a football game, keeps the campus looking like a park. Anyone who tends even the smallest lawn or garden knows how difficult that task is.

# Introduction

Barbara J. Hellenthal

To those who live, work, or visit the University of Notre Dame, its campus landscape, including site, natural features, buildings, and plants, is a defining element of the university. The overall effect that the campus presents is the result of a balance struck between the functional needs of the university–scholarly, spiritual, recreational–and the aesthetic goals. Within the landscape, the woody plants are the most prominent component in both size and numbers.

Twenty-seven years ago Peter E. Hebert, C.S.C., compiled a list of trees, shrubs, and vines–the woody plants–growing on the Notre Dame campus. The woody plants are a logical focus for a study of the campus flora because they are visible throughout all seasons and remain in place for years, limited only by changing human needs or environmental factors. Much changes in twenty-seven years, however, and Father Hebert's list has become out of date.

During 1990, the Sesquicentennial Committee began planning special events, programs, and projects that would celebrate the university's 150th anniversary in ways that documented its past, reflected its present outlook, and, strengthened by these introspections, encouraged new scholarly contributions from the university community. In this spirit, the committee recognized that a new survey

1

of the campus's woody plants could provide a unique perspective–one that would document the university's environment and its historical development while also providing a basis from which decisions directing its future growth could be made. This book is an outgrowth of that broader, more comprehensive, project. Father Hebert had described 1,657 actual plant sites on the campus (a site was either an individual plant or a group of plants counted as a unit, i.e., a hedge or clump). The new survey checked the status of each of those twenty-seven-year-old sites (determining whether each was still present or had disappeared) and added newly defined sites for the plantings around new buildings and the changes to existing structures. The number of defined sites, new plus old, rose to 3,571. Of the old sites, 765 have been altered.

During the campus survey, specimens of the many kinds of plants being documented were collected. This Sesquicentennial reference collection, numbering about 2,000 specimens, is housed in the Greene-Nieuwland Herbarium in the Galvin Life Science Center. Father Hebert's personal collection, containing specimens from his own campus collections that began around 1923 and ended with his death in 1974, is also housed in Notre Dame's herbarium.

Herbarium

A herbarium is a unique, specialized museum. It is a collection of preserved plants that is systematically arranged, much like a library. Scientists in many fields, including botany, genetics, ecology, evolution, and biogeography, use the herbarium as a research and educational tool. Most herbarium specimens are pressed, dried, mounted on paper of a standard size, labelled, and filed in closed cabinets. The term *herbarium* can mean either the preserved plant collection or the building (or room) in which it is housed. Although now obsolete, the term originally referred to an illustrated herbal rather than to a collection of real plants.

The two surveys of Notre Dame's woody plants, with their attendant reference collections and computer-stored data bases, provide a unique opportunity for study of the campus flora. Comparing current and twenty-seven-year-old information allows us to describe how and why the campus flora has changed with time. This is the beginning of a permanent, ongoing, and systematic documentation of planting activities on the campus that can be used to aid decision making. Decisions about what to plant, and where, can be guided by knowledge of what has been here, but has disappeared, paired with the reasons for disappearance.

The new additions to the campus flora are almost exclusively the result of deliberate planning and planting around new buildings and of alterations to existing sites. The losses are the result of several factors. Some plants have proved not hardy, others have succumbed to insects or diseases, still others have been removed when they became too large for their sites or when they stood in the way of construction. The greatest losses in the number of kinds of plants on the campus have occurred in two large areas. The first is the golf course, which has changed considerably since earlier years. Almost all low shrubbery has been removed, leaving only free-standing trees that do not hide errant golf balls. Cedar Grove Cemetery has undergone a similar transformation. There the number of trees has been reduced (including removal of many of the cedars for which it was named), and almost all shrubs, except some evergreens (mostly yews), have been removed.

The second large area of loss to the diversity of the campus flora is the area around and between the lakes, including the buildings along the lake margins. Here, there has been a general thinning of the vegetation, in some areas for pedestrian safety. In 1992 the university designated both lakes and the wooded areas surrounding them as natural areas, which protects them from further encroachment. The two keys to maintaining diversity within the campus flora are the designation of protected areas and the kind of extensive survey of the campus, site by site, that is documented here.

For example, in 1991 a small maintenance shed just west of the health services building was enlarged and remodelled to accommodate the new mail distribution center. The old shed, which had been built in 1900, was flanked on the south and the west by a small pocket of woods, part of which was cleared to make way for the larger building and for a sand pit for volleyball. Questions that can be answered now, but that could not be answered in 1991 are, "What is unique about this woods?" or, "Are there any plants here that should be saved?" According to Father Hebert, this was the only site on the campus of two native tree species, pawpaw (*Asimina triloba*) and sassafras (*Sassafras albidum*). When surveyed in 1992, only the sassafras remained. One other unique tree that grows in that pocket of woods is the only sour cherry tree (*Prunus cerasus*) found on campus. If construction of the mail distribution center occurred today, this information about rarity could have been considered during the construction planning process. In the extreme case, if the actual tree had historical value (no historical information about this one exists), the decision may have been made to preserve it where it stood. Less extreme measures would be to try to save the tree by transplanting it to a safer site or plant new trees of the same species in another appropriate site to counteract the loss. This option, of course, is still available. New pawpaw trees, and any other kinds of plants that have disappeared from the campus flora, can always be planted.

Many of the kinds of plants growing on the campus are native to this part of the country and can be found growing wild in Michigan, Indiana, or Illinois. But many more are native to other areas of the world. One characteristic shared by all of the kinds of plants on the campus is a tolerance for the climate found here, which is a reminder that

Changes

geographically distant areas can have similar growing conditions.

Notre Dame lies in the Midwest, where temperatures are hot during summer and cold during winter. This is a result of latitude, which means greater solar radiation during summer than during winter. Proximity to Lake Michigan moderates somewhat the temperature extremes as well as their timing and duration. The lake water warms and cools more slowly than the surrounding land, which results in a lag in rising temperatures in the spring and, also, a lag in the onset of cooler temperatures in autumn. These lags are reflected in the air temperature over nearby land. During winter, air passing over the lake from the west also brings added moisture, often in the form of the familiar "lake effect" snow.

At this latitude, the most critical environmental factor in determining whether or not a plant will thrive is temperature, especially the annual minimum temperature. Other factors include rainfall and soil moisture, day length, amount of solar radiation, soil type and acidity, and many more. The U.S. Department of Agriculture has used average annual minimum temperature to divide North America into eleven plant hardiness zones. Each zone represents a ten degree (Fahrenheit) range of minimum temperatures. Zone 1 (in parts of Alaska and Canada) reaches -50°F. Zone 11 (the Florida Keys, coastal Southern California, parts of Hawaii, and southern Mexico) does not drop below 40°F. Zones 3 through 9 encompass most areas of the United States.

For increased accuracy in guiding plant growers, zones 2 through 10 are each subdivided into two halves, each spanning five degrees. Because of its proximity to Lake Michigan, Notre Dame lies in a disjunct section of the warmer Zone 5b (-15° to -10°F), which includes all parts of the Lower Peninsula of Michigan and of northwestern Indiana that are moderated by the Great Lakes. The area just south of Notre Dame, including the Kankakee River and central Indiana ranging south to the northern edge of Indianapolis, is in the colder Zone 5a (-20° to -15°F). It is subjected to colder prevailing winter winds that sweep across the plains of Illinois, Iowa, and Wisconsin from the west and northwest without the moderating effect of Lake Michigan. In contrast, the very eastern edge of Lake Michigan, stretching from just west of Notre Dame in Indiana's Porter and LaPorte counties and northward into the Michigan counties of Berrien and Van Buren through Leelanau, is even warmer than Notre Dame. That area is a disjunct piece of Zone 6b (-5° to 0°F), which is found, otherwise, only in southern Indiana along the Ohio River and southward.

Climate

Growth zones

## NOMENCLATURE

The plants described in this book are referred to by their scientific names, which are based on the Latin language. Although common, vernacular names can be used in nontechnical literature, any gardener or plant scientist quickly learns that common names are not precise to a degree that ensures that everyone–writer, scientist, or his or her audience–knows with certainty which plant is being discussed.

Common names frequently describe some feature of the plant, but that feature may be descriptive of more than one kind of plant. An example is the name "ironwood," which says something about the hardness of the wood. This name is used for some very different kinds of trees in different parts of the world including six completely different trees found in the United States. Just as frequently, the problem lies with too many common names for the same plant. For example, Indiana's state tree (*Liriodendron tulipifera*), which also grows on the campus, is known as tulip tree, yellow-poplar, tulip poplar, white-poplar, and whitewood. These names each describe a distinctive feature of the tree's flowers, which look like tulips, or its wood, which is soft like that of the poplar trees and pale.

The solution to the name problem was first outlined clearly by the Swedish botanist Carl Linnaeus (1707–1778) in his 1753 reference work about plants of the world, *Species plantarum*. His work placed plants in twenty-four classes (sorted by stamen number, union, and length). Each kind of plant was given, in Latin, a broader generic name (the genus) and a specific epithet that, when combined with the genus, formed the name of a species (the binomial). These names are not in classical Latin (as used by Cicero), but in what is called botanical Latin, which is derived from the form of Latin that was spoken and written by scholars during the Middle Ages. The rules for describing and naming those plants that are found growing and reproducing naturally in the wild are set down in the *International Code for Botanical Nomenclature*, which is published by the members of the International Association for Plant Taxonomy. These two-part scientific names, with corresponding Latin descriptions, for each kind of plant are recognized and understood by scientists worldwide.

The genus (plural genera), the broader category used by Linnaeus, is represented in the scientific name by the first word, which is always capitalized. In plants, the genus is loosely defined as an entity comprised of one or more species that all have some features or characters in common or that are similar. Most frequently, these similarities are in the reproductive parts (flowers and fruits), but they also may be in features of vegetative parts like leaves, stems, or roots. Also, at a more fundamental level, all of the species belonging to a genus show genetic relationships. A nonspecialist can group plants into genera by recognizing conspicuous features that are similar among the members of the genus. For example, even people who have no technical training can recognize that the maples, all members of the genus *Acer*, seem to be related because of their similar fruits (paired, winged, and keylike). Many, but not all, of the maple species also have similar leaves that lead to the comment, "It looks like a maple."

Genus

But the nonspecialist also can see that all of the maples are not completely alike. They have distinct features (characters) that separate them into species. The species (plural also species) is a fundamental, but difficult to define, unit of classification. The species name is comprised of the genus, which is capitalized, followed by the specific epithet, which is not capitalized. This two-part name is either under-lined or italicized, for example, *Acer rubrum* (red maple). The individuals within a species all resemble each other and their ancestors in essential features. The common features of a species are self-perpetuating throughout a population that is isolated by environment, geographic distribution, and, more or less, by genetics. Although there are exceptions, the members of a species are able to breed and produce viable offspring among themselves, but not with members of another species.

**Species**

A species may be subdivided into even smaller units at the discretion of the scientist who is studying the plants. The most commonly used categories, in descending order within the species, are subspecies (subsp.), variety (var.), and form or forma (f.). The decision to assign a name at one of these levels is based on evidence of stable differences that the scientist has recognized in some subpopulation of the species. The level that the scientist assigns the plants with this set of differences is a matter of the degree of difference that he or she perceives these features to be from the norm as described in the definition of the species. The definitions of these three categories overlap somewhat.

The subspecies, the broadest category, has structural differences and, often, is distributed in a distinct geographic area that is separate from any other subspecies of the same species (but within the broader range described for the species). An example that is growing on the campus is the black maple (*Acer saccharum* subsp. *nigrum*), which is distinct in both its leaf form and its geographic distribution. Whereas the leaf of the sugar maple (*A. s.* subsp. *saccharum*) is flat with three to five lobes and has widely spaced teeth along its margin, that of the black maple (*A. s.* subsp. *nigrum*) is drooping, three-lobed, and smooth-edged without teeth. The species *A. saccharum* is widely distributed from eastern Canada through Texas. The black maple subspecies is found in a more limited area from Quebec through Iowa and North Carolina.

**Subspecies**

The variety is more commonly assigned in botany than are the other lower categories. As with subspecies, a variety is structurally distinct within the broader species description. The variety may or may not have its own geographical distribution and, if it does, that distribution may or may not be shared by or overlap the distributions of other varieties within the same species. This definition is vague, but the description and limits of an actual variety, when a name is assigned, are spelled out clearly by the author of the name. Many plants with scientific names defined to the level of variety have been

**Variety**

planted on the campus. A conspicuous example of species and variety is the honeylocust (*Gleditsia triacanthos*), which has large, often branched, thorns on both trunk and branches, and its thornless variety, *G. t.* var. *inermis.* The absence of thorns and a more slender growth habit distinguish the variety.

The lowest rank within a species is the forma (or form). It is used when the variation from the norm is trivial, occurs sporadically within the "normal" population, and involves one or a very few traits such as leaf shape, fruit color, or flower color. Examples of the rank of forma are common on the campus, although most of them have been planted. One that occurs sporadically in the woods around the lakes is the white-flowered form of bitter nightshade (*Solanum dulcamara* f. *albiflorum*), a weedy, scrambling shrub that usually has purple flowers. Father Hebert included both the species and the white forma in his campus woody plant list twenty-seven years ago. No plants with white flowers were seen on the campus during the most recent survey so only the species is now included.

Forma

Another category that appears throughout this book is the cultivar. The word is a contraction of "cultivated variety." The cultivar name is always capitalized and never appears in italics. It is either preceded by cv. or enclosed in single quotation marks, as it is in this book. The cultivar category is used exclusively in the world of cultivated plants (in horticulture rather than in botany). It is defined as a variant that has been selected for further propagation because of some desirable characteristic. While a botanical variety must have the ability to maintain its distinctive characteristics through successive generations by natural reproductive means in the wild, a cultivar can be maintained through completely artificial or vegetative means such as by divisions, rooted cuttings, or grafting.

Cultivar

Cultivar names are governed by the *International Code of Nomenclature for Cultivated Plants*. Since 1959, these names have been "fancy names" that are distinctly different from the botanical Latin names of species and varieties. This rule results in descriptive cultivar names such as 'Sea Green' and 'Old Gold' (both cultivars of *Juniperus chinensis* that have distinctive leaf colors). The cultivar may be a selection of a botanical variety. One example that has been planted on the campus is *Gleditsia triacanthos* var. *inermis* 'Shademaster,' which is a cultivar of the thornless honeylocust. The cultivar has an upright growth habit and very few fruits (fruits can be messy in lawns).

Another plant category that appears in the campus flora is the hybrid. This is most often the offspring of two sexually crossed species within a single genus (an interspecific hybrid). This type of hybrid is given its own unique, collective name, similar to a specific epithet, but it is preceded by a multiplication sign. For example, *Platanus × acerifolia*, the London planetree, is the result of a cross between *P. occidentalis* and *P. orientalis*. Intergeneric hybrids (crosses

Hybrid

between species in different genera) also exist, although there are no examples on the campus. An intergeneric hybrid is given a name derived from the two (sometimes three) genera involved in the cross. That name is preceded by a multiplication sign. For example, the popular, evergreen Leyland cypress is written × *Cupressocyparis leylandii*. Its parents are Monterey cypress, *Cupressus macrocarpa*, and Nootka falsecypress, *Chamaecyparis nootkatensis*. Some hybrids occur spontaneously in nature. Hybridization is quite common in the wild within oaks, willows, hawthorns, and honeysuckles, for example. Other hybrids are the result of deliberate crosses that are carried out to develop a plant that bears desirable traits of the parent plants.

In botanical literature, but not always in that of gardening, the species name (or the subspecies or lower category) is followed by the name of the author who described it. This is done for precision. It allows other scientists to find, read, and understand the description of that species in the scientific literature. The practice places both previous and current scientists on common ground. In this book, the author's names are included in the chapter that catalogs the campus flora and have been omitted in the three text chapters and the plant site list. For brevity, the author names follow the standardized abbreviations found in the "Authors Cited" section of Bailey's *Hortus Third*.

## BIBLIOGRAPHY

### Plant Identification and General Information

Bailey, L. H. 1928. *The Cultivated Evergreens*. New York: Macmillan.

Bailey, L. H. 1939. *The Standard Cyclopedia of Horticulture*. 3 vols. New York: Macmillan.

Bailey, L. H., Hortorium Staff. 1976. *Hortus Third*. New York: Macmillan.

Barnes, B. V., and W. H. Wagner, Jr. 1981. *Michigan Trees*. Ann Arbor, Mich.: University of Michigan Press.

Blackburn, B. 1971. *Trees and Shrubs in Eastern North America*. New York: Oxford University Press.

Chadwick, L. C., and R. A. Keen. 1976. *A Study of the Genus Taxus*. Research bulletin no. 1086. Wooster: Ohio Agricultural Research and Development Center.

Chittendon, F. J., ed. 1951. *The Royal Horticultural Society Dictionary of Gardening*. 4 vols. London: Oxford University Press.

Cope, E. A. 1986. *Native and Cultivated Conifers of Northeastern North America, a Guide*. Ithaca, N.Y.: Cornell University Press.

Dirr, M. A. 1990. *Manual of Woody Landscape Plants: Their Identification, Ornamental Characters, Culture, Propagation and Uses.* Champaign, Ill.: Stipes Publishing.

Eichenlaub, V. L., et al. 1990. *The Climatic Atlas of Michigan*. University of Notre Dame Press.

Fernald, M. L. 1950. *Gray's Manual of Botany*. New York: D. Van Nostrand.

Gleason, H. A. 1952. *The New Britton and Brown Illustrated Flora of the Northeastern United States and Adjacent Canada*. 3 vols. Bronx: The New York Botanical Garden.

Gleason, H. A. & A. Cronquist. 1991. *Manual of Vascular Plants of Northeastern United States and Adjacent Canada*. Bronx: The New York Botanical Garden.

Hebert, P. E., C.S.C. 1966. *Trees, Shrubs and Vines on Notre Dame Campus*. Biology Department, University of Notre Dame.

Huxley, A., ed. 1992. *The New Royal Horticultural Society Dictionary of Gardening.* 4 vols. New York: Stockton Press.

Johnson, H. 1979. *The Principles of Gardening.* New York: Simon & Schuster.

Mabberley, D. J. 1987. *The Plant Book.* England: Cambridge University Press.

Petrides, G. A. 1972. *A Field Guide to Trees and Shrubs.* Boston: Houghton Mifflin.

Rehder, A. 1951. *Manual of Cultivated Trees and Shrubs.* New York: Macmillan.

Sargent, C. S. 1922. *Manual of the Trees of North America.* 2 vols. New York: Dover.

Taylor, N., ed. 1948. *Taylor's Encyclopedia of Gardening, Horticulture and Landscape Design.* Boston: Houghton Mifflin.

U. S. D. A. *Plant Hardiness Zone Map.* 1990. Agricultural Research Service Miscellaneous Publication no. 1475. U.S. Dept. of Agriculture.

Voss, E. G. 1985. *Michigan Flora, Part II Dicots.* Cranbrook Institute of Science Bulletin no. 59. Ann Arbor: Cranbrook Institute of Science and University of Michigan.

Wyman, D. 1969. *Shrubs and Vines for American Gardens.* New York: Macmillan.

Wyman, D. 1986. *Wyman's Gardening Encyclopedia.* New York: Macmillan.

Wyman, D. 1990. *Trees for American Gardens.* New York: Macmillan.

## Poisonous Plants

Frankel, E. 1991. *Poison Ivy, Poison Oak, Poison Sumac, and Their Relatives.* Pacific Grove, Calif.: Boxwood Press.

Hardin, J. W., and J. M. Arena, M.D. 1974. *Human Poisoning from Native and Cultivated Plants.* Durham, N.C.: Duke University Press.

Kingsbury, J. M. 1964. *Poisonous Plants of the United States and Canada.* Englewood Cliffs, N.J.: Prentice-Hall.

Lewis, W. H., and M. P. F. Elvin-Lewis. 1977. *Medical Botany.* New York: John Wiley & Sons.

## Plant Taxonomy and Systematics

Brickell, C. D., ed. 1980. *International Code of Nomenclature for Cultivated Plants. Regnum Vegetabile,* Vol. 104. International Association for Plant Taxonomy. Utrecht: Bohn, Scheltema & Hollema.

Coombs, A. J. 1985. *Dictionary of Plant Names.* Portland: Timber Press.

Greuter, W., et al., eds. 1988. *International Code of Botanical Nomenclature. Regnum Vegetabile,* Vol. 118. International Association for Plant Taxonomy. Königstein, Germany: Koeltz Scientific Books.

Lawrence, G. H. M. 1951. *Taxonomy of Vascular Plants.* New York: Macmillan.

Porter, C. L. 1967. *Taxonomy of Flowering Plants.* San Francisco: W. H. Freeman.

Smith, A. W. 1972. *A Gardener's Dictionary of Plant Names.* New York: St. Martin's Press.

Stearn, W. T. 1983. *Botanical Latin.* North Pomfret, Vt.: David & Charles.

Woodland, D. W. 1991. *Contemporary Plant Systematics.* Englewood Cliffs, N.J.: Prentice-Hall.

## History of Plants and People

Christensen, C. M. 1984. *E. C. Stakman, Statesman of Science.* St. Paul: American Phytopathological Society.

Coats, P. 1970. *Flowers in History.* New York: Viking Press.

Gourlie, N. 1953. *The Prince of Botanists, Carl Linnaeus.* London: H. F. & G. Witherby, Ltd.

Peattie, D. C. 1950. *A Natural History of Trees of Eastern and Central North America.* Boston: Houghton Mifflin.

Spongberg, S. A. 1990. *A Reunion of Trees.* Cambridge, Mass.: Harvard University Press.

*Webster's Biographical Dictionary.* 1953. Springfield, Mass.: G. & C. Merriam.

# Before Notre Dame du Lac

## Robert P. McIntosh

When Father Edward Sorin arrived at the place he named Notre Dame du Lac on a cold November day in 1842, the year we celebrate in the Sesquicentennial of the University of Notre Dame, he was in some senses a late comer. Twelve years earlier Father Stephen Badin had purchased 524 acres of the very recently surveyed Section 36, Township 38N, Range 2E in the northernmost tier of townships of the new State of Indiana, and thereon built a log chapel on the shore of what we now know as St. Mary's Lake. Father Badin could have celebrated a near sesquicentennial of the building in 1686 of an earlier log chapel on the same shore by Father Claude Allouez. According to Father Sorin, Father Allouez would have arrived on the heels of Father Louis Hennepin and Robert Sieur de La Salle who, less than a "league" (*ca.* 3 miles) to the west in December of 1679, had sought a portage from the River of the Miami, later the St. Joseph River, to the River Seignelay, or Kankakee River, and hence to the Mississippi. On a later trip in 1681, La Salle met there with the then resident Miami Indians by tradition under a large open grown burr oak tree, later known as the Council Oak. That tree remained a landmark until August of 1991 when the remaining branches broke away from the approximately 400-year-old trunk. Two offspring of the Council Oak, grown from acorns, still thrive in the area just west of Sacred Heart Church above the Grotto on the Notre Dame campus.

The "Miami, Mascouten and Oiatinon" encountered by LaSalle in 1679 occupied a village just west of the St. Joseph River according to Father Hennepin who, in 1683, documented the journey. Miami were familiar to the French travellers from previous encounters in the vicinity of Green Bay on northern Lake Michigan along the approaches to alternate routes to the Mississippi. The Iroquois had driven them and other tribes from most of the area at the south end of Lake Michigan and LaSalle's treaty was designed to unite these tribes with the French against the Iroquois and English. The Potawatomi had occupied the valley of the St. Joseph River in the sixteenth century, fishing, hunting, and raising corn, beans, and squash, but those encountered by Father Badin in the 1830s had returned to the region from the Green Bay area. Their renewed occupancy was also temporary for in 1838 most of them were involuntarily moved westward.

These tribes of written history, however sparsely recorded, followed a long lineage of even less well-documented residents or transients. Their immediate predecessors had occupied the area from 1000 A.D. to 1500 A.D. Woodland peoples had lived in the area, introducing agriculture and building characteristic mounds in the Kankakee valley, leaving as evidence pottery and copper artifacts, the latter part of an extensive trade in copper. For nearly 12,000 years before the mound builders, smaller populations of nomadic hunters, the earliest following close upon the retreating ice sheets of what were questionably the last of the several Pleistocene glaciers, pursued herds of mammoth, mastodon, musk ox, and elk. Their presence is indicated by ubiquitous and characteristically fluted stone spearheads and evidence of butchering on skeletal remains of mastodon.

The site for a mission, originally purchased by Father Badin, was received by Father Sorin from the Bishop of Vincennes for the purpose of building a university. It was located on terrain created millenia earlier by retreating glaciers. An early post-glacial antecedent of Lake Michigan, dammed to the north by ice, was substantially higher than modern Lake Michigan and drained south down the then much larger Kankakee River. It was joined at the eventual site of South Bend by a similarly large flow from an antecedent of Lake Huron. The valley was and is bordered by morainal hills also deposited by retreating glaciers. The immediate landscape of the university of Father Sorin's vision was an extensive plain of poorly drained sands deposited by outwash from the melting glaciers and pocked by lakes formed in depressions once occupied by residual blocks of glacial ice, in effect terrestrial icebergs. Such is the history of St. Mary's and St. Joseph's lakes. A low ridge formed that separated the drainages of the modern St. Joseph and Kankakee rivers establishing the narrow span of the continental divide over which LaSalle sought the shortest portage.

After the ice of the Wisconsin glaciation retreated about 13,000 years ago, during this previous experience with global warming, the barren landscape was covered by open parkland of scattered spruce trees, similar to that found in modern Arctic Canada and Alaska, until about 10,000 years before present (B.P. in common paleontological usage). At about this time the forests became predominantly pine, which lasted until 8,000 years B.P., when they were replaced by deciduous forests of various types not much different from those encountered by early European travellers. The numerous species comprising these migrating forests returned from diverse places to which they had retreated before the glaciers. These included the Atlantic Coastal Plain from New Jersey to Texas and the unglaciated mountains of the southeastern United States. The omnipresent lakes, bogs, and marshes of the region provide evidence of these travels in the form of residual distributions of living organisms now largely departed to the north, macrofossils of plants and animals, and, particularly, vertical layers of well-preserved microfossil pollen, beginning at the bottom with the pollens of spruce and other plants now associated with the Arctic and followed by that of pine and hardwood trees in turn. The general sequence of these events was clear from early studies of pollen taken from cores in deposits in lakes and bogs; it was not until the atomic era following World War II that radioactive carbon ($C^{14}$) dating provided a relatively precise chronology (give or take a century or so) of the events described above.

Perhaps the most distinctive events of post-glacial history for this region were one or more warm dry periods, one extending from 6,500 B.P. to 3,000 B.P. During such periods grassland plants and animals that we associate largely with the Dakotas, Kansas, and Iowa migrated eastward into Wisconsin, Illinois, Michigan, and Indiana. The valley of the St. Joseph River and the lake shore occupied sequentially by Fathers Allouez, Badin, and Sorin were located at this geological, climatic, biological, and cultural crossroads that had witnessed millenia of historical traverses of plants, animals, and humans—north to south, east to west, and return. The landscape encountered by Father Sorin one and one half centuries ago was the consequence of this complex history.

The site of Father Sorin's prospective university rested on the northeastern edge of what came to be called the "Prairie Peninsula," an extension of western grassland east of the Mississippi River penetrating the western edge of the eastern deciduous forest as far as Ohio. This "Peninsula" included the Grand Prairie, which occupied most of central Illinois and west-central Indiana with continuous extensions northeast along the Kankakee River, breaking up around the St. Joseph River at South Bend into islands of prairie interspersed with forest (Figure 1). Prairie areas, marked by distinctive dark soils, were at first suspect to northern Europeans because no trees grew on them. However, the early settlers quickly recognized their superior merit for crops. The great agricultural heartland of America was established on these prairie soils, but only after the problem of breaking the prairie sod was resolved. Familiar place names in northern Indiana, such as LaPorte, derived from the metaphorical door leading through the eastern forest edge to the prairie. The word "prairie" was adopted from the French to describe these treeless areas for which English had no good equivalent. Had the earliest European visitors been Ukrainian or Hungarian, who came from similar landscapes, they would have felt more at home and would have had a vernacular name for these grasslands. The most common early explanation of European settlers for the existence of prairie was fire since the grasslands were subject to regular burning either by naturally set fires or by fires set by Indians to drive game. It remained the favorite explanation until one sage observer noted that it was necessary to have a prairie before there could be a prairie fire and wondered which came first. Current explanations for the distribution of prairie are a complex of historical changes in climate, frequency of drought, incidence of fire, and a topography and soils that influence the availability of water.

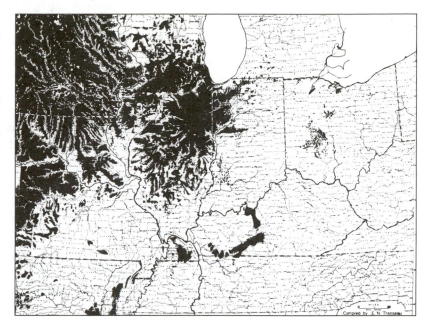

Figure 1. The "Prairie Peninsula," a concept developed by the ecologists C. C. Adams and H. A. Gleason and represented here in a map published by E. N. Transeau. Map courtesy of *Ecology* published by the Ecological Society of America.

What the area in which Notre Dame was founded was like in 1679 or 1842 is hard to reconstruct. Anthropological evidence documents the millenia of Native American cultures regionally, but relatively little of it is specific to the square mile or so that we associate with the University of Notre Dame. An archaeological dig near the site of the original chapel on the south shore of St. Mary's Lake produced stone artifacts including a complete knife or spear point, indicating prehistoric use of the area by Native Americans between 4000 and 3000 B.P. The earliest written documentation is that of Father Louis Hennepin, who travelled on the River of the Miamis (St. Joseph River) with LaSalle in December 1679. They missed the portage to the Kankakee River and went farther up the River of the Miamis, which would bring them to the vicinity of South Bend and Mishawaka. Hennepin records that LaSalle got lost pursuing a deer, in all probability on the west side of the river where he would have been scouting for the portage. LaSalle lost the deer but returned with two fat possums hanging from his belt. They eventually located the portage and Father Hennepin described "a great plain" about one-half mile west of the river, on the edge of which was located an Indian village, in the area of the modern Riverview and Highland cemeteries. Buffalo horns, carcasses, and boats made of buffalo skins indicated that buffalo were plentiful in the area. Hennepin described fires set by the Indians to drive buffalo to slaughter. They sometimes killed as many as one hundred twenty in a day. The women were then notified of the kill and sent to bring home the meat in backpacks up to "three hundred pounds weight," with a child on top for good measure, according to Hennepin who described the buffalo and their use by the Indians in detail. One familiar legacy of the buffalo is an area around the site of South Bend, just east of the St. Joseph River, known to the French as "Parc aux Vauches." This term, bastardized to Parkovash, appears in the earliest land titles in South Bend and is perpetuated in the name of a street and small park a half-mile west of the university. It joins other reminders of this era in streets named LaSalle, Tonti, and Ribourde for the French travellers, plus Wakewa, Ostemo, and Pokagon for the Native American residents.

Although the portage was no doubt used by Europeans during the next century and a half, there are few specific records of the immediate vicinity of the future site of Father Sorin's university. Father Pierre Charlevoix used the St. Joseph–Kankakee portage in 1721. Charlevoix described the Portage Prairie, which he called "Ox-Head Prairie," ". . . as a great prairie, all sprinkled with little tufts of woodland." This was an apt description as later, more detailed information suggests. Father Badin arrived on the shore of St. Mary's Lake in 1830 and built a log building, a story and one-half high, presumably using logs from the immediate vicinity. In 1834, when Badin constructed another building, Col. L. M. Taylor, one of the founders of South Bend, debited to his account 4,936 ft. of lumber at $49.26. Badin also purchased 6,000 shingles and paid $40.00 for getting out timber from an unspecified location. In 1838 Father Benjamin Petit, whose mission included Badin's chapel on St. Mary's Lake, referred to Indians moving along the shores of the lake and on paths in the forest on their way to chapel. Father Petit and his predecessor, Father Louis De Seille, were suspected of urging the resident Potawatomi to resist the efforts of the United States government to persuade them to sell their land and move west. If so, their efforts failed. The rights of the Potawatomi to their lands in Indiana were extinguished and in September 1838, most of the Potawatomi, numbering fewer than one thousand, began their trip west with a guard of volunteer troops under the command of General John Tipton appointed by Indiana's governor, David Wallace. Father Petit joined them on this sad journey and died on his return trip. He is buried at Notre Dame.

Father Sorin, in his Chronicles, described the site of the university as having 10 acres of cultivated land in 1842. The remaining 514 acres, except for the lakes, he described as virgin forest. In the chronicle on the farm, Father Sorin wrote that an additional 50 acres were cleared in 1843 and he resolved that 100 acres more would be cleared in 1844. Apparently it happened, for Brother John Garnier quoted a letter from Sorin to Father Moreau in 1845 saying that a handful of brothers had cleared 200 acres in two years and 105 acres were then in wheat. He also mentioned that in 1843, 200 trees were planted near the lake and in 1845, 300 peach trees were planted. One early log building, 46 by 20 feet, was constructed from logs carted to the place but it is not clear from where. Another building, somewhat later, required 60,000 ft. of lumber. A small creek, which runs along or through much of the northern part of modern Notre Dame, did supply power for a saw mill before the creek ran into the St. Joseph River. Whether that mill supplied the lumber is not known. Another small stream running from St. Mary's Lake to the St. Joseph River supported a carding machine and fulling mill for the preparation of cloth, which suggests early sheep grazing in the area.

In 1849 visitors to the first commencement were described as coming northeast through the woods from South Bend although the site of the university was largely cleared for farmland. Only the island (the area now between the lakes) was said to retain an old grove of trees; although Father Sorin, while on a retreat on the island, had cut some trees. No mention was made of kinds, sizes, or numbers of trees. One of the few specific references is to poplar boards, to make a coffin, that were hauled some forty miles. The South Bend *Times* for February 18, 1917, asserted that the margin of the lake was originally graced with majestic oaks and hickories but only a few well-rotted stumps remained. However, the source and accuracy of that information is not clear. The earliest visitors and residents of the site of the University of Notre Dame occasionally noted the beauty of the setting but said very little about the vegetation. Most of them, being recent arrivals from Europe, probably knew little enough about the local flora or fauna in any case.

The only specific documentation of the vegetation in the vicinity of the site of the original chapel and the later university comes from the land survey records made by William Brookfield in 1829, just before the arrival of Father Badin and nearly a century and a half after Father Allouez. These early land surveys were done under contract with the office of the Surveyor General, an office established by the United States government in 1796. The surveys of public land in the Northwest Territory replaced both the tenuous boundaries of the several Indian tribes and the French measures of leagues or arpents with land divisions in a regular pattern of townships that are six miles on a side, each subdivided into 36 sections that are one mile square, each including 640 acres. This pattern is reflected in the modern road network of any reasonably level area. The 524 acres purchased by Father Badin in 1830 constituted most all of section 36 in the extreme southeast corner of Township 38N, Range 2E, of the recently organized St. Joseph County just east of the St. Joseph River. The University of Notre Dame subsequently acquired much of the adjacent section 25 to the north, also in Township 38N, Range 2E, and sections 31 and 30 in Township 38N, Range 3E immediately east of the original site (Figure 2).

Starting from a base line, the surveyors initially surveyed the outer boundaries of the township and then subdivided it into sections. The surveyor's "chain" (66 ft.) was 80 to the mile and at 40 chains (quarter section corner) and 80 chains (section corner) the surveyor set a post and recorded the species, diameter, compass direction, and distance of two trees (usually), which were blazed with an axe. These were known as "bearing" or "witness" trees. Distances to the trees were given in "links," a surveyor's unit of 7.92 inches. These data provide the most useful part of the surveyors' records. In addition they recorded the species and size of any tree ("line tree") encountered on the section lines and noted streams, roads, trails, and any change in the landscape or vegetation. Their notes at each section corner rated the land 1st, 2nd, or 3rd rate and briefly described the type of vegetative cover, and sometimes soil or other landscape features. When there were no trees near a corner, the surveyor made a mound of earth, clear evidence that the area was prairie. In their descriptions in St. Joseph County, the surveyors recognized two types of prairie, wet and dry, both marked by tall grasses and, in the wet prairies, no doubt, by sedges and rushes which were not distinguished by the surveyors. The grasses of a wet prairie of a county south of St. Joseph County were described by the surveyor as tall enough to be tied over the head of a man on horseback. St. Joseph County at this time had much more of the now rapidly disappearing wetlands than at present. One estimate was that 20.5% of the county was permanently ponded and another 13.5% was seasonally ponded. Much of this was in wet prairie that has since been drained for agriculture or development.

Land surveying had a long history in the American Colonies and the United States. George Washington and Thomas Jefferson were surveyors in their time. Since land was the principal form of wealth, surveying was a significant profession and surveyors were usually

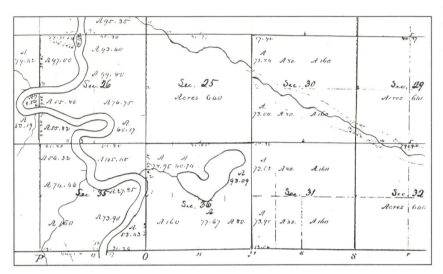

Figure 2. A composite map from the original surveyor's record of section 36, the original area granted to Father Sorin, and adjacent sections showing the St. Joseph River in sections 35 and 26. Juday Creek is the diagonal line across sections 30 and 25. Courtesy of the State Archives, Indiana Commission on Public Records.

capable and knowledgeable men. Numerous studies, several in Indiana, have exploited surveyor's records to determine the character of the landscape before extensive European influence occurred.  The early surveyors were excellent botanists listing between 73 and 80 tree species in Indiana surveys and 49 species in the 25 northern counties of Indiana. Charles Deam's comprehensive *Trees of Indiana* included numerous smaller trees, which would not usually reach the size used by surveyors. If these tree species and varieties are excluded, there are about 90 tree species native to Indiana. Thus, the surveyors recognized the majority of tree species known from Indiana, including some relatively uncommon ones. Even many of the notoriously difficult oaks were recognized, although the surveyors of St. Joseph County wisely lumped the hickories together. In Indiana it was quite clear that the vegetation of the northern tier of counties, particularly in the northwest, differed from that to the south and east.

In 1829 surveyor William Brookfield surveyed Township 38N, Ranges 2 and 3E, which included section 36 and adjacent sections currently occupied by Notre Dame (Figure 2). The south boundary of section 36 is now marked by Angela Boulevard from a point just west of St. Joseph's High School. It continues on a line through the Cedar Grove Cemetery to the junction of Edison and Old Juniper roads. Old Juniper Road follows the east boundary north past the football stadium and the North Dining Hall to its junction with Douglas Road at the Notre Dame Credit Union. The north boundary is marked by Douglas Road, west across Highway 33, and the old Michigan Central Railroad on the St. Mary's College campus, to the northwest corner near the greenhouse end of the Science Building. The west boundary extends south, intersecting the St. Joseph River near the outfall of the now buried outlet from the Notre Dame lakes and back to near Angela Boulevard.

Brookfield encountered a road leading NW at 9.00 chains and a trail leading N at 74.11 chains as he went east on the south boundary of section 36. Going north on the east boundary he found a road leading NE at 4.25 chains. At 65.00 chains N of the south boundary he noted a lake, 10 chains W of the east boundary, that he estimated as 20 chains wide and about 40 chains long. Brookfield's final map outlined one lake some 30 chains, N-S, at its widest point and about 60 chains E-W. The dimensions in his notes approximate the dimensions of the east end of the lake, now St. Joseph's Lake. The number of lakes at Notre Dame is confounded by dual names. Father Allouez reportedly had called the mission Ste-Marie-des Lacs implying more than one lake. Father Sorin called it Notre Dame du Lac, which remains the official title of the university and implies only one lake. It is not clear if Brookfield entered the section, although his map shows a stream flowing from the west end of the lake he outlined to the St. Joseph River. In addition to his duties as surveyor, Brookfield was in 1830 a

Trees
| | |
|---|---|
| Beech | *Fagus grandifolia* |
| Black ash | *Fraxinus nigra* |
| Black walnut | *Juglans nigra* |
| Cedar | *Juniperus virginiana* |
| Cherry | *Prunus serotina* |
| Elm | *Ulmus* spp. |
| Hickory | *Carya* spp. |
| Ironwood | *Ostrya virginiana* |
| Lynn | *Tilia americana* |
| Maple | Acer rubrum or |
| | *A. saccharinum* |

Oaks
| | |
|---|---|
| Burr | *Quercus macrocarpa* |
| Black | *Q. velutina* |
| Jack | *Q. ellipsoidalis* |
| Red | *Q. rubra* |
| Swamp | *Q. bicolor* |
| White | *Q. alba* |
| Yellow | *Q. muehlenbergii* |
| Pepperage | *Nyssa sylvatica* |
| Poplar | *Liriodendron tulipifera* |
| Sugar | *Acer saccharum* |
| Swamp ash | *Fraxinus pennsylvanica* |
| Sycamore | *Platanus occidentalis* |
| White ash | *Fraxinus americana* |
| White walnut | *Juglans cinerea* |

Shrubs or small trees
| | |
|---|---|
| Hazel | *Corylus* spp. |
| Pawpaw | *Asimina triloba* |
| Spice bush | *Lindera benzoin* |

Herbs
| | |
|---|---|
| Compass plant | *Silphium* |
| | *terebinthinaceum* |
| Whole-leaf rosin | |
| weed | *S. integrifolium* |

Table 1. Scientific names of tree and shrub or small tree species mentioned by the surveyor.

local resident who, as bonded county agent, supervised land sales. The county commission met at his house in section 27 near the portage from the St. Joseph River. It is likely that Brookfield, as a resident of the area from 1827, county surveyor, and a justice, was familiar with the interior of section 36. He platted the never developed town of St. Joseph on the site of the famous portage as a prospective county seat but was forestalled by Alexis Coquillard and Lathrop M. Taylor, for whom Brookfield surveyed the town of South Bend, which became and remains the county seat. Brookfield left the state soon afterward, but his mark remains indelibly in the surveyor's notes and maps that he drew in 1829. Brookfield's notes were inscribed in an elegant script with appropriate flourishes that would be the envy of any nineteenth-century schoolboy and, no doubt, had endeared him to his teachers.

The immediate setting of Father Sorin's university in section 36 may be further abstracted from Brookfield's notes. He recorded trees as small as 3 inches in diameter. On the boundaries of section 36 he listed 27 individual trees of six species: 11 white oak, 9 yellow oak, 4 black oak, 1 red oak, 1 hickory, and 1 pepperage (scientific names are given in Table 1).

The smallest was a hickory 3 inches in diameter, the largest a 42-inch white oak, the latter at the SE section corner. More than half of the trees were between 11 and 21 inches in diameter. The trees recorded illustrate a familiar problem of using surveyor's records—the positive identification of their tree species. Brookfield's yellow oak is not entirely clear. Two species (*Quercus velutina* and *Q. muehlenbergii*) have been called yellow oak. It is impossible that these would have been mistaken for each other because their leaves are very different. Brookfield recognized black and yellow oaks, both of which occur in this area. On the west boundary of section 36, he recorded several yellow oaks near the ravine on the St. Mary's College campus where the outlet from the Notre Dame lakes joins the St. Joseph River. Now yellow oaks (*Q.*

*muehlenbergii*) grow in the vicinity. Although they are not clearly the same ones identified by Brookfield, it seems reasonable that he was identifying yellow oak correctly. Black oak (*Q. velutina*) and red oak (*Q. rubra*) are also found locally but it seems unlikely that Brookfield was recognizing some black oaks as yellow oaks, as one Indiana botanist (J. Potzger) suggested might be the case. It is probable that other oaks (*Q. coccinea, Q. ellipsoidalis*) also occurred in the area. The group of oaks including these several species is notoriously difficult and some even form hybrids. Professor Richard Jensen of St. Mary's College, a recognized expert on oaks, is still working to sort these all out so the surveyors of the 1820s should not be faulted.

Another look at section 36 can be abstracted from the surveyor's descriptions at its corners. The SW corner (on low ground west of the St. Joseph High School) was described as: "Land swampy, Timber Swamp ash and Lynn Undergrowth hazel" and an unknown shrub. The SE corner (now the junction of Old Juniper and Edison roads) was: "Land rolling, 3rd rate, Timber oak." The NE corner (now at the Notre Dame Credit Union) was: "Land 3rd rate, timber oak, No undergrowth." The NW corner (now on St. Mary's campus) was: "Land gently rolling—Good Barrens, W(hite), B(lack), Y(ellow) oak and hickory." Barrens did not describe bare or non-fertile land. In fact, it characterized some of the best agricultural land in the county marked by scattered trees, usually oaks, on open grassland. It was also known as oak opening or, later, oak savannah because of the widely spaced trees (Figure 3).

Anecdotal accounts of the forest in the 1840s sometimes described it as virgin or dense. Virgin or undisturbed forest was often an illusion

Figure 3. A view of a pastured oak opening a few miles west of Notre Dame illustrating the much branched, widely spaced trees. In an original oak opening the prairie grasses would be much taller.

of late European arrivals who discounted the effects of their Native American predecessors. The distances given by the surveyors from the corners to the two nearest trees can, with some caution, be used to estimate average tree density as number per acre. Most trees in section 36 were over 30 links (20 ft.) from the corner, two were over 70 links (46 ft.) distant. The average of the 18 distances available for section 36 was 37.4 links (25.6 ft.). One conventional method of estimating tree density is to assume that each tree occupies an area determined by squaring this average distance to give an area per tree (655.4 sq. ft.) and dividing this estimate of area occupied by each tree into the number of square feet in one acre (43,560). This requires an assumption that trees are evenly distributed as on a checkerboard, which is not true. However, as a rough approximation it indicates that the density of trees in the vicinity of section 36 was about 66 trees per acre. This suggests a relatively open woodland as indicated by the surveyor's corner descriptions. Closed canopied forests now growing on the campus have 150-200 trees per acre based on average distances of 17 to 14.5 feet.

As the university grew, it came to occupy most of the three sections adjacent to section 36 west to Ironwood Road and north to what is now Judy, or Juday, Creek but which was unceremoniously shown on earlier maps as State Ditch. If the trees on the boundaries of these sections are tabulated, the vegetation in the vicinity of the prospective university remains essentially the same. Thirty-seven additional trees included no additional species or individuals of unusual size. The trees were 17 white oak, 11 yellow oak, 7 hickory, 1 black oak, and 1 red oak. The hickories were all small, the largest 12 inches in diameter. Of the total of 64 trees recorded for the four sections, 55 (86%) were oak with 28 (43%) of those being white oak. The notes at the corners of the adjacent sections provided no surprises, often simply stating, "Land as Before" or, in one case, "Thinly timbered." The density of trees per acre remained essentially the same based on data for all four sections. It is likely that other species occurred in the swampy area around the lake(s) although no records of this exist.

If a somewhat larger area of the surveyor's records is examined, the nature of the general area around section 36 in 1829 becomes clearer. In four sections immediately west of Notre Dame, in Range 2E and mostly west of the St. Joseph River, 56 trees included principally oaks (72%) but included a new species of oak, burr oak, nearly equal in number (14) to white oak (15). Corners along the river included additional tree species, lynn (basswood), sycamore, black walnut, elm, maple (probably silver maple), and cedar (red cedar or juniper), the species that had marked the location of the portage for LaSalle. At three corners the surveyor noted "mound" because no trees were nearby and, at one corner, the surveyor noted "Burr Oak 12 no other tree handy." Burr oak is commonly associated with prairie in "oak openings," or what the surveyors described as "Barrens." The trees of oak openings are distinctive in having low spreading branches, or knobs remaining from these, which indicate that the tree grew in open country as in figure three. The same species in a forest grows straight up without low branches. The sections to the east of Notre Dame were also dominated by oaks, which comprised 46 of 51 trees (90%). Two miles east of Notre Dame the surveyors again noted that they were entering prairie and marked corners by mounds. On the south boundary of section 34 (T38N, R3E) the surveyor's notes described a "Timber Island," a reminder of Charlevoix's "tufts of woodland," surrounded by a sea of prairie. The site of Notre Dame was in fact surrounded by prairie at the northeast edge of the Prairie Peninsula, with Portage Prairie to the west, Harris Prairie to the east, and Sumption Prairie to the southwest.

An anomaly among the early buildings at Notre Dame was a "Sugar House" reported by Thomas Schlereth in his account of the development of the campus. Previous studies of the surveyor's records showed no "sugar" trees, as the surveyors designated sugar maple, in Range 38N and only small amounts in Range 37N, although its usual associate, beech, increased substantially. The surveyor's notes on the east boundary of Township 37N Range 2E, which extends for six miles south of Notre Dame, showed 7 oaks in the first mile; 3 oaks, 2 hickories, and 1 maple (silver or red) in the second mile; 8 oaks in the third mile; 3 oaks, 1 hickory, 1 beech, 1 ironwood, and 1 black ash in the fourth mile. The field note on the SE corner of that section (24), however, recorded: "Timber oak, beech, sugar, undergrowth hazel, ironwood and spice bush." The fifth mile produced 2 beeches, 2 elms, 1 hickory, and 2 large sugar trees (30 and 36 inches in diameter, respectively). The corner note read: "Timber sugar, walnut, elm, undergrowth ash, spice bush, pawpaw." These are all species characteristic of a much richer, more dense forest. The last section, six miles south, produced 3 beeches, 2 hickories, 1 cherry, and 3 sugar trees (27, 30 and 38 inches in diameter, respectively). On other boundaries this far south the surveyors recorded sugar and beech and added black walnut (2 measuring 60 inches in diameter) and white walnut (butternut) and several poplar (yellow poplar or tulip tree), the largest 48 inches in diameter, a white ash also 48 inches in diameter, and a red oak 36 inches in diameter. A short haul from the forest at the south side of modern South Bend in the morainal hills at Rum Village and south of Dragoon Trail would have produced ample maple sap for the sugar house. The dense forests of the southeastern part of the county on heavier loam and siltloam soils were similar to those of central Indiana and quite different from those in the northwestern part of St. Joseph County. A sample of thirty-two distances to trees in this forest gave a mean distance of 14.1 ft. and a tree density approximating 220 trees per acre. These and other hardwood forests in southern Michigan offered timber for later industries such as Studebaker wagons and Singer sewing machines that developed in South Bend.

The establishment of the university introduced new forces into the landscape, producing wheat fields, pastures, orchards, and avenues of trees, some evident to the present. The residual areas of forest on the Notre Dame campus are small and unlike those encountered by the surveyors in 1829 or by Father Sorin in 1842. Any area that was not cleared, grazed, burned, or built on began the inexorable process of succession because of seed germination and growth of trees either of the original species in the area or of new species introduced during decades of disturbance. The smallest of three areas of old forest is on the west shore of St. Joseph's Lake rising to the road leading to St. Joseph Hall in the original section 36 granted to Father Sorin. There are paths leading to Stations of the Cross but the sizes of the larger trees, which are forest grown, suggest considerable age. Two black oaks that stood at the upper edge of this stand were cut in 1987. The annual ring counts of these stumps dated their origins to approximately 1841 and 1847, respectively. A white oak in the same area, also cut in 1987, dated to about 1836. The second largest area of residual old-growth forest is immediately north of the Loftus Center in Section 31. An open-grown white oak near the west edge indicated that the modern remnant began in a relatively open area. Ring counts of larger white oaks made in 1970 by Clark W. Ashby, of Southern Illinois University, date the oldest of these trees to 1852 and recruitment continued through the 1850s to 1910 suggesting that it was not cleared during that interval although there are a few large oak stumps. This area is shown as forest in a map drawn in 1902 of the university's farmlands. The largest trees in the forest are black oaks but their ages are not known. The modern forest remains principally oak (black 27%, white 20%) with an understory largely of red maple and black cherry, which were not frequently recorded in the area by the surveyors in 1829. The average distance to trees was 17.1 ft. or a density of about 150 trees per acre.

The largest remaining forested area containing older trees, nearly 10 acres, is at the corner of Douglas Road and the road to Married Student Housing in the SW quarter of section 25. The map of the university farms in 1902 shows the area as pasture and it is likely that the area, even as forest, was grazed, which is the fate of most forests associated with farms. Nevertheless, the present stand is the most diverse including large red, white, and black oaks (3 to 3.5 ft. diam.), hickories, ash, and some fair-sized maple trees all of unknown age but clearly constituting the oldest and best stand of forest dating to the origins of the university.

The historical context of the University of Notre Dame was a landscape traversed by multiple glaciations, subjected to different climates, covered by varied vegetations, grazed by herds of long extinct animals, and hunted for millennia by peoples eventually misnamed Indians by European invaders. In one sense, they were not entirely wrong since the Indians of the seventeenth century were descendants of Asian people, if not of the Indies as envisioned by the hopeful early explorers. The vagaries of postglacial climate and human occupancy formed the immediate mix of oak forest, oak savannah, and prairie in which Notre Dame was founded. As late as the 1960s a few lonely plants of familiar prairie species, whole-leafed rosin weed and prairie dock, were collected from the north shore of St. Joseph's Lake by Father Hebert who inspired this volume. The remnant stands of oak forest are a more conspicuous legacy for the Sesquicentennial of the University of Notre Dame du Lac.

## BIBLIOGRAPHY

### History of Notre Dame

Beirne, K., C.S.C. 1966. *From Sea to Shining Sea: The Holy Cross Brothers in the United States.* Valatie, N.Y.: Holy Cross Press.

Hope, A. J., C.S.C. 1948. *Notre Dame: One Hundred Years.* Rev. ed. University of Notre Dame Press.

Lyons, J. A., ed. 1869. *Silver Jubilee of the University of Notre Dame, June 23rd, 1869.* Chicago: E. B. Myers.

McAvoy, T. T. undated. Manuscript PNDPIOL0-2, Archives, University of Notre Dame.

McAvoy, T. T. 1933. "Father Badin Comes to Notre Dame." *Indiana Magazine of History* 29:7-16.

Schlereth, T. J. 1977. *The University of Notre Dame: A Portrait of Its History and Campus.* University of Notre Dame Press.

Sorin, E., C.S.C. 1895. "Chronicles of Notre Dame Du Lac from the Year 1841." Trans. J. M. Toohey, C.S.C. Mss. Archives, University of Notre Dame. Now published as *Chronicles of Notre Dame du Lac.* Ed. and annotated by James T. Connelly, C.S.C. University of Notre Dame Press, 1992.

Wack, J. T. 1967. "The University of Notre Dame Du Lac: Foundation, 1842–1857." Ph.D. Dissertation, University of Notre Dame.

### General Regional History and Description

Bartlett, C. H., and R. H. Lyon. 1899. *La Salle in the Valley of the St. Joseph.* South Bend, Ind.: Tribune Printing.

Charlevoix, P. 1844. *Journal d'un voyage, fait par adre du roi dans l'Amerique Septentrionale.* Paris: Chez Rollin Fils.

Clifton, J. 1984. *The Pokagons, 1863-1983.* Lanham, Md.: University Press of America.

Hennepin, L. 1683. *A Description of Louisiana.* Trans. J. G. Shea. 1880; New York: John G. Shea.

Howard, T. E. 1907. *A History of St. Joseph County, Indiana.* Vol. 1. Chicago: Lewis Publishing.

Lindsey, A. A., ed. 1966. *Natural Features of Indiana.* Indianapolis: Indiana Academy of Science, Indiana State Library.

McKee, I. 1941. *The Trail of Death: Letters of Benjamin Marie Petit.* Indianapolis: Indiana Historical Society.

Peckham, H. H. 1978. *Indiana: A Bicentennial History.* New York: W. W. Norton.

Schurr, M. R. 1991. "Exploring the Foundations of Notre Dame: The 1991 Archaeological Field School Investigations at the Old College Site (12SJ228), Saint Joseph County, Indiana."

Taylor, R. M., Jr., E. W. Stevens, M. A. Ponder, and P. Brockman. 1989. *Indiana: A New Historical Guide.* Indianapolis: Indiana State Historical Society.

## Surveyors Records and Studies of Vegetation

Anderson, R. C. 1991. "Illinois Prairies: A Historical Perspective." *Illinois Natural History Survey Bulletin* 34:384–391.

Archives, State Library, Indianapolis. General Land Office Survey Records for Indiana, 1799–1834. Vols. 1–8.

Bourdo, E. A. 1956. "A Review of the General Land Office Survey and of Its Use in Quantitative Studies of Former Forests." *Ecology* 37:754–768.

Deam, C. H. 1918. *Trees of Indiana*. Bulletin No. 3. Indianapolis: State Board of Forestry of Indiana.

Finley, D., and J. E. Potzger. 1952. "Characteristics of the Original Vegetation in Some Prairie Counties of Indiana." *Butler University Botanical Studies* 10:114–118.

Hicks, D. J., and M. Yoder. 1987. "Original Vegetation and Contemporary Landscape Patterns in Southern Elkhart County." *Proceedings of the Indiana Academy of Science* 97:244.

Homoya, M. A., D. B. Abrell, J. R. Aldrich, and T. W. Post. 1984. "The Natural Regions of Indiana." *Proceedings of the Indiana Academy of Science* 94:245–287.

Kapp, R. O., D. L. Cleary, G. G. Snyder, and D. C. Fisher. 1990. "Vegetational and Climatic History of the Crystal Lake Area and the Eldridge Mastadon Site, Montcalm County, Michigan." *American Midland Naturalist* 123:47–63.

Lindsey, A. A. 1961. "Vegetation of the Drainage-aeration Classes of Northern Indiana Soils in 1830." *Ecology* 42:432–436.

Lindsey, A. A., W. B. Crankshaw, and S. A. Qadir. 1965. "Soil Relations and Distribution Map of the Vegetation of Presettlement Indiana." *Botanical Gazette* 126:155–163.

Potzger, J. E., M. E. Potzger, and J. McCormick. 1956. "The Forest Primeval of Indiana as Recorded in the Original U.S. Land Surveys and an Evaluation of Previous Interpretations of Indiana Vegetation." *Butler University Botanical Studies* 13:95–111.

Rohr, F. W., and J. E. Potzger. 1951. "Forest and Prairie in Three Northwestern Indiana Counties." *Butler University Botanical Studies* 10:61–70.

Spurr, S. H. 1951. "George Washington, Surveyor and Ecological Observer." *Ecology* 32:544–549.

Transeau, E. N. 1935. "The Prairie Peninsula." *Ecology* 16:423–437.

# A Place, Its Plantsmen,
# and Its Plants

Thomas J. Schlereth

"On the 28 of August last year the spot where the University and all the surrounding buildings now stand," reported M. R. Keegan to the readers of Philadelphia's *Catholic Herald* in 1844, "was a complete wilderness." In the hyperbole typical of nineteenth-century American journalism, Keegan, the *Herald's* Midwest correspondent, went on to describe the changes that the founders of Notre Dame had initiated on their recently acquired (1842) northern Indiana 524-acre land parcel: "The surrounding forest resounds with the echoes of the ax, saw, and anvil . . . . What a change in seventeen months. Out of several hundred acres of which the farm consists, one hundred and forty are cleared, grubbed, ploughed, and ninety-six are now in wheat; a spacious college of four stories, seven workshops for mechanical trades, a novitiate (two stories) erected. The face of the whole country changed, the savage wilderness giving place in the short space of time to civilization."

Keegan's dispatch, its obvious bravado notwithstanding, reveals several things about the early landscape of the University of Notre Dame: it was relatively isolated, wooded, multifunctional, and, to a certain extent, a planned environment. Such features characterized numerous American nineteenth-century denominational college campuses. In fact, the American campus, by the 1840s, had become a unique type of space. While indebted to the Campus Martius of ancient Rome for its name and often influenced by the Gothic quadrangles of medieval Britain for its design, the American university, particularly as it evolved in the nineteenth century, developed a new landscape. This space was usually pastoral, sometimes in a deliberately segregated rural location; it often began with a single "Main Building" from which other structures followed; it had residential quarters for students and faculty, frequently possessed some overall site design; and it had a penchant for traditional architecture. It usually included formal and informal arrangements of trees, shrubs, and herbaceous plants on its grounds. In the words of architect Robert Stern: "American campus—ideal, independent villages, socially and culturally coherent communities for learning and research—are among the greatest dream places of our civilization and a distinctly American invention."

Notre Dame's campus, from its origins, shared in this American tradition of landscape and architectural history. It also bears the influence of French planning and planting practices, plus the imprint of a century and a half of surveyors, botanists, gardeners, arborists, and plantsmen. These individuals, many of whom go unnoticed in most of the University's published histories, continually manipulated and maintained, uprooted and replanted, designed and redesigned the Notre Dame site, altering it from an environment of oak-opening forest (described by Robert McIntosh above) to one which now possesses less than a twentieth of its early nineteenth-century natural vegetation.

Notre Dame, *ca.* 1848, showing (l. to r.) first Sacred Heart Church, first Main Building, and (foreground) Manual Labor Training School, porter's lodge, and entrance road. Courtesy University of Notre Dame Archives [UNDA].

This change of place took place most dramatically and most frequently at two places: at the campus's immediate center and on its ever-widening perimeters. This evolution of landscape philosophy and practice proceeded in four overlapping stages that can be summarized as: (1) a college yard including an intimate *cour d'honneur*; (2) a campus mall with a Victorian arboretum and a grand avenue; (3) a Collegiate-Gothic campus featuring quadrangles combining residential and academic structures; and, finally, (4) a public university complex of functionally zoned activities.

*First Planners and Landscapers*

The preference of American college founders for a country (as opposed to a city) setting for their institutions began with Thomas Jefferson's influential designs (1817–1826) for the University of Virginia. Jefferson conceived of the American campus as a pastoral "academic village," a rural retreat removed from the turmoil and temptations of city life.

Notre Dame's founder and first president, Edward Frederick Sorin, C.S.C. (1814–1893) had no choice but to start his school in rural Indiana. In 1842 he and his religious community, the *Congregatio a Sancta Cruce* or Congregation of the Holy Cross (C.S.C.) that had been founded in 1837 by Reverend Basil Anthony Moreau in Le Mans, France, were given 524 acres of largely wooded land in St. Joseph County, Indiana, by the Bishop of Vincennes. In return for this property, Sorin and his colleagues agreed to reopen the area's Catholic mission station that had been sporadically manned by French clerics beginning in 1686; establish a novitiate for Holy Cross brothers who would teach in the bishop's diocesan schools; and to build a college. Two campus structures—the "Old" College built in 1843 and a log chapel/cabin reconstructed in 1906 to represent the missioner's dwelling Sorin found when he first arrived on the site in November 1842—survive as artifacts of Notre Dame's frontier existence in those first years. A squat, two-story structure (later expanded to four stories), the Old College housed classrooms, a student dormitory, refectory, a dormitory for faculty (brothers), a recreation room, and a kitchen.

The Old College served as Notre

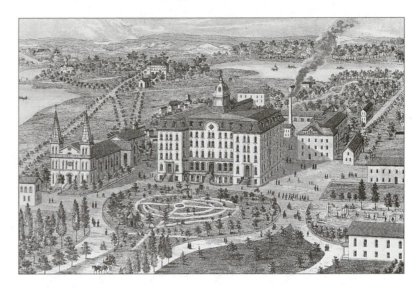

Notre Dame, *ca.* 1866, bird's-eye-view illustrating (l. to r.) Sacred Heart Church, Main Building II (constructed 1864–66), infirmary, exhibition and recreation halls, and (center) the *cour d'honneur* garden park. Courtesy UNDA.

Notre Dame, *ca.* 1888, university catalogue engraving depicting, with minor spatial distortions, the campus mall and its principal structures (l. to r.) Sorin Hall (projected design), Sacred Heart Church II (constructed 1871-88), Main Building III (constructed 1879-88), Washington Hall, and Science Hall (now La Fortune Student Center). Courtesy UNDA.

Dame's first Main Building. If it had continued as such, the campus would possibly have developed in quite a different direction. The university might have been more closely clustered around one or both of its two lakes, a design scheme appropriate to its incorporated (1844) title as the University of Notre Dame du Lac. Instead, the university's Council of Administration decided, in the early summer of 1843, to depart the lake site and locate its main campus on a north-south axis with the lakes at its flank rather than its front. Over the next century, houses of religious formation such as seminaries and novitiates were built around both St. Mary's and St. Joseph's lakes, but no major university structures were constructed. What did occur was that the university's principal buildings took their spatial orientation from the land rather than from the lakes.

While the academic and cultural activities of the university developed elsewhere, agricultural and industrial Notre Dame centered around the original founding landscape. Rich marl deposits west of this site yielded raw materials for brick production, which began as early as 1843. A year later lime kilns were also in operation. Until the early 1880s the university kilns produced the lime (vital for plaster, mortar, and as fertilizer) and the distinctive yellow-buff "Notre Dame brick" (by 1858 one-half million were produced annually for sale) used in all Notre Dame's buildings erected during that period. The first university farm expanded east and south from the Old College and the Log Chapel, which were eventually surrounded by a complex of agricultural structures that grew from a half dozen in the 1860s to over twenty by the 1890s.

University Farms, 1865–88, engraved view showing six buildings surrounding the Old College farmstead (center foreground) and appropriate livestock grazing in split-railed pastures. Courtesy UNDA.

Behind the Old College was an ice house, farther up the hill a slaughter house and a huge pigsty. A large cow barn, several animal sheds, and a three-story (80' × 40') hay barn occupied the present site of Howard and Morrissey Halls. Adjacent to the Old College and just beyond the Founders' Monument were a horse shed and implement barn. Where the Architecture Building now stands was a large wagon shed, tool house, another stable, and a windmill, and beyond that stood a wheat granary and corncribs. East of the corncribs was the Manual Labor and Industrial School complex (a vocational school that taught eight trades, including farming, to boys serving apprenticeships from age twelve to twenty-one). The university bakery, with its adjoining storage buildings for wood, coal, and grain, completed this lakeside landscape.

In addition to its heavily utilitarian land use (grain crops, feed lots, pasturage, vegetable fields), the university plotted a more formal landscape around its first Main Building. An early student left a diary account of how this area looked in 1846: "The yard in front of the college contained about half an acre, with here and there a fine oak, while thence on to South Bend was a dense forest. . . . The front yard fence was flanked by two small one-story cottages, one occupied by Mr. Stever as a little general store; the other by the good old porter, Brother Cyprian, who was the shoemaker of the community. Southwest of the college, stood the Manual Labor establishment, having a tailor shop under the care of Brother Augustus and a printing office under Brother Joseph. . . . Still a little further back stood the carpenter shop, a log building under Brother William. To the east of it stood the blacksmith shop and the gardener's house."

Brother Peter Fitzpatrick, C.S.C., with surveying equipment. Courtesy UNDA.

Edward Sorin, president of Notre Dame, and Brother Peter Fitzpatrick, C.S.C. , Professor of Astronomy and Civil Engineering, were the principal creators of this landscape. Sorin, who admired European planning schemes that used long *alleés* to enliven a structure's visual interest and public symbolism, envisioned in the 1840s a tree-lined "Grand Avenue" leading to his Main Building. Brother Peter, who also taught surveying, platted this boulevard as a vertical axis connecting the university and the outskirts of the neighboring communities of Lowell and South Bend. In his correspondence with the I. M. Thorton Nursery in New York in 1859, Sorin hoped to parallel both sides of Notre Dame's Avenue with "a stately, straight range of white cedars" in order to create an evergreen entrance to the university. He ultimately settled, however, for a hardwood corridor, first of red oak, then sugar maples. At the north terminus of his French boulevard, Sorin had Fitzpatrick build a white picket fence in order to enclose a college yard. The yard was expanded (approximately an acre) when the university built a second Main Building at the site of its first college. At the south end of the yard one found the university's porter's lodge and its federal post office secured through the efforts of Senator Henry Clay in 1851. Within the college yard were two circular structures—a Victorian gazebo and the university's first observatory. Formal and naturalistic plantings of trees (for example, sycamore and catalpa) and shrubs (for example, spiraea and hydrangea) could likewise be found here, along with cast-iron fountains and flower urns. Shrub and tree "thickets" combining a variety of plant species and forms also figured in this mid-century environment. Tall pyramidal and conical trees such as cedar and spruce were placed in the center or rear of the thicket with smaller shrubs such as lilac or mock orange surrounding them.

In the decade after its erection, Main Building II's south landscape took on more space and symbolism. The idea of a campus yard yielded to one of *cour d'honneur*, a small park setting inspired by French landscape practice. The planting pattern within the *cour d'honneur* resembled the Divine Heart, the *Sacre-Coeur*, a religious symbol prominent in the devotional practice of nineteenth-century French Catholicism and an emblem adopted by the Holy Cross community. The Sacred Heart was also the patron of the university's main church. In 1893, a statue of the Sacred Heart of Jesus by Robert Cassiani was placed in the heart of the heart-garden.

The plants in the college yard's heart garden served as a "botanical garden" for Celestine Basile Carrier, C.S.C., and his biology classes. *The Scholastic*, the university's weekly magazine begun in 1865, reported in the spring of 1873 that Carrier periodically revamped its format and contents. A frequent traveller abroad, Carrier often returned to Notre Dame with seeds and plants, particularly from France.

Published guides to the university in 1858 and 1865 note (but unfortunately do not describe in detail) the Botanical Garden. They allude to numerous other flower gardens connected with the houses of religious formation encircling the western shores of St. Mary's and St. Joseph's lakes. The most elaborate formal garden of this type was located between the two lakes in front of St. Joseph's Novitiate and the Our Lady of the Angels chapel. Before it was drained and filled, this lowland between the lakes frequently flooded, thereby creating an "Island" (really a peninsula), which the Holy Cross community saw as a natural cloister for religious contemplation. Here, in a formal garden with serpentine walks, statuary, and parterre arrangements of rose beds, they erected a shrine to the Blessed Virgin patterned after the Portiuncula established by St. Francis at Assisi.

*Brother Philip Neri Kunze, C.S.C., Horticulturist (1844–1929)*

Brother Philip Kunze, C.S.C., Professor of German, chief landscaper and custodian of campus grounds and gardens, 1870–1926. Courtesy UNDA.

In 1861 seventeen-year-old Robert Kunze, a native of Silesia, spent his novitiate as a Holy Cross brother on the "Island" in St. Joseph's Hall. After teaching in the Holy Cross parochial schools in Cincinnati, he joined the Notre Dame faculty as a professor of German. A talented calligrapher whose work in German and English script was widely published, he also taught penmanship in the university's preparatory (high school) department. Although deft with pen, Kunze's greatest forte was with plants. His enormous impact on Notre Dame came not in its classrooms but on its landscape. Although nothing in his familial or personal background prepared him for the task, he became in the mid-1870s the campus's chief custodian, landscaper, and plantsman. Fifty years later he was still at work on its grounds and gardens.

During Kunze's long career at Notre Dame, the university assumed a new identity. This change in institutional status was reflected in its treatment of physical space. By the beginning of Kunze's tenure, Notre Dame faculty members and students more frequently spoke of the physical environment around the building compound of Sacred Heart Church, Main Building III (begun in 1879), and the Academy of Music as a campus. This Latinism, invented at colonial Princeton was, by the mid-nineteenth century, becoming the most popular term for American college grounds. The word replaced an earlier usage, the college yard, that had been the enclosed landscape that surrounded earlier Notre Dame Main buildings. By 1890 a different environment had emerged in front of Main Building III. In place of the fenced, cloister-like French *cour d'honneur* of park and botanical garden, we find an open-ended campus mall containing a large arboretum. This mall, with the Main Building at its north end, featured two rows of buildings facing each other across its expanse. It contained a dual carriageway that joined a straight, tree-lined (Notre Dame) avenue leading to South Bend.

This Notre Dame campus plan also had American precedents. Paul Turner, in *Campus: An American Architectural Tradition* (1985), suggests the concept appeared as early as 1795 at the University of North Carolina at Chapel Hill but was never fully executed there. However South Carolina College (now the University of South Carolina) did, suggests Turner, "construct several structures around a

University Mall, 1912, looking south to Notre Dame Avenue with (foreground) specimens of Brother Kunze's yucca collection. Courtesy UNDA.

University Mall, winter 1914, showing the university arboretum's geometrical walkways and formal plantings. Courtesy T. J. Schlereth Collection, UNDA.

pattern that came to be called `the horseshoe,' but which was in effect a mall–two rows of buildings facing one another across a greensward, with the president's house at the center of one end, and the entrance from town at the other end."

A wide mall, often with a main building (or equally important structure such as a library or chapel) at its terminus, became a popular American campus plan. Thomas Jefferson's design for the University of Virginia is but the most famous instance of its application. Others can be found at the University of Alabama at Tuscaloosa, University of Wisconsin at Madison, and Wilberforce University in Ohio.

Notre Dame's mall never came to be called or thought of as such. Two factors may account for this. First the space between the two lines of buildings–those to the east devoted to academic work (Science, Engineering, Business, Law) and those to the west designed for residential life (Sorin, Walsh, Alumni halls)–was never a verdant greensward. Since the 1850s it contained trees and shrubs in both formal and informal plantings. Second, the next type of campus planning that the university would adopt, in the 1920s, involved creating Gothic quadrangles inspired by British university architecture. This "Collegiate Gothic" style influenced the twentieth-century development of the university's north and south quadrangles. As the parlance of South Quad and North Quad became established, it also became common (if technically incorrect) to speak of the space in front of the Main Building as the Main Quad.

Philip Kunze decided to plant the university's mall with every genus and species of tree, shrub, and vine that was indigenous to the North American continent or that would grow in the northern Indiana climate. His particular love was trees. Like Alexander Smith, Kunze believed "a man does not plant a tree for himself; he plants it for posterity." In the arboretum itself, Kunze introduced fifty-three tree species, among them shingle oak (*Quercus imbricaria*), European beech (*Fagus sylvatica*), paper birch (*Betula papyrifera*), Camperdown elm (*Ulmus × vegeta*), Schwedler maple (*Acer platanoides* 'Schwedleri'), and the saucer magnolias (*Magnolia × soulangiana*). As a general scheme he reserved the central spine of the mall for a double row of deciduous trees that he flanked with assorted evergreens planted randomly.

## Parks and Pastures

To the modern eye the Victorian lawn, garden, or park often appears cluttered, excessive, and eclectic. Carpet-beds, plants with large, coarse-textured leaves, exotic, "weeping" tree and shrub forms, plus numerous garden ornaments (deer, stags, dogs, lions, boars, and classical figures), fountains and urns, benches and seats, hitching posts and mounting blocks, lamp posts and birdhouses filled the late nineteenth-century landscape. Notre Dame had two such environments during this period: the campus mall park in front of its 1879 Main Building and a smaller park space in front of its 1882 St. Edward's Hall. Brother Kunze oversaw the horticultural nature and nurture of both.

The most impressive features of the campus mall park were its variety of trees and its curving carriage ways. In the same spirit that Frederick Law Olmsted and other landscape architects created huge pleasure parks for American cities such as New York's Central Park, Chicago's Lincoln Park, or San Francisco's Golden Gate Park, Brother Kunze landscaped, on a much smaller scale, Notre Dame's most public space. At its formal entrance was erected, in 1906, a statue of Edward Sorin, the institution's first campus planner. A dual carriageway wound its way through the park's trees, past university buildings devoted to engineering, science, and music. Stopping at the steps of the Main Building one could survey the garden park at its horticultural height: urns planted with geraniums and snapdragons; carpet-beds executed with patterns of marigolds, verbenas, centauria, and dwarf cannas. Two large fountains flanked the statue

St. Edward's Park, *ca.* 1890. Courtesy UNDA.

of the Sacred Heart. Centerstage was Brother Kunze's prize yucca-plant collection, two hundred of which were exhibited at the St. Louis World's Fair in 1904. Even in winter photographers thought the mall worthy of attention.

In St. Edward's Park, Kunze crafted a cameo Victorian landscape. In a miniature (400 ft. × 100 ft) space for the Minim students, he designed another heart-shaped garden, complete with a statue of St. Edward, flower urns, water fountains, several large, raised floral displays defined in plantings of echeveria, alternanthera, pyrethrum, and ageratum, including two spelling out "Ave Maria" and "St. Edward's Park." When a playhall was added to the combination grade school, dormitory, library, chapel, and music hall that was St. Edward's Hall, Brother Kunze, in turn, added an oval of deciduous trees to grace the playhall's southern exposure.

As Brother Kunze transformed Notre Dame's ornamental horticultural displays, another Holy Cross confrere, Brother Leo Donovan, introduced new agricultural practices to the university's farms. At the turn of the century most of the Notre Dame farm buildings, formerly located east of the Old College, came to be concentrated in the southwestern corner of the present South Quad as well as a larger tract (St. Joseph's Farm in Granger, Indiana) eight miles northeast of the campus. The Brothers of Holy Cross staffed these various university farms that, at their greatest

Brother Leo Donovan, C.S.C. and one ("Champ") of his prized Belgian draft horses. Courtesy UNDA.

University Farms, *ca.* 1900, seen from northeast with Manual Labor Training School Building (lower right, now Badin Hall) and other farm structures: residences for brothers and hired men, the university horse and dairy barns, circular swine barn, hennery, and several grain-storage buildings. Courtesy UNDA.

extent, covered over 3,500 acres and produced everything from peat for fireplaces to tobacco for faculty cigars.

The Notre Dame farm consisted of approximately 1,100 acres that in 1900 practically ringed the campus on all sides. By that date most farm buildings were located on a site now occupied by Fisher and Pangborn Halls, the South Dining Hall, and the current ninth, tenth, and eleventh holes of the W. J. Burke Memorial Golf Course. The farm complex included several farmhouses for the brothers and hired hands, the university horse barn and livery, a dairy barn with a large Holstein herd, a circular barn and surrounding sties for raising over 700 Hampshire hogs, a hennery, and several grain-storage buildings. Fields of corn, alfalfa, and wheat stretched beyond these structures to the South Bend city limits.

When Brother Donovan took over as director of the farm in 1900, this land's fertility was practically exhausted due to a lack of knowledge of the benefits of rotating crops, planting legumes, or using fertilizers. Donovan, a local Lakeville farmer before joining the brothers' community in 1897, eventually persuaded John Zahm, the Holy Cross Provincial, to permit him to take courses at the Universities of Iowa and Illinois in order to find a solution to the farm's declining productivity. After learning new agricultural techniques, which he coupled with his own experimentation, he began to apply manure, limestone, and huge amounts of rock phosphate (twelve freight carloads went on the present golf course) to his fields. Yields increased tremendously. A thirty-acre field (formerly extending south of the present Law Building) produced 300 bushels of potatoes before Donovan's experiments and 8,200 bushels after he fertilized it. A record for wheat productivity in the state was set in 1918 when the harvest yielded 6,000 bushels per 200-acre plot.

Brother Donovan, who supervised the Notre Dame farms from 1900 to 1940, also excelled in breeding livestock. By 1910 he had introduced hog and cattle feedlots to the campus. His increased corn yields enabled him to feed beef cattle, which, in turn, produced manure for his fields. In 1912 he first took his beef to the International Stock Show in Chicago, winning first prize for the best grain-fed cattle in the Hereford class. For the next thirty-five years he exhibited prime beef, Hampshire hogs, and Belgian stock horses at state fairs and stock shows. Named Indiana State Champion Feeder in 1937, he supplied and slaughtered (in structures formerly behind Moreau Seminary) all the beef and pork for the university kitchens and shipped the surplus to the Chicago stockyards.

Donovan became such an expert on cattle breeding and Indiana soils that he was invited to lecture at agricultural institutes and schools as well as contribute to agricultural journals. He was a major force behind Notre Dame's establishment of an agricultural school in 1917.

The first Catholic university to offer two-year and four-year degrees in agriculture, Notre Dame's program was expanded in 1919 to award a bachelor of science in seven agricultural areas. Although the "Aggie" school never reached its anticipated 300-student enrollment, it did continue in a modified form until it was discontinued in 1932.

As demands for other uses of university land increased in the late 1920s, the farms were moved from the South Quad to land along Bulla Road and then entirely to Granger, Indiana, where the brothers' community still operates a 1,900-acre farm on land purchased by Edward Sorin in 1867.

Rev. Julius Nieuwland, C.S.C., Professor of Botany, Biology, and Chemistry, founder (1909) of the *American Midland Naturalist* and collector of Notre Dame's Nieuwland Herbarium. Courtesy UNDA.

## Botany at Notre Dame

Robert Kunze never taught any of the life sciences at the university although he was qualified to teach ornamental horticulture and, quite probably, arboriculture and general botany. Others, however, did; formal instruction in plant science began in 1844, two years after the university's founding. Early minutes of the Council of Professors record that Brother Augustine, C.S.C., was appointed to teach botany and zoology. Thereafter laymen such as J. E. Tallon, M.D., and clerics, such as Civil War chaplain Louis Neyron, taught botany, medicine, chemistry, and anatomy. By 1864, the sciences organized into a formal Scientific Department wherein Thomas L. Vagnier, C.S.C., taught the botany course. The university's College of Science dates its origin from this date.

Several Holy Cross priests, including Celestine Basile Carrier, C.S.C. (1832-1904), John Augustine Zahm, C.S.C. (1851-1921), and Alexander Marion Kirsch, C.S.C. (1855-1923), pursued or encouraged botanical studies within the College: Carrier as the creator of the university's first Botanical Garden, Zahm as director of the Science Department and its museum and the planner and builder of its first campus building (presently La Fortune Student Center), and Kirsch as the university's first professor of biology (the term biology appears for the first time in the university's academic Bulletin for the school year 1894-95 as Kirsch's scholarly specialty). Several of these scientists, Carrier (Master of Arts and Licentiate in Science) and Kirsch (Louvain, Belgium), for example, were either European-trained or the sons (Zahm) of northern European immigrant parents. The Old World leadership of the College continued under both its most famous early twentieth-century scientist, Julius Arthur Nieuwland, C.S.C. (1878-1936), born in Hansbeke, Belgium, and Francis Joseph Wenninger, C.S.C. (1888–1940), born at Pamhagen, Austria, its dean from 1923 to 1940.

In 1904 Julius Nieuwland became professor of botany in the College, a position he held until 1921 when he joined the chemistry faculty. While it was in this latter role that Nieuwland became famous for his pioneering research in acetylene chemistry and the development of synthetic rubber, he maintained a life-long interest in natural history and botany. Nieuwland took his doctorate in chemistry at Catholic University in Washington, D.C., in 1904 but, as M. W. Lyon notes in *Father Nieuwland the Botanist* (1937), wished he had specialized in botany.

During his doctoral studies, Nieuwland came under the influence of Edward Lee Greene (1843-1915) who, at the turn of the century, was a major force in western plant taxonomy. Robert McIntosh's biography of Greene, in the 1983 publication of Greene's *Landmarks of Botanical History*, also recognizes him as "the premier student of the history of botany." Nieuwland was influential in recruiting Greene to the Notre Dame faculty late in 1914. Greene transferred his entire botanical library and herbarium to the university. Unfortunately his career at Notre Dame ended with his death the following November. He is buried in the Holy Cross cemetery in the lay "Faculty Row," a stone's throw from the grave of Nieuwland, his student and supporter. There James Burns, C.S.C., the Holy Cross Provincial at the time of Greene's death, erected a monument with an inscription selected from the botanist's own description of a colleague:

Edward Lee Greene. Courtesy UNDA.

> A man whom nature in all her phases attracted and engaged and
> for whom she opened a door leading unto the house of God.

Nieuwland, at the suggestion of Greene, founded the *Midland Naturalist* in 1909, later (with the fifth issue of Volume 1) renamed the *American Midland Naturalist*. Nieuwland, notes McIntosh, a later editor of the scholarly publication and writing "Life History of a Journal" (Vol. 123:5), was principally "interested in taxonomy of vascular plants and assembled a considerable herbarium, largely of midwestern plants. Many of these he collected, others were purchased at 10 cents per specimen or by swapping the equivalent in issues of the *American Midland Naturalist*. Nieuwland also studied morphology of lower plants, particularly algae, and organography of higher plants. By means of a substantial business, making and selling botanical slides, he secured funds for purchase of natural history books. Some of the rare classical publications of the early American naturalists, C. S. Rafinesque and J. E. LeConte, were reprinted and offered for sale in the early volumes of the journal."

Notre Dame's Nieuwland Herbarium continues to grow in numbers of specimens, particularly in its Midwest holdings. As required by the conventions of botany, scientists must deposit "voucher specimens" in official repositories as proof of research that has been carried out or to document geographic range extensions. For example, this latter information is in the form of "new county records" for the official Flora of Indiana. Notre Dame's Nieuwland Herbarium is one of Indiana's three official repositories for such records.

Since scientists also deposit voucher specimens documenting their research projects on other state or region's flora, a collection such as the Nieuwland also assists later researchers. For instance, in their ongoing *Michigan Flora* project at the University of Michigan, Edward Voss and his colleagues at the University of Michigan have made extensive use of Notre Dame's herbarium specimens that were collected in areas of the Upper Peninsula and southwestern lower Michigan, amassed by Nieuwland and others such as Peter Hebert, C.S.C. The Voss research will result in a three-volume publication of which two volumes are complete.

Nieuwland's botanical collecting had several nineteenth-century precedents at Notre Dame. The President of the French Institute, sent the first major botanical collection of European plants to the university. Reverend S. Barthos, a missionary, donated valuable New Zealand specimens, particularly ferns. As noted earlier, Fathers Carrier (who also collected in Canada) and Kirsch augmented the North American collections such that by 1877 the first herbarium contained between 4,000 and 5,000 specimens.

Unfortunately this collection, housed as it was in the university's Main Building Museum, was destroyed when that structure and four other university buildings burnt to the ground in a disastrous campus fire on April 23, 1879. Carrier, by then a professor of natural sciences at a Holy Cross sister institution, the College St. Laurent, Montreal, Canada, renewed his collecting of Canadian specimens for Notre Dame. His work received an award (a diploma of merit) at the Chicago Columbian Exposition (where university herbarium specimens were also displayed as part of Notre Dame's collegiate exhibition) in 1893. A year before Carrier received similar recognition for his Canadian collection at the Provincial Exhibition of Montreal. The bulk of both collections eventually came to Notre Dame.

Kirsch also began recollecting specimens of plant material lost in the Great Fire; he took particular interest in tropical woods and fruits. Nieuwland, when he returned from his graduate studies in 1904, made the herbarium his passion. Even after he became a professor of organic chemistry in 1918, he continued collecting especially in the summers when he taught summer courses in botany. The Nieuwland collection presently contains approximately 200,000 specimens. Nieuwland's most spectacular collecting coup, however, was securing the private herbarium of E. L. Greene, and that botanist's library for Notre Dame. The gift was brought about through Nieuwland's personal and professional friendship with Greene. The Greene library, containing several pre-Linnaean works in botany, was a superb reference resource for scientific research in the history of the discipline. The Greene Herbarium, although smaller (65,000 specimens) than the Nieuwland, was no less significant since it represented a major collection of western North American plants.

Greene, a prolific botanist who had been an Episcopalian minister and missionary in the American West (1885-1895) and who had been awarded an honorary doctorate of law degree from Notre Dame (1894), described as new to science or recombined and redefined from earlier workers' findings over 4,500 plant species. The Greene collection contains most of the actual plant specimens he used to carry out this work. As the original specimens, called "type" specimens, these are very important to current researchers studying western American botany. (Scientists must refer to the original specimens to verify their own interpretations of the early written plant descriptions). The Greene collection has yet another unique feature. It was the first herbarium in North America to computerize the information contained on its mounted specimens and their labels. The information was computerized in 1969-1971 with the financial support of the National Science Foundation and served as a pilot project for the botanical community and set standards for many other North American herbarium computerization projects.

*Father Peter Hebert (1886-1974): Self-Taught Notre Dame Naturalist*

Notre Dame's Greene-Nieuwland Herbarium presently contains approximately 265,000 specimens, making it the second largest herbarium in the state after Indiana University's in Bloomington. Peter Hebert, C.S.C., contributed numerous specimens to the collection over a fifty-year collecting career focused mainly in Michigan and Indiana. In the estimate of Clifton Keller, previously a botanist at Andrews University who received his doctorate in botany at Notre Dame, Hebert's collection "represents a nearly if not complete record of native plants to be found in St. Joseph County, Indiana, and Berrien County, Michigan." Hebert's collection numbered over 6,000 specimens, representing 5,484 species in 711 genera.

As other Notre Dame naturalists before him, Hebert contributed to the campus flora, particularly wild flowers and aquatic plants. "Into vacant spots around Notre Dame's campus," notes Keller, "he planted not only to beautify but to have close at hand plants he wanted to study." For example, he introduced the water lily, *Nelumbo lutea*, to St. Mary's Lake and planted a Kentucky coffeetree (*Gymnocladus dioica*) outside his room near the northwest corner of Corby Hall.

Rev. Peter Hebert, C.S.C., *ca.* 1930, Professor of Greek and Latin, on a "botanizing" walk around the Notre Dame lakes. Courtesy UNDA.

Rev. Peter Hebert, C.S.C., author of the first catalogue (1966) of *Trees, Shrubs, and Vines on the Notre Dame Campus*. Courtesy of the Herbarium.

An eccentric whose friends included the Irish author Shawn Leslie and South Bend capitalist Joseph Oliver (both of whom he took "botanizing" among Michigan's bogs and dunes), he also published research in the *American Midland Naturalist*, attempted to get the university to endow a professorship in botany, and compiled the first edition (1966) of *Trees, Shrubs, and Vines on the Notre Dame Campus*.

Hebert's family background, in part, prepared him for his avocational life as an amateur naturalist. Born January 24, 1886, on a farm near Pinnebog not far from Bad Axe in the extreme northern thumb of Michigan, Peter was one of twelve children of a French-Canadian couple who had moved to Michigan. In sparsely populated Huron county, Hebert, along with his father and his brother, Alfred, spent a childhood in the woods–hunting geese and ducks, trapping fox and rabbits. Hebert later recalled his father had predetermined outdoor careers for both him and his brother; Alfred would be a commercial fisherman, Peter was to take over the family farm. Before assuming either of these occupations, the elder Hebert also decided that both sons would be educated. He sent both to Notre Dame in 1901 where, although neither ever lost his love of lake and land, both ultimately became fishers of men.

Anticipating returning to his father's farm, Peter, age fifteen, enrolled in the university's Manual Labor School. By 1905, however, Hebert felt he should become a priest; that year he received a novice's habit for the Congregation of Holy Cross priest community. Between 1906 and 1910 he completed a Notre Dame baccalaureate degree as a Holy Cross seminarian. While a collegian, Hebert was a man of words: a member of *The Scholastic's* Board of Editors; an intercollegiate debater (he and Michael A. Mathis defeated Ohio State in a famous 1908 tournament); a frequent contributor of poetry to *The Scholastic's* literary columns. He was selected as one of the three 1910 class graduates to deliver the traditional Bachelors' Orations at his June 13, 1910, commencement. Hebert addressed the assembly on "The Ordinance of God."

On June 26, 1914, Peter Hebert became Father Hebert, a Holy Cross priest, the same year his brother and alter ego, Alfred, was also ordained to the clergy for the Diocese of Detroit. The following September young Hebert began a teaching career which, with the exception of a year (1918-1919) at the University of Portland, had but one location, the University of Notre Dame, and one academic specialty, the Greek and Roman classics. Residing in the priest's quarters of Corby Hall, Hebert taught Latin for the next four decades until he retired from the faculty in 1958.

Although long, Hebert's was not a distinguished academic career. While he headed the university's Classics department for a brief (1931-1939) stint, he wrote a single volume in his field: *Selections From the Latin Fathers* published by Ginn and Company in 1924 as part of their

College Series of Latin Authors. A reprint edition was issued by Caratzas Brothers in 1982. His annotations on the texts taken from Jacques Paul Migne's *Patrologia Latina* (1844-64) were drawn largely from his classroom notes. He based his selections (Tertullian to St. Augustine) on the premise they were "at once representative of their authors and of the period in which they wrote and helpful in developing character in the American college man."

A personable but low-keyed teacher, Hebert's ministry had a similar character. Neither an eloquent preacher, a profound theologian, nor a revered confessor, he was something of a private priest, a quiet man known and loved by a few: Holy Cross confreres such as Cornelius Hagerty, Leo R. Ward, and Julius Nieuwland; faculty friends such as Professor John Cooney (a fellow birdwatcher) and Professor Rufus W. Rauch, (a fellow Latinist), naturalist colleagues such as Frederick J. Hermann, Professor of Botany at the University of Michigan, assorted undergraduate students, and women religious (particularly from Michigan) who pursued advanced degrees in Notre Dame's summer graduate program. The influence of one such Sister, Lucy Marie, O.P. (Marceline Horton), may have prompted Hebert's first serious efforts at "botanizing" which, in turn, led to his becoming the university's best-known amateur naturalist and the compiler of the first systematic listing of its campus flora.

Hebert himself never specifically accounted for his fascination with the natural world. His rural and agrarian boyhood contributed to it, to be sure; so did his early friendship with Julius Nieuwland who provided him with a scientific exemplar to imitate and the taxonomic expertise to do so. Some Hebert biographers, like Fathers Haggerty and Leo R. Ward, attribute his interest in botany to his desire to teach more successfully Virgil and Homer, whose pastoral texts are filled with references to nature. There may have been still another factor. One of Father Hebert's sisters, Adele, had joined a Dominican community of women religious in Grand Rapids, Michigan. She always advised her Dominican sisters to look up her brother when they came to study in Notre Dame's summer graduate school. Hebert proved always the congenial host.

One of these Dominican women, Lucy Marie, O.P. (Marceline Horton), who had studied botany at the University of Michigan, taught at Aquinas College in Grand Rapids, and who came to Notre Dame in the 1920s, may have also contributed to Hebert's avocation. "In the summer of 1923," Sister Evangeline recalled "Father Peter seemed to need something besides his work." Her friend, Sr. Lucy Marie, was at Notre Dame in summer school studying botany. "By some design of Providence," Sr. Evangeline continues, "she [Sr. Lucy] initiated Father into the mysteries of botany. He remarked later that for him that spelled salvation. How much he enjoyed the numerous field trips with Father Nieuwland, Sister, and the other devotees of

God's natural beauty." In a letter Hebert wrote to Frederick Hermann many years later (May 15, 1961) he recalled with much pleasure "botanizing" with Sister Lucy and Father Nieuwland.

Whatever the cause of his conversion to "botanizing," Father Hebert–whom his friend Leo Ward remembered never doing anything half-heartedly be it bidding at bridge or counting sedges– became an ardent naturalist. He followed Nieuwland whenever he went into the field adopting his mentor's book plate motto, *Considerate lilia agri* (John: 1:7), "Consider the lilies of the field, they neither sow nor reap, yet the Heavenly Father cares for them" as his own. He poured over the Greene Herbarium making comparative analyses with specimens he collected in the Midwest. He associated with other Indiana botanists such as Charles Deam, author of *The Trees of Indiana* (1918) and Raymond Friesner, Secretary for the Indiana Academy of Science. Friesner was particularly impressed with Hebert's field methods and herbarium mountings. When adding two of Hebert's sedge collections (*Carex acutiformis* and *C. scabrata*) as new county records to the Indiana flora, Friesner complimented him for "how excellently you make your specimens and do your work."

Two terrains became Hebert's special botanical province: southwestern Michigan (particularly Berrien County) and the University of Notre Dame campus. To those who noticed, he cut something of a campus figure. Usually dressed in long black cassock (plus the Holy Cross community's cape in cold weather) and topped with a three-cornered biretta, and at times clad in galoshes or hip boots, he ventured forth from Corby Hall daily (often twice during March through November) to see what plants or birds he could identify and study. He began his own herbarium (now a part of the Nieuwland Herbarium with his first collections in 1923). At age 85, he was still tramping the Notre Dame lakes in search of new plant material. Father Leo Ward recalled one such lake trek when Hebert "spying something special . . . leaned too far and went splash into the water. Two boys going by pulled him out, and he landed victorious with the plant in his hand."

Two individuals, however, pushed Hebert to share his growing botanical knowledge with others. Each also pressed him into three periods of intense collecting, although he gathered new specimens yearly for his herbarium. Nieuwland the professional nurtured Hebert the amateur during the 1920s and until Nieuwland's death in 1936. In the late 1940s Frederick J. Hermann befriended him because of their mutual interest in aquatic plants and thus began Hebert's longest personal and professional contact with a professional scientist outside of Notre Dame. Hebert, a man with no academic publications or research grants to his name, lobbied continually in the early 1950s to persuade the University Administration to seek funding from the National Science Foundation to support a Notre Dame biology department project that would do a definitive flora of the State of Michigan. Hermann, then at the University of Maryland and the Washington headquarters of the U.S. Department of Agriculture, would head up the research and publication team. He would also occupy a chair of botany at Notre Dame. Unlike Nieuwland who successfully enticed Greene to come to the university in 1914, Hebert could not convince Notre Dame officials to act similarly regarding Hermann. A final scholarly irony resulted when the first volumes of *Michigan Flora*, under the direction of E. G. Voss at the University of Michigan, came to be published based, in part, on the botanical research of both Hermann and Hebert.

Hermann probably deserves credit for Hebert's only scholarly journal article, "New County Records of Sedges in Michigan and Indiana," published in the *American Midland Naturalist* (1956). He and Hermann corresponded frequently, often monthly, trading botanical specimens, citations, and gossip. Hermann had his friend's collections deposited in the National Herbarium. Hebert took Hermann's daughter, a postulant at St. Mary's Holy Cross Sister's novitiate, under his care. The two men also shared another of nature's pleasures, ornithology. Hebert's interest in birds seems to have paralleled his growing intrigue with plants for as early as 1928 he began keeping detailed records of every bird he saw every day. For example, his papers in the University Archives contain a cache of 3×5 cards whereon Hebert recorded his daily entries. Thirty years later he was still keeping tabs on Notre Dame's bird population and its bird watchers. To wit, an excerpt from a letter of January 13, 1959, to Hermann: "A Mrs. Rea of South Bend who conducts bird watching for this county and takes a bird census every year about Christmas time, reports Lapland Longspurs and Myrtle Warblers for Dec. 30. Well–Maybe so. But I have had an eye open for birds in this vicinity since 1928, and I have never seen a longspur at any time, much less myrtle warblers in December. I don't know whether I'm getting incredulous or just getting old! Then too, is a new bird rarer than a new plant?"

*The Hebert Guide: An Intellectual History of a Natural History*

Born in the north woods, Hebert delighted in returning to them often. When possible he did so in the company of his priest brother. "Al," wrote a eulogist, "would drive Peter wherever he wanted to go botanize and he would bring along his shot-gun, rifle, bow and arrow and fishing pole, depending upon the season." Hebert also made botanical forays to Oregon and to a Notre Dame property of 7345 acres including 30 lakes on both sides of the state line between Wisconsin and Michigan's Upper Peninsula in Vilas County (Wisconsin) and Gogebic County (Michigan). Now known as the University of Notre Dame Environmental Research Center (UNDERC), much of this site was donated to the university in the 1940s by Martin Gillen, an enthusiastic supporter of field biology and a benefactor who saw the biological sciences as a key to the longtime preservation and research use of the property. Hebert, like many Holy Cross priests, vacationed at the Gillen estate. Predictably he could not resist botanizing while there. At some time in the early 1960s he made a preliminary survey of the plant material on the property and sent a copy to the university president, Theodore M. Hesburgh, C.S.C.

At Father Hesburgh's suggestion (he apparently sent Hebert a listing of trees and shrubs on the Notre Dame campus done by an unknown source), Hebert also began to prepare a compendium of information (botanical name, common name, site where the plant was growing in 1966) on trees and woody plants that he knew existed within the university's environs. As his main scholarly references, he used Alfred Rehder, *Manual of Cultivated Trees and Shrubs Hardy in North America* (1940); Charles Sprague Sargent, *Manual of the Trees of North America* (1905); Liberty Hyde Bailey, *Manual of Cultivated Plants Commonly Grown in the Continental United States and Canada* (1949); Liberty Hyde Bailey, *The Cultivated Conifers in North America* (1933).

By early summer he had his data in sufficient form to write President Hesburgh on June 29, 1966: "The list of trees and shrubs on our campus to which you referred quite some time ago has never reached me, so I was presumptuous enough to attempt one myself. I have added some woody vines which belong naturally in this category and which I knew you would want included." Hebert went on: "I have indicated briefly, yet definitely enough, where a specimen or specimens of all plants listed can be readily located. Identifications were not always easy," the self-taught taxonomist admitted but, with his typical modesty concluded, "hoping they are right I want to give due thanks for the delights experienced in doing this little job."

In his letter of reply Father Hesburgh praised Hebert's efforts and asked him to talk with two other Holy Cross priests, James McGrath in the Biology department and Jerome J. Wilson, Vice-President for Business Affairs, and the university official in charge of campus buildings and grounds. The impressive number of campus genera prompted Hesburgh to say he was "most interested in seeing the number of these enlarged." The president concluded, in words reminiscent of Brother Philip Neri's original aim for a Notre Dame arboretum: "My main idea is that this campus could be a living botanical garden containing all of the species possible for this climate."

Hesburgh sent Hebert's manuscript to Wilson who wrote (July 26, 1966) Hebert he thought the plant inventory a "truly remarkable job." He agreed to the idea of further collaboration with himself, Father McGrath, and Dr. Earl Savage, a biology faculty member with a specialty in plant pathology, as to future tree and herbaceous plantings on the Notre Dame campus. Wilson sent (July 29, 1966) Hebert's manuscript on to McGrath who, upon receiving it, decided it should have a wider circulation than university administrative circles. He thought it should be published. He spoke to Hebert about the idea. Hebert was skeptical; he considered it only a locational checklist. McGrath persisted, Hebert resisted but eventually agreed–provided he could make revisions. With these completed by July 1967, the volume was "published" by the Notre Dame Biology Department in a mimeograph format and spiral-bound by the Ave Maria Press. The first edition was 100 copies. Now a collector's item, copies of that first printing were largely distributed gratis to university administrators, faculty, and Hebert's friends. Some went to other naturalists and various herbaria. Thereafter subsequent reprintings–the printing work done by McGrath and the printing costs subsidized by the Biology Department–were sold in the Notre Dame Bookstore. I remember buying my copy for $2.00 in 1972, the year I joined the faculty. After a time, the "Hebert guide" (as it was usually called) went out of print. In 1974 its author died of a heart attack, a month after he had celebrated the 60th anniversary of his ordination with a jubilee Mass offered–the liturgical changes of the Second Vatican Council notwithstanding–in Latin.

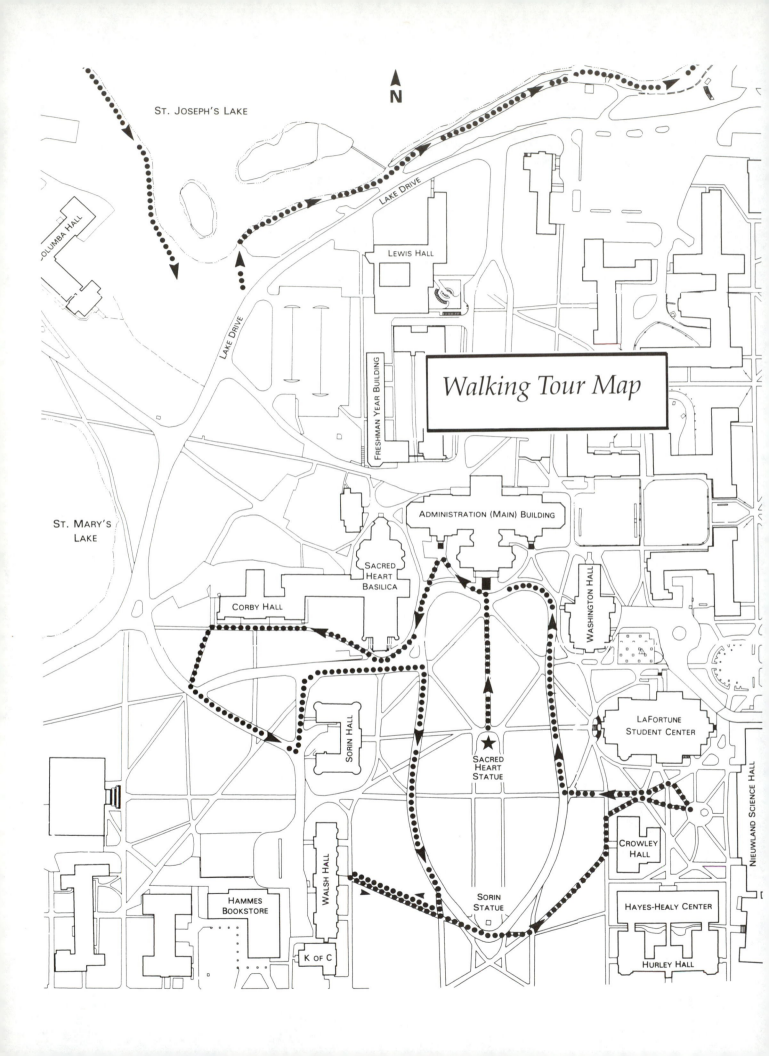

N

ST. JOSEPH'S LAKE

LAKE DRIVE

LAKE DRIVE

COLUMBA HALL

LEWIS HALL

FRESHMAN YEAR BUILDING

*Walking Tour Map*

ST. MARY'S LAKE

ADMINISTRATION (MAIN) BUILDING

SACRED HEART BASILICA

CORBY HALL

WASHINGTON HALL

LaFORTUNE STUDENT CENTER

SORIN HALL

★ SACRED HEART STATUE

CROWLEY HALL

NIEUWLAND SCIENCE HALL

HAMMES BOOKSTORE

WALSH HALL

SORIN STATUE

HAYES-HEALY CENTER

K OF C

HURLEY HALL

# Walking Tour

Barbara J. Hellenthal

The walking tour highlights some of the plants you encounter as you walk around the Main Quad or around St. Joseph's Lake. Other trees and shrubs can be identified through the Site catalogue.

### Main Quad

Begin at the Sacred Heart statue, facing the Sorin statue to the south. Much of the shade along the central walks between the two statues is cast by maple trees, with their familiar open hand-shaped leaves and vivid autumn color. Those of sugar maple (*Acer saccharum*) have smooth-edged lobes, those of red (*A. rubrum*) have teeth along the lobes, and those of Norway (*A. platanoides*) are similar to sugar but exude milky juice when broken and turn color much later in the autumn. On the right (west) of the Sacred Heart statue is a large sugar maple. On the left (east) is a red maple with a

Norway maple

Paper birch

– PLATE I –

Saucer magnolia

Yew

Norway
spruce

Copper beech

young Norway maple just south of it. Norways are not as vivid during autumn.

Also on your left, farther east than the maples, is the distinctive white trunk of a paper birch (*Betula papyrifera*). This tree is the largest of its species known in the state of Indiana. It grows in cool, northern forests. Its normal range just dips into northern Indiana. The cool shade of the Main Quad has allowed it to grow this large here, although it is not thriving. This is the only record-sized tree on the campus.

Turning north to face the Dome, you can see the dark green outlines of many tightly pruned evergreen yews (*Taxus* spp.). They are recognized by their flat, one-inch-long needles. At this end younger plants form a low hedge, while along the sides of the path older plants make an evergreen wall.

A pair of saucer magnolias (*Magnolia* × *soulangiana*) flanks this end of the walk. These magnolias have large, pink, cup-shaped flowers that bloom in late April. The one on the left (west) is a commemorative planting.

Walking toward the Dome along this central walk, you can see two eastern redcedars (*Juniperus virginiana*) among the yews on your left (west). Their short, sharp, silvery needles stand in contrast to the dark green yew needles. Redcedars and other junipers are common throughout the older areas of the campus.

On the east (right) side of the walk stands another evergreen, a tall Norway spruce (*Picea abies*) with its characteristically drooping branches and sharp-tipped needles that are square in cross section (those of yew are flat).

On either side, set farther out from the walk, are copper beeches (*Fagus sylvatica* 'Atropunicea') with smooth, gray bark and coppery red leaves. These trees, magnificent in old age, are popular in the parks of Europe.

Near the end of the path is another pair of saucer magnolias. The eastern (right) tree died and was replaced in 1992 with a large, new, commemorative tree

– PLATE II –

that will grow to fill its space. The view of the Dome with the blooming magnolias in the foreground is one of the most frequently photographed sights on the campus.

From the front steps of the Administration building, follow the wide, curving walkway west, toward Sacred Heart Basilica. You will see more maples in the lawn on your left. The closer tree is a sugar maple and the more distant tree is a Norway maple. On your right is a triangular bed of dwarf plants, mostly evergreens, west of the main steps to the Administration building. This bed is dominated by a central tree with a rugged outline and evergreen scales arranged on small, fan-shaped branches. This tree, and another like it in the bed just east of the main steps, is a dwarf Hinoki falsecypress (*Chamaecyparis obtusa* 'Nana Gracilis'). The two trees are about 50 years old and will grow to be only about 8 feet tall. They were brought from Oregon and planted here in 1991.

Hinoki falsecypress

Tricolor European beech

Dawn redwood

Behind (north) the triangular bed, tucked against the wall of the Administration building and sheltered by a large yew, is a European beech (*Fagus sylvatica* 'Tricolor') with mottled pink, white, and green leaves. It is a smaller cultivar of the same species as the copper beeches, with the same smooth bark, but with even more striking leaves.

Another unusual tree is located just to the right of the west wing stairs. This tall, pyramidal tree with small, feathery needles and shreddy, red bark is a dawn redwood (*Metasequoia glyptostroboides*). It loses its needles in winter. In 1941, 5-million-year-old fossils of this tree species were discovered in Japan. Later that year, living trees were found in China, a find that caused much excitement in the botanical world. Seeds from these trees were brought to the United States in 1947-48. Most of the dawn redwoods growing on college campuses today have been raised from those seeds. The native bald cypress is similar, but does not have red bark and has its needles scattered along the branches or alternate, whereas those of dawn redwood are arranged in opposite pairs along the small branches.

Japanese maple

– PLATE III –

Colorado blue spruce

Eastern redbud

Callery pear

Weeping Nootka falsecypress

Turning toward the church (west), you will see another copper beech just left of the east door.

Following the wide, curving walk to the left (south) along the east wall of the church you will see two red-leaved Japanese maples (*Acer palmatum*) with fan-shaped leaves on graceful branches.

Towering over the maples is a Colorado blue spruce (*Picea pungens*). It has sharp, square needles like Norway spruce, but does not have the drooping branches. Colorado blue spruce needles vary from green to blue to silver. Examples of all color forms can be found throughout the campus.

Continue around to the front (south) of Sacred Heart. The two broadly conical, needle-leaved trees that stand at each outer corner of the building are Serbian spruce (*Picea omorika* 'Nana'), which has blunt, flat needles that are not characteristic of most spruce species.

On either side of the central doorway are two other entrances, each flanked by two upright, columnar Norway spruce (*Picea abies* 'Cupressina').

Continue west (left) down the sidewalk to Corby. South (left) of the walk stands a globe-shaped Callery pear (*Pyrus calleryana*), with its glossy leaves that turn dark red in late autumn. It has masses of white blooms in April.

To the right (north) of the walk is a redbud (*Cercis canadensis*) with its simple, heart-shaped leaves and red purple buds in April and May.

Behind the redbud, on the west side of the church, is a group of hemlocks (*Tsuga canadensis*) with small, evergreen needles.

On the west end of this lawn, behind the St. Jude statue, stand three tall, evergreen, weeping Nootka falsecypress (*Chamaecyparis nootkatensis* 'Pendula') and two Japanese lilacs (*Syringa reticulata*), which bloom later in the spring than the common lilacs. One tree lilac is behind the falsecypress and the other is at the SE corner of Corby.

– PLATE IV –

A horsechestnut (*Aesculus hippocastanum*) stands just left of the walk beyond the SE corner of Corby. It has palmately compound leaves, each with five to seven leaflets like fingers on an open palm.

Continue west along the front of Corby. After you pass the main stairway you will see, in the lawn behind the Corby statue, two tall European larches (*Larix decidua*) with their needles in clusters of up to 30. They lose their needles during winter.

Horsechestnut

As you reach the west end of Corby, look down the hill to your right to see a huge sycamore (*Platanus occidentalis*) with a forked trunk. It has large leaves and distinctive bark that peels to reveal patches of green, white, and tan.

Turn left on the angled path. Pausing about midway to the road, you will see in the center of the lawn on your right a Kentucky coffeetree (*Gymnocladus dioica*). It has large twice-compound leaves, thick pods, and a rugged, stark outline in the winter. Father Hebert, who lived in Corby, planted this tree. The species was one of his favorites.

European larch

Continue on the sidewalk until you meet the road. Straight ahead, across the road, is a cucumber tree (*Magnolia acuminata*). The leaves are large, simple, and look tropical. The greenish, upright flowers produce pinkish fruits in October that vaguely resemble small cucumbers. A second cucumber tree is in the lawn to the left of the first.

Cucumber tree

Turning east, follow the road toward Sorin hall. On your right, the tree with the forked trunk, immediately east of the second cucumber tree, is a river birch (*Betula nigra*). It has shaggy, tan bark. River birch is more common on the newer, east side of the campus.

The bushlike tree next on your right, in the center of the lawn, is a fernleaf beech (*Fagus sylvatica* 'Laciniata') with finely divided leaves.

River birch

– PLATE V –

Japanese
pagodatree

Maple-leaf panax

Common
lilac

Mugo pine

As you pass the sidewalk to Corby, on your left, you can see a Japanese pagodatree (*Sophora japonica*) with its branches of lacey, compound leaves overarching the walk. It blooms in midsummer with upright clusters of pealike flowers that are followed by yellow pods.

Continue on the drive to the back of Sorin, then turn left (north). The tall tree on your right is a shingle oak (*Quercus imbricaria*), with its leathery, simple, unlobed leaves that do not look like those of oak.

On your left, in the triangular bed, are two cork-trees (*Phellodendron amurense*). They have long, compound leaves of up to 13 leaflets and corky bark.

Turn back toward the Main Quad, pausing at the lawn north of Sorin, which faces Sacred Heart. In the center of this lawn stands a rounded tree with glossy, star-shaped leaves that look like those of sweetgum or maple, but much larger. This is a maple-leaf panax (*Kalopanax pictus*). A second, smaller tree of the same species but a different variety stands just to the west. They bloom in late summer.

Rejoin the wide, main walkway of the Main Quad by passing between beds of old-fashioned lilacs (*Syringa vulgaris*) on your left and a bed of bushy, but tall, mugo pines (*Pinus mugo*) on your right (at lamppost 58).

At this intersection, as you turn south on the main walkway, you will see on your right (west) another dawn redwood with its red, shreddy bark and feathery needles.

On your left, it is impossible to overlook the weeping, almost monstrous, form of the Camperdown elm (*Ulmus × vegeta* 'Camperdownii') with its branches almost touching the ground. This weeping form has been grafted onto an upright trunk. The graft union is the thickened section of trunk just below the branches at about eye level.

Continuing south, on your right (west) are three

– PLATE VI –

shrubby evergreens with flat, scalelike leaves arranged on horizontal, fanlike branches. These are American arborvitae (*Thuja occidentalis*).

As you meet the central sidewalk to Sorin Hall, on your right (west), flanking the steps of Sorin, are a pair of vase-shaped American elms (*Ulmus americana*). Most of the elm species look very similar and can be distinguished most easily by comparing their small, winged fruits that appear in May. Most species are susceptible to Dutch Elm Disease. The vigilant pruning of diseased branches by our groundskeepers has allowed the campus to remain shaded by elms.

On your left (east), north of the intersection of the paths, stands a sweetgum (*Liquidambar styraciflua*), with its star-shaped leaves that turn rich red during autumn. Its prickly fruits (ball-shaped) drop throughout autumn and winter.

Next is a low bed of azaleas (*Rhododendron* sp.), which must be protected by a windbreak during the winter, but then produce a bright display of red flowers in early May.

Just south of the azaleas, on the other side of the crosswalk, is a young hackberry (*Celtis occidentalis*). Its leaves are similar to those of elm, but it has small, pea-shaped fruits and distinctive, warty bark, which is most obvious on younger trees.

On your right at the SE corner of Sorin stand four trees in a triangular area bordered by walks. The two smaller trees with toothed and three-lobed leaves are amur maples (*Acer ginnala*), a small, shrubby maple that tolerates shade. The two larger trees with heart-shaped leaves (also with toothed edges) are lindens. The double-trunked tree just north of the lamppost and closer to you is a pendent silver linden (*Tilia petiolaris*), which has leaves that are white and hairy below. The farther one, closer to Sorin, is a small-leaved European linden (*Tilia cordata*). Its leaves are smooth and blue green below.

Continuing on the wide north-south walk, on your

American arborvitae

Sweetgum

Amur maple

Azalea

– PLATE VII –

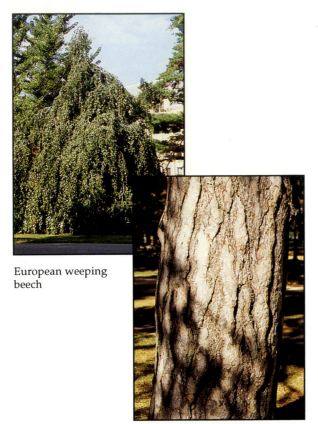

European weeping beech

Austrian pine

White pine

Scotch pine

left, just south of the east-west walk, is a large red oak (*Quercus rubra*) with pointed leaf lobes.

On the right (west), are two elms. Between them, farther from the path, you can see a white oak (*Quercus alba*), with rounded leaf lobes.

Moving south, you can see the fantastic form of another weeping tree. This is a European weeping beech (*Fagus sylvatica* 'Pendula'). This is a weeping cultivar of the same species as the copper beeches.

After you pass the weeping beech, you can see southwest of it another unusual tree, a ginkgo (*Ginkgo biloba* 'Laciniata') with fan-shaped leaves on stiff-looking, sparse branches. This species, like dawn redwood, is ancient. It was native to China, but is extinct in the wild and only can be found growing in cultivation.

A short side trip down the sidewalk to Walsh Hall shows several interesting plants. Three species of pine are scattered throughout this area. On your right is a towering, irregularly branched white pine (*Pinus strobus*), a tree native to North America. It has soft needles grouped in fives.

Next, on your left (south of the path to Walsh), is an Austrian pine (*Pinus nigra*), which has long, stiff needles in groups of two and bark that separates into light gray and tan plates and vertical ridges.

On your right (north of the path to Walsh) is a Scotch pine (*Pinus sylvestris*) with shorter, twisted needles in twos and dark bark that is orange on the upper, younger branches.

On your left (south) is a young English oak (*Quercus robur*) with its small, blunt-lobed leaves.

Each of Walsh Hall's three stairways is flanked by a pair of smaller trees. These are flowering dogwoods (*Cornus florida*) with white petal-like bracts that bloom in May.

– PLATE VIII –

The large shrubs between the dogwoods are witch-hazel (*Hamamelis vernalis*). They are the earliest woody plants to bloom here, from late winter into March. Their spidery, yellow flowers are small, but welcome when nothing else is blooming.

Following the path from Walsh back (east) to the wide, main walk, you will pass between two pin oaks (*Quercus palustris*). They have deeply lobed, sharp-pointed leaves.

Flowering dogwood

As you face the Sorin statue, the trees on either side are red maples. Turning around to face the South Quad, you have an excellent view of the vase-shaped American elms on the far side. Planted in the 1920s, these trees line the east-west sidewalks from O'Shaughnessy to the Rockne Memorial.

This vista is framed in the foreground by the drooping branches of a pair of Norway spruce. Just north of the eastern (left) spruce is a tulip tree (*Liriodendron tulipifera*), Indiana's state tree. It has a dark, straight, finely-furrowed trunk, lyre-shaped leaves, and green and orange tulip-shaped flowers.

Pin oak

At this point, leave the wide main walkway to follow the smaller curving walkway that passes under the tulip tree. Looking east, the first building along the east side of the Main Quad is Hurley Hall. The section of lawn between you and Hurley contains more pines like those in front of Walsh. The large deciduous tree growing on the northern end of this section is a honeylocust (*Gleditsia triacanthos*) with its trunk bristling with large, branched thorns.

Still looking east, down the sidewalk that runs between the honeylocust on your right and evergreen spruce and pine on your left, you can see, along the wall of Hayes-Healy, two American holly trees (*Ilex opaca*) with their typical holly leaves, glossy and spiny, and red berries that remain in winter.

Honeylocust

Continue north, on the smaller curving walkway, to the north end of Crowley. Just beyond the NW

Witch-hazel

– PLATE IX –

Spruce

American holly

Baldcypress

Carolina allspice

corner is a baldcypress (*Taxodium distichum*). It has small, feathery needles that drop during autumn. It can be distinguished from dawn redwood by its leaves that are scattered and alternate along the stems. It also has darker, gray brown bark. In the wild it grows in swamps, where it produces "knees" that protrude from the water around its base.

Turn right (east) between Crowley and LaFortune. On your right at the north wall of Crowley is a multi-trunked small tree with smooth, dark, blue gray bark. This is an American hornbeam (*Carpinus caroliniana*). Its other common name is "musclewood," which describes the appearance of the branches: corded like the muscles along a human arm.

Next along the NE wall of Crowley is a purple-leaved smoketree (*Cotinus coggygria*), which gets its name from the clouds of small flowers that appear like smoke in summer.

Heading toward the fountain (east) on your left is a large Oriental beech (*Fagus orientalis*), which resembles the European beeches of the Main Quad, but has shorter leaves that are hairy below.

Red oaks stand on each side of the fountain. A row of pin oaks runs along the west wall of Nieuwland. Pin oak leaves are smaller and more deeply lobed than those of red.

Following the path to LaFortune, with the Oriental beech on the right, you can see two limber pines (*Pinus flexilis*) on your left. These have dark, "crackled" bark and needles grouped in fives like white pine. Take the path between the pines and turn left toward the Main Quad.

On your right are three mixed beds of shrubs. None of the species in the beds has very distinctive leaves, but two have other ornamental features. The first bed contains Carolina allspice (*Calycanthus floridus*), which stands out in early May because of its red brown flowers with a sweet, fruity fragrance. The second

– PLATE X –

species, in the second and third beds, is winterberry (*Ilex verticillata*), whose bare branches are covered by a cloud of red berrylike fruits all winter after the leaves have fallen.

In the lawn area extending toward the Main Quad from the third bed, you will see a small yellowwood (*Cladrastis kentukea*) behind (east) the west-facing bench. This tree was planted in 1991 by the University's Sesquicentennial subcommittee on exhibitions and permanent legacy. It replaces a state record-sized yellowwood that stood at the site until it fell during a storm. Yellowwood has white, pealike flowers during summer and fine, gray bark.

In front of the west-facing bench, across the sidewalk from it, stand two large oaks. The nearer one is a black oak (*Quercus velutina*), with leaves similar to those of red oak but with deeply cut, sharp lobes. North of it is a shingle oak.

Continuing west on the sidewalk you will pass on your left a north-facing bench and then a pin oak. As you reach the main walkway you will be standing between two more oaks. The one on the left (south) is a bur oak (*Q. macrocarpa*) with lyreshaped leaves and blunt lobes. The one on the right (north) is a chestnut oak (*Q. muehlenbergii*). It has egg-shaped leaves with no lobes but sharp teeth like those on the leaves of chestnut.

Straight ahead, on the west side of the main walkway is the massive, broken trunk of a tree-of-heaven (*Ailanthus altissima*). Tree-of-heaven has weak wood but can survive in harsh, city conditions, where it is often seen sprouting through pavement or in empty lots where any greenery is welcome.

Walking north on the wide ·main walkway, on your left are two European larches. The large shrub on your left just north of the larches is a bottlebrush buckeye (*Aesculus parviflora*), so named because its flower spikes of summer look like brushes. It has large hand-shaped leaves.

Sycamore maple

Winterberry

Yellowwood

Ornamental Crabapple

– PLATE XI –

Purpleleaf
cherry-plum

Washington
hawthorn

Allegheny serviceberry

Boston ivy

Just west of the buckeye you can see the paper birch. The next tree, near the crosswalk, is a Crimean linden (*Tilia × euchlora*). It has weeping branches, shiny, heart-shaped leaves, and a smooth, evenly furrowed trunk.

On your right, east of the main walkway, stands a sycamore maple (*Acer pseudoplatanus*), which has scaly bark and rather large leaves, for a maple, that resemble those of sycamore.

Continue north to the point where the sidewalks from Washington Hall and LaFortune join to meet the main walkway. Looking east you will see a lawn area planted with three small, flowering trees. The two low-spreading trees are flowering crabapples (*Malus* sp.). The upright tree with purple leaves is a cherry-plum (*Prunus cerasifera* 'Mt. St. Helens'). All bloom in April.

Looking east down the Washington Hall sidewalk, without walking over there, you can see the thornless honeylocusts that are shading the picnic tables on the plaza.

To the right of the plaza, seven Washington hawthorns (*Crataegus phaenopyrum*) line the ramp at the north entrance to LaFortune. They have white flowers in May, followed by red fruits that persist into winter.

Turning back to the Main Quad, on your left (west) are two low beds. The first is purple and red azaleas (*Rhododendron* sp.) and the second is bordered by the sword-shaped leaves of Adam's needle yucca (*Yucca filamentosa*). Yuccas are uncommon on campus today, but were a popular feature during the early 1900s.

Follow the outer circle north along Washington Hall. Just north of the wrought iron staircase on the west wall of Washington is a small flowering tree with graceful form and simple leaves. It is a serviceberry (*Amelanchier laevis*). It has white flowers with strap-shaped petals that bloom in April, before most of the other flowering trees. The edible fruits are eaten by birds long before people find them.

Follow the curved sidewalk back around to the

– PLATE XII –

Administration building, where the east and south walls support three species of vines. On the south wall of the east wing grows Boston ivy (*Parthenocissus tricuspidata*), with its three-lobed, glossy leaves that turn bright red during autumn. This is a common vine found on many buildings across campus.

Just right of the main steps there is another vine clinging to the Boston ivy on the south wall. It is a Grecian silkvine (*Periploca graeca*), which has been growing in that spot since at least 1909 when Father Nieuwland first documented its presence. It has rather small, but striking, maroon and green flowers in midsummer that are a reward for careful observers. The flowers are followed by pods similar to those of milkweed, to which it is related.

On the left side of the main steps grows trumpetvine (*Campsis radicans*), with trumpet-shaped orange flowers in midsummer.

### St. Joseph's Lake Tour

As it is difficult to describe the exact locations of trees in wooded settings, this tour will give general comments about what can be found along the path with mention of the sites of specific plants that grow near recognizable landmarks (i.e., stairways, lampposts, the swimming beach).

The tour begins at the southwest corner of the lake at the broad opening just across the street from the entrance to the parking lot west of Lewis Hall. As you approach you will see on the lake edge a silver maple (*Acer saccharinum*). It has the familiar "maple" leaves, but they are more deeply divided and silver white on the back. To the left of the maple is a large cottonwood (*Populus deltoides*) with deeply fissured bark and triangular leaves that flutter in the slightest breeze. The shoreline between the trees is a tangled mass of vines of several species. Growing thickly near the silver maple and climbing by coiled tendrils is grape (*Vitis*

Trumpetvine

Grecian silkvine

Poison ivy

Poison ivy

– PLATE XIII –

Sycamore Bark

Honeysuckle

Honeysuckle

Cranberrybush

*riparia*) with simple, sharp-lobed leaves and black fruits. At the base of the cottonwood and climbing straight up its trunk by the use of aerial roots is poison ivy (*Toxicodendron* spp.) with its familiar three leaflets and white fruits. Poison ivy, which causes a skin rash for many people, is extremely common around the lakes. It is important to stay on the path. A third vine here is Virginia creeper (*Parthenocissus quinquefolia*), which has five leaflets on each leaf, blue black fruits, and climbs by using tendrils tipped with adhesive disks. It often turns a deep maroon red in autumn.

Turning to your right and starting counterclockwise around the lake, you will see on both sides of the path a tangle of several species of shrubs. Each stands out at a different time of the year. In spring the honeysuckles (*Lonicera* spp.) have pairs of tubular flowers that are white, pink, or yellow. In midsummer pairs of juicy red berries form. The cranberrybushes (*Viburnum opulus*) have flat clusters of many white flowers in spring that are followed by red fruits in late summer. Both of these shrub species are common around the lake.

The trees on your right as you head east on the path are, first, sycamore (*Platanus occidentalis*) with its mottled bark, and second, white ash (*Fraxinus americana*), younger trees with dark brown buds and opposite, compound leaves.

Scattered along the more open lake shore are silver maples and white mulberries (*Morus alba*). The mulberries often have more than one main trunk with yellow bark. Their leaves are toothed and irregularly lobed. In this open area you also have a good view of the nearest island. There, the trees with conspicuous white trunks and silver leaves are white poplar (*Populus alba*).

The next section of the path, as you re-enter the woods, is lined with many large black walnuts (*Juglans nigra*). They are slow to leaf out in the spring and have large, compound leaves. Their green fruits, larger than ping pong balls, drop in late summer.

– PLATE XIV –

Continue on the path to the small brick building on your right. On both sides of this building are young boxelder trees (*Acer negundo*). This is a species of maple with uncharacteristic leaves, divided into three leaflets. The young stems are green like the leaves.

In the area around the next broad path to your right are red and white oaks. The red oak (*Quercus rubra*) has sharply pointed leaf lobes, and the white oak (*Quercus alba*) has rounded leaf lobes.

At the stairway leading up to the road, you will see a white oak at the base of the stairs. Across the path on your left is a catalpa (*Catalpa speciosa*). It has large heart-shaped leaves, showy white flowers in June, and long pods that remain visible on the tree during winter.

After passing the stairway you will see on your right, growing next to the path and near the fire hydrant, a very large sycamore. Continue on the path and you will see a second large sycamore, next to the path and below the power plant. Around the second sycamore are young American basswood (*Tilia americana*). Basswood has large heart-shaped leaves with toothed edges and dark, finely ridged bark.

Just before the cleared, grassy slope to the cooling tower on your right stands a shagbark hickory (*Carya ovata*). It has bark that peels in long, broad strips and leaves with five leaflets.

After passing the cooling tower, you will pass through a stretch of the path with a canopy of large cottonwoods and an understory of plums and cherries (*Prunus* spp.). They are noticeable when blooming (white flowers) in early spring, but blend into the hillside during other times.

Past the beach, on the right, are more red and white oaks. The shrubs at their bases, with large white flowers in May followed by shiny black fruits, are Japanese jetbead (*Rhodotypos scandens*). The fruits remain in winter.

As you near the path to Holy Cross House, the ground is covered with periwinkle (*Vinca minor*). The

White mulberry

Choke-cherry

Plum

Boxelder

– PLATE XV –

Japanese jetbead

Staghorn sumac

Yellow willow

Red sassafras

leaves are evergreen and the flowers are lilac blue.

On your left are occasional stands of shrubby staghorn sumac (*Rhus hirta*), which gets its name from the velvety hairs covering the branches. The compound leaves turn bright orange to red in autumn. The branches end in red fruit clusters that remain through the winter.

On the wide, sloping lawn of Moreau Seminary, just left of the first steps, is a red oak with two redbuds (*Cercis canadensis*) growing in its shade. The bright red purple buds of redbud light up the entire lake shore in early spring.

At the water's edge below the lawn, a row of yellow willows (*Salix alba* var. *vitellina*) trail their weeping branches into the water.

After passing the lawn of Moreau, you enter a long wooded stretch. At the base of the first lamppost, on your right, and in the area around it are sapling sassafras (*Sassafras albidum*) with irregular, lobed or mitten-shaped leaves.

At the second lamppost, at the base of the steps that lead to St. Joseph Hall, and stretching along the path is a grove of Chinese evodia trees (*Evodia daniellii*). They have gray bark, leaves similar to those of ash (compound with 7 to 11 leaflets), and masses of white flowers that appear in midsummer. These trees, native to China and Korea, are unusual in this "natural" setting and must be seeding themselves.

The path eventually emerges from the woods, curving around to the open lawn by Columba Hall, which is dominated by several very large sycamores. Continuing around the curve, the island is in sight on your left. Cranberrybush covers the island. It has bright red fruits and the leaves turn dark red in autumn.

Shading the path on your right is a large dense Norway maple (*Acer platanoides*). On the left by the water is a double-trunked silver maple. The open shore along this final stretch contains more tree species that have been described earlier.

– PLATE XVI –

# THE BOTANICAL CATALOGUE

# Description of Campus Flora Database

With the exception of the three introductory chapters and walking tour, each of the sections of this book was generated by computer programs from a relational database. The database was developed to permit continuous documentation of the Notre Dame Campus flora, a process that need not stop with the publication of this work. Because of the database format, it is possible to monitor changes in the campus flora over time and to assess gains or losses in the overall diversity of the flora. The section of this work that lists the flora by campus landmark and site is feasible only because of the computerized structure of the information.

A relational database may be thought of as a group of logically linked tables. Each table has columns (fields) that correspond to the kinds of information contained in the database and rows (records) that correspond to individual observations. For example, one of the tables in the database documents the names of the plants contained in the campus flora. In this table the fields contain the name, taxonomic level of the name (e.g., family, genus, species, subspecies, cultivar, form, variety, etc.), corresponding vernacular name, author of the name, name used by Hebert in his 1967 work, distinguishing and descriptive characteristics, etc. The table has a single record for each name included in the flora regardless of type. Thus the family, genus, species, and variety names for a single kind of plant each are represented as separate records.

A second table in the database contains information about plantings. In this table there are fields corresponding to the reference location or landmark, the specific site of the planting, the number of specimens at the site, whether the site was documented by Hebert in 1967, the status of the site (whether the plants are still there), whether herbarium mounts or field notes were made from specimens at the site, whether the planting is commemorative, etc. In this table there is a single record for each planting site for each kind of plant on the campus. The two tables (name and planting site) are linked through a key field that is common to both. In this case the name table has a field that contains a unique code for each kind of plant. The site table uses this key (rather than the plant name) to identify the kind of plant at a specific location. There is a one-to-many relationship between the name and planting site tables. Each planting site record is associated with only one kind of plant, but a single kind of plant can be present at many planting sites.

An additional table in the database contains information on commemorative plantings. It has fields for the kind of commemoration, the individual or group responsible for the planting, whether the site is labeled with a plaque, etc. This table contains two keys, one for the plant name, and the second for the planting site.

The Notre Dame Campus Flora database is maintained as dBASE III™ (Borland International, Inc.) format files on an IBM PC™-compatible microcomputer in the University of Notre Dame Greene-Nieuwland Herbarium. Compiled computer programs written in the Clipper™ (Computer Associates, Inc.) programming language produced lists of the flora organized by botanical names and campus sites, lists of commemorative plantings and plants lost from the campus since 1967, and concordance files for indices. Output files produced in stripped ASCII format were converted to WordPerfect® (WordPerfect Corp.) format using the document conversion utility program Word-for-Word™ (MasterSoft®). Within WordPerfect, macros were used to produce the document in camera-ready format. The index was generated by WordPerfect from concordance files extracted from the database. Final copy was printed on an HP LaserJet IV™ printer using the Complete Font Library (Pacific Data Products, Inc.) data cartridge. The typeface used is CG Palacio. The campus map that follows was created using Adobe® Illustrator™ on an Apple® Macintosh® computer.

## Alphabetical List of Campus Buildings and Sites

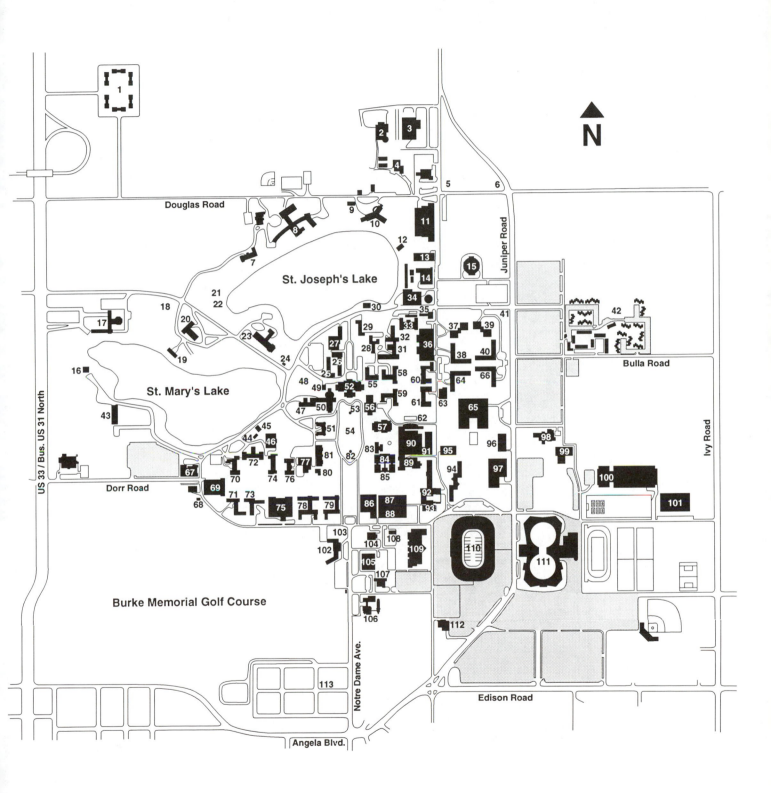

N

St. Joseph's Lake

Douglas Road

St. Mary's Lake

US 33 / Bus. US 31 North

Dorr Road

Juniper Road

Bulla Road

Ivy Road

Burke Memorial Golf Course

Notre Dame Ave.

Edison Road

Angela Blvd.

# Botanical Names with Descriptions

Barbara J. Hellenthal

This catalogue contains information about every kind of woody plant that is growing on the campus and describes the planting sites. The plants are grouped by plant families, which are broad categories of genera that share recognized fruit and flower characteristics. The families are arranged by botanical similarity, ordered from the evolutionarily most primitive to most advanced. The family names appear in large, bold, capital letters. Within each family, the genera are listed alphabetically. Below each genus, its species, subspecies, varieties, forms, and cultivars are listed alphabetically.

Each genus entry begins with its name (in italics), the author first describing it (abbreviated), and one or more common names (in brackets). The genus entry is divided into two paragraphs. The first contains general information about its history, economic uses, horticultural characteristics, natural distribution, and poisonous properties, if present. The second paragraph in each genus entry is a brief description of its structural features. The order in which these features appear is unvarying with a general description first, followed by branch and leaf characteristics, flower and fruit characteristics, and, last, botanical information that can be used to distinguish the genus from other similar kinds of plants (key characters).

The species and hybrid entries are listed alphabetically below each genus. The specific epithet appears in italics. Names of hybrids are preceded by "×" and followed by the parent species. In either, the name is followed by the author (abbreviated) and one or more common names (in brackets). The name of the species, when written, is actually a combination of the genus name, as listed above, followed by the specific epithet. The species (or hybrid) entry includes descriptive characteristics that distinguish it from all other species (or hybrids) within that genus that are found on the campus plus information on appearance and culture, native distribution, the year of first horticultural use, poisonous properties, and maximum height attained under normal cultivation. The subspecies (subsp.), variety (var.), form (f.), and cultivar (in single quotes) entries are listed, below the appropriate species. The information included for a subspecies, variety, form, or cultivar is limited to that which separates it from the species.

The site information is listed in an indented paragraph below the plant name. Sites are organized by primary landmarks (usually buildings). The primary landmarks are listed alphabetically and appear in small capital letters. Each is followed by a list of more specific site descriptions (i.e., which side of the building) and, in brackets, the number or approximate quantity (few, many, clump, hedge, etc.) of plants found at that site. An asterisk within the brackets means that the site was included also in Father Hebert's list twenty-seven years ago. The term **"Commem."** appears in the brackets if that tree has been planted to commemorate a person or event. Further information about the commemorative plants can be found in the Commemorative Plantings section that begins on page 269. The classification system here follows Arthur Cronquist, *An Integrated System of Classification of Flowering Plants* (1981).

## GINKGOACEAE [GINKGO FAMILY]

*Ginkgo* L. [**Ginkgo; Maidenhair Tree**]

Brought to Europe from Japan, where it was being cultivated, by the Dutch East India Company in the early 1700s, the ginkgo is the only living example of an otherwise extinct family (including at least 6 genera) known from the fossil record. Fossils of early ginkgo relatives are found in rock over 200 million years old and remains of leaves identical to living ginkgoes are found in 65-million-year-old deposits. Ginkgo is native to eastern China, but believed to be extinct in the wild and maintained only through cultivation. Called silver apricot in China, the kernel is edible after the fleshy outer coat has been removed. The oily outer pulp gives off the rancid butter odor of butyric acid and can cause severe dermatitis in some people. Because of the offensive odor of the fruit produced by female trees, male trees are frequently planted and available commercially as distinct cultivars. The ginkgo is a good tree for city conditions that has no known disease or insect problems. It is rather slow-growing, but can become too large for small yards.

Broad-leaved tree: deciduous, dioecious. Unusual fan-shaped leaves with veins long and parallel as they divide, arise from stubby spur shoots that branch from long shoots. Leaves arranged alternately or clustered at ends of spur shoots. Female trees produce plumlike kernels, each with fleshy outer coat and bony inner coat. Although *Ginkgo* is grouped with the gymnosperms because of its "naked" seeds, its reproductive characteristics are more closely related to those seen in primitive plants like the cycads and ferns.

*biloba* L. [**Ginkgo; Maidenhair Tree**]

Deciduous tree. Leaf veins parallel, fan-shaped; spur shoots present on stems. Street and lawn tree; golden foliage; picturesque silhouette. Ornamental in summer, autumn, winter. Introduced, native to eastern China. In horticulture since 1784. Outer pulp of fruit causes dermatitis. Maximum height 80 ft.

KNOTT HALL: S wing, E side, S end [2]; SW lawn [1]; W wing, S side [1]. MOREAU SEMINARY: Chapel, E side [1*]. PASQUERILLA HALL EAST: W door [3]. PASQUERILLA HALL WEST: E door [2]. RILEY HALL OF ART AND DESIGN: S side [1].

'Laciniata' [**Split-leaf Ginkgo**]

Deciduous tree. Leaves deeply divided.

ADMINISTRATION (MAIN) BUILDING: N lawn [1*]. CORBY HALL: E wing, N, lawn above Grotto [1]. FISHER HALL: W side [1*]. PRESBYTERY: NW corner, W 10yd [2]. PROVINCE ARCHIVES CENTER: SE corner [1]. WALSH HALL: Main entrance, E 40yd [1*].

## TAXACEAE [YEW FAMILY]

*Taxus* L. [**Yew**]

The hard, strong, elastic wood of the slow-growing yews is used in bows, knife handles, and furniture. Yews are very common in yards and gardens because of their winter hardiness, compact growth, resistance to diseases and pests, and good color year-round. Shrub forms are more common than trees in the United States. Female plants, with red arils visible during winter, are more showy. Yews are native to temperate regions from Europe to central Malaysia and Mexico. Bark of the Pacific yew, *T. brevifolia* which is native to the Pacific Coast from Alaska to California and to the Sierra Nevada and Rocky Mountains, yields taxol. Taxol is used for the treatment of ovarian cancer, but it is not a cure. The branches, leaves, and seeds are poisonous to humans and domesticated livestock, but not to deer or birds. The toxic principle is the alkaloid taxine.

Needle-leaved tree or shrub: evergreen, coniferous, dioecious. Branches alternate; leaves soft, 0.5-1.25 in. long, arranged spirally on twigs or appearing 2-ranked. Male and female flowers borne on separate plants. Red berrylike structure that develops on female plant is not a fruit, but actually a hard seed only partially enclosed by the fleshy aril. This single, exposed seed with its red, berrylike cover distinguishes the yew from all other conifers, which usually bear woody cones that hold the naked seeds (junipers have blue or brown berrylike fruits). The species of yews are very difficult to tell apart, even by trained botanists.

*baccata* L. [**English Yew**]

Evergreen tree. Leaf tip long, tapering; bud scales blunt, only slightly keeled. Leaves dark, shiny green. Introduced, native to northern Africa, western Asia, Europe. Entire plant toxic to humans and livestock when eaten. Maximum height 60 ft.

BROWNSON HALL: Court, SE corner [1]; Court, SW corner [1]. JUNIPER ROAD: E, opposite Galvin, fence, E side [2]; North Gate, fence, roadside [7]; ROTC stoplight, fence, campus-side [2]; W, Library circle N [2]; W, Library circle N, N planting [3]; W, Library circle N, S planting [2]; W, Library circle S [2]; W, Library circle S, fence, campus-side [5]; W, at Bulla Rd [21]; W, at Galvin, fence, campus-side [4]. ZAHM HALL: NW sign [4].

### 'Aurea' [Golden Yew; Irish Yew]

Evergreen tree. Growth compact, yellow but fades to green; hardier than the species. Developed in England.

HESBURGH CENTER: Court, NW bed [6]; Court, SE bed [6].

### 'Fastigiata' [English Yew]

Evergreen tree. Columnar-oval shape; branches rigid, upright; needles large, dark. Developed in Fermanagh, Ireland. In horticulture since 1760. Maximum height 30 ft.

JUNIPER ROAD: N at Douglas Rd, entrance sign [2]; S at Edison Rd, entrance sign [2].

### 'Fastigiata Aurea' [Golden English Yew]

Evergreen tree. Growth slow; young growth yellow; more winter hardy than the species.

JUNIPER ROAD: Pedestrian entrances, flanking [many].

### 'Pendula' [Weeping Yew]

Evergreen tree. Spreading outline; branches slender, drooping.

ARCHITECTURE BUILDING: NW corner, E [1*].

### 'Repandens' [Spreading Yew]

Evergreen shrub. Dwarf, spreading; branch tips droop; leaves form V on twig; female plants only. Low, wide-spreading; olive green lower leaf surface visible; hardy. Developed in America. In horticulture since 1887. Maximum height 10 ft.

ADMINISTRATION (MAIN) BUILDING: E front end [1*]. ARCHITECTURE BUILDING: NE corner [2*]. GROTTO OF OUR LADY OF LOURDES: Above, St. Francis statue, N 8yd [1*]. HOWARD HALL: N wing, E end [3*]; S wing, E end [2*].

### 'Stricta' [Irish Yew]

Evergreen tree. Growth columnar; leaves dark, scattered around stem, not 2-ranked. Picturesque, formal shape; dark green foliage. Developed in Ireland. In horticulture since 1780.

HOLY CROSS HOUSE: Cornerstone [1*].

### 'Stricta Aurea' [English Yew]

Evergreen tree. Growth columnar; leaves yellow.

JUNIPER ROAD: Pedestrian entrances, flanking [many].

### *cuspidata* Siebold & Zucc. [Japanese Yew]

Evergreen tree. Leaf broad, yellow bands below, midrib raised; bud scales keeled. Dark green, shrubby tree for planting in formal or informal sites. Introduced, native to Japan, Korea, Manchuria. In horticulture since 1853. Entire plant toxic to humans and livestock when eaten. Maximum height 40 ft.

ALUMNI HALL: N side [18]. ARCHITECTURE BUILDING: NW corner [2]. CARROLL HALL: SW corner, W 40yd [2]. COLUMBA HALL: Front entrance [hedge]; Front, fountain [1]; N side, smokestack, above parking lot [5]; NE corner, lawn [1]; NE, along road [hedge]. CORBY HALL: N side [12]. FRESHMAN YEAR BUILDING: SW corner, SW 20yd [1]. GALVIN LIFE SCIENCE CENTER: W side, SW edge [hedge]. GROTTO OF OUR LADY OF LOURDES: N side, along steps [hedge]; SE, steps [hedge]; SW corner, Thomas Dooley statue [2]; SW corner, Thomas Dooley statue [2]. HOLY CROSS HOUSE: Douglas rd, along [hedge]; S, hedge [hedge]. HOWARD HALL: S entrance, E side [2]; SE corner [few]. LEWIS HALL: NE door [5*]; NW corner [1*]. MOREAU SEMINARY: Holy Cross House, walk between [hedge]. OUTDOOR WAY OF THE CROSS: Station 1, N 10ft [4*]. PRESBYTERY: SW corner [1]. SACRED HEART BASILICA: Sacristy, S side

[1].

### 'Capitata' [Japanese Yew]

Evergreen tree. Pyramidal, erect form. Size can be controlled by pruning. Maximum height 50 ft.

KNOTT HALL: S wing, E side [4]. PASQUERILLA HALL EAST: N wing, E side [2]. SIEGFRIED HALL: W door [2].

### 'Densa' [Japanese Cushion Yew]

Evergreen shrub. Low, dense shrub; leaves very dark green. Good form; slow growth. Maximum height 4 ft.

FISHER HALL: NE corner [7*]. HESBURGH LIBRARY: Pool, S, SE, SW ends [beds*]. LEWIS HALL: E, main entrance, N of walk [7*]. PANGBORN HALL: N, main entrance, flanking [14*]. WALSH HALL: Front [20*].

### 'Erecta' [Japanese Upright Yew]

Evergreen tree. Columnar form; upright growth.

COLUMBA HALL: NE lawn [11*]; NW lawn [12*].

### 'Expansa' [Japanese Saucer Yew]

Evergreen shrub. Spreading, vase-shaped outline with low, open center.

ARCHITECTURE BUILDING: SE corner [2*]. HOLY CROSS ANNEX: S lawn [5*]; SE lawn [5*].

### 'Fastigiata' [Japanese Pyramidal Yew]

Evergreen shrub. Dwarf, columnar form; leaves yellow.

CORBY HALL: E front entrance, flanking [2*]. FATIMA RETREAT HOUSE: Fatima shrine, flanking [4*]; Fatima shrine, front [5*]. HOLY CROSS ANNEX: S lawn [18*]. LEWIS HALL: E side [7*].

### 'Intermedia' [Japanese Compact Yew]

Evergreen shrub. Dense, slow-growing; dwarf, rounded outline. Developed by Robert Brown of Queens, Long Island.

ALUMNI HALL: E side [11*]. CAVANAUGH HALL: SE corner [8*]. CENTER FOR CONTINUING EDUCATION: S end [4*]; W entrance, N side [9*]; W entrance, S side [9*]. ZAHM HALL: E side [1*].

### 'Nana' [Japanese Dwarf Yew]

Evergreen tree. Dense, wide-spreading; slow growth; leaves broad, dull green. Introduced, native to Japan. Maximum height 20 ft.

ADMINISTRATION (MAIN) BUILDING: E front end [1*]; W front [2*]. FARLEY HALL: N end [4*].

### × *media* Rehd.: *T. baccata* × *T. cuspidata* [Anglojapanese Yew]

Evergreen tree. Branchlets remain green for 2 years, then brown; leaves 2-ranked; bud scales blunt. Usually shrubby with central stem. Developed by Alfred Rehder, Arnold Arboretum, Harvard University. In horticulture since 1923. Entire plant toxic to humans and livestock when eaten. Maximum height 20 ft.

BROWNSON HALL: Court, SE, SW corners [21]. BURKE MEMORIAL GOLF COURSE: Maintenance center [6]. COLUMBA HALL: S side, steps [many]. CORBY HALL: SW corner [1]. CROWLEY HALL OF MUSIC: W side [6]. DECIO FACULTY HALL: E plaza [hedge]; W plaza [hedge]. DILLON HALL: N side [20]. FATIMA RETREAT HOUSE: W side [hedge]. FITZPATRICK HALL OF ENGINEERING: SE corner planter [2]; SW corner planter [3]. FRESHMAN YEAR BUILDING: S [hedge]. GALVIN LIFE SCIENCE CENTER: NW end [hedge]; W side [beds]. HOWARD HALL: E side, arches [beds]; SE corner [2]. HURLEY HALL OF BUSINESS ADMINISTRATION: E end [hedge]; W side [few]. KEENAN HALL:

Stanford, front [hedge]. LAFORTUNE STUDENT CENTER: NE, Fieldhouse Mall, W edge [hedge]. LAW SCHOOL: S entrance [2]. O'SHAUGHNESSY HALL: W side [hedge]; W side, plaza [hedge]. RILEY HALL OF ART AND DESIGN: E side [hedge]. SNITE MUSEUM OF ART: Court [many]. SORIN HALL: E side [hedge]. SOUTH DINING HALL: N, main entrance [1*].

'Brownii' [**Brown's Yew**]

Evergreen tree. Plants male; erect, conical form; leaves dense, short. Good for shearing because of dense growth. Developed by T. D. Hatfield of Wellesley, Massachusetts. Maximum height 12 ft.

BREEN-PHILLIPS HALL: W side [8*]. CORBY HALL: Main entrance, flanking [2*]. FARLEY HALL: Front [8*]. UNIVERSITY HEALTH SERVICES: SE [hedge].

'Cole' [**Cole Yew**]

Evergreen shrub. Growth dense, low-spreading. Developed by Cole Nursery Co. of Painesville, Ohio.

HESBURGH CENTER: Court, E border [4]; Court, N border [4]; Court, NW bed [16]; Court, SE bed [16]; Court, planter N1 [2]; Court, planter N2 [2]; Court, planter N3 [2]; Court, planter N4 [2]; N side, E entrance to residences [2]; N side, residences, main entrance [6]. HESSERT AEROSPACE RESEARCH CENTER: S side [4]. JUNIPER ROAD: E, ROTC stoplight, fence [5]; E, opposite Galvin, at fence [4]; W, Library circle N [1]; W, Library circle N, S fence [2]; W, Library circle N, fence [2]; W, Library circle S [1]; W, Library circle S, fence, campus-side [4]; W, at Galvin, fence [4].

'Densiformis' [**Anglojapanese Yew**]

Evergreen tree. Dense, shrublike form to 6 ft. wide. Maximum height 4 ft.

JOYCE ATHLETIC AND CONVOCATION CENTER: Gate 10 [beds]; Gate 2 [4]. KNOTT HALL: N walk, E end [16].

'Hatfieldii' [**Hatfield's Yew**]

Evergreen tree. Plants male; dense, broadly pyramidal form; leaves spiral on twigs. Good growth form. Developed by Alfred Rehder, Arnold Arboretum, Harvard University. In horticulture since 1923. Maximum height 10 ft.

MOREAU SEMINARY: Patio, front [12*].

'Hicksii' [**Hicks' Yew**]

Evergreen tree. Plants female; growth erect, branches ascending; old shrubs broad. Red fruits frequently abundant. Ornamental in winter.

ADMINISTRATION (MAIN) BUILDING: Sacred Heart Statue, walk, N end, sides [2*]; Sacred Heart Statue, walk, S end, sides [2*]. KNOTT HALL: S wing, E side [7]; S wing, W side [4]; W wing, S side [7]. MORRIS INN: E, main beds, W edge [bed]. PASQUERILLA HALL EAST: N wing, NE corner [bed]; N wing, W side [bed]. PASQUERILLA HALL WEST: N wing, E side [beds]; W door [2]. SIEGFRIED HALL: E wing, S side [3]; S wing, E side [4]; SE door, flanking [4]; W door [10]. SNITE MUSEUM OF ART: S, flanking walk [hedge]. SOUTH DINING HALL: N, main entrance, W [1*].

# ARAUCARIACEAE [ARAUCARIA FAMILY]

*Araucaria* Juss. [**Araucaria**]

*Araucaria* and *Agathis* are the pines of the Southern Hemisphere. They are very tall, important, timber-producing trees that bear cones but have evergreen leaves that are broad or awl-shaped rather than the needles of the Northern

Hemisphere pines. *Araucaria heterophylla*, native to Norfolk Island between New Caledonia and New Zealand, is the popular indoor plant of conservatories and shopping malls. It grows outdoors in Hawaii and can reach 200 ft. tall where it is native.

Tall tree, leaves awl-shaped: evergreen, coniferous, dioecious. Branches arranged in strict whorls along trunk, 5 branches per whorl in *A. araucana*. Leaves stiff, overlapping on stem. Female cones large, woody, with only 1 ovule per bractless cone scale. Scales on the cones of Northern Hemisphere pines contain bracts and 2 ovules.

*araucana* (Mol.) C. Koch [**Monkey-puzzle Tree; Chilean Pine**]

Evergreen tree. Stiff, lance-shaped, overlapping leaves to 2 in. long; branches whorled, 5 per whorl. Unique, gaunt appearance. Introduced, native to Chile, Argentina. In horticulture since 1795. Maximum height 80 ft.

SUPPORT SERVICES BUILDING: N bed [1].

## PINACEAE [PINE FAMILY]

*Abies* Mill. [**Fir**]

The symmetrical, pyramidal, and slow-growing firs require a cool, moist climate. They are not well suited to pruning. Topping destroys the pyramidal form and the lower branches will not regrow if removed. Firs are an important commercial Christmas tree crop in the cooler, moist regions of the United States and in Europe. Balsam fir produces the resin Canada balsam, which is used as a fixative for microscope slide mounts. Firs are native to the higher elevation forests from Europe through Central America.

Large needle-leaved tree: evergreen, coniferous, monoecious. Branches grow in whorls along main trunk. Needles grow singly on the branches, are rather flat with 2 white bands on the lower surface and blunt tips (usually). Female cones grow upright on branches, mature in one year with the scales falling, leaving only the central axis on the tree. Firs can be separated from other evergreens by their single, flat, white-banded, blunt-tipped needles that leave only a round, smooth, disklike scar on the branch when removed and, also, by their upright cones that disintegrate when mature.

*balsamea* (L.) Mill. [**Balsam Fir**]

Evergreen tree. Twig with gray hairs, not grooved; leaf with 2 white bands below. Leaves fragrant, smell of balsam. Native to northeastern North America. In horticulture since 1696. Maximum height 75 ft.

GROTTO OF OUR LADY OF LOURDES: Above, surrounding [13*]; Sides [2*].
LOG CHAPEL: NW corner [2*].

'Nana' [**Dwarf Balsam Fir**]

Evergreen shrub. Compact, mounded form; needles short, dark green above, silver below. Maximum height 2 ft.

CARROLL HALL: S side [4].

*concolor* (Gord. & Glendinning) Lindl. ex Hildebr. [**White Fir; Colorado Fir**]

Evergreen tree. Twig not hairy, smooth; both leaf surfaces with white bands. Leaves silvery; soft appearance. Native to western North America. In horticulture since 1872. Maximum height 50 ft.

CARROLL HALL: SE corner, E 35yd [1*]. GRACE HALL: SW door plaza [1]. GROTTO OF OUR LADY OF LOURDES: Above [2*]; Corby, midway, W of walk [1 **Commem.**]. PRESBYTERY: Porch, S 5yd [1*]. SORIN HALL: SE 60yd [1*].

ZAHM HALL: N side [1*].

*nordmanniana* (Steven) Spach [**Nordmann Fir; Caucasian Fir**]

> Evergreen tree. Twig hairy; leaf white below, crowded, points forward on twig. Tall, stately form, to 200 ft. in the wild; needles very dark green. Introduced, native to Greece, Caucasus Mountains, Asia Minor. In horticulture since 1848. Maximum height 60 ft.
>
> ZAHM HALL: S 15yd [1*].

*Cedrus* Trew [**Cedar**]

> The true cedars are striking, even exotic, tall trees in the landscape. They are conical when young, becoming more open and with broadly horizontal or weeping branches at maturity. They are important timber trees in their native North Africa and Asia, where they grow in the mountains. The distinctly flat-topped Cedar of Lebanon, *C. libani*, was used to build Solomon's temple. Solomon was King of Israel during the tenth century, B.C. The Atlas and Cyprus cedars, *C. atlantica* and *C. brevifolia*, are very similar to *C. libani* and considered by many botanists to be only geographically defined subspecies of *C. libani*.
>
> Needle-leaved tall tree: evergreen, coniferous, either monoecious or dioecious. Needles 4-angled in cross section, scattered on long shoots or whorled, 8-40 together, on rough spur shoots. Male cones erect, female smaller, remaining on tree 2-3 years.

*atlantica* (Endl.) G. Mannetti ex Carrière [**Blue Atlas Cedar; Atlas Cedar**]

> Evergreen tree. Leaf 1 in. long, blue green, square in cross section; twig hairy; branch tips upright. Needles may be blue, gray, or silver. Introduced, native to the Atlas Mountains of Algeria and Morocco. In horticulture since 1840. Maximum height 60 ft.

'Glauca Pendula' [**Weeping Blue Atlas Cedar**]

> Evergreen tree. Weeping form; main trunk and branches drooping; leaves blue. Needs staking to remain upright; branches look like waterfalls.
>
> SUPPORT SERVICES BUILDING: N bed [1].

*Larix* Mill. [**Larch**]

> The shape of the larch is broadly pyramidal, but its foliage is open and casts only a light shade. The leaves are a pleasing light green in spring, turning yellow before they fall in autumn. Larch grows in the highly acid water of northern bogs in the United States and in cool areas across the Northern Hemisphere. The wood of larch, strong when in contact with water, has been used in shipbuilding in North America. Tannin from the bark is used in tanning leather.
>
> Needle-leaved tree: deciduous, coniferous, dioecious. Branches whorled on main trunk. Short, slow-growing spur shoots marked by annual growth rings are present on older branches. Most needles in clusters of 12-40 on spur shoots. Female cones erect and woody, not conspicuous when needles are present. True larch and golden-larch are the only needle-leaved trees with deciduous needles that grow in clusters on spur shoots. The woody cones of true larch are smaller and remain through winter, those of golden-larch are larger and disintegrate before winter.

*decidua* Mill. [**European Larch**]

> Deciduous tree. Needles grow in clusters of 12-40; each 1.25 in., flat above; cone to 1.5 in. long. Light green, feathery foliage. Ornamental in spring. Introduced,

native to central Europe through Siberia. Maximum height 75 ft.

> BURKE MEMORIAL GOLF COURSE: SW area [few*]. CORBY HALL: Front, Corby statue [2*]. FISHER HALL: Pangborn, between [1*]. LAFORTUNE STUDENT CENTER: SW 30yd, lamppost 53, W 10yd [2*]. MOREAU SEMINARY: N of indoor basketball court [1*].

*laricina* (Du Roi) C. Koch [**Tamarack; Eastern Larch**]

Deciduous tree. Needles in clusters of 12-30, to 1.25 in. long, angled midrib above; cone 0.75 in. long. Grows in wet, boggy areas; leaves turn yellow. Ornamental in autumn. Native to northern North America. In horticulture since 1737. Maximum height 80 ft.

> PRESBYTERY: W side, in grove above Grotto [6].

*Picea* A. Dietr. [**Spruce**]

Young spruce trees are pyramidal and formal in appearance. As they age or become crowded and shaded, they lose lower branches and can become scraggly. They need well-drained, moderately moist soil and grow poorly in the South. Spruce wood is light and strong, often used for pulp. Spruce is native to the cooler, mountainous regions of the Northern Hemisphere.

Needle-leaved tree: evergreen, coniferous, monoecious. Branches whorled along main trunk. Needles solitary, square in cross-section, attached to branchlets by woody leaf bases, which remain as rough pegs on stem after needles fall. Female cones hang from branch tips. Cone scales papery and not dropping at maturity. Spruce can be separated from other evergreens by the presence of woody pegs on the stems and by the square needles, which can be felt when rolled between finger and thumb. Hemlock and fir have flat needles.

*abies* (L.) Karst. [**Norway Spruce**]

Evergreen tree. Branches droop; first year leaves point forward, 0.75 in. long, dark; hairless orange twig. Graceful, sweeping branches; dark appearance. Introduced, native to north and central Europe. Maximum height 60 ft.

> ADMINISTRATION (MAIN) BUILDING: Sacred Heart Statue, walk, midway E side [1*]; W front, S 12yd [1]. ALUMNI HALL: E side [1]; NE corner [1*]. ARCHITECTURE BUILDING: E, at steps [4*]. BROWNSON HALL: E side [2*]. BURKE MEMORIAL GOLF COURSE: S central area [many]. CARROLL HALL: SW corner [4*]. CAVANAUGH HALL: NW corner [1*]. CORBY HALL: Dining room, NW [7*]; SW 20yd [3*]; SW corner, S 10yd [1*]. CROWLEY HALL OF MUSIC: W 15-30yd [6*]. DILLON HALL: E court [1]. GROTTO OF OUR LADY OF LOURDES: Above [4*]. HAGGAR HALL: W end [1*]. HOLY CROSS ANNEX: S [1*]. LAFORTUNE STUDENT CENTER: NW corner [1]. LAW SCHOOL: NW corner [1*]; W entrance [1*]. LOG CHAPEL: W end [1]. MORRISSEY HALL: Main entrance, E side [2*]. PRESBYTERY: S 15yd [1*]. SORIN HALL: SE corner [2*]; SW corner [1*]. ST. EDWARD'S HALL: SW corner, W [1]. STADIUM: W, gate 14 [2]. WALSH HALL: SE corner, at Knights of Columbus Hall [6*]. WASHINGTON HALL: W side [1].

'Columnaris' [**Columnar Spruce**]

Evergreen tree. Growth narrowly columnar; branches very short.

> UNIVERSITY HEALTH SERVICES: S, at road turn [1*].

'Cupressina' [**Norway Spruce**]

Evergreen tree. Broadly columnar form; branches upturned; young growth reddish.

> HESBURGH CENTER: Court, E border [4]; Court, N border [4]. SACRED HEART

BASILICA: Main entrance, flanking E door [2]; Main entrance, flanking W door [2]; N, flanking door [2]. SNITE MUSEUM OF ART: Court, planters [2]. SUPPORT SERVICES BUILDING: S bed [2].

### 'Nidiformis' [Bird's Nest Spruce]

Evergreen shrub. Broad, low, dense, rounded with hollow, nestlike center. Maximum height 6 ft.

ADMINISTRATION (MAIN) BUILDING: Front, E bed [1]; Front, W bed [1]. HESBURGH CENTER: Court, NW bed [13]; Court, SE bed [13]. SESQUICENTENNIAL COMMONS: S central outer bed, E and W ends [30]. SUPPORT SERVICES BUILDING: N bed [1]; S bed [2].

### 'Pendula' [Weeping Norway Spruce]

Evergreen tree. Branches drooping but main stem upright.

ADMINISTRATION (MAIN) BUILDING: Front, E bed [1]. MORRIS INN: Main entrance, E beds [beds]. SUPPORT SERVICES BUILDING: N bed [1]; S bed [2].

### 'Pumila' [Dwarf Norway Spruce]

Evergreen shrub. Growth dwarf, dense, broadly rounded; leaves blue green. Maximum height 4 ft.

ADMINISTRATION (MAIN) BUILDING: Front, E bed [3]; Front, W bed [2]. ECK TENNIS PAVILION: S [4]. HESSERT AEROSPACE RESEARCH CENTER: N plaza [4]. ST. MICHAEL'S LAUNDRY: NE corner [8]. SUPPORT SERVICES BUILDING: S bed [1]. ZAHM HALL: NW sign [2].

### 'Repens' [Dwarf Norway Spruce]

Evergreen shrub. Dwarf, spreading form; mounded at the center when mature. ADMINISTRATION (MAIN) BUILDING: Front, E bed [1]; Front, W bed [1].

### *alcoquiana* (J. G. Veitch ex Lindl.) Carrière [Alcock Spruce]

Evergreen tree. Current growth points forward, 0.75 in., gray above, dark below, stiff; reddish twig hairy. Symmetrical habit; silvery appearance. Introduced, native to Japan. Maximum height 75 ft.

### 'Howell's Dwarf' [Alcock Spruce]

Evergreen shrub. Growth dwarf, wide; leaves light blue below, look striped.

ADMINISTRATION (MAIN) BUILDING: Front, E bed [2]; Front, W bed [2]. SACRED HEART BASILICA: E side door, N side [6]. SUPPORT SERVICES BUILDING: S bed [1].

### *glauca* (Moench) Voss [White Spruce]

Evergreen tree. Current leaves grow at right angle, straight, flexible, not sharp; twig shiny yellow brown. Spirelike form with age; needles blue or gray green. Native to northeastern North America. In horticulture since 1700. Maximum height 60 ft.

ARCHITECTURE BUILDING: E along walk to Sorin, N side [5*]; E along walk to Sorin, S side [4*]. FARLEY HALL: E side [3*].

### 'Conica' [Conical White Spruce]

Evergreen tree. Dwarf, dense, pyramidal form; leaves light green. Native to Alberta, Canada, found growing wild. In horticulture since 1904. Maximum height 10 ft.

KOONS REHEARSAL HALL: NW corner [1]. SUPPORT SERVICES BUILDING: S bed (spiral topiary) [2].

### 'Conica Rainbows End' [Rainbows End Spruce]

Evergreen tree. Tufts of golden yellow needles at branch tips. Developed at Iseli Nursery, Boring, Oregon. Maximum height 6 ft.

SUPPORT SERVICES BUILDING: N bed [1].

*omorika* (Panc.) Purk. [**Serbian Spruce**]

> Evergreen tree. Current leaves point forward, flat in cross section, 0.5 in. long, gray green; twig hairy. Narrow, upright form. Introduced, native to southeastern Europe. In horticulture since 1880. Maximum height 60 ft.

'Nana' [**Dwarf Serbian Spruce**]

> Evergreen tree. Growth dwarf, irregularly conical; leaves dense, 0.4 in. long. Maximum height 10 ft.
>
>> ADMINISTRATION (MAIN) BUILDING: Front, E bed [1]; Front, W bed [1]. HESBURGH CENTER: SW Plaza, outer section, corner [36]. JUNIPER ROAD: E, opposite Galvin, N end of planting [3]; North Gate, S end of planting [3]; ROTC stoplight, E planting, S end [3]; W, Library circle N, N end [1]; W, Library circle N, S end [2]; W, Library circle S, N end [3]; W, Library circle S, S end of planting [3]; W, at Bulla Rd, N section, N end [3]; W, at Bulla Rd, S section, S end [3]; W, at Galvin, ends of planting [4]. SACRED HEART BASILICA: Main entrance, flanking [2]. SUPPORT SERVICES BUILDING: S bed [1].

*orientalis* (L.) Link [**Oriental Spruce**]

> Evergreen tree. Current leaves pressed to red gray, hairy twig, 0.4 in. long, blunt or notched tip, shiny. Slow, dense growth; dark needles; branches horizontal, graceful. Introduced, native to Asia. In horticulture since 1827. Maximum height 60 ft.

'Skylands' [**Oriental Spruce**]

> Evergreen tree. Growth dwarf; form narrow; leaves yellow above.
>
>> SUPPORT SERVICES BUILDING: NE bed [1].

*pungens* Engelm. [**Colorado Blue Spruce**]

> Evergreen tree. Current leaves at right angle to twig, 1.5 in., straight, stiff, sharp; twig smooth, tan. Needles blue or gray green, effect can be striking. Native to western North America, Rocky Mountains. In horticulture since 1862. Maximum height 60 ft.
>
>> ADMINISTRATION (MAIN) BUILDING: W front, iron stairs, W [1*]. DEBARTOLO CLASSROOM BUILDING: E side, S of NE door [4]; E side, central lawn [1]. ECK TENNIS PAVILION: SE corner [1]; SW corner [2]. FARLEY HALL: E side [1*]; N end [1*]. GRACE HALL: E side [2]; SW door plaza [2]. HAMMES BOOKSTORE: W wing, NW corner [1*]. HESBURGH CENTER: E side, NE corner, NW [2]; W side, service drive, N [3]; W side, service drive, S [3]. HESBURGH LIBRARY: NW corner [1*]. HESSERT AEROSPACE RESEARCH CENTER: N plaza [9]; S side [4]. JOYCE ATHLETIC AND CONVOCATION CENTER: Gate 2, N of walk [3]. JUNIPER ROAD: N at Douglas Rd, entrance sign [5]; S at Edison Rd, entrance sign [15]. KEENAN HALL: SW corner, S [1*]. KNOTT HALL: N side, along walk [6]; N wing, W end [3]; S wing, S end [2]; W door [3]; W wing, S side [4]. LAFORTUNE STUDENT CENTER: W entrance, N side [1*]. O'SHAUGHNESSY HALL: E side [2]. PASQUERILLA HALL WEST: E wing, E end [3]; E wing, S side [7]; E wing, S walk, end [5]. SACRED HEART BASILICA: E side [1]. SIEGFRIED HALL: E wing, E end [4]; E wing, N side, W end [5]; N, along walk [7]; S wing, S end [2]; SE lawn [2]. SNITE MUSEUM OF ART: S side [4]. ST. EDWARD'S HALL: SW corner, S 12yd [1*]. UNIVERSITY HEALTH SERVICES: SW corner [3*]. ZAHM HALL: SW corner [1*].

'Argentea' [**Colorado Silver Spruce**]

> Evergreen tree. Leaves light blue to silvery white.
>
>> MORRISSEY HALL: SW corner [1*].

'Baby Blue-eyes' [**Colorado Blue Spruce**]

> Evergreen tree. New growth very blue at tips of branches. Ornamental in spring.
> DEBARTOLO CLASSROOM BUILDING: W side, N and S ends [4].

'Glauca' [**Blue Spruce; Colorado Blue Spruce**]

> Evergreen tree. Leaves blue green.
> ADMINISTRATION (MAIN) BUILDING: W front [3*]. BADIN HALL: N door, N 20yd [1*]. COLUMBA HALL: Main entrance, 10yd [1*]. DEBARTOLO CLASSROOM BUILDING: E side, flanking central doors [9]; W side, flanking doors [2]. FATIMA RETREAT HOUSE: Outdoor Station 12 [5*]. HOLY CROSS ANNEX: S lawn [3*]. HOLY CROSS HOUSE: E 40yd, Sacred Heart statue [5*]. HOWARD HALL: N [1*]. JUNIPER ROAD: ROTC stoplight, E parking lot fence [1]. MORRISSEY HALL: Main entrance, E side [1*]. SACRED HEART BASILICA: SE [2*]. ST. EDWARD'S HALL: W side [2*].

'Hoopsii' [**Colorado Spruce**]

> Evergreen tree. Growth fast; form broad and dense; leaves blue white.
> DEBARTOLO CLASSROOM BUILDING: E side, S central area [2]. HESSERT AEROSPACE RESEARCH CENTER: SE corner [2]. SUPPORT SERVICES BUILDING: E side, S end, along wall [2].

'Koster' [**Koster Weeping Blue Spruce**]

> Evergreen tree. Form conical; branchlets drooping; leaves bluish.
> BADIN HALL: NW corner, N 15yd [1*]. DILLON HALL: Main entrance [1*].

'Montgomery' [**Colorado Blue Spruce**]

> Evergreen shrub. Growth dwarf; rounded, bushy form becoming conical with age; leaves silver blue.
> PASQUERILLA HALL EAST: W wing, W end, NW plaza [1]. PASQUERILLA HALL WEST: W door [1]. SUPPORT SERVICES BUILDING: N bed [1]; S bed [1].

'Prostrate Green' [**Colorado Spruce**]

> Evergreen shrub. Growth low, spreading; leaves green.
> ADMINISTRATION (MAIN) BUILDING: Front, E bed [2]; Front, W bed [2]. SACRED HEART BASILICA: Main entrance, E door [5]; Main entrance, W door [5]. SUPPORT SERVICES BUILDING: N bed [1].

'Viridis' [**Colorado Green Spruce**]

> Evergreen tree. Leaves dull, green.
> KEENAN HALL: S, basement stairway [1*].

*purpurea* M. T. Mast. [**Purple Cone Spruce**]

> Evergreen tree. This year's leaves point forward on twig, 0.75 in. long, dark green; twig orange, hairless. Introduced, native to western China. In horticulture since 1910. Maximum height 100 ft.
> SUPPORT SERVICES BUILDING: N bed [2]; S bed [3].

*rubens* Sarg. [**Red Spruce**]

> Evergreen tree. Leaves twisted, crowded above twig, incurved, 0.5 in., dull green; twig red brown, hairy. Native to northeastern North America. In horticulture since 1750. Maximum height 70 ft.
> HAGGAR HALL: N parking lot, N [1*].

*Pinus* L. [**Pine**]

> Among the 90-100 species of pine, there are species that can grow in areas with almost any environmental condition found in North America, ranging from the poor, thin soil at the timberline to the salt spray and wind-subjected areas of the

coasts. Most pines are trees that reach considerable heights, but the shorter species and cultivars are suitable for smaller gardens. The overall pyramidal shape disappears with age. Worldwide, pines are the most important group of lumber trees. Some species are the sources of turpentine, edible pine nuts (pine seeds), and rosin. The Scotch pine, *P. sylvestris*, is the most common Christmas tree grown in the Midwest. Pines are widely distributed in temperate North America, South and Central America, Sumatra, and Java. Six states have designated pines as their state trees. The white pine (*P. strobus*) of Maine and Minnesota and Montana's ponderosa pine (at least the hardier *P. ponderosa* var. *scopulorum*) can be found on the Notre Dame campus.

Needle-leaved tree: evergreen, coniferous, monoecious. Branches whorled on main stem. Needles in bundles (fascicles) arising from papery sheaths attached to branchlets. Female cones produce woody scales that take 2-3 years to mature before opening to release winged seeds. Pines are distinguished from all other needle-leaved conifers by their fascicled needles. All other conifers bear solitary needles that are arranged either singly along the branches, like fir, spruce, hemlock, and yew; or clustered in large numbers at the ends of short spur-shoots as in larch. The many pine species can be separated by cone characteristics and by determining the number of needles in each fascicle, whether grouped in twos, threes, or fives. On the Notre Dame campus *P. aristata*, *P. flexilis*, *P. parviflora*, and *P. strobus* have needles grouped in fives; *P. rigida* has needles in threes; *P. ponderosa* var. *scopulorum* and *P. pungens* have needles variably in twos or threes; and *P. banksiana*, *P. densiflora*, *P. leucodermis*, *P. mugo*, *P. nigra*, *P. resinosa*, *P. sylvestris*, and *P. thunbergii* have needles in twos.

*aristata* Engelm. [**Bristlecone Pine**]

Evergreen tree. Leaves in 5s, 1.75 in. long, edge smooth, sticky resin spots cling to leaves; cone spiny. Growth extremely slow; use in rock garden or as an accent. Native to the western United States. In horticulture since 1861. Maximum height 20 ft.

SUPPORT SERVICES BUILDING: NE bed [1].

*banksiana* Lamb. [**Jack Pine**]

Evergreen tree. Leaf 1 in. long, in groups of 2, papery sheath at leaf base 0.1 in. long. Hardy tree found in sandy soil in the wild. Native to arctic Canada through northeastern United States. In horticulture since 1783. Maximum height 50 ft.

CARROLL HALL: NW 70yd [4*].

*densiflora* Siebold & Zucc. [**Japanese Red Pine**]

Evergreen tree. Leaf 3-5 in. long, in groups of 2, flexible; twig slender; bark orange. Usually shrubby. Introduced, native to Japan. In horticulture since 1854. Maximum height 60 ft.

'Umbraculifera' [**Dwarf Japanese Red Pine**]

Evergreen tree. Dwarf form; broad, dense, umbrellalike outline. Maximum height 9 ft.

LEWIS HALL: E, main entrance, S along wall [3].

*flexilis* James [**Limber Pine**]

Evergreen tree. Leaf 1-3 in. long, in groups of 5, edges smooth, soft, sheath at leaf base deciduous. Irregular, open habit; slow growth; dark blue green foliage. Native to the Rocky Mountains of North America. In horticulture since 1861. Maximum height 50 ft.

CARROLL HALL: E lawn [1]. HAGGAR HALL: N, parking lot, NW corner [1*]. LAFORTUNE STUDENT CENTER: S central door, SSE 20yd [2*].

*leucodermis* Ant. [**Bosnian Pine; Graybark Pine**]

Evergreen tree. Leaves in 2s, to 2.5 in. long, very dark green; sheath 0.13 in. long; bud scale tips pale. Slow-growing; upright form. Introduced, native to Italy, the Balkan Peninsula. Maximum height 90 ft.

'Shira' [**Bosnian Pine; Graybark Pine**]

Low, mounded form.

SUPPORT SERVICES BUILDING: N bed [1]; S bed [1].

*mugo* Turra [**Mugo Pine; Swiss Mountain Pine**]

Evergreen tree. Leaf 0.75-2 in. long, in groups of 2, papery sheath at leaf base 0.1 in. long. Usually shrubby but becomes tall. Introduced, native to central and southern Europe. In horticulture since 1779. Maximum height 20 ft.

ARCHITECTURE BUILDING: E side, N of steps [1]. DILLON HALL: E court [1]. FLANNER HALL: NW, junction of roads [5]. SACRED HEART BASILICA: SE 20yd, lamppost 58 [6*]. SORIN HALL: W central side, W [1]. ST. EDWARD'S HALL: N entrance [1].

*nigra* Arnold [**Austrian Pine**]

Evergreen tree. Leaf to 6.5 in. long, in groups of 2, stiff, will fold but not break when bent; buds brown. Handsome bark in old age, ridged and mottled gray brown. Introduced, native to southcentral Europe, Asia Minor. In horticulture since 1759. Maximum height 60 ft.

BURKE MEMORIAL GOLF COURSE: Dorr Road, S side, along [many]. CARROLL HALL: W [1]. CORBY HALL: W end, W 45yd [1]; W, lakeside [1]. CROWLEY HALL OF MUSIC: NE at walk [1]; SW corner, W 35yd [1]; SW corner, W 50yd [1]. DILLON HALL: SE corner, S 50yd [1]. HURLEY HALL OF BUSINESS ADMINISTRATION: Sorin statue, between [6*]; W side, N [3*]; W side, center [1]; W side, center, W 10yd [1]. JOYCE ATHLETIC AND CONVOCATION CENTER: W, along wall at gate 1 [2]. KNIGHTS OF COLUMBUS COUNCIL HALL: NW corner [1]. KNOTT HALL: S wing, W side [2]; SW lawn [2]; W wing, S side [2]. LAFORTUNE STUDENT CENTER: S side at walks [1]; SW corner, S 15yd [1*]. MORRISSEY HALL: Chapel, E side [1]. O'SHAUGHNESSY HALL: E side [1]. PANGBORN HALL: SW corner, SW [1]; W side [9]. SORIN STATUE: NNE 30yd [1]. ST. MARY'S LAKE: SE edge [1]. WALSH HALL: E 20 yd, between S and central doors [3*]; E central entrance, SE 30yd [1]; E central entrance, SE 50yd [1]. ZAHM HALL: SE courtyard door, 25yd [1].

*parviflora* Siebold & Zucc. [**Japanese White Pine**]

Evergreen tree. Leaf to 2.5 in. long, in groups of 5, edge toothed; twig sparsely hairy. Growth slow; pyramidal, dense form, becomes broad, flat-topped. Introduced, native to Japan, Taiwan. In horticulture since 1861. Maximum height 50 ft.

'Glauca' [**Japanese White Pine**]

Evergreen tree. Leaves twisted, silver blue. Maximum height 45 ft.

FISHER HALL: NE corner [1]. JUNIPER ROAD: S at Edison Rd, entrance sign [4]. SUPPORT SERVICES BUILDING: N bed [1]. ZAHM HALL: N side [1].

*ponderosa* Dougl. ex P. & C. Laws. [**Western Yellow Pine; Ponderosa Pine**]

Evergreen tree. Leaf 5-11 in. long, in groups of 3; cone scale with outward-turned prickle. Grows best where found in the wild. Native to western North America. In horticulture since 1827. Maximum height 100 ft.

var. *scopulorum* Engelm. [**Rocky Mountain Ponderosa Pine**]

Evergreen tree. Leaf 3-6 in. long; branches drooping; shorter than the species. Columnar form; hardier than the species.

ARCHITECTURE BUILDING: NE corner, E 65yd [1]; SE corner, E 55yd [1*].
BADIN HALL: NW corner, W 10yd [1*]. OLD COLLEGE: W [1*]. SOUTH DINING
HALL: E entrance [2*]; NW corner [1*]; SW corner [1]. ST. EDWARD'S HALL:
W side [7*].

*pungens* Lamb. [**Table Mountain Pine**]

Evergreen tree. Leaf 2.5 in. long, in groups of 2-3, coarse, stiff, twisted; cones in
groups of 3. Rarely planted. Native to New Jersey through Georgia. Maximum
height 50 ft.

ST. MARY'S LAKE: NE corner, E side [1].

*resinosa* Ait. [**Red Pine; Norway Pine**]

Evergreen tree. Leaf 5-6 in. long, in groups of 2, stiff, will break or snap when
bent. Tolerates poor soil. Native to northeastern North America. In horticulture
since 1756. Maximum height 80 ft.

CARROLL HALL ANNEX: SW [1]. CORBY HALL: W, lakeside [1*]. DECIO
FACULTY HALL: W, service entrance, N side [2]. GALVIN LIFE SCIENCE CENTER:
W side, N of entrance [3]. HOLY CROSS ANNEX: S, Statue of Little Flower [1].
LOG CHAPEL: N, 10yd [1*]. O'SHAUGHNESSY HALL: N entrance, SE [1]. OLD
COLLEGE: N, lakeside [1*]. PANGBORN HALL: SW corner, S [1].

'Globosa' [**Dwarf Red Pine**]

Evergreen tree. Compact, globe-shaped form; needles shorter.

HAGGAR HALL: E [1*]. SOUTH DINING HALL: SE corner [4*].

*strobus* L. [**Eastern White Pine**]

Evergreen tree. Leaf 2-5 in. long, in groups of 5, edge toothed, flexible; twigs
smooth. Graceful, soft habit; form pyramidal but irregular in old age. Native to
eastern North America. In horticulture since 1705. Maximum height 100 ft.

ANGELA BOULEVARD: Notre Dame Ave campus entrance [8]. CENTER FOR
CONTINUING EDUCATION: E side [6]. FATIMA RETREAT HOUSE: NW [many].
FITZPATRICK HALL OF ENGINEERING: SE corner, E lawn [5]. FLANNER HALL:
NW corner [1]. GALVIN LIFE SCIENCE CENTER: SE corner [5]. GRACE HALL: N
side [4]. HESBURGH LIBRARY: SW corner [8*]. HURLEY HALL OF BUSINESS
ADMINISTRATION: W entrance [3*]. JOYCE ATHLETIC AND CONVOCATION
CENTER: Gate 3 [5]; Gate 8, S side [2]; Gate 9, S side [3]; N side [7]; W, S of
gate 11 [2]; W, between gates 1 and 11 [3]. KNIGHTS OF COLUMBUS COUNCIL
HALL: SE corner, E 15yd [1*]. LYONS HALL: SE front [5*]. PASQUERILLA HALL
EAST: N wing, E side [9]. PASQUERILLA HALL WEST: N wing, N end [3]. POST
OFFICE: SE corner [3]. SORIN STATUE: SW 30yd [1*]. STADIUM: E, gate 3 [5];
E, gate 7 [5]; NE, gates 1 and 2 [4]; SE, gate 9 [3]. STEPAN CENTER: S side,
flanking door [6]. UNIVERSITY CLUB: N side [2]. WALSH HALL: Main entrance,
E 15yd [1*]. ZAHM HALL: N [1].

'Blue Shag' [**Eastern White Pine**]

Evergreen shrub. Dwarf; globe-shaped form to 4.0 ft. wide; needles very dense.
Maximum height 3 ft.

HAMMES BOOKSTORE: W wing, S [2]. PASQUERILLA HALL EAST: W wing, W
end, NW plaza [2]. SUPPORT SERVICES BUILDING: N bed [4]; S bed [4].

'Fastigiata' [**Pyramidal White Pine**]

Evergreen tree. Narrowly columnar form when young; branches ascending.

CAVANAUGH HALL: Breen-Phillips, between [2*]. HURLEY HALL OF BUSINESS
ADMINISTRATION: E end, N [2*]. KNIGHTS OF COLUMBUS COUNCIL HALL: Sorin
statue, between [3*]. NIEUWLAND SCIENCE HALL: LaFortune, between [few*].
RILEY HALL OF ART AND DESIGN: W side [1*]. WALSH HALL: Chapel, E 10yd

[1*].

*sylvestris* L. [**Scotch Pine**]

Evergreen tree. Leaf 1.5-3 in. long, in groups of 2, twisted; papery sheath at leaf base to 0.1 in. long. Introduced, native to Europe through northern Asia. Maximum height 60 ft.

Burke Memorial Golf Course: NW area [1]; NW area, near W fence [10]; Sollitt shelter, E path [1]. Carroll Hall: SW corner, W [4]. Columba Hall: SE corner, SE [1]. Corby Hall: SW corner, SW 20yd [1]. Dillon Hall: S side, E [1]. Farley Hall: Breen-Phillips, between [1]. Flanner Hall: SW corner [2]; W side [3]; W wing, NW corner [1]; W wing, NW corner, N 50yd [few]. Galvin Life Science Center: SE [1]; SE corner [1]. Hayes-Healy Center: NW corner, W 50yd [1]. Joyce Athletic and Convocation Center: Gate 8, flanking [2]; W, along N wall at gate 2 [3]; W, along wall at gate 1 [2]. Old College: NE corner, NE 35yd, lakeside [1]. Post Office: NW corner, N 10yd [3]. Radiation Research Building: SW corner [3]. Rockne Memorial: W, along Dorr Rd, S side [few*]. St. Mary's Lake: Architecture Bldg, N at lake margin [1]; N edge [1]. Stepan Chemistry Hall: NE corner, NE, 20yd [4]. Walsh Hall: Hurley Hall, between [4*]; NE corner, NE 30yd [1*].

'Fastigiata' [**Pyramidal Scotch Pine**]

Evergreen tree. Columnar, very narrow form; branches upright. Maximum height 25 ft.

Center for Social Concerns: SW corner [1*]. Hesburgh Library: S, main entrance [few*].

'Pendula' [**Weeping Scotch Pine**]

Evergreen tree. Branches drooping.

Carroll Hall: E lawn [1*]. Corby Hall: W, lakeside [1*].

var. *rigensis* Loud. [**Upright Scotch Pine**]

Evergreen tree. Bark very red; crown conical.

Corby Hall: Main entrance, S 35yd, S of road [2*]. Grotto of Our Lady of Lourdes: Above [1*].

'Watereri' [**Waterer Scotch Pine**]

Evergreen tree. Growth dwarf, dense; conical form, becomes broad and flat with age. Maximum height 10 ft.

Fisher Hall: W side [2*]. Hesburgh Library: Pool, NE corner, lamppost C18, SE 5yd [1*].

*thunbergiana* Franco [**Japanese Black Pine**]

Evergreen tree. Leaf 2-5 in. long, in groups of 2, stiff; bud white, not resinous. Buds conspicuous against shiny dark green leaves. Introduced, native to Japan. In horticulture since 1855. Maximum height 80 ft.

Carroll Hall: W side, center, W 60yd [2*]. LaFortune Student Center: S central door, S 30yd [1]. St. Mary's Lake: N edge [1*].

*Pseudolarix* Gord. [**Golden-larch**]

Golden-larch is a rarely grown tree that deserves more attention. It grows slowly, becoming only 45 ft. tall in 100 years. Its broadly pyramidal outline makes it suitable for growing in a parklike setting. The name golden-larch refers to the beautiful autumn color of the needles before they fall. It was brought to England from China in 1854 by Robert Fortune, a Scotsman who worked as a botanical and horticultural collector for the Horticultural Society of London and, later, for the East India Company. He transported living plants to England from the Orient by sealing them in soil-filled wood and glass cases that allowed them to survive aboard ship without the loss of moisture to drying winds, which had thwarted previous importation efforts. Golden-larch is native to the mountains of eastern China.

Needle-leaved tree: deciduous, coniferous, monoecious. Branches whorled on main trunk. Branches of 2 types: long and thin with solitary needles or slow-growing spur shoots marked by annual constrictions or rings. Most needles grow in clusters of 15-30 that appear whorled at ends of spur shoots. Male and female flowers on separate branches of same plant. Female cones at ends of branches. Golden-larch can be distinguished from true larch (*Larix*) both by its larger cones, which look like artichokes and disintegrate at the end of the growing season, and by its longer, broader needles.

*kaempferi* Gord. [**Golden-larch**]

Deciduous tree. Leaves in groups of 15-30, 1.5-2.5 in. long; cones erect. Leaves turn golden yellow. Ornamental in autumn. Introduced, native to eastern China. In horticulture since 1854. Maximum height 50 ft.

'Nana' [**Dwarf Golden-larch**]

Deciduous tree. Dwarf form.

SACRED HEART BASILICA: W side [1].


*Pseudotsuga* Carrière [**Douglas-fir**]

One of the most important timber trees, Douglas-fir also is used as a Christmas tree. It is the state tree of Oregon. Its common name refers to David Douglas (1799-1834), who introduced this tree to England after visiting the Pacific Northwest in the 1820s as a plant explorer for the Horticultural Society of London. Douglas-fir, with its medium growth rate, is popular as an evergreen ornamental tree wherever it is not too windy and dry. It can tolerate pruning, which even allows its use as a hedge. The Douglas-firs are native to eastern Asia and western North America, ranging from British Columbia to Texas and Mexico.

Tall needle-leaved tree: evergreen, coniferous, monoecious. Branches whorled along main trunk. Needles grow singly on branches and are soft but sharp-pointed with 2 white bands beneath. Female cones hang from branches and bear protruding, papery, three-pronged bracts. Douglas-fir can be separated from all other evergreens by these distinctive hanging cones, the sharp-pointed and shiny, chestnut brown buds at the tips of the branchlets, and the soft needles.

*menziesii* (Mirbel) Franco [**Douglas-fir**]

Evergreen tree. Leaf 1-1.5 in. long; cone hanging, with protruding 3-pronged bracts; bud long-pointed. Form tall and stately. Native to the Pacific Coast and Rocky Mountains. In horticulture since 1827. Maximum height 80 ft.

ARCHITECTURE BUILDING: SE corner, E 35yd [1*]. FIRE STATION: NE corner [1*]. HAMMES BOOKSTORE: SE corner [1]. LAFORTUNE STUDENT CENTER: N side [1*]; S side [1*]; SW corner [1*]. LAW SCHOOL: SW door, S [1]. LOG CHAPEL: S side [9*]. MORRIS INN: NE corner, N 20yd [1]. MORRISSEY HALL: SE corner [1*]. SORIN HALL: SE 45yd [4*]. WASHINGTON HALL: Sacred Heart statue, midway [1*].

*Tsuga* Carrière [**Hemlock**]

Many people think hemlocks are the most beautiful of all needle-leaved evergreens. They tolerate shade but are intolerant of drought and strong winds. They can be grown as specimen trees or pruned and used in hedges. Although the common name is hemlock, this is not the poison hemlock that Greek philosopher and teacher Socrates (d. 399 B.C.) was forced to drink when condemned to death for "impiety and corrupting youth." He drank a draft made from *Conium maculatum*, an herbaceous plant in the parsley family that is native to Europe. Although the two plants are not even remotely related, the hemlock tree acquired its common name apparently because its feathery branching pattern bears a vague resemblance to the pinnately compound leaves of poison hemlock. Tannin extracted from hemlock tree bark is used for tanning leather, and hemlock wood has been used as paper pulp. Hemlocks are native to eastern Asia and temperate North America. The eastern hemlock, *T. canadensis*, is the state tree of Pennsylvania.

Needle-leaved tree: evergreen, coniferous, monoecious. Slender, flexible branches give a graceful appearance. Needles solitary, short, flat, blunt or rounded and attached to branchlets by small, but distinct, leaf stalks or petioles. Female cones small, hanging from tips of branchlets. Hemlocks can be differentiated from the firs by the small, pendant cones and the rough projections remaining on the branches when the needles are removed. Hemlocks can be separated from the spruces, which also have hanging cones, although larger, by the mode of attachment of the needles to the branchlets. Hemlock needles are constricted at the base and have a distinct leaf stalk or petiole. Spruce needles are not narrow at the base and are not attached by a leaf stalk to the branchlets.

*canadensis* (L.) Carrière [**Eastern Hemlock**]

Evergreen tree. Leaf to 0.75 in. long, toothed, narrowing to rounded tip; cone small, to 0.75 in., hanging. Graceful, feathery appearance. Native to eastern North America. Maximum height 70 ft.

CALVARY [3*]. CARROLL HALL: SW corner, [10*]. GROTTO OF OUR LADY OF LOURDES: N side, steps, N side [1*]; S side [2*]. HOLY CROSS ANNEX: S [7*]; S side [2*]. PRESBYTERY: NW corner [1*]; SW corner [1*]. SACRED HEART BASILICA: Sacristy, S side [5*].

'Dawsoniana' [**Eastern Hemlock**]

Evergreen tree. Growth slow; compact form, broader than tall; needles dark green. Developed in Wellesley, Massachusetts. In horticulture since 1920.

SUPPORT SERVICES BUILDING: S bed [1].

'Golden Splendor' [**Eastern Hemlock**]

Evergreen tree. Upright form; leaves yellow.

SUPPORT SERVICES BUILDING: S bed [1].

'Jeddeloh' [**Eastern Hemlock**]

Evergreen shrub. Growth dwarf; mounded, spreading form; branches drooping. Maximum height 1 ft.

DEBARTOLO CLASSROOM BUILDING: N side, below windows [15]. PASQUERILLA HALL EAST: N wing, W side [9]; W wing, N side [10]. PASQUERILLA HALL WEST: E wing, N side, W of door [8].

'Pendula' [**Eastern Hemlock**]

Evergreen tree. Form wider than tall; branches drooping.

SACRED HEART BASILICA: W side [1]. SUPPORT SERVICES BUILDING: S bed [1].

# TAXODIACEAE [TAXODIUM FAMILY]

*Metasequoia* Miki [**Dawn Redwood**]

A fast-growing, pyramidal tree with a soft feathery appearance, dawn redwood grows best in moist, slightly acid soil where it is protected from early autumn frosts. In northern areas it often does better in warmer hillside and upland sites than in low areas and ravines. It is an ancient tree genus that was discovered in Japan as a fossil in 1941 from Pliocene sediments 5 million years old. Living trees were found in eastern Szechwan Province, China, that same year, causing much excitement in the botanical world. Seeds from these trees were gathered in 1947-48 during a special expedition sponsored by the Arnold Arboretum of Harvard University at Cambridge, Massachusetts. The seeds were shared with interested botanists and horticulturists at universities and arboreta around the world. Trees grown from these seeds can be seen on many college campuses and in public gardens.

Needle-leaved tree: deciduous, coniferous, monoecious. Branches of 2 kinds, either persistent or deciduous. Persistent branches bright red-brown. Deciduous branches thin, bearing 50-60 needles each, dropping with leaves during autumn. Female cones small, dark brown, hanging on long stalks (peduncles). Dawn redwood may be confused with baldcypress (*Taxodium*). Both have short, soft, flat needlelike leaves growing on deciduous branches and reddish, shreddy bark. But the needles of dawn redwood are arranged in pairs, opposite each other along the branchlets; those of baldcypress are alternately arranged along the stems.

*glyptostroboides* H. H. Hu & Cheng [**Dawn Redwood**]

Deciduous tree. Leaves to 1.5 in. long; cones to 1.25 in. long. Pyramidal outline; feathery foliage. Ornamental in summer. Introduced, native to China. In horticulture since 1948. Maximum height 100 ft.

ADMINISTRATION (MAIN) BUILDING: S side, SW inner corner [1]. MOREAU SEMINARY: E court [1]. MORRIS INN: NE corner [1]. SACRED HEART BASILICA: Main entrance, SE 30yd [1]. ST. JOSEPH HALL: W end, N 60yd [1*].

*Sciadopitys* Siebold & Zucc. [**Umbrella-pine**]

This is an unusual, slow-growing tree that appears pinelike. It does not lose its lower branches with age and has no serious diseases or insect pests. It does poorly in hot dry situations. The name umbrella-pine refers to the spokelike arrangement of the needles. Although today this tree is found only in one valley in Honshu, a central island of Japan, it was much more widespread during the Tertiary period (1,000,000-70,000,000 years ago) of the Cenozoic era and is found as fossilized remnants in the brown coal of Europe. Its wood is used for shipbuilding and oils are extracted for use in varnish.

Scale-leaved and needle-leaved tree: evergreen, coniferous, monoecious. Branches horizontal, arranged in whorls along main stem. Scale leaves scattered spirally along twigs, crowded near tips. Needlelike leaves (fused pairs of leaves with central groove) in whorls of 20-30 along twigs. Female cones, maturing in 2 years, grow either upright or horizontally or hang from branches and bear broad scales with 5-9 seeds per scale.

*verticillata* (Thunb.) Siebold & Zucc. [**Umbrella-pine**]

Evergreen tree. Leaves 2-5 in. long, in groups of 20-30; cones 1.75-4 in. long.

Unusual foliage and texture for use as an accent tree. Introduced, native to Japan. In horticulture since 1861. Maximum height 30 ft.

Sacred Heart Basilica: W side [1]. Support Services Building: S bed [1].

### *Taxodium* L. Rich. [**Baldcypress**]

A tall, pyramidal tree that casts light shade, baldcypress is appropriate in a large parklike setting where moisture is available. The familiar "knees" that form around the trunk when baldcypress is growing in its native swampy habitat in the southern United States do not form when it is grown in upland sites or gardens. Its wood is highly rot resistant even when water-saturated and, consequently, is valuable as timber for wet conditions. Baldcypress is native to eastern North America and the central highland plateau of Mexico.

Needle-leaved tree: deciduous, coniferous, monoecious. Branches of 2 types present. Early branches persistent, turning brown. Later branches remaining green, deciduous, dropping with needles during autumn. Cones small, short-stalked with thick shield-shaped scales; purplish early, turning brown with age. Baldcypress resembles dawn redwood, but can be distinguished by the manner in which the needles are arranged on the branches. Baldcypress needles are arranged alternately along the stem whereas dawn redwood needles are in opposite pairs along the stem.

### *distichum* (L.) L. Rich. [**Baldcypress**]

Deciduous tree. Leaves 1 in. long; cones 0.5 in. long; bark shredding. Stately tree for wet sites. Native to southcentral and southeastern United States. In horticulture since 1640. Maximum height 70 ft.

Grotto of Our Lady of Lourdes: W, St. Mary's Lake, between [1*]. LaFortune Student Center: SW 30yd [1]. Snite Museum of Art: SW corner [2]. Washington Hall: Cavanaugh, between [2].

## CUPRESSACEAE [CYPRESS FAMILY]

### *Chamaecyparis* Spach [**Falsecypress**]

Falsecypress is native to regions of North America and Asia that have humid, moist climates, but it is being introduced gradually into the dryer areas of the midwestern United States. Tree forms become very tall, but numerous dwarf, well-formed cultivars have been developed. Some species of falsecypress are used for timber. Many are grown as ornamentals because of the great variety in size and form.

Scale-leaved (awl-shaped on some juvenile forms) tree: evergreen, coniferous, monoecious. Leaves arranged in opposite pairs around stem, resulting in square cross-sectional outline. Branches and branchlets form flexible, flattened sprays. Separating falsecypress from *Thuja* and *Platycladus* is difficult without comparing their cones. Falsecypress cones are spherical with 6-12 shield-shaped, woody scales that are pointed at the center; whereas *Thuja* cones are longer than wide and have overlapping scales. *Platycladus* cones are ovoid with 6-8 scales, each terminating in a hook. The leaves of either *Chamaecyparis* or *Platycladus* may be grooved. This central groove appears only on alternating pairs (those in only one plane) or not at all on *Platycladus*, but is found on the paired leaves growing in both planes in *Chamaecyparis*.

### *nootkatensis* (D. Don) Spach [**Nootka Falsecypress; Alaska-cedar**]

Evergreen tree. Leaves sharp, keeled, spreading, seam hidden, length equal, green below; twig 4-angled. Native to western United States, Alaska to Oregon. In horticulture since 1853. Maximum height 45 ft.

### 'Glauca Compacta' [**Nootka Falsecypress**]

Evergreen tree. Leaves bluish; form conical with dense growth.

> HESBURGH CENTER: S side, SW edge [3]; SE corner, W [3]; W side, S section, in bed [3].

### 'Pendula' [**Weeping Nootka Falsecypress**]

Evergreen tree. Branches drooping.

> CORBY HALL: E side, S end [3*]. HESBURGH CENTER: Court, S bed [1]; Court, W bed [1]; Court, middle bed [3]; E side, NE corner [3]; SE corner [3]. SUPPORT SERVICES BUILDING: E, along wall [6].

### *obtusa* (Siebold & Zucc.) Endl. [**Hinoki Falsecypress**]

Evergreen tree. Leaf blunt, pressed to stem, not keeled, side leaf longer than face leaf, seam not visible. Introduced, native to Japan. In horticulture since 1861. Maximum height 75 ft.

> MORRIS INN: E, along building, N of main entrance [2]. PASQUERILLA HALL WEST: E wing, N side [4]; N wing, E side [1]; W door [2].

### 'Aurea' [**Hinoki Falsecypress**]

Evergreen tree. Leaves at ends of branches yellow.

> ADMINISTRATION (MAIN) BUILDING: Front, E bed [1]. HESBURGH CENTER: SE corner, W 10yd [2]; W side, N section, middle, W 10yd [2].

### 'Crippsii' [**Hinoki Falsecypress**]

Evergreen tree. Broadly pyramidal form; growth slow; branchlets fernlike, incurved; foliage yellow at ends.

> MORRISSEY HALL: N side [2]. SUPPORT SERVICES BUILDING: S bed [1].

### 'Fernspray Gold' [**Hinoki Falsecypress**]

Evergreen shrub. Growth dwarf; leaves yellow; branches twisted.

> SUPPORT SERVICES BUILDING: N bed (standard) [1].

### 'Nana Gracilis' [**Hinoki Falsecypress**]

Evergreen tree. Dwarf, bushy pyramidal form; growth at branch tips dense, twisted. Maximum height 6 ft.

> ADMINISTRATION (MAIN) BUILDING: Front, E bed [1]; Front, W bed [1]. MORRIS INN: E, along building, N of main entrance [1]. PASQUERILLA HALL EAST: N wing, E side [2]; N wing, W door [2]; W wing, N side [2]. SUPPORT SERVICES BUILDING: S bed [1]; S bed (standard) [2].

### 'Nana Lutea' [**Hinoki Falsecypress**]

Evergreen shrub. Dense, broadly pyramidal form to 4 ft. wide; branches twisted; leaves dark green, thick. Maximum height 6 ft.

> SUPPORT SERVICES BUILDING: S bed [1].

### 'Pygmaea Aurescens' [**Hinoki Falsecypress**]

Evergreen tree. Dwarf, broad form; leaves bronze above.

> HESSERT AEROSPACE RESEARCH CENTER: E side [4]. MAINTENANCE CENTER: E, between ND Press and Transportation [2]. MORRIS INN: E, along building, N of main entrance [6]. PASQUERILLA HALL EAST: N wing, E side [1]. PASQUERILLA HALL WEST: W door [1]. SUPPORT SERVICES BUILDING: N bed (Blue Carpet juniper graft below) [1]. ZAHM HALL: NW sign [2].

### *pisifera* (Siebold & Zucc.) Endl. [**Sawara Falsecypress**]

Evergreen tree. Leaves sharp, keeled, spreading, white-marked below, side leaves shorter; twig round. Introduced, native to Japan. In horticulture since 1861. Maximum height 70 ft.

> ALUMNI HALL: Chapel, W end, S tree [1*]; W court, S side [1*]. BROWNSON HALL: Court [3*]. BURKE MEMORIAL GOLF COURSE: NW area [1]. DILLON HALL: NE corner [1*]. MORRISSEY HALL: E wing, N 15yd [1*].

### 'Boulevard' [Sawara Falsecypress]

Evergreen tree. Leaves silver blue; form irregularly conical; growth slow. Maximum height 10 ft.

> GRACE HALL: SW door plaza [9]. MORRIS INN: Main entrance, E beds [20]. PASQUERILLA HALL EAST: N wing, E side [5]. PASQUERILLA HALL WEST: W door [5]. SUPPORT SERVICES BUILDING: S bed [1].

### 'Filifera Aurea Nana' [Sawara Falsecypress]

Evergreen shrub. Dwarf form; branches in threadlike sprays; leaves awl-shaped, yellow.

> MORRIS INN: Main entrance, E beds [beds].

### 'Filifera Nana' [Sawara Falsecypress]

Evergreen tree. Growth dwarf; leaves awl-shaped.

> JOYCE ATHLETIC AND CONVOCATION CENTER: Gate 2, N of walk [5].

### 'Golden Mop' [Sawara Falsecypress]

Evergreen tree. Dwarf growth; round to conical form; branches drooping; leaves yellow.

> ECK TENNIS PAVILION: S side [9]. HESSERT AEROSPACE RESEARCH CENTER: E side [12]; N plaza, SE corner [3]. JUNIPER ROAD: N at Douglas Rd, entrance sign [6]; S at Edison Rd, entrance sign [6]. PASQUERILLA HALL EAST: W wing, W end, NW plaza [12]. SUPPORT SERVICES BUILDING: N bed [5]; S bed [4]. ZAHM HALL: NW sign [2].

## *Juniperus* L. [Juniper]

Very common and popular ornamentals, junipers grow in many forms including pyramidal trees, shrubs of various habits, and low mat-forming ground covers. They are tolerant of most soil, pollution, and moisture conditions, but need sun. Only female bushes bear the decorative bluish, berrylike fruits. The junipers should not be grown near many woody plants of the rose family, including serviceberry, hawthorn, and crab apple, because they are the alternate host of a fungus disease called cedar apple rust, which has a complex 2-part life cycle. One part of the cycle is spent on junipers, where fleshy orange growths with hornlike appendages form. These growths form spores that travel by air to deciduous woody plants of the rose family where they form distinctive flat spots with orange, red and yellow rings on the leaves. These spots are aesthetically unappealing and, in humid years when they are numerous, can limit photosynthesis and weaken the plant. Extracts from juniper fruits are found in varnish and medicinal preparations and are used as the flavoring in gin and some foods, especially meat or poultry dishes. The wood is used in panelling, pencils, and fencing. The aromatic wood found in cedar chests comes from *J. virginiana*, which is native to eastern North America. Junipers are native to broad regions of the Northern Hemisphere, growing as far north as the Arctic.

Needlelike or scale-leaved shrub or small tree: evergreen, coniferous, dioecious or monoecious. Leaves arranged in opposite pairs (usually) along stem. Leaves always needlelike on young plants. Both needlelike and scale leaves on old plants. Fruit a small, pea-sized cone of fleshy scales united to appear berrylike, each with 1-12 seeds. The only other needle-leaved evergreen with berrylike fruit is *Taxus*, which differs in its red fruits.

Those of juniper are purple brown to blue black.

*chinensis* L. [**Chinese Juniper**]

> Evergreen tree. Scale leaves usually blunt but some may be sharp and grouped in threes; fruit brown. Often shrubby. Introduced, native to eastern Asia. In horticulture since 1767. Maximum height 60 ft.
>
> > BURKE MEMORIAL GOLF COURSE: NE area [few]; Sollitt shelter, E [1]. CORBY HALL: NW, Grotto lawn, S edge [4*]; W 40ft [3*]. O'SHAUGHNESSY HALL: NW corner, S 10yd [1*]; NW corner, S 10yd [1].

'Arbuscula' [**Chinese Arborescent Juniper**]

> Evergreen tree. Dense, conical form; leaves bright green.
>
> > BURKE MEMORIAL GOLF COURSE: Scattered throughout [15*]. FATIMA RETREAT HOUSE: Fatima shrine, flanking [hedge*].

'Columnaris' [**Chinese Columnar Juniper**]

> Evergreen tree. Growth fast; narrow, conical form; leaves needlelike.
>
> > O'SHAUGHNESSY HALL: W entrance [1*].

'Globosa' [**Chinese Globe Juniper**]

> Evergreen tree. Growth dwarf; dense, rounded form. Developed in Japan. Maximum height 7 ft.
>
> > ALUMNI HALL: Chapel, W end [7*]. DILLON HALL: Chapel, E end [5*].

'Keteleeri' [**Keteleer Juniper**]

> Evergreen tree. Pyramidal form; stiff trunk; foliage open, loose; leaves scalelike, sharp. In horticulture since 1905. Maximum height 20 ft.
>
> > MOREAU SEMINARY: NW, S of fuel tanks [1*].

'Mas' [**Robert Fortune Juniper**]

> Evergreen tree. Male trees only; broadly columnar form; growth dense. Maximum height 30 ft.
>
> > DILLON HALL: E court [7*]; W court [6*].

'Old Gold' [**Chinese Juniper**]

> Evergreen tree. Growth compact; leaves yellow to bronze. Maximum height 4 ft.
>
> > ADMINISTRATION (MAIN) BUILDING: Front, E bed [3]. DEBARTOLO CLASSROOM BUILDING: E side, N end along S wall [9]; E side, SE corner [28]; N side, NE corner [25]; W side, NW corner [8]; W side, SW corner [8]. HESBURGH CENTER: E side, NE corner [12]; SE corner [12]. HESSERT AEROSPACE RESEARCH CENTER: N plaza [12]. JUNIPER ROAD: N at Douglas Rd, entrance sign [6]; S at Edison Rd, entrance sign [6]; W, Library circle N, S planting [4]. SUPPORT SERVICES BUILDING: E side, flanking door [19].

'Pfitzeriana' [**Pfitzer Juniper**]

> Evergreen shrub. Branches wide-spreading, tips nodding; leaves bright green. Most commonly planted juniper cultivar. Maximum height 10 ft.
>
> > HOLY CROSS ANNEX: W, tool shed, SW 15yd [3*]. LAFORTUNE STUDENT CENTER: W entrance, NW 5yd [2*].

var. *sargentii* A. Henry [**Sargent Juniper**]

> Evergreen shrub. Broadly mounded form; leaves blue green, waxy. Introduced, native to Japan. In horticulture since 1892. Maximum height 2 ft.
>
> > MOREAU SEMINARY: E end, steps [2*].

'Sea Green' [**Chinese Juniper**]

> Evergreen shrub. Compact, spreading form; branches arching; leaves bright to dark green. Maximum height 6 ft.
>
> > HESBURGH CENTER: E side [12]; S side [36]. JOYCE ATHLETIC AND CONVOCATION CENTER: N at B2 parking lot [bed]; W side, between gates 1

and 2 [beds]. JUNIPER ROAD: N at Douglas Rd, entrance sign [bed]; S at Edison Rd, entrance sign [bed]; W, at Bulla Rd, N section, campus-side [5]; W, at Bulla Rd, S section, campus-side [5]. SIEGFRIED HALL: SE door plaza, planter [bed].

### 'Shimpaku' [Chinese Juniper]

Evergreen shrub. Irregular, low form.

HESSERT AEROSPACE RESEARCH CENTER: E side [10]. JOYCE ATHLETIC AND CONVOCATION CENTER: W wall, center, between gates 1 and 2 [bed]. JUNIPER ROAD: W, Library circle S, fence, roadside [2]; W, at Bulla Rd, middle section, roadside [12]. ST. MICHAEL'S LAUNDRY: E side, N of walk, along wall [9]. SUPPORT SERVICES BUILDING: S bed [1].

### 'Torulosa' [Clustered Juniper]

Evergreen shrub. Branches tufted, cordlike; growth rapid. Sometimes 25 ft. tall and treelike. Maximum height 6 ft.

CARROLL HALL: S, parking lot, W end [8*]. FISHER HALL: S end, near road [7*]. HOLY CROSS HOUSE: Moreau Seminary, midway between [1*].

### 'Torulosa Variegata' [Variegated Clustered Juniper]

Evergreen shrub. Upright form; growth slow; foliage splashed with white or yellow blotches. Marks on foliage striking; used as accent plant.

SUPPORT SERVICES BUILDING: N bed [2].

### communis L. [Common Juniper]

Evergreen tree. Leaves needlelike, wide white band above, not fused along twig, joined at discrete point. Native to North America, Europe, Asia. Maximum height 15 ft.

### 'Effusa' [Common Juniper]

Evergreen ground cover. Wide-spreading form; growth open; leaves needlelike, silvery above, rich green below. Maintains leaf color in winter. Maximum height 1 ft.

ADMINISTRATION (MAIN) BUILDING: Front, E bed [3]; Front, W bed [2]. DEBARTOLO CLASSROOM BUILDING: N side, NW door, flanking [42]. HESBURGH CENTER: Court, E border [12]; Court, N border [30]; Court, square planter [20]; N side, residence patios [51]. SACRED HEART BASILICA: E side door, S side [6]. SUPPORT SERVICES BUILDING: N bed (standard) [1]; S bed [1]; S bed (standard) [1].

### conferta Parl. [Shore Juniper]

Evergreen shrub. Leaf needlelike, upper thin white band hidden in deep groove, each joins twig at one point. Tolerates salt and dry, sandy soil. Introduced, native to Japan. In horticulture since 1915. Maximum height 2 ft.

### 'Blue Pacific' [Shore Juniper]

Evergreen ground cover. Leaves very short, densely spaced. Leaves blue green; hardier than the species. Maximum height 1 ft.

DEBARTOLO CLASSROOM BUILDING: E side, N of doors [38]; E side, S of doors [38]; W side, N of doors [16]; W side, S of doors [20].

### horizontalis Moench [Creeping Juniper]

Evergreen ground cover. Most leaves scalelike, blue green; twigs with pleasant odor when crushed. Widely used to cover hot, rocky slopes. Native to North America. In horticulture since 1836. Maximum height 2 ft.

ECK TENNIS PAVILION: S side, flanking walk [beds]. KNOTT HALL: W door, central bed [bed]. KOONS REHEARSAL HALL: E side [18]. PASQUERILLA CENTER: S side, flanking door [beds]. PASQUERILLA HALL EAST: W wing, W end, NW plaza [beds]. SNITE MUSEUM OF ART: Court [bed].

### 'Blue Chip' [**Creeping Juniper**]

Evergreen ground cover. Spreads 10 ft. wide; leaves stay blue during summer, purple-tipped in winter. Developed by Hill Nursery Company. In horticulture since 1940. Maximum height 0.8 ft.

> SESQUICENTENNIAL COMMONS: E inner bed [58]; N inner beds [40]; S inner beds [40]; W inner bed [58].

### 'Plumosa' [**Andorra Juniper**]

Evergreen ground cover. Wide-spreading, dense form; growth rapid; leaves purplish in winter. Developed by Andorra Nurseries, Philadelphia, Pennsylvania. In horticulture since 1907. Maximum height 2 ft.

> DeBARTOLO CLASSROOM BUILDING: S side [10]. FATIMA RETREAT HOUSE: Outdoor Stations [beds*]; W, Highway 31 entrance, center [bed*]. JUNIPER ROAD: North Gate, fence, at benches [5]; ROTC stoplight, E parking lot fence [4].

### 'Youngstown' [**Creeping Juniper**]

Evergreen ground cover. Growth very low; leaves green.

> JUNIPER ROAD [beds].

### *procumbens* (Endl.) Miq. in Sieb. & Zucc. [**Creeping Juniper**]

Evergreen ground cover. Leaves needlelike, fused along twig, 2 white spots at base above, waxy. Introduced, native to Japan. In horticulture since 1843. Maximum height 2 ft.

### 'Nana' [**Creeping Juniper**]

Evergreen ground cover. Mounded, spreading form; growth dense; leaves blue green, purplish in winter. Maximum height 2.5 ft.

> ADMINISTRATION (MAIN) BUILDING: Front, E bed [2]; Front, W bed [1]; Main steps, E bed [2]. SUPPORT SERVICES BUILDING: N bed (standard) [1].

### *sabina* L. [**Savin Juniper**]

Evergreen shrub. Leaves scalelike, dark green; twig with unpleasant odor when crushed. Stiff, vase-shaped habit. Introduced, native to western Asia, Europe. In horticulture since 1580. Maximum height 6 ft.

> ADMINISTRATION (MAIN) BUILDING: Front, SE corner [1*]. HOLY CROSS ANNEX: S, lake steps, flanking [6*]. OUTDOOR WAY OF THE CROSS: Station 1, E 10yd [1*].

### 'Blue Danube' [**Savin Juniper**]

Evergreen ground cover. Semi-upright, more horizontal than species; crowded twigs curve up; awl and scale leaves. Spreads to 12 ft.; leaves gray blue. Maximum height 4 ft.

> SESQUICENTENNIAL COMMONS: E outer bed [50]; SE outer bed [18]; SW outer bed [18]; W outer bed [50].

### 'Tamariscifolia' [**Tamarix Savin**]

Evergreen shrub. Growth low, rapid; leaves needlelike, bright green. Maximum height 1.5 ft.

> CENTER FOR SOCIAL CONCERNS: E side [hedge*]. GROTTO OF OUR LADY OF LOURDES: SE, steps, N [1*]. PASQUERILLA HALL WEST: N wing, W side, planter [6].

### 'Variegata' [**Hoarfrost Savin**]

Evergreen shrub. Growth dwarf; branches drooping at tips; leaves scalelike, white-streaked. Maximum height 3 ft.

> DeBARTOLO CLASSROOM BUILDING: W side, S of doors [16]; W side, between

doors [34]. FATIMA RETREAT HOUSE: Fatima shrine, flanking [beds*]. JOYCE ATHLETIC AND CONVOCATION CENTER: W side, corners between gates 1 and 2 [beds]. SUPPORT SERVICES BUILDING: N bed [1]; S bed [1].

### *scopulorum* Sarg. [**Rocky Mountain Juniper**]

Evergreen tree. Leaves scalelike, some sharp and opposite; twig odorless; fruit blue; bark loose. Popular for its pyramidal habit and steel blue leaves. Native to the North American Rocky Mountains. In horticulture since 1836. Maximum height 40 ft.

### 'Skyrocket' [**Rocky Mountain Juniper**]

Evergreen tree. Narrowest columnar form available, may be only 2 ft. wide when 15 ft. tall.

JUNIPER ROAD: ROTC stoplight, E parking lot fence [3].

### 'Table Top' [**Rocky Mountain Juniper**]

Evergreen shrub. Flat-topped form; growth dwarf; leaves silver blue. Maximum height 6 ft.

HESBURGH CENTER: Court, planter N1 [8]; Court, planter N2 [8]; Court, planter N3 [8]; Court, planter N4 [6]. SUPPORT SERVICES BUILDING: N bed [1]; S bed [1].

### *squamata* D. Don [**Singleseed Juniper**]

Evergreen shrub. Leaves in threes, needlelike, fused along twig, green without white bands. Introduced, native to Asia. In horticulture since 1836. Maximum height 10 ft.

MAINTENANCE CENTER: E, between ND Press and Transportation [6]. MORRIS INN: E, main beds flanking walk [20]; E, main beds, N & S [12].

### 'Blue Carpet' [**Singleseed Juniper**]

Evergreen ground cover. Low, creeping form; leaves dense, blue gray to green. Maximum height 1 ft.

HESBURGH CENTER: Court, E entrance [2]. SUPPORT SERVICES BUILDING: E side, flanking door (standards) [2].

### 'Blue Star' [**Singleseed Juniper**]

Evergreen shrub. Low, irregular, rounded form; growth dense; leaves silver blue. In horticulture since 1950. Maximum height 3 ft.

ADMINISTRATION (MAIN) BUILDING: Front, E bed [2]; Front, W bed [2]. HESBURGH CENTER: Court [beds]; E side, SE entrance, flanking [23]; N side [beds]; S side, W corner, near plaza [35]; SE corner, W [14]; SW Plaza, outer section, NW corner [8]; SW Plaza, outer section, SE corner [8]; W side, S section [32]. JUNIPER ROAD: North Gate, fence, at benches [2]. SUPPORT SERVICES BUILDING: N bed (Prince of Wales graft below) [1].

### 'Holger' [**Singleseed Juniper**]

Evergreen shrub. Spreading form; new growth yellow, turning gray green. Maximum height 3 ft.

ADMINISTRATION (MAIN) BUILDING: Front, E bed [3]; Front, W bed [4]. SUPPORT SERVICES BUILDING: N bed [2].

### 'Meyeri' [**Meyer's Blue Juniper**]

Evergreen shrub. Dense form; branches erect; leaves needlelike, blue white above. Developed by F. N. Meyer. In horticulture since 1910. Maximum height 6 ft.

PROVINCE ARCHIVES CENTER: NW, roadside [hedge*].

### *virginiana* L. [**Eastern Redcedar**]

Evergreen tree. Leaves scalelike, some sharp and opposite; twig odorless when crushed. Native to eastern and central North America. In horticulture since 1664. Maximum height 50 ft.

> CEDAR GROVE CEMETERY: N, E of shed [1]. DILLON HALL: E court, S side [1]; E court, entrance [1]. WASHINGTON HALL: W side [1*].

'Albospica' [**Silvery Redcedar**]

Evergreen tree. Leaves at twig tips vary from green to creamy white.

> SOUTH DINING HALL: SW corner, parking lot, W [1*].

'Burkii' [**Steel-blue Redcedar**]

Evergreen tree. Conical form; leaves steel blue, purplish in winter. Maximum height 25 ft.

> O'SHAUGHNESSY HALL: W, main entrance, N [2*]; W, main entrance, S 20yd [1*]; W, main entrance, S 6yd [1].

'Canaertii' [**Canaert Redcedar**]

Evergreen tree. Narrow columnar to conical form; twigs cordlike, tufted at ends of branches. Maximum height 35 ft.

> COMMUNITY CEMETERY: S end, Cross [1*]. FATIMA RETREAT HOUSE: NE 100yd, St. Joseph statue, rear [3*]; NE corner [1*]; NW corner [1*]. MOREAU SEMINARY: NE side [3*].

'Glauca' [**Silver Redcedar**]

Evergreen tree. Narrowly columnar form; leaves silver blue, fading to silver green. Maximum height 25 ft.

> ADMINISTRATION (MAIN) BUILDING: Sacred Heart Statue, walk, midway W side [2*]. FRESHMAN YEAR BUILDING: S [1*].

'Globosa' [**Globose Redcedar**]

Evergreen tree. Compact, rounded form; twigs dense but thin. Maximum height 15 ft.

> CORBY HALL: SE corner [1*].

'Kosteri' [**Koster Juniper**]

Evergreen shrub. Mounded, bushy form; growth spreading, feathery at tips. Maximum height 4 ft.

> HAGGAR HALL: S [hedge*].

'Schottii' [**Schott's Redcedar**]

Evergreen tree. Narrow, pyramidal form; growth dense, slow. In horticulture since 1875. Maximum height 35 ft.

> DILLON HALL: SW entrance, S side [2*]. FATIMA RETREAT HOUSE: Mission House, W entrance, N side [1*]; W side [12*]. MOREAU SEMINARY: N entrance, W side [1*]. O'SHAUGHNESSY HALL: NW corner [1*]; Vita Dulcedo Spes entrance, S 5yd [1*].

'Tripartita' [**Fountain Redcedar**]

Evergreen shrub. Dwarf, irregular form; dense, stout growth; branches stiff. Maximum height 4 ft.

> SACRED HEART BASILICA: Sacristy, S side [3*].

'Venusta' [**Glossy Redcedar**]

Evergreen tree. Conical form; leaves ash gray. Developed in the United States. In horticulture since 1915.

> O'SHAUGHNESSY HALL: Vita Dulcedo Spes entrance, S [3*]. SOUTH DINING HALL: S parking lot, midway to Fisher at road [7*].

*Platycladus* Spach [**Oriental Arborvitae**]

This is the most commonly grown ornamental evergreen in the southern and western United States. The many cultivars provide a variety of sizes, shapes and leaf colors. Oriental arborvitae is native to Korea and northern China. Until recently *Platycladus* was considered just one species in the genus *Thuja*, but the morphological differences between it and all other species of *Thuja* are great enough so that it has been segregated as a distinct genus.

Scale-leaved shrub or tree: evergreen, coniferous, monoecious. Branchlets form sprays that grow in distinctly vertical planes, a characteristic that separates them from *Thuja*, which has horizontal sprays. Scale leaf pairs in *Thuja* are all of equal length and width, but those of *Platycladus* are of two distinct types: the lateral pairs, when viewed from above, are longer; the vertical pairs are shorter. *Thuja* cones are longer than wide with overlapping, papery scales. The scales of *Platycladus* cones, which are of similar size and shape, end in hooks that are not found on *Thuja*. Seeds in *Platycladus* cone scales are wingless, those of *Thuja* are winged.

*orientalis* (L.) Franco [**Oriental Arborvitae**]

Evergreen tree. Leaf triangular, blunt, grooved on back, not pressed to stem; branchlets in vertical plane. Does not thrive in the North Central states, better south and west. Introduced, native to northern China, Korea. In horticulture since 1737. Maximum height 25 ft.

ALUMNI HALL: S side [3*]. CARROLL HALL: SE, along road [9]; SW corner, lawn [30*]. CEDAR GROVE CEMETERY: N, W of shed [many]. CORBY HALL: N 15yd [1*]. DILLON HALL: S side [9*].

'Aurea' [**Golden Dwarf Oriental Arborvitae**]

Evergreen shrub. Compact, low, rounded form; leaves yellow.

COLUMBA HALL: NW corner, lawn [6*].

*Thuja* L. [**Arborvitae**]

Arborvitae is commonly grown as an ornamental. It is broadly pyramidal in outline and has a single trunk. With age, the trees become scraggly at their bases. Although evergreen, the leaves of some cultivars turn reddish or yellow brown during winter, colors not appreciated by everyone. Arborvitae is native to eastern Asia and North America. Within North America, *T. occidentalis* grows in the east and *T. plicata* in the west. Both are used for hedges or windbreaks and for lumber. The wooden shingles common in the west are made from *T. plicata*.

Scale-leaved tree: evergreen, coniferous, monoecious. Branchlets form flattened sprays that grow in horizontal planes. This characteristic, although partially blurred by the flexible, drooping habit of the branchlets, distinguishes arborvitae from Oriental arborvitae (*Platycladus*), which has vertical sprays. The scalelike leaves of *Thuja* are opposite and overlapping with tips more blunt than those of *Chamaecyparis*. Scales are only as long as wide in *Thuja*, whereas in *Platycladus* the lateral scale leaf pairs, when viewed from above, are longer than wide. *Thuja* cones are longer than wide with overlapping, papery scales. The cone scales of *Platycladus*, although of similar size and shape, end in hooks. Those of *Thuja* do not. Seeds in *Thuja* cone scales are winged, whereas those in *Platycladus* cone scales are wingless.

*occidentalis* L. [**American Arborvitae; Northern White Cedar**]

Evergreen tree. Leaves overlapping, short-pointed with glands, bright green; branchlet in horizontal plane. Leaves turn bronze in winter; used as specimen plant or hedge. Native to eastern North America. In horticulture since 1536. Maximum height 60 ft.

> BURKE MEMORIAL GOLF COURSE: Scattered throughout [many*]. COLUMBA HALL: NW 10yd [1]. FRESHMAN YEAR BUILDING: W side [4*]. GROTTO OF OUR LADY OF LOURDES: SE, steps, N [1*]. HESBURGH CENTER: N side, at court gate [5]; W side, service drive, N edge [11]. LAW SCHOOL: S entrance [15]. LOFTUS SPORTS CENTER: W side, N end, flanking door [15]; W side, S end, flanking door [15]. OLD COLLEGE: NW 35yd, lakeside [1]. PRESBYTERY: W 15yd [1*]. SIEGFRIED HALL: E door, flanking [5].

### 'Conica' [Conical Arborvitae]

Evergreen tree. Conical form.

> HOLY CROSS HOUSE: E wing, N side [7*]; E wing, N side [1]. MOREAU SEMINARY: N, Douglas Rd entrance [7*]; N, Douglas Rd entrance, W [1].

### 'Emerald Green' [Emerald Green Arborvitae]

Evergreen tree. Narrow, conical, compact form; leaves bright green. Tolerates heat and extreme cold. In horticulture since 1950. Maximum height 15 ft.

> DEBARTOLO CLASSROOM BUILDING: E side, around central plaza [62]; W side, along walk [139].

### 'Europe Gold' [Golden Arborvitae]

Evergreen tree. Conical form; leaves yellow.

> HESSERT AEROSPACE RESEARCH CENTER: E side [2].

### 'Fastigiata' [Columnar Arborvitae]

Evergreen tree. Columnar form; branches short, crowded.

> CARROLL HALL: SE [5*].

### 'Globosa' [Globe Arborvitae]

Evergreen shrub. Dwarf, rounded form. Maximum height 6 ft.

> CAMPUS SECURITY BUILDING: N, Carroll Hall sign, lakeside [1*]. DECIO FACULTY HALL: E, edge of plaza [hedge]; W, edge of plaza [hedge]. KNOTT HALL: S wing, E door [2]; W wing, N side, flanking walk [39]; W wing, W plaza, flanking door [6]. SIEGFRIED HALL: N, flanking walk [36].

### 'Golden Globe' [Golden Globe Arborvitae]

Evergreen shrub. Growth dwarf; rounded form; foliage yellow.

> GRACE HALL: NE door plaza [29]. SUPPORT SERVICES BUILDING: S bed [1].

### 'Pyramidalis' [Pyramidal Arborvitae]

Evergreen tree. Pyramidal form; leaves green, soft-textured.

> COMMUNITY CEMETERY: N end [12*]. HOLY CROSS HOUSE: N side [7*].

### 'Rheingold' [American Arborvitae]

Evergreen shrub. Conical form, rounded when young; growth slow; leaves yellow gold. Maximum height 5 ft.

> ADMINISTRATION (MAIN) BUILDING: Front, E bed [2]; Front, W bed [3]. MORRIS INN: E, beds flanking walk [8]. SUPPORT SERVICES BUILDING: N bed [1]; S bed [2]; S bed (standard) [1].

### 'Robusta' [Siberian Arborvitae]

Evergreen tree. Conical form; growth slow, upright.

> SORIN HALL: E, roadside [3*].

### 'Techny' [American Arborvitae]

Evergreen tree. Growth slow; dense, pyramidal form; foliage stays green during winter. Maximum height 15 ft.

> SUPPORT SERVICES BUILDING: N end [22]; S end [9].

## MAGNOLIACEAE [MAGNOLIA FAMILY]

*Liriodendron* L. [**Tulip Tree**]

Tulip trees are native to eastern North America and China. *L. tulipifera* is the official state tree of both Indiana and Tennessee and the unofficial state tree of Kentucky and North Carolina, where it has been chosen by popular vote, but has not been so designated by state legislative action. It is the tallest hardwood tree of the North American forest, reaching 200 feet tall in the southern Appalachians. Its long, straight, lightweight logs were used by Native Americans and pioneers to build homes and canoes. Daniel Boone used a tulip log canoe that was 60 feet long. The tulip tree is difficult to transplant, except when young, because of its tap root, but will grow quickly when established. Although large, it casts dappled, open shade. The flowers resemble tulips.

Tall, broad-leaved tree: deciduous. Branchlets ringed at each node by a scar left by the deciduous stipules found at the base of each leaf petiole. Leaves alternate, smooth-edged but lobed, the 4 lobes making the leaves appear lyre-shaped. The solitary, tulip-shaped orange-banded green flowers grow upright at the ends of the twigs, appearing just as the leaves expand in spring. Fruit a conelike mass of carpels, each bearing a winged nutlet, that remains over winter.

*tulipifera* L. [**Tulip Tree; Yellow-poplar**]

Deciduous tree. Leaf 3-8 in. long, apex straight, 3-4 lobes each side; bud 0.5 in. long, 2 waxy scales. Conical form; open shade; leaves turn golden yellow. Ornamental in autumn. Native to eastern United States. In horticulture since 1663. Maximum height 90 ft.

DILLON HALL: W court [4*]. FLANNER HALL: N 25yd [1*]; S side [1]; SW corner [1]. HESBURGH CENTER: E side, NE corner, E 10yd [1]; SE corner, SE 10yd [1]; SE corner, SW 15yd [1]. HESSERT AEROSPACE RESEARCH CENTER: SE corner [1]. RADIATION RESEARCH BUILDING: S side [5*]. SACRED HEART STATUE: SE 35yd [1*]. SORIN HALL: SE at walk [1]. ST. JOSEPH HALL: NW corner, N 45yd [1].

*Magnolia* L. [**Magnolia**]

Magnolias are grown for their spectacular spring flowers. Hardly a picture of Notre Dame's Main building is taken in the spring without the two large, pink-flowered saucer magnolias framing the view. This post card view may be the most familiar scene of the campus. Magnolias are native from eastern North America to Central America and Venezuela and, in Asia, from the Himalayas to Japan. The evergreen species are not hardy in the Midwest and the flowers of even the deciduous species are sensitive to frost. Both tree and shrub forms, suitable for large or small gardens, are available. The wood is fine-grained and satiny but soft. That of *M. hypoleuca* is used in Japan to make lacquer ware. Linnaeus named this genus in honor of Pierre Magnol (1638-1715), a French physician and professor of botany who also was the director of the botanical garden at Montpellier. Directing a botanical garden was not an unusual occupation for a doctor of that time. It reflects the intense interest and reliance by the medical world in the medicinal properties of plants. Linnaeus credits Magnol with introducing him to the idea of classifying plants by families.

Broad-leaved tree or shrub: deciduous or evergreen. Leaves alternate, simple, smooth-margined. The large, showy flowers produce conelike fruits of congested carpels. The red or orange seeds are suspended briefly from the carpels at maturity by slender threads before dispersing.

*acuminata* L. [**Cucumber Tree**]

> Deciduous tree. Leaf large, 4-10 in. long, petiole long; flower yellow green, 3 in. long. Tall, widely spreading tree. Ornamental in spring, summer. Native to eastern United States, New York to Georgia, Illinois to Arkansas. In horticulture since 1736. Maximum height 80 ft.
>
> > CORBY HALL: SW corner, SW 50yd [2*].

× *proctoriana* Rehd.: *M. salicifolia* × *M. stellata* [**Chinese Magnolia**]

> Deciduous tree. Branchlets green purple, blotchy; bud hairless; leaf to 3.5 in. long, pointed. Cylindrical, single-stemmed form; flowers white. Ornamental in spring. Maximum height 25 ft.
>
> > BADIN HALL: W side [2*]. CORBY HALL: E front entrance, S roadside [1*]. HOWARD HALL: Chapel, W end [1*]. ST. JOSEPH HALL: N 40yd [1].

× *soulangiana* Soul.-Bod.: *M. heptapeta* × *M. quinquepeta* [**Saucer Magnolia**]

> Deciduous tree. Leaf to 6 in. long, petiole short; fewer than 12 flower petals. Multistemmed, shrubby form; flower large, white to purple. Ornamental in early May. Developed by M. Soulange-Bodin of Fromont, France. In horticulture since 1826. Maximum height 30 ft.
>
> > ADMINISTRATION (MAIN) BUILDING: Front, S of stairs, E of walk [1 **Commem.**]; Front, S of stairs, W of walk [1*]. BROWNSON HALL: Court [2*]. GALVIN LIFE SCIENCE CENTER: W, front walk, N side [1 **Commem.**]. GROTTO OF OUR LADY OF LOURDES: NW walk entering, E side [1*]; NW walk, S 10yd [1]; W, roadside [1]. LAFORTUNE STUDENT CENTER: E entrance, S [1]. MOREAU SEMINARY: W wing, S [1*]. SACRED HEART STATUE: N, E of walk [1]; N, W of walk [1 **Commem.**].

'Rubra' [**Scarlet Magnolia**]

> Deciduous shrub. Flower light purple to rose red; loose, shrubby growth. Ornamental in spring.
>
> > SACRED HEART STATUE: NW [1*].

*stellata* (Siebold & Zucc.) Maxim. [**Star Magnolia**]

> Deciduous shrub. Leaf to 4 in. long, blunt, petiole short; flower petals 12-25, each strap-shaped. Flowers numerous, white, fragrant. Ornamental in early spring to the middle of April. Introduced, native to Japan. In horticulture since 1862. Maximum height 20 ft.
>
> > FATIMA RETREAT HOUSE: Main entrance, W 10yd [1*]; Mission House, N side [1*]. GALVIN LIFE SCIENCE CENTER: S end, S of walk [1 **Commem.**]. MOREAU SEMINARY: E end [1*]. PANGBORN HALL: NE corner [1*]. PASQUERILLA CENTER: N side, bed E of door [2]; S side, bed W of door [2]. SORIN HALL: E side [2*].

# CALYCANTHACEAE [STRAWBERRY-SHRUB FAMILY]

*Calycanthus* L. [**Sweetshrub; Allspice**]

> The common names for this genus of shrubs are clues to its most conspicuous features. The dark maroon flowers that appear during May through July give off a sweet, fruity fragrance that smells like a combination of pineapple, strawberry,

and banana. The leaves, bark, wood, and roots smell like camphor. The bark was used as a substitute for cinnamon during earlier times. The genus contains only two species. One is native to the eastern United States and the other grows in the Southwest. The eastern species, *Calycanthus floridus*, is hardy in Indiana. The seeds of both species are poisonous.

Broad-leaved, aromatic shrub: deciduous. Leaves opposite, simple, surface hairy and pale below. Flowers formed at tips of branchlets, maroon to red brown, outer sepals and inner petals both straplike and look identical (called tepals for this reason). Fruit resembles an urn or capsule, contains many one-seeded achenes.

*floridus* L. [**Carolina Allspice; Common Sweetshrub**]

Deciduous shrub. Leaf egg-shaped, to 5 in. long, hairy below; flower maroon, 2 in. wide, tepals straplike. Broad, mounded shrub grown for fragrant flowers. Ornamental in May into July. Native to Virginia through Florida. In horticulture since 1726. Seeds poisonous when eaten. Maximum height 9 ft.

LAFORTUNE STUDENT CENTER: Crowley, bed at walk between [bed].

## LAURACEAE [LAUREL FAMILY]

*Sassafras* Trew [**Sassafras**]

Sassafras is found in eastern North America and eastern Asia. The North American species is a pioneer tree that forms dense colonies in abandoned fields. It is used ornamentally in naturalized plantings because of its striking foliage. All plant parts have a spicy aromatic odor and taste. This quality caused both Native Americans and European settlers to hope that sassafras held medicinal and curative powers. Oil from the bark of the roots was used in medicines, insecticides, soaps, and perfumes. Interest has waned as the plant has failed to live up to expectations. Sassafras tea is still brewed from the roots, but recent studies suggest that these extracts may be carcinogenic.

Broad-leaved, aromatic tree: deciduous, either monoecious or dioecious. Young twigs vivid light green. Leaves alternate, simple, variably shaped with 1-3 irregular lobes or none. The asymmetrical 1-lobed leaves are "mitten-shaped." Flowers inconspicuous, yellow, frequently unisexual; fruit a small, dark blue drupe on a bright red stalk.

*albidum* (Nutt.) Nees [**Red Sassafras**]

Deciduous tree. Leaf shape variable, can be egg-shaped, mitten-shaped or 3-lobed, bright green. Leaves turn yellow, orange, scarlet or purple. Ornamental in autumn. Native to Maine to Michigan, south to Florida and Texas. Maximum height 60 ft.

MAIL DISTRIBUTION CENTER: W side [26*]. ST. JOSEPH'S LAKE: N shore [few].

## SAURURACEAE [LIZARD'S-TAIL FAMILY]

*Houttuynia* Thunb. [**Houttuynia**]

A recently developed cultivar of this low-growing plant is gaining interest because of its multicolored foliage. The leaf margins are irregularly blotched with yellow, bronze and red. The colors are brightest in sunny locations. It is most effective in large raised beds and containers where moisture is dependable.

Houttuynia is native from Japan south to the mountains of Java and Nepal. Young shoots are eaten as a vegetable in China.

Broad-leaved, scarcely woody, perennial ground cover: deciduous. Leaves alternate along stem, heart-shaped, palmately veined, edge smooth. Flowers tiny with no petals, on short spikes; fruit a dry 3-5 seeded capsule.

*cordata* Thunb. [**Houttuynia**]

Perennial ground cover. Leaf egg-shaped, base heart-shaped, 5 veins from the leaf base, surface dotted with glands. Prefers wet soil or standing water; neat growth habit. Introduced, native to Japan, south to Java and Nepal. Maximum height 1.3 ft.

'Chamaeleon' [**Houttuynia**]

Perennial ground cover. Leaves splotched with red, dark green, and creamy white. Ornamental in summer.

HESBURGH CENTER: Court, E border [bed]; Court, E entrance [bed]; Court, N border [bed]; Court, between planters E1 & E2 [bed]. JOYCE ATHLETIC AND CONVOCATION CENTER: Gate 10, flanking [beds]; Gate 2 [beds]; W, along wall at gate 1 [bed]. JUNIPER ROAD: W, Library circle N, N fence [bed]; W, Library circle N, S fence [bed]. KNOTT HALL: W wing, N walk, central planter [bed]. PASQUERILLA CENTER: N side door, E [bed]; S side, W of door [bed]. SIEGFRIED HALL: N walk, central planter [bed].

# RANUNCULACEAE [BUTTERCUP FAMILY]

*Clematis* L. [**Virgin's Bower; Clematis**]

Clematis vines are grown for their small to large showy flowers, either bell-shaped or opening flat, that bloom from midsummer into autumn. The feathery heads of the fruit clusters also are ornamental. The roots need cool soil, which can be accomplished by planting east or north of a structure, by placing the clematis behind other perennials, or by mulching the plant's base. The soil should not be acid. Clematis is native to temperate areas of both hemispheres and to tropical Africa. Some people develop a skin rash from handling or pruning the vines, especially in the spring. The native virgin's bower, *C. virginiana*, is one species that has been mentioned as causing this problem.

Broad-leaved woody, climbing vine or perennial herb (some woody or semi-woody): deciduous. Leaves either simple or compound, grow in pairs (opposite) along stem. Leaf stalks aid climbing by curling around slender twigs or trellises. Flowers range from solitary to paniculate. Petals absent, 4-8 petallike sepals. Fruits numerous small achenes, terminated by feathery styles, that grow in heads.

*dioscoreiflora* Lév. & Vaniot [**Korean Clematis**]

Deciduous vine. Flowers white, small, to 0.6 in. wide, fragrant. Flowers bloom late. Ornamental in late summer. Introduced, native to Korea. Foliage causes dermatitis in some people.

'Robusta' [**Korean Clematis**]

Deciduous vine. Flowers white, larger than the species, to 1.25 in. wide. Flowers bloom late. Ornamental in late summer.

CORBY HALL: W end, W of walk [2].

× *jackmanii* T. Moore: *C. lanuginosa* × *C. viticella* [**Jackman Clematis**]

Deciduous vine. Flowers large, to 6 in. wide, 4 sepals, grow in groups of 3; leaf

pinnately compound. Flowers lavendar or white to purple, showy. Ornamental in June. Foliage causes dermatitis in some people. Maximum height 18 ft.
>    Fatima Retreat House: E side, court, trellis [2].

*spp.* [**Clematis**]
>    Deciduous vine. Leaf simple or compound, lobed or smooth; flower petals absent, sepals large, stamens many. Flowers showy, white to purple, may be fragrant; fruit feathery. Ornamental in summer, autumn. Foliage causes dermatitis in some people.
>    Corby Hall: SW corner [1]. Holy Cross House: SW, trellis [1].

## BERBERIDACEAE [BARBERRY FAMILY]

*Berberis* L. [**Barberry**]
>    Frequently grown as a hedge or specimen plant that tolerates drought, barberry has attractive flowers and fruit. Cultivars with red to purple leaves are popular. Because of its spines, it can be used as a barrier plant. Yellow dye is extracted from the roots and inner bark. In Europe the edible fruits are used in preserves and jam. One species that was introduced to North America from Europe and became naturalized, *B. vulgaris*, is the alternate host of a rust fungus (*Puccinia graminis*) that seriously affects wheat and other cereal grains. Part of the fungus' complex life cycle is lived out on barberry, part on the cereal grasses. In 1917 North Dakota outlawed barberry from all land within its jurisdiction in an effort to break the wheat stem rust fungus' 2-part life cycle. By 1918 13 major wheat-producing states, including Indiana and Michigan, had jointly launched a massive barberry eradication program. Their slogan was, "Free The 13 States From The Menace Of The Red Tyrant!" Everyone participated including Boy and Girl Scout troops, women's groups, and garden clubs. The campaign, spearheaded by E. C. Stakman, Professor of Plant Pathology at the University of Minnesota, was largely successful. By the early 1940s 300 million bushes had been destroyed. While most barberry in the wild is now gone, the disease still occurs because the fungus produces spores on wheat stems that can overwinter in soil and re-infect wheat without going through the barberry phase of its life cycle. The most common ornamental species, Japanese barberry or *B. thunbergii*, does not harbor the wheat rust fungus. Barberries are native to South America, eastern Asia, Europe, North America, and northern Africa.
>    Broad-leaved, spiny shrub: deciduous or evergreen (some southern species). Wood and inner bark of all species are yellow. Branches yellow or red to black when young, armed with 3-branched spines, and grooved. Leaves alternate but may appear whorled on short shoots, simple, margins either smooth, toothed, or with minute spines. Flowers yellow to orange, solitary or in various panicles or racemes; form red, yellow, or black berries.

× *mentorensis* L. Ames: *B. julianae* × *B. thunbergii* [**Mentor Barberry**]
>    Deciduous shrub. Stem grooved, spines 3-parted; leaf to 2 in. long, spine-tipped; fruit dark red, rare. Uniform growth, good barrier plant; holds leaves late in autumn. Developed by M. Horvath of Mentor, Ohio. In horticulture since 1942. Maximum height 5 ft.
>    Pasquerilla Hall East: W wing, SW corner [8]. Sorin Statue:

Surrounding [hedge].

*thunbergii* DC. [**Japanese Barberry**]

Deciduous shrub. Stem red brown, grooved, spines 1-parted; leaf to 1 in. long, wide at apex, tip blunt. Bright red fruit persistent, showy. Ornamental in winter. Introduced, native to Japan. In horticulture since 1864. Maximum height 6 ft.

CAMPUS SECURITY BUILDING: S side [hedge*]. CORBY HALL: NW, road, N side [hedge*]. FARLEY HALL: N wing, E side [1]. KNOTT HALL: S wing, E side [8]. PASQUERILLA HALL WEST: N wing, N end [5]. SIEGFRIED HALL: W door [8]. SORIN HALL: N end [hedge*].

'Atropurpurea' [**Japanese Bronze-leaf Barberry**]

Deciduous shrub. Leaf dark red to purple. Ornamental in summer. Developed in Orleans, France. In horticulture since 1926. Maximum height 6 ft.

DECIO FACULTY HALL: E door [hedge]; E plaza [hedge]; W door [hedge]; W plaza [hedge]. FATIMA RETREAT HOUSE: Outdoor Station 3 [3*]. GROTTO OF OUR LADY OF LOURDES: W, roadside [hedge*]. NIEUWLAND SCIENCE HALL: S entrance (Riley Hall door), flanking [hedge*].

'Crimson Pygmy' [**Dwarf Japanese Barberry**]

Deciduous shrub. Dwarf, dense form; purple leaves. Ornamental in summer. Developed by Van Eyck in Boskoop, Holland. In horticulture since 1942. Maximum height 2 ft.

ADMINISTRATION (MAIN) BUILDING: Front, E bed [6]; Front, W bed [6]. ECK TENNIS PAVILION: S side [15]. JUNIPER ROAD: E, ROTC stoplight, fence [10]; E, opposite Galvin, at fence, W side [12]; Library Circle, N section, fence [7]; Library Circle, S, flanking drive [10]; North Gate, fence, roadside [16]; W, Library circle N, at fence [14]; W, at Bulla Rd, fence, roadside [46]; W, at Galvin, fence, roadside [10]. SUPPORT SERVICES BUILDING: N bed [3]; S bed [4].

*Mahonia* Nutt. [**Oregon Grape**]

*Mahonia* is native to North and Central America and Asia. It survives in the Midwest if placed out of hot, sunny, and windy areas. The plants are interesting year-round because of their fragrant yellow flowers that bloom in April, followed by blue black berries, and their glossy leaves that remain through winter. The genus *Mahonia* was named for an early American horticulturist, Bernard M'Mahon (1775-1816), by Thomas Nuttall, who was Professor of Botany at Harvard, an ornithologist, and an explorer. The fruits are edible.

Broad-leaved thornless shrub, some almost treelike: evergreen. Leaves alternate along the stem, odd-pinnately compound (leaflets in pairs along the central axis with one at the apex); leaflets usually spiny-toothed, as in holly. Flowers bright yellow and usually in racemes, panicles, or umbels. Fruit a dark, blue black berry covered with a waxy bloom, resembling a grape.

*aquifolium* (Pursh) Nutt. [**Oregon Grape**]

Evergreen shrub. Leaf pinnately compound, 5-9 leaflets, each spine-tipped; flowers in 3 in. wide clusters. Glossy dark green leaves; bright yellow flowers; blue black fruit. Ornamental in spring, autumn, winter. Native to northwestern North America. In horticulture since 1823. Maximum height 6 ft.

ALUMNI HALL: E side [beds]; W court [beds*]. CUSHING HALL OF ENGINEERING: N, main entrance, E [beds*]. DILLON HALL: NW corner [bed*]; W court [beds*]. FATIMA RETREAT HOUSE: Mission House, NW corner [1]. HOLY CROSS HOUSE: N side [beds*]. LAW SCHOOL: Cushing, between

[many]. MOREAU SEMINARY: W end, lake slope [beds*]. PANGBORN HALL: N, main entrance, W [3*].

## MENISPERMACEAE [MOONSEED FAMILY]

*Menispermum* L. [**Moonseed**]

Grown for its glossy, large leaves, moonseed should be planted only where it can be controlled because it spreads by underground suckers. It will resprout even if pruned to the ground in winter. Moonseed is native to eastern North America and eastern Asia. Both the common name moonseed and the genus *Menispermum* refer to the crescent or moon-shaped seeds. The rootstocks contain bitter alkaloids. The fruits are poisonous and have been mistaken for wild grapes, but the plants can be differentiated by their seeds. Moonseed has one crescent-shaped seed in each fruit, whereas a grape has several smaller seeds.

Broad-leaved twining vine: deciduous. Leaves shield-shaped, palmately-lobed with 3-7 lobes, arranged alternately along stem. Flowers green yellow, in long-stalked racemes. Fruit a berry-like waxy, black drupe.

*canadense* L. [**Common Moonseed**]

Deciduous vine. Leaf 10 in. long, lobes shallow, long petiole attached in blade, not at base; fruit black. Unusual, distinctive leaves. Ornamental in summer. Native to eastern North America. In horticulture since 1646. Fruit poisonous when eaten. Maximum height 15 ft.

FATIMA RETREAT HOUSE: Calvary, in hedge [1]. GROTTO OF OUR LADY OF LOURDES: NE, steps, E [1]. ST. JOSEPH'S LAKE: NW woods [few*]; S edge, N of University Health Services [many].

## CERCIDIPHYLLACEAE [KATSURA TREE FAMILY]

*Cercidiphyllum* Siebold & Zucc. [**Katsura Tree**]

The katsura tree is grown in North America as a handsome, well-shaped, wide-spreading shade tree that grows 50 feet tall. In temperate areas of China and Japan, where it is native, it grows to 100 feet tall. It is the largest deciduous tree found in either country. Its timber is used for panelling and cabinetry. Here it has no serious disease or insect problems.

Broad-leaved tree: deciduous, dioecious. Leaves opposite or sub-opposite, simple, wavy-edged or scalloped. The second-year growth produces short spurs that bear the flowers and solitary leaves. Flowers without petals, the female flower produces a dry podlike follicle that splits along one seam to release many seeds. *Cercidiphyllum* resembles *Cercis*, or redbud, but can be distinguished by its scalloped leaf margins and opposite, paired leaves along its twigs. *Cercis* leaves are smooth-margined and arranged alternately along the stems.

*japonicum* Siebold & Zucc. [**Katsura Tree**]

Deciduous tree. Leaf almost round, base heart-shaped, tip blunt, margin wavy. Young leaves red purple, turning blue green, then yellow to orange. Ornamental in spring, summer, autumn. Introduced, native to China, Japan. In horticulture since 1865. Maximum height 60 ft.

BADIN HALL: E, 2 each wing [4*]. DECIO FACULTY HALL: W side, NW lawn [1 **Commem.**]. DILLON HALL: NW corner [3*]. FISHER HALL: Pangborn, between [5*]. LOG CHAPEL: Old College, midway [1 **Commem.**]. MORRISSEY HALL: E side [2*].

'Pendula' [**Weeping Katsura Tree**]

Deciduous tree. Weeping branches; blue green leaves. Maximum height 25 ft.
HESBURGH LIBRARY: Pool, W side [1 **Commem.**]. HESSERT AEROSPACE RESEARCH CENTER: E side [1]; N plaza [1]. SUPPORT SERVICES BUILDING: N bed [1].

# PLATANACEAE [PLANETREE FAMILY]

*Platanus* L. [**Sycamore**]

The bark of the sycamores is unmistakable with its white to gray-yellow outer layer peeling off to reveal large patches of olive and brown. A huge, oddly shaped sycamore stands on the Grotto lawn, north of Corby Hall. Its girth is 241 in. Many students have had their pictures taken while seated on its low, spreading branches. It has been referred to as the "Legend Sycamore," but the actual legend is a poorly documented story about visits to the tree by an elderly Potawatomi chief. He was visiting the site where, many years earlier, his friend, while fishing on the lake, had been stabbed and killed by a white man. The sycamore is supposed to have grown at the spot where the fisherman fell. The broad, low limbs appear, to some viewers, like an open hand "begging for mercy." Sycamore occurs in north temperate areas of the Northern Hemisphere. The species can be differentiated by fruit arrangement. The native sycamore, *P. occidentalis*, has solitary fruit "balls" and the hybrid London planetree has 2-3 "balls" per stalk that hang like beads on a string. The native sycamore is very susceptible to a fungus, anthracnose, which disfigures buds and newly developed leaves during cool, wet springs and causes them to drop. The trees then send out another growth of leaves, but this takes time during which they present a bleak appearance. The London planetree is more resistant to anthracnose. In the wild, sycamore grows along rivers and lakes and in bottom lands. At one time, its massive trunks were sawed into broad panels that were used to make the wooden Pullman rail cars. The fruits were the favorite food of the now extinct Carolina paroquet, the only bird of the parrot family that was native to the United States.

Broad-leaved tree: deciduous, monoecious. Twig encircled by leaf scars at the base of each bud. Leaves very large, palmate, 3-5 lobes. Small female flowers on long stalk; fruit a ball of nutlets covered by downy hair that disintegrates over winter.

× *acerifolia* (Ait.) Willd.: *P. occidentalis* × *P. orientalis* [**London Planetree**]

Deciduous tree. Leaf lobes deep, to middle of blade; fruit heads grow in 2s on each stalk. Needs a large, open site; interesting, mottled bark. Developed in London, an accidental hybrid. In horticulture since 1663. Maximum height 100 ft.
FIELDHOUSE MALL: LaFortune to library, flanking walks [many]; S side, E end [1 **Commem.**]. KNOTT HALL: W wing, N walk, central planter [1].

*occidentalis* L. [**Sycamore; Buttonwood; American Planetree**]

    Deciduous tree. Leaf lobes shallow, each wider than long; fruit heads solitary, 1 per stalk. Very large; interesting, mottled bark. Native to Main and Ontario to Florida and Texas. In horticulture since 1640. Maximum height 100 ft.

        ALUMNI HALL: E side [2*]. ANGELA BOULEVARD: Notre Dame Ave campus entrance [2]. FARLEY HALL: E court [3*]. GROTTO OF OUR LADY OF LOURDES [13*]. HAGGAR HALL: Fieldhouse Mall, between [12*]. HESBURGH LIBRARY [many*]. JOYCE ATHLETIC AND CONVOCATION CENTER: Gate 4, S side [1]; Gate 7, S side [3]. KNOTT HALL: W wing, S side [1]. SACRED HEART STATUE: SW lawn [2]. SIEGFRIED HALL: E wing, N walk, central planter [1]; SE lawn [2]. SNITE MUSEUM OF ART: S side [3]. ST. JOSEPH'S LAKE: Shore [many]. STADIUM: E, gate 3 [3]; NE, gates 1 and 2 [1]; S, gate 10 [1]; SE, gate 9 [6]. WALSH HALL: E at main walkway [2].

# HAMAMELIDACEAE [WITCH-HAZEL FAMILY]

*Hamamelis* L. [**Witch-hazel**]

    Witch-hazels are native to temperate eastern North America and eastern Asia. Their primary ornamental appeal is their fragrant flowers that bloom from late fall to early winter or during late winter. The flowers have yellow to red crumpled, strap-shaped petals that appear in stark contrast to the bare winter branches. Time of flowering varies by species. *H. vernalis* blooms during late winter and the native *H. virginiana* blooms during late autumn. An aromatic extract of witch-hazel bark and leaves is combined with alcohol and used as an astringent.

    Broad-leaved shrub: deciduous. Leaves alternate, simple, toothed. Flower clusters at leaf axils along stem; fruit a woody capsule that opens a year later to forcibly expel black seeds.

× *intermedia* Rehd.: *H. japonica* × *H. mollis* [**Witch-hazel**]

    Deciduous shrub. Flowers red to yellow, blooms late winter into spring; leaves vary with each cultivar. Growth vigorous; loose branching habit; leaves turn yellow to red. Ornamental in late winter to March, autumn. Developed at the Arnold Arboretum of Harvard University. In horticulture since 1945. Maximum height 20 ft.

'Diane' [**Witch-hazel**]

    Deciduous shrub. Flowers copper red; leaves turn yellow, orange, and red. Flowers showy on bare branches, but leaves linger to hide effect. Ornamental in March, autumn.

        DEBARTOLO CLASSROOM BUILDING: E side, S of N end doors [2]. HESSERT AEROSPACE RESEARCH CENTER: N plaza [3]. JOYCE ATHLETIC AND CONVOCATION CENTER: Gate 11, S side [6]. SUPPORT SERVICES BUILDING: N bed [1]; S bed [1].

*vernalis* Sarg. [**Vernal Witch-hazel**]

    Deciduous shrub. Flowers with 4 yellow to red 0.5 in. long petals, bloom late winter to early spring. Unusual flowering time. Ornamental in very early spring. Native to Missouri through Louisiana to Oklahoma. In horticulture since 1908. Maximum height 10 ft.

        CARROLL HALL: W 30yd, hedge [1*]. WALSH HALL: Front [6*].

*virginiana* L. [**Witch-hazel**]

> Deciduous tree. Flowers with 4 yellow, strap-like petals, bloom in October and November. Often has multiple stems. Ornamental in autumn. Native to eastern North America. In horticulture since 1736. Maximum height 20 ft.
>
> > ALUMNI HALL: N, main entrance, W [1*]; NE corner [1*]. GRACE HALL: NE door [2]. LAW SCHOOL: E side, SE corner [1]. WASHINGTON HALL: N entrance, W side [1*].

*Liquidambar* L. [**Sweetgum**]

Sweetgum is an excellent lawn and street tree with a broadly pyramidal outline, beautiful yellow, purple, and red fall color and interesting fruits that remain on the branches after the leaves fall. The fruits litter the ground during winter to some homeowners' dismay. Native to North America and Asia, it is both a valuable timber tree and the source for the aromatic balsam (storax) used in perfumes and medicines. *L. orientalis*, grown in Asia Minor, was the source of Levant storax, the balm of Gilead of the Bible.

> Broad-leaved tree: deciduous. Leaves alternate, toothed, palmate with 5-7 lobes (star-shaped). Flowers inconspicuous; with male flowers on upright stalks at the ends of branches, female flowers hanging on slender stalks below. Fruit a dense ball of spiny capsules that open to dispense brown, winged seeds.

*styraciflua* L. [**Sweetgum**]

> Deciduous tree. Leaf star-shaped with 5-7 lobes; fruit a spiny ball, persistent on twigs. Leaves turn brilliant orange, yellow, and red, all on same tree. Ornamental in autumn. Native to Connecticut to Florida and Central America. In horticulture since 1681. Maximum height 75 ft.
>
> > ADMINISTRATION (MAIN) BUILDING: E front end, stairs, E side [1*]. CENTER FOR SOCIAL CONCERNS: E and W, flanking building [2*]. DeBARTOLO CLASSROOM BUILDING: E side, SE corner [1]. DECIO FACULTY HALL: W side [1]. FATIMA RETREAT HOUSE: N end, W 4yd [1]. GROTTO OF OUR LADY OF LOURDES: Lakeside, near, Columba Hall Rd [1*]; S walk, N side [1*]. MOREAU SEMINARY: Front [1]. O'SHAUGHNESSY HALL: Decio, between [1*]. PASQUERILLA HALL EAST: N wing, E side [1]; N wing, W side [2]. SORIN HALL: SE corner, E 50yd [1*].

*Parrotia* C. A. Mey. [**Parrotia**]

*Parrotia* has fine foliage and early, but not showy, flowers. The flowers have bright red stamens but no petals, a reward for the observant garden visitor during March. With age, the trunk develops peeling, lacy bark with green, brown, gray, and white patches. The genus was named for its discoverer, F. W. Parrot (1792-1841), a German naturalist and traveler, first, and, later, professor of medicine at the University in Tartu, Estonia. *Parrotia* is native to Iran, the region Parrot was exploring in 1829 when he made history as the first person to reach the summit of Mount Ararat (16,945 ft. above sea level) just across the border in eastern Turkey.

> Broad-leaved small tree or large shrubs: deciduous. Leaves alternate along stem, smooth above but with star-shaped (stellate) hairs below, edge wavy-toothed near apex. Flowers clustered in dense heads, with no petals, but with red stamens surrounded by hairy bracts; fruit a small 2-celled capsule with one seed in each cell.

*persica* C. A. Mey. [**Persian Parrotia**]

> Deciduous tree. Leaf 5 in. long, oval-oblong, coarse teeth above middle, sparse hair below, wavy surface. Striking bark peels when matures to show gray, green, white, brown. Ornamental in winter. Introduced, native to Iran. In horticulture since 1840. Maximum height 40 ft.
>
> > Support Services Building: NE bed [1].

## ULMACEAE [ELM FAMILY]

*Celtis* L. [**Hackberry**]

> Because they grow well in hot, windy, dry conditions, hackberries are common in the plains states. As elms were lost to Dutch elm disease and the search began for a suitable replacement, hackberries became more popular. However, hackberry is susceptible to a fungus and a mite that both attack and deform the buds. This results in numerous small twigs growing from the ends of branches in unsightly bunches, often referred to as "witches' brooms." The fruit is edible and quite sweet, but the pulp is thin and harbors a very hard seed. Wildlife and birds eat them. Hackberries are native to temperate areas of the Northern Hemisphere, although a few species are tropical.
>
> Broad-leaved tree: deciduous, dioecious. Leaves alternate, simple, toothed along margins, asymmetrical at base. Flowers small, inconspicuous, either male or perfect (male and female parts in a single flower). Fruit a small, pea-sized drupe (like a cherry pit), any of several colors, hanging on slender stalk. Hackberry looks very much like elm except that the round fruit is unlike the flat, winged samara of elm.

*occidentalis* L. [**Hackberry**]

> Deciduous tree. Leaf smooth, edge toothed, base asymmetrical, to 5 in. long; fruit gray, pealike. Grows under adverse conditions. Native to Quebec to North Carolina and Alabama. In horticulture since 1636. Maximum height 60 ft.
>
> > Calvary: St. Joseph's Lake, W 75yd, area [many*]. Campus Security Building: W wing, N 30yd [3*]. Carroll Hall: NE corner, E 120yd, lakeside [1*]; NW 20yd [1*]. Lewis Hall: NE corner, NE 40yd, lakeside [1*]. Sorin Hall: E side, SE 35yd [1*]. St. Mary's Lake: W end, Highway 31, between [7*].

*Ulmus* L. [**Elm**]

> Because of its graceful arching silhouette, the American elm was the premier lawn and street tree in much of North America until the onset of Dutch elm disease, a fungus spread by elm bark beetles. The fungus clogs the tree's vascular system, stopping nutrient transport within it. Notre Dame's South Quad, the walks of which are lined by American elms that were planted during the 1920s, is a good example of the kind of planting that dominated city and town settings during the first 60 years throughout the eastern and midwestern United States. Maintaining an American elm today requires diligent pruning of dead wood or spraying. No elm species is completely unaffected by Dutch elm disease, but *U. pumila*, *U. parvifolia*, some hybrids of these, and some cultivars of *U. carpinifolia* are resistant to the disease. *U. pumila*, the Siberian elm, and *U. parvifolia*, the Chinese elm, are both small-leaved species that frequently are

confused in nurseries. Ornamentally, *U. parvifolia* is superior. It blooms in the fall and holds its glossy, dark green leaves longer than most trees. It also has very interesting lacy bark. Elms are native to north temperate North America and similar habitats in Europe and Asia. The American elm is the state tree of both Massachusetts and Nebraska. Elm timber has been used for furniture, tool handles, coffins, and even for water pipes in London before metal and plastic became available.

Broadleaved tree: deciduous (rarely evergreen). Leaves alternate, simple, double-toothed along margins with asymmetrical outline at base. Flowers inconspicuous and perfect (male and female parts in one flower). Fruit a flat, 1-seeded samara, with a notched wing surrounding a nutlet.

*americana* L. [**American Elm**]

Deciduous tree. Leaf double-toothed, hairy in teeth clefts, rough above, 6 in. long; fruit margin hairy. Spreading, vase-shaped shade tree; susceptible to Dutch elm disease. Native to eastern and central North America. In horticulture since 1752. Maximum height 80 ft.

BADIN HALL: NE corner, N 15yd [1]. BURKE MEMORIAL GOLF COURSE: Sollitt shelter, E [many]. CAVANAUGH HALL: S door, W 20yd [1]. CORBY HALL: Main entrance, S 40yd, roadside [1*]; N side, kitchen, N 20yd [1]; SW corner, W 25yd [1]. DILLON HALL: S [1]. ECK TENNIS PAVILION: SE corner [1]. HAMMES BOOKSTORE: Front [3*]. HOLY CROSS HOUSE: E 20yd [1]; N 50yd, Douglas Rd, N [1]; SE 15yd [1]; Tool shed, NW corner, W 3yd [1]. HOWARD HALL: W 6yd [1]. LAFORTUNE STUDENT CENTER: NE corner, E [1*]. LOFTUS SPORTS CENTER: SW corner [1]. LYONS HALL: E 15yd [1]. MORRISSEY HALL: Front [2*]; Main entrance, SE 20yd [1]; S 20yd, W of front door [1]; S 8yd, E of front door [1]; S 8yd, W of front door [1]. ROCKNE MEMORIAL: O'Shaughnessy, along walks between [40*]. SORIN HALL: E side [2*]. STADIUM: E, gates 4 and 5 [1]; N, gates 18 and 19 [2]; S, gate 10 [1]; W, gate 14 [1]. STANFORD HALL: NW corner [1].

*carpinifolia* Ruppius ex Suckow [**Smooth-leaf Elm**]

Deciduous tree. Leaf double-toothed, not rough, 2-3 in. long, fewer than 12 vein pairs along midrib. Pyramidal; ascending branches; some resistance to Dutch elm disease. Introduced, native to Europe, North Africa, western Asia. In horticulture since 1850. Maximum height 90 ft.

CORBY HALL: Main entrance, steps, SW 4yd [1*]; SW corner, W 15yd, just N of walk [1*].

*davidiana* Planch. [**Japanese Elm**]

Deciduous tree. Leaf double-toothed, hair tufts below; stem bumpy corky; shoot hairy; fruit edge smooth. Susceptible to Dutch elm disease. Introduced, native to northern China. Maximum height 90 ft.

var. *japonica* (Rehd.) Nakai [**Japanese Elm**]

Deciduous tree. Vase-shaped form, broad crown; young branches drooping; seed placed above center in fruit. May be more tolerant to Dutch elm disease than the species. Introduced, native to northern Asia. Maximum height 90 ft.

CORBY HALL: SW corner, W 15yd, 4yd N of walk [1*].

*glabra* Huds. [**Wych Elm; Scotch Elm**]

Deciduous tree. Leaf double-toothed, hairless along margin, rough; fruit hairless. Susceptible to elm leaf miner and Dutch elm disease. Introduced, native to Great Britain to Siberia. Maximum height 100 ft.

CORBY HALL: Main entrance, steps, SE lawn [1*]. LAFORTUNE STUDENT

CENTER: W entrance, W 15yd [1*].

### 'Cornuta' [Horned Elm]

Deciduous tree. Larger leaves than the species with 3-5 projection or lobes at the apex. Susceptible to Dutch elm disease.

SACRED HEART BASILICA: E front entrance, S 35yd [1*].

### *parvifolia* Jacq. [Lacebark Elm; Chinese Elm]

Deciduous tree. Leaf single-toothed, to 2 in. long, shiny above, hairy below; shoot hairy; autumn flowers. Resistant to Dutch elm disease; beautiful bark; holds leaves late. Ornamental in autumn, winter. Introduced, native to north and central China, Korea, Japan. In horticulture since 1794. Maximum height 50 ft.

BURKE MEMORIAL GOLF COURSE: SE area [2*]; Sollitt Shelter, E 40yd [1*]. CARROLL HALL: S 25yd [1*]; SE corner, E in lawn [1*].

### *pumila* L. [Siberian Elm]

Deciduous tree. Leaf toothed, 1.5-3.5 in. long; shoots become smooth; flowers in spring. Inferior tree, weak branches; many pests, resists Dutch elm disease. Introduced, native to eastern Siberia, northern China to Korea. In horticulture since 1860. Maximum height 70 ft.

BURKE MEMORIAL GOLF COURSE: Rockne Memorial, W 50yd [1]. CARROLL HALL: N side [8*]. COLUMBA HALL: Basketball court, N side [1*]. COMMUNITY CEMETERY: SW corner [1*]. LYONS HALL: S end [3*]. STADIUM: NE, gates 1 and 2 [2]; SW, gate 12 [2]; W, gate 14 [1].

### *rubra* Muhlenb. [Slippery Elm]

Deciduous tree. Leaf double-toothed, edge hairy, rough, wide below middle; fruit hairy at middle only. Becomes weedy; susceptible to Dutch elm disease. Native to southeastern Canada to Florida and Texas. In horticulture since 1830. Maximum height 60 ft.

CARROLL HALL: W 30yd, hedge [1*]. CUSHING HALL OF ENGINEERING: NE corner, NE 15yd [1*].

### *thomasii* Sarg. [Rock Elm; Cork Elm]

Deciduous tree. Branch corky-winged; leaf double-toothed, rough above, hairy below; fruit edge hairy. Susceptible to Dutch elm disease; wood very hard and heavy. Native to Quebec to Tennessee and Nebraska. In horticulture since 1875.

STANFORD HALL: NW corner, W [5*].

### × *vegeta* (Loud.) Lindl.: *U. carpinifolia* × *U. glabra* [Huntingdon Elm]

Deciduous tree. Leaf double-toothed, 5-6 in. long, smooth above, 14-18 vein pairs. Branches ascending; susceptible to Dutch elm disease.

CORBY HALL: Main entrance, SE of steps [1*]; Main entrance, steps, W [1*].

### 'Camperdownii' [Camperdown Elm]

Deciduous tree. Branches drooping. Susceptible to Dutch elm disease.

SACRED HEART BASILICA: SE 35yd, junction of walks [1*].

## MORACEAE [MULBERRY FAMILY]

### *Maclura* Nutt. [Osage Orange]

Osage orange, native only to a small region of Arkansas, Texas, and Oklahoma, is used as a windbreak or hedge plants in the Midwest. It can withstand the extreme cold and heat of the region. The fruits dropping from female trees can be a nuisance. They are not poisonous, just sticky and inedible. Today its rot resistant wood makes excellent fence posts, but during the 1800s settlers used the thorny shrubs as living hedges that were impenetrable to livestock. It was the only practical means of fencing farms until the gradual introduction of wire fencing around 1875. Two remnant examples of osage orange hedges can still be seen at Notre Dame. They are a reminder that much of the land was farmed during earlier days. One hedge grows along the north edge of the golf course between the Security building and U.S. Highway 33. The second hedge is along Douglas Road, just north of the Maintenance Center (or south of the Notre Dame Credit Union). Other stretches of early osage orange hedges can be seen east of the campus along Douglas Road between Juniper and Ironwood roads. The bark of the roots produces a yellow dye that was used early in the twentieth century, but has been supplanted by synthetic compounds. Osage orange is in the same plant family as mulberry and has been used to feed silkworms in Europe.

Broad-leaved, spiny tree: deciduous, dioecious. Branches exude milky juice when cut. Leaves alternate, simple, smooth along margins. Female flowers produce large, globose pulpy aggregate fruits (syncarps) in which small achenes are embedded. Fruit superficially resembles a grapefruit in size and color and exudes milky juice when cut.

*pomifera* (Raf.) C. K. Schneid. [**Osage Orange**]

> Deciduous tree. Branches thorny; fruit globe-shaped, to 6 in. wide, yellow green, bumpy. Rugged, tolerates extreme conditions, used as barrier. Native to Arkansas to Texas. In horticulture since 1818. Maximum height 40 ft.
>
> > BURKE MEMORIAL GOLF COURSE: Sollitt Shelter, W 10yd [1*]. CAMPUS SECURITY BUILDING: Dorr Road, N side [hedge*]. ROCKNE MEMORIAL: W, Dorr Rd, along S side [23*].

*Morus* L. [**Mulberry**]

Because of its salt and drought tolerance, ability to grow in rocky soil, and rapid growth, mulberry is useful in some situations. However, unless a fruitless cultivar has been planted, the falling fruits can become messy on sidewalks and pavement. The fruit is edible and favored by birds. Mulberries are native to North and South America, Africa, and Asia. The leaves of *M. alba* are the food of the silkworm, *Bombyx mori*, in China. A large-leaved cultivar, 'Macrophylla,' has been developed to increase leaf volume and silk production.

Broad-leaved tree: deciduous, monoecious. Leaves alternate, simple, often irregularly lobed and toothed along margins. Female flowers produce a fleshy aggregate fruit (syncarp) that resembles a blackberry.

*alba* L. [**White Mulberry**]

> Deciduous tree. Leaf smooth, lustrous above, shape variable with both lobed and not lobed forms on a tree. Tolerates drought and gravely soil. Introduced, native to China. Maximum height 50 ft.
>
> > BURKE MEMORIAL GOLF COURSE: S central area [1]. CAMPUS SECURITY BUILDING: E wing, N 5yd [1]; N, parking lot, NW 10yd [1]; SW corner [2]. COLUMBA HALL: SE corner, SE 40yd [1]. CORBY HALL: NW corner, N [2]. FISCHER GRADUATE RESIDENCE COMPLEX: N, woods [1]. GRACE HALL: E side [1]. HOLY CROSS ANNEX: SW area [many]. HOLY CROSS HOUSE: N 50yd, Douglas Rd, N, shed, NW 20yd [1]; NE corner, N 30yd [1]. LEWIS HALL: N, 5yd [1]. LOFTUS SPORTS CENTER: SW corner [1]. MORRISSEY HALL: Chapel, W side [1*]. SOUTH DINING HALL: SW corner, golf course fence, S [2]. ST.

Joseph's Lake: Shore [many].

'Tatarica' [**Russian Mulberry**]

> Deciduous tree. Tree and fruit smaller than the species. Extremely hardy.
> Architecture Building: W [hedge*]. Lyons Hall: S [hedge*].


## JUGLANDACEAE [WALNUT FAMILY]

*Carya* Nutt. [**Hickory**]

> The long taproot of hickory makes this a difficult tree to transplant, limiting its landscape value. It is a valued forest tree, native from eastern North America to Central America, with rugged bark and leaves that turn golden brown during autumn. Shagbark hickory, *C. ovata*, is unmistakable in local woods. Its bark hangs in long, loose, curling patches on the trunk. Shagbark hickory can be seen at Notre Dame along the edge of the woods on the east side of the road leading to University Village just north of Douglas Road. This wooded area is one of several that have been set aside as campus natural areas. Use of these areas is restricted to observation and education. The pecan wood and nuts of commerce are from *C. illinoinensis*. Hickory wood is valued as a fuel and is used for smoking meats. It is also made into baseball bats and handles for tools because of its shock-absorbing qualities.
>
> Broad-leaved large tree: deciduous, monoecious. Leaves alternate along stem, pinnately compound with an odd number of leaflets, usually 3-17, with largest at leaf apex. Male flowers grow in drooping catkins, female flowers form racemes at ends of branches. Fruit a hard-shelled nut enclosed in a thick husk that splits into 4 parts. Hickory resembles walnut, but the pith in the twigs is solid, rather than chambered as it is in walnut.

*laciniosa* (Michx. f.) Loud. [**Shellbark Hickory**]

> Deciduous tree. Bud brown, blunt, with 4 scales; leaf 2 ft. long, 7 leaflets, dark olive green; twig tan. Native to New York through Oklahoma. In horticulture since 1800. Maximum height 80 ft.
> St. Joseph Hall: W road, N of turnoff, E side [1].

*ovalis* (Wangenh.) Sarg. [**Sweet Pignut**]

> Deciduous tree. Bark in small strips; bud 0.5 in. long; leaf 1 ft. long, 5-7 leaflets, hairless; twig gray. Native to eastern United States. In horticulture since 1800. Maximum height 50 ft.
> Community Cemetery: NE, edge of woods [many*]. Eck Tennis Pavilion: SE corner [8]. Fischer Graduate Residence Complex: N, woods [1]. Holy Cross Annex: NE corner, N [1]. Holy Cross House: SW slope [2]. Loftus Sports Center: N, woods [many*]; SW corner [3]. Province Archives Center: N, Douglas Rd, N side [1*]. St. Joseph Hall: SW [many]. St. Joseph's Lake: Boat house, S 35yd [1]; Boat house, S 90yd [1]; SE margin [many*].

var. *obcordata* Sarg. [**Obcordate Pignut**]

> Deciduous tree. Nut angled, broader than high, inversely heart-shaped.
> Ave Maria Press: Main entrance, E [1*]. Carroll Hall Annex: SE 10ft [1*]. Community Cemetery: N central area [1*]. Fire Station: E end [1*]. Moreau Seminary: SW corner, lake slope [4*]. Sacred Heart Statue: SW 40yd [1*].

var. *obovalis* Sarg. [**Obovate Pignut**]
>> Deciduous tree. Nut flattened, base rounded, apex rounded or pointed.
>>> HOLY CROSS ANNEX: NW, woods [many*]. LOFTUS SPORTS CENTER: N, woods [many*].

var. *obovalis* f. *acuta* Sarg. [**Stipitate Pignut**]
>> Deciduous tree. Bark tight, not loose; nut pointed at both ends. Native to midwestern United States.
>>> ST. JOSEPH'S LAKE: NW woods [1*].

*ovata* (Mill.) C. Koch [**Shagbark Hickory**]
>> Deciduous tree. Bark shaggy; bud large; leaf 14 in. long, 5 leaflets, hairy teeth; olive green; twig gray. Native to Quebec through Florida and Texas. In horticulture since 1629. Maximum height 80 ft.
>>> ST. JOSEPH HALL: SW 100yd, road, E side [1]. ST. JOSEPH'S LAKE: Boat house, S 35yd [1*]; NW woods [2*].

*Juglans* L. [**Walnut**]
>> The black walnut is a prime timber tree, but may be too coarse and large for most landscape plantings. The English walnut is smaller, but less reliably hardy. Walnut roots produce juglone, an allelopathic compound that is toxic to many other plants in the landscape and garden. The nuts of all walnuts are edible, but the walnut of commerce is the English walnut. The black walnut also is eaten in the United States. The fine-grained wood of walnut is valued for cabinetry and furniture-making. Walnuts are native to North and South America, Europe, and eastern Asia.
>> Broad-leaved large tree: deciduous, monoecious. Leaves alternate along stem, large and pinnately compound with an odd number of leaflets, as many as 23. Flowers inconspicuous; male appear on previous year's wood, female on new wood. Fruit a nut enclosed in a thick husk that does not fall away at maturity. Pith in walnut stems is chambered or cross-partitioned; pith in hickory twigs is solid.

*ailantifolia* Carrière [**Japanese Walnut**]
>> Deciduous tree. Leaflets 11-17, hairy, toothed, 6 in. long; bark rough; fruit pointed, sticky-hairy. Introduced, native to Japan. In horticulture since 1860. Maximum height 60 ft.
>>> BURKE MEMORIAL GOLF COURSE: S central area, shelter, NE corner [few*].

var. *cordiformis* (Maxim.) Rehd. [**Heart Nut**]
>> Deciduous tree. Nut heart-shaped, flattened, thin-shelled. Introduced, native to Japan.
>>> BURKE MEMORIAL GOLF COURSE: Rockne Memorial, SW 100yd [4*].

× *bixbyi* Rehd.: *J. cinerea* × *J. ailantifolia* [**Japanese Rough-shelled Walnut**]
>> Deciduous tree. Leaflets toothed; bark not smooth; nut shell rough, but ridges shallow and blunt. In horticulture since 1903.
>>> BURKE MEMORIAL GOLF COURSE: S central area, birdhouse, S [1*].

*nigra* L. [**Black Walnut**]
>> Deciduous tree. Leaflets 15-23, smooth, toothed; bark very rough, grooved; fruit rounded, not sticky. Native to eastern United States. In horticulture since 1686. Maximum height 75 ft.
>>> ALUMNI SENIOR BAR: W side [19*]. BURKE MEMORIAL GOLF COURSE: NW area fence [1]; Tee 10, N 10ft [1]. CARROLL HALL: NE, along walk [100*]. CORBY HALL: N, lawn above Grotto [1*]. GROTTO OF OUR LADY OF LOURDES: N,

outer walk, along N edge [14]. JUNIPER ROAD: Edison Rd intersection, E of sign [1]. LEWIS HALL: N, lakeside, along path [40*]. LOFTUS SPORTS CENTER: SW corner [1]. ROCKNE MEMORIAL: N side, grove [85*].

*regia* L. [**English Walnut**]
> Deciduous tree. Leaflets 5-9, not toothed; bark smooth, light gray. Introduced, native to southeastern Europe through China. Maximum height 60 ft.
> MOREAU SEMINARY: W 20yd [1*].

## MYRICACEAE [SWEET GALE FAMILY]

*Myrica* L. [**Bayberry**]
> Although only semi-evergreen in this region, bayberry is certainly hardy. It is native to temperate and subtropical regions of both hemispheres. The most decorative feature is the waxy white fruit that remains through the winter. It does well in poor, sandy soil but is adaptable to heavier soils, and tolerates salt and sun or partial shade. The fruits yield both the aromatic wax used in bayberry candles and palmitic acid used in soap production.
>
> Broad-leaved shrub or small tree: deciduous or semi-evergreen. Leaves alternate, simple, narrow but usually broader above middle; petioles short. Flowers inconspicuous, of only one sex; male and female usually on separate plants. Fruits of female plant small, distinctive with gray white covering; seed bony.

*pensylvanica* Loisel. [**Bayberry**]
> Deciduous shrub. Leaf toothed near tip, surface dotted with aromatic glands; fruit gray, waxy. Leaves aromatic, shiny, leathery; fruit persistent. Ornamental in summer, winter. Native to Nova Scotia through Alabama and Florida. In horticulture since 1725. Maximum height 12 ft.
> DECIO FACULTY HALL: W, service drive, N side [1]. HESBURGH LIBRARY: W, Moses statue, S [beds*].

## FAGACEAE [BEECH FAMILY]

*Castanea* Mill. [**Chestnut**]
> The American chestnut, once common and valuable for its decay resistant wood and delicious fruits, has been devastated by the fungus *Endothia parasitica*. It clogs the cambium layer of the wood, halting nutrient transport within the tree. The disease arrived on the East Coast from Asia around 1904 and rapidly spread westward. By the 1950s the entire chestnut tree population of eastern North America was dead. Stumps of dead trees in eastern forests still send up shoots, but these shoots are not resistant to the disease and short-lived. The Japanese, *C. crenata*, and Chinese, *C. mollissima*, chestnuts are resistant to the disease, but do not have timber and nut qualities as desirable as those of the susceptible American (*C. dentata*) and Spanish (*C. sativa*) chestnuts. Researchers are hybridizing the resistant and susceptible species, with the hope of improving their commercial qualities. The chestnuts of commerce are nuts of *C. sativa*, imported from Italy. Scientists also are studying biological control of the fungus by a virus that slows fungal growth, giving the tree time to wall off the invader.

Chestnut species grow throughout north temperate regions.

Broad-leaved large tree or shrub: deciduous, monoecious. Leaves alternate, simple, toothed along their margins. Female flowers form at the base of the male catkins or in separate leaf axils. The prickly fruit husk splits at maturity to shed 1-7 large nuts.

*mollissima* Blume [**Chinese Chestnut**]

> Deciduous tree. Leaf to 6 in. long with bristlelike teeth, shiny above, hairy below; bud and twig hairy. Introduced, native to China, Korea. In horticulture since 1853.
>
> > DECIO FACULTY HALL: O'Shaughnessy, E 25yd [1]. FRESHMAN YEAR BUILDING: W parking lot, NE corner [1]; W parking lot, SE corner [1]. PROVINCE ARCHIVES CENTER: SW corner, W 30yd [1].

*Fagus* L. [**Beech**]

> Beeches are large, magnificent trees appropriate in parklike settings. Two large copper beeches, *F. sylvatica* 'Atropunicea' with their red leaves, flank the walk between Sacred Heart statue and the Main building. One of Sir Arthur Conan Doyle's Sherlock Holmes mysteries is titled "The Copper Beeches." The story takes place in an English country house of the same name in rural Hampshire. Beeches have low-spreading branches that, unless pruned, completely shade out grass and weeds. In Europe, they are commonly pruned into hedges. They are not suitable as street trees because of their shallow, broadly spreading fibrous roots. Beech wood is important in furniture making. The edible nuts were the favorite food of the now extinct passenger pigeon. Both beech and passenger pigeon were common in eastern North America until vast areas of the beech-oak woodlands were cleared for farming during the 1800s. This eliminated food and nesting sites, contributing to the extinction of the birds. The last passenger pigeon died in the Cincinnati Zoo on September 1, 1914. Beeches grow throughout the North Temperate Zone.

Broadleaved large trees: deciduous, monoecious. Bark unusually smooth, gray, acquires an "elephant hide" appearance with age in some species. The distinctive brown winter buds at the ends of the twigs are very long, slender, and sharply pointed. Female flowers grow in clusters of 2 or 3. The prickly fruit husks enclose 1 or 2 three-angled nuts.

*grandifolia* J. F. Ehrh. [**American Beech**]

> Deciduous tree. Leaf coarse-toothed, 11-15 straight vein pairs, shiny above, hair tufts below. Native to eastern North America. In horticulture since 1800. Maximum height 70 ft.
>
> > DILLON HALL: S side [1*]. HESBURGH LIBRARY: W side [1*]. HOLY CROSS HOUSE: Douglas Rd, between [1*].

*orientalis* Lipsky [**Oriental Beech**]

> Deciduous tree. Leaf wavy-edged, 7-10 curved vein pairs, silky hairs below. Introduced, native to eastern Europe. In horticulture since 1904. Maximum height 100 ft.
>
> > CROWLEY HALL OF MUSIC: E 15yd [1*]. LAFORTUNE STUDENT CENTER: SE corner, S 13yd [1*].

*sylvatica* L. [**European Beech**]

> Deciduous tree. Leaf wavy-edged, shiny dark green above, pale below, twice as long as wide. Beautiful specimen that needs a large site. Introduced, native to Europe. Maximum height 60 ft.

KNOTT HALL: SW lawn [1]. SORIN STATUE: NE [1].

### 'Atropunicea' [Copper Beech; Purple Beech]

Deciduous tree. Leaves purple, gradually fading to green. Developed in Hanleiter Forest, Sonderhausen, Thuringia. In horticulture since 1772.

ADMINISTRATION (MAIN) BUILDING: Main entrance, S 40yd [2*]. CARROLL HALL: NW corner, N 20yd [1]. COLUMBA HALL: NE corner [1*]. CORBY HALL: N bird bath [1]. HOLY CROSS HOUSE: N 35yd [1*]; W 30yd [1*]. MOREAU SEMINARY: W end, S side [1*]. PROVINCE ARCHIVES CENTER: W 5yd [1*]. SACRED HEART BASILICA: E side door, S side [1*].

### 'Fastigiata' [European Pyramidal Beech]

Deciduous tree. Narrow, columnar form.

ALUMNI HALL: NE corner [1]. HESBURGH CENTER: SW Plaza, outer section, edge [6].

### 'Laciniata' [Fernleaf Beech; Cutleaf Beech]

Deciduous tree. Leaf lobes deep or shallow, 7-9 lobes; leaf shaped normally otherwise. In horticulture since 1792.

ARCHITECTURE BUILDING: E, on walkway [1].

### 'Pendula' [European Weeping Beech]

Deciduous tree. Branches drooping.

WALSH HALL: Main entrance, E 45yd [1*].

### 'Roseo-marginata' [Rose-pink European Beech]

Deciduous tree. Leaves purple with irregular pink borders. Leaves may scorch in full sun. In horticulture since 1883.

SUPPORT SERVICES BUILDING: N bed [1].

### 'Tricolor' [Tricolor European Beech]

Deciduous tree. Leaves white with green spots, edged with pink. Leaves may scorch when grown in full sun. Ornamental in summer.

ADMINISTRATION (MAIN) BUILDING: S side, SW inner corner [1].

## *Quercus* L. [Oak]

The earliest historical records show that oaks were the dominant trees on the land that was to become Notre Dame. Many oak species have ornamental features that are valued in the landscape. They are tall, suitable for specimen plantings. The first records of red oaks being planted at Notre Dame date from the 1870s. Those species that are native to North America are more colorful during autumn than the nonnative species. Oaks are susceptible to some insect and disease problems. Oak wilt, a fungus disease spread from tree to tree by root grafts and insects, is a serious problem of red oaks in the Midwest. However, red oaks grow faster and are easier to transplant than white oaks. Pin oaks show leaf yellowing (chlorosis) as a result of an iron deficiency in the soil. This condition can be made worse by heavy lawn watering, which causes the iron to leach from soil near the roots. Oaks are sensitive to soil compaction and changing soil depth over their roots. Tree decline is seen frequently around construction sites because of this. The oaks are the most important trees of commerce in North America. The wood, hard and strong, is used in shipbuilding, construction, flooring, furniture, and cabinetry. The wood of shingle oak (*Q. imbricaria*) was used to produce shingles and clapboards. Some species produce tannins for the leather industry. Cork for flooring, floats, bottle corks, and insulation comes from the cork oak, *Q. suber*, which is grown commercially in Portugal. Oaks grow throughout the North Temperate Zone and at high elevations in the tropics. The importance of oaks, both commercially and as a feature in the landscape, is reflected in the number of states that have chosen them as state trees. Either red or white oaks are designated as such in Connecticut, Illinois, Iowa, Maryland, and New Jersey.

Broadleaved tree or shrub: deciduous (some evergreen species in the South), monoecious. Leaves alternate, margins toothed, lobed (either sharp-pointed or blunt lobes) or entire. Male flowers form drooping catkins; female flowers solitary or in spikes. The fruit, or acorn, is a nut surrounded by a cuplike husk (involucre). The many species of oak are distinguished by differences in leaf, bud, and acorn characters.

*acutissima* Carruth. [**Sawtooth Oak**]

Deciduous tree. Leaf not lobed but bristle-toothed, 12-16 parallel vein pairs, rsembles a chestnut leaf. Broad, pyramidal to oval form; leaf stays green into November. Introduced, native to China, Japan, Korea. In horticulture since 1862. Maximum height 45 ft.

GROTTO OF OUR LADY OF LOURDES: NW walk, near W entrance [1].

*alba* L. [**White Oak**]

Deciduous tree. Leaf oblong with 5-9 blunt lobes, surface blue green above, smooth below. Stately in old age. Native to eastern United States. In horticulture since 1724. Maximum height 80 ft.

ANGELA BOULEVARD: Old Juniper Rd, W side [1]. BURKE MEMORIAL GOLF COURSE: NE area [1]. COLUMBA HALL: NE corner [1*]. CORBY HALL: SW 35yd [1*]. CROWLEY HALL OF MUSIC: NW corner, W 60yd [1*]. ECK TENNIS PAVILION: SE corner [2]. HOLY CROSS ANNEX: W side, S 15yd [1]. LEWIS HALL: NE corner [5*]. LOFTUS SPORTS CENTER: SW corner [3]. MOREAU SEMINARY: S, lake slope [1*]. SORIN HALL: SE corner, SE 40yd [1*]. ST. JOSEPH HALL: Holy Cross Annex, woods between [many*]. ST. JOSEPH'S LAKE [many].

*bicolor* Willd. [**Swamp White Oak**]

Deciduous tree. Leaf with 6-9 blunt teeth on each side, velvety and white or gray green below. Drought tolerant. Native to Quebec through Georgia and Arkansas. In horticulture since 1800. Maximum height 60 ft.

MOREAU SEMINARY: N side [4*]; NE, parking lot, S end [3*].

*coccinea* Muenchh. [**Scarlet Oak**]

Deciduous tree. Leaf 6 in., ovate, 7 bristled lobes, teeth many, sinus C-shaped, hair tufts at veins below. Difficult to transplant. Native to eastern United States, west to Minnesota and Missouri. In horticulture since 1691. Maximum height 75 ft.

CORBY HALL: SW [1]. HAMMES BOOKSTORE: N basketball court, NW corner [1*].

*ellipsoidalis* E. J. Hill [**Northern Pin Oak**]

Deciduous tree. Leaf 5 in., rounded, 5-7 bristled lobes, teeth few, very deep round sinuses, pale below. Native to Quebec through Georgia to Arkansas. In horticulture since 1902. Maximum height 60 ft.

ANGELA BOULEVARD: Notre Dame Ave, Juniper Rd, between [1*]. O'SHAUGHNESSY HALL: N [1*].

*imbricaria* Michx. [**Shingle Oak**]

Deciduous tree. Leaf margin wavy, not lobed, 1 bristle at apex, pale green or brown and hairy below. Tolerates urban conditions. Native to central United

States. In horticulture since 1724. Maximum height 60 ft.

> Grotto of Our Lady of Lourdes: NW walk, near W entrance [1]. LaFortune Student Center: WSW 15yd [1*]. Sorin Hall: N wing, W end [1*].

*macrocarpa* Michx. [**Bur Oak; Mossy-cup Oak**]

Deciduous tree. Leaf lyre-shaped, white below, lobes blunt, upper 5 shallow, 3 at base deep. Native to Nova Scotia to Texas. In horticulture since 1811. Maximum height 80 ft.

> Burke Memorial Golf Course: Sollitt shelter, E [1]. Corby Hall: N [2]. Crowley Hall of Music: NW 40yd [1]. Rockne Memorial: W end [2*].

*muehlenbergii* Engelm. [**Chestnut Oak**]

Deciduous tree. Leaf narrow oblong, 8-13 sharp teeth each side, yellow green above, white-hairy below. Much taller in the wild. Native to eastern United States through Texas to Mexico. In horticulture since 1822. Maximum height 50 ft.

f. *alexanderi* (Britt.) Trel. [**Alexander's Chestnut Oak**]

Deciduous tree. Leaf egg-shaped, wider at apex.

> LaFortune Student Center: SW 30yd, lamppost 53, S 10ft [1*].

*palustris* Muenchh. [**Pin Oak**]

Deciduous tree. Leaf with 5-7 bristled lobes, deep U-shaped sinuses, base wedge-shaped, hairless below. Most common landscape oak. Native to central and midwestern United States. In horticulture since 1770. Maximum height 70 ft.

> Burke Memorial Golf Course: Sollitt Shelter, W [1]. Corby Hall: S [1]. Eck Tennis Pavilion: S lawn, E of walk [1]; SW corner [1]. Juniper Road: ROTC stoplight, E parking lot fence [1]. Knott Hall: S wing, W side, S end [1]. LaFortune Student Center: Riley, between [7]. North Dining Hall: NE corner [1*]. Pasquerilla Center: S side [2]. Pasquerilla Hall East: N wing, NW corner [1]. Radiation Research Building: NE and NW corners [5]. Sacred Heart Statue: NE and NW [2]; S 15yd [1]. Snite Museum of Art: E [4*]. Sorin Statue: SE 15yd [1]; W 20yd [1]; W 30yd [1]. Stadium: E, gate 3 [1]; E, gates 4 and 5 [2]. Walsh Hall: Main entrance, E, walk to main road, end [1*].

*robur* L. [**English Oak**]

Deciduous tree. Leaf with 3-7 blunt lobes each side, basal 2 earlike, dark green above, blue green below. Taller in Europe, sensitive to weather extremes here. Introduced, native to Europe, North Africa, western Asia. Maximum height 60 ft.

> Sorin Hall: S wing, E end [1*]. Walsh Hall: E lawn [1].

'Fastigiata' [**Columnar English Oak**]

Deciduous tree. Narrow, columnar form; may be only 15 ft. wide at maturity. Maximum height 60 ft.

> DeBartolo Classroom Building: S side, SW corner, flanking door [2].

*rubra* L. [**Red Oak; Northern Red Oak**]

Deciduous tree. Leaf with 7-11 bristled lobes, pale and smooth below with tufts of brown hair at veins. Good street and lawn tree; grows rapidly. Native to eastern North America. In horticulture since 1800. Maximum height 75 ft.

> Ave Maria Press: E side [2*]. Burke Memorial Golf Course: NE area [4]; SW central area, near birdhouse [2]. Carroll Hall: E lawn, 80yd ESE [4]. Corby Hall: Entrance, W 50ft [1]. DeBartolo Classroom Building: SE corner [1]. Eck Tennis Pavilion: S central lawn [1]; S lawn, W of walk [1];

SE corner [2]. HAYES-HEALY CENTER: LaFortune, between [4]. KNOTT HALL: SW lawn [4]. KOONS REHEARSAL HALL: W [1 **Commem.**]; W, along walk [3]. LOFTUS SPORTS CENTER: SW corner [9]. MOREAU SEMINARY: NE, parking lot [14]; W end, lake slope, flanking steps [1*]. O'SHAUGHNESSY HALL: NW corner [3]. PASQUERILLA CENTER: S side [1]. SORIN HALL: SE 20yd [1*]. ST. JOSEPH HALL: W end, N 40yd [1*].

*velutina* Lam. [**Black Oak**]

Deciduous tree. Leaf with 2-9 sharp lobes, sinuses deep, base wedge-shaped, brownish hair below. Difficult to transplant; uncommon in horticulture. Native to eastern and central United States. In horticulture since 1800. Maximum height 60 ft.

BURKE MEMORIAL GOLF COURSE: Sollitt shelter, SW corner, W 25yd [1]. CARROLL HALL: NW corner, NW 30yd [1]. CAVANAUGH HALL: N lawn, N of door [1 **Commem.**]. COLUMBA HALL: Garage, ENE 20yd [1]. HOLY CROSS ANNEX: N end, N 10yd [1*]; SW 50yd [many*].

f. *dilaniata* Trel. [**Cutleaf Black Oak**]

Deciduous tree. Leaf shape resembles a turkey foot, lobes narrow, sinuses deep and much broader.

AVE MARIA PRESS: SW corner [1*].

f. *macrophylla* Trel. [**Broadleaf Black Oak**]

Deciduous tree. Leaves larger, lobes broad, sinuses narrow and shallow.

HAGGAR HALL: NW corner, NW 10yd [1*]; NW corner, NW 20yd [1*].

f. *pagodaeformis* Trel. [**Pagoda Black Oak**]

Deciduous tree. Leaf pagoda-shaped with deep, broad, rounded sinuses.

HAGGAR HALL: NW corner, W [1*]. LAFORTUNE STUDENT CENTER: SW 20yd [1*].

# BETULACEAE [BIRCH FAMILY]

*Betula* L. [**Birch**]

These graceful landscape trees with multiple trunks, have interesting, peeling bark that, depending on the species, may be white or light to medium red brown. Their glossy green leaves turn yellow in autumn. All birches are native to the Northern Hemisphere. The white-barked paper birch, *B. papyrifera*, which stands out in contrast to the evergreens in cool northern forests reaching almost to the Arctic Circle, is susceptible to attack by an insect, the bronze birch borer, when planted in the warmer soil of Indiana. This causes trees to die back from the top. It is, consequently, at the southern limit of its natural range in northwestern Indiana. Indiana's largest paper birch is growing at Notre Dame on the Main Quad just west of LaFortune Student Center. The Indiana Department of Natural Resources Big Tree Register of 1980 described it as 53 ft. tall with a crown spread of 41 ft. and a trunk circumference of 66 in. (4.5 ft. above the ground). No larger candidates have been reported since the 1980 publication. Its size can be attributed to the shady site, which keeps the soil at its roots cooler, but the stress induced by Indiana's climate is evident in the frequent death of branches. The paper birch is the state tree of New Hampshire, where the climate is cooler. The river birch with its red brown bark, which is native to river bottoms and flood plains of the eastern United States but ranging south to eastern Texas, is better able to thrive in warm temperatures. Birch bark, impervious to water, was made into canoes. Birch wood is used for furniture, plywood, and skis.

Broad-leaved tree or shrub: deciduous, monoecious. Leaves alternate, simple, toothed along margins. Pendulous male catkins form in summer, remain visible through following winter. Female flowers upright and conelike on stems, appear in April. Fruits maintain conelike appearance as they form 3-lobed scales that shelter numerous small nutlets. Catkins shatter and fall to ground when nuts are ripe. This feature distinguishes birch from alder, whose catkins are similar to birch, but do not shatter and fall at maturity.

*nigra* L. [**River Birch; Black Birch**]

Deciduous tree. Bark red brown to tan or silver pink, peeling; leaf to 3 in. long, gray below. Hardiest birch in warm areas, less susceptible to insect borers. Ornamental in winter. Native to eastern United States, Minnesota through Florida. In horticulture since 1736. Maximum height 40 ft.

ALUMNI HALL: S wing, W side [1*]. BURKE MEMORIAL GOLF COURSE: SW corner [4]. FISHER HALL: Pangborn, between [1*]. GRACE HALL: W side [2]. HESBURGH LIBRARY: Stadium, between [18*]; W side, Moses statue, NW [2]. JOYCE ATHLETIC AND CONVOCATION CENTER: Gate 10 [2]; Gate 3 [1]; Gate 8, S side [1]; N side [5]. SORIN HALL: SW 30yd [1*]. SORIN STATUE: NE 30yd [1]. UNIVERSITY CLUB: N side [4].

*papyrifera* Marsh. [**Paper Birch; Canoe Birch**]

Deciduous tree. Bark chalk white, peeling in sheets; leaf to 4 in. long, green below. Needs cool, shaded soil; leaves turn clear yellow. Ornamental in autumn, winter. Native to northern North America. In horticulture since 1750. Maximum height 70 ft.

ALUMNI HALL: Dillon, between, S roadside [1*]. BURKE MEMORIAL GOLF COURSE: Caddy shack, S [1]; NW corner [1]. LAFORTUNE STUDENT CENTER: Sacred Heart Statue, between [1*]. PRESBYTERY: NW corner [1].

*populifolia* Marsh. [**Gray Birch**]

Deciduous tree. Bark dull white, black patch below each branch; leaf 3 in. long, triangular with long tip. Usually with multiple trunks; short-lived. Native to Nova Scotia through Delaware. In horticulture since 1780. Maximum height 40 ft.

UNIVERSITY HEALTH SERVICES: E side [1*].

*Carpinus* L. [**Hornbeam**]

These slow-growing trees, appropriate for small gardens, provide good shade, interesting branching patterns, and smooth gray bark with a "muscled" appearance. Hornbeam has no serious disease or insect problems, but it requires moisture during the growing season. The European hornbeam withstands heavy pruning and is often used to form the pleached alleys or screens of European formal gardens. Pleaching is a highly stylized pruning and training technique in which parallel rows of identical trees are clipped and woven into flat planes of foliage arising from stiltlike trunks. *Carpinus* has been called ironwood because of its extremely dense hard wood, which is used in tool-making, piano sound mechanisms, pulleys, and butchers' chopping blocks. It is called blue beech or musclewood because of its smooth, beechlike, blue gray bark that forms long "muscles" like those of a human arm.

Broad-leaved small or medium-sized tree: deciduous, monoecious. Leaves alternate, simple, toothed along margins, with 7-24 pairs of distinctly parallel veins. Female catkins hang from twig tips, developing 3-lobed leafy bracts that surround small, nutlike fruits. The leafy bracts help distinguish *Carpinus* from *Ostrya*, which has nutlets completely enclosed in bladderlike bracts.

*betulus* L. [**European Hornbeam**]

Deciduous tree. Bud large, to 0.3 in. long; leaf thick, veins impressed; fruit bract 3-lobed, 2 in. long. Often used in Europe for formal, clipped hedges. Introduced, native to Europe through Iran. Maximum height 60 ft.

HESBURGH LIBRARY: Pool, E side [1*]; Pool, W side [1*]. LAW SCHOOL: W side [2]. LEWIS HALL: Patio [1*].

'Fastigiata' [**European Hornbeam**]

Deciduous tree. Branches develop in an upright or fanlike habit without a central leader. In horticulture since 1883. Maximum height 40 ft.

DEBARTOLO CLASSROOM BUILDING: N side [5].

'Pendula' [**Weeping European Hornbeam**]

Deciduous tree. Growth shrubby; branches drooping.

SUPPORT SERVICES BUILDING: N bed [1].

*caroliniana* Walt. [**American Hornbeam; Blue Beech**]

Deciduous tree. Bud small, to 0.25 in. long; leaf veins flat; fruit bract 3-lobed, 1 in. long. Shrubby; bark smooth, blue gray; stem fluted; leaf turns orange. Ornamental in autumn, winter. Native to New England through Minnesota and Arkansas. In horticulture since 1812. Maximum height 30 ft.

ALUMNI HALL: SE corner, S side [1]. CROWLEY HALL OF MUSIC: N 5yd [1*].

*Corylus* L. [**Hazelnut; Filbert**]

The shrubby American hazelnut, appropriate in naturalistic settings, can become large. In the wild it grows in thickets, pastures, or on hillsides, where squirrels feed on the nuts. Turkish hazelnut is a large tree that withstands drought. The male flowers (catkins) appear very early, before the leaves, to add interest in the spring. The fruits that follow are edible. Commercial filberts are harvested from *C. avellana* and *C. maxima*, which are native to Europe. Worldwide, *Corylus* is found throughout north temperate areas.

Broadleaved, small to large tree or shrub: deciduous, monoecious. Leaves alternate, simple, with toothed margins. Female flowers form clusters of nuts enclosed in leafy husks at the ends of the branches.

*americana* Walt. [**American Hazelnut; American Filbert**]

Deciduous shrub. Petiole 0.5 in. long, leaf oval, curved to thin point, length 1.5 times width, hairy below. Use in naturalized settings. Native to eastern North America. In horticulture since 1798. Maximum height 18 ft.

CALVARY: Cross, sides [2*]. ST. JOSEPH HALL: W in woods, along path, N side [few]. ST. JOSEPH'S LAKE: NW woods [many*].

*avellana* L. [**European Hazel**]

Deciduous shrub. Petiole to 0.5 in. long, leaf wide oval, almost lobed, to 4 in. long, veins hairy below. Forms thickets by sending shoots from roots. Introduced, native to Europe, Asia, northern Africa. Maximum height 20 ft.

'Contorta' [**European Hazel**]

Deciduous shrub. Branches and leaves extremely twisted and curled. Grafted on roots of species, which send suckers that need pruning. Ornamental in winter.

Developed in Gloucestershire, England. In horticulture since 1863. Maximum height 10 ft.

> GROTTO OF OUR LADY OF LOURDES: W [1 **Commem.**]. SACRED HEART BASILICA: W side [1].

*colurna* L. [**Turkish Hazelnut**]

> Deciduous tree. Petiole to 1 in. long, leaf wide oval, may be lobed, to 6 in. long, veins hairy below. Formal, pyramidal form; tolerates drought. Introduced, native to southeastern Europe, western Asia. In horticulture since 1852. Maximum height 50 ft.
>
> > BURKE MEMORIAL GOLF COURSE: NE central area [1*]. ROCKNE MEMORIAL: S, practice green, SE corner [1*].

*Ostrya* Scop. [**Hophornbeam**]

The hophornbeams are attractive, slow-growing, hardy trees that can withstand dry, exposed conditions and have no serious insect or disease problems. The common name refers to the similarity of their hanging fruits and those of the hops used in beer-making. It is a superficial resemblance. The beer hops are from a nonwoody plant, *Humulus lupulus*, of the hemp family. Eastern hophornbeam wood is the second hardest of our native trees. Only dogwood is harder. The hophornbeams are native to the Northern Hemisphere.

> Broad-leaved small tree: deciduous, monoecious. Leaves alternate, simple, toothed along margins, with veins not as straight and parallel as those of *Carpinus*. Female catkins form hanging fruit clusters of nutlets enclosed in green or pale yellow bladderlike bracts, which are unique to *Ostrya*.

*virginiana* (Mill.) C. Koch [**Eastern Hophornbeam; Ironwood**]

> Deciduous tree. Leaf to 5 in. long, veins hairy above, forked at ends. Pyramidal form; good for urban sites. Native to eastern North America. In horticulture since 1690. Maximum height 40 ft.
>
> > ROCKNE MEMORIAL: W, golf maintenance center, NW corner [1*].

## THEACEAE [TEA FAMILY]

*Stewartia* L. [**Stewartia**]

The stewartias are ornamental trees and shrubs that have both beautiful white, camellialike flowers that appear in midsummer and striking bark that flakes in irregular pieces to reveal lighter inner bark. This feature is especially effective in winter. Stewartia grows in rich, moist soil in areas with light shade during midday. It is difficult to transplant when mature. Stewartias are native to eastern Asia and eastern North America. The genus was named by Linnaeus, but using an older spelling, in honor of John Stuart (1713-1792), 3rd Earl of Bute (southwestern Scotland), British Prime Minister in 1762-1763, and patron of botany and horticulture.

> Broad-leaved small tree or shrub: deciduous. Leaves alternate, simple, edged with widely spaced teeth. Flowers large, solitary, white; a woody, 5-celled capsule that opens to disperse 1-4 seeds from each cell.

*koreana* Nakai ex Rehd. [**Korean Stewartia**]

> Deciduous tree. Leaf 3 in., wrinkled above, wavy-toothed, teeth incurved, thick;

flower 3 in., opens flat. Showy white flowers; leaves turn purple; bark flakes gray and brown. Ornamental in midsummer through winter. Introduced, native to Korea. In horticulture since 1917. Maximum height 30 ft.

> GROTTO OF OUR LADY OF LOURDES: W lawn, N of walk [1]. HESBURGH CENTER: E side, SE entrance, flanking [2]; S side, SW edge, near plaza [1]; S side, entrance [2]; SW Plaza, outer section, NW corner [1]; SW Plaza, outer section, SE corner [1]; W side, S section, SW corner of bed [1]; W side, entrance [2].

*pseudocamelia* Maxim. [**Japanese Stewartia**]

Deciduous tree. Leaf 3.5 in., smooth above, faint wavy-toothed, scalloped edge; flower cup-shaped, 2.5 in.. Flower white; flaking, red brown bark; leaf turns yellow, deep red. Ornamental in midsummer through winter. Introduced, native to Japan. In horticulture since 1874. Maximum height 40 ft.

> DEBARTOLO CLASSROOM BUILDING: E side, between central doors [7]. SUPPORT SERVICES BUILDING: N bed [1].

# CLUSIACEAE [MANGOSTEEN FAMILY]

*Hypericum* L. [**St. Johnswort**]

The ornamental species are shrubs and evergreen ground covers grown for their bright yellow flowers of midsummer. The St. Johnswort of the Midwest, *H. frondosum*, is a medium-sized, stout shrub with peeling red brown bark. *Hypericum* is a large genus native to temperate North America and to the mountainous tropics. Plants of the genus are poisonous to livestock. They cause photosensitization when eaten. This becomes a problem when the weedy species get into hay.

Broad-leaved shrub, tree, or perennial herb: deciduous or evergreen. Leaves in opposite pairs on 2-winged stems, simple, glossy, blue green, dotted on both surfaces with small oil glands, smooth-edged. Flowers large, yellow, appear in June and July, each with 5 petals and a dense brush made up of numerous stamens; fruit a 3-celled capsule with many seeds.

*prolificum* L. [**Shrubby St. Johnswort**]

Deciduous shrub. Bark gray brown, tight; leaf blue green, to 3 in. long; flower to 1 in. wide, sepals small. Flowers bright yellow, showy. Ornamental in summer. Native to Ontario to Georgia, Minnesota, and Louisiana. In horticulture since 1750. Foliage causes photosensitivity when eaten as forage by livestock. Maximum height 4 ft.

> LAW SCHOOL: S wing, SW corner [3]; S wing, W side [2].

# TILIACEAE [LINDEN FAMILY]

*Tilia* L. [**Basswood; Linden; Lime**]

The family name of the Swedish naturalist and father of systematic taxonomy, Carl Linnaeus (1707-1778), was derived from the Swedish name *Lind* for the linden or lime tree. Linnaeus' ancestors were yeoman farmers who owned and worked their land. By tradition they formed their names by adding "son" to their fathers' first names. Nils Ingemarsson (b. 1674), Carl Linnaeus' father, was forced to take a surname when he enrolled in the university on his way to becoming a Lutheran clergyman. He chose the name Linnaeus, a reference to a huge linden tree that was growing on his family's ancestral land. At about the same time, other branches of Linnaeus' family took the names Tiliander and Lindelius, also in reference to the ancestral linden tree. The lindens are some of the best shade and street trees. They are tolerant of urban conditions and provide dense shade with regular, pyramidal outlines. They are native to temperate regions of the Northern Hemisphere. The American basswood, *T. americana*, is taller and has larger, coarser leaves than the European species. It is almost too large for most urban sites, but magnificent in its natural eastern North American mixed deciduous forest setting. In Europe lindens frequently line avenues. *Unter den Linden*, the famous avenue in Berlin, Germany, is shaded by *T. × europaea* 'Pallida', a large-leaved cultivar of the naturally occurring hybrid European linden. The Europeans also use lindens for formally pruned hedges. The fragrant flowers of linden are pollinated by bees. Basswood honey is prized for its flavor in North America. The term basswood refers to the bass or bast fibers, used in rope making, which are obtained from the inner bark. The soft white wood is used to make inexpensive furniture, piano keys, or excelsior, and for wood carving. It was used by Grinling Gibbons (1648-1720), the English woodcarver and sculptor who was employed by architect Sir Christopher Wren, when he carved the stalls in St. Paul's and other London churches.

Broad-leaved tall tree: deciduous. Leaves alternate along stem, simple, margin toothed, asymmetrically heart-shaped. Flowers small but fragrant, yellow white, hanging in cymes of up to 10 flowers each; fruit small, gray, nutlike, each with 1-3 seeds, hangs below distinctive strap-shaped papery bract. This fruit arrangement is unique to the genus *Tilia*.

*americana* L. [**American Basswood; American Linden**]

Deciduous tree. Leaf to 8 in. long, coarse, smooth below with hair tufts; shoot and petiole smooth. Too large for many urban sites, used in golf courses and parks. Native to eastern Canada through Texas. In horticulture since 1752. Maximum height 80 ft.

BURKE MEMORIAL GOLF COURSE: S central area [7]; Sollitt shelter, E [1]. CALVARY: Woods [many*]. CAMPUS SECURITY BUILDING: NE corner, E 35yd [1*]. HESBURGH LIBRARY: Stepan Chemistry, walk between, S side [2]. ST. JOSEPH'S LAKE [many]. ST. MARY'S LAKE: N central edge, 10 yd N of path [1]. WASHINGTON HALL: S, main entrance, SE 5yd [1*].

*cordata* Mill. [**Small-leaved European Linden**]

Deciduous tree. Leaf to 3 in. long, teeth blunt, dull above, blue green and smooth below; twig brown. Good shade tree. Introduced, native to Europe. Maximum height 70 ft.

PASQUERILLA HALL EAST: N wing, E side [1]. PASQUERILLA HALL WEST: N wing, N end [2]. SORIN HALL: SE corner, ESE 30yd [1*].

'DeGroot' [**Small-leaved European Linden**]

Deciduous tree. Upright habit with compact head. Grows more slowly than most lindens; leaves glossy, dark green. Maximum height 40 ft.

DEBARTOLO CLASSROOM BUILDING: S side, center, at walk [2].

× *euchlora* C. Koch: *T. ? cordata* × *T. dasystyla* [**Crimean Linden**]
>    Deciduous tree. Weeping form; leaf 4 in. long, shiny above, brown hair tufts below, toothed; twig green. Maximum height 60 ft.
>> LaFortune Student Center: Sacred Heart Statue, midway [1*].

*heterophylla* Venten. [**White Basswood**]
>    Deciduous tree. Leaf to 6 in. long, feltlike hairs below, base heart-shaped; shoot and petiole smooth. Introduced, native to Europe. Maximum height 100 ft.
>> Burke Memorial Golf Course: SW central area [many]. Stadium: NE, gates 1 and 2 [1]; NW, gate 16 [1].

× *moltkei* F. L. Spaeth: *T. ? americana* × *T. ? petiolaris* [**Moltke's Linden**]
>    Deciduous tree. Weeping; leaf gray-hairy below when young, no tufted hairs, petiole and shoot smooth.
>> Burke Memorial Golf Course: SW area [many*].

*petiolaris* DC. [**Pendent Silver Linden**]
>    Deciduous tree. Weeping; leaf to 4.5 in. long, white-hairy below, petiole long and hairy; shoot hairy. Graceful form; leaves flutter in the wind. Introduced, native to southeastern Europe, western Asia. In horticulture since 1840. Maximum height 75 ft.
>> Sorin Hall: SE corner, SSE 15yd, E of lamppost 57 [1*].

## MALVACEAE [MALLOW FAMILY]

*Hibiscus* L. [**Rose-of-Sharon; Hibiscus; Mallow**]
>    Hibiscus is a vase-shaped shrub or small tree grown for its large flowers that bloom during middle to late summer when few other shrubs bloom. The flowers can be single or double. They range from white, blue, and purple to red, almost always with red at their centers. Most species grow in the tropics, but rose-of-Sharon, *H. syriacus*, is a warm temperate species that has been introduced into gardens of the East and Midwest. The colorful giant hibiscus of the tropics is *H. rosa-sinensis*.
>    Broad-leaved tree, shrub, or perennial herb: deciduous (tropical species evergreen). Leaves alternate along stem, simple, toothed, palmately lobed, each with 3 lobes. Flowers large, bell-shaped, 5-petalled, upright, solitary on the current season's growth; fruit a dry 5-celled capsule that splits to dispense 3 or more seeds from each cell, capsule remains through winter.

*syriacus* L. [**Shrub-althea; Rose-of-Sharon**]
>    Deciduous shrub. Erect, upright branches; flower to 4 in. wide, 5 petals. Showy white, red, purple flowers bloom when few others are blooming. Ornamental in July through September. Introduced, native to China, India. In horticulture since 1600. Maximum height 12 ft.
>> Brownson Hall: Court, SW corner [2]. Corby Hall: Front, Corby statue, SE 30yd [1*]. Holy Cross House: W [4]. Knott Hall: S wing, W side [2]. Moreau Seminary: W end, along walk [4*]. Pasquerilla Hall East: N wing, SE corner [3]. Pasquerilla Hall West: N wing, W side [3]. Siegfried Hall: S wing, E side [2].

'Blushing Bride' [**Shrub-althea; Rose-of-Sharon**]
>    Deciduous shrub. Flowers light pink, petals double.
>> Support Services Building: S bed [3].

## SALICACEAE [WILLOW FAMILY]

*Populus* L. [**Poplar; Cottonwood; Aspen**]

Poplars have been used widely in landscaping because they are vigorous growers. This makes them suitable for windbreaks in the plains. However, in urban areas their popularity is declining for several reasons. Their shallow roots can raise sidewalks and clog water pipes and sewers, causing many cities to disallow them as street trees by ordinance. Their brittle wood breaks readily during wind and snowstorms. The Lombardy poplar, *P. nigra* 'Italica', is the distinctively narrow upright tree introduced during colonial times from Italy. It is susceptible to a canker-causing fungus disease that causes it to die back from the top. The fluttering leaves of cottonwood, poplar, and aspen (including quaking aspen) are the result of the weak, flattened petioles. Just as drinking straws lose strength and rigidity when flattened, so do the petioles of *Populus*, allowing the leaves to flutter in the slightest breeze. *Populus* wood is used for pulp. The name cottonwood refers to the "cotton" attached to the seeds of *P. deltoides*. Cottonwood is the state tree of Kansas, South Dakota, and Wyoming. Quaking aspen, *P. tremuloides*, is the state tree of Nevada. The clear yellow autumn leaves of quaking aspen define "fall color" in the Rocky Mountains. Poplars grow throughout the Northern Hemisphere.

Broad-leaved large or small tree: deciduous, dioecious. Leaves alternate, simple, broad, either lobed or toothed, but always with long, flattened petioles. Flowers appear before leaves in long, drooping catkins; male and female grow in separate catkins on same tree. Fruit a small capsule covering hairy seeds.

*alba* L. [**White Poplar; Silverleaf Poplar**]

Deciduous tree. Leaf densely white-hairy below, petiole not flat. Leaves not quaking, very white; roots can clog plumbing pipes. Introduced, native to Europe, Asia; naturalized in North America. In horticulture since 1784. Maximum height 70 ft.

COLUMBA HALL: NE, lakeside [1*]; SE 60yd [2*]. ST. JOSEPH'S LAKE: W end [10*]. ST. MARY'S LAKE: W end [few].

*deltoides* Bartr. ex Marsh. [**Cottonwood**]

Deciduous tree. Leaf triangular, smooth below, edge thin, clear, hairy, 2 glands at base; petiole flat. Leaves quake in the wind; messy, limbs weak, damaged by wind. Native to Quebec through Florida and Texas. In horticulture since 1750. Maximum height 100 ft.

BROWNSON HALL: W side [1*]. BURKE MEMORIAL GOLF COURSE: NE area [2]. CARROLL HALL: N, lakeside [8*]; SE 50yd [1]. FATIMA RETREAT HOUSE: E 50yd [many]; S, lakeside [2]; SE 50yd, lakeside [1]. GRACE HALL: Flanner, between [1]; SW corner [2]. HOLY CROSS HOUSE: N 40yd, Douglas Rd, N [1*]; SE, lakeside [3*]. OUTDOOR WAY OF THE CROSS: Station 1, E 15yd [1*]; Station 1, NE 30yd [1*]. PASQUERILLA HALL EAST: Pasquerilla Hall West, midway [2*]; W wing, N of W end [1]. ST. JOSEPH HALL: NW corner, N 40yd [1]; NW corner, N 50yd [1]. ST. JOSEPH'S LAKE: Power plant, 75yd NW [2]; SW, at walk to island [1]. ST. MARY'S LAKE: W end, ravine [6*].

*grandidentata* Michx. [**Bigtooth Aspen**]

Deciduous tree. Leaf not hairy, rounded, edge thick, 5-15 dull teeth per side, petiole flat. Quaking; fast-growing but of little ornamental value. Native to

Ontario through Nova Scotia and eastern United States. In horticulture since 1772. Maximum height 70 ft.

> Carroll Hall: Tennis courts, N, lakeside [8*]. Grotto of Our Lady of Lourdes: W, lakeside [1*].

## *Salix* L. [**Willow**]

Often grown for erosion control, willows thrive in the wet ground along lakes and streams. In the northern United States, the most hardy and reliable of the weeping forms are *S. alba*, with its yellow stems, and the hybrid *S.* × *blanda*, which has glossy leaves. The willows are difficult to tell apart and many, including these two, are sold in nurseries under the name *S. babylonica*, which is not hardy this far north. Many yellow willows, *S. alba* var. *vitellina*, grow along the shores of Notre Dame's lakes. Their weeping yellow branches are visible during the winter. Willow bark is the original source for salicin (salicylic acid) or aspirin, which is now produced synthetically. The long, flexible branches that are characteristic of the genus are used in basketry and weaving for furniture. The roots yield blue red dyes. The true weeping willow, *S. babylonica*, was the inspiration for the "blue willow" or "willow" china pattern. The pussy willow of the spring floral industry comes from this genus. Many species are native to the temperate and colder regions of the Northern Hemisphere; only a few species are found in the Southern Hemisphere.

Broad-leaved tree or shrub: deciduous, dioecious. Leaves alternate, simple, toothed, usually long and narrow. Each winter bud covered by a single scale rather than the multiple, overlapping scales more commonly seen on woody plants. Flowers small; male and female borne in dense catkins on separate trees. Fruit, on female trees, a small capsule enclosing hairy seeds.

### *alba* L. [**White Willow**]

Deciduous tree. Twig yellowish; leaf silky below, narrow, 4 in. long, with narrow stipules at leaf base. Branches weeping. Introduced, native to North Africa, Asia, Europe. Maximum height 100 ft.

#### var. *vitellina* (L.) J. Stokes [**Yellow Willow**]

Deciduous tree. Young twigs egg yolk yellow; leaf chalk white below.

> Carroll Hall: Kitchen, NE, lakeside [1]; Kitchen, NE, lakeside [1]; N side, N 40 yd [1]; N, lakeside [1]; NE corner, E 100yd, lakeside [1]; NE corner, E 125yd, lakeside [1]; NNW, E of Carroll Hall Annex [1]. Columba Hall: Basketball court, N [1]; Basketball court, W 10yd, lakeside [4]. Community Cemetery: SW corner, S 60yd [1]. Fatima Retreat House: SE, lakeside [3]. Grotto of Our Lady of Lourdes: N, 100yd [1]; WSW, St. Mary's Lake margin [1]. Lyons Hall: NW basketball court, N, lakeside [2]. Moreau Seminary: S, lakeside [6]. St. Joseph's Lake: Lewis Hall, N 15 yd [1]; Power plant, NW 100yd [2]; S side, central area [1]; SW corner, along road [1]; SW corner, along road, ENE 12yd [1]; SW corner, along road, ENE 32yd [1]. St. Mary's Lake: N central edge [3]; NW edge [many].

### *amygdaloides* Anderss. [**Peachleaf Willow**]

Deciduous shrub. Twig green brown; leaf glossy above, pale below, to 1 in. wide, tip sharp, thick. May be treelike. Native to North America. Maximum height 30 ft.

> Holy Cross House: SE corner, lakeside [1*]. Moreau Seminary: NE [1*].

*bebbiana* Sarg. [**Bebb's Willow**]

> Deciduous shrub. Leaf densely hairy below, dull green above, 2-3 times longer than wide. Native to North America. Maximum height 30 ft.
>
> > FATIMA RETREAT HOUSE: E 40yd [1]. MOREAU SEMINARY: NW corner, W [1].

× *blanda* Anderss.: *S. ? babylonica* × *S. ? fragilis* [**Niobe Willow; Wisconsin Willow**]

> Deciduous tree. Twig red green; leaf shiny above, hairless below, thick, teeth on edge dull. Branches pendulous but not truly weeping. Developed through hybridization. In horticulture since 1867. Maximum height 40 ft.
>
> > NORTH DINING HALL: E side [1*].

*caprea* L. [**Goat Willow**]

> Deciduous tree. Leaf silver green below, edge toothed and curly, base wedge-shaped, tip abruptly pointed. Showy, more disease resistant than the native pussy willow. Ornamental in spring. Introduced, native to Europe. Maximum height 25 ft.
>
> > COMMUNITY CEMETERY: Mission House, between [1]. ST. JOSEPH'S LAKE: Boat house, E [many].

*discolor* Muhlenb. [**Pussy Willow**]

> Deciduous shrub. Leaf silver below, edge with widely spaced teeth, tip long-pointed. The true, native pussy willow; susceptible to disease. Ornamental in spring. Native to eastern North Ameriac. Maximum height 20 ft.
>
> > HOLY CROSS HOUSE: E end, S, lakeside [1].

*exigua* Nutt. [**Sandbar Willow**]

> Deciduous shrub. Leaf very narrow, dull above, densely hairy below, widely spaced teeth along edge. Native to Alaska through Louisiana. Maximum height 10 ft.
>
> > ST. MARY'S LAKE: S margin, E end [many*].

*fragilis* L. [**Brittle Willow; Crack Willow**]

> Deciduous tree. Leaf pale below, narrow, to 7 in. long, with round stipules at base. Introduced, native to Europe, Asia. Maximum height 60 ft.
>
> > CARROLL HALL: E, lakeside [few*]. COLUMBA HALL: Basketball court, WNW, 25yd [1]. GROTTO OF OUR LADY OF LOURDES: W, lakeside [1]. OLD COLLEGE: N, lakeside [2*].

*matsudana* G. Koidz. [**Hankow Willow**]

> Deciduous tree. Leaf narrow, 3 in. long, white below, edge sharp-toothed; twig olive green. Introduced, native to northern Asia. Maximum height 50 ft.

'Tortuosa' [**Corkscrew Willow; Dragon-claw Willow**]

> Deciduous tree. Twigs and leaves contorted or twisted. Unusual appearance, considered bizarre by some people. Ornamental in winter. Developed in China. In horticulture since 1923. Maximum height 30 ft.
>
> > BROWNSON HALL: Court, NE corner [1]. ST. MARY'S LAKE: E edge [1].

*nigra* Marsh. [**Black Willow**]

> Deciduous tree. Leaf very narrow, 5 in. long, not glossy, many fine teeth along edge; twig yellow. May be shrubby. Native to eastern United States through nothern Mexico. Maximum height 35 ft.
>
> > HOLY CROSS HOUSE: SW, lakeside [1*]. ST. MARY'S LAKE: SE edge, NW of road intersection [3].

*purpurea* L. [**Purpleosier Willow; Basket Willow**]

> Deciduous shrub. Leaf waxy white below, blue green above, very narrow, toothed near tip; shoots red purple. Dense, rounded form; purple shoots gradually turn gray. Introduced, native to Europe and North Africa through

central Asia and Japan. Maximum height 10 ft.

'Pendula' [**Purpleosier Willow; Basket Willow**]

Deciduous shrub. Wide-spreading form; branches slender, drooping. Often grafted on a standard to raise weeping branches in the air.

SUPPORT SERVICES BUILDING: N bed [1].


## ERICACEAE [HEATH FAMILY]

*Arctostaphylos* Adans. [**Bearberry**]

Bearberry is an extremely hardy, tough, low shrub for sandy, rocky sites. It grows in acid or limestone soils, but either must be well drained and low in nutrients. Most species are native to western North America, but two are circumpolar. The edible fruits were ground into a meal in earlier days.

Broad-leaved, low-growing shrub: evergreen. Leaves alternate along stem, small, simple, glossy, edge smooth but curled under. Flowers small, pink to white, nodding, bell-shaped, in racemes at branch ends, in April and May; fruit a small, red, berrylike drupe holding 4-10 nutlets.

*uva-ursi* (L.) K. Spreng. [**Bearberry; Kinnikinick**]

Evergreen ground cover. Leaf to 1 in. long, glossy above, pale below, edge curled under. Hardy when established, but difficult to transplant; fruit red. Ornamental in late summer through winter. Native to North Ameriac, Europe, northern Asia. In horticulture since 1800. Maximum height 1 ft.

'Massachusetts' [**Bearberry; Kinnikinick**]

Evergreen ground cover. Leaf small; flowers abundant; disease resistant; low growing form. Developed in Oregon from Massachusetts seed.

HESBURGH CENTER: Court, NW bed [bed]; Court, SE bed [bed].


*Gaultheria* L. [**Gaultheria; Wintergreen**]

These small ornamental shrubs are grown for their nodding flowers, which bloom from May through September, and for their evergreen foliage. The low-growing *G. procumbens* is useful as a creeping, 6 in. tall ground cover where the soil is acidic, moist, and highly organic. This native eastern North American species was the original source of medicinal wintergreen, which is now extracted from cherry or sweet birch, *Betula lenta*. Gaultherias are native to the South American Andes, North and Central America, and from Asia through Australia. No records of poisoning are known for this genus and the fruits have been eaten.

Broad-leaved, erect or prostrate shrub, rarely a small tree: evergreen. Leaves alternate along stem, simple, either wavy-edged or toothed, the teeth often bristly. Flowers nodding, pink to white, bell-shaped, solitary in leaf axils; fruit a berrylike 5-celled, seed-bearing capsule enclosed by a fleshy, bright-colored calyx.

*procumbens* L. [**Wintergreen**]

Evergreen ground cover. Leaf 1.5 in. long with bristly teeth, wintergreen odor when crushed. Fruit red; leaves turn red. Ornamental in winter. Native to eastern North America. In horticulture since 1762. Maximum height 0.5 ft.

HESBURGH CENTER: SE corner, W [beds]. JOYCE ATHLETIC AND CONVOCATION CENTER: W, between gates 1 and 2, at benches [bed]. SUPPORT SERVICES BUILDING: N bed [75].

*Leucothoe* D. Don [**Leucothoe; Fetterbush**]

These shrubs are grown for their handsome, large, evergreen leaves and numerous small, white flowers. As do many other plants in the heath family, leucothoe requires moist but well-drained, acidic soil with a high organic content. It can withstand full sun if not subjected to drought or drying winds. Leucothoe is native to North and South America and eastern Asia. All parts of the plant should be considered poisonous, as are so many plants in the heath family, although information is scarce in the literature.

Broad-leaved shrub: evergreen or rarely deciduous. Leaves long, alternate along stem, simple, edge toothed or hairy. Flowers small, white, pitcher-shaped with margins edged with 5 small teeth, clustered in racemes hanging from leaf axils; fruit an inconspicuous 5-celled, many-seeded capsule.

*axillaris* (Lam.) D. Don [**Downy Leucothoe; Fetterbush**]

Evergreen shrub. Leaf leathery, dark glossy green, edge with wide teeth; flower clusters 3 in. long. Clusters of small, white flowers are showy. Ornamental in early spring. Native to southeastern United States. In horticulture since 1765. Many closely related Rhododendron Family plants are poisonous. Maximum height 6 ft.

FATIMA RETREAT HOUSE: Mission House, N side [1*].

*Oxydendrum* DC. [**Sourwood; Sorrel Tree**]

Sourwood is one of only a few heath family plants that reach tree size. It is native to the eastern United States. Its leaves, sour when chewed, were used to quench thirst during earlier times. The glossy laurel-like leaves turn vivid pink to red during autumn. The small but abundant white flowers that form at the tips of the branches are showy during June and July. This medium-sized, pyramidal tree is suitable for specimen planting. It has good features during all seasons.

Broad-leaved tree: deciduous. Leaves alternate, simple, margin toothed. Flowers small, white, fragrant, numerous in drooping clusters at tips of branches; fruit a 5-valved capsule that persists into winter.

*arboreum* (L.) DC. [**Sourwood; Sorrel Tree**]

Deciduous tree. Leaf simple, 3-8 in. long, toothed, shiny dark green above, pale with hairy veins below. White flowers in drooping clusters at branch tips; leaves turn red. Ornamental in June to July, autumn. Native to Pennsylvania to Illinois, south to Florida and Louisiana. In horticulture since 1747. Maximum height 30 ft.

SUPPORT SERVICES BUILDING: N bed [1]; S bed [1].

*Pieris* D. Don [**Pieris**]

Pieris are native to eastern North America, eastern Asia, and the Himalayas. They are grown for their handsome flowers and foliage that is bronze when young. The plants can be used as medium-sized specimens or massed in shrub borders. They tolerate sun or partial shade but need protection from wind. The soil must be well-drained but need not be as acidic as that required by most other plants of the heath family. All parts of the plants should be considered poisonous if eaten although reports of poisoning are rare.

Broad-leaved shrub or small tree: evergreen. Leaves alternate along stem, simple, edge wavy or toothed. Flower small, white, urn-shaped, hanging in long narrow panicles at branch tips; fruit a small, dehiscent, 5-celled capsule. A distinctive feature of pieris is its flower buds, which form during the summer and remain conspicuous through the following winter. Flowers open in March and April.

*japonica* (Thunb.) D. Don [**Lily-of-the-valley Bush**]

Evergreen shrub. Flower buds form summer before flowering, visible during winter; flower cluster 6 in. long. Young leaves bronze to vivid red; flowers remain for 2-3 weeks. Ornamental in early spring. Introduced, native to Japan. In horticulture since 1870. Many closely related Rhododendron Family plants are poisonous. Maximum height 12 ft.

KEENAN HALL: SE entrance [2]. MORRISSEY HALL: S, intersection of walks [1]. PANGBORN HALL: N, main entrance, W [bed]. UNIVERSITY HEALTH SERVICES: N side [1].

*Rhododendron* L. [**Rhododendron; Azalea**]

The rhododendrons and azaleas, with their large vividly-colored flowers, have been the subject of one of the most intense and prolonged horticultural "improvement" efforts in history, activity that reached its height in nineteenth century Great Britain. The only other plants that possibly have engendered such heightened activity are the roses, *Rosa*, during the same period in history and the tulips, *Tulipa*, that have been cultivated in Iran since the thirteenth century and in Europe since the sixteenth century. Tulips were introduced to Europe by Charles Lécluse (1526-1609), better known as Clusius, a French physician and botanist who also introduced the potato to Europe. There are almost 900 species of *Rhododendron*. Most of these are native to temperate regions of the Northern Hemisphere, especially to the Himalayas, to southeastern Asia, and to the Malaysian mountains (155 species are found in New Guinea alone). Only one species is found in Australia and none is found in either Africa or South America. While rhododendrons and azaleas are in the same genus, they can be roughly separated into two groups defined by leaf and flower characteristics. Rhododendrons usually have glossy, evergreen, scaly, leaves and larger clusters of large, bell-shaped flowers each with 10 or more (up to 20) stamens at its center. Azaleas usually have deciduous leaves that may be hairy, but never scaly, and smaller, funnel-shaped flowers with only 5 stamens. Although smaller, azalea flowers are abundant and can completely cover the bushes at their blooming peak. In the harsh climate of the Midwest, *Rhododendron* plants require light shade (either from trees or from placement on the north side of a building) and well-drained acid soil that is mulched to maintain an even temperature. If not placed in appropriate sites and protected from desiccation, the evergreen leaves of the rhododendrons can suffer winter wind and sun burn. The deciduous azaleas do not have this problem. The low, evergreen P.J.M. rhododendrons, with their lavender pink flowers, are reliable in the Midwest as are the extremely hardy and colorful 'Northern Lights' hybrid azaleas (white or yellow to rose pink) that were introduced by the University of Minnesota in 1979 from crosses made in 1957 by the late Dr. Albert G. Johnson. Rhododendron and azalea leaves, twigs, flowers, and pollen contain andromedotoxin, a resinoid that is poisonous when eaten.

Broad-leaved tree or shrub: evergreen or deciduous. Leaves alternate along stem, either evergreen and scaly or deciduous with a smooth or hairy surface. Flowers funnel or bell-shaped, with either 5 or 10-20 stamens, clustered at branch ends in most species, but at leaf axils in some species; fruit a woody, dehiscent, 5-valved capsule that opens to disperse many small seeds.

*catawbiense* Michx. [**Catawba Rhododendron**]

Evergreen shrub. Leaf 6 in. long, leathery, pale below, base rounded; flower 2.5 in. wide, in 6 in. cluster. May. Ornamental in All parts poisonous when eaten. Native to the southern Appalachians through Georgia and Alabama. In horticulture since 1809. Maximum height 10 ft.

BROWNSON HALL: Court, NE corner [3]. HOLY CROSS HOUSE: N side [11*]. MOREAU SEMINARY: S central side [2].

*obtusum* (Lindl.) Planch. [**Hiryu Azalea**]

Evergreen shrub. Leaf glossy, 1.25 in. long; flower 1 in. wide, usually rose red, growing in threes. Dense, spreading form; many cultivars available. Introduced, native to Japan. In horticulture since 1844. All parts are poisonous when eaten. Maximum height 6 ft.

WASHINGTON HALL: LaFortune, crosswalk between, W [1].

f. *Hinomoyo* 'Amoenum' [**Japanese Pink Azalea**]

Evergreen shrub. Flowers pink, funnel-shaped.

HOLY CROSS HOUSE: S entrance, E [1*].

f. *Yayegiri* 'Amoenum' [**Japanese Salmon-red Azalea**]

Evergreen shrub. Flowers salmon red, funnel-shaped.

FARLEY HALL: W door, S [1]. WASHINGTON HALL: LaFortune, crosswalk between, W [1].

*spp.* [**Rhododendron; Azalea**]

Evergreen shrub. Evergreen or deciduous; flower bell or funnel-shaped, color varies. Grown for glossy foliage and showy flowers. Ornamental in spring. Native to eastern United States, Japan, China; found on all continents. All parts are poisonous when eaten.

FARLEY HALL: W central door, S side [hedge]. FISHER HALL: N entrance, E [bed]. HESBURGH CENTER: Court, S bed [11]; Court, W bed [19]; Court, middle bed [16]. JOYCE ATHLETIC AND CONVOCATION CENTER: W, between gates 1 and 11 [26]. SNITE MUSEUM OF ART: Court [10]. SORIN HALL: E at crosswalk [bed]. WASHINGTON HALL: SW, bed at intersection [bed].

'P.J.M.' [**P.J.M. Rhododendron**]

Evergreen shrub. Leaf small, to 2.5 in. long, hairless, leathery, rusty below. Flowers lavendar pink, profuse; leaves turn purple. Ornamental in early spring, autumn. Developed in Massachusetts. In horticulture since 1943. Maximum height 6 ft.

HESBURGH CENTER: N side, E entrance, S [7]. JUNIPER ROAD: W at Bulla Road, S fence, roadside [3]. SUPPORT SERVICES BUILDING: N bed [1]; S bed [2].

'Ramapo' [**Ramapo Rhododendron**]

Evergreen shrub. Compact form; leaf with white, waxy coating; flowers bright red pink. Ornamental in April.

DEBARTOLO CLASSROOM BUILDING: E side, between central doors [32]; NE corner, E side at doors [11]. HESBURGH CENTER: Court, S bed [bed]; Court, W bed [bed]; Court, middle bed [bed]; SW Plaza [15]. JUNIPER ROAD: N at Douglas Rd, entrance sign [bed]; S at Edison Rd, entrance sign [bed]. SESQUICENTENNIAL COMMONS: S central outer bed, center [18]. SUPPORT SERVICES BUILDING: E, flanking door [12]; N bed [2]; S bed [2].

## STYRACACEAE [STORAX FAMILY]

*Halesia* L. [**Silverbell**]

The native North American silverbells are understory trees of eastern and southern forests. Other species are native to eastern China. Ornamentally, they are used as lawn trees or placed in woodland or shrub border. Their white, bell-like flowers appear in April and May. They tolerate sun or partial shade and need acidic or neutral, rich, well-drained soil. They have no insect or disease problems.

Broad-leaved, medium-sized tree or shrub: deciduous. Leaves alternate along stems, simple, smooth-edged, surface smooth above but hairy below. Flowers white, 4-lobed bell-shaped, hanging in 2-5 flowered cymes along stems; fruit a 4-winged, dry, green to brown drupe with 2-3 seeds.

*carolina* L. [**Carolina Silverbell; Snowdrop-tree**]

Deciduous tree. Leaf to 5 in. long. tip long-tapered, hairy below; flowers bell-shaped. Flowers bloom just before leaves appear and persist two weeks. Ornamental in April to early May. Native to West Virginia through Florida and Texas. In horticulture since 1756. Maximum height 40 ft.

BURKE MEMORIAL GOLF COURSE: 17th tee, halfway to 17th green [1*]; SW area, SW of green 8 [1*].

*Styrax* L. [**Snowbell**]

The snowbells of the temperate regions are grown for their early summer display of white, fragrant flowers that hang in drooping clusters on loosely branching, open shrubs. *Styrax* is native to broad areas of the Mediterranean, southeastern Asia, western Malaysia, and tropical America. The bark of the tropical species of southeastern Asia provide a water soluble balsamic resin, benzoin, that is used in incense, perfumes, ointments, cough treatments, and antiseptics.

Broad-leaved shrub or low tree: deciduous, tropical species are evergreen. Leaves alternate along stem, simple, margin smooth or slightly toothed, surface smooth above but with tufts of hair at the vein axils below. Flower hanging, 5-lobed, bell-like, in 3-6 flowered racemes; fruit a small, dry, 1-seeded drupe.

*japonicus* Siebold & Zucc. [**Japanese Snowbell**]

Deciduous tree. Leaf elliptic, 3.5 in. long, pointed, faint teeth on edge, hair tufts below in vein axils. Branches low on trunk, wide-spreading; graceful; bell-like flowers. Ornamental in May to June. Introduced, native to Japan, China. In horticulture since 1862. Maximum height 30 ft.

DEBARTOLO CLASSROOM BUILDING: E side, NW corner [1]; E side, flanking central doors [2].

## HYDRANGEACEAE [HYDRANGEA FAMILY]

*Deutzia* Thunb. [**Deutzia**]

Deutzia is grown for its showy white to pink spring flowers, but it is rather inconspicuous during the remaining seasons. It is native to temperate Asia, Mexico, and the mountains of Central America.

Broad-leaved shrub: deciduous. Leaves opposite along stem, simple, toothed. Flowers, in panicles or racemes, produce capsules of tiny seeds. Deutzia can be confused with *Philadelphus*. Deutzia buds are visible at the bases of the leaf stalks along the stem whereas *Philadelphus* buds are hidden. Deutzia leaves are rough like sandpaper because of their covering of star-shaped hairs, *Philadelphus* leaves are smooth.

*gracilis* Siebold & Zucc. [**Japanese Slender Deutzia**]

Deciduous shrub. Leaf 3 in. long, toothed, some starlike hairs above, smooth deep green below; smooth bark. White flowers profuse, in 3 in. long clusters. Ornamental in late May. Introduced, native to Japan. In horticulture since 1880. Maximum height 4 ft.

ALUMNI HALL: NE corner, at walk [hedge*]. FARLEY HALL: E court [hedge]. FISHER HALL: W side [hedge]. FRESHMAN YEAR BUILDING: Brownson court, SW [1]. LAW SCHOOL: NW corner, at walk [hedge*]. MORRIS INN: S end [hedge*].

× *lemoinei* Hort. Lemoine ex Bois: *D. gracilis* × *D. parviflora* [**Lemoine Deutzia**]

Deciduous shrub. Leaf 4 in. long, toothed, green above, starlike hairs below; bark peeling, brown. White flowers forming 3 in. long upright clusters; very hardy. Ornamental in late May. Developed by M. Lemoine of Nancy, France. In horticulture since 1891. Maximum height 7 ft.

FARLEY HALL: E court [20*].

× *magnifica* (Hort. Lemoine) Rehd.: *D. scabra* × *D. vilmoriniae* [**Clustered Deutzia**]

Deciduous shrub. Leaf 3 in. long, hairy and gray green below; flowers white, double. Flowers showy, form 3 in. long clusters. Ornamental in May to June. Developed by M. Lemoine of Nancy, France. In horticulture since 1909. Maximum height 10 ft.

CAMPUS SECURITY BUILDING: NE corner, E side [2*].

*scabra* Thunb. [**Double-flowering Scabrid Deutzia**]

Deciduous shrub. Leaf 4 in. long, both surfaces like sandpaper with starlike hairs; bark peeling, brown. Flowers white, forming 6 in. long upright clusters. Ornamental in early June. Introduced, native to Japan, China. In horticulture since 1822. Maximum height 10 ft.

'Candidissima' [**Double-flowering Scabrid Deutzia**]

Deciduous shrub. Flowers white, with double petals.

FRESHMAN YEAR BUILDING: W parking lot, SW [1]. HOWARD HALL: N wing, W end [1].

*Hydrangea* L. [**Hydrangea**]

Hydrangeas have long been popular in the landscape because of their showy clusters of white, pink, or blue flowers. These appear during midsummer and often remain on the plants through the winter. The shrubs tolerate shade and are easy to grow. University records dating from the 1880s and 1890s describe new beds of hydrangeas that were being planted in front of the Main building. Although these beds are no longer present, many others can be found on campus. Hydrangeas are native to eastern Asia and both North and South America.

Broad-leaved vine or shrub, may be treelike: deciduous. Leaves opposite along the stems with toothed margins. The flower clusters, either rounded or pyramidal, are composed of small fertile flowers at the center with large, showy sterile flowers around the margin or crowning the fertile ones. The sterile flowers have 3-5 large petallike sepals, but lack all other flower parts. Fruit is a dehiscent capsule of many small seeds.

*arborescens* L. [**Wild Hydrangea**]

Deciduous shrub. Leaf toothed, not lobed, broad, 8 in. long, dark green above, few sparse hairs below. Flowers white in flat clusters with large sterile ones at rim. Ornamental in June through September. Native to eastern and central United States. In horticulture since 1736. Leaves and buds poisonous when eaten. Maximum height 5 ft.

'Grandiflora' [**Snowball Hydrangea**]

Deciduous shrub. Flowers white, all sterile and large, form 8 in. wide clusters.
KNOTT HALL: W wing, N side [8]. OUTDOOR WAY OF THE CROSS: Station 9, N [1]. PASQUERILLA HALL WEST: E wing, E end [3]. SIEGFRIED HALL: E wing, N side [7].

*macrophylla* (Thunb.) Ser. [**Large-leaf Hydrangea**]

Deciduous shrub. Leaf toothed, not lobed, broad, 8 in. long, slippery, glossy green above, hairless. Flower clusters large, soil pH regulates color from blue to pink. Ornamental in July, August. Introduced, native to Japan. Leaves and buds poisonous when eaten. Maximum height 6 ft.
FISHER HALL: N side [1]. PRESBYTERY: Front [10*].

*paniculata* Siebold [**Panicle Hydrangea**]

Deciduous tree. Leaf toothed, not lobed, narrow, 6 in. long, dark green above, hairy veins below. Flowers yellowish but with a few larger white or pink sterile ones. Ornamental in July through summer. Introduced, native to China, Japan. In horticulture since 1861. Leaves and buds poisonous when eaten. Maximum height 25 ft.

'Grandiflora' [**Peegee Hydrangea**]

Deciduous tree. Flowers mostly large and sterile, color changes from white to pink to bronze. Flowers persistent. Ornamental in summer through autumn.
CORBY HALL: Dining room, N end [1*]. PRESBYTERY: E, main entrance, flanking [2].

*quercifolia* Bartr. [**Oak-leaf Hydrangea**]

Deciduous shrub. Leaf toothed, lobed, 8 in. long, dark green above, brown-hairy below. Flowers white, pink to brown, outer ones showy, clusters upright. Ornamental in late June, July. Native to southeastern United States. In horticulture since 1803. Leaves and buds poisonous when eaten. Maximum height 6 ft.
CAVANAUGH HALL [beds*]. KEENAN HALL: W side [beds*]. KNOTT HALL: W wing, N side [4]. LYONS HALL: SE corner [1]. NORTH DINING HALL: N end [6]. SIEGFRIED HALL: E wing, N side [3]. SNITE MUSEUM OF ART: Court [many]. STANFORD HALL: Surrounding [beds*].

*Philadelphus* L. [**Mock Orange**]

Mock orange is a popular shrub that was a very familiar ornamental plant to European gardeners. They continued to grow it after immigrating to the United States. Early university records frequently mention its presence on the campus. It is native to North America, Europe, and eastern Asia, and is grown for the fragrant white flowers that appear in late spring. Pruning, which is rarely needed, should be carried out immediately after the flowers fade because the next year's flower buds will form during summer.

Broad-leaved shrub: deciduous. Leaves opposite, simple, either toothed or smooth-edged. Flowers white, solitary or in clusters; fruit a dry capsule containing many small seeds. Mock orange is frequently confused with another flowering shrub, *Deutzia*. The buds along the stem of mock orange are completely hidden in the bases of the leaf stocks but visible in *Deutzia*. The leaves of mock orange are smooth, those of *Deutzia* feel like sandpaper because their surfaces are covered by tiny star-shaped hairs.

*coronarius* L. [**Sweet Mock Orange**]
> Deciduous shrub. Leaf 4 in. long, toothed, wider below middle, vein axils hairy below. Flowers white, 1.5 in. long, very fragrant, in clusters of 5-7. Ornamental in May to June. Introduced, native to southwestern Asia, Europe. In horticulture since 1560. Maximum height 12 ft.

'Zeyheri' [**Zeyher Mock Orange**]
> Deciduous shrub. Erect form; flowers solitary on stem, each 1 in. wide. Flowers white, showy, fragrant. Ornamental in May to June. Maximum height 6 ft.
>> FRESHMAN YEAR BUILDING: W parking lot, SE [2]; W parking lot, W [4]. HOLY CROSS ANNEX: NW corner, N 40yd, road, N [few*]. LYONS HALL: NW basketball court, N, lakeside [1]. MAIL DISTRIBUTION CENTER: N end, W [1]; SW corner, W 7yd [1]. ST. JOSEPH'S LAKE: Freshman Year W parking lot, N [1].

× *cymosus* Rehd.: *P. ? × P. ?* [**Cymose Mock Orange**]
> Deciduous shrub. Leaf 4.5 in. long, widest at middle, smooth below; some flowers double, clusters of 1-5. Showy white flowers. Ornamental in May to June. Maximum height 7 ft.
>> MAINTENANCE CENTER: SW corner, W 50yd [1].

*inodorus* L. [**Large-flowering Mock Orange**]
> Deciduous shrub. Leaf 4 in. long, not toothed, hairs on veins below; flower 2 in. wide, in clusters of 1-3. Not fragrant but large. Ornamental in June. Native to Pennsylvania through Alabama. Maximum height 10 ft.

var. *grandiflorus* (Willd.) A. Gray [**Large-flowering Mock Orange**]
> Deciduous shrub. Leaf 4 in. long, toothed, some hairs above, more at vein axils below. Flowers bell-shaped, flat, petals round, opening oblong, no odor. Ornamental in May to June. Native to Virginia through Alabama.
>> CALVARY: SW 15yd [few*].

*lewisii* Pursh [**Lewis Mock Orange**]
> Deciduous shrub. Leaf 3 in. long, rarely toothed, some hairs each side; flower 2 in. wide, clustered 3-11. Fragrant. Ornamental in May to June. Native to western North America. Maximum height 10 ft.
>> SNITE MUSEUM OF ART: Court [many].

× *nivalis* Jacq.: *P. coronarius × P. pubescens* [**Snowy Mock Orange**]
> Deciduous shrub. Leaf margin toothed, few hairs below; flower 1.5 in. wide, clustered 5-8. Showy white flowers. Ornamental in May to June.
>> ST. EDWARD'S HALL: S, flanking archway [4*].

× *virginalis* Rehd.: *P. ? × P. ?* [**Virginal Mock Orange**]
> Deciduous shrub. Leaf to 3 in. long, thin silver-hairy below; flowers double, clustered 3-7. May to June.
>> ADMINISTRATION (MAIN) BUILDING: Main entrance, W side [1]. CARROLL HALL ANNEX: NW, 20yd [1]. FATIMA RETREAT HOUSE: W side [1]. FRESHMAN YEAR BUILDING: W parking lot, stop sign, SE 20yd [1]. HOWARD HALL: N [hedge]; S wing, NE corner, N [1]. HURLEY HALL OF BUSINESS ADMINISTRATION: SW corner [1]. LAW SCHOOL: N [4]. LYONS HALL: N, lakeside [1]. ROCKNE MEMORIAL: SE corner, S [hedge*]. ST. EDWARD'S HALL: S side, E arch, front

[2].

# GROSSULARIACEAE [CURRANT FAMILY]

*Ribes* L. [**Currant; Gooseberry**]
These low shrubs, native to temperate regions of the Northern Hemisphere and to the Andes, are grown for their edible fruits or as ornamentals. Native Americans used the fruit of *R. aureum* to make pemmican, a long-lasting staple in their diets. The fruits were pulverized with dried buffalo meat to make a paste that was formed into cakes. Fruits of unarmed cultivars of the native prickly gooseberry, *R. cynosbati*, are made into pies. The European blackcurrant, *R. nigrum*, is used for making jams, jellies, and cassis, the liqueur. Because of its high vitamin C content, the blackcurrant has been used in a traditional tonic for treating colds. *Ribes* species are the alternate host of a fungus, *Cronartium ribicola* (white pine blister rust), with a complex life cycle involving separate phases on white pine and on *Ribes*. This disease causes serious economic losses to the lumber industry. *Ribes* plants are banned from white pine habitats. Male plants of the ornamental alpine currant, *R. alpinum*, are said to be immune to rust.
Broad-leaved, prickly shrubs: deciduous. Leaves alternate along stem, palmately veined, usually lobed. Female flowers produce juicy berries of various colors. The species with spines are usually called gooseberries. Those lacking spines are called currants.

*alpinum* L. [**Alpine Currant; Mountain Currant**]
Deciduous shrub. Twig not spiny; leaf 3-lobed, longer than wide, not woolly below, base rounded or flat. Male plants usually available; a good hedge plant. Introduced, native to Europe. In horticulture since 1588. Maximum height 6 ft.
CENTER FOR CONTINUING EDUCATION: NE corner [hedge*]. FATIMA RETREAT HOUSE: Fatima shrine, rear [1]; Mission House, S side [1*]. LAW SCHOOL: N entrance, E [1]; NW corner [1]. NIEUWLAND SCIENCE HALL: N wing, N side [hedge]. PASQUERILLA CENTER: N, flanking walk [hedge]; S side, along walk [hedge].

'Aureum' [**Alpine Currant**]
Deciduous shrub. Dwarf form; leaves yellow. In horticulture since 1881. Maximum height 3 ft.
DeBARTOLO CLASSROOM BUILDING: E side, S of N end doors [2].

*aureum* Pursh [**Golden Currant**]
Deciduous shrub. Twig not spiny; leaf 3-lobed, base flat, sides of middle lobe parallel, not diverging. Fruit purple black, smooth. Native to Washington through Montana to California. Maximum height 6 ft.
JOYCE ATHLETIC AND CONVOCATION CENTER: Gate 10, W [5]; Gate 9, W [6]; NW corner, gate 3.[5]. SUPPORT SERVICES BUILDING: N bed [1]; S bed [1].

*sanguineum* Pursh [**Winter Currant**]
Deciduous shrub. Twig not spiny; leaf wider than long, 3-5 lobed, white hairy below, base heart-shaped. Fruit blue black with white, waxy coat. Native to British Columbia through northern California. In horticulture since 1818. Maximum height 12 ft.

'Pulborough Scarlet' [**Scarlet Currant**]
Deciduous shrub. Flowers intensely medium pink; fruit blue black, waxy-coated. Maximum height 6 ft.

JOYCE ATHLETIC AND CONVOCATION CENTER: Gate 10, N [5]; NW corner, gate 3 [5]. SUPPORT SERVICES BUILDING: S bed [2].

## ROSACEAE [ROSE FAMILY]

*Amelanchier* Medic. [**Serviceberry**]

Most serviceberries are native to North America, but a few species are found in Europe and Asia. They are grown here for their masses of small white flowers of early spring, their early summer fruits, and their yellow to red leaves of autumn. They are appropriate in naturalized plantings or as specimen trees. The fruits are edible, but quickly eaten by birds. *Amelanchier* is susceptible to attack by several insects and a bacterial disease, fire blight. Other common names applied to this genus are shadblow, reflecting the time of flowering that corresponds to the shad run in New England rivers, and Juneberry, proclaiming the time of fruit formation.

Broad-leaved small tree or shrub: deciduous. Leaves alternate along stem, simple, toothed along margin. Flowers white, starlike, with 5 narrow petals; fruit a dark red, purple, or black berrylike pome with 5-10 seeds.

*arborea* (Michx. f.) Fern. [**Downy Serviceberry; Juneberry**]

Deciduous shrub. Leaf egg-shaped, 3-5 in. long, gray green when young, remains hairy; fruit purple black. Multiple stems, may be treelike; fruit attracts birds. Native to eastern North America through Louisiana and Oklahoma. In horticulture since 1746. Maximum height 25 ft.

CUSHING HALL OF ENGINEERING: W side [many]. GROTTO OF OUR LADY OF LOURDES: N, along outer walk [2]. JOYCE ATHLETIC AND CONVOCATION CENTER: Gate 10 [7]. KNIGHTS OF COLUMBUS COUNCIL HALL: S entrance, W [1]. KOONS REHEARSAL HALL: W side [6]; W side, N of door, along walk [3]. PASQUERILLA CENTER: N side, bed E of door [1]; NW corner [2]; S side, bed W of door [1]. SNITE MUSEUM OF ART: Court, SE corner [1]; Court, W side [4].

'Cole Select' [**Downy Serviceberry**]

Deciduous tree. Multistemmed, shrubby form; leaves turn red. Ornamental in autumn.

DEBARTOLO CLASSROOM BUILDING: E side, along walls [19]; S side, central windows [5].

*interior* E. L. Nielson [**Inland Juneberry; Shadbush**]

Deciduous shrub. Leaf oval, 2-3 in. long, base heart-shaped, tip short-pointed, hairy when young. Multiple stems but treelike. Native to Michigan and Wisconsin through Iowa. Maximum height 30 ft.

FLANNER HALL: NW door, flanking [4]. GRACE HALL: NE door [2].

*laevis* Wieg. [**Allegheny Serviceberry**]

Deciduous shrub. Leaf egg-shaped, 3-5 in. long, purple when young, then green, never hairy; fruit black. May be treelike; fruit attracts birds. Native to eastern North America. In horticulture since 1870. Maximum height 30 ft.

CUSHING HALL OF ENGINEERING: N side, W [2]. FATIMA RETREAT HOUSE: St. Joseph statue [2]. LAW SCHOOL: SE corner [2]. WASHINGTON HALL: W entrance, N [1].

*Chaenomeles* Lindl. [**Flowering Quince**]

These upright shrubs native to eastern Asia are grown for their beautiful flowers that appear briefly during spring. Flower color ranges from white through pink and apricot to shades of red. With their tangled branches, thorns and leaves that do not change color before falling, spring is their most ornamental season. The edible fruits, which are produced only by cross-pollination from a second plant, are made into preserves.

Broad-leaved thorny shrub: deciduous or semi-evergreen. Leaves alternate along stem, simple, margin toothed or wavy. Two large round, leaflike stipules grow at each leaf base. Flowers in clusters of 2-4 on last year's wood; fruit an applelike pome, usually yellow green and very fragrant.

*japonica* (Thunb.) Lindl. ex Spach [**Japanese Floweringquince**]

Deciduous shrub. Short spines; leaf 2 in., wide above middle, teeth coarse-wavy, 2 leafy stipules at base. Flowers orange red, 1.5 in. wide; fruit green yellow, fragrant. Ornamental in early April, October. Introduced, native to Japan. In horticulture since 1874. Maximum height 3 ft.

JOYCE ATHLETIC AND CONVOCATION CENTER: W side, S of gate 10 [6].

*speciosa* (Sweet) Nakai [**Japanese Quince**]

Deciduous shrub. Twig spiny, leaf to 3.5 in. long, glossy, sharp-toothed, 2 leaflike stipules at base. Flowers showy but sensitive to spring frost; many colors available. Ornamental in April. Introduced, native to China. In horticulture since 1800. Maximum height 10 ft.

CAVANAUGH HALL: S end [hedge*]. DILLON HALL: N wing, W end [10*]; W court [10*]. FARLEY HALL: S end [hedge*]. FATIMA RETREAT HOUSE: Fatima shrine, rear [1]. KNOTT HALL: S wing, W side [3]; W wing, S side [2]. PASQUERILLA HALL EAST: W wing, W end [3]. PASQUERILLA HALL WEST: E wing, S side [3]. SIEGFRIED HALL: E wing, S side [2]; S wing, E side [3]. ST. EDWARD'S HALL: NW corner [hedge].

'Texas Scarlet' [**Japanese Quince**]

Deciduous shrub. Spreading, compact form; flowers tomato red.

SUPPORT SERVICES BUILDING: N bed [1].

*Cotoneaster* Medic. [**Cotoneaster**]

These ornamental shrubs are grown for their glossy leaves and for their colorful fruits that remain through the winter. Some species form low masses of branches that are effective as a ground cover on banks and hillsides. They are native to the temperate regions of Europe, Asia, and northern Africa.

Broad-leaved shrub: deciduous or evergreen. Leaves alternate along stem, simple with smooth margins. Flowers white or pink, in short-stalked clusters; fruit a small red to black pome bearing 2-5 nutlets.

*acutifolius* Turcz. [**Pekinese Cotoneaster**]

Deciduous shrub. Erect; leaf 2 in. long, 1 in. wide, dull green, hairy. Introduced, native to northern China. In horticulture since 1883. Maximum height 10 ft.

LYONS HALL: Archway, NW side [bed*].

*adpressus* Bois [**Nan Shan Cotoneaster**]

Deciduous shrub. Low, stem creeping and rooting; leaf to 1 in. long, scoop-shaped or wavy. Showy red fruits. Ornamental in winter. Introduced, native to western China. In horticulture since 1896. Maximum height 1.5 ft.

var. *praecox* Bois & Berthault [**Nan Shan Cotoneaster**]

> Deciduous shrub. Taller; fruit larger than the species. Introduced, native to China. In horticulture since 1905. Maximum height 3 ft.
>
> Moreau Seminary: SW corner [1*].

*apiculatus* Rehd. & E. H. Wils. [**Cranberry Cotoneaster**]

> Deciduous shrub. Low; leaf to 1 in. long, flat, edge hairy, bristle-tipped. Compact, mounded growth; used as a cover for banks. Introduced, native to western China. In horticulture since 1910. Maximum height 3 ft.
>
> Hesburgh Library: S, main entrance, bed either side [2]. Knott Hall: W wing, N side, flanking walk [beds]; W wing, W plaza, flanking door [beds]. LaFortune Student Center: S side [hedge]. Loftus Sports Center: W side [beds]. Lyons Hall: Archway, NW, central bed facing lake [bed]. Morris Inn: Main entrance, E beds [many]. Pasquerilla Hall East: N wing, E side [bed]; W wing, W end, NW plaza [beds]. Radiation Research Building: W side [bed]. Siegfried Hall: E door plaza [beds]; N, along walk [beds]. Support Services Building: N bed [1].

*dammeri* C. K. Schneid. [**Bearberry Cotoneaster**]

> Evergreen ground cover. Low, stem trailing, rooting; leaf 1 in. or longer, glossy above, waxy below. A dense, flat ground cover. Introduced, native to central China. In horticulture since 1900. Maximum height 1.5 ft.
>
> Snite Museum of Art: Court [many].

'Coral Beauty' [**Bearberry Cotoneaster**]

> Evergreen ground cover. Fruits coral red; leaves glossy; growth vigorous. Maximum height 2.5 ft.
>
> Support Services Building: S bed [2].

'Walter's Red' [**Bearberry Cotoneaster**]

> Evergreen ground cover. Fruit abundant, bright red.
>
> Hessert Aerospace Research Center: E side, flanking steps [2]. Pasquerilla Hall West: N wing, E side [bed]; SW corner [2]. Support Services Building: N bed [1].

*divaricatus* Rehd. & E. H. Wils. [**Spreading Cotoneaster**]

> Deciduous shrub. Erect, arching; leaf to 1 in. long, glossy dark green above, paler below. Glossy green leaves turn intense yellow, red, and purple. Ornamental in autumn. Introduced, native to China. In horticulture since 1907.
>
> Alumni Hall: W wing, S end [bed*]. Cushing Hall of Engineering: NE corner [1*]. Dillon Hall: S side, E of ramp [3*]. Joyce Athletic and Convocation Center: S corner at gate 8 [beds]; W side, gate 3 [hedge]; W, along N wall at gate 2 [hedge]; W, along wall at gate 1 [beds]. Lewis Bus Shelter: N side [bed]. Pasquerilla Hall East: N wing, N end [1]; N wing, NE corner [bed]. Pasquerilla Hall West: N wing, NE corner [bed].

*horizontalis* Decne. [**Rock Cotoneaster**]

> Deciduous ground cover. Low; shoots in stiff, fishbone pattern; leaf to 1 in. long, flat, not wavy. Introduced, native to western China. In horticulture since 1880. Maximum height 3 ft.
>
> Morris Inn: Main entrance, E beds, behind benches [beds]. Pasquerilla Hall East: N wing, E side [bed]; N wing, W door [bed]. Pasquerilla Hall West: W door [beds].

*multiflorus* Bunge [**Arching Cotoneaster**]

> Deciduous shrub. Erect, arching; leaf 2 in. long, gray green and hairless below. Introduced, native to western China. In horticulture since 1900. Maximum height

12 ft.

var. *calocarpus* Rehd. & E. H. Wils. [**Arching Cotoneaster**]
> Deciduous shrub. Leaf narrower, flowers more abundant, fruit larger than the species. Introduced, native to western China.
>> ALUMNI HALL: E side [3]; W court [many*]. ARCHITECTURE BUILDING: SW corner, W 10yd [2*]. CUSHING HALL OF ENGINEERING: N side [beds]; N, main entrance, E side [1*]. DILLON HALL: NW corner [5*].

*Crataegus* L. [**Hawthorn; Haw; Thorn**]
> The hawthorns, although dense and thorny, are popular ornamentals because of their distinctive horizontal, flat-topped branching patterns, showy spring flowers, and red fruits. They can be used as barrier plants or clipped to form hedges and screens. Some species are especially attractive. The Washington hawthorn, *C. phaenopyrum*, has a delicate appearance and keeps its bunches of small, red berries through the winter. The beauty of hawthorns is tempered by the many disease and insect pests that they harbor. Their foliage rarely reaches late summer without being marred by these pests. In the wild, hawthorns are common in thickets, bordering the edges of forests, and along fencerows. They are native to the North Temperate Zone. The majority of the species are native to North America. Hawthorn fruits are edible, but few species are flavorful.
>
> Broad-leaved, thorny shrub or small tree: deciduous. The thorns are modified stems that may even sprout leaves. Leaves alternate along branches, lobed or simple, margin toothed. Flowers white or pink to red, growing in clusters (corymbs); fruit a small applelike pome with 1-5 single-seeded nutlets.

*arnoldiana* Sarg. [**Arnold Hawthorn**]
> Deciduous tree. Branches zigzag, thorns 3 in.; leaf 2 in. long, egg-shaped, 3-5 toothed lobes, hairy below. Most conspicuous and earliest fruit of the hawthorns. Ornamental in middle of August. Native to Connecticut, Massachusetts. Maximum height 20 ft.
>> ALUMNI HALL: S side, at ramp [1*].

*calpodendron* (J. F. Ehrh.) Medic. [**Pear Hawthorn**]
> Deciduous tree. Few thorns, 1.5 in. long; leaf 5 in. long, egg-shaped, 3-5 shallow lobes, hairy below. Fruit dull orange red, pear-shaped. Native to Ontario and Minnesota through Georgia. Maximum height 20 ft.
>> FATIMA RETREAT HOUSE: Mission House, garage, SE corner [1*].

*coccinoides* Ashe [**Kansas Hawthorn**]
> Deciduous tree. Very thorny; leaf egg-shaped, lobes shallow, edge wavy. Young leaves red, then green; turn orange, scarlet; fruit dark red. Ornamental in spring, autumn, winter. Native to Indiana through Kansas and Arkansas. Maximum height 20 ft.
>> HESBURGH LIBRARY: Pool, NW corner, W 20yd [1*]; SE corner [2*]. RADIATION RESEARCH BUILDING: W end [1*]. SOUTH DINING HALL: E side [2*].

*crus-galli* L. [**Cockspur Hawthorn; Cockspur-thorn**]
> Deciduous tree. Slender thorns 3 in. long; leaf obovate, 4 in. long, few teeth, leathery, glossy green. Native to Quebec through Kansas and North Carolina. In horticulture since 1656. Maximum height 30 ft.
>> ALUMNI HALL: NE corner [1]; SE, Law School, walk between [1]. CENTER FOR CONTINUING EDUCATION: S end [1]. CENTER FOR SOCIAL CONCERNS: SW corner [1*]. DECIO FACULTY HALL: W side [3]. FISHER HALL: SW corner [1].

FLANNER HALL: S side [1]. GALVIN LIFE SCIENCE CENTER: NE corner [1]. GRACE HALL: SW door plaza [2]. HESBURGH LIBRARY: Pool, W [1*]; SE corner [3*]. JOYCE ATHLETIC AND CONVOCATION CENTER: Gate 11, flanking [2]; Gate 4 [1]; Gate 7, flanking [2]; Gate 9, E side [1]; NW corner, gate 3, flanking [2]. NIEUWLAND SCIENCE HALL: NW door, NW [2]. NORTH DINING HALL: SE corner [1*]. O'SHAUGHNESSY HALL: E side [1]. PANGBORN HALL: S wing, E door [2]. SNITE MUSEUM OF ART: S side [3]. SOUTH DINING HALL: W side [6*].

### var. *pachyphylla* (Sarg.) Palmer [Thick-leaved Cockspur-thorn]

Deciduous tree. Leaves very thick and leathery with veins impressed above. Native to Indiana and Missouri.

FISHER HALL: W side [1*]. STEPAN CHEMISTRY HALL: NE corner, E 15yd [3].

### × *disperma* Ashe: *C. crus-galli* × *C. punctata* [Two-seeded Hawthorn]

Deciduous tree. Leaf elliptic, wider above middle, fine-toothed, leathery dark green with impressed veins. Native to Pennsylvania through Virginia to Iowa. Maximum height 24 ft.

NORTH DINING HALL: NE corner [2*].

### *laevigata* (Poir.) DC. [English Hawthorn]

Deciduous tree. Thorns 1 in. long; leaf 2.5 in., 3-5 broad, toothed lobes, blunt or pointed, dark green. Introduced, native to Europe, northern Africa, western Asia. Maximum height 20 ft.

### 'Paulii' [Double-flowering English Hawthorn]

Deciduous tree. Flowers intensely rose red with double petals. Developed by Mr. Paul of Princeton, New Jersey. In horticulture since 1858.

CUSHING HALL OF ENGINEERING: N side, W end [1*].

### × *lavallei* Herincq: *C. crus-galli* × *C. pubescens* [Lavalle Hawthorn]

Deciduous tree. Thorns 2 in. long; leaf 4 in., oblong, pointed, toothed, not lobed, hairy below on veins. Leaves turn bronze to red; fruits persistent. Ornamental in autumn, winter. In horticulture since 1880. Maximum height 30 ft.

DEBARTOLO CLASSROOM BUILDING: W side, NW corner [1]; W side, SW corner [1]. JOYCE ATHLETIC AND CONVOCATION CENTER: N at B2 parking lot [2]. SUPPORT SERVICES BUILDING: S bed [1].

### *mollis* (Torr. & A. Gray) Scheele [Downy Hawthorn]

Deciduous tree. Few 2 in. curved thorns; leaf 4 in., broad, 4-5 short lobes, double teeth, hairy below. Native to Ontario through Mississippi. In horticulture since 1683. Maximum height 30 ft.

FATIMA RETREAT HOUSE: E, lakeside [1]. HOLY CROSS HOUSE: SE, lake steps, S [1]. LYONS HALL: SW corner [1].

### *monogyna* Jacq. [Oneseed Hawthorn; English Hawthorn]

Deciduous tree. Thorns 1 in. long; leaf egg-shaped, 3-7 lobes, few teeth at tip, shiny green above. Introduced, native to Europe, Asia, northern Africa. Maximum height 30 ft.

FATIMA RETREAT HOUSE: W, along Highway 31 [1]. SOUTH DINING HALL: SE corner [1*].

### *phaenopyrum* (L. f.) Medic. [Washington Hawthorn]

Deciduous tree. Thorns 1-3 in. long; leaf broadly triangular, 3-5 sharp-toothed lobes, shiny, pale below. Native to southeastern and central United States. In horticulture since 1738. Maximum height 30 ft.

ALUMNI HALL: E side [1]; SE [1*]. ANGELA BOULEVARD: Notre Dame Ave campus entrance [7]. CENTER FOR CONTINUING EDUCATION: NE corner [1]; W side [2]. CORBY HALL: SE corner, S 15yd [1]. DILLON HALL: Main entrance,

W [1*]. FATIMA RETREAT HOUSE: S side, central SE corner [1]. FITZPATRICK HALL OF ENGINEERING: SE corner planter [1]; SW corner planter [1]. GALVIN LIFE SCIENCE CENTER: NE corner [4]. GRACE HALL: E side [3]. HAGGAR HALL: S [7*]. HESBURGH LIBRARY: S, main entrance plaza, flanking [6]; S, main entrance plaza, flanking [6]. HOLY CROSS HOUSE: S, slope [1]. HOWARD HALL: E side [2]. JOYCE ATHLETIC AND CONVOCATION CENTER: Gate 9, W side [1]. KNOTT HALL: S wing, W side, S end [2]; W wing, W plaza door [5]. LAFORTUNE STUDENT CENTER: N side [7]. LAW SCHOOL: NW corner [2]; SE corner [1]; SW corner [2*]. LYONS HALL: Archway, SW, 15yd [2]. NIEUWLAND SCIENCE HALL: NE corner [3]. RILEY HALL OF ART AND DESIGN: SW corner [2*]. SIEGFRIED HALL: SE lawn [1]. SOUTH DINING HALL: E entrance [1*]. ST. EDWARD'S HALL: N side [2]. STEPAN CHEMISTRY HALL: NE corner, N [3]. UNIVERSITY CLUB: NW corner [1]; SW corner [1]. ZAHM HALL: Cavanaugh, SW between [3].

*pruinosa* (H. L. Wendl.) C. Koch [**Frosted Hawthorn**]

> Deciduous tree. Many thorns; leaf egg-shaped, teeth sharp, lobes 3-5 each side, blue green, hairless. Native to Newfoundland through Arkansas. Maximum height 25 ft.
>
> FATIMA RETREAT HOUSE: W, along Highway 31 [few*]. HOLY CROSS ANNEX: SW slope [1*]. LYONS HALL: Archway, SE [1].

*punctata* Jacq. [**Dotted Hawthorn**]

> Deciduous tree. Thorns rare; leaf 4 in. long, obovate, lobed and toothed near tip, hairy below. Native to eastern Canada through Indiana and Iowa. Maximum height 35 ft.
>
> BURKE MEMORIAL GOLF COURSE: Maintenance center, W [1]. FATIMA RETREAT HOUSE: W, along Highway 31 [1*].

var. *pausiaca* (Ashe) Palmer [**Olive-shaped Haw**]

> Deciduous tree. Leaf 2.5 in., oblong, toothed above middle, dark olive green above, veins hairy below. Native to Pennsylvania, New York. Maximum height 25 ft.
>
> CORBY HALL: SW corner, W 15yd [1*]. ST. JOSEPH'S LAKE: NW woods [1*].

*putnamiana* Sarg. [**Putnam Hawthorn**]

> Deciduous tree. Thorny; leaf triangular or egg-shaped, teeth sharp, 3-4 faint lobes each side, hairless. Native to Ohio, Kentucky, Indiana, and Illinois. Maximum height 30 ft.
>
> FRESHMAN YEAR BUILDING: W parking lot, SW corner, W 10yd [1*].

*submollis* Sarg. [**Emerson's Thorn**]

> Deciduous tree. Thorny; leaf egg-shaped or elliptic, teeth coarse, 4-5 faint lobe pairs, faint hairs below. Native to eastern Canada through New York. Maximum height 30 ft.
>
> FATIMA RETREAT HOUSE: W, along Highway 31 [many*]. MORRISSEY HALL: Chapel, N end [3*].

*succulenta* Link [**Fleshy Hawthorn**]

> Deciduous tree. Thorny; leaf 3 in. long, leathery, teeth sharp, lobes shallow, 4-5 pairs. Native to southeastern Canada through Colorado and Arizona. Maximum height 25 ft.
>
> MOREAU SEMINARY: Basketball court, SE corner [1*].

*Kerria* DC. [**Japanese Rose**]

> *Kerria* is a spreading shrub native to temperate eastern Asia that has arching branches. It is grown for its ornamental, bright yellow flowers that appear in April and May. It does best when grown in partial shade.
>
> Broad-leaved shrub: deciduous. Leaves alternate along stem, simple, double-toothed. Flowers five-petalled, bright yellow; fruit an inconspicuous, dry achene.

*japonica* (L.) DC. [**Japanese Rose**]

> Deciduous shrub. Leaf 4 in. long, egg-shaped, double toothed, bright green above, pale and hairy below. Native to China, Japan. In horticulture since 1834. Maximum height 6 ft.
>
> Support Services Building: N bed [1].

'Pleniflora' [**Japanese Globeflower**]

> Deciduous shrub. Flowers yellow gold with double petals, last longer than those of the species. Maximum height 8 ft.
>
> Brownson Hall: Court [1].

*Malus* Mill. [**Apple**]

> These broad, many-branched trees are native to the North Temperate Zone. The state tree of Michigan is, simply, "apple." The genus *Malus* contains both the species grown commercially for its large edible fruits, *M. pumila*, and the small-fruited crabapple species and hybrids, grown for ornament. Defined roughly by fruit size, the crabapples include those species (most frequently *M. baccata*) and hybrids with fruits smaller than 2 in. in diameter. The spring buds and flowers of crabapples are spectacular. Many cultivars keep their small, colorful fruits into the winter. They are more cold tolerant than the large-fruited species. Some crabapples are made into jelly. Although all apples are edible, the small seeds are poisonous. They contain amygdalin, a cyanogenic glycoside that breaks down to form hydrocyanic acid (HCN) during digestion. The ornamental crabapples suffer from many serious disease and insect pests. However, with so many cultivars available, it is possible to select one that is more resistant to disease and pests. Also, the best cultivars bear flowers in profusion consistently every year while less desirable ones tend to produce flowers in abundance only every other year. In 1931, Arthur D. Slavin published the description of a new ornamental cultivar of the native American crabapple, *M. coronaria*. The new cultivar that he introduced was 'Nieuwlandiana,' named for Julius A. Nieuwland, C.S.C., professor of botany and chemistry at Notre Dame, founder of the University's research and teaching herbarium, and founding editor of the scientific journal *The American Midland Naturalist*, which is still published at Notre Dame with Robert P. McIntosh as editor. Arthur Slavin was an employee of the Rochester, New York, Bureau of Parks. His father, Bernard H. Slavin, who was Superintendent of the Rochester Parks, had selected the Nieuwland crabapple from seedlings raised by his department in 1928. The younger Slavin earned a Master's degree in biology at Notre Dame in 1929 with Fr. Nieuwland as his advisor. He named the new crabapple in honor of his former professor and advisor. He published the new plant's description in *The American Midland Naturalist* while Fr. Nieuwland was still its editor. Arthur Slavin described the Nieuwland crabapple as having rose red buds opening to fragrant pink flowers

2.25 in. across with double petals. The fruits were yellow to light green, 1.75 in. across, waxy, and fragrant when mature. He went on to say that a "most satisfactory" jelly, clear yellow with a high pectin content and a "peculiar but very pleasant tasting quality" could be made from the fruit. Rev. Peter Hebert's 1966 flora of the Notre Dame campus lists one Nieuwland crabapple growing on a site west of the Moreau Seminary chapel. That tree has disappeared, but efforts to acquire another for the campus continue.

Broad-leaved small tree: deciduous. Leaves alternate, simple, margin toothed and sometimes lobed. Side branches, bearing leaves and flowers, often stunted or spurlike with visible annual "rings" indicating their age. Flowers produce the familiar apple fruit (pome) with a core of 5 seed-bearing papery carpels surrounded by edible flesh. *Malus* is sometimes included within the pear genus, *Pyrus*. The differences between the two genera are not conspicuous except for the lack in *Malus* of the gritty stone cells that give pear fruit its distinctive texture.

*floribunda* Siebold ex Van Houtte [**Japanese Flowering Crabapple**]

Deciduous tree. Stem arched, hairy; leaf 3 in. long, egg-shaped to oblong, lobes rare, teeth sharp. Rounded form, dense growth; flowers deep pink, turn pale; red fruit. Ornamental in spring, late summer to autumn. Introduced, native to Japan. In horticulture since 1862. Maximum height 25 ft.

DeBartolo Classroom Building: E side, SE corner [3]; N side, NE corner [3]. Fatima Retreat House: Fatima shrine, W, flanking walk [2]. St. Michael's Laundry: E, flanking front walk [2].

*pumila* Mill. [**Common Apple**]

Deciduous tree. Leaf 4 in., elliptic to oval, lobes rare, veins fade before margin, green and hairy below. Fruit edible, larger than 2 in. across. Introduced, native to Europe, western Asia. Maximum height 40 ft.

Corby Hall: NW, walk to Grotto [1]. Cushing Hall of Engineering: N, main entrance, W side [1*]. Fatima Retreat House: Fatima shrine, NE 45yd [1]; S side, SE corner [1]. Fisher Hall: SW corner, SE 10yd [2*]. Mail Distribution Center: SW corner [3*].

*sargentii* Rehd. [**Sargent Crabapple**]

Deciduous shrub. Stem horizontal; leaf 3 in. long, egg-shaped, sharp-toothed, not lobed, base heart-shaped. Low, broad with dense branches; flowers red, turn white, fragrant. Ornamental in spring. Introduced, native to Japan. Maximum height 8 ft.

O'Shaughnessy Hall: W side [1]. Pasquerilla Hall West: N wing, W parking circle [1]. Snite Museum of Art: S entrance, S 15yd at street [3]; S side, at building, along walk [6].

*spp.* [**Ornamental Crabapple hybrids**]

Deciduous tree. Variable, leaf surfaces usually hairy, teeth sharp on margin; winter bud hairy. Flowers often showy, fragrant; fruit smaller than 2 in., persistent. Ornamental in spring, autumn, winter. Introduced, native to eastern Asia. Maximum height 50 ft.

Alumni Hall: Dillon, between, N [2*]. Breen-Phillips Hall: E side, center [1]. Burke Memorial Golf Course: S central area, water fountain, NE 30yd [2]; S central area, water fountain, SE 10yd [1]; SE area [1]. Cavanaugh Hall: Administration Bldg, along walk between [7]. Cedar Grove Cemetery: N, W of shed, S of road [1]. Center for Continuing Education: E side [2]. Community Cemetery: Mission House, between [4]. Computing Center and Math Building: N door, E side [1*]. Corby Hall: NW 30yd,

Grotto lawn [3*]; NW corner, N 25yd [1*]. CUSHING HALL OF ENGINEERING: N side, E [1]. DECIO FACULTY HALL: E entrance, S 30yd [1]; E entrance, near plaza [8]; E side [5]; NW corner [2]; W side [4]; W side [2]. DILLON HALL: N side [1*]; S side, ramp [1*]. ECK TENNIS PAVILION: S [5]. FARLEY HALL: S entrance, flanking [2]. FATIMA RETREAT HOUSE: Main entrance, N 30yd [1]; N end, NE [1]. FLANNER HALL: SE corner [6]. FRESHMAN YEAR BUILDING: W parking lot, SW corner, W 15yd [1]. GALVIN LIFE SCIENCE CENTER: NE corner [3]; NW corner [1]; SE corner [1]; W, main entrance, S 10yd [1 **Commem.**]; W, main entrance, SW 50yd [1]; W, main entrance, W 15yd, S of walk [1 **Commem.**]. GRACE HALL: S side [4]; W side [1]. HAGGAR HALL: E 20yd [3]. HESBURGH LIBRARY: Pool to Stadium [many*]; Pool, SW corner, SW 20yd [4]; SW 30yd, midway to Radiation Bldg [1 **Commem.**]. HOLY CROSS HOUSE: NE side [1]; SW slope [1]. HURLEY HALL OF BUSINESS ADMINISTRATION: Main entrance, flanking [2*]. KNIGHTS OF COLUMBUS COUNCIL HALL: SW corner [1]. KNOTT HALL: N walk, flanking central bed [4]; S wing, E side [2]; S wing, S end [3]; SW lawn [15]; W door, central bed [4]. KOONS REHEARSAL HALL: E [1]. LAFORTUNE STUDENT CENTER: NW lawn [2]. MOREAU SEMINARY: N wing, NE corner, E side [1]; NE corner [1]; S side, W door [1]; SW end, W 10yd [1]. MORRIS INN: N end, N 20yd [1*]. NIEUWLAND SCIENCE HALL: N wing, N side [6]. NORTH DINING HALL: N end [2*]; W side [3]. O'SHAUGHNESSY HALL: E side [1]. PASQUERILLA CENTER: NE corner, E side [2]; NW corner, W side [1]; SE corner [9]; SW corner [3]. PASQUERILLA HALL EAST: N wing, E entrance, parking circle [1 **Commem.**]; N wing, E side [3]; NE corner [1]; NE side [1]; W wing, S side [1]. PASQUERILLA HALL WEST: N wing, W parking circle [1]; N wing, W side [3]. PRESBYTERY: E, main entrance, flanking [2]. RADIATION RESEARCH BUILDING: SE corner, S 30yd [2]. ROCKNE MEMORIAL: E side, flanking door [2]. SIEGFRIED HALL: E wing, N side, along walk [4]; S wing, S end [1]; S wing, W side [2]; SE door plaza, planter [4]; SE lawn [13]. SNITE MUSEUM OF ART: Court [8]; W side, window, W [1*]. SORIN HALL: E side [1]; S end [1]; S end [1]. SOUTH DINING HALL: NW corner, W [1*]; SW corner, W 30yd near Fisher S end [1*]. ST. EDWARD'S HALL: N side [3].

## 'Christmas Holly' [**Christmas Holly Crabapple**]

Deciduous tree. Spreading form; buds red; flowers white, single; fruit small, bright red, firm. Fruit showy, remains on tree for extended time. Ornamental in autumn into January. Maximum height 15 ft.

MAINTENANCE CENTER: E, between ND Press and Transportation [2].

## 'Coral Beauty' [**Coral Beauty Crabapple**]

Deciduous tree. Small, upright form; flowers coral red.

MORRIS INN: Main entrance, E beds [4].

## 'Dolgo' [**Dolgo Crabapple**]

Deciduous tree. Flower bud pink, opens to white, fragrant. Fruit vivid red purple, forms earlier than most, made into jelly. Ornamental in early May, August. Developed at the South Dakota Agricultural Experiment Station. In horticulture since 1917. Maximum height 40 ft.

HESBURGH CENTER: E side [3]. JUNIPER ROAD: Pedestrian entrances [many]. ST. MICHAEL'S LAUNDRY: NE corner [1].

## 'Profusion' [**Profusion Flowering Crab**]

Deciduous tree. Bud deep red, flower red purple, fading to pink, fruit dark red. Buds showy; fruit persistent. Ornamental in spring, winter. Maximum height 15 ft.

MORRIS INN: W entrance, W [1 **Commem.**].

'Red Jade' [**Red Jade Crabapple**]

Deciduous tree. Graceful form; weeping branches; buds deep pink, opening white; fruit shiny, red. Flowering is more profuse during alternate years. Maximum height 15 ft.

PASQUERILLA CENTER: S side [1 **Commem.**].

'Robinson' [**Robinson Crabapple**]

Deciduous tree. Bud deep crimson, flower deep pink, single. Disease resistant. Developed by C. M. Hobbs of Indianapolis, Indiana. Maximum height 25 ft.

HESBURGH CENTER: S side, middle, corner [4]. JUNIPER ROAD: S at Edison Rd, entrance sign [4]; W, Library circle N, fence, campus-side [2].

'Snowdrift' [**Snowdrift Crabapple**]

Deciduous tree. Vigorous growth; rounded form; glossy, dark leaves; buds pink, opening white; fruit orange. Flowers abundant every year. Ornamental in spring. Maximum height 20 ft.

ROCKNE MEMORIAL: E side, flanking steps [2 **Commem.**].

*yunnanensis* (Franch.) C. K. Schneid. [**Veitchii Crabapple**]

Deciduous tree. Leaf 5 in. long, broadly egg-shaped, teeth sharp, double, 3-5 lobes, densely hairy below. Flower white to pink, single; fruit red with white dotted surface. Introduced, native to western China. Maximum height 40 ft.

DEBARTOLO CLASSROOM BUILDING: N side, NW door, flanking [6]; S side, flanking windows [2]. ST. MICHAEL'S LAUNDRY: E side, S end [5].

var. *veitchii* Rehd. [**Veitchii Crabapple**]

Deciduous tree. Flowers white; leaf coarsely textured, heart-shaped. Upright, egg-shaped outline. Introduced, native to central China. Maximum height 20 ft.

HESBURGH CENTER: N side, residence patios [6].

*Potentilla* L. [**Cinquefoil**]

This large genus contains many nonwoody, low plants and a few shrubby species. The shrubs are grown for their roselike yellow, white, or orange flowers that bloom throughout the summer when few other shrubs are in flower. Native to north temperate, boreal, and arctic areas, and to temperate regions of the Southern Hemisphere, they are extremely cold hardy and very tolerant of dry and alkaline soils. They are small with an informal appearance that makes them appropriate for low hedges, foundation plantings, and borders. They have no serious disease or insect problems. The common name, cinquefoil, refers to the five leaflets per leaf that are found in most species. This is an old name. In Middle English it was *cincfoil*, in Old French *cincfoille*, and in Latin *quinquefolium*.

Broad-leaved shrub: deciduous. Stem slender; leaves alternate, pinnately compound with 3-7, usually 5, lobes, growing on slender stems. Flowers roselike, usually yellow, either solitary or in small clusters on new growth; fruit an inconspicuous, dry achene.

*fruticosa* L. [**Shrubby Cinquefoil**]

Deciduous shrub. Leaf 1 in. long, with 3-7 but usually 5 small, silky leaflets. Flowers bright yellow, bloom over a long period. Ornamental in June until frost. Native to temperate Northern Hemisphere. Maximum height 4 ft.

HESBURGH LIBRARY: W, Moses statue, S bed [beds*]. MAINTENANCE CENTER: S side [7].

*Prunus* L. [**Cherry; Plum; Peach; Chokecherry**]

The fruit trees of this genus are of tremendous economic importance. In addition, many species are highly ornamental with fleeting but beautiful spring flowers. Several species have beautiful, shiny bark. *Prunus* is native to temperate regions, especially of the Northern Hemisphere, but reaches the Andes. Fruits of both native and introduced species are popular food for birds. The ornamental species tolerate the hot, dry summers of the Midwest. Most are small to medium-sized trees that are both short-lived and prone to disease and insect pests. The native black cherry, *P. serotina*, has been prized for furniture making since Colonial times, but has almost disappeared from forests as a result. The double-flowering Oriental cherries that bloom along the Tidal Basin in Washington, D.C., each spring are *P. serrulata* 'Kwanzan', also called 'Sekiyama.' The first two trees were planted in 1912 by Mrs. William Howard Taft and Viscountess Chinda, wife of the Japanese Ambassador. Today those have been increased to 3,000 trees. The twigs, leaves, and bony seeds, but not the flesh of the fruit, are poisonous when eaten. They contain amygdalin, a cyanogenic glycoside that breaks down to form violently toxic hydrocyanic acid (HCN) during digestion.

Broad-leaved tree or shrub: usually deciduous. Leaves alternate along stem, simple, and toothed along margin. Leaf often with glands at the base of the blade where it meets the petiole. Flowers usually white to pink; fruit a drupe with a bony pit enclosed in juicy flesh, of variable size.

*americana* Marsh. [**American Plum**]

Deciduous shrub. Thorny; leaf wide above middle, gray below, sharp double teeth, petiole hairy, glandless. Often grows in colonies in the wild; may be treelike; fruit edible. Native to New England through Florida and New Mexico. In horticulture since 1874. Cherry pits and foliage may be poisonous. Maximum height 25 ft.

HOLY CROSS HOUSE: S, lake slope [1]. ST. JOSEPH'S LAKE: Boat house beach fence, SE corner, SE [1].

*avium* (L.) L. [**Mazzard; Sweet Cherry**]

Deciduous tree. Leaf wide below middle, dull, bumpy above, hairy below, dull teeth, red glands on petiole. Peeling, red brown bark; flowers showy; fruit edible. Ornamental in April. Introduced, native to Europe, western Asia; naturalized in North America. Cherry pits and foliage may be poisonous. Maximum height 40 ft.

CARROLL HALL: W 30yd, hedge, E side [6*]. GRACE HALL: Chapel, NE [4]; E side [1]. MOREAU SEMINARY: E end [1*]; St. Joseph Hall, slope between [1]; St. Joseph Hall, woods between [1]. ST. JOSEPH'S LAKE: Boat house beach fence, SE corner, E [1]; Boat house, N [few].

*cerasifera* J. F. Ehrh. [**Cherry-plum**]

Deciduous tree. Leaf thin, wide below middle, tip sharp, dull above, green below, 5-6 veins, blunt teeth. Often shrubby; rounded form. Introduced, native to Asia; naturalized in Europe and North America. In horticulture since 1700. Fruit pits and foliage may be poisonous. Maximum height 30 ft.

GRACE HALL: NW corner [1 **Commem.**]. KNIGHTS OF COLUMBUS COUNCIL HALL: S entrance, W of walk [1 **Commem.**]. MOREAU SEMINARY: Chapel entrance, W [1].

'Atropurpurea' [**Purpleleaf Cherry-plum**]

> Deciduous tree. Dense, upright form with purple leaves and small, light pink flowers. Leaf color best when grown in full sun. Ornamental in summer. Developed in Persia (Iran). In horticulture since 1880.
>
>> ALUMNI HALL: SE entrance, flanking [2*]. COLUMBA HALL: SW, along road [6]. ECK TENNIS PAVILION: S [2]. FATIMA RETREAT HOUSE: NW lawn [2*]. MOREAU SEMINARY: Chapel, W side, corner entrance [1]. STEPAN CENTER: S side, flanking door [2]. WASHINGTON HALL: NW corner [1]. ZAHM HALL: S end, flanking [3].

'Mt. St. Helens' [**Purpleleaf Cherry-plum**]

> Deciduous tree. Straight trunk, round form; leaves appear early, purple through summer; flowers light pink. More vigorous than parent 'Newport;' leaf larger, deeper purple. Ornamental in summer. Developed by J. Frank Schmidt. Maximum height 20 ft.
>
>> LaFORTUNE STUDENT CENTER: NW lawn [1].

'Newport' [**Purpleleaf Cherry-plum**]

> Deciduous tree. Shrubby form; leaves bronze, becoming dark purple; flowers white pink; fruit purple. Ornamental in summer. Maximum height 20 ft.
>
>> KNOTT HALL: W wing, N side, flanking walk [2]. PASQUERILLA HALL EAST: N wing, E side [1]. SIEGFRIED HALL: N, flanking walk [2].

'Thundercloud' [**Purpleleaf Cherry-plum**]

> Deciduous tree. Flowers pink, single, appear before leaves; leaves remain purple all summer. Ornamental in summer. Developed by Housewearts Nursery, Woodburn, Oregon. In horticulture since 1937. Maximum height 20 ft.
>
>> DeBARTOLO CLASSROOM BUILDING: E side, midway N and S of doors [2]; W side, midway N and S of doors [2]. HESBURGH CENTER: W side, N section, NW corner [1]; W side, N section, middle [1]; W side, S section, S [1].

*cerasus* L. [**Sour Cherry**]

> Deciduous tree. Leaf thick, wide below middle, tip pointed, shiny gray green above, teeth blunt. Grown for fruit: the cherries of pie filling; fruit sets in shade. Introduced, native to western Asia, southeastern Europe; naturalized in the United States. Cherry pits and foliage may be poisonous. Maximum height 30 ft.
>
>> UNIVERSITY HEALTH SERVICES: N side, W 40yd [1*].

*laurocerasus* L. [**Common Cherrylaurel**]

> Evergreen tree. Leaf shiny, thick, evergreen, with few or no teeth, 2 glands on leaf at base. Shrubby; a good hedge plant, withstands shearing; tolerates shade. Introduced, native to southeastern Europe, southwestern Asia. In horticulture since 1576. Fruits and foliage may be poisonous. Maximum height 18 ft.

'Schipkaensis' [**Schip Laurel**]

> Evergreen shrub. Growth less coarse than the species; leaf narrow, dark green. Hardiest of the cherrylaurels; tolerates shearing and shade. Developed at Shipka Pass, Bulgaria; where it was found in the wild. Maximum height 5 ft.
>
>> DeBARTOLO CLASSROOM BUILDING: N [10]. HESBURGH CENTER: N side, E entrance to residences [2]; N side, E entrance, N [2]; W side, N section, N end [3]. ST. MICHAEL'S LAUNDRY: S end [14]. SUPPORT SERVICES BUILDING: E side [2]; N bed [1].

*mahaleb* L. [**Mahaleb Cherry**]

> Deciduous tree. Leaf egg-shaped, wide below middle, tip blunt, teeth blunt, alternating with glands. Rare as ornament, used as rootstock for better fruiting cherries. Introduced, native to Europe, western Asia. Cherry pits and foliage may

be poisonous. Maximum height 30 ft.

CARROLL HALL: W 30yd, hedge [1].

*munsoniana* W. F. Wight & Hedr. [**Wild Gooseplum; Munson Plum**]

Deciduous tree. Leaf V-shaped in cross section, veins hairy or smooth below, teeth dull, petiole hairy. Native to Ohio through Kansas and Texas. Fruits and foliage may be poisonous. Maximum height 30 ft.

POWER PLANT: NW 75yd, slope [1*].

*sargentii* Rehd. [**Sargent Cherry**]

Deciduous tree. Leaf white below, glands on petiole, tip and teeth abruptly sharp, base rounded or cordate. Flower single, pink; young leaves purple bronze, turn yellow to red. Ornamental in spring, autumn. Introduced, native to Japan. In horticulture since 1890. Foliage and fruit pits may be poisonous. Maximum height 50 ft.

'Accolade' [**Sargent Cherry**]

Deciduous tree. Open, spreading form; flowers pink, semidouble, 12-15 petals. Maximum height 25 ft.

DEBARTOLO CLASSROOM BUILDING: E side, midway N and S of doors [4]; W side, midway N and S of doors [4].

*serotina* J. F. Ehrh. [**Blackcherry; Wild Black Cherry**]

Deciduous tree. Leaf wide below middle, shiny green above, light below and hairy midrib, small thick teeth. Too aggressive and weedy for the garden, but important for timber. Native to Nova Scotia through North Dakota, Texas, and Florida. In horticulture since 1629. Foliage and fruit pits are poisonous. Maximum height 60 ft.

BURKE MEMORIAL GOLF COURSE: NW area [1*]; S central area [1]. CARROLL HALL: SW corner, WSW 100yd [1]. COMMUNITY CEMETERY: NE corner, NE 45yd [2*]. LOFTUS SPORTS CENTER: SW corner [12]. OUTDOOR WAY OF THE CROSS: Woods [1*]. ST. JOSEPH HALL: Holy Cross Annex, woods between [many*]. ST. JOSEPH'S LAKE: NW woods, N end [many*].

*serrulata* Lindl. [**Japanese Flowering Cherry**]

Deciduous tree. Leaf teeth long, bristled, spreading; base round to wedged, 4 glands; tip abruptly pointed. Flowers showy. Ornamental in spring. Introduced, native to Japan, China, Korea. Foliage and fruit pits may be poisonous. Maximum height 75 ft.

var. *lannesiana* (Carrière) Mak. [**Japanese Double-flowering Cherry**]

Deciduous tree. Leaf teeth long, bristlelike; flowers pink. Ornamental in spring.

BROWNSON HALL: Court [1]. DECIO FACULTY HALL: NE corner, S [2].

*subhirtella* Miq. [**Higan Cherry**]

Deciduous tree. Leaf dark, shiny above, veins hairy below, sharp double teeth; petiole hairy, glandular. Flowers very early. Ornamental in spring. Introduced, native to Japan. Fruit pits and foliage may be poisonous. Maximum height 25 ft.

'Snofozam' [**Snow Fountain Weeping Higan Cherry**]

Deciduous tree. Dwarf, weeping form; flowers white, single, profuse. Ornamental in spring. Maximum height 15 ft.

LEWIS HALL: E, main entrance, N of walk [1 **Commem.**]. MORRIS INN: Main entrance, E beds [2].

*tomentosa* Thunb. [**Nanking Cherry**]

Deciduous tree. Twig hairy; leaf hairy below, wide above middle, teeth short-pointed. Bark shiny red, peeling; flowers fragrant. Ornamental in spring, winter. Introduced, native to China, Japan. In horticulture since 1870. Foliage and fruit pits may be poisonous. Maximum height 10 ft.

CALVARY: W, in woods [1*].

### *virginiana* L. [**Chokecherry**]

Deciduous tree. Leaf wide above middle, shiny above, gray below, teeth small, sharp, petiole with glands. Flowers white; fruit made into jam, jelly, and wine. Native to Newfoundland through North Carolina, Missouri, and Kansas. In horticulture since 1724. Foliage and fruit pits may be poisonous. Maximum height 30 ft.

BURKE MEMORIAL GOLF COURSE: SW area [many*]. CALVARY: Woods [many*]. FISCHER GRADUATE RESIDENCE COMPLEX: N, woods [1]. HOLY CROSS HOUSE: S, ascending path, S [1]. MOREAU SEMINARY: S, lake slope [many*]. ST. JOSEPH'S LAKE: Boat house, S [1]; Distribution Center, N, lakeside [few].

### 'Shubert Select' [**Shubert Select Chokecherry**]

Deciduous tree. Pyramidal, dense form; leaves turn from green to red and then remain red through summer. Ornamental in late spring through summer. Developed by O. H. Will Nurseries, Bismarck, North Dakota. In horticulture since 1950. Maximum height 30 ft.

DECIO FACULTY HALL: S wing, E side lawn [1 **Commem.**]. HESBURGH CENTER: Court, square planter [4]. JUNIPER ROAD: ROTC stoplight, fence, campus-side [2].

### *Pyracantha* M. J. Roem. [**Firethorn**]

These stiff-branched shrubs native to Asia and southeastern Europe are grown for their red, orange, or yellow fruits that remain through the winter. Pyracantha can be used as a barrier plant, loose hedge, or espaliered on a trellis. *P. coccinea* is the only species hardy in the northern states and even within this species some cultivars are more reliably hardy and disease resistant than others. Fruit production is heavier when the plants are grown in full sun. Pruning can be done at any time. The thorns of *Pyracantha* differentiate the genus from *Cotoneaster*, which is thornless.

Broad-leaved, usually thorny shrub: evergreen to semi-evergreen. Leaves alternate, simple, with margin smooth, wavy, or toothed. Flowers white, in short-stalked, branched clusters that form on last year's twigs, not on the current year's growth; fruit a small, applelike pome.

### *coccinea* M. J. Roem. [**Firethorn**]

Deciduous tree. Stem glossy brown; leaf shiny green, wavy-toothed, petiole hairy. Fruit abundant, orange red, persistent. Ornamental in September through winter. Introduced, native to Italy through the Caucasus Mountains. In horticulture since 1629. Maximum height 18 ft.

PASQUERILLA HALL WEST: E wing, S side [4]. SIEGFRIED HALL: S wing, E side [3].

### 'Lalandei' [**Laland Firethorn**]

Evergreen shrub. Fruit bright orange red; growth vigorous with longer shoots, leaf edge wavy. In horticulture since 1874. Maximum height 15 ft.

ADMINISTRATION (MAIN) BUILDING: Main entrance, W side [1]. FARLEY HALL: NW corner [1*]; SW corner [1*]. FATIMA RETREAT HOUSE: Outdoor Station 10, W [hedge*]; Outdoor Station 11, S [hedge*]; Outdoor Station 5, W [hedge*]. HOWARD HALL: Front [1]. HURLEY HALL OF BUSINESS ADMINISTRATION: Court [1]. MOREAU SEMINARY: Chapel, SE and SW corners [4*]. PANGBORN HALL: N side, E [1].

× *spp.*: *P.* 'Orange Glow' × *P. rogersiana* 'Flava' [**Firethorn**]
> Evergreen shrub. Hardy; free-flowering; fruit orange red; grown on walls as espalier. Ornamental in winter. Maximum height 10 ft.

'Teton' [**Firethorn**]
> Evergreen shrub. Upright form; fruit yellow orange. Maximum height 16 ft.
>> HESBURGH CENTER: SW Plaza, outer section, inside edge S [5]; SW Plaza, outer section, inside edge W [5].

*Pyrus* L. [**Pear**]
> Pears long have been grown for their fruits in Eurasia, the Mediterranean, and northern Africa, where they are native. More recently, a few species have been promoted for their ornamental characteristics. *P. calleryana* and, especially, its spineless cultivar 'Bradford' have become popular street trees with a neatly pyramidal outline that becomes broader with age. The white flowers bloom early in the spring. The glossy green leaves turn yellow to wine red or purple during autumn. They turn color later than most trees and can be hit by frost before they reach peak coloration here in the North. Pear bark has antibacterial properties. The wood is used in carving.
>
> Broad-leaved, sometimes spiny, small tree: deciduous or semi-evergreen. Leaves alternate along branches, simple, wavy-margined or almost toothed. Flowers appear in spring before leaves or at the same time; fruit a fleshy pome, like apple, with 5 papery, seed-bearing carpels at its core. The ornamental fruits are small, like crabapples, and not pear-shaped.

*calleryana* Decne. [**Callery Pear**]
> Deciduous tree. Leaf broadly oval, glossy, leathery, teeth rounded or wavy-edged. Flowers white; leaves turn red to deep purple; disease resistant. Ornamental in spring, late fall. Introduced, native to Korea, China. In horticulture since 1908. Maximum height 50 ft.
>> BADIN HALL: W door, N [1]. COMMUNITY CEMETERY: Mission House, between [4]. CORBY HALL: Architecture Bldg, between [3]. ECK TENNIS PAVILION: S side, flanking walk [6]. FIELDHOUSE MALL: Flanking walks around fountain [many]. JOYCE ATHLETIC AND CONVOCATION CENTER: W wall, between gates 1 and 2 [8]. KNOTT HALL: S wing, E door circle [6]; S wing, E side, S end [1]; W wing, N side, flanking walk [10]; W wing, W plaza, flanking door [18]. KOONS REHEARSAL HALL: N side, NE corner [2]; SE court [6]. LEWIS HALL: E, main entrance [1]. LOFTUS SPORTS CENTER: W side, N door [2]; W side, S door [2]. MORRIS INN: W side [1 **Commem.**]. NORTH DINING HALL: N end [2]; S end [2]; W side, N [2]; W side, S [2]. O'SHAUGHNESSY HALL: W side, plaza [7]. PASQUERILLA CENTER: E side, S end [2]; N side, at entrance [2]. PASQUERILLA HALL EAST: W wing, W end, NW plaza [8]. SACRED HEART BASILICA: Main entrance, W lawn [1 **Commem.**]. SIEGFRIED HALL: E door plaza [12]; N, flanking walk [14]; S wing, W side [1]; W door, circle [6]. SOUTH DINING HALL: NW corner [1 **Commem.**]. ST. EDWARD'S HALL: S lawn [1 **Commem.**]. STEPAN CHEMISTRY HALL: E and W sides [10]. WALSH HALL: E lawn between main doors [1 **Commem.**].

'Aristocrat' [**Callery Pear**]
> Deciduous tree. Broadly pyramidal with horizontal branches; leaves shiny green, wavy-edged. Leaf color variable, yellow to red; susceptible to fire blight. Ornamental in autumn. Maximum height 50 ft.

DeBartolo Classroom Building: E side, between central doors [11]; W side, between doors [4].

### 'Chanticleer' [Chanticleer Pear]

Deciduous tree. Narrow, upright, pyramidal form. Heavy flowering; leaves turn red purple; disease resistant. Ornamental in spring, midautumn.

Dillon Hall: N side [1 **Commem.**]. Hessert Aerospace Research Center: E side [2]. Joyce Athletic and Convocation Center: N at B2 parking lot [2]. St. Michael's Laundry: E side [3]. Support Services Building: S bed [1].

### 'Redspire' [Callery Pear]

Deciduous tree. Open, pyramidal form; leaf thick, shiny, dark green. Leaves turn yellow then red; susceptible to fire blight. Developed by Princeton Nurseries, New Jersey. Maximum height 40 ft.

Architecture Building: NE corner, E lawn [1 **Commem.**]. Hesburgh Center: Court, NW bed [3]; Court, SE bed [3]. Lewis Hall: E, main entrance [2]. Washington Hall: E plaza [2].

### communis L. [Common Pear]

Deciduous tree. Leaf egg-shaped to elliptic, firm, wavy-toothed; fruit large, fleshy. Fruit edible; extremely susceptible to fire blight. Introduced, native to Europe, western Asia; naturalized in the United States.

Fatima Retreat House: Community Cemetery, between [2]. Fischer Graduate Residence Complex: N, woods [1].

### Rhodotypos Siebold & Zucc. [Jetbead]

Jetbead is a tough shrub of loose, open habit, native to central China and Japan, that is grown for its white flowers and bright green foliage. It tolerates shade, poor soil, and urban pollution. The shiny black, pea-sized fruits are grouped 3-4 at the ends of the flower branches. They are not large enough to be showy, but remain throughout winter to add some interest to the garden. The fruits are poisonous. They contain amygdalin, a cyanogenic glycoside that breaks down to form the violently toxic hydrocyanic acid (HCN) after being eaten.

Broad-leaved shrub: deciduous. Leaf simple, double-toothed with conspicuously parallel veins, arranged in opposite pairs along stem. This is the only genus in the rose family that does not have alternate leaves. Flowers white, solitary and roselike at branch ends; fruit a black drupe with a bony seed enclosed in a fleshy covering.

### scandens (Thunb.) Mak. [Japanese Jetbead]

Deciduous shrub. Leaf veins straight, parallel, appear ribbed. Flowers white; fruit black, shiny, persistent. Ornamental in early summer through winter. Introduced, native to Japan, China. In horticulture since 1866. Maximum height 6 ft.

Calvary: St. Joseph Hall, woods between [many*]. Campus Security Building: E side [4*]. Carroll Hall: W 30yd, hedge [2*]. Cushing Hall of Engineering: NE corner [3*]. Hayes-Healy Center: S side, SW corner [1]. Sorin Hall: E, main entrance, E 20yd [1].

### Rosa L. [Rose]

Because of their beautiful flowers, roses have been grown ornamentally, hybridized, and improved since ancient times. They are native to north temperate areas and to tropical mountains. *R. carolina* and *R. multiflora* are both found in the wild growing along fences in pastures. The first is native; the second, introduced from China, has escaped from cultivation. *R. hugonis* is named for Father Hugh Scallan (Pater Hugo), a missionary who discovered the plant growing in northwestern China. Roses are frequently attacked by many insects and diseases. *R. rugosa*, called the salt spray rose, tolerates windy, saline, dry conditions and has become naturalized along the sandy ocean shores of the Northeast. It can be used in areas subjected to winter road salt. The fruits or hips of roses are edible and very high in vitamin C. The flowers of some species are the source for essential oils used in the perfume industry.

Broad-leaved, prickly, upright or climbing shrub: deciduous or evergreen. Leaves alternate along stem, usually odd-pinnately compound and toothed. Flowers with 5 petals in wild species; fruit a red, fleshy receptacle called a hip, that holds small, hairy achenes.

*carolina* L. [**Pasture Rose; Wild Rose**]

Deciduous shrub. Leaflets 5-7, teeth sharp, coarse; stipules narrow; prickles paired or scattered, bristly. Flowers pink, single; fruit red, pear-shaped, persistent. Ornamental in June through winter. Native to Maine through Wisconsin to Texas and Florida. In horticulture since 1826. Maximum height 6 ft.

HOLY CROSS HOUSE: S slope [many*]. ST. JOSEPH'S LAKE: SW margin [1].

*hugonis* Hemsl. [**Father Hugo Rose**]

Deciduous shrub. Small leaflets 5-13, blunt, no hairs; stipules unlobed; scattered, stout prickles, bristly. Flowers bright yellow, single, abundant. Ornamental in May to June. Introduced, native to central China. In horticulture since 1899. Maximum height 8 ft.

LYONS HALL: NE corner, N, at wood fence [1].

*multiflora* Thunb. ex J. Murr. [**Japanese Multifloral Rose; Baby Rose**]

Deciduous shrub. Leaflets 9, pointed, shiny, hairy; long, fingerlike stipules; prickles paired, hooked. Flowers white, abundant, fragrant; fruit red, egg-shaped; weedy. Ornamental in June into winter. Introduced, native to Japan, Korea; escaped in the United States. In horticulture since 1868. Maximum height 10 ft.

ST. JOSEPH'S LAKE: W end, junction of walks [many*]. ST. MARY'S LAKE: S edge, N of Campus Security Bldg [1]; S margin, N of Campus Security Bldg [1]; W end, ravine, N side [hedge*].

*Rubus* L. [**Blackberry**]

This genus is distributed worldwide, but concentrated in the Northern Hemisphere, ranging to the Arctic Circle. In the wild they can be found growing in woodland under the trees. Plants of this genus are grown for their edible fruits, not for ornament. The blackberry, cloudberry, loganberry, raspberry, dewberry, and boysenberry of commerce are all species, hybrids, and improved cultivars of *Rubus*.

Broad-leaved, usually prickly, shrub: deciduous. Leaves alternate, toothed, and either simple and lobed or pinnately compound. Stems, usually prickly, grow for 2 years, producing white flowers and fruit during the second year, then die. Fruit an aggregate of drupelets, each juicy and single-seeded.

*frondosus* Bigel. [**Leafy-bracted Blackberry**]

Deciduous shrub. Canes not purple; leaflets toothed, hairy but green below; prickles slightly curved. Fruit edible. Native to southern Canada, eastern and

central United States.
>    CALVARY: Woods [many*]. ST. JOSEPH'S LAKE: Boat house, rear walk, E side [many*].

*occidentalis* L. [**Black Raspberry; Blackcap**]
>    Deciduous shrub. Canes purple, coated waxy-white; leaflets 3, double-toothed, white below, prickles stout. Fruit edible. Native to eastern and central North America. Maximum height 5 ft.
>    CALVARY: St. Mary's Lake, woods between [many*]; Woods [many*]. ST. JOSEPH'S LAKE: Boat house, rear walk, E side [many*]; W end, 15yd NW of Station #9 [1]. ST. MARY'S LAKE: W end, ravine, S side [many*].

*Sorbus* L. [**Mountain-ash**]
These small trees are grown for their autumn displays of masses of small orange, red, or yellow applelike fruits. Their only drawback is a susceptibility to stem borers that can weaken or kill even mature trees. They are native to the Northern Hemisphere. The American mountain-ash, *S. americana*, is an understory tree of the far northern forests that is hardy to temperatures as low as -50°F. The fruits are an important food of grouse and ptarmigan. In France and Italy people eat the fruits after they have been left for a period of controlled decay that softens them, a process called bletting, or else the fruits are made into cider.
>    Broad-leaved small tree or shrub: deciduous. Leaves alternate along stem, odd-pinnately compound, margin toothed. Small, white flowers grow in flat-topped clusters (corymbs) at branch ends; fruit a small, applelike pome bearing 2-5 carpels, each with 1-2 seeds.

*aucuparia* L. [**European Mountain-ash**]
>    Deciduous tree. Buds hairy; leaflets 9-15, margin toothed near apex. Fruit orange red, abundant in bright clusters, attracts birds. Ornamental in August, September. Introduced, native to Europe, western Asia, Siberia; naturalized in North America. Maximum height 40 ft.
>    BREEN-PHILLIPS HALL: W lawn, main entrance, S [1 **Commem.**]. CUSHING HALL OF ENGINEERING: W end [1*]. FATIMA RETREAT HOUSE: Fatima shrine, rear [1*].

'Cardinal Royal' [**European Mountain-ash**]
>    Deciduous tree. Symmetrical, narrowly oval form; leaves dark green above, silver below; fruit red. Fruit very showy, brilliant red. Ornamental in August, September. Developed by Michigan State University. Maximum height 35 ft.
>    HESBURGH CENTER: N side, parking area [3]. JOYCE ATHLETIC AND CONVOCATION CENTER: W side, W of gate 2 [1]. LAW SCHOOL: W side, center [1 **Commem.**].

*Spiraea* L. [**Spiraea; Bridal-wreath**]
Spiraea is an old-fashioned flowering shrub, popular in gardens since Victorian times. At Notre Dame during the 1880s, extensive hedges were planted along the sides of St. Edward's Hall. The Minim students, who lived in the hall during that time, periodically carried the flowering branches during May processions (the first, third, or fourth Sundays in May). Spiraeas are medium to small-sized shrubs grown for their masses of small white to rose pink flowers. The flowers bloom in spring or early summer. Spiraeas need sun and moisture to thrive.

These shrubs, native to the Northern Hemisphere, have graceful, arching branches. They should be pruned to control size, not to alter their shape. Some species bloom early from buds formed the previous season. Others bloom on the new growth. Those that bloom early on last year's wood should be pruned immediately after flowering. Delayed pruning will cause the buds of next year's flowers to be cut off. The species that bloom later on the current year's wood should be pruned in early spring before the flower buds are formed.

Broad-leaved shrub: deciduous. Leaves alternate along stems. Flowers bloom in flat or drooping clusters along stems; fruit an inconspicuous, flat, dry follicle that splits along a single seam to release tiny, oblong seeds.

× *bumalda* Burv.: *S. albiflora* × *S. japonica* [**Anthony Waterer Spiraea**]

Deciduous shrub. Leaf sharply double-toothed, dull green, hairless, base rounded; shoot angled. White to bright purple pink flowers in clusters. Ornamental in early summer. In horticulture since 1891. Maximum height 4 ft.

BURKE MEMORIAL GOLF COURSE: Maintenance center, E [hedge]. CORBY HALL: W end, W 50yd [2]. CUSHING HALL OF ENGINEERING: NE corner [3]. DECIO FACULTY HALL: E door [hedge]; W door [hedge]. KNOTT HALL: S wing, E door, N side [10]; S wing, SE corner [4]; S wing, W side [10]; W wing, NW corner [7]; W wing, S side [4]. O'SHAUGHNESSY HALL: E side, N end [many]. PASQUERILLA HALL EAST: N wing, W side [bed]. PASQUERILLA HALL WEST: E door [beds]; E wing, E end [2]. SIEGFRIED HALL: E door, flanking [10]; E wing, N side [2]; E wing, S side [1]; S wing, E side [10]; S wing, S end [5]; W door [4].

'Goldflame' [**Goldflame Spiraea**]

Deciduous shrub. Leaf rich bronze red turning yellow green, then green; flowers faded pink. Very heat tolerant. Ornamental in spring. Maximum height 4 ft.

DEBARTOLO CLASSROOM BUILDING: E side, along walls [22]; SE corner, S of E door [20]; SW corner, flanking S door [30]. ECK TENNIS PAVILION: S side [6]. HESBURGH CENTER: SW Plaza, outer section, inner area S [19]; SW Plaza, outer section, inner area W [19]; W side, N section, middle [7]. HESSERT AEROSPACE RESEARCH CENTER: S side [9]. JOYCE ATHLETIC AND CONVOCATION CENTER: Gate 11, S side [12]; Gate 9, flanking [20]. ST. MICHAEL'S LAUNDRY: E, flanking front walk [8]. SUPPORT SERVICES BUILDING: N bed [2]; S bed [2].

'Limemound' [**Limemound Spiraea**]

Deciduous shrub. Dense, mounded form; mature leaves lime green. Young leaves yellow, become lime green, then turn orange red. Ornamental in spring through autumn. Maximum height 3 ft.

DEBARTOLO CLASSROOM BUILDING: E side, S of N end doors [5]. ECK TENNIS PAVILION: S side [6]. GALVIN LIFE SCIENCE CENTER: W, main entrance, S bed [8]. HAMMES BOOKSTORE: W wing, S [11]. ST. MICHAEL'S LAUNDRY: E side, N of walk, along wall [3]. SUPPORT SERVICES BUILDING: S bed [1].

*japonica* L. f. [**Japanese Spiraea**]

Deciduous shrub. Leaf toothed or double toothed, gray green with hairy veins below, base round; shoot round. Flowers rose pink. Introduced, native to eastern Asia. Maximum height 6 ft.

HAYES-HEALY CENTER: W side [bed]. MORRISSEY HALL: NW corner [2].

var. *fortunei* (Planch.) Rehd. [**Robert Fortune Spiraea**]

Deciduous shrub. Flowers deep pink in large clusters. Developed in China. In horticulture since 1849. Maximum height 5 ft.

HURLEY HALL OF BUSINESS ADMINISTRATION: S side [3*]. LOG CHAPEL: W end

[4*]. MORRISSEY HALL: E end [2*].

### 'Ruberrima' [Chinese Spiraea]

Deciduous shrub. Mounded form; flowers dark rose, hairy. Maximum height 3 ft.

CORBY HALL: W end [1*].

### *nipponica* Maxim. [Nippon Spiraea]

Deciduous shrub. Leaf edge smooth or scalloped, tip blunt, blue green below; bud flattened; shoot not hairy. Flowers white. Introduced, native to the mountains of Japan. Maximum height 8 ft.

SNITE MUSEUM OF ART: Court [4].

### 'Snowmound' [Snowmound Nippon Spiraea]

Deciduous shrub. Leaves blue green; flowers white; dense form. Ornamental in May to June. Maximum height 5 ft.

BURKE MEMORIAL GOLF COURSE: Maintenance center, E [few]. MAIL DISTRIBUTION CENTER: SW corner [many]. O'SHAUGHNESSY HALL: E side [many].

### *prunifolia* Siebold & Zucc. [Double Bridal-wreath]

Deciduous shrub. Leaf toothed, tip pointed, shiny, dark green above, fine hairs below. Flowers white, double, in clusters of 3-6, appear before the leaves. Ornamental in late April. Introduced, native to China, Korea, Formosa. In horticulture since 1864. Maximum height 9 ft.

ST. EDWARD'S HALL: S side, W arch, front [2]. WALSH HALL: N end, W side [2*].

### *trichocarpa* Nakai [Korean Spiraea]

Deciduous shrub. Leaf toothed only at pointed tip, dull above; bud flat, slipper-shaped; branches ridged. Flowers white, in rounded clusters. Introduced, native to Korea. Maximum height 5 ft.

CARROLL HALL: W 30yd, hedge, center [1].

### × *vanhouttei* (C. Briot) Zab.: *S. cantoniensis* × *S. trilobata* [Vanhoutte Spiraea]

Deciduous shrub. Leaf 3-5 lobed, toothed, dull blue green above, waxy white below. Fountainlike form. In horticulture since 1862. Maximum height 8 ft.

CARROLL HALL: NW corner, W 30yd [1*]. CORBY HALL: SW corner, SW 5yd [1]. CROWLEY HALL OF MUSIC: E side [16*]. FIELDHOUSE MALL: N side, along [hedge]. HOLY CROSS ANNEX: NE corner [1]. LYONS HALL: S entrance, W [2]. MORRIS INN: N end [6*]. MORRISSEY HALL: E end [2]. O'SHAUGHNESSY HALL: E side [few]. OLD COLLEGE: SE corner [7*]. PASQUERILLA HALL EAST: N wing, E parking area [bed]. WALSH HALL: NE corner [2*]. WASHINGTON HALL: S, main entrance, W side [3*]; SW corner, W 10yd [26*].


## *Stephanandra* Siebold & Zucc. [Stephanandra; Lace Shrub]

These shrubs, native to temperate eastern Asia, are grown for their graceful, arching habit that is low enough in the cultivar 'Crispa' to be used as a ground cover or bank cover. The leaves are lacy because of their deeply cut lobes. The flowers are spiraealike, but too small to be conspicuous. Stephanandra may suffer some branch dieback during extreme winters in the Midwest unless planted in a sheltered site away from extremes of sun and wind.

Broad-leaved shrub: deciduous. Leaves alternate along zigzag, brown stem, deeply lobed, toothed. Flowers small, yellow to white, in clusters; fruit an inconspicuous follicle that opens to release seeds.

*incisa* (Thunb.) Zab. [**Lace Shrub**]
> Deciduous shrub. Leaf lobes deep, toothed, bright green, veins hairy below, stipules at leaf base. Useful cover for banks; flowers inconspicuous. Introduced, native to Japan, Korea. In horticulture since 1872. Maximum height 7 ft.
>> GALVIN LIFE SCIENCE CENTER: N side [beds]. HURLEY HALL OF BUSINESS ADMINISTRATION: W side [bed].

## CAESALPINIACEAE [CAESALPINIA FAMILY]

*Cercis* L. [**Redbud**]
> These graceful, ornamental trees are grown for their showy spring flowers that are red purple or magenta in bud and open to red pink. The common name refers to the vivid flower buds. Redbuds tolerate all but the wettest soil. They are found in North America, southern Europe, and Asia. The native eastern redbud (*C. canadensis*), which is Oklahoma's state tree, is more reliably hardy than *C. chinensis*. The species that grows from the western Mediterranean to eastern Bulgaria, *C. siliquastrum*, is called Judas-tree in the mistaken belief that this was the tree on which Judas Iscariot hanged himself. The confusion surrounds the similarity of the actual Latin phrase *Arbor Judaeae*, which means Judaea tree or tree of Jerusalem (where the tree is frequently grown), with the phrase as it has been transformed by legend and time, *Arbor Judae*, which would mean Judas tree when translated, implying tree of Judas, rather than Jerusalem.
>
> Broad-leaved small tree or shrub: deciduous. Leaf heart-shaped, simple, smooth-edged, alternate along zigzag stem. Flowers almost pealike, in clusters of 4 to 8 on old wood, bloom before leaves appear; fruit a thin, pealike pod that hangs on tree into winter. The redbud looks like another small ornamental tree, the katsura tree or *Cercidiphyllum japonicum*, but they are not closely related. The differences are small but distinct: leaves alternate and smooth-edged in redbud, but opposite and wavy or scallop-edged in katsura tree.

*canadensis* L. [**Eastern Redbud; Judas-tree**]
> Deciduous tree. Leaf base only slightly heart-shaped, edge thin, gray beneath; flower 0.5 in. long. Flowers abundant, intensely red purple fading to pink purple. Ornamental in March to April. Native to eastern United States through northern Mexico. In horticulture since 1641. Maximum height 30 ft.
>> DECIO FACULTY HALL: NE corner [3]. FIELDHOUSE MALL: W [few]. GALVIN LIFE SCIENCE CENTER: W, main entrance, S bed [2]; W, main entrance, WSW 20yd at crosswalk [1 **Commem.**]. HOWARD HALL: Morrissey Hall, midway [1*]. JUNIPER ROAD: E, opposite Galvin, at fence, E side [2]; North Gate, planting [3]; W, at Bulla Rd, N section, S end [1]; W, at Bulla Rd, S section, N end [1]; W, at Galvin, fence, campus-side [2]. LEWIS HALL: N, lakeside [3*]. LYONS HALL: N, parking lot, N edge [1 **Commem.**]; NW basketball court, W end [1*]. RILEY HALL OF ART AND DESIGN: Hurley, between [4]. ROCKNE MEMORIAL: NW corner [3*]. SACRED HEART BASILICA: SW corner [2*]. SORIN HALL: SE corner, SE 15yd [1*]. ST. JOSEPH'S LAKE: Holy Cross House, SW 50yd lakeside [1]. STADIUM: E, gate 3 [1]; E, gate 7 [3]; NE, gates 1 and 2 [1].

'Forest Pansy' [**Eastern Redbud**]
> Deciduous tree. Young leaves bright red purple, gradually turning dark red

green. May be less hardy than the species, also blooms later.
> DECIO FACULTY HALL: S end [1]; W side, NW lawn, W edge [2].

*Gleditsia* L. [**Honeylocust**]

This broad-ranging genus is native to eastern North America, South America, the Caspian Sea, India, and from Japan to the Philippines. The thornless, ornamental honeylocusts are graceful with open shade and a tolerance for urban pollution, which has made them popular as landscape and street trees. The long pods, filled with a sweet pulp and seeds, remain after the leaves have fallen. The abundant, branched thorns on the trunks and lower branches of wild trees are spectacular. They can be 1 ft. long. They are so hard and sharp that during the Civil War, the Confederates used them like pins to hold their ragged uniforms together. At Notre Dame, these sharp thorns can be seen arming the trunk of the large honeylocust that is growing on the Main Quad west of the Hurley Hall of Business Administration.

Broad-leaved, spiny tree: deciduous. Thorns arise deep within the bark, firmly anchored to the wood. Leaves alternate, pinnately or bipinnately compound with 30 or more leaflets per leaf. Flowers green yellow, not conspicuous, fragrant; fruit a long, thin pod, pulp sweet, seeds very hard.

*triacanthos* L. [**Honeylocust**]

Deciduous tree. Multibranched, 4 in. thorns on trunk and stem; leaf bipinnately compound; pod 1.5 ft.. Casts open shade, feathery appearance; suffers from many pests. Native to the eastern and central United States. Maximum height 135 ft.
> CARROLL HALL: St. Mary's Lake, road-walk junction, NE [1*]. HAYES-HEALY CENTER: NW corner, W 30yd [1*]. MORRISSEY HALL: NW corner [1*].

var. *inermis* Willd. [**Thornless Honeylocust**]

Deciduous tree. Thorns absent from trunk and stem; fruit formation rare. Salt tolerant; suffers from many pests. In horticulture since 1700. Maximum height 70 ft.
> BURKE MEMORIAL GOLF COURSE: Cedar Grove Cemetery, N of NW corner [1]. CEDAR GROVE CEMETERY: NE entrance, at Notre Dame Ave [1]. DEBARTOLO CLASSROOM BUILDING: E, at street [8]; E, flanking central doors [2]. DECIO FACULTY HALL: E plaza [5]; E plaza [6]; SW corner [3*]; W plaza [6]; W plaza [6]. DILLON HALL: SW corner, W [2*]. FATIMA RETREAT HOUSE: Mission House, E side [1*]; Mission House, W side [2*]. FIELDHOUSE MALL: W end plaza [14]. FISHER HALL: E end, S [6*]. FLANNER HALL: NW door plaza [2]; S side [1]; W side [2]. GRACE HALL: NE door plaza [2]; W side [1]. HOLY CROSS HOUSE: E wing [2*]. JOYCE ATHLETIC AND CONVOCATION CENTER: NW corner, gate 3 [3]. JUNIPER ROAD: W at Bulla Rd, middle section, roadside [3]. MOREAU SEMINARY: N lawn [4*]. PASQUERILLA HALL WEST: N wing, W side, planter [1]. PROVINCE ARCHIVES CENTER: N 7yd [1*]. SOUTH DINING HALL: SE corner, S [3*]; W side [3*]. SUPPORT SERVICES BUILDING: E parking lot, S end [3]. WALSH HALL: W side [4*].

var. *inermis* 'Shademaster' [**Thornless Honeylocust**]

Deciduous tree. Upright form, branches not spreading; stem thornless; fruit rare. Maximum height 45 ft.
> WASHINGTON HALL: E plaza [15].

*Gymnocladus* Lam. [**Kentucky Coffeetree**]

This is an interesting, rugged tree free of insect and disease problems, but its large pods and leaves can be messy during autumn. Some species are native to eastern Asia. The Kentucky coffeetree grows in moist bottomlands, ravines, and slopes in the eastern United States. Its low branching pattern has kept it from being used as a commercial timber tree, but it has been used locally for fence posts. The early settlers used its large seeds, roasted and ground, as a coffee substitute, although the taste is not similar. The pulp and seeds contain the alkaloid cytisine and are poisonous. The toxic principle, apparently, is destroyed by roasting, but this is not well understood. The Kentucky coffeetree was the favorite tree of Peter E. Hebert, C.S.C., whose 1966 checklist, *Trees, Shrubs and Vines on Notre Dame Campus*, is the cornerstone of knowledge of the campus' flora. He planted the Kentucky coffeetree standing beyond the southwest corner of Corby Hall, where he lived.

Broad-leaved large tree: deciduous. Leaves large, bipinnately compound, alternate along stem. Flowers fragrant, green white, clustered in pyramidal, many-flowered panicles; fruit a large, thick pod holding several large, hard seeds within a sticky pulp.

*dioica* (L.) C. Koch [**Kentucky Coffeetree**]

Deciduous tree. Leaf very large, 3 ft. long, bipinnately compound; pod 10 in. long; large hard brown seeds. Very tough tree for large, open areas. Native to eastern and central United States. In horticulture since 1748. Seeds and pulp in pods poisonous when eaten. Maximum height 75 ft.

BURKE MEMORIAL GOLF COURSE: SW corner [1]. CORBY HALL: SW corner, SW 20yd [1*]. CROWLEY HALL OF MUSIC: N end [1*]; NE corner [1*]; S end [1*]. RADIATION RESEARCH BUILDING: SE corner, E 35yd [1*].

## FABACEAE [PEA FAMILY]

*Caragana* Fabr. [**Pea-tree**]

Pea-trees are grown in North America for their showy yellow flowers. They can be used as hedges and windbreaks in harsh, dry conditions. *Caragana* is native to eastern Europe and from central Asia to China. In treeless areas such as Mongolia and Siberia these shrubby plants are a valuable fuel source.

Broad-leaved, sometimes thorny, shrub or small tree: deciduous. Leaves alternate along stem, with paired spines at each leaf base, even-pinnately compound with 8-12, smooth-edged leaflets. Flowers yellow, pealike, solitary or in fascicles of 4; fruit a small pod with 3-5 seeds, that opens with a popping sound in mid-to late summer to release seeds.

*arborescens* Lam. [**Siberian Pea-tree**]

Deciduous shrub. Leaf to 3 in. long, pinnately compound, spine-tipped stipules at base. Used for screens and windbreaks; tolerates poor soil and drought. Introduced, native to Siberia, Mongolia. In horticulture since 1752. Maximum height 20 ft.

LAW SCHOOL: SW corner [2*]. SOUTH DINING HALL: SW corner [4*].

*Cladrastis* Raf. [**Yellowwood**]

Two mature yellowwoods grow along the south side of the Grotto. A record-sized yellowwood stood beyond the southwest corner of LaFortune Student Center. It is now gone, a victim of age and severe weather. The Indiana Department of Natural Resources 1980 Big Tree Register listed it as the largest of its species known in the state at 70 ft. tall, 106 in. circumference, and 46 ft. crown spread. A young yellowwood now stands at the LaFortune site. It was presented to the University in 1991 by Notre Dame's Sesquicentennial subcommittee on exhibitions and permanent legacy. Yellowwood is native to eastern North America and temperate eastern Asia. It is a spreading, low-branched, medium-sized tree with good ornamental qualities that is suitable for smaller landscapes. It has showy white, fragrant flower clusters in the spring, but flowers are abundant only every other year or even every third year. The leaves are bright green, turning golden yellow in autumn. It has no serious disease or insect problems. It has always been a rare tree in the wild. It was used to make a yellow dye and its fine-grained wood was carved into gun stocks.

Broad-leaved tree: deciduous. Leaves odd-pinnately compound, alternate along stem. Flowers white, pealike, hanging like wisteria; fruit a brown pod with 4-6 flat, brown seeds.

*kentukea* (Dum.-Cours.) Rudd [**Yellowwood; Virgilia**]

Deciduous tree. Leaf to 1 ft. long, pinnately compound; bud on stem enclosed by leaf base, not visible. Broad, rounded form; clusters of white, fragrant flowers; gray bark. Ornamental in May to June. Native to southeastern and central United States. In horticulture since 1812. Maximum height 50 ft.

CORBY HALL: NW corner, N 35yd at Grotto walk [1*]. GROTTO OF OUR LADY OF LOURDES: SE, steps [1*]. LAFORTUNE STUDENT CENTER: SW 10yd [1* **Commem.**].

*Robinia* L. [**Locust**]

Locust is rarely cultivated in North America, where it is native, because of its extreme susceptibility to the locust borer. Borers riddle the trees, making the wood worthless. In Europe, where locust has escaped from cultivation and the borer is not as common, the ornamental and fine timber qualities have been improved by plant breeding. The wood is so hard that it looks varnished when only sanded and polished. It is the most durable of the hardwoods, even surpassing white oak. During the days of wooden ships, locust was the source for superior treenails, the wooden pegs used to fasten hull timbers. The nails swelled when wet for an extremely tight hold. During the War of 1812, the British partially attributed their defeat by the United States' naval forces on Lake Champlain, between New York and Vermont, to the superior performance of the locust wood used in the U.S. fleet. Locust was still unavailable at that time in Britain for ship-building. Bees, attracted to the fragrant locust flowers, produce a fine honey. Two poisonous compounds, a glycoside and a phytotoxin, that are found in young leaves, inner bark, and seeds, produce severe symptoms when the plant parts are eaten.

Broad-leaved, often spiny, tree or shrub: deciduous. Stems with pairs of short, stiff thorns at each leaf node. Leaves alternate along stem, odd-pinnately compound with 7-19 smooth-edged leaflets. Flowers white, pealike, hanging in many-flowered racemes; fruit a many-seeded large pod that stays on tree in winter.

### *pseudoacacia* L. [**Black Locust**]

Deciduous tree. Stem with paired 0.5 in. long spines at leaf nodes; leaf pinnately compound, 14 in. long. Tough tree for severe conditions; has many disease and insect pests. Native to eastern and central United States. In horticulture since 1635. Inner bark, leaves and seeds poisonous when eaten. Maximum height 50 ft.

ARCHITECTURE BUILDING: N side [1*]. CAMPUS SECURITY BUILDING: N side, E of parking lot [5*]. FIRE STATION: SE corner [1*]. FISCHER GRADUATE RESIDENCE COMPLEX: N, woods [few]. LOG CHAPEL: NW, along road and SE [8*].

### *Sophora* L. [**Pagodatree**]

The pagodatree is a spreading tree suitable for a large urban site. The white or yellowish pealike flowers, in large, upright, pyramidal clusters, bloom from July through mid-August. This is the latest blooming time of any tree grown for its showy flowers. The genus contains many species that are native to temperate and tropical regions of both hemispheres. It is frequently found growing around Buddhist temples in Japan and Korea, resulting in its common name. Some species have poisonous seeds, but the toxicity of the seeds of pagodatree is not known.

Broad-leaved tree or shrub: deciduous (a few evergreen). Leaves alternate, odd-pinnately compound, each with 7-17 smooth-edged leaflets. Flowers pealike, white, fragrant, in large, many-flowered, pyramidal panicles; fruit a pod that turns yellow, then brown, and remains on tree during winter.

### *japonica* L. [**Japanese Pagodatree**]

Deciduous tree. Leaf 10 in. long, pinnately compound, shiny, bright green above, waxy white, hairy below. Broad form; open shade; fragrant white flowers in 12 in. clusters. Ornamental in July and August. Introduced, native to China, Korea. In horticulture since 1747. Seeds may be poisonous if eaten. Maximum height 75 ft.

CORBY HALL: Main entrance, S 50yd [1*]. HESBURGH LIBRARY: Pool, SW [1 **Commem.**].

### *Wisteria* Nutt. [**Wisteria**]

These vigorous vines, native to eastern Asia and eastern North America, are grown for their showy, pealike, lilac blue, pink, or white spring flowers. They need strong support. The flowers are spectacular, but may not appear for 7 or more years after a vine is planted. The genus was named in 1818 by the American botanist Thomas Nuttall in honor of Caspar Wistar, a Philadelphia physician and professor of anatomy at the University of Pennsylvania. *W. floribunda*, which climbs in a clockwise fashion around its support, is most common. *W. sinensis*, which climbs counterclockwise, is also planted. The seeds and pods are poisonous when eaten. The toxic principle is unknown.

Broad-leaved, twining vine: deciduous. Leaves alternate along stem, odd-pinnately compound, each with up to 19 smooth-edged leaflets. Flowers pealike, hanging in many-flowered racemes; fruit a velvety, several-seeded pod that opens in winter.

*floribunda* (Willd.) DC. [**Japanese Wisteria**]
> Deciduous vine. Leaflets 13-19; flowers on 1 in. long stalks; pod velvety-hairy. Showy violet flowers hang on 20 in. long clusters, slight fragrance. Ornamental in April to May. Introduced, native to Japan. In horticulture since 1830. Maximum height 35 ft.
>> BROWNSON HALL: Court, W side [1]. SNITE MUSEUM OF ART: Court, W wall [1].

## ELAEAGNACEAE [OLEASTER FAMILY]

*Elaeagnus* L. [**Oleaster; Silverberry**]
> These small trees and shrubs have striking silvery foliage that can provide contrast in the landscape. Their flowers are inconspicuous but very fragrant in May. One species is native to North America. Many more are native to southern Europe and Asia, where they tolerate salt, drought, and wind. These species were brought to the United States for use in windbreaks and along highways where salt builds up in the soil. Unfortunately, the fruits are spread by birds and the plants have become weedy and invasive. They also are subject to insect and disease problems that make them short-lived.
>
> Broad-leaved, sometimes spiny, small tree or shrub: deciduous or evergreen. Leaves alternate along stem, simple, smooth-edged, both surfaces covered by silvery scales. Flowers small, fragrant, yellow, with a calyx tube but no petals, in clusters of 1-3 in leaf axils; fruit a small, drupelike achene covered with silvery scales.

*angustifolia* L. [**Russian Olive; Oleaster**]
> Deciduous tree. Leaf oblong, to 3 in. long, dull green and scaly above, silver scales below; fruit silver. Striking silver leaves; flowers small but fragrant; salt tolerant. Ornamental in May through summer. Introduced, native to Europe, western Asia. Maximum height 20 ft.
>> KEENAN HALL: NW corner [1*]. MOREAU SEMINARY: SW corner, W 25yd [1*].

*umbellata* Thunb. [**Japanese Silverberry; Autumn Oleaster**]
> Deciduous shrub. Leaf elliptic or egg-shaped, 4 in. long, bright green above, silver below; fruit red. Spreading form; used to control erosion in dry soil; becomes weedy. Introduced, native to China, Japan, Korea. In horticulture since 1830. Maximum height 18 ft.
>> PARIS HOUSE: E hedge, S end [1*].

## THYMELAEACEAE [MEZEREUM FAMILY]

*Daphne* L. [**Daphne**]
> Daphne, grown for its flowers and restrained habit, is native to Asia and Europe. *D. cneorum* has masses of fragrant, rose pink flowers in April and May. The spicy scent, like carnation, attracts butterflies. It is evergreen and low-growing, appropriate as a groundcover or accent in a rock garden. The beauty is tempered by the plant's toxicity. Daphne was one of the earliest plants to be recorded as poisonous. The Greek physician Dioscorides, in the first century A.D., mentioned its poisonous qualities in his *De Materica Medica*, which

remained the authority in botany and medical remedies for 1500 years. The toxic principle is dihydroxycoumarin, the aglycone component of a glycoside that is found in all parts of the plant. The toxic effects are numerous and severe. The small berrylike fruits are attractive to children.

Broad-leaved shrub: deciduous or evergreen. Leaves simple, alternate but crowded along stem. Flowers rose pink, bloom April and May, sometimes again in late summer, with no petals but calyx tube ends in 4 spreading, petallike lobes, in umbels of 6-8; fruit a leathery or fleshy 1-seeded drupe.

*cneorum* L. [**Rose Daphne; Garland Flower**]

Evergreen ground cover. Leaf to 2 in. long, shiny dark green above, waxy below. Dense clusters of fragrant, rose pink flowers. Ornamental in April and May. Introduced, native to the mountains of Europe. In horticulture since 1752. Plant extremely poisonous if small amount eaten, especially fruits. Maximum height 1 ft.

'Ruby Glow' [**Rose Daphne; Garland Flower**]

Evergreen ground cover. Flowers dark pink, foliage dark green. Developed at Lake County Nursery, Perry, Ohio. Maximum height 1 ft.

MORRIS INN: Main entrance, E beds [few]. ZAHM HALL: N side, at door [5].


## NYSSACEAE [TUPELO FAMILY]

*Nyssa* L. [**Tupelo; Sourgum**]

Tupelo is a medium-sized tree valued for brilliant autumn color (yellow red to wine red) that is consistent from year to year, and for an interesting, abruptly pyramidal silhouette. The shape makes it conspicuous during winter. The fruits attract birds through early winter. The native North American species grow in swampy woods, on dry hillsides, or in abandoned fields. Others are native to China and Indomalaysia. Their taproots make them easier to transplant when young or from container-grown stock. They have no serious disease or insect problems.

Broad-leaved tree: deciduous, some dioecious. Leaves alternate along stem, simple, mostly smooth-edged, glossy above. Flowers small, male and female may be on separate trees, 2-4 flowers clustered at leaf base; fruit an oblong, blue black drupe.

*sylvatica* Marsh. [**Black Tupelo; Blackgum; Sourgum**]

Deciduous tree. Leaf simple, elliptic, to 6 in. long, shiny above, waxy below with some hairs on veins. Pyramidal; horizontal branches; leaves turn yellow to red, purple. Ornamental in autumn. Native to eastern North America. In horticulture since 1750. Maximum height 50 ft.

ARCHITECTURE BUILDING: N side [2*]. COMPUTING CENTER AND MATH BUILDING: S door, E side [2*]. CORBY HALL: Old College, midway [1*]. HESBURGH LIBRARY: SW corner, S [2*]. JOYCE ATHLETIC AND CONVOCATION CENTER: Gate 2 [1]; Gate 8, S side [1]; Gate 9, S side [1]. KOONS REHEARSAL HALL: E, flanking parking lot [4]. PANGBORN HALL: S side, S 5yd [1]. RADIATION RESEARCH BUILDING: E end [1*].

## CORNACEAE [DOGWOOD FAMILY]

*Cornus* L. [**Dogwood**]

The pink or white native dogwoods are extremely popular small accent trees that signify spring to many gardeners when they bloom. In the wild, they are graceful understory or forest edge trees that light up the woods with their flat, horizontal sprays of white-bracted flowers before the shade of summer develops. In recent years a fungus disease, dogwood anthracnose or *Discula*, has increased in severity. Infected trees develop characteristic leaf spots and branch death, resulting in eventual death of the tree. Although no resistant strains are known, the possibility of infection can be reduced by planting flowering dogwoods where they receive adequate moisture and sunlight. Mulching at the base also conserves moisture. The lush growth produced by high nitrogen lawn fertilizers also is more vulnerable to infection. The Korean dogwood, which is very similar to our native large-flowered species, is slightly more resistant to the disease. Dogwoods are native to North America, Europe, and Asia, plus a few species in Africa and South America. Flowering dogwood is the state tree of both Missouri and Virginia, illustrating their broad distribution in the United States. The flowering dogwoods are the most showy, but several other shrubby species have a place in the garden. The cornelian cherry, *C. mas*, with its small yellow flowers, is one of the earliest woody plants to bloom. Its fruits can be used for jam and syrup. The bright red or yellow stems of *C. alba* and *C. sericea* are very striking against the winter snow. Bunchberry, *C. canadensis*, is a low-growing ground cover for shady, acid soil, a hint of its native northern forest habitat.

Leaves usually in opposite pairs but some species alternate; simple, smooth-edged, veins distinctively parallel. A fresh dogwood leaf grasped between the hands and pulled apart will exhibit trailing "strings" between the veins across the gap of the torn edges. Flowers small, clustered, surrounded by white or pink bracts, not petals; fruit a 2-seeded drupe, juicy in some species.

*alba* L. [**Tartarian Dogwood**]

Deciduous shrub. Leaf rough blistery above, waxy green below; stem red with long oval lenticels, pith white. Stems bright red. Ornamental in winter. Introduced, native to Siberia, northern China, northern Korea. In horticulture since 1741. Maximum height 10 ft.

'Argenteo-marginata' [**Tartarian Dogwood**]

Deciduous shrub. Leaf margin marked irregularly with white; stem red. Ornamental in summer through winter.

FATIMA RETREAT HOUSE: E side, E 15yd [1*]. HESSERT AEROSPACE RESEARCH CENTER: N plaza [3]. JOYCE ATHLETIC AND CONVOCATION CENTER: Gate 11 [3]. PASQUERILLA HALL EAST: N wing, W side, N end [12]. PASQUERILLA HALL WEST: N wing, W side [5]. STEPAN CENTER: S side, W [2].

*alternifolia* L. [**Alternate-leaf Dogwood; Pagoda Dogwood**]

Deciduous tree. Leaves alternate but crowded at end of stem; large shrub or tree; fruit blue black. Broadly horizontal growth; branches form tiers. Native to southern Canada, Minnesota through Georgia. In horticulture since 1760. Maximum height 25 ft.

CORBY HALL: N side, kitchen, N walk to Grotto [1*].

*amomum* Mill. [**Pale Dogwood**]

Deciduous shrub. Leaf green and silky-hairy below; stem smooth purple, pith brown. Native to eastern North America. In horticulture since 1658. Maximum height 10 ft.

subsp. *obliqua* (Raf.) J. S. Wilson [**Pale Dogwood**]

Deciduous shrub. Leaf waxy gray and bumpy with flat hairs below; stem smooth and yellow red to purple.

FISCHER GRADUATE RESIDENCE COMPLEX: N, woods [many].

*canadensis* L. [**Bunchberry**]

Perennial ground cover. Leaves alternate but clustered with 4 or 6 at stem tip; stems horizontal, low-growing. Slow-growing, needs shady acid soil; bracts and red fruit showy. Ornamental in May through early winter. Native to Greenland through Alaska to West Virginia through California. Maximum height 0.8 ft.

MORRIS INN: Main entrance, E beds [beds].

*florida* L. [**Flowering Dogwood**]

Deciduous tree. Leaf dark green above, waxy and hairy-veined below; bud hidden by leaf base; fruit red. Broad horizontal, tiered form; white bracts, dark red leaves showy. Ornamental in spring, autumn. Native to eastern United States through Kansas and Texas. In horticulture since 1731. Maximum height 40 ft.

ALUMNI HALL: SE corner [5*]; SE, main gate, W 15yd [1 **Commem.**]; SE, main gate, just W [1 **Commem.**]. CAVANAUGH HALL: Main entrance [2*]; S, basketball court, E edge [1 **Commem.**]. CORBY HALL: S 60yd [3*]. CUSHING HALL OF ENGINEERING: Law School, plaza between [2]. FATIMA RETREAT HOUSE: Calvary, NE [1]. FISHER HALL: N entrance, E [1 **Commem.**]. FRESHMAN YEAR BUILDING: SW [2]. GALVIN LIFE SCIENCE CENTER: SW corner, W [1]. GROTTO OF OUR LADY OF LOURDES: N [4*]. HESBURGH LIBRARY: Pool, S and E [4*]; Pool, SW [1*]. HESSERT AEROSPACE RESEARCH CENTER: E side [2]. HOWARD HALL: N side, NE 8 yd [1*]. KEENAN HALL: SE entrance, flanking [2]. KOONS REHEARSAL HALL: W side, S end [2]. PASQUERILLA CENTER: NW corner [1]; SE corner [1]; SW corner [3]. PRESBYTERY: NE corner [1*]. SNITE MUSEUM OF ART: Court [3*]; Court, entrance, E 10yd [3]. STADIUM: Galvin, midway, parking circle, E end [1 **Commem.**]. WALSH HALL: E flanking steps [6]; E side, flanking steps [6]. ZAHM HALL: W side [3].

'Rubra' [**Red-flowering Dogwood**]

Deciduous tree. Flower bracts pink to rose red. Flower buds slightly less hardy than those of the species. Ornamental in spring.

BURKE MEMORIAL GOLF COURSE: Sollitt Shelter, E [1*]; Tee 1, E [3*]. CUSHING HALL OF ENGINEERING: NE corner [1*]. FATIMA RETREAT HOUSE: Calvary, NW [1]. FRESHMAN YEAR BUILDING: W parking lot, S [1*]. GROTTO OF OUR LADY OF LOURDES: W [1 **Commem.**].

*kousa* Hance [**Kousa Dogwood**]

Deciduous tree. Leaf opposite, dark above, 2-5 veins, waxy below with brown hair tufts; red, stalked fruit. Broadly horizontal branches; showy white flower bracts last 6 weeks. Ornamental in June. Introduced, native to China, Korea, Japan. In horticulture since 1875. Maximum height 30 ft.

DEBARTOLO CLASSROOM BUILDING: NE corner, E side at doors [3]. FISHER HALL: N entrance, E [1]. JOYCE ATHLETIC AND CONVOCATION CENTER: W side, W of gate 10 [1]. ZAHM HALL: NW end, N [1].

*mas* L. [**Cornelian Cherry**]

Deciduous tree. Leaf egg-shaped, shiny dark green above, long hairs below; stem hairy, red green; bud seen. Shrubby; small balls of yellow flowers very early; showy fruit red. Ornamental in March, August. Introduced, native to central and southern Europe, western Asia. Maximum height 25 ft.

> FISHER HALL: N entrance, W [1*]. GALVIN LIFE SCIENCE CENTER: W, main entrance, flanking [3]. PASQUERILLA HALL EAST: N wing, W side [1]. POST OFFICE: N side [2].

*purpusii* Koehne [**Silky Dogwood; Pale Dogwood**]

Deciduous shrub. Leaf waxy green and bumpy below, hairs flat; stem smooth, yellow red to purple, pith brown. Native to Quebec through Kansas. Maximum height 10 ft.

> CARROLL HALL: Swimming pier (former) [1*]. MOREAU SEMINARY: E end, S, lakeside [1*].

*racemosa* Lam. [**Gray Dogwood**]

Deciduous shrub. Leaf narrow, 3-4 veins, dark gray green above, flat hairs below; stem red tan; bud visible. White fruit attracts birds; pink fruit stalks remain showy. Ornamental in autumn, winter. Native to Ontario and Minnesota through Georgia and Oklahoma. In horticulture since 1758. Maximum height 15 ft.

> FRESHMAN YEAR BUILDING: W parking lot, W [many*].

*sanguinea* L. [**Bloodtwig Dogwood**]

Deciduous shrub. Leaf woolly-hairy on both sides, paler below; stem purple red, hairy, pith white. Forms dense, coarse colonies by sucker growth. Introduced, native to Europe. Maximum height 15 ft.

> CORBY HALL: SW corner [1*]. DILLON HALL: S side [1*]. HURLEY HALL OF BUSINESS ADMINISTRATION: S side [7*]. LYONS HALL: Chapel, S side [5*]. ST. MARY'S LAKE: S edge [many*].

*sericea* L. [**Red-osier Dogwood**]

Deciduous shrub. Leaf waxy gray, bumpy above, few hairs below; stem red with lenticels, pith white. Provides a mass of red color; used for erosion control. Ornamental in winter. Native to North America. In horticulture since 1656. Maximum height 9 ft.

> ECK TENNIS PAVILION: S side [3]. LYONS HALL: Archway, SE [1]. MORRISSEY HALL: SW corner, S 35yd [3]. PASQUERILLA CENTER: NW corner [hedge]; SE corner [hedge]; SW corner [hedge]. ST. MARY'S LAKE: S edge [many*]. SUPPORT SERVICES BUILDING: N bed [4].

'Flaviramea' [**Goldentwig Dogwood**]

Stems bright yellow. Ornamental in winter.

> ECK TENNIS PAVILION: S side [3]. HESSERT AEROSPACE RESEARCH CENTER: N plaza [2]. LOFTUS SPORTS CENTER: W side, center [10]. SUPPORT SERVICES BUILDING: N bed [4].

## CELASTRACEAE [STAFF-TREE FAMILY]

*Celastrus* L. [**Bittersweet**]

Bittersweet is grown for its showy orange fruits that are visible through the winter outdoors and used in dried arrangements. Its growth is rampant, but suitable for covering trellises and fences where it can be kept constrained. In North and South America, Oceania, eastern Asia, and Madagascar, where it is native, it can be found in the wild engulfing small trees and shrubs, killing them by girdling their stems. The plant should be considered poisonous, but the poisonous principle is not yet described.

Broad-leaved twining vine or shrub: deciduous, often dioecious. Leaves toothed, simple, alternate along stem. Male and female flowers on separate plants; fruit a 3-5 celled capsule with 2 seeds in each cell, enclosed by a fleshy, yellow to red aril.

*orbiculatus* Thunb. [**Oriental Bittersweet**]

Deciduous vine. Leaf rounded, wider above the middle, to 5 in. long; flowers and fruit form at leaf axils. Introduced, native to Japan, China; naturalized in the eastern United States. In horticulture since 1870. Seeds may be poisonous when eaten in large quantities. Maximum height 40 ft.

FRESHMAN YEAR BUILDING: Brownson court, S wall [1].

*scandens* L. [**American Bittersweet**]

Deciduous vine. Leaf egg-shaped to oblong, wider below middle, to 4 in. long; flower and fruit at stem tip. Plant can cover and kill small trees and shrubs; orange fruit showy. Native to Quebec through North Carolina, to New Mexico. Seed may be poisonous when eaten in large quantities. Maximum height 25 ft.

LEWIS HALL: NE 60yd, lakeside [few*].


*Euonymus* L. [**Spindletree; Euonymus**]

*Euonymus* is a diverse genus with most species native to Asia, but some also found in Europe, North America, Africa, and Australia. Some species have corky wings along their stems, others have glossy evergreen leaves and are grown as ground covers, still others have showy orange, pink, or red fruits. All species are highly susceptible to attack by the euonymus scale, an insect that feeds on foliage and stems causing discoloration, decline, or death. The plants of all species should be considered poisonous. An unnamed poisonous principle, present in bark, leaves, and fruits, has caused problems in humans and horses in Europe, but not in North America.

Broad-leaved tree, shrub, or vine (rarely): deciduous or evergreen. Leaves simple, toothed, in opposite pairs along 4-angled, often green, stems. Flowers small, green white, bloom in June and July; fruit a pendent, 3-5 celled capsule, seeds enclosed by orange, pink, purple, or red fleshy arils.

*alata* (Thunb.) Siebold [**Winged Burningbush; Winged Spindletree**]

Deciduous shrub. Upright; leaf dull; twig corky-winged; fruit divided podlike, capsule purple, aril orange. Ornamental in autumn through winter. Introduced, native to eastern Asia. In horticulture since 1860. All parts poisonous when eaten. Maximum height 20 ft.

ALUMNI HALL: W wing, S end [2*]. CORBY HALL: Main entrance, E side [15*]. CUSHING HALL OF ENGINEERING: N, main entrance, E [3]. DILLON HALL: E wing, S end [3*]. FATIMA RETREAT HOUSE: Mission House, S side [hedge*]. FISHER HALL: E end [1*]. FLANNER HALL: E side [hedge]. HAMMES BOOKSTORE: W wing, S [11]. HOLY CROSS HOUSE: S side [2*]. HOWARD HALL: Front [2*]; N wing, W end [1*]. JOYCE ATHLETIC AND CONVOCATION CENTER: W, between gates 1 and 2, at benches [14]. KEENAN HALL: Front [3*]. KNOTT HALL: S wing, E side [3]; S wing, W side, S end [5]. LEWIS BUS SHELTER: E end [1*]. MAINTENANCE CENTER: S side [5]. NORTH DINING HALL: W side [few]. O'SHAUGHNESSY HALL: E side [many]. PASQUERILLA CENTER: E [hedge]; N [hedge]. PASQUERILLA HALL EAST: W wing, S side [13].

Pasquerilla Hall West: E wing, S side [10]. Province Archives Center: SE corner [1]. Sacred Heart Basilica: Crypt, E side [2*]. Siegfried Hall: E wing, N side [2]; S wing, W side [3]. Sorin Hall: S end [13*]. St. Michael's Laundry: E side, N of walk, along wall [11]. Stepan Center: S side, E of door [1]. University Club: NE lawn [hedge]. Walsh Hall: SW [1].

### var. *aptera* Regel [**Wingless Burningbush; Wingless Spindletree**]

Deciduous shrub. Twig only slightly winged or not at all; branches looser, not as stiff.

Grotto of Our Lady of Lourdes: N side, steps, N side [1*].

### 'Compacta' [**Narrow-winged Burningbush**]

Deciduous shrub. Branches more slender but dense; corky wings on twigs less pronounced. Less hardy than species; needs no pruning when used as a hedge. Maximum height 10 ft.

Fatima Retreat House: Fatima shrine, SE [2*]. Hesburgh Center: N side, residences, NE corner [5]; N side, residences, NW corner [5]; SW Plaza, outer section, S side [11]; SW Plaza, outer section, W side [11]. Hesburgh Library: SW corner [1*]; W, Moses statue, S shrubbery [1*]. Juniper Road: E, ROTC stoplight, fence [7]; E, opposite Galvin, at fence, W side [5]; North Gate, S end [4]; North Gate, fence, roadside [3]; ROTC stoplight, E parking lot [4]; W, Library circle N, planting [12]; W, Library circle N, roadside [3]; W, Library circle S, fence, S end [4]; W, Library circle S, roadside [4]; W, at Bulla Rd, N section, N end [5]; W, at Bulla Rd, S section, S end [5]; W, at Galvin, fence, roadside [8]. Moreau Seminary: Basketball court, NE corner [2*]; Basketball court, SE corner [1*]; NE corner, fire hydrant [3*]. Morris Inn: Main entrance, E beds, NW [12]; Main entrance, E beds, SW [12]. Support Services Building: E, along S entrance wall [14]; N bed [4]; S bed [3].

### *bungeana* Maxim. [**Winterberry Spindletree**]

Deciduous tree. Leaf waxy, petiole 1 in.; twig wingless; capsule deep-lobed and yellow pink, aril orange. Showy in fruit. Ornamental in September to October. Introduced, native to northern China, Manchuria. In horticulture since 1883. All parts poisonous when eaten. Maximum height 24 ft.

Burke Memorial Golf Course: Main building, E [many*]. Howard Hall: SW corner, SW [1]. Morris Inn: NW corner, N 25yd [1*].

### *europaea* L. [**European Spindletree**]

Deciduous tree. Leaf dull, veins raised below, petiole short; twig wingless; capsule pink red, aril orange. Best when used in groups; showy only when in fruit. Ornamental in September to November. Introduced, native to Europe, western Asia. All parts poisonous when eaten. Maximum height 30 ft.

Administration (Main) Building: NE corner, N side [2]. Burke Memorial Golf Course: SW central area [many]; Sollitt Shelter, W [1]; Sollitt shelter, E [1]. Fatima Retreat House: Fatima shrine, NE 60yd [2]. Law School: NW corner [1]. Morrissey Hall: SW corner [12*].

### var. *atrorubens* Rehd. [**Crimson-fruited Spindletree**]

Deciduous tree. Fruit capsule intensely crimson.

Carroll Hall: W 30yd, hedge [many*].

### *fortunei* (Turcz.) Hand.-Mazz. [**Chinese Winter-creeper**]

Deciduous ground cover. Low or climbing, not self-supporting; leaf shiny, small, often 1 in. long. Can grow as a vine, 40-70 ft. long; cultivars variable. Introduced, native to central and western China. In horticulture since 1907. All parts poisonous when eaten. Maximum height 3 ft.

> ALUMNI HALL: S side, ramp [bed]. BADIN HALL: E side [bed]. CAVANAUGH HALL: SW [bed]. CUSHING HALL OF ENGINEERING: NE corner [2]. DILLON HALL: E court [bed]. GALVIN LIFE SCIENCE CENTER: N side [bed]. HOWARD HALL: N wing, SW corner [1]; SE corner [4]. KEENAN HALL: Front [1]; N side, W [beds]. KOONS REHEARSAL HALL: N, along wall [beds]. POST OFFICE: N side [hedge]. SNITE MUSEUM OF ART: Court [4]. SOUTH DINING HALL: W entrance, N, on wall [1]. ST. JOSEPH HALL: Lake slope, top of steps [bed*]. ZAHM HALL: N side, at door, flanking walk [2].

'Carrierei' [**Carriere's Winter-creeper**]

Evergreen shrub. Shrubby habit; leaf glossy dark green; heavy fruit, capsule green red, aril yellow orange. Maximum height 8 ft.

> ALUMNI HALL: W court, N entrance [1*]. DILLON HALL: E court, N entrance [1*].

var. *radicans* (Siebold ex Miq.) Rehd. [**Common Winter-creeper**]

Evergreen vine. Climbing or trailing form; leaf egg-shaped to broadly elliptic, toothed, thick, 2 in. long.

> ALUMNI HALL: W wing, S end [bed*]. DILLON HALL: E wing, SE end [bed*].

var. *radicans* f. *reticulata* (Regel) Rehd. [**White-veined Winter-creeper**]

Evergreen vine. Trailing form; leaf variegated with white along the veins.

> ST. JOSEPH HALL: Lake slope, top of steps, E [1*].

var. *vegeta* (Rehd.) Rehd. [**Fruitful Winter-creeper**]

Evergreen shrub. Spreading form; leaf broadly elliptic to round, thick, wavy-toothed; fruit abundant. Can be trained as a vine. Maximum height 5 ft.

> HOWARD HALL: N wing, SW corner [bed*].

*hamiltoniana* Wallich [**Yeddo Spindletree**]

Deciduous tree. Leaf elliptic to oblong, dull, veins hairy below; capsule yellow, aril orange, seed white. Introduced, native to the Himalayas. All parts poisonous when eaten. Maximum height 40 ft.

var. *yedoensis* (Koehne) Blakelock [**Yeddo Spindletree**]

Deciduous tree. Leaf wide above middle; fruit capsule lobed, pink purple, aril orange, seed white. Introduced, native to China, Japan. In horticulture since 1865. Maximum height 15 ft.

> HOLY CROSS HOUSE: W end, lake slope [many*].


## AQUIFOLIACEAE [HOLLY FAMILY]

*Ilex* L. [**Holly**]

Hollies are native to temperate and tropical Asia and North and South America. The broadleaved, evergreen hollies, either *I. opaca* of North America, which is the state tree of Delaware, or the English holly, *I. aquifolium*, with red fruits, have long been associated with celebration. Christians use holly as a household decoration during Christmas celebrations, but even earlier, it was associated with the ancient Roman Festival of Saturn. Both the evergreen and deciduous hollies are used ornamentally. The masses of bright red fruits crowding the stems of the leafless hollies, *I. verticillata* and *I. decidua*, are striking in winter. Both male and female plants must be planted. Fruit will form after pollination on the female plants. The white wood of holly is smooth and hard. It is used for inlay, musical instruments and veneers, and as an ebony substitute when dyed. Although hollies are not considered poisonous, their leaves and fruits contain alkaloids that can cause physiological disturbances when eaten, especially by children. The leaves of some species have been used as a tea substitute.

Broad-leaved tree or shrub: deciduous or evergreen, often almost completely dioecious. Leaves alternate along stem, simple, smooth-edged or toothed, teeth often ending in spines in the evergreen species. Flowers small, white, in clusters at leaf axils along stem. Female plants form fruit, each a red, berrylike, stony-seeded drupe.

*cornuta* Lindl. & Paxt. [**Chinese Holly**]

Evergreen shrub. Leaf thick, leathery, very shiny, with 5-9 spines along margin. Not very hardy; red fruit showy, abundant on female plants. Ornamental in winter. Introduced, native to eastern China, Korea. In horticulture since 1846. Berries poisonous when eaten. Maximum height 10 ft.

'China Boy' [**Chinese Holly**]

Evergreen shrub. Rounded, compact form; leaf margin turned under or cupped. No fruit, pollinator for 'China Girl;' cold hardy, heat tolerant. Developed by Mrs. F. Leighton Meserve. Maximum height 10 ft.
    Howard Hall: SW corner [1].

'China Girl' [**Chinese Holly**]

Evergreen shrub. Rounded, compact form; leaf margin turned under or cupped. Red fruit abundant, pollinated by 'China Boy;' heat and cold hardy. Ornamental in winter. Developed by Mrs. F. Leighton Meserve. Maximum height 10 ft.
    Howard Hall: SW corner [2].

*crenata* Thunb. [**Japanese Holly**]

Evergreen shrub. Leaf thick, leathery, shiny dark green, margin toothed but not spiny; fruit black. Good hedge or foundation plant; needs no pruning. Introduced, native to Japan, Korea. In horticulture since 1864. Berries poisonous when eaten. Maximum height 10 ft.
    Fatima Retreat House: Mission House, E side [9*]; Mission House, N side [1*]. Snite Museum of Art: Court [5].

*glabra* (L.) A. Gray [**Inkberry**]

Evergreen shrub. Leaf thin, few blunt teeth near tip or none; fruit black. Good shrub for hedge or foundation in moist, acidic soil. Native to Nova Scotia through Florida to Texas. In horticulture since 1759. Maximum height 8 ft.
    Koons Rehearsal Hall: E side [10]; W side, N of door, along walk [16]; W side, S end [8]. Pasquerilla Center: N side door, E, along wall [22]; N side, W of door, along wall [16].

*opaca* Ait. [**American Holly**]

Evergreen tree. Leaf thick, leathery but dull, with about 13 large spines along margin. Abundant red fruits on female plant, needs male pollinator plant. Ornamental in winter. Native to Massachusetts to Florida, Missouri, and Texas. In horticulture since 1744. Berries poisonous when eaten. Maximum height 50 ft.
    Hayes-Healy Center: W side, along foundation [2]. Keenan Hall: E entrance, SE corner [2]. Moreau Seminary: Chapel, E court [1]; O'Rourke Bell W, E court [2*]. Morrissey Hall: Main entrance, E [2*]. Pangborn Hall: N, main entrance, W [1].

*verticillata* (L.) A. Gray [**Winterberry**]

Deciduous shrub. Leaf thin, not evergreen, dark green above, hairy below, margin toothed but not spiny. Adundant red fruits on female plant, needs male pollinator plant. Ornamental in winter. Native to Newfoundland through Minnesota, Texas, and Georgia. In horticulture since 1736. Berries poisonous when eaten. Maximum height 10 ft.

JOYCE ATHLETIC AND CONVOCATION CENTER: Gate 3, N [10]; W side, gate 3 [4]. LAFORTUNE STUDENT CENTER: Crowley, crosswalk between, N side [bed].

## BUXACEAE [BOX FAMILY]

*Buxus* L. [**Box; Boxwood**]

Box is frequently used for clipped formal hedges and edgings in the gardens of Europe and North America. It withstands shearing and can be formed into topiaries and fanciful shapes, but also has an elegant form when allowed to grow unpruned. Box is native to western Europe, the Mediterranean, temperate eastern Asia, the West Indies, and Central America. It is the hardest, heaviest tree in Britain. It has been used to make rulers, musical instruments, inlay for furniture, and was carved into engraving blocks during the 1800s.

Broad-leaved shrub or small tree: evergreen. Leaves in opposite pairs along stem, simple, smooth-edged, glossy. Flowers fragrant, creamy, without petals, bloom April-May; fruit a small, dry capsule in 3 sections, each with 2 seeds.

*microphylla* Siebold & Zucc. [**Korean Boxwood**]

Evergreen shrub. Leaf small, 1 in. long, wider above the middle; flowers form at leaf axils and stem tips. Flowers small but fragrant; good hedge plant, withstands pruning. Introduced, native to Japan. In horticulture since 1860. Leaf or twig may be poisonous when eaten, leaf may cause skin rash. Maximum height 4 ft.

SUPPORT SERVICES BUILDING: S bed [1].

'Wintergreen' [**Korean Boxwood**]

Evergreen shrub. Leaf light green, small. Very winter hardy. Developed by Scarff Nursery Company, New Carlisle, Ohio.

HESBURGH CENTER: Court, planter E1 [6]; Court, planter E2 [5]; Court, planter E3 [5]; Court, planter E4 [6]; SW Plaza, inner section, edge [27]. SESQUICENTENNIAL COMMONS: E inner bed, W edge [24]; N inner beds, S edges [40]; S inner beds, N edges [40]; W inner bed, S edge [24].

*Pachysandra* Michx. [**Pachysandra; Spurge**]

Japanese pachysandra is used in the landscape as a low-growing, evergreen groundcover. It can grow in deep shade, but can be burned by winter wind and sun when grown in exposed sites. Pachysandra is native to North America and eastern Asia.

Broad-leaved shrub or herbaceous perennial: evergreen. Leaves alternate along stem but crowded, appearing whorled at stem tip, edge toothed. Flowers white, bloom in March-April, males above females; fruits white, berrylike drupes, rare.

*terminalis* Siebold & Zucc. [**Japanese Pachysandra; Japanese Spurge**]

Evergreen ground cover. Leaves clustered at stem tip; leaf wider above middle, toothed above middle, 3 veins. Good ground cover for deep shade under trees with shallow roots. Introduced, native to Japan. In horticulture since 1882. Maximum height 1 ft.

FATIMA RETREAT HOUSE: Flanking [beds*]. MOREAU SEMINARY: N side, E court [beds*]. MORRIS INN: Main entrance, E beds [beds]. SNITE MUSEUM OF ART: Court [beds].

'Variegata' [**Japanese Pachysandra**]

Evergreen ground cover. Leaves edged and marked with white. Grows more slowly and less vigorously than the species.

HESBURGH CENTER: SW Plaza, inner section, beds [bed].


# RHAMNACEAE [BUCKTHORN FAMILY]

*Rhamnus* L. [**Buckthorn**]

The most common buckthorns, *R. cathartica* and *R. frangula*, were brought from Europe for ornament, but have escaped in the eastern and central United States. Today, these shrubs are rarely used ornamentally although they can grow in harsh urban environments. *R. cathartica* is the host for one stage in the life cycle of a fungus disease, *Puccinia coronata*, crown rust of oats and some other grasses. Consequently, the shrubs are banned where these crops are economically important. Buckthorns are native to temperate areas of the Northern Hemisphere, Brazil, and South Africa. The berries have been the source for green and yellow dyes and pigments in southern Europe and Asia. Poisoning after eating the fruits and leaves of buckthorn has been reported in Europe. The toxic principle has not been described. *R. purshiana*, of the Pacific Northwest, is the source for cascara sagrada, a laxative. Several species contain glycosides from which the purgative anthraquinone is obtained.

Broad-leaved sometimes spiny shrub or small tree: deciduous, some evergreen. Leaves either in opposite pairs or alternate along stem, veins conspicuously parallel, edge toothed or smooth. Flowers inconspicuous, green, in early summer, clustered in leaf axils. Flowers on a plant may be male, female, perfect (male and female parts all in one flower), or in any combination of the 3 conditions. Fruit, formed by female or perfect flowers, a small blue to black berrylike drupe.

*frangula* L. [**Glossy Buckthorn; Alder Buckthorn**]

Deciduous shrub. Leaf edge smooth or merely wavy, 2.5 in. long, 8-9 vein pairs; fruit red. Introduced, native to Europe, northern Africa, Asia; escaped in the United States. Leaves and fruit poisonous when eaten. Maximum height 12 ft.

CALVARY: St. Joseph Hall, woods lakeside [many*]. CARROLL HALL: NE 75yd, lakeside [many*]. COMMUNITY CEMETERY: Mission House, between [1]. MORRISSEY HALL: Main entrance, E [1]; NW corner, lakeside [few]. OLD COLLEGE: N, lakeside [few*]. OUTDOOR WAY OF THE CROSS: Station 5 [many*]. SNITE MUSEUM OF ART: Court [4]. ST. MARY'S LAKE: W end [many*].


# VITACEAE [GRAPE FAMILY]

*Parthenocissus* Planch. [**Woodbine**]

This genus contains the most common ornamental vines, most frequently seen covering the walls of buildings or growing on arbors. They provide shade through the summer and brilliant orange, red, or yellow color in early autumn.

The native Virginia creeper is slightly hardier than Boston ivy, also called Japanese creeper, which is native to Japan and central China. The blue black berries are attractive to children and should be considered poisonous, although the poisonous principle has not been defined.

Broad-leaved tendril-bearing vine: deciduous, rarely evergreen. Leaves alternate along stem, either simple and lobed or palmately compound, edges of both toothed. Tendrils usually branched and disk-tipped. Flowers inconspicuous, greenish, in clusters (cymes or panicles) opposite leaves; fruit a small, blue black berry with 1-4 seeds. The adhesive disks at the tips of the tendrils separate *Parthenocissus* from the very similar vines of *Vitis*, the grapes, which have tendrils with thinly pointed tips.

*inserta* (A. Kern.) K. Fritsch [**Glossy Virginia Creeper**]

Deciduous vine. Leaf glossy above, 5 palmate leaflets; tendrils tapering, not disk-tipped. Will not cling to walls, but clambers over walls and buildings. Native to Quebec through Arizona.

CALVARY: Woods [1*]. CARROLL HALL: NW path, S side [1].

*quinquefolia* (L.) Planch. [**Virginia Creeper**]

Deciduous vine. Leaf with 5 palmate leaflets; stem round; tendrils long, 5-8 branches with adhesive disks. Very hardy; leaves turn purple to crimson red. Ornamental in autumn. Native to New England through Florida into Mexico. In horticulture since 1622. Berries may be poisonous when eaten; reports poorly documented. Maximum height 50 ft.

ADMINISTRATION (MAIN) BUILDING: N wing, NE corner [1*]. CALVARY: Woods [many*]. FARLEY HALL: NE corner, E wall [1*].

*tricuspidata* (Siebold & Zucc.) Planch. [**Boston Ivy**]

Deciduous vine. Leaf 3-lobed, glossy; stem square; tendrils short, 5-12 branches with disk tips. Less hardy than Virginia creeper but still common; turns rich red. Ornamental in autumn. Introduced, native to Japan, China. In horticulture since 1862. Maximum height 50 ft.

ADMINISTRATION (MAIN) BUILDING: S wall, E of main steps [few]. ARCHITECTURE BUILDING: Walls, all sides [many*]. BREEN-PHILLIPS HALL: NE corner [1*]. BROWNSON HALL: E side, on wall [many]. CAVANAUGH HALL: W end, wall [many*]. FARLEY HALL: SW corner [1*]. NORTH DINING HALL: E side [1*]. O'SHAUGHNESSY HALL: W, main entrance, N side [1]. PRESBYTERY: SE corner [1*]. SNITE MUSEUM OF ART: Court [many]. ST. EDWARD'S HALL: Wall [1]. WASHINGTON HALL: W side [1*].

*Vitis* L. [**Grape**]

Grapes are well known for their fruits, eaten fresh or dried as raisins and currants, and used in making wine. They also are used ornamentally to cover walls and arbors. Their autumn color is striking. They grow throughout the Northern Hemisphere, found in the wild climbing trees and other supports in open woodland and along riverbanks.

Broad-leaved tendril-bearing vine or shrub (uncommon): deciduous. Leaves palmately lobed, alternate along stem, with branched or simple tendrils (modified inflorescences). Flowers 5-petalled, in narrow panicles; fruit a juicy berry with small pear-shaped seeds. Differences in the tendrils separate *Vitis* from closely related *Parthenocissus*. The tendrils on *Vitis* grasp by coiling, their tips are thin and pointed. The tendrils of *Parthenocissus* adhere to surfaces by their flat, adhesive, disklike tips.

*aestivalis* Michx. [**Silver-leaf Grape**]
>>Deciduous vine. Leaf with 3-5 deep lobes, woolly-hairy below; tendril and flower absent beside third leaf. Fruit black with waxy white bloom. Native to New England through Florida and Kansas to Texas.

>var. *argentifolia* (Munson) Fern. [**Silver-leaf Grape**]
>>Deciduous vine. Leaf white below, hair only on veins below.
>>>CALVARY: Community Cemetery, walk between, N side [many*]. LOFTUS SPORTS CENTER: N, woods [1].

*riparia* Michx. [**River-bank Grape; Frost Grape**]
>>Deciduous vine. Leaf with 3-5 lobes, each tapering, hairs only on veins below. Fruit black with a waxy white bloom. Native to Nova Scotia through Manitoba to Texas.
>>>BURKE MEMORIAL GOLF COURSE: SW corner, fence [1]. LYONS HALL: N wing, SE corner [1*]. MORRIS INN: Service door, W, golf course fence [1*]. ROCKNE MEMORIAL: S, golf course fence [few*]. ST. JOSEPH HALL: Moreau, between [many*]. ST. MARY'S LAKE: N, old swimming pier, N in hedge [1*]; S edge, N of Campus Security Bldg [1]; W end, near Carroll Hall [many].

## STAPHYLEACEAE [BLADDERNUT FAMILY]

*Staphylea* L. [**Bladdernut**]
>The shrubby native American bladdernut is grown for its interesting inflated, papery fruit capsules, the "bladders" of its common name. Its rounded, dense, suckering form is appropriate for a sunny or partially shaded, informal or woodland site. The genus is native to temperate areas of the Northern Hemisphere.

>Broad-leaved shrub or small tree: deciduous. Leaves compound with 3 toothed leaflets on each, in opposite pairs along stem. Flowers bell-shaped, green white, in small panicles at ends of branches; fruit a papery, 3-lobed capsule, each lobe inflated and containing 1-2 seeds. The leaves of bladdernut are similar to those of poison ivy, but the two can be differentiated by the following characteristics. Bladdernut leaves grow in opposite pairs along the stems, poison ivy leaves are arranged alternately. Bladdernut leaflets are finely and closely toothed along their edges, poison ivy leaves are smooth-edged or have irregular and widely spaced teeth or lobes. Bladdernut fruits are large, papery capsules that hang from the ends of the branches, poison ivy fruits are small, whitish berries that grow in branched clusters arising from the leaf axils. Bladdernut is a dense, tall and wide shrub, never a vine. Poison ivy grows as a low, weak shrub or as a vine, climbing trees, posts, and fences.

*trifolia* L. [**American Bladdernut**]
>>Deciduous shrub. Leaf with 3 leaflets, only the middle one stalked, edge sharply toothed. Inconspicuous foliage; fruit changes from green to light brown. Ornamental in September. Native to eastern United States, Canada. In horticulture since 1640. Maximum height 15 ft.
>>>ARCHITECTURE BUILDING: Log Chapel, midway [1*]. ST. EDWARD'S HALL: S lawn [1*].

## HIPPOCASTANACEAE [HORSECHESTNUT FAMILY]

*Aesculus* L. [**Horsechestnut; Buckeye**]

The Ohio buckeye, *A. glabra*, is the state tree of Ohio. Campus legend at Notre Dame says that Ohio State University students planted an Ohio buckeye near or between Alumni and Dillon halls in 1935, when their team met Notre Dame on the football field. If planted, that tree has disappeared. However, there is a horsechestnut, *A. hippocastanum*, growing at the south side of Alumni Hall. Horsechestnut is a coarser tree than the buckeye. It is unlikely that the two species were confused, although they have similar appearances. The wood from the native buckeyes of North America was used to make artificial limbs, baby cradles, and shipping crates, where its light weight was an advantage. Other species are found in southeastern Europe, India, and eastern Asia. *Aesculus* trees are tall and coarse, interesting, but too large for small yards. They are too messy to be used as street trees because of dropping flowers, fruits, leaves, and twigs. The nuts, young growth, and sprouts contain a glycoside, aesculin, that is poisonous to humans and livestock. Bookbinders have used this toxic quality to their advantage by employing a starchy paste made from the nuts in their bindings to deter insects. Native Americans ate a nutritious ground meal derived from the nuts, but only after roasting, mashing, and washing to extract the poisonous principle.

Broad-leaved tree or shrub: deciduous. Leaves large, toothed, palmately compound, in opposite pairs along stem. Flowers large, showy, upright panicles in mid-May; fruit a large, leathery (spiny in some species) capsule that splits to reveal 1-2 large, shiny brown seeds.

*hippocastanum* L. [**Horsechestnut**]

Deciduous tree. 5-7 stalkless leaflets, 10 in. long, double-toothed; bud gummy; fruit spiny. Needs a large area; striking when given enough room. Introduced, native to the Balkan Peninsula. In horticulture since 1756. Young shoots, leaves, flowers and seeds poisonous when eaten. Maximum height 75 ft.

ALUMNI HALL: S side [1*]. BURKE MEMORIAL GOLF COURSE: NE area [3]. CORBY HALL: SE corner, SE 10yd [1*]; W 10yd [1*]. GROTTO OF OUR LADY OF LOURDES: Corby kitchen, walk, W side [1*]. MOREAU SEMINARY: SW corner [1*]. SIEGFRIED HALL: Pasquerilla Hall West, between [1]. SORIN HALL: SE corner, E 60yd [1*].

*octandra* Marsh. [**Yellow Buckeye; Sweet Buckeye**]

Deciduous tree. 5 short-stalked leaflets, fine-toothed, yellow below; fruit smooth, pear-shaped. Flowers yellow. Ornamental in May. Native to Pennsylvania through Georgia to Illinois and Alabama. In horticulture since 1764. Young shoots, leaves, flowers, and seeds poisonous when eaten. Maximum height 75 ft.

HOLY CROSS HOUSE: NE lawn [1].

*parviflora* Walt. [**Bottlebrush Buckeye**]

Deciduous shrub. 5-7 short-stalked leaflets, 8 in. long, wavy-toothed, gray-hairy below; pear-shaped fruit. Wide-spreading form; tolerates shade; large, white flower clusters. Ornamental in June to July. Native to South Carolina, Florida, and Alabama. In horticulture since 1785. Young shoots, leaves, flowers, and seeds poisonous when eaten. Maximum height 15 ft.

CORBY HALL: E wing, N, lawn above Grotto [1*]. LAFORTUNE STUDENT CENTER: Sacred Heart Statue, midway, roadside [1*].

## ACERACEAE [MAPLE FAMILY]

*Acer* L. [**Maple**]

To most North Americans the maples are the most readily recognized trees. The sugar maples lining Notre Dame Avenue are one of the first sights to greet a campus visitor. Records show that maples have been planted on the campus since the turn of the century. Maples are native to north temperate regions and to the mountains of the Tropics. They provide brilliant autumn color in the northern hardwood forests as well as maple syrup and lumber for indoor uses such as cabinetry, musical instruments, and flooring. The sugar maple, *A. saccharum*, is the state tree of Rhode Island, Vermont, West Virginia, and Wisconsin; and the unofficial, but popularly selected, state tree of New York. Maples are the most popular urban lawn and street trees. Their flowers are small but conspicuous because they appear in early spring, before the leaves. Maintaining a healthy lawn under maple trees is difficult because the trees cast dense shade and have shallow roots that rob the topsoil of the same nutrients needed for lawn growth. The native red and sugar maples provide the most colorful autumn display. Norway maple, native to Europe, is less colorful, but the most tolerant maple to urban pollution. Norway maple was first brought to America from Europe at about the time of the Revolutionary War by William Hamilton, a wealthy Philadelphian who developed his 300-acre estate, The Woodlands, into a horticultural showplace. The native silver maple grows very quickly, but has lost favor in landscaping because of its weak wood, which becomes dangerous during ice or wind storms. The smaller Japanese maples and shrubby maples are used as accent plants. They have graceful silhouettes, colorful fruit, or interesting bark and leaf forms. Maple bark is very thin, with the living layer near the surface. For the first few winters, maple trunks should be wrapped to protect this layer from sudden warming by the sun followed by refreezing, resulting in cracks that allow the introduction of diseases and insects.

Broad-leaved tree or shrub: deciduous (some evergreen). Leaves in opposite pairs on stem, either palmately lobed or pinnately compound, both often with toothed edges. Flowers red, yellow, or bright green, in hanging raceme or upright corymb. Fruit a pair of long-winged samaras, called a schizocarp, each with a nutlet.

*circinatum* Pursh [**Vine Maple; Oregon Vine Maple**]

Deciduous tree. Leaf round, 5-9 shallowly palmate lobes, double-toothed; samara wings spread horizontally. Shrubby; stems twisted; flowers white and purple; samaras red. Ornamental in spring, summer, autumn. Native to British Columbia through northern California. In horticulture since 1826. Maximum height 20 ft.

'Little Gem' [**Vine Maple; Oregon Vine Maple**]

Deciduous shrub. Compact, rounded form; leaves smaller than the species. SUPPORT SERVICES BUILDING: S bed [1].

*ginnala* Maxim. [**Amur Maple**]

Deciduous tree. Form often shrubby; leaf palmately 3-lobed, central lobe longer. Leaves glossy green, turning yellow to red; winged fruits red. Ornamental in summer, autumn. Introduced, native to Japan, Manchuria, China. In horticulture since 1860. Maximum height 20 ft.

> BURKE MEMORIAL GOLF COURSE: Scattered throughout [many*]. COLUMBA HALL: Basketball court, NW corner [1]; E wing, SE corner, SE [4]; NE corner, E lawn [1]. FISCHER GRADUATE RESIDENCE COMPLEX: N, woods [1]. HOLY CROSS ANNEX: SW [1]. JUNIPER ROAD: W, at Bulla Rd, S section, roadside [3]. PROVINCE ARCHIVES CENTER: SW corner, S [1]. SORIN HALL: SE corner, SE 15yd [2*].

### *negundo* L. [**Boxelder**]

Deciduous tree. Leaf pinnately compound, 3-5 leaflets; stem green with waxy bloom. Fast growth; cold and drought tolerant; can be weedy. Native to Canada, United States. In horticulture since 1688. Maximum height 50 ft.

> BURKE MEMORIAL GOLF COURSE: NW area [many*]. CAMPUS SECURITY BUILDING: SW corner [6*]. LOG CHAPEL: NW 50yd, lakeside [1*]. ROCKNE MEMORIAL: S, practice green, E side [8]. ST. JOSEPH HALL: W, woods [many*]. UNIVERSITY HEALTH SERVICES: N, near lake [many*].

### *palmatum* Thunb. [**Japanese Maple**]

Deciduous tree. Leaf deeply 5-9 lobed, lobe lance-shaped, edge double-toothed. Graceful habit, often shrubby; delicate leaves. Ornamental in summer. Introduced, native to Korea, China, Japan. In horticulture since 1820. Maximum height 25 ft.

> GROTTO OF OUR LADY OF LOURDES: Above, N side [1*]. HESBURGH CENTER: Court, S bed [1]; Court, W bed [1]. HOLY CROSS HOUSE: Moreau Seminary, S of walk between [3*]. JUNIPER ROAD: W, at Bulla Rd, N section, roadside [3]. MORRIS INN: Court, NW corner [1*]; Court, SW corner [1*]; Main entrance, E beds [2]. PASQUERILLA HALL EAST: W wing, W end, NW plaza [1]. PROVINCE ARCHIVES CENTER: S side, center [1]. SACRED HEART BASILICA: E side [2*].

### 'Atropurpureum' [**Bloodleaf Japanese Maple**]

Deciduous tree. Leaves 5-7 lobed, red. Good red color, but may fade to green later. Ornamental in spring, autumn.

> SUPPORT SERVICES BUILDING: S bed [1].

### f. *dissectum* Maxim. [**Threadleaf Japanese Maple**]

Deciduous tree. Leaf with 7-9 lobes, each narrow and threadlike.

> HESBURGH CENTER: Court, middle bed [2]. WASHINGTON HALL: SW corner [2]; W side [2].

### f. *dissectum* Maxim. 'Crimson Queen' [**Japanese Maple**]

Deciduous tree. Growth mounded; leaf deep red in full sun, lobes finely dissected. Maximum height 4 ft.

> HESBURGH CENTER: SW Plaza, inner section, corner [1].

### f. *dissectum* Maxim. 'Everred' [**Threadleaf Japanese Maple**]

Deciduous tree. Leaf threadlike, deep red fading to green during summer. Maximum height 4 ft.

> ADMINISTRATION (MAIN) BUILDING: Front, E bed [2]; Front, W bed [1].

### f. *dissectum* Maxim. 'Germaine's Gyration' [**Threadleaf Japanese Maple**]

Deciduous tree. Leaf dissected, green turning yellow; side branches twisted. Developed by Bob Vandermoss. Maximum height 7 ft.

> HESBURGH CENTER: Court [2]. SUPPORT SERVICES BUILDING: S bed [1].

### f. *dissectum* Maxim. 'Red Select' [**Japanese Maple**]

Deciduous tree. Dense, rounded form; leaves deep red. Leaves hold color throughout the summer. Maximum height 4 ft.

PASQUERILLA HALL EAST: W wing, W end, NW plaza [2].

### 'Sango Kaku' [Japanese Maple]

Deciduous tree. Leaf 5-7 lobed, margin double-toothed; 1 and 2 year old branches red. Leaves turn yellow red or coral; stems remain red. Ornamental in autumn, winter. Maximum height 25 ft.

SUPPORT SERVICES BUILDING: S bed [1].

### 'Sharp's Pygmy' [Japanese Maple]

Deciduous tree. Dense form; small leaves. Leaves turn deep red. Ornamental in autumn. Maximum height 3 ft.

ADMINISTRATION (MAIN) BUILDING: Front, E bed [1]; Front, W bed [1].

### 'Shishigashira' [Japanese Maple]

Deciduous tree. Dwarf growth; leaf deep green, crinkled. Leaves turn orange. Ornamental in autumn.

HESBURGH CENTER: Court, NW bed [1]; Court, SE bed [1].

### 'Willow Leaf' [Japanese Maple]

Deciduous tree. Leaf black red, lobes narrow and separated. Graceful form. Maximum height 8 ft.

MORRIS INN: Main entrance, E beds [2].

### *platanoides* L. [Norway Maple]

Deciduous tree. Leaf broad, 5-lobed; lobes long-pointed; sap milky. Broad, round shade tree. Ornamental in summer. Introduced, native to Norway, Europe to northern Iran. Maximum height 60 ft.

ARCHITECTURE BUILDING: Corby Hall, between [3]. BURKE MEMORIAL GOLF COURSE: Scattered throughout [many]. CARROLL HALL: SE and SW corners [2]. CAVANAUGH HALL: Main entrance, 50ft [1*]; Main entrance, NW 50ft [1]; NW corner [1 **Commem.**]. FLANNER HALL: S side [3]. FRESHMAN YEAR BUILDING: W side, SW [3]. GALVIN LIFE SCIENCE CENTER: S [3]. GRACE HALL: NE corner [2]; W side [2]. KNIGHTS OF COLUMBUS COUNCIL HALL: Walsh Hall, midway [1*]. KNOTT HALL: S wing, E side [2]. KOONS REHEARSAL HALL: S side [8]. MAINTENANCE CENTER: S side [3]. NORTH DINING HALL: NW entrance [2]. O'SHAUGHNESSY HALL: Vita Dulcedo Spes entrance, S [1]. PASQUERILLA CENTER: NE corner [1]; NW corner [3]; SW corner [1]. SNITE MUSEUM OF ART: Court [1]; S side [6]. ST. JOSEPH'S LAKE: W lawn [1]. STADIUM: E, gate 7 [1]; NE, gates 1 and 2 [1]; NW, gate 16 [1]; SE, gate 8 [1]. STEPAN CENTER: S, walk to Flanner [11]. WALSH HALL: NE corner [1*]. ZAHM HALL: E [3*].

### 'Columnare' [Columnar Norway Maple]

Deciduous tree. Columnar form, 15-20 ft. wide at maturity; leaf smaller with shallower lobes than species. Maximum height 60 ft.

JOYCE ATHLETIC AND CONVOCATION CENTER: S side, parking lots [many].

### 'Crimson King' [Norway Maple]

Deciduous tree. Leaves deep maroon throughout season. Ornamental in summer. Developed in Orleans, France. In horticulture since 1946. Maximum height 50 ft.

COLUMBA HALL: SE, at St. Mary's Lake [1 **Commem.**]. CUSHING HALL OF ENGINEERING: O'Shaughnessy, midway [1 **Commem.**]. JOYCE ATHLETIC AND CONVOCATION CENTER: Gate 3 [3]; S side, parking lots [many]. ST. MARY'S LAKE: E end, W of Grotto [1 **Commem.**]. UNIVERSITY VILLAGE: Playground [1 **Commem.**].

'Crimson Sentry' [**Norway Maple**]

>Deciduous tree. Dense, columnar habit. Leaves dark purple; growth slow. Ornamental in spring, summer. Developed by Princeton Nurseries, New Jersey. Maximum height 25 ft.
>
>>DEBARTOLO CLASSROOM BUILDING: E side, flanking central doors [4].

'Emerald Queen' [**Norway Maple**]

>Deciduous tree. Rounded to oval form; leaves leathery, dark green. Tolerates urban conditions; leaves turn bright yellow. Ornamental in autumn. Maximum height 50 ft.
>
>>JOYCE ATHLETIC AND CONVOCATION CENTER: S, along Edison Rd [many].

'Rubrum' [**Crimson Norway Maple**]

>Deciduous tree. Leaves green turning red. Ornamental in summer, autumn.
>
>>ADMINISTRATION (MAIN) BUILDING: NW corner [1]. CARROLL HALL: W lawn [2*]. FATIMA RETREAT HOUSE: Mission House, garage, midway to lake [1*]; W, Highway 31 entrance, S side [1*]; W, Highway 31 exit, N side [2*]. HOLY CROSS HOUSE: S side [2*]. MOREAU SEMINARY: E side [1].

'Schwedleri' [**Schwedler's Maple**]

>Deciduous tree. Leaves red turning bronzish dark green, then red. Ornamental in summer, autumn.
>
>>ADMINISTRATION (MAIN) BUILDING: Washington Hall, midway [1*]. SACRED HEART BASILICA: E 25yd [1*].

*pseudoplatanus* L. [**Sycamore Maple**]

>Deciduous tree. Leaf 5-lobed; lobe broadly egg-shaped, edge wavy-toothed. Conspicuous winged fruit clusters; salt tolerant. Ornamental in summer. Introduced, native to Europe, western Asia. Maximum height 60 ft.
>
>>CAVANAUGH HALL: Washington Hall, midway [1*]. WASHINGTON HALL: Sacred Heart statue, midway [1*].

'Spaethii' [**Sycamore Maple**]

>Deciduous tree. Leaves purple red below, petioles red. Leaves turn bright red; growth vigorous; susceptible to aphids. Ornamental in Summer, autumn.
>
>>DEBARTOLO CLASSROOM BUILDING: S side, S of E door [1].

*rubrum* L. [**Red Maple**]

>Deciduous tree. Leaf 3-5 lobed, lobes triangular, inner and outer edges toothed. Leaves turn yellow or red. Ornamental in autumn. Native to eastern Canada through Texas. In horticulture since 1860. Maximum height 60 ft.
>
>>BROWNSON HALL: E side [3*]. BURKE MEMORIAL GOLF COURSE: SW corner [3]; SW corner [1]. DILLON HALL: S [3]. FATIMA RETREAT HOUSE: SE corner, E [1]; W side, N [1]. FIELDHOUSE MALL: SE [4]. FITZPATRICK HALL OF ENGINEERING: S side [2]. GALVIN LIFE SCIENCE CENTER: N side lawn, N 30yd [5]; W, main entrance, S of walk [1]. NORTH DINING HALL: NW corner [2]; SW corner [4]. PANGBORN HALL: S [3]. RILEY HALL OF ART AND DESIGN: NE corner [1]. SACRED HEART STATUE: E 10yd [1]. SNITE MUSEUM OF ART: Court [1]. STADIUM: SE, gate 8 [1]; SW, gate 12 [1]. WASHINGTON HALL: W 15yd [1*]; W 25yd [1*].

'Columnare' [**Columnar Red Maple**]

>Deciduous tree. Columnar to pyramidal form.
>
>>HESBURGH LIBRARY: Pool, S, near lamppost C10 [3*].

'Red Sunset' [**Red Maple**]

>Deciduous tree. Pyramidal to rounded form. Good color, leaves orange to red; very hardy; a superior cultivar. Ornamental in autumn. Maximum height 50 ft.

DeBARTOLO CLASSROOM BUILDING: E side, S of N end doors [1]. KNOTT HALL: S wing, S end [2]. SESQUICENTENNIAL COMMONS: E outer bed [2]; SE outer bed [1]; SW outer bed [1]; W outer bed [2].

*saccharinum* L. [**Silver Maple; Soft Maple**]

Deciduous tree. Leaf 5-lobed, lobes deeply divided, silver white below. Leaves silvery in the wind; graceful, weeping but weak branches. Ornamental in summer. Native to Quebec through Florida, west to Oklahoma. In horticulture since 1725. Maximum height 90 ft.

CARROLL HALL: E, along road [3]. CAVANAUGH HALL: NE corner [1]. COLUMBA HALL: Garage, NE [many*]. FATIMA RETREAT HOUSE [many]. FRESHMAN YEAR BUILDING: W parking lot, N [few*]. POST OFFICE: Morris Inn, midway [4]. SORIN HALL: W side, W center, 30yd [1]. ST. JOSEPH HALL: W side, SW 30yd [1]. ST. JOSEPH'S LAKE: Shore [many].

'Laciniatum' [**Cutleaf Silver Maple**]

Leaf deeply divided, lobes narrow.

RADIATION RESEARCH BUILDING: S [1].

'Wieri' [**Wier's Cutleaf Maple**]

Deciduous tree. Leaf deeply divided, lobes narrow, sharp-pointed; branches drooping. Developed by D. B. Wier. In horticulture since 1873.

ARCHITECTURE BUILDING: E 25yd, N of walk [1]; E 25yd, S of walk [1].

*saccharum* Marsh. [**Sugar Maple; Hard Maple**]

Deciduous tree. Leaf 3-5 lobed, lobe margins faintly, widely toothed. Leaves turn yellow, orange or red. Ornamental in autumn. Native to eastern Canada through Texas. In horticulture since 1753. Maximum height 75 ft.

ADMINISTRATION (MAIN) BUILDING: Main entrance, steps, SE 10yd [1*]; NE corner, N, along road [4]. ALUMNI HALL: SE corner, S [3]. ARCHITECTURE BUILDING: Corby Hall, midway [1]. BURKE MEMORIAL GOLF COURSE: Scattered throughout [many]. CAVANAUGH HALL: E side [4]. GALVIN LIFE SCIENCE CENTER: NW corner, N 30yd [2]; SW corner, W 50yd [1]. HESBURGH LIBRARY: E entrance, E [1]. JUNIPER ROAD: ROTC stoplight, N sect., campus-side [4]. KEENAN HALL: SW corner [2]. O'SHAUGHNESSY HALL: Vita Dulcedo Spes entrance, S [1]. PANGBORN HALL: SW corner, SW [1]. SACRED HEART BASILICA: E side door, NE 10yd [1*]. SACRED HEART STATUE: W [2*]. SOUTH DINING HALL: SW corner, S [1]. ST. EDWARD'S HALL: N [1]; S, statue, flanking [2]. STADIUM: E, gate 6 [1]; N, gates 18 and 19 [1]; NE, gates 1 and 2 [1]; SE, gate 9 [1]; SW, gate 12 [1]. WASHINGTON HALL: W entrance, W 20yd [1*].

subsp. *nigrum* (Michx. f.) Desmarais [**Black Maple**]

Deciduous tree. Leaf 3-lobed, drooping, not toothed, yellow green and hairy below. Native to Quebec through Iowa and North Carolina.

CARROLL HALL: SE corner, along walk to lake, N side [1*]; SE corner, along walk to lake, S side [2*]. DECIO FACULTY HALL: SE corner, E 20yd [1]. DILLON HALL: W wing, S, golf course fence, S side [1*]. HESBURGH LIBRARY: E entrance, SE [1]. SACRED HEART STATUE: NW 25yd [1*]. ST. EDWARD'S HALL: N [1].

## ANACARDIACEAE [CASHEW FAMILY]

*Cotinus* Mill. [**Smoketree**]

Smoketree gets its name from its unique appearance during and after flowering. The individual flowers are inconspicuous, but so abundant that they form large panicles. As the floral structures mature, the flower stalks of the sterile flowers, which are covered with long, silky hairs, elongate and appear like clouds of pinkish smoke engulfing the branches. This effect persists from June into August or September. It tolerates dry, rocky soil. Some popular cultivars have purple leaves and purple hairs. *Cotinus* is native to the southeastern United States and from southern Europe to southwestern China.

Broad-leaved shrub or small tree: deciduous, often dioecious. Leaves alternate along stem, simple, smooth-edged with distinctly parallel veins diverging from the central vein. Flowers small, long-stalked, abundant in cloudlike panicles; fruit a small, flattened, kidney-shaped drupe.

*coggygria* Scop. [**Smoketree; Smokebush**]

Deciduous shrub. Leaf oval, 3.5 in. long, blue green, edge smooth, veins parallel. Flowers small, but hairy flower stalks remain, cloudlike, over bush. Ornamental in June to September. Introduced, native to southern Europe to Asia. In horticulture since 1656. Maximum height 15 ft.

Crowley Hall of Music: NE corner [1*]; SE corner [3*]. Sorin Hall: Architecture Building, midway [3*]; NE corner [1*]. Stadium: SE, Angela and Juniper intersection [7*].

'Royal Purple' [**Smoketree; Smokebush**]

Deciduous shrub. Leaves and inflorescences rich purple red. Ornamental in summer, autumn.

Support Services Building: S bed [1].

*Rhus* L. [**Sumac**]

The sumacs are vigorous, broadly colonizing shrubs that are suited to mass plantings on hillsides or in naturalized settings where the soil is well-drained. They offer early, spectacular orange to red autumn color, which is a common sight along railroads and highways. The red, hairy, densely packed fruit panicles at the ends of the branches remain showy from August into winter. These edible fruits are used to make a lemonadelike beverage. Dyes and tanning compounds are derived from many species. Sumac is native to temperate and tropical regions of both hemispheres. Poison ivy and related poisonous species have been transferred from *Rhus* to a separate genus, *Toxicodendron*.

Broad-leaved shrub or clinging vine: deciduous (some evergreen), usually dioecious. Leaves large, odd-pinnately compound with 3-31 leaflets, alternate along stout stems. In *R. hirta* the twigs are extremely hairy, resembling velvety stag's horns. Flowers in panicles; female panicles denser, male larger and loose; fruit a red, hairy drupe.

*aromatica* Ait. [**Fragrant Sumac**]

Deciduous shrub. 3 leaflets, center one stalked, edge toothed above middle; fruit red, in terminal clusters. Fruit hairy, showy; leaves aromatic when crushed; controls erosion. Ornamental in September through autumn. Native to Ontario through Minnesota, Texas, and Florida. In horticulture since 1759. Maximum height 6 ft.

ALUMNI HALL: W court [10*]. ST. JOSEPH'S LAKE: NW, path to Calvary, W side [1].

### *glabra* L. [**Smooth Sumac**]

Deciduous shrub. Stem smooth; 11-31 toothed, smooth leaflets with red central stalk, deep green, waxy below. Leaves turn vivid orange to red; red fruit clusters persistent. Ornamental in autumn, winter. Native to temperate eastern North America. In horticulture since 1620. Maximum height 20 ft.

ST. JOSEPH'S LAKE: Boat house, E [few].

### *hirta* (L.) Sudw. [**Staghorn Sumac**]

Deciduous shrub. 13-27 leaflets, edge toothed, surface dense-hairy; stem velvety-hairy; fruit red. Red fruit clusters showy; leaves turn bright orange to scarlet. Ornamental in autumn through winter. Native to eastern North America. In horticulture since 1629. Maximum height 25 ft.

HOLY CROSS HOUSE: S, lakeside [many*]. POWER PLANT: NW, lakeside [many*]. ST. JOSEPH'S LAKE: NW woods [many*]. UNIVERSITY HEALTH SERVICES: N, slope to lake [many*].

### f. *dissecta* (Rehd.) Reveal [**Cutleaf Staghorn Sumac**]

Deciduous shrub. Teeth on edge of leaflets deeply divided, look slashed between teeth. Leaves delicate and fernlike. Ornamental in summer.

SNITE MUSEUM OF ART: S entrance, E of walk [4].

### *Toxicodendron* Mill. [**Poison Ivy**]

All of the species in this genus are poisonous, causing some degree of dermatitis in one of every two people who come in contact with any part of a plant. The reaction can be severe when droplets of the irritating compound carried by smoke from brush fires are inhaled. The toxic principle is the oleoresin urushiol. The running sores do not spread the rash as some people believe, but it is possible to repeatedly reinfect oneself by handling gardening tools, gloves, or even pets that have been in contact with the plant. The lacquer for the beautiful black lacquerware made in China and Japan comes from one of the toxic plants of this genus, *T. verniciflua*, the varnish or lacquer tree. The toxic principle is extremely difficult to remove from the skin simply with soap because, when in contact with air, it oxidizes and becomes gummy, not unlike the lacquer of the related species. However, flushing with large amounts of cool water as quickly as possible is still helpful in limiting the reaction. The admonition "leaflets three, let it be," is helpful in identifying poison ivy, but sweeps some innocent plants into its net. These can be differentiated by various combinations of morphological features. Strawberries, blackberries, and raspberries all have leaves made of 3 leaflets (trifoliolate) like poison ivy, but also have familiar edible fruits and may have spines, which poison ivy never has. Bladdernut (*Staphylea trifolia*), boxelder (*Acer negundo*), and some young ashes (*Fraxinus* spp.) all have similar trifoliolate leaves, but they are definitely trees or vigorous, large shrubs with papery or winged seeds, never vines or low weak shrubs like poison ivy, which has white, berrylike fruits. Also, bladdernut, boxelder, and the ashes all have leaves arranged in opposite pairs along the stems whereas those of poison ivy are arranged alternately. The vine form of poison ivy is the only vining plant with short, fuzzy aerial roots that attach it to tree trunks. The *Parthenocissus* vines, both Boston ivy and Virginia creeper, do not have these fuzzy aerial roots. They grasp by small round disks. Poison ivy usually climbs in a straight line whereas most other vines twine around the branches on which they climb. Another vine with aerial roots is English ivy, *Hedera*. Its leaves are lobed, never composed of 3 separate leaflets like poison ivy. During winter, vines with fuzzy aerial roots should be viewed with suspicion as should any low, leafless woody plants on the forest floor with fuzzy buds that are stalked and alternately arranged along the stems. Poison ivy is broadly distributed in temperate and subtropical regions. It is an opportunistic plant found in disturbed sites where it is carried by people, animals, and birds. It may not be found deep in an undisturbed forest, but it is often abundant along paths and trails of state or national parks, which might look pristine, but are subjected to constant foot traffic. The poison ivy of the Midwest is two separate species, the climbing *T. radicans* and the low-growing *T. rydbergii*, which was defined as a separate species by Edward Lee Greene, whose most important work was his lifelong study of the flora of western North America. He named more than 4,000 new species of plants during his career, which ended with his death in 1915. Greene's priceless herbarium and collection of rare botanical books are housed at Notre Dame.

Broad-leaved shrub, small tree, or clinging vine: deciduous (some evergreen). Leaves alternate along climbing (by aerial roots) or low-growing stems, compound with 3 leaflets (trifoliolate) that each may be irregularly lobed or toothed. Flowers small, green white, in several-flowered panicles at leaf axils; fruit a white, 1-seeded, berry-like drupe.

*radicans* (L.) Kuntze [**Poison Ivy**]
> Deciduous vine. 3 leaflets, margin and surface variable; aerial roots on stem; fruit white, in leaf axils. Native to temperate North America. All parts poisonous if touched or eaten. Maximum height 10 ft.
>> HOLY CROSS ANNEX: St. Joseph Hall, woods between [many*]. ST. JOSEPH'S LAKE: Lakeside [many]. ST. MARY'S LAKE: Lakeside [many].

*rydbergii* (Small ex Rydb.) Greene [**Poison Ivy**]
> Deciduous shrub. 3 leaflets, edge wavy-toothed, folded along axis, hairy veins below; no aerial roots. Native to North America west to Arizona and British Columbia. All parts poisonous if touched or eaten. Maximum height 2 ft.
>> HOLY CROSS ANNEX: St. Joseph Hall, woods between [many*]. ST. JOSEPH'S LAKE: Lakeside [many]. ST. MARY'S LAKE: Lakeside [many].

## SIMAROUBACEAE [QUASSIA FAMILY]

*Ailanthus* Desf. [**Ailanthus; Tree-of-heaven**]
> *Ailanthus* is native from Asia to Australia. One species, *A. altissima*, is naturalized in North America and from central to southern Europe. Here it is found in disturbed, inhospitable, or neglected urban sites. It is vigorous and tenacious, found sprouting in gaps in pavement, along foundations, or any other impossible situation. Although it provides greenery where nothing else will grow, it has weak wood, causes heaved sidewalks, and its male flowers have an objectionable odor. The tree-of-heaven was brought to Europe by French Jesuit missionaries who found it growing in China. In 1784 it was first planted in America by William Hamilton. At that time, it was an exotic novelty of tropical

appearance that was assigned to the gardens and estates of the wealthy.

Broad-leaved tall tree: deciduous, usually dioecious. Leaves alternate on stem, pinnately compound, each with 13-25 leaflets. Flowers yellow green, borne in long panicles during mid-June, female flowers odorless, male flowers called "vile." Fruit a samara, like maple, but with seed or nutlet centered between 2 wings. The leaves are similar to those of the ashes, but the bases of *Ailanthus* leaflets are notched.

*altissima* (Mill.) Swingle [**Tree-of-heaven**]

Deciduous tree. Leaflets 11-25, edge smooth, 1-4 large teeth at base; twig yellow or red brown, stout. Weedy tree that tolerates extreme environmental conditions. Introduced, native to China; naturalized in the United States. In horticulture since 1784. May cause a skin rash on some people. Maximum height 60 ft.

CAMPUS SECURITY BUILDING: N side, E of parking lot [8]; NW 60yd, along road [2*]. PASQUERILLA HALL EAST: W wing, NW corner [5]. SACRED HEART STATUE: SE 50yd [1*].

# RUTACEAE [RUE FAMILY]

*Evodia* J. R. Forst. & G. Forst. [**Evodia**]

The evodias are uncommon small trees with aromatic bark. Ornamentally, they have abundant small white flowers that bloom from late June or July through August, when few other trees are flowering; glossy, dark green, ashlike leaves; and red to black fruits that remain through November. Evodia needs full sun and rich, moist but well-drained soil. Diseases and insects are not serious problems. They are native to Madagascar, eastern Asia through Australia, and Polynesia.

Leaves in opposite pairs on stem, odd-pinnately compound with 7-11 leaflets. Flowers small, white appear in masses (corymbs) on the current season's growth during midsummer; fruit a red to black capsule that splits to release shiny blackish seeds. The leaves resemble those of the more common ashes, but ash is not aromatic when stem or leaves are rubbed; and the winged fruits (samaras) of ash are distinctly different. Another less common tree that can be confused with evodia is *Phellodendron*. They are differentiated by their buds. Those of evodia are visible on the stem at the base of the leaf petiole. *Phellodendron* buds are surrounded and hidden by the base of the leaf petiole.

*danielii* (Benn.) Hemsl. [**Chinese Evodia**]

Deciduous tree. Leaf 15 in. long, 7-11 leaflets, hairy below; bud exposed and visible at leaf base on stem. Open tree for small lawns; white flowers in clusters, bloom late. Ornamental in June to August. Introduced, native to northern China, Korea. In horticulture since 1905. Maximum height 30 ft.

COMPUTING CENTER AND MATH BUILDING: E side [1]. ST. JOSEPH HALL: Lakeside, base of steps [40*].

*Phellodendron* Rupr. [**Cork-tree**]

These trees are grown ornamentally for their foliage, rugged appearance, and corky bark. In their native eastern Asia, they are used medicinally and grown for timber. Although the cork-tree is not tall, it is too wide-spreading for use in small lawns. It has no disease or insect problems and is quite hardy.

Broad-leaved tree: deciduous, dioecious. Leaves in opposite pairs on stem, odd-pinnately compound with 5-11 leaflets. Small, yellow green female flowers bloom in late spring, in panicles; fruit an aromatic, juicy, berrylike black drupes. While the leaves look very much like those of the ashes, they can be separated by the presence of corky bark, aromatic foliage, and juicy fruits in *Phellodendron*. Another, more uncommon, tree that is similar is *Evodia*. *Phellodendron* buds are completely hidden in the base of the leaf petiole. The buds of *Evodia* are visible on the stem at the base of the leaf petiole.

*amurense* Rupr. [**Cork-tree**]

> Deciduous tree. Leaf 15 in. long, 5-13 leaflets; bud hidden under base of leaf petiole on stem. Beautiful, corklike bark develops in old age. Introduced, native to Japan, China. In horticulture since 1856. Maximum height 45 ft.
>
> > BURKE MEMORIAL GOLF COURSE: S central area, W of cemetery [2]; Tee 4 [1].
> > SORIN HALL: W, triangle of shrubbery [2*].

# ARALIACEAE [GINSENG FAMILY]

*Hedera* L. [**Ivy**]

These evergreen vines, especially English ivy, may be the most readily recognized of all plants in Western culture due, in part, to their use as indoor plants. They are native to Europe, the Mediterranean, and western Asia. In the landscape, they are used as ground covers for shady areas and to cover walls and masonry. The aerial roots that form along the stems attach themselves to surfaces. The familiar lobed leaves are actually a juvenile form. The unlobed mature leaves and flowering branches may form only after many years or not at all. The leaves and rarely seen fruits are poisonous. They contain hederagenin, a saponic glycoside that affects red blood cells after absorption.

> Broad-leaved vine or shrub (rare): evergreen. Leaves alternate along aerial root-bearing stems, usually 3-5 lobed and smooth-edged. Flowers rare, green white, in umbels; fruit a small, berrylike black drupe with 3-5 seeds.

*helix* L. [**English Ivy**]

> Evergreen vine. Stem climbs by aerial rootlets; leaf 3-5 lobed, becomes egg-shaped in old age. Can cover walls or be used as a low ground cover. Introduced, native to Europe, western Asia, northern Africa. Leaves and fruit poisonous when eaten. Maximum height 90 ft.
>
> > BROWNSON HALL: E side [1*]. FITZPATRICK HALL OF ENGINEERING: S side, E door, E planter [bed]; S side, W door, E planter [bed]. HESBURGH LIBRARY: S, main entrance plaza, flanking [beds*]. SACRED HEART BASILICA: Sacristy, N entrance, E side [1*].

*Kalopanax* Miq. [**Ornamental Panax**]

*Kalopanax* provides uncommon, medium-sized, rounded shade trees. They are taller in the wild in their native China, Manchuria, and Japan. The large leaves, resembling maple or sweetgum, give them an almost tropical appearance. The prickles on the branches disappear with age. The stems are stout, even clublike, which makes them appear coarse in winter, especially when young. There are no serious disease or insect problems. Many plants in the Araliaceae, the ginseng family, are ingested as tonics by people worldwide. During the 1984 Moscow Olympics, the Russian Olympic team drank a tonic made from one of these plants in a closely related genus. It was *Acanthopanax senticosus* or Siberian ginseng. In the literature of medical botany, this species and the more well known genus of ginseng, *Panax*, are discussed as panaceas, those compounds, usually tonics, used by healthy people to make them feel even better. While pharmacologically or physiologically active components are found in some tonics (glycosides in *Panax*), they have not been fully characterized and their effects are difficult to quantify. The desire by many to profit, either directly or financially, from the use of ginseng has resulted in the almost complete extirpation from the wild of the small, shade-loving, slow-growing North American ginseng, *P. quinquefolius*.

Broad-leaved, often hairy or prickly tree: deciduous. Leaves alternate along stem, palmately 5-7 lobed, margin toothed. Flowers small, white, in July and August, in small ball-like clusters grouped in larger panicles; fruit a small black drupe.

*pictus* (Thunb.) Nakai [**Maple-leaf Panax**]

Deciduous tree. Stem stout, yellow brown, prickly; leaf palmate, 5-7 toothed lobes, hairy veins below. Uncommon but fine shade tree. Introduced, native to China, Korea, Japan. In horticulture since 1865. Maximum height 60 ft.

var. *magnificus* (Zab.) Nakai [**Maple-leaf Panax**]

Deciduous tree. Prickles rare to absent on stem; leaf dense-hairy below, lobes egg-shaped.

SORIN HALL: N end, NNW 5yd [1*].

var. *maximowiczii* (Van Houtte) Hara [**Prickly Panax**]

Deciduous tree. Leaf hairy below, lobes oblong, deeply cut beyond middle of leaf.

SORIN HALL: N end, NNE 5yd [1*].


# APOCYNACEAE [DOGBANE FAMILY]

*Vinca* L. [**Periwinkle; Myrtle**]

Periwinkle is a popular evergreen ground cover for sunny or shady areas. It has glossy leaves and pleasing, but not spectacular, lilac to blue flowers in April. It is native to Europe, northern Africa, and central Asia, but it has escaped from cultivation in North America and can often be found on the floor of woods.

Broad-leaved trailing shrub: evergreen. Leaves in opposite pairs along trailing stem, simple, glossy, edge smooth. Flower slightly funnel-shaped with 5 broad, reflexed lobes; fruit, rarely formed in cultivation, a dry, cylindrical follicle, opens at 1 seam to drop 6-8 seeds.

*minor* L. [**Common Periwinkle; Running Myrtle**]

Evergreen ground cover. Leaf simple, oblong to egg-shaped, shiny dark green above, lighter below. Flower lilac blue, 1 in. wide, attractive. Introduced, native to Europe, western Asia; escaped from cultivation in the United States. Maximum height 0.5 ft.

ARCHITECTURE BUILDING: E entrance, N side [bed]. COMMUNITY CEMETERY: Cross, base [bed*]. CORBY HALL: Front, Corby statue [bed*]; Main entrance, flanking [beds*]. GALVIN LIFE SCIENCE CENTER: W [beds]. GROTTO OF OUR LADY OF LOURDES: SW corner [bed]. HESBURGH LIBRARY: Pool, S end, flanking [beds*]. MORRISSEY HALL: E, along wall [bed]. OLD COLLEGE: Main entrance [bed*]. SNITE MUSEUM OF ART: Court [beds]. ST. JOSEPH'S LAKE [many].

## ASCLEPIADACEAE [MILKWEED FAMILY]

*Periploca* L. [**Silkvine**]

Silkvine is grown on arbors and trellises as a twining ornamental for its fragrant, green to purple flowers of June or August and for its glossy leaves. The name silkvine refers to the tufts of long, silky hairs attached to the seeds. The seeds of milkweed, which is in the same family, are similar. Silkvine is native to the Mediterranean, eastern Asia, and tropical Africa. At Notre Dame, a silkvine grows on the south side of the Main Building. It cannot attach itself to the building, but uses the Boston ivy, which is clinging to the bricks, for its support. The vine has been there growing since at least 1909. Julius Nieuwland, C.S.C., botanist and chemist at Notre Dame, collected a sample from the plant on June 8, 1909. That specimen can be found in his herbarium, which is housed in the Galvin Life Science Center. Diverging somewhat from his usually professional, unemotional manner in matters of botany, Father Nieuwland wrote on the paper on which the specimen is mounted, "Cultivated. Said to have been transplanted from St. Joseph River Bank by the N.D. gardener. Certainly a mistake!!" But his interest in the plant did not seem to wane for he collected another sample from the same plant on June 10, 1929. This time he simply labelled it with date collected and location. Father Hebert's herbarium also holds a specimen that he collected eight days after Father Nieuwland in 1929. The two priests were certainly enjoying their shared passion for botany and plant collection during that time.

Broad-leaved twining vine: deciduous. Leaves in opposite pairs on twining stems, simple, smooth-edged, glossy dark green above and paler below. Flowers green purple, in long-stalked cymes; fruit a many-seeded long, thin podlike follicle.

*graeca* L. [**Grecian Silkvine**]

Deciduous vine. Leaf simple, to 5 in. long, egg-shaped or oblong, dark green, shiny. Climbs by twining; flower 1 in. wide, deep maroon and green. Introduced, native to southeastern Europe, western Asia. Maximum height 40 ft.

ADMINISTRATION (MAIN) BUILDING: SE corner, wall [1*].

## SOLANACEAE [NIGHTSHADE FAMILY]

*Lycium* L. [**Matrimony-vine**]

Matrimony-vine is a clambering shrub with thorny, arching branches. It was popular during earlier times because its branches become loaded with small, bright red fruits in autumn. It has lost favor because of its coarse, rank growth. It is native to tropical and warm temperate regions of both hemispheres. It has been poisonous to cattle and sheep after large quantities were eaten.

Broad-leaved, often thorny, shrub: deciduous or evergreen. Leaves alternate but closely clustered along thorny stem, small, gray green, simple, smooth-edged. Flowers small but numerous, solitary or clustered at leaf axils, lilac-colored, bell-shaped, 3-5 lobed; fruit a small, red, juicy berry with several seeds.

*halimifolium* Mill. [**Matrimony-vine**]
>Deciduous shrub. Stem spiny; leaf narrow, 2.5 in. long; 1-3 flowers at each leaf node. Branches arching; berries orange red, small. Introduced, native to Europe, Asia; naturalized in the United States. Poisonous to grazing livestock. Maximum height 10 ft.
>>PARIS HOUSE: E hedge, S end [1*].

*Solanum* L. [**Nightshade**]
>This genus, distributed worldwide, contains some important food plants (potato and eggplant), many ornamental shrubs that are hardy only in frost-free regions, some medicinal plants, and some aggressively weedy species that have escaped from cultivation and become naturalized in North America. One shrubby, climbing species commonly weedy in northern Indiana woodlands, riverbanks, and gardens is bitter nightshade, *S. dulcamara*. All parts of the plant, but especially the unripe green berries, should be considered poisonous. The toxic principle is the glyco-alkaloid solanine, which, when eaten, results in both nervous symptoms and more direct irritation of the gastrointestinal system. Several plants within the genera *Solanum* and *Atropa* bear the common name nightshade. They are all poisonous to varying degrees.
>Broad-leaved tree, shrub, vine, or herbaceous plant: deciduous. Leaves alternate along sprawling stems, simple or 3-5 lobed. Flowers violet, 5-lobed, wheel or bell-shaped like tomato and eggplant; fruit a small, juicy, red, several-seeded berry.

*dulcamara* L. [**Bitter Nightshade**]
>Deciduous vine. Leaf to 4 in. long with 1-3 lobes at base; flower purple; fruit red. Can be shrubby or climbing. Introduced, native to Europe, Asia. Unripe berries poisonous when eaten. Maximum height 15 ft.
>>LEWIS HALL: N, lakeside [few*]. ST. JOSEPH'S LAKE: N slope at St. Joseph Hall [many].

# VERBENACEAE [VERBENA FAMILY]

*Callicarpa* L. [**Beautyberry**]
>Beautyberry is an apt name for these ornamental shrubs. The tight, many-fruited clusters of berrylike fruits turn bright bluish lilac in late autumn, standing out in sharp contrast to the yellowing leaves. *Callicarpa* is native to the tropics and subtropics of Asia, Australia, and North and Central America. One species, *C. americana*, reaches the United States, ranging from Virginia to Texas.
>Broad-leaved tree or shrub: evergreen or deciduous. Leaves in opposite pairs, simple. Flowers pink, white, blue, or purple, 4-lobed, in dense cymes at leaf axils; fruit purple, a 4-celled, berrylike drupe.

*bodinieri* Lév. [**Bodinier Beautyberry**]
>Deciduous shrub. Branches erect; leaf narrow-elliptic, 5 in. long, toothed, hairy below. Flowers lilac; fruit blue lilac, in dense clusters. Ornamental in July to October. Introduced, native to central, western China. In horticulture since 1887. Maximum height 10 ft.
>>SUPPORT SERVICES BUILDING: N bed [2].

## OLEACEAE [OLIVE FAMILY]

*Forsythia* Vahl. [**Forsythia**]

Forsythia is popular as a very early spring flowering shrub. The bright yellow flowers form on long arching branches. The graceful form is lost if the bushes are pruned. Forsythias are effective in massed, hillside plantings and when seen in flower from a distance. They are undistinguished during the remainder of the year. They are native to southeastern Europe and eastern Asia and barely hardy here. The flower buds on all branches above the snow line are frequently killed during winters when temperatures reach -10° to -15°F. As they flower in the spring, they are extremely sensitive to late frosts, which can be disappointing to the gardener.

Broad-leaved shrub: deciduous. Leaves in opposite pairs on stem, simple or 3-lobed, margins toothed, at least near tip. Flowers bright yellow, trumpet-shaped, each with 4 recurved lobes, bloom before leaves appear in March and April; fruit a small, brown capsule with many winged seeds.

× *intermedia* Zab.: *F. suspensa* × *F. viridissima* [**Border Forsythia**]

Deciduous shrub. Stem brown, internode chambered, node solid; leaf to 5 in. long, toothed above middle. Yellow flowers very showy and early, but susceptible to late frost. Ornamental in early spring. In horticulture since 1885. Maximum height 10 ft.

KNOTT HALL: W wing, S side [8]. LAFORTUNE STUDENT CENTER: SE, fountain, N side [8]. NORTH DINING HALL: S door, W [many]. OUTDOOR WAY OF THE CROSS: Station 2 [10*]; Station 8 [1*]. PASQUERILLA HALL EAST: N wing, E side [8]; W door [bed]; W wing, S side [5]. PASQUERILLA HALL WEST: E door [bed]; E wing, S side [3]; N wing, W side [11]. SIEGFRIED HALL: E wing, N side [3]; E wing, S side [6]; S wing, S end [5].

'Vitellina' [**Vitelline Forsythia**]

Deciduous shrub. Flowers deep yellow, 1 in. long; growth upright. Developed by Späth Nurseries, Berlin, Germany.

HOWARD HALL: S wing, E end [3*].

*suspensa* (Thunb.) Vahl [**Weeping Forsythia**]

Deciduous shrub. Stem brown, internode hollow, node solid; leaf toothed, often lobed at base. Branches arching or spreading. Introduced, native to China. Maximum height 10 ft.

HURLEY HALL OF BUSINESS ADMINISTRATION: S entrance, E [1]. OUTDOOR WAY OF THE CROSS: Station 10, S, along walk [1*].

*viridissima* Lindl. [**Greenstem Forsythia**]

Deciduous shrub. Stem green, internode and node chambered; leaf 6 in. long, wider and toothed above middle. Flowers yellow green, 1 in. wide, less showy than other forsythias. Introduced, native to China. In horticulture since 1845. Maximum height 10 ft.

WASHINGTON HALL: S side [1].

*Fraxinus* L. [**Ash**]

The ashes are popular street and shade trees of vigorous, upright growth that can tolerate harsh conditions after they are established. They are native to temperate areas, especially of North America, with a few species reaching the tropics. The Green ash, *F. pennsylvanica*, is the state tree of North Dakota, where it tolerates extremely cold and dry conditions.   Ash is important for timber. Baseball bats, hockey sticks, and other sports equipment is made of white ash because it is tough, slightly pliant, and not too heavy. Green ash, which is slightly heavier but otherwise similar, is used for oars. Blue ash, which grows to 120 feet tall in the Wabash River valley, is the heaviest of the native species, but still used for spade and shovel handles. The common name refers to its sap, which turns blue when exposed to air. The inner bark was used by the pioneers to make a blue dye. Blue ash twigs are distinctive among the ashes because they are square in cross section, the result of corky wings. The seedless male trees are preferred in the landscape.

Broad-leaved medium or tall tree: deciduous, usually dioecious. Leaves in opposite pairs on stem, odd-pinnately compound. Male and female flowers usually on separate trees. Only one species, *F. ornus* of Europe and Asia, has showy flowers with petals. The other species are inconspicuous in flower. Fruit a 1-seeded, winged samara.

*americana* L. [**White Ash**]

Deciduous tree. Leaflet stalked, dark green above, waxy white below; shoot and petiole hairless; bud brown. Too large for small yards; leaves turn yellow to maroon. Ornamental in early autumn. Native to eastern North America to Texas. In horticulture since 1724. Maximum height 80 ft.

BURKE MEMORIAL GOLF COURSE: SE corner, SE [few]. COLUMBA HALL: Front, W of road [3*]. HOLY CROSS HOUSE: SE, lake slope [many*]. MOREAU SEMINARY: W end, S [1]. PARIS HOUSE: S, front yard [1]. ST. JOSEPH'S LAKE: NW woods [4*]. STADIUM: E, gate 6 [1]; E, gates 4 and 5 [2]; S, gate 11 [1]; SE, gate 8 [1].

'Ascidiata' [**Pitcher Ash**]

Deciduous tree. Base of each leaflet funnel-shaped, resembles the lip of a pitcher. In horticulture since 1910.

PRESBYTERY: NE corner [1*].

'Autumn Blaze' [**White Ash**]

Deciduous tree. Oval form; leaves turn purple. Tolerates harsh, cold, and dry conditions. Ornamental in early autumn.

ZAHM HALL: N side [1].

'Autumn Purple' [**White Ash**]

Deciduous tree. Male tree; pyramidal to rounded form; leaves turn red purple, lasting 2-4 weeks. Ornamental in autumn. Maximum height 45 ft.

ZAHM HALL: NW end, N [2].

f. *iodocarpa* Fern. [**Purple-fruited Ash**]

Deciduous tree. Fruit conspicuously red purple in summer.

COMPUTING CENTER AND MATH BUILDING: SW corner, SW 100yd [1*].

*angustifolia* Vahl [**Eurasian Ash**]

Deciduous tree. Lower leaflets not stalked, upper stalked and hairless; bud brown, dome-shaped. Introduced, native to southern Europe, North Africa, western Asia. In horticulture since 1800. Maximum height 75 ft.

UNIVERSITY CLUB: NW, SW, flanking parking lot [4].

*nigra* Marsh. [**Black Ash**]

Deciduous tree. Lower leaflets not stalked, upper stalked and hairy; bud dark brown, pointed, conical. Very hardy; narrow form; open shade. Native to Newfoundland through Iowa to Arkansas. In horticulture since 1800. Maximum height 50 ft.

ST. MARY'S LAKE: NW corner, W 8yd [1].

*pennsylvanica* Marsh. [**Green Ash**]

Deciduous tree. All leaflets stalked, rusty or green-hairy below; shoot and petiole hairy; bud brown. Pyramidal when young, becoming irregular; leaves turn yellow. Ornamental in autumn. Native to Nova Scotia through Manitoba to Texas and Florida. In horticulture since 1824. Maximum height 60 ft.

BURKE MEMORIAL GOLF COURSE: NW area [few]. CALVARY: St. Joseph Hall, woods between [many*]. COMPUTING CENTER AND MATH BUILDING: S door, E side [1]. FRESHMAN YEAR BUILDING: W parking lot, N end, W 20yd, roadside [1*]. GALVIN LIFE SCIENCE CENTER: S end, Juniper road, E side [1]. HAGGAR HALL: NW corner, N 15yd [1*]. HAMMES BOOKSTORE: N basketball court, N [2]. KNIGHTS OF COLUMBUS COUNCIL HALL: S entrance, W side [1*]. KNOTT HALL: S wing, E door circle [1]. LOFTUS SPORTS CENTER: W side, center [3]. SIEGFRIED HALL: W door, circle [1]. ST. JOSEPH HALL: Calvary, woods between [few*]. ST. JOSEPH'S LAKE: NE at base of steps [1*]; NW woods [many*]; SW end, Calvary, junction of walks [1*].

'Marshall's Seedless' [**Green Ash**]

Deciduous tree. Male, seedless tree; leaf shiny, dark green. Leaves turn yellow. Ornamental in Autumn. Developed by Marshall Nurseries, Arlington, Nebraska. In horticulture since 1959. Maximum height 50 ft.

MORRIS INN: E [2]. NORTH DINING HALL: N end, E [2]; S end, E [3].

'Summit' [**Green Ash**]

Deciduous tree. Upright, symmetrical form with straight central trunk; tree female and seed-producing. Leaves turn yellow. Ornamental in autumn. Developed by Summit Nurseries, Stillwater, Minnesota. In horticulture since 1948. Maximum height 45 ft.

JUNIPER ROAD: North Gate to Joyce Athletic and Convocation Center, flanking Juniper Rd [38].

*quadrangulata* Michx. [**Blue Ash**]

Deciduous tree. Twig square, 4 corky wings along stem; leaflets stalked; bud gray to red brown. Tolerates drought and limestone soils; leaves turn pale yellow. Ornamental in autumn. Native to Michigan through Arkansas and Tennessee. In horticulture since 1823. Maximum height 70 ft.

CORBY HALL: Old College, midway [1*]. FRESHMAN YEAR BUILDING: Brownson court [1*]. MOREAU SEMINARY: W end, lakeside [1*].

*Ligustrum* L. [**Privet**]

The privets can withstand heavy pruning and are most frequently grown as clipped hedges, in which case the flowers are rarely seen. The white flowers that form nodding clusters in early summer are fragrant, but one component of the odor is trimethylamine, which smells like ammonia. Many people find it offensive. The privets are native to Europe, northern Africa, and from eastern and southeastern Asia to Australia. The blue black fruits remain on the shrubs until winter, when they are eaten by birds. Although the berries have been reported to be poisonous, the toxic principle is unknown.

Broad-leaved shrub or small tree: deciduous or evergreen. Leaves in opposite pairs on stem, simple, margins may be hairy. Flowers creamy white, funnel-shaped, small upright panicles at leaf axils; fruit a blue black, berry-like drupe with 1-4 seeds.

*amurense* Carrière [**Amur Privet**]

> Deciduous shrub. Stem, petiole, midrib below densely hairy; leaf narrow, elliptic; branches stiff, upright. Used for hedges, withstands severe pruning. Introduced, native to northern China. In horticulture since 1860. Fruit may be poisonous when eaten. Maximum height 15 ft.
>
> > HOLY CROSS HOUSE: NW side [hedge].

*obtusifolium* Siebold & Zucc. [**Border Privet**]

> Deciduous shrub. Stem and leaf lower surface hairy; leaf elliptic to oblong; branches spreading, horizontal. Used as a screen or hedge. Introduced, native to Japan. In horticulture since 1860. Fruit may be poisonous when eaten. Maximum height 12 ft.
>
> > BADIN HALL: N wing, N side [10*]. FATIMA RETREAT HOUSE: Calvary, SW 15yd [1]. ROCKNE MEMORIAL: E, front entrance, S [1].

var. *regelianum* (Koehne) Rehd. [**Regel's Privet**]

> Deciduous shrub. Leaf more hairy than that of the species; branches grow in horizontal planes. Maximum height 5 ft.
>
> > KNOTT HALL: W wing, N walk, flanking central planter [hedge]. SIEGFRIED HALL: N, flanking central bed [hedge].

*ovalifolium* Hassk. [**California Privet**]

> Deciduous shrub. Stem hairless when mature; leaf shiny dark green above, yellow green below. Introduced, native to Japan. In horticulture since 1847. Fruit may be poisonous when eaten. Maximum height 15 ft.
>
> > CUSHING HALL OF ENGINEERING: NE corner [1]. LAFORTUNE STUDENT CENTER: W entrance, W 30yd [3*].

*vulgare* L. [**Common Privet; European Privet**]

> Deciduous shrub. Stem hairy; leaf narrowly elliptic, not hairy below, thick but not leathery. Introduced, native to Europe, northern Africa; naturalized in the United States. Fruit may be poisonous when eaten. Maximum height 15 ft.
>
> > LYONS HALL: S [hedge]. O'SHAUGHNESSY HALL: E side [15*]. ZAHM HALL: SW corner [hedge*].

'Chlorocarpum' [**Green-fruited Privet**]

> Deciduous shrub. Fruit greenish yellow.
>
> > CARROLL HALL: NW, lakeside [many].


*Syringa* L. [**Lilac**]

> The lilacs, with their showy, fragrant panicles of white to purple, but usually lilac flowers, are some of the most popular and familiar ornamental shrubs grown. Hundreds of cultivars with single or double petals and various colors have been developed through horticultural breeding programs. Pruning should be done immediately after flowering in late spring because the next year's flower buds begin forming by early summer and would be removed by later pruning. The most serious problem of lilac is powdery mildew, a gray fungus that can coat the leaves during warm, humid summers or where air circulation is restricted around the shrubs. Growing plants in the open and removing the oldest branches at the base of the plant to improve air circulation and light penetration can help slow the disease, which will weaken the plant over time. Lilacs are common in North American gardens, but they are native only to southeastern Europe and eastern Asia.
>
> Broad-leaved shrub or small tree: deciduous. Leaves opposite on stem, simple,

smooth-edged, usually hairless on both surfaces. Flower a tube with 4 reflexed lobes, fragrant, in panicles; fruit a dry, leathery capsule that splits along 2 seams to release winged seeds.

× *chinensis* Willd.: *S. persica* × *S. vulgaris* [**Chinese Lilac**]
Deciduous shrub. Shoot hairless; leaf 3 in. long, medium to dark green, hairless. Flower lilac to purple, fragrant, less coarse than common lilac. Ornamental in middle of May. Developed in Rouen, France. In horticulture since 1777. Maximum height 15 ft.
CROWLEY HALL OF MUSIC: E [1]. WASHINGTON HALL: NW corner [2].

*meyeri* C. K. Schneid. [**Meyer Lilac**]
Deciduous shrub. Shoot hairy; leaf 1.75 in., shiny dark green above, pale with hairs below on veins at base. Dense, evenly rounded form with masses of fragrant, lilac flowers. Ornamental in May. Introduced, native to northern China, but now unknown in the wild. In horticulture since 1908. Maximum height 8 ft.
GALVIN LIFE SCIENCE CENTER: NW corner [hedge].

'Palibin' [**Meyer Lilac**]
Deciduous shrub. Compact growth, broader than tall, to 7 ft. wide; flower buds red purple, open light pink. Flower clusters dense, cover plant when in bloom. Ornamental in May. Maximum height 5 ft.
DEBARTOLO CLASSROOM BUILDING: W side, midway N and S of doors [8]. SUPPORT SERVICES BUILDING: N bed (standard) [1].

*reticulata* (Blume) Hara [**Japanese Tree Lilac**]
Deciduous tree. Shoot not hairy; leaf 5.5 in., dark above, gray green and veiny below; stem dotted, brown. Bark cherrylike; flowers white, fragrant, remaining 2 weeks. Ornamental in middle of June, winter. Introduced, native to Japan. In horticulture since 1876. Maximum height 30 ft.
BROWNSON HALL: S, court entrance [2]. CORBY HALL: SE corner [2*]. HOWARD HALL: N wing, E end, S [1]. LEWIS HALL: Patio [6*]. MORRIS INN: N parking lot [1]. PANGBORN HALL: SE corner, golf course fence, S [1]. SUPPORT SERVICES BUILDING: E, flanking parking lot [2]; S bed [1].

*vulgaris* L. [**Common Lilac**]
Deciduous shrub. Shoot and leaf hairless; leaf 5 in. long, blue green; stem brown, ridged, with small dots. Flowers lilac, very fragrant; plant insect and disease prone. Ornamental in early to middle of May. Introduced, native to southern Europe. In horticulture since 1563. Maximum height 20 ft.
ADMINISTRATION (MAIN) BUILDING: SW corner [few]. CORBY HALL: Architecture Bldg, midway [2*]. CROWLEY HALL OF MUSIC: SW corner [1*]. FATIMA RETREAT HOUSE: NE corner, N [1*]. FISHER HALL: S wing, E side [10*]. FRESHMAN YEAR BUILDING: W parking lot, SW corner [1]. HOLY CROSS ANNEX: W, hedge [hedge*]. KOONS REHEARSAL HALL: N, flanking E-W walk [6]. MORRISSEY HALL: SE corner [1]. OUTDOOR WAY OF THE CROSS: Station 2, E, lakeside [1*]. SACRED HEART BASILICA: SE corner, E 40yd [1*]. SORIN HALL: E, roadside [1*]. ST. EDWARD'S HALL: E end, NE corner [hedge]. ST. JOSEPH'S LAKE: N side [many]. WALSH HALL: W side [2]. WASHINGTON HALL: SW corner [few].

'Alba' [**White Lilac**]
Deciduous shrub. Taller than the species; flowers white, not double-petalled.
BREEN-PHILLIPS HALL: SE corner [10*].

'Purpurea' [**Purplish Red Lilac**]
Deciduous shrub. Flowers purple red.

HOWARD HALL: N wing, SE corner [4*]. MOREAU SEMINARY: SW corner [many*].

*wolfi* C. K. Schneid. [**Manchurian Lilac**]

Deciduous shrub. Shoot hairy; leaf to 6 in. long, veins hairy below. Flowers lilac, fragrant, in 1 ft. long clusters. Ornamental in May. Introduced, native to Manchuria, Korea. Maximum height 20 ft.

BROWNSON HALL: S end [3*]. FRESHMAN YEAR BUILDING: W 70yd, roadside [3*]. HAYES-HEALY CENTER: N entrance, E side [1*].

## BIGNONIACEAE [BIGNONIA FAMILY]

*Campsis* Lour. [**Trumpet-creeper**]

These vines are found in eastern Asia and the eastern United States. The trumpet-creeper that is native in the United States is a rampant vine that climbs by aerial rootlike holdfasts that cling to walls and arbors. The large orange to red trumpet-shaped flowers bloom from mid-summer to September. Some people develop a blistery rash when in contact with the foliage.

Broad-leaved climbing vine: deciduous. Leaves alternate along stem, large, odd-pinnately compound with toothed leaflets. Flowers 5-lobed, orange to red, trumpet-shaped, in cymes at branch ends; fruit a long podlike capsule with many small 2-winged seeds.

*radicans* (L.) Seem. [**Trumpet-creeper; Trumpet-vine**]

Deciduous vine. Leaf compound with 5-11 toothless leaflets, hairy below; flower 2 in. wide, shallow-lobed. Vigorous vine for screening or sturdy trellis; orange red flowers. Ornamental in late June to September. Native to Pennsylvania through Illinois to Texas. In horticulture since 1640. Contact with foliage or flowers may cause skin irritation. Maximum height 40 ft.

ADMINISTRATION (MAIN) BUILDING: NE corner [1*]; NW corner [1*]. BROWNSON HALL: NE corner [1*]. MORRISSEY HALL: NE corner [1*]. SESQUICENTENNIAL COMMONS: Pergola, climbing arches [25]. ST. JOSEPH'S LAKE [many*].

× *tagliabuana* (Vis.) Rehd.: *C. grandiflora* × *C. radicans* [**Hybrid Trumpet-creeper**]

Deciduous vine. Leaf pinnately compound, 7-11 leaflets, veins hairy below; flower 2.5 in. wide, deep-lobed. Vigorous vine for screen or sturdy trellis; flowers orange and red. Ornamental in July to September. Developed by the Tagliabue brothers of Milan, Italy. In horticulture since 1858. Contact with foliage or flowers may cause skin irritation. Maximum height 30 ft.

'Madame Galen' [**Madame Galen Trumpet-creeper**]

Deciduous vine. Flower color deep, apricot orange; leaflets egg-shaped, tips pointed. Flowers profuse, showy. Ornamental in July to September. Developed in French nurseries. In horticulture since 1889. Maximum height 25 ft.

SESQUICENTENNIAL COMMONS: Pergola, climbing arches [25].

*Catalpa* Scop. [**Catalpa**]

The catalpas are large trees, mostly native to North America but with a few species in eastern Asia, that are used as street trees and for shade in lawns and parks. They are popular because of their showy white, bell-shaped flowers dotted with purple that appear in May and June. Their fruit capsules, which may be 20 inches long, often remain visible through winter. Catalpas tolerate extreme environmental conditions. They are not desirable in the landscape because of their weak wood, short life, and coarse features. Their lesser qualities were disregarded by gardeners in earlier years, who valued their utility as shade trees. During the nineteenth century many catalpas were planted on the Notre Dame campus for shade, especially on what is now the Main Quad.

Broad-leaved tree: deciduous, rarely evergreen. Leaves usually in opposite pairs along stem or grouped in whorls of 3 or more, large, simple, heart-shaped, smooth-edged. Flowers large, white, bell-shaped ending in 2 ruffled lobes, in May and June, in large, branched panicles; fruit a very long podlike 2-celled capsule with numerous seeds, each with tufts of hairs at both ends.

*bignonioides* Walt. [**Southern Catalpa; Common Catalpa**]

Deciduous tree. Leaf to 8 in. long, abruptly sharp-pointed, veins hairy below, foul odor when crushed. Broadly rounded, irregular form; branches short and crooked. Native to Georgia through Louisiana. In horticulture since 1726. Flowers may cause skin irritation. Maximum height 40 ft.

FATIMA RETREAT HOUSE: S, lakeside [1*]. OUTDOOR WAY OF THE CROSS: Station 7 [1*]. PRESBYTERY: Freshman Year W parking lot, midway [3*]. SORIN STATUE: NW 50yd [1*]. WALSH HALL: N end [2*].

*speciosa* Warder ex Engelm. [**Northern Catalpa**]

Deciduous tree. Leaf to 1 ft. long, long-pointed, dense-hairy below, odorless when crushed. Narrow, irregular form; appears coarse in landscape. Native to southern Illinois and Indiana through Tennessee and Arkansas. In horticulture since 1754. Flowers may cause skin irritation. Maximum height 60 ft.

COLUMBA HALL: NW corner, N 70yd [few]. HOLY CROSS HOUSE: SE corner, NE 25yd [1]. MOREAU SEMINARY: S, lakeside [1].


# CAPRIFOLIACEAE [HONEYSUCKLE FAMILY]

*Lonicera* L. [**Honeysuckle**]

The honesuckles are native to broad areas of the Northern Hemisphere, ranging south to Mexico and the Philippines. They are popular, vigorous ornamental shrubs and ground covers that often have numerous sweet-smelling flowers, followed by red to black berries that attract birds. The flowers of several species are pollinated by hawkmoths (members of the Sphingidae or sphinx moth family) that are attracted by scent to the night-opening flowers, which extend their floral organs beyond the petal margins to act as landing stages for the moths.

Broad-leaved shrub or vine: deciduous, some evergreen. Leaves in opposite pairs on stem, simple, smooth-edged. Flower tubular, 2-lipped or 5-lobed, usually white to yellow, in pairs at leaf axils (usually); fruit a few to many-seeded juicy berry, usually red.

× *amoena* Zab.: *L. korolkowii* × *L. tatarica* [**Honeysuckle**]

Deciduous shrub. Leaf egg-shaped, 2 in. long, gray green; flower 0.75 in. long, paired, crowded at stem tip. Flowers pink or white. Ornamental in early summer. Maximum height 9 ft.

'Rosea' [**Honeysuckle**]

Deciduous shrub. Flowers pink turning yellow, fragrant.

CARROLL HALL: Tool shed, N side [12*]. MAIL DISTRIBUTION CENTER: N, lakeside [1*].

× *bella* Zab.: *L. morrowii* × *L. tatarica* [**Belle Honeysuckle**]

Deciduous shrub. Stem light, hollow brown pith; leaf egg-shaped, blue green, veins hairy. Hardy; branches arching; flowers pink, white turn yellow; fruit red. Ornamental in middle of May. Developed at Münden Botanic Garden, Germany. In horticulture since 1889. Maximum height 10 ft.

FATIMA RETREAT HOUSE: Sacred Heart shrine, SW 15yd [1]. FRESHMAN YEAR BUILDING: W parking lot, N, lakeside [1]; W parking lot, SW exit [1]. HOLY CROSS ANNEX: NW 40yd, in thicket [1*]; SE 50yd [1*]. MAINTENANCE CENTER: SW corner, W 50yd [1]. ST. EDWARD'S HALL: S side, W arch [1]. ST. MARY'S LAKE: SW corner, woods [3].

*fragrantissima* Lindl. & Paxt. [**Winter Honeysuckle**]

Deciduous shrub. Stem waxy blue or brown, hairless, pith solid white; leaf edge hairy. Small cream white flowers, lemon-scented; fruit dark red, in pairs. Ornamental in March to early April. Introduced, native to eastern China. In horticulture since 1845. Maximum height 10 ft.

BURKE MEMORIAL GOLF COURSE: Cedar Grove Cemetery, at W fence [1]. HAGGAR HALL: S wall [hedge*]. PASQUERILLA HALL WEST: NW corner, hedge [3].

*japonica* Thunb. [**Japanese Honeysuckle**]

Deciduous vine. Twining; top leaves not fused; shoot and both leaf surfaces hairy; leaf pale green below. Evergreen where warm; flowers yellow white, fragrant; fruit black. Ornamental in June to November. Introduced, native to Japan, China, Korea; escaped in the United States. In horticulture since 1806. Maximum height 30 ft.

CALVARY: E, 45yd [1]. FATIMA RETREAT HOUSE: E side, SE beds [1].

*maackii* (Rupr.) Maxim. [**Amur Honeysuckle**]

Deciduous shrub. Stem hairy, hollow, pith brown; leaf tapering to long tip, veins hairy on both surfaces. Flowers white to yellow; fruit red; weedy in the South. Ornamental in May to June. Introduced, native to Manchuria, Korea. In horticulture since 1855. Maximum height 15 ft.

CALVARY: E, 60yd [many]. FATIMA RETREAT HOUSE: SW corner, S, lakeside [many]. FISCHER GRADUATE RESIDENCE COMPLEX: N, woods [1].

*morrowii* A. Gray [**Morrow Honeysuckle**]

Deciduous shrub. Stem gray, hairy, hollow brown pith; leaf dense-hairy below; bud blunt, hairy. Flowers white to yellow, in pairs; fruit red. Ornamental in May. Introduced, native to Japan. In horticulture since 1975. Maximum height 8 ft.

HOLY CROSS ANNEX: Tool shed, N walk, W side [4*]. LYONS HALL: Chapel, S side [5*]; S wing, 15yd NE [1*]. ST. EDWARD'S HALL: S side, W arch, W [4*]. ST. JOSEPH HALL: SW 50yd, woods [1].

*ruprechtiana* Regel [**Ruprecht Honeysuckle**]

Deciduous shrub. Leaf 4 in. long, oblong, narrow, pale green and hairy below; flowers in pairs; fruit red. Flowers white to yellow; fruit red and transparent. Ornamental in late spring. Introduced, native to northeastern Asia, Manchuria, China. Maximum height 12 ft.

HOLY CROSS ANNEX: W, road to tool shed, N end, E [2*]; W, road to tool shed, N end, W [3*]. HOLY CROSS HOUSE: SE, lakeside at culvert [3*].

*tatarica* L. [**Tatarian Honeysuckle**]

Deciduous shrub. Stem hairless, hollow brown pith; leaf hairless, blue green, waxy white below; fruit red. Flowers pink to white, in pairs. Ornamental in May.

Introduced, native to central Asia, Russia. In horticulture since 1752. Maximum height 12 ft.

CALVARY: E, 30yd [1]. CAVANAUGH HALL: NW corner [1]. CEDAR GROVE CEMETERY: Chapel, NW corner, NW [1]. CORBY HALL: NW, lakeside [1*]. FISCHER GRADUATE RESIDENCE COMPLEX: N, woods [1]. FRESHMAN YEAR BUILDING: SW corner, NW [1]; W parking lot, stop sign, SE 20yd [1]. HOLY CROSS ANNEX: W [hedge]. HOLY CROSS HOUSE: E, Sacred Heart statue, N [many]. HOWARD HALL: N [hedge]. O'SHAUGHNESSY HALL: E side [1]. OLD COLLEGE: N, lakeside [3*]. PASQUERILLA HALL WEST: E wing, S side [5]; N wing, NW corner [3]. SIEGFRIED HALL: E wing, S side [4]. UNIVERSITY HEALTH SERVICES: N, lakeside cabin, W side [1].

### 'Alba' [Tatarian White Honeysuckle]
Deciduous shrub. Flowers pure white.

FRESHMAN YEAR BUILDING: W parking lot, NW corner, NW 50yd [1*].

### 'Latifolia' [Tatarian Large-leaved Honeysuckle]
Deciduous shrub. Leaf larger than species, to 4 in. long and 2 in. wide.

HOLY CROSS ANNEX: Tool shed, E end [3*]. HOWARD HALL: NW corner [2*].

### f. *leroyana* (Zab.) Rehd. [Leroy Honeysuckle]
Deciduous shrub. Dwarf form; flowers sparse. Maximum height 3 ft.

UNIVERSITY HEALTH SERVICES: N, lakeside cabin, SE corner [1*].

### var. *parvifolia* (Hayne) Jaeg. [Hayne Honeysuckle]
Deciduous shrub. Flowers white.

ST. JOSEPH'S LAKE: Boat house, top of slope, NE [many*].

### 'Rosea' [Regelian Honeysuckle]
Deciduous shrub. Flowers rose pink outside, light pink inside.

HOLY CROSS ANNEX: NW 40yd [1*].


## *Sambucus* L. [Elder]

The elders are large, coarse, multistemmed shrubs that are found growing in wet sites in the wild. They are native to temperate and subtropical regions of the Northern Hemisphere. In the landscape they should be placed where their sprawling nature is an advantage, such as along roadsides or naturalized areas where soil moisture is high. The fruits are attractive to birds and used to make jellies and wine when ripe. However, the remainder of the plant and the unripe berries contain poisonous alkaloids and cyanogenic glycosides.

Broad-leaved shrub or small tree: deciduous. Leaves in opposite pairs on stout, pithy stems, large, odd-pinnately compound, usually with 7 toothed leaflets. Flowers small, creamy white, in June and July, form flat-topped many-flowered cymes; fruit a purple black, juicy, berrylike drupe with 3-5 nutlets.

### *canadensis* L. [American Elder]
Deciduous shrub. Large pinnate leaf, 7 toothed leaflets; stem coarse, yellow gray, dotted with lenticels. Flat clusters of white flowers; purple black berries attract birds. Ornamental in June to July. Native to eastern North America through Texas. In horticulture since 1761. Maximum height 12 ft.

CAMPUS SECURITY BUILDING: N, St. Mary's Lake margin [1*]. HOLY CROSS ANNEX: Tool shed, S side [many*]. ST. JOSEPH'S LAKE: NW woods [few*].

*Symphoricarpos* Duh. [**Snowberry**]

The white fruits, visible from September into November, of the snowberries are more ornamental than the inconspicuous flowers. The plants are dense, shade-tolerant, and tend to spread or colonize by suckers, which makes them appropriate for erosion control but not for small sites. The snowberries are native to North America and western China.

Broad-leaved shrub: deciduous. Leaf in opposite pairs on stem, simple, usually smooth-edged (sometimes slightly lobed). Flowers small, white or pink in inconspicuous spikes, in June; fruit a white, 2-seeded drupe.

*rivularis* Suksd. [**Common Snowberry**]

Deciduous shrub. Leaf 1.25 in. long, elliptic; fruit white, round. Flowers small but numerous, white to pink; fruit showy. Native to Alaska to California and Montana. Maximum height 10 ft.

GROTTO OF OUR LADY OF LOURDES: N, outer walk, along S edge [few]. MORRISSEY HALL: NE corner [1*]; NW corner [few*].


*Viburnum* L. [**Viburnum**]

The viburnums are a large, diverse group of popular ornamentals that can provide a plant for almost any purpose. They have showy fragrant flowers and colorful fruits that are attractive to birds. Some but not all of the species have edible fruits (*V. opulus*, *V. lentago*, and *V. prunifolium* are edible, among others). *V. carlesii* has extremely fragrant balls of pink to white flowers in spring. The wood of *V. acerifolium* and *V. dentatum* was used to make arrows in earlier times. Viburnums are native to North America, Europe, and Asia.

Broad-leaved shrub or small tree: deciduous, some semi-evergreen. Leaves in opposite pairs on stem, usually simple and toothed along margin but palmately lobed in some species (similar to maple leaves). Flower small, tubular, 5-lobed pink to white, in many-flowered clusters (umbel-like cymes or panicles), either flat-topped or in hemispherical "snowballs."  Many of the ornamental viburnums have larger sterile flowers, either encircling the smaller fertile flowers or completely replacing them. Fruits formed by fertile flowers are 1-seeded, berrylike drupes.

*acerifolium* L. [**Maple-leaf Viburnum**]

Deciduous shrub. Leaf 3-lobed, teeth coarse, dense hairs and black dots below, petiole hairy without glands. Fruit black; withstands shade. Native to New Brunswick through Minnesota to North Carolina and Georgia. In horticulture since 1736. Maximum height 6 ft.

CALVARY: Woods [many*].

× *bodnantense* Aberc.: *V. farreri* × *V. grandiflorum* [**Bodnant Viburnum**]

Deciduous shrub. Leaf 4 in., edge toothed, smooth above, hair tufts in vein axils below; fruit red to black. Early, fragrant flowers, buds deep pink, in 3 in. clusters. Ornamental in winter to early spring. Developed at Bodnant Gardens, Wales. Maximum height 11 ft.

'Pink Dawn' [**Bodnant Viburnum**]

Deciduous shrub. Leaves green, pubescent, with deep veins; flower buds rose pink, opening pink. Erect form; flowers fragrant, opening very early; fruit dark blue. Ornamental in late autumn to early spring. Developed at Bodnant Gardens, Wales. Maximum height 10 ft.

DEBARTOLO CLASSROOM BUILDING: E side, S of N end doors [4]. HAMMES BOOKSTORE: W wing, S [6]. SUPPORT SERVICES BUILDING: N bed [3]; S bed [2].

× *burkwoodii* Hort. Burkw. & Skipw.: *V. carlesii* × *V. utile* [**Burkwood Viburnum**]

Deciduous shrub. Leaf veins reach edge, brown hairs below; petiole 0.5 in. long, bud naked showing leaves. Heat and cold tolerant; flowers pink to white, fragrant. Ornamental in spring. Developed in England. In horticulture since 1924. Maximum height 10 ft.

> JOYCE ATHLETIC AND CONVOCATION CENTER: Gate 2, N of walk [4]; S of gate 10 [7]. PASQUERILLA HALL WEST: E wing, N side [2]; N wing, E side [3]. ST. MICHAEL'S LAUNDRY: N side [3].

*carlesii* Hemsl. [**Fragrant Viburnum**]

Deciduous shrub. Leaf veins reach toothed edge, both sides hairy, petiole 0.5 in. long; bud scaleless. Flower buds pink, form 3 in. balls of white flowers, spice-scented. Ornamental in April to May. Introduced, native to Korea. In horticulture since 1812. Maximum height 8 ft.

> FATIMA RETREAT HOUSE: Fatima shrine, E, flanking E drive [6*]; NE corner, at parking lot [hedge*]. GROTTO OF OUR LADY OF LOURDES: N side [1*]. LOG CHAPEL: E, flanking entrance [2*]. LYONS HALL: Archway, S side [8]; Archway, SE [few*]. MORRISSEY HALL: SE corner [2]. NORTH DINING HALL: N end [7]; S end, center [6].

*dentatum* L. [**Arrowwood Viburnum**]

Deciduous shrub. Leaf veins reach toothed edge, star-shaped hairs on petiole; bud with scales; fruit blue. Used as a screen, very hardy. Native to New Brunswick and Minnesota to Texas through Georgia. In horticulture since 1736. Maximum height 15 ft.

> KNOTT HALL: S wing, E side [6]; S wing, W side [4]; W wing, N side [10]. SIEGFRIED HALL: E wing, N side [11]; S wing, E side [11]; S wing, W side [5]. SNITE MUSEUM OF ART: SW corner [7]. ST. EDWARD'S HALL: N wing, NE corner [2].

*lentago* L. [**Nannyberry; Sweet Viburnum**]

Deciduous shrub. Leaf veins fade at toothed edge, hairy below, petiole winged; bud long, gray, 2 scales. Good shrub for border or naturalizing; attracts birds. Native to Hudson Bay, Canada, through Georgia. In horticulture since 1761. Maximum height 18 ft.

> BURKE MEMORIAL GOLF COURSE: Fisher Hall, S of fence [many*]. CARROLL HALL: W 30yd, hedge [1*]. DECIO FACULTY HALL: W, service entrance [1]. FATIMA RETREAT HOUSE: E side [1]; NW corner, NW 30yd [1]; W, along parking drive [many]. FISHER HALL: N side, E center [1]. HAMMES BOOKSTORE: SE corner [3]. LYONS HALL: NW corner [7*]. ROCKNE MEMORIAL: SE corner, S [1*].

*opulus* L. [**Cranberrybush; Guelder-rose**]

Deciduous shrub. Leaf 3-lobed, toothed, hairy below, petiole narrowly V-grooved, stalkless glands at blade. Showy white flowers and red fruit. Ornamental in May, September through October. Introduced, native to Europe, northern Africa, northern Asia. Maximum height 12 ft.

> DECIO FACULTY HALL: S end, E 5yd [2]. FATIMA RETREAT HOUSE: E [1]. FLANNER HALL: N side [2]. LEWIS HALL: N, woods [many*]. LYONS HALL: S, in hedge [1]. NORTH DINING HALL: N end [9]. ROCKNE MEMORIAL: NW corner, N 400yd, lakeside [few]. SNITE MUSEUM OF ART: Court [8]. ST. JOSEPH'S LAKE: Islands, both [many*]. ST. MARY'S LAKE: Island, N of Campus Security Bldg [many*]. ST. MICHAEL'S LAUNDRY: E, flanking main door [2].

'Compactum' [**Cranberrybush**]

Deciduous shrub. Low, dense form; flowers and fruit abundant. Ornamental in May, September through October. Maximum height 6 ft.

JUNIPER ROAD: ROTC stoplight, E and W sides [4]; W, Galvin fence, roadside [6]; W, Library circle N, fence, roadside [3]; W, Library circle S, fence, roadside [3]; W, at Bulla Rd, N section, roadside [6]; W, at Bulla Rd, S section, roadside [6]; W, at Galvin, fence, campus-side [6].

'Nanum' [**Dwarf Cranberrybush**]

Deciduous shrub. Dwarf form; few flowers or fruit. Used as a low filler plant. Maximum height 2 ft.

HAMMES BOOKSTORE: W wing, S [2]. HESBURGH CENTER: N side, residence patios, inside wall [23]. HESSERT AEROSPACE RESEARCH CENTER: N plaza [9]. JUNIPER ROAD: E, opposite Galvin, fence, W side [15]; North Gate, fence, N end [16]; ROTC stoplight, fence, campus-side [12]; W, Galvin fence, campus-side [12]; W, Library circle N, fence [2]; W, Library circle N, fence, campus-side [8]; W, Library circle S, fence [2]; W, Library circle S, fence, campus-side [18]. SNITE MUSEUM OF ART: S side, W of walk [hedge]. SUPPORT SERVICES BUILDING: E side, flanking door [6]. WASHINGTON HALL: E plaza [hedge].

'Roseum' [**Snowball; Snowball-bush**]

Deciduous shrub. Showy, sterile flowers are bright apple green, turning white to pink. Ornamental in middle of May. Maximum height 12 ft.

LYONS HALL: NW basketball court, N, lakeside [2*]. ST. MARY'S LAKE: N edge [few*].

*plicatum* Thunb. [**Japanese Snowball**]

Deciduous shrub. Leaf veins reach even-toothed edge; leaf and flower 2-ranked on stem; bud scales present. Flowers white, sterile, not forming fruit. Ornamental in May to June. Introduced, native to China, Japan. In horticulture since 1844. Maximum height 15 ft.

HOWARD HALL: N wing, E end [11*]. LYONS HALL: E side, S of arch [1*].

f. *tomentosum* (Thunb.) Rehd. [**Doublefile Viburnum**]

Deciduous shrub. Flower heads flat, outer large flowers sterile, inner small ones fertile; fruit red black. Elegant shrub used as a specimen, in border or massed for screening. Ornamental in May. Introduced, native to China, Japan. In horticulture since 1865. Maximum height 10 ft.

ALUMNI HALL: S side, ramp [3*]. CORBY HALL: N side, court [1]. DILLON HALL: E court, N entrance [1*]; E court, NE corner [3]; E court, SE [2*]; S wing, NE entrance [10*]. FATIMA RETREAT HOUSE: NW front door, E, corner [1]. HAYES-HEALY CENTER: N entrance, NE 20yd [1]. JOYCE ATHLETIC AND CONVOCATION CENTER: N side [13]. LOFTUS SPORTS CENTER: W side, N door [6]; W side, S door [6]. ST. EDWARD'S HALL: E end, NE corner, N 20yd [1].

f. *tomentosum* (Thunb.) Rehd. 'Mariesii' [**Doublefile Viburnum**]

Deciduous shrub. Distinctively horizontal branches with large white flowers raised above the branches. In horticulture since 1875.

HESBURGH CENTER: Court, E border [10]; Court, N border [10]; E side [12]; E side, NE corner, S [4]; S side, middle, inner corner [3]. HESSERT AEROSPACE RESEARCH CENTER: E [6]. SUPPORT SERVICES BUILDING: S bed [1].

*prunifolium* L. [**Blackhaw; Sweethaw**]

Deciduous tree. Leaf hairless, veins fade at fine-toothed edge, petiole wingless; bud pointed, 2 scales. Used as a small specimen tree; flowers creamy white. Native to Connecticut through Florida to Texas. In horticulture since 1727.

Maximum height 15 ft.

> MAIL DISTRIBUTION CENTER: SW corner [7*]. PASQUERILLA HALL EAST: N wing, W door, flanking [4]; N wing, W side [1]; W wing, W end [2]. PASQUERILLA HALL WEST: E door, flanking [4]; N wing, E side [2]. ST. JOSEPH HALL: SE, lake slope, flanking steps to pier [few*].

*recognitum* Fern. [**Arrowwood**]

Deciduous shrub. Leaf veins reach coarse-toothed edge, few hairs below, petiole hairless; bud with scales. Blue black fruit attracts birds. Native to eastern North America. Maximum height 12 ft.

> HOLY CROSS HOUSE: S entrance, E [1]; W end [1]. MORRIS INN: NE corner, E side [1]; SE corner [1].

*rhytidophyllum* Hemsl. [**Rugose Viburnum**]

Evergreen shrub. Leaf oblong, wrinkled dark green above, yellow gray and hairy below, veins reach wavy edge. Interesting broad-leaved evergreen, leaves lost in severe weather. Introduced, native to central and western China. In horticulture since 1900. Maximum height 15 ft.

> CARROLL HALL: W 30yd, hedge [4*]. DEBARTOLO CLASSROOM BUILDING: N side, NW door, E side [2]; N side, between windows [12]. FATIMA RETREAT HOUSE: W side [1*]. FITZPATRICK HALL OF ENGINEERING: S side, E door, W planter [2]; S side, W door, W planter [1]. HESBURGH CENTER: E side [1]. KNOTT HALL: S wing, E side, S of door [1]; S wing, W side, S end [6]; W wing, N side [2]; W wing, SW corner [3]. KOONS REHEARSAL HALL: S side, W end [14]. LAFORTUNE STUDENT CENTER: SW entrance, flanking [2]. PASQUERILLA HALL EAST: W wing, S side [4]; W wing, W end [3]. PASQUERILLA HALL WEST: E wing, E end [2]; E wing, S side [3]. RILEY HALL OF ART AND DESIGN: SE corner [3]. SACRED HEART BASILICA: E side door, N side [3*]. SIEGFRIED HALL: E wing, SE corner [3]; W door [1].

*sieboldii* Miq. [**Siebold Viburnum**]

Deciduous shrub. Leaf veins reach toothed edge, leaf not 2-ranked, base wedged, foul odor; bud with scales. Masses of creamy white flowers; fruit rose red to black. Ornamental in May, August through October. Introduced, native to Japan. In horticulture since 1880. Maximum height 20 ft.

> CARROLL HALL: NW [many]; W 30yd, hedge [3*].

*trilobum* Marsh. [**American Cranberrybush Viburnum**]

Deciduous shrub. Leaf 3-lobed, few teeth, hairless, petiole groove broad, flat with stalked glands at base. Showy white flowers and red fruit; leaves turn yellow to red purple. Ornamental in May through autumn. Native to northern North America. In horticulture since 1812. Maximum height 12 ft.

'Alfredo' [**American Cranberrybush Viburnum**]

Deciduous shrub. Dwarf form with dense, broad habit. Leaves turn red. Ornamental in autumn. Maximum height 6 ft.

> PASQUERILLA CENTER: NW corner, S and E ends [hedge]; SE corner, N and W ends [hedge]; SW corner, N and E ends [hedge]. WASHINGTON HALL: E side, plaza [8].

*Weigela* Thunb. [**Weigela**]

These straggly shrubs have pleasing bright rose red (some are white, pink, or lavender) flowers during May and June with some sporadic flowering again during late summer. Weigela grows in full sun, but should be placed in a shrub border to draw attention away from its coarse, ratty winter appearance. It can suffer winter dieback, but some hardier cultivars have been developed. It is an "old-fashioned" shrub, like rose-of-Sharon, that is frequently seen growing in older sections of cities. It is native to eastern Asia.

Broad-leaved shrub: deciduous. Leaves in opposite pairs on stem, simple, margin toothed. Flowers funnel-shaped, ending in 5 spreading lobes, solitary or in few-flowered cymes at leaf axils; fruit a small, dry 2-valved woody capsule that opens from the top to disperse the seeds.

*florida* (Bunge) A. DC. [**Flowering Weigela**]

Deciduous shrub. Leaf toothed, long-pointed, medium green above, veins hairy below. Flowers funnel or bell-shaped, red pink. Ornamental in May to June. Introduced, native to Japan. In horticulture since 1860. Maximum height 9 ft.

HAYES-HEALY CENTER: N side [4*]. HOLY CROSS HOUSE: S entrance, E [1]. HURLEY HALL OF BUSINESS ADMINISTRATION: E end [3*]. SACRED HEART BASILICA: SE corner, E 35yd [14*].

## AGAVACEAE [CENTURY-PLANT FAMILY]

*Yucca* L. [**Yucca**]

The most visible yucca is the Joshua Tree, *Y. brevifolia*, of the southwestern North American desert. It stands 40 ft. tall with stilettolike leaves bunched at the sparse branch tips. The yuccas that are hardy in the Midwest are low and bushy with long, swordlike leaves arising at soil level. The genus is a minor element of the Notre Dame campus today, but during the early 1900s Brother Robert Kunze's yucca collection, which included both tender and hardy species, was a conspicuous feature of the landscape in front of the Main Building. In the Midwest, yuccas bloom during July and August. The white flowers are pollinated at night by the small, white yucca moth, *Tegeticula yuccasella*. The female moth gathers balls of the sticky pollen, flies to a flower stalk on another plant, inserts her eggs into the sides of the ovaries, and then packs pollen into the stigmas. This activity ensures cross-pollination of the plants and a ready food supply (the forming seeds) for the developing moth larvae. Yuccas are native to the warmer areas of North America. Strong fibers for rope or kraft paper and newspaper fibers are harvested from the stiff leaves. A foaming agent used in beverage making is derived from the base of the plant. The flowers and fruit of some species are eaten.

Broad-leaved tree or shrub: evergreen. Leaves clustered at ends of branches in some species or at ground level in stemless species, stiff and swordlike, margin often with long, curly, hanging threads. Flowers usually white, clustered on flower stalk to 6 ft. tall; fruit a dry capsule with black seeds.

*filamentosa* L. [**Adam's-needle Yucca**]

Evergreen shrub. Leaf stiff, erect, to 2.5 ft. long, curling hairs along edge; flower stalk to 6 ft. tall. Flowers yellow white, flower stalk striking. Ornamental in July to August. Native to South Carolina and Mississippi to Florida. In horticulture since 1675. Maximum height 2 ft.

BROWNSON HALL: S wall, W, court entrance [1]. LEWIS HALL: SW corner [1]. SORIN HALL: E, bed at intersection [many]. WASHINGTON HALL: SW, bed at intersection [9].

## SMILACACEAE [CATBRIER FAMILY]

*Smilax* L. **[Greenbrier]**
In the Midwest greenbrier is not used as an ornamental, but is found growing as a shrub or climber in woods and natural habitats. *Smilax* grows worldwide in temperate and tropical areas. Sarsaparilla, the flavoring and medicine or tonic of earlier days, comes from the dried roots of some tropical species of *Smilax*. The foliage of *S. lanceolata*, called Jackson brier, is grown in Florida for limited use in floral arrangements, but the common, feathery "smilax" of the cut flower industry, which resembles the foliage of the vegetable asparagus, is the lily family plant *Asparagus asparagoides*.

Broad-leaved vine: deciduous or evergreen, dioecious. Climbs by paired tendrils found at base of each leaf petiole. Stems often prickly, especially those low on plant. Leaves alternate along stem with 3-9 long, parallel veins arising from leaf base. Flowers green, white, or yellow and inconspicuous. Fruit a small blue to black berry.

*hispida* Muhlenb. **[Bristly Greenbrier]**
Deciduous vine. Twining; stems prickly; leaf egg-shaped to round, edge toothed, veins parallel. Berries black; impenetrable in thickets in the wild. Native to eastern and central United States, southern Canada. Maximum height 30 ft.

POWER PLANT: NW, slope [1*]. ST. JOSEPH'S LAKE: Boat house, S 45yd [1*]; NW woods [few*].

# Planting Sites

This catalogue of the plants on the campus is organized by primary campus landmark (usually a building). It is intended as a guide to the plants found around each building. The botanical and horticultural information about the plants, as described in the previous chapter, is excluded here for brevity, but referred to by the page number that follows each family name. Here, the primary landmarks are listed alphabetically. Each is followed by a list of the actual plants found at that landmark. The plants are listed alphabetically by plant family and, within each family, by genus, species, subspecies (subsp.), variety (var.), form (f.), and cultivar (within single quotation marks). The symbol "×" designates the hybrids. Each plant has been identified to the lowest level possible. Cultivar names are included when known. Common names are listed in brackets. Each common name is followed by a list of the locations of the specific planting sites (from one to many) with respect to the primary landmark. Each site includes a terse description of its location and, within brackets, a count of the number of specimens at the site (either a number or an estimate such as many, few, clump, etc.). An asterisk is included in the brackets if the planting also was documented by Father Hebert twenty-seven years ago. Commemorative plantings are marked by "**Commem**." Additional information is included in the Commemorative Plantings section, which follows on page 269.

## ADMINISTRATION (MAIN) BUILDING

**ACERACEAE [MAPLE FAMILY]**, p. 161

*Acer palmatum* f. *dissectum* 'Everred' [**Threadleaf Japanese Maple**]: Front, E bed [2]; Front, W bed [1].

*Acer palmatum* 'Sharp's Pygmy' [**Japanese Maple**]: Front, E bed [1]; Front, W bed [1].

*Acer platanoides* 'Rubrum' [**Crimson Norway Maple**]: NW corner [1].

*Acer platanoides* 'Schwedleri' [**Schwedler's Maple**]: Washington Hall, midway [1*].

*Acer saccharum* [**Sugar Maple; Hard Maple**]: Main entrance, steps, SE 10yd [1*]; NE corner, N, along road [4].

**ASCLEPIADACEAE [MILKWEED FAMILY]**, p. 172

*Periploca graeca* [**Grecian Silkvine**]: SE corner, wall [1*].

**BERBERIDACEAE [BARBERRY FAMILY]**, p. 86

*Berberis thunbergii* 'Crimson Pygmy' [**Dwarf Japanese Barberry**]: Front, E bed [6]; Front, W bed [6].

**BIGNONIACEAE [BIGNONIA FAMILY]**, p. 179

*Campsis radicans* [**Trumpet-creeper; Trumpet-vine**]: NE corner [1*]; NW corner [1*].

**CELASTRACEAE [STAFF-TREE FAMILY]**, p. 151

*Euonymus europaea* [**European Spindletree**]: NE corner, N side [2].

**CUPRESSACEAE [CYPRESS FAMILY]**, p. 72

*Chamaecyparis obtusa* 'Aurea' [**Hinoki Falsecypress**]: Front, E bed [1].

*Chamaecyparis obtusa* 'Nana Gracilis' [**Hinoki Falsecypress**]: Front, E bed [1]; Front, W bed [1].

*Juniperus chinensis* 'Old Gold' [**Chinese Juniper**]: Front, E bed [3].

*Juniperus communis* 'Effusa' [**Common Juniper**]: Front, E bed [3]; Front, W bed [2].

*Juniperus procumbens* 'Nana' [**Creeping Juniper**]: Front, E bed [2]; Front, W bed [1]; Main steps, E bed [2].

*Juniperus sabina* [**Savin Juniper**]: Front, SE corner [1*].

*Juniperus squamata* 'Blue Star' [**Singleseed Juniper**]: Front, E bed [2]; Front, W bed [2].

*Juniperus squamata* 'Holger' [**Singleseed Juniper**]: Front, E bed [3]; Front, W bed [4].

*Juniperus virginiana* 'Glauca' [**Silver Redcedar**]: Sacred Heart Statue, walk, midway W side [2*].

*Thuja occidentalis* 'Rheingold' [**American Arborvitae**]: Front, E bed [2]; Front, W bed [3].

**FAGACEAE [BEECH FAMILY]**, p. 98

*Fagus sylvatica* 'Atropunicea' [**Copper Beech; Purple Beech**]: Main entrance, S 40yd [2*].

*Fagus sylvatica* 'Tricolor' [**Tricolor European Beech**]: S side, SW inner corner [1].

**GINKGOACEAE [GINKGO FAMILY]**, p. 54

*Ginkgo biloba* 'Laciniata' [**Split-leaf Ginkgo**]: N lawn [1*].

**HAMAMELIDACEAE [WITCH-HAZEL FAMILY]**, p. 90

*Liquidambar styraciflua* [**Sweetgum**]: E front end, stairs, E side [1*].

**HYDRANGEACEAE [HYDRANGEA FAMILY]**, p. 117

*Philadelphus* × *virginalis* [**Virginal Mock Orange**]: Main entrance, W side [1].

**MAGNOLIACEAE [MAGNOLIA FAMILY]**, p. 82

*Magnolia* × *soulangiana* [**Saucer Magnolia**]: Front, S of stairs, E of walk [1 **Commem.**]; Front, S of stairs, W of walk [1*].

**OLEACEAE [OLIVE FAMILY]**, p. 174

*Syringa vulgaris* [**Common Lilac**]: SW corner [few].

**PINACEAE [PINE FAMILY]**, p. 59

*Picea abies* [**Norway Spruce**]: Sacred Heart Statue, walk, midway E side [1*]; W front, S 12yd [1].

*Picea abies* 'Nidiformis' [**Bird's Nest Spruce**]: Front, E bed [1]; Front, W bed [1].

*Picea abies* 'Pendula' [**Weeping Norway Spruce**]: Front, E bed [1].

*Picea abies* 'Pumila' [**Dwarf Norway Spruce**]: Front, E bed [3]; Front, W bed [2].

*Picea abies* 'Repens' [**Dwarf Norway Spruce**]: Front, E bed [1]; Front, W bed [1].

*Picea alcoquiana* 'Howell's Dwarf' [**Alcock Spruce**]: Front, E bed [2]; Front, W bed [2].

*Picea omorika* 'Nana' [**Dwarf Serbian Spruce**]: Front, E bed [1]; Front, W bed [1].

*Picea pungens* [**Colorado Blue Spruce**]: W front, iron stairs, W [1*].

*Picea pungens* 'Glauca' [**Blue Spruce; Colorado Blue Spruce**]: W front [3*].

*Picea pungens* 'Prostrate Green' [**Colorado Spruce**]: Front, E bed [2]; Front, W bed [2].

**ROSACEAE [ROSE FAMILY]**, p. 122

*Pyracantha coccinea* 'Lalandei' [**Laland Firethorn**]: Main entrance, W side [1].

**TAXACEAE [YEW FAMILY]**, p. 55

*Taxus baccata* 'Repandens' [**Spreading Yew**]: E front end [1*].

*Taxus cuspidata* 'Nana' [**Japanese Dwarf Yew**]: E front end [1*]; W front [2*].

*Taxus × media* 'Hicksii' [**Hicks' Yew**]: Sacred Heart Statue, walk, N end, sides [2*]; Sacred Heart Statue, walk, S end, sides [2*].

**TAXODIACEAE [TAXODIUM FAMILY]**, p. 71

*Metasequoia glyptostroboides* [**Dawn Redwood**]: S side, SW inner corner [1].

**VITACEAE [GRAPE FAMILY]**, p. 157

*Parthenocissus quinquefolia* [**Virginia Creeper**]: N wing, NE corner [1*].

*Parthenocissus tricuspidata* [**Boston Ivy**]: S wall, E of main steps [few].


## ALUMNI HALL

**ACERACEAE [MAPLE FAMILY]**, p. 161

*Acer saccharum* [**Sugar Maple; Hard Maple**]: SE corner, S [3].

**ANACARDIACEAE [CASHEW FAMILY]**, p. 166

*Rhus aromatica* [**Fragrant Sumac**]: W court [10*].

**BERBERIDACEAE [BARBERRY FAMILY]**, p. 86

*Mahonia aquifolium* [**Oregon Grape**]: E side [beds]; W court [beds*].

**BETULACEAE [BIRCH FAMILY]**, p. 103

*Betula nigra* [**River Birch; Black Birch**]: S wing, W side [1*].

*Betula papyrifera* [**Paper Birch; Canoe Birch**]: Dillon, between, S roadside [1*].

*Carpinus caroliniana* [**American Hornbeam; Blue Beech**]: SE corner, S side [1].

**CAPRIFOLIACEAE [HONEYSUCKLE FAMILY]**, p. 180

*Viburnum plicatum* f. *tomentosum* [**Doublefile Viburnum**]: S side, ramp [3*].

**CELASTRACEAE [STAFF-TREE FAMILY]**, p. 151

*Euonymus alata* [**Winged Burningbush; Winged Spindletree**]: W wing, S end [2*].

*Euonymus fortunei* [**Chinese Winter-creeper**]: S side, ramp [bed].

*Euonymus fortunei* 'Carrierei' [**Carriere's Winter-creeper**]: W court, N entrance [1*].

*Euonymus fortunei* var. *radicans* [**Common Winter-creeper**]: W wing, S end [bed*].

**CORNACEAE [DOGWOOD FAMILY]**, p. 149

*Cornus florida* [**Flowering Dogwood**]: SE corner [5*]; SE, main gate, W 15yd [1 **Commem.**]; SE, main gate, just W [1 **Commem.**].

**CUPRESSACEAE [CYPRESS FAMILY]**, p. 72

*Chamaecyparis pisifera* [**Sawara Falsecypress**]: Chapel, W end, S tree [1*]; W court, S side [1*].

*Juniperus chinensis* 'Globosa' [**Chinese Globe Juniper**]: Chapel, W end [7*].

*Platycladus orientalis* [**Oriental Arborvitae**]: S side [3*].

**FAGACEAE [BEECH FAMILY]**, p. 98

*Fagus sylvatica* 'Fastigiata' [**European Pyramidal Beech**]: NE corner [1].

**HAMAMELIDACEAE [WITCH-HAZEL FAMILY]**, p. 90

*Hamamelis virginiana* [**Witch-hazel**]: N, main entrance, W [1*]; NE corner [1*].

HIPPOCASTANACEAE [HORSECHESTNUT FAMILY], p. 160
Aesculus hippocastanum [**Horsechestnut**]: S side [1*].
HYDRANGEACEAE [HYDRANGEA FAMILY], p. 117
Deutzia gracilis [**Japanese Slender Deutzia**]: NE corner, at walk [hedge*].
PINACEAE [PINE FAMILY], p. 59
Picea abies [**Norway Spruce**]: E side [1]; NE corner [1*].
PLATANACEAE [PLANETREE FAMILY], p. 89
Platanus occidentalis [**Sycamore; Buttonwood; American Planetree**]: E side [2*].
ROSACEAE [ROSE FAMILY], p. 122
Cotoneaster divaricatus [**Spreading Cotoneaster**]: W wing, S end [bed*].
Cotoneaster multiflorus var. calocarpus [**Arching Cotoneaster**]: E side [3]; W court [many*].
Crataegus arnoldiana [**Arnold Hawthorn**]: S side, at ramp [1*].
Crataegus crus-galli [**Cockspur Hawthorn; Cockspur-thorn**]: NE corner [1]; SE, Law
School, walk between [1].
Crataegus phaenopyrum [**Washington Hawthorn**]: E side [1]; SE [1*].
Malus spp. [**Ornamental Crabapple hybrids**]: Dillon, between, N [2*].
Prunus cerasifera 'Atropurpurea' [**Purpleleaf Cherry-plum**]: SE entrance, flanking [2*].
TAXACEAE [YEW FAMILY], p. 55
Taxus cuspidata [**Japanese Yew**]: N side [18].
Taxus cuspidata 'Intermedia' [**Japanese Compact Yew**]: E side [11*].


## ALUMNI SENIOR BAR

JUGLANDACEAE [WALNUT FAMILY], p. 96
Juglans nigra [**Black Walnut**]: W side [19*].


## ANGELA BOULEVARD

FAGACEAE [BEECH FAMILY], p. 98
Quercus alba [**White Oak**]: Old Juniper Rd, W side [1].
Quercus ellipsoidalis [**Northern Pin Oak**]: Notre Dame Ave, Juniper Rd, between [1*].
PINACEAE [PINE FAMILY], p. 59
Pinus strobus [**Eastern White Pine**]: Notre Dame Ave campus entrance [8].
PLATANACEAE [PLANETREE FAMILY], p. 89
Platanus occidentalis [**Sycamore; Buttonwood; American Planetree**]: Notre Dame Ave
campus entrance [2].
ROSACEAE [ROSE FAMILY], p. 122
Crataegus phaenopyrum [**Washington Hawthorn**]: Notre Dame Ave campus entrance [7].


## ARCHITECTURE BUILDING

ACERACEAE [MAPLE FAMILY], p. 161
Acer platanoides [**Norway Maple**]: Corby Hall, between [3].
Acer saccharinum 'Wieri' [**Wier's Cutleaf Maple**]: E 25yd, N of walk [1]; E 25yd, S of walk
[1].
Acer saccharum [**Sugar Maple; Hard Maple**]: Corby Hall, midway [1].
APOCYNACEAE [DOGBANE FAMILY], p. 171
Vinca minor [**Common Periwinkle; Running Myrtle**]: E entrance, N side [bed].

FABACEAE [PEA FAMILY], p. 144
 *Robinia pseudoacacia* [**Black Locust**]: N side [1*].
FAGACEAE [BEECH FAMILY], p. 98
 *Fagus sylvatica* 'Laciniata' [**Fernleaf Beech; Cutleaf Beech**]: E, on walkway [1].
MORACEAE [MULBERRY FAMILY], p. 94
 *Morus alba* 'Tatarica' [**Russian Mulberry**]: W [hedge*].
NYSSACEAE [TUPELO FAMILY], p. 148
 *Nyssa sylvatica* [**Black Tupelo; Blackgum; Sourgum**]: N side [2*].
PINACEAE [PINE FAMILY], p. 59
 *Picea abies* [**Norway Spruce**]: E, at steps [4*].
 *Picea glauca* [**White Spruce**]: E along walk to Sorin, N side [5*]; E along walk to Sorin, S side [4*].
 *Pinus mugo* [**Mugo Pine; Swiss Mountain Pine**]: E side, N of steps [1].
 *Pinus ponderosa* var. *scopulorum* [**Rocky Mountain Ponderosa Pine**]: NE corner, E 65yd [1]; SE corner, E 55yd [1*].
 *Pseudotsuga menziesii* [**Douglas-fir**]: SE corner, E 35yd [1*].
ROSACEAE [ROSE FAMILY], p. 122
 *Cotoneaster multiflorus* var. *calocarpus* [**Arching Cotoneaster**]: SW corner, W 10yd [2*].
 *Pyrus calleryana* 'Redspire' [**Callery Pear**]: NE corner, E lawn [1 **Commem.**].
STAPHYLEACEAE [BLADDERNUT FAMILY], p. 159
 *Staphylea trifolia* [**American Bladdernut**]: Log Chapel, midway [1*].
TAXACEAE [YEW FAMILY], p. 55
 *Taxus baccata* 'Pendula' [**Weeping Yew**]: NW corner, E [1*].
 *Taxus baccata* 'Repandens' [**Spreading Yew**]: NE corner [2*].
 *Taxus cuspidata* [**Japanese Yew**]: NW corner [2].
 *Taxus cuspidata* 'Expansa' [**Japanese Saucer Yew**]: SE corner [2*].
VITACEAE [GRAPE FAMILY], p. 157
 *Parthenocissus tricuspidata* [**Boston Ivy**]: Walls, all sides [many*].

## AVE MARIA PRESS

FAGACEAE [BEECH FAMILY], p. 98
 *Quercus rubra* [**Red Oak; Northern Red Oak**]: E side [2*].
 *Quercus velutina* f. *dilaniata* [**Cutleaf Black Oak**]: SW corner [1*].
JUGLANDACEAE [WALNUT FAMILY], p. 96
 *Carya ovalis* var. *obcordata* [**Obcordate Pignut**]: Main entrance, E [1*].

## BADIN HALL

CELASTRACEAE [STAFF-TREE FAMILY], p. 151
 *Euonymus fortunei* [**Chinese Winter-creeper**]: E side [bed].
CERCIDIPHYLLACEAE [KATSURA TREE FAMILY], p. 88
 *Cercidiphyllum japonicum* [**Katsura Tree**]: E, 2 each wing [4*].
MAGNOLIACEAE [MAGNOLIA FAMILY], p. 82
 *Magnolia* × *proctoriana* [**Chinese Magnolia**]: W side [2*].
OLEACEAE [OLIVE FAMILY], p. 174
 *Ligustrum obtusifolium* [**Border Privet**]: N wing, N side [10*].
PINACEAE [PINE FAMILY], p. 59
 *Picea pungens* 'Glauca' [**Blue Spruce; Colorado Blue Spruce**]: N door, N 20yd [1*].

*Picea pungens* 'Koster' [**Koster Weeping Blue Spruce**]: NW corner, N 15yd [1*].
*Pinus ponderosa* var. *scopulorum* [**Rocky Mountain Ponderosa Pine**]: NW corner, W 10yd [1*].
ROSACEAE  [ROSE FAMILY], p. 122
*Pyrus calleryana* [**Callery Pear**]: W door, N [1].
ULMACEAE  [ELM FAMILY], p. 92
*Ulmus americana* [**American Elm**]: NE corner, N 15yd [1].


## BREEN-PHILLIPS HALL

OLEACEAE  [OLIVE FAMILY], p. 174
*Syringa vulgaris* 'Alba' [**White Lilac**]: SE corner [10*].
ROSACEAE  [ROSE FAMILY], p. 122
*Malus* spp. [**Ornamental Crabapple hybrids**]: E side, center [1].
*Sorbus aucuparia* [**European Mountain-ash**]: W lawn, main entrance, S [1 **Commem.**].
TAXACEAE  [YEW FAMILY], p. 55
*Taxus × media* 'Brownii' [**Brown's Yew**]: W side [8*].
VITACEAE  [GRAPE FAMILY], p. 157
*Parthenocissus tricuspidata* [**Boston Ivy**]: NE corner [1*].


## BROWNSON HALL

ACERACEAE  [MAPLE FAMILY], p. 161
*Acer rubrum* [**Red Maple**]: E side [3*].
AGAVACEAE  [CENTURY-PLANT FAMILY], p. 187
*Yucca filamentosa* [**Adam's-needle Yucca**]: S wall, W, court entrance [1].
ARALIACEAE  [GINSENG FAMILY], p. 170
*Hedera helix* [**English Ivy**]: E side [1*].
BIGNONIACEAE  [BIGNONIA FAMILY], p. 179
*Campsis radicans* [**Trumpet-creeper; Trumpet-vine**]: NE corner [1*].
CUPRESSACEAE  [CYPRESS FAMILY], p. 72
*Chamaecyparis pisifera* [**Sawara Falsecypress**]: Court [3*].
ERICACEAE  [HEATH FAMILY], p. 113
*Rhododendron catawbiense* [**Catawba Rhododendron**]: Court, NE corner [3].
FABACEAE  [PEA FAMILY], p. 144
*Wisteria floribunda* [**Japanese Wisteria**]: Court, W side [1].
MAGNOLIACEAE  [MAGNOLIA FAMILY], p. 82
*Magnolia × soulangiana* [**Saucer Magnolia**]: Court [2*].
MALVACEAE  [MALLOW FAMILY], p. 109
*Hibiscus syriacus* [**Shrub-althea; Rose-of-Sharon**]: Court, SW corner [2].
OLEACEAE  [OLIVE FAMILY], p. 174
*Syringa reticulata* [**Japanese Tree Lilac**]: S, court entrance [2].
*Syringa wolfi* [**Manchurian Lilac**]: S end [3*].
PINACEAE  [PINE FAMILY], p. 59
*Picea abies* [**Norway Spruce**]: E side [2*].
ROSACEAE  [ROSE FAMILY], p. 122
*Kerria japonica* 'Pleniflora' [**Japanese Globeflower**]: Court [1].
*Prunus serrulata* var. *lannesiana* [**Japanese Double-flowering Cherry**]: Court [1].

SALICACEAE [WILLOW FAMILY], p. 110
    *Populus deltoides* [**Cottonwood**]: W side [1*].
    *Salix matsudana* 'Tortuosa' [**Corkscrew Willow; Dragon-claw Willow**]: Court, NE corner [1].
TAXACEAE [YEW FAMILY], p. 55
    *Taxus baccata* [**English Yew**]: Court, SE corner [1]; Court, SW corner [1].
    *Taxus* × *media* [**Anglojapanese Yew**]: Court, SE, SW corners [21].
VITACEAE [GRAPE FAMILY], p. 157
    *Parthenocissus tricuspidata* [**Boston Ivy**]: E side, on wall [many].


## BURKE MEMORIAL GOLF COURSE

ACERACEAE [MAPLE FAMILY], p. 161
    *Acer ginnala* [**Amur Maple**]: Scattered throughout [many*].
    *Acer negundo* [**Boxelder**]: NW area [many*].
    *Acer platanoides* [**Norway Maple**]: Scattered throughout [many].
    *Acer rubrum* [**Red Maple**]: SW corner [3]; SW corner [1].
    *Acer saccharum* [**Sugar Maple; Hard Maple**]: Scattered throughout [many].
BETULACEAE [BIRCH FAMILY], p. 103
    *Betula nigra* [**River Birch; Black Birch**]: SW corner [4].
    *Betula papyrifera* [**Paper Birch; Canoe Birch**]: Caddy shack, S [1]; NW corner [1].
    *Corylus colurna* [**Turkish Hazelnut**]: NE central area [1*].
CAESALPINIACEAE [CAESALPINIA FAMILY], p. 142
    *Gleditsia triacanthos* subsp. *inermis* [**Thornless Honeylocust**]: Cedar Grove Cemetery, N of NW corner [1].
    *Gymnocladus dioica* [**Kentucky Coffeetree**]: SW corner [1].
CAPRIFOLIACEAE [HONEYSUCKLE FAMILY], p. 180
    *Lonicera fragrantissima* [**Winter Honeysuckle**]: Cedar Grove Cemetery, at W fence [1].
    *Viburnum lentago* [**Nannyberry; Sweet Viburnum**]: Fisher Hall, S of fence [many*].
CELASTRACEAE [STAFF-TREE FAMILY], p. 151
    *Euonymus bungeana* [**Winterberry Spindletree**]: Main building, E [many*].
    *Euonymus europaea* [**European Spindletree**]: SW central area [many]; Sollitt Shelter, W [1]; Sollitt shelter, E [1].
CORNACEAE [DOGWOOD FAMILY], p. 149
    *Cornus florida* 'Rubra' [**Red-flowering Dogwood**]: Sollitt Shelter, E [1*]; Tee 1, E [3*].
CUPRESSACEAE [CYPRESS FAMILY], p. 72
    *Chamaecyparis pisifera* [**Sawara Falsecypress**]: NW area [1].
    *Juniperus chinensis* [**Chinese Juniper**]: NE area [few]; Sollitt shelter, E [1].
    *Juniperus chinensis* 'Arbuscula' [**Chinese Arborescent Juniper**]: Scattered throughout [15*].
    *Thuja occidentalis* [**American Arborvitae; Northern White Cedar**]: Scattered throughout [many*].
FAGACEAE [BEECH FAMILY], p. 98
    *Quercus alba* [**White Oak**]: NE area [1].
    *Quercus macrocarpa* [**Bur Oak; Mossy-cup Oak**]: Sollitt shelter, E [1].
    *Quercus palustris* [**Pin Oak**]: Sollitt Shelter, W [1].
    *Quercus rubra* [**Red Oak; Northern Red Oak**]: NE area [4]; SW central area, near birdhouse [2].
    *Quercus velutina* [**Black Oak**]: Sollitt shelter, SW corner, W 25yd [1].
HIPPOCASTANACEAE [HORSECHESTNUT FAMILY], p. 160
    *Aesculus hippocastanum* [**Horsechestnut**]: NE area [3].

JUGLANDACEAE [WALNUT FAMILY], p. 96
  *Juglans ailantifolia* [**Japanese Walnut**]: S central area, shelter, NE corner [few*].
  *Juglans ailantifolia* var. *cordiformis* [**Heart Nut**]: Rockne Memorial, SW 100yd [4*].
  *Juglans × bixbyi* [**Japanese Rough-shelled Walnut**]: S central area, birdhouse, S [1*].
  *Juglans nigra* [**Black Walnut**]: NW area fence [1]; Tee 10, N 10ft [1].
MORACEAE [MULBERRY FAMILY], p. 94
  *Maclura pomifera* [**Osage Orange**]: Sollitt Shelter, W 10yd [1*].
  *Morus alba* [**White Mulberry**]: S central area [1].
OLEACEAE [OLIVE FAMILY], p. 174
  *Fraxinus americana* [**White Ash**]: SE corner, SE [few].
  *Fraxinus pennsylvanica* [**Green Ash**]: NW area [few].
PINACEAE [PINE FAMILY], p. 59
  *Larix decidua* [**European Larch**]: SW area [few*].
  *Picea abies* [**Norway Spruce**]: S central area [many].
  *Pinus nigra* [**Austrian Pine**]: Dorr Road, S side, along [many].
  *Pinus sylvestris* [**Scotch Pine**]: NW area [1]; NW area, near W fence [10]; Sollitt shelter,
    E path [1].
ROSACEAE [ROSE FAMILY], p. 122
  *Crataegus punctata* [**Dotted Hawthorn**]: Maintenance center, W [1].
  *Malus spp.* [**Ornamental Crabapple hybrids**]: S central area, water fountain, NE 30yd [2];
    S central area, water fountain, SE 10yd [1]; SE area [1].
  *Prunus serotina* [**Blackcherry; Wild Black Cherry**]: NW area [1*]; S central area [1].
  *Prunus virginiana* [**Chokecherry**]: SW area [many*].
  *Spiraea × bumalda* [**Anthony Waterer Spiraea**]: Maintenance center, E [hedge].
  *Spiraea nipponica* 'Snowmound' [**Snowmound Nippon Spiraea**]: Maintenance center, E
    [few].
RUTACEAE [RUE FAMILY], p. 169
  *Phellodendron amurense* [**Cork-tree**]: S central area, W of cemetery [2]; Tee 4 [1].
SALICACEAE [WILLOW FAMILY], p. 110
  *Populus deltoides* [**Cottonwood**]: NE area [2].
STYRACACEAE [STORAX FAMILY], p. 117
  *Halesia carolina* [**Carolina Silverbell; Snowdrop-tree**]: 17th tee, halfway to 17th green [1*];
    SW area, SW of green 8 [1*].
TAXACEAE [YEW FAMILY], p. 55
  *Taxus × media* [**Anglojapanese Yew**]: Maintenance center [6].
TILIACEAE [LINDEN FAMILY], p. 107
  *Tilia americana* [**American Basswood; American Linden**]: S central area [7]; Sollitt shelter,
    E [1].
  *Tilia heterophylla* [**White Basswood**]: SW central area [many].
  *Tilia × moltkei* [**Moltke's Linden**]: SW area [many*].
ULMACEAE [ELM FAMILY], p. 92
  *Ulmus americana* [**American Elm**]: Sollitt shelter, E [many].
  *Ulmus parvifolia* [**Lacebark Elm; Chinese Elm**]: SE area [2*]; Sollitt Shelter, E 40yd [1*].
  *Ulmus pumila* [**Siberian Elm**]: Rockne Memorial, W 50yd [1].
VITACEAE [GRAPE FAMILY], p. 157
  *Vitis riparia* [**River-bank Grape; Frost Grape**]: SW corner, fence [1].


# CALVARY

BETULACEAE [BIRCH FAMILY], p. 103
  *Corylus americana* [**American Hazelnut; American Filbert**]: Cross, sides [2*].

CAPRIFOLIACEAE [HONEYSUCKLE FAMILY], p. 180
    *Lonicera japonica* [**Japanese Honeysuckle**]: E, 45yd [1].
    *Lonicera maackii* [**Amur Honeysuckle**]: E, 60yd [many].
    *Lonicera tatarica* [**Tatarian Honeysuckle**]: E, 30yd [1].
    *Viburnum acerifolium* [**Maple-leaf Viburnum**]: Woods [many*].
HYDRANGEACEAE [HYDRANGEA FAMILY], p. 117
    *Philadelphus inodorus* var. *grandiflorus* [**Large-flowering Mock Orange**]: SW 15yd [few*].
OLEACEAE [OLIVE FAMILY], p. 174
    *Fraxinus pennsylvanica* [**Green Ash**]: St. Joseph Hall, woods between [many*].
PINACEAE [PINE FAMILY], p. 59
    *Tsuga canadensis* [**Eastern Hemlock**]: [3*].
RHAMNACEAE [BUCKTHORN FAMILY], p. 157
    *Rhamnus frangula* [**Glossy Buckthorn; Alder Buckthorn**]: St. Joseph Hall, woods lakeside
        [many*].
ROSACEAE [ROSE FAMILY], p. 122
    *Prunus tomentosa* [**Nanking Cherry**]: W, in woods [1*].
    *Prunus virginiana* [**Chokecherry**]: Woods [many*].
    *Rhodotypos scandens* [**Japanese Jetbead**]: St. Joseph Hall, woods between [many*].
    *Rubus frondosus* [**Leafy-bracted Blackberry**]: Woods [many*].
    *Rubus occidentalis* [**Black Raspberry; Blackcap**]: St. Mary's Lake, woods between [many*];
        Woods [many*].
TILIACEAE [LINDEN FAMILY], p. 107
    *Tilia americana* [**American Basswood; American Linden**]: Woods [many*].
ULMACEAE [ELM FAMILY], p. 92
    *Celtis occidentalis* [**Hackberry**]: St. Joseph's Lake, W 75yd, area [many*].
VITACEAE [GRAPE FAMILY], p. 157
    *Parthenocissus inserta* [**Glossy Virginia Creeper**]: Woods [1*].
    *Parthenocissus quinquefolia* [**Virginia Creeper**]: Woods [many*].
    *Vitis aestivalis* var. *argentifolia* [**Silver-leaf Grape**]: Community Cemetery, walk between,
        N side [many*].

## CAMPUS SECURITY BUILDING

ACERACEAE [MAPLE FAMILY], p. 161
    *Acer negundo* [**Boxelder**]: SW corner [6*].
BERBERIDACEAE [BARBERRY FAMILY], p. 86
    *Berberis thunbergii* [**Japanese Barberry**]: S side [hedge*].
CAPRIFOLIACEAE [HONEYSUCKLE FAMILY], p. 180
    *Sambucus canadensis* [**American Elder**]: N, St. Mary's Lake margin [1*].
CUPRESSACEAE [CYPRESS FAMILY], p. 72
    *Thuja occidentalis* 'Globosa' [**Globe Arborvitae**]: N, Carroll Hall sign, lakeside [1*].
FABACEAE [PEA FAMILY], p. 144
    *Robinia pseudoacacia* [**Black Locust**]: N side, E of parking lot [5*].
HYDRANGEACEAE [HYDRANGEA FAMILY], p. 117
    *Deutzia* × *magnifica* [**Clustered Deutzia**]: NE corner, E side [2*].
MORACEAE [MULBERRY FAMILY], p. 94
    *Maclura pomifera* [**Osage Orange**]: Dorr Road, N side [hedge*].
    *Morus alba* [**White Mulberry**]: E wing, N 5yd [1]; N, parking lot, NW 10yd [1]; SW
        corner [2].
ROSACEAE [ROSE FAMILY], p. 122
    *Rhodotypos scandens* [**Japanese Jetbead**]: E side [4*].

SIMAROUBACEAE [QUASSIA FAMILY], p. 168
   *Ailanthus altissima* [**Tree-of-heaven**]: N side, E of parking lot [8]; NW 60yd, along road [2*].
TILIACEAE [LINDEN FAMILY], p. 107
   *Tilia americana* [**American Basswood; American Linden**]: NE corner, E 35yd [1*].
ULMACEAE [ELM FAMILY], p. 92
   *Celtis occidentalis* [**Hackberry**]: W wing, N 30yd [3*].


# CARROLL HALL

ACERACEAE [MAPLE FAMILY], p. 161
   *Acer platanoides* [**Norway Maple**]: SE and SW corners [2].
   *Acer platanoides* 'Rubrum' [**Crimson Norway Maple**]: W lawn [2*].
   *Acer saccharinum* [**Silver Maple; Soft Maple**]: E, along road [3].
   *Acer saccharum* subsp. *nigrum* [**Black Maple**]: SE corner, along walk to lake, N side [1*]; SE corner, along walk to lake, S side [2*].
CAESALPINIACEAE [CAESALPINIA FAMILY], p. 142
   *Gleditsia triacanthos* [**Honeylocust**]: St. Mary's Lake, road-walk junction, NE [1*].
CAPRIFOLIACEAE [HONEYSUCKLE FAMILY], p. 180
   *Lonicera* × *amoena* 'Rosea' [**Honeysuckle**]: Tool shed, N side [12*].
   *Viburnum lentago* [**Nannyberry; Sweet Viburnum**]: W 30yd, hedge [1*].
   *Viburnum rhytidophyllum* [**Rugose Viburnum**]: W 30yd, hedge [4*].
   *Viburnum sieboldii* [**Siebold Viburnum**]: NW [many]; W 30yd, hedge [3*].
CELASTRACEAE [STAFF-TREE FAMILY], p. 151
   *Euonymus europaea* var. *atrorubens* [**Crimson-fruited Spindletree**]: W 30yd, hedge [many*].
CORNACEAE [DOGWOOD FAMILY], p. 149
   *Cornus purpusii* [**Silky Dogwood; Pale Dogwood**]: Swimming pier (former) [1*].
CUPRESSACEAE [CYPRESS FAMILY], p. 72
   *Juniperus chinensis* 'Torulosa' [**Clustered Juniper**]: S, parking lot, W end [8*].
   *Platycladus orientalis* [**Oriental Arborvitae**]: SE, along road [9]; SW corner, lawn [30*].
   *Thuja occidentalis* 'Fastigiata' [**Columnar Arborvitae**]: SE [5*].
FAGACEAE [BEECH FAMILY], p. 98
   *Fagus sylvatica* 'Atropunicea' [**Copper Beech; Purple Beech**]: NW corner, N 20yd [1].
   *Quercus rubra* [**Red Oak; Northern Red Oak**]: E lawn, 80yd ESE [4].
   *Quercus velutina* [**Black Oak**]: NW corner, NW 30yd [1].
HAMAMELIDACEAE [WITCH-HAZEL FAMILY], p. 90
   *Hamamelis vernalis* [**Vernal Witch-hazel**]: W 30yd, hedge [1*].
JUGLANDACEAE [WALNUT FAMILY], p. 96
   *Juglans nigra* [**Black Walnut**]: NE, along walk [100*].
OLEACEAE [OLIVE FAMILY], p. 174
   *Ligustrum vulgare* 'Chlorocarpum' [**Green-fruited Privet**]: NW, lakeside [many].
PINACEAE [PINE FAMILY], p. 59
   *Abies balsamea* 'Nana' [**Dwarf Balsam Fir**]: S side [4].
   *Abies concolor* [**White Fir; Colorado Fir**]: SE corner, E 35yd [1*].
   *Picea abies* [**Norway Spruce**]: SW corner [4*].
   *Pinus banksiana* [**Jack Pine**]: NW 70yd [4*].
   *Pinus flexilis* [**Limber Pine**]: E lawn [1].
   *Pinus nigra* [**Austrian Pine**]: W [1].
   *Pinus sylvestris* [**Scotch Pine**]: SW corner, W [4].
   *Pinus sylvestris* 'Pendula' [**Weeping Scotch Pine**]: E lawn [1*].
   *Pinus thunbergiana* [**Japanese Black Pine**]: W side, center, W 60yd [2*].

*Tsuga canadensis* [**Eastern Hemlock**]: SW corner, [10*].
RHAMNACEAE  [BUCKTHORN FAMILY], p. 157
    *Rhamnus frangula* [**Glossy Buckthorn; Alder Buckthorn**]: NE 75yd, lakeside [many*].
ROSACEAE  [ROSE FAMILY], p. 122
    *Prunus avium* [**Mazzard; Sweet Cherry**]: W 30yd, hedge, E side [6*].
    *Prunus mahaleb* [**Mahaleb Cherry**]: W 30yd, hedge [1].
    *Prunus serotina* [**Blackcherry; Wild Black Cherry**]: SW corner, WSW 100yd [1].
    *Rhodotypos scandens* [**Japanese Jetbead**]: W 30yd, hedge [2*].
    *Spiraea trichocarpa* [**Korean Spiraea**]: W 30yd, hedge, center [1].
    *Spiraea* × *vanhouttei* [**Vanhoutte Spiraea**]: NW corner, W 30yd [1*].
SALICACEAE  [WILLOW FAMILY], p. 110
    *Populus deltoides* [**Cottonwood**]: N, lakeside [8*]; SE 50yd [1].
    *Populus grandidentata* [**Bigtooth Aspen**]: Tennis courts, N, lakeside [8*].
    *Salix alba* var. *vitellina* [**Yellow Willow**]: Kitchen, NE, lakeside [1]; Kitchen, NE, lakeside
        [1]; N side, N 40 yd [1]; N, lakeside [1]; NE corner, E 100yd, lakeside [1]; NE corner,
        E 125yd, lakeside [1]; NNW, E of Carroll Hall Annex [1].
    *Salix fragilis* [**Brittle Willow; Crack Willow**]: E, lakeside [few*].
TAXACEAE  [YEW FAMILY], p. 55
    *Taxus cuspidata* [**Japanese Yew**]: SW corner, W 40yd [2].
ULMACEAE  [ELM FAMILY], p. 92
    *Celtis occidentalis* [**Hackberry**]: NE corner, E 120yd, lakeside [1*]; NW 20yd [1*].
    *Ulmus parvifolia* [**Lacebark Elm; Chinese Elm**]: S 25yd [1*]; SE corner, E in lawn [1*].
    *Ulmus pumila* [**Siberian Elm**]: N side [8*].
    *Ulmus rubra* [**Slippery Elm**]: W 30yd, hedge [1*].
VITACEAE  [GRAPE FAMILY], p. 157
    *Parthenocissus inserta* [**Glossy Virginia Creeper**]: NW path, S side [1].

## CARROLL HALL ANNEX

HYDRANGEACEAE  [HYDRANGEA FAMILY], p. 117
    *Philadelphus* × *virginalis* [**Virginal Mock Orange**]: NW, 20yd [1].
JUGLANDACEAE  [WALNUT FAMILY], p. 96
    *Carya ovalis* var. *obcordata* [**Obcordate Pignut**]: SE 10ft [1*].
PINACEAE  [PINE FAMILY], p. 59
    *Pinus resinosa* [**Red Pine; Norway Pine**]: SW [1].

## CAVANAUGH HALL

ACERACEAE  [MAPLE FAMILY], p. 161
    *Acer platanoides* [**Norway Maple**]: Main entrance, 50ft [1*]; Main entrance, NW 50ft [1];
        NW corner [1 **Commem.**].
    *Acer pseudoplatanus* [**Sycamore Maple**]: Washington Hall, midway [1*].
    *Acer saccharinum* [**Silver Maple; Soft Maple**]: NE corner [1].
    *Acer saccharum* [**Sugar Maple; Hard Maple**]: E side [4].
CAPRIFOLIACEAE  [HONEYSUCKLE FAMILY], p. 180
    *Lonicera tatarica* [**Tatarian Honeysuckle**]: NW corner [1].
CELASTRACEAE  [STAFF-TREE FAMILY], p. 151
    *Euonymus fortunei* [**Chinese Winter-creeper**]: SW [bed].

CORNACEAE [DOGWOOD FAMILY], p. 149
> *Cornus florida* [**Flowering Dogwood**]: Main entrance [2*]; S, basketball court, E edge [1 **Commem.**].

FAGACEAE [BEECH FAMILY], p. 98
> *Quercus velutina* [**Black Oak**]: N lawn, N of door [1 **Commem.**].

HYDRANGEACEAE [HYDRANGEA FAMILY], p. 117
> *Hydrangea quercifolia* [**Oak-leaf Hydrangea**]: [beds*].

PINACEAE [PINE FAMILY], p. 59
> *Picea abies* [**Norway Spruce**]: NW corner [1*].
> *Pinus strobus* 'Fastigiata' [**Pyramidal White Pine**]: Breen-Phillips, between [2*].

ROSACEAE [ROSE FAMILY], p. 122
> *Chaenomeles speciosa* [**Japanese Quince**]: S end [hedge*].
> *Malus spp.* [**Ornamental Crabapple hybrids**]: Administration Bldg, along walk between [7].

TAXACEAE [YEW FAMILY], p. 55
> *Taxus cuspidata* 'Intermedia' [**Japanese Compact Yew**]: SE corner [8*].

ULMACEAE [ELM FAMILY], p. 92
> *Ulmus americana* [**American Elm**]: S door, W 20yd [1].

VITACEAE [GRAPE FAMILY], p. 157
> *Parthenocissus tricuspidata* [**Boston Ivy**]: W end, wall [many*].


## CEDAR GROVE CEMETERY

CAESALPINIACEAE [CAESALPINIA FAMILY], p. 142
> *Gleditsia triacanthos* subsp. *inermis* [**Thornless Honeylocust**]: NE entrance, at Notre Dame Ave [1].

CAPRIFOLIACEAE [HONEYSUCKLE FAMILY], p. 180
> *Lonicera tatarica* [**Tatarian Honeysuckle**]: Chapel, NW corner, NW [1].

CUPRESSACEAE [CYPRESS FAMILY], p. 72
> *Juniperus virginiana* [**Eastern Redcedar**]: N, E of shed [1].
> *Platycladus orientalis* [**Oriental Arborvitae**]: N, W of shed [many].

ROSACEAE [ROSE FAMILY], p. 122
> *Malus spp.* [**Ornamental Crabapple hybrids**]: N, W of shed, S of road [1].


## CENTER FOR CONTINUING EDUCATION

GROSSULARIACEAE [CURRANT FAMILY], p. 121
> *Ribes alpinum* [**Alpine Currant; Mountain Currant**]: NE corner [hedge*].

PINACEAE [PINE FAMILY], p. 59
> *Pinus strobus* [**Eastern White Pine**]: E side [6].

ROSACEAE [ROSE FAMILY], p. 122
> *Crataegus crus-galli* [**Cockspur Hawthorn; Cockspur-thorn**]: S end [1].
> *Crataegus phaenopyrum* [**Washington Hawthorn**]: NE corner [1]; W side [2].
> *Malus spp.* [**Ornamental Crabapple hybrids**]: E side [2].

TAXACEAE [YEW FAMILY], p. 55
> *Taxus cuspidata* 'Intermedia' [**Japanese Compact Yew**]: S end [4*]; W entrance, N side [9*]; W entrance, S side [9*].

## CENTER FOR SOCIAL CONCERNS

CUPRESSACEAE [CYPRESS FAMILY], p. 72
   *Juniperus sabina* 'Tamariscifolia' [**Tamarix Savin**]: E side [hedge*].
HAMAMELIDACEAE [WITCH-HAZEL FAMILY], p. 90
   *Liquidambar styraciflua* [**Sweetgum**]: E and W, flanking building [2*].
PINACEAE [PINE FAMILY], p. 59
   *Pinus sylvestris* 'Fastigiata' [**Pyramidal Scotch Pine**]: SW corner [1*].
ROSACEAE [ROSE FAMILY], p. 122
   *Crataegus crus-galli* [**Cockspur Hawthorn; Cockspur-thorn**]: SW corner [1*].


## COLUMBA HALL

ACERACEAE [MAPLE FAMILY], p. 161
   *Acer ginnala* [**Amur Maple**]: Basketball court, NW corner [1]; E wing, SE corner, SE [4];
      NE corner, E lawn [1].
   *Acer platanoides* 'Crimson King' [**Norway Maple**]: SE, at St. Mary's Lake [1 **Commem.**].
   *Acer saccharinum* [**Silver Maple; Soft Maple**]: Garage, NE [many*].
BIGNONIACEAE [BIGNONIA FAMILY], p. 179
   *Catalpa speciosa* [**Northern Catalpa**]: NW corner, N 70yd [few].
CUPRESSACEAE [CYPRESS FAMILY], p. 72
   *Platycladus orientalis* 'Aurea' [**Golden Dwarf Oriental Arborvitae**]: NW corner, lawn [6*].
   *Thuja occidentalis* [**American Arborvitae; Northern White Cedar**]: NW 10yd [1].
FAGACEAE [BEECH FAMILY], p. 98
   *Fagus sylvatica* 'Atropunicea' [**Copper Beech; Purple Beech**]: NE corner [1*].
   *Quercus alba* [**White Oak**]: NE corner [1*].
   *Quercus velutina* [**Black Oak**]: Garage, ENE 20yd [1].
MORACEAE [MULBERRY FAMILY], p. 94
   *Morus alba* [**White Mulberry**]: SE corner, SE 40yd [1].
OLEACEAE [OLIVE FAMILY], p. 174
   *Fraxinus americana* [**White Ash**]: Front, W of road [3*].
PINACEAE [PINE FAMILY], p. 59
   *Picea pungens* 'Glauca' [**Blue Spruce; Colorado Blue Spruce**]: Main entrance, 10yd [1*].
   *Pinus sylvestris* [**Scotch Pine**]: SE corner, SE [1].
ROSACEAE [ROSE FAMILY], p. 122
   *Prunus cerasifera* 'Atropurpurea' [**Purpleleaf Cherry-plum**]: SW, along road [6].
SALICACEAE [WILLOW FAMILY], p. 110
   *Populus alba* [**White Poplar; Silverleaf Poplar**]: NE, lakeside [1*]; SE 60yd [2*].
   *Salix alba* var. *vitellina* [**Yellow Willow**]: Basketball court, N [1]; Basketball court, W 10yd,
      lakeside [4].
   *Salix fragilis* [**Brittle Willow; Crack Willow**]: Basketball court, WNW, 25yd [1].
TAXACEAE [YEW FAMILY], p. 55
   *Taxus cuspidata* [**Japanese Yew**]: Front entrance [hedge]; Front, fountain [1]; N side,
      smokestack, above parking lot [5]; NE corner, lawn [1]; NE, along road [hedge].
   *Taxus cuspidata* 'Erecta' [**Japanese Upright Yew**]: NE lawn [11*]; NW lawn [12*].
   *Taxus* × *media* [**Anglojapanese Yew**]: S side, steps [many].
ULMACEAE [ELM FAMILY], p. 92
   *Ulmus pumila* [**Siberian Elm**]: Basketball court, N side [1*].

## Community Cemetery

APOCYNACEAE [DOGBANE FAMILY], p. 171
  *Vinca minor* [**Common Periwinkle; Running Myrtle**]: Cross, base [bed*].
CUPRESSACEAE [CYPRESS FAMILY], p. 72
  *Juniperus virginiana* 'Canaertii' [**Canaert Redcedar**]: S end, Cross [1*].
  *Thuja occidentalis* 'Pyramidalis' [**Pyramidal Arborvitae**]: N end [12*].
JUGLANDACEAE [WALNUT FAMILY], p. 96
  *Carya ovalis* [**Sweet Pignut**]: NE, edge of woods [many*].
  *Carya ovalis* var. *obcordata* [**Obcordate Pignut**]: N central area [1*].
RHAMNACEAE [BUCKTHORN FAMILY], p. 157
  *Rhamnus frangula* [**Glossy Buckthorn; Alder Buckthorn**]: Mission House, between [1].
ROSACEAE [ROSE FAMILY], p. 122
  *Malus* spp. [**Ornamental Crabapple hybrids**]: Mission House, between [4].
  *Prunus serotina* [**Blackcherry; Wild Black Cherry**]: NE corner, NE 45yd [2*].
  *Pyrus calleryana* [**Callery Pear**]: Mission House, between [4].
SALICACEAE [WILLOW FAMILY], p. 110
  *Salix alba* var. *vitellina* [**Yellow Willow**]: SW corner, S 60yd [1].
  *Salix caprea* [**Goat Willow**]: Mission House, between [1].
ULMACEAE [ELM FAMILY], p. 92
  *Ulmus pumila* [**Siberian Elm**]: SW corner [1*].

## Computing Center and Math Building

NYSSACEAE [TUPELO FAMILY], p. 148
  *Nyssa sylvatica* [**Black Tupelo; Blackgum; Sourgum**]: S door, E side [2*].
OLEACEAE [OLIVE FAMILY], p. 174
  *Fraxinus americana* f. *iodocarpa* [**Purple-fruited Ash**]: SW corner, SW 100yd [1*].
  *Fraxinus pennsylvanica* [**Green Ash**]: S door, E side [1].
ROSACEAE [ROSE FAMILY], p. 122
  *Malus* spp. [**Ornamental Crabapple hybrids**]: N door, E side [1*].
RUTACEAE [RUE FAMILY], p. 169
  *Evodia danielii* [**Chinese Evodia**]: E side [1].

## Corby Hall

APOCYNACEAE [DOGBANE FAMILY], p. 171
  *Vinca minor* [**Common Periwinkle; Running Myrtle**]: Front, Corby statue [bed*]; Main entrance, flanking [beds*].
BERBERIDACEAE [BARBERRY FAMILY], p. 86
  *Berberis thunbergii* [**Japanese Barberry**]: NW, road, N side [hedge*].
CAESALPINIACEAE [CAESALPINIA FAMILY], p. 142
  *Gymnocladus dioica* [**Kentucky Coffeetree**]: SW corner, SW 20yd [1*].
CAPRIFOLIACEAE [HONEYSUCKLE FAMILY], p. 180
  *Lonicera tatarica* [**Tatarian Honeysuckle**]: NW, lakeside [1*].
  *Viburnum plicatum* f. *tomentosum* [**Doublefile Viburnum**]: N side, court [1].
CELASTRACEAE [STAFF-TREE FAMILY], p. 151
  *Euonymus alata* [**Winged Burningbush; Winged Spindletree**]: Main entrance, E side [15*].

CORNACEAE [DOGWOOD FAMILY], p. 149

    *Cornus alternifolia* [**Alternate-leaf Dogwood; Pagoda Dogwood**]: N side, kitchen, N walk to Grotto [1*].

    *Cornus florida* [**Flowering Dogwood**]: S 60yd [3*].

    *Cornus sanguinea* [**Bloodtwig Dogwood**]: SW corner [1*].

CUPRESSACEAE [CYPRESS FAMILY], p. 72

    *Chamaecyparis nootkatensis* 'Pendula' [**Weeping Nootka Falsecypress**]: E side, S end [3*].

    *Juniperus chinensis* [**Chinese Juniper**]: NW, Grotto lawn, S edge [4*]; W 40ft [3*].

    *Juniperus virginiana* 'Globosa' [**Globose Redcedar**]: SE corner [1*].

    *Platycladus orientalis* [**Oriental Arborvitae**]: N 15yd [1*].

FABACEAE [PEA FAMILY], p. 144

    *Cladrastis kentukea* [**Yellowwood; Virgilia**]: NW corner, N 35yd at Grotto walk [1*].

    *Sophora japonica* [**Japanese Pagodatree**]: Main entrance, S 50yd [1*].

FAGACEAE [BEECH FAMILY], p. 98

    *Fagus sylvatica* 'Atropunicea' [**Copper Beech; Purple Beech**]: N bird bath [1].

    *Quercus alba* [**White Oak**]: SW 35yd [1*].

    *Quercus coccinea* [**Scarlet Oak**]: SW [1].

    *Quercus macrocarpa* [**Bur Oak; Mossy-cup Oak**]: N [2].

    *Quercus palustris* [**Pin Oak**]: S [1].

    *Quercus rubra* [**Red Oak; Northern Red Oak**]: Entrance, W 50ft [1].

GINKGOACEAE [GINKGO FAMILY], p. 54

    *Ginkgo biloba* 'Laciniata' [**Split-leaf Ginkgo**]: E wing, N, lawn above Grotto [1].

HIPPOCASTANACEAE [HORSECHESTNUT FAMILY], p. 160

    *Aesculus hippocastanum* [**Horsechestnut**]: SE corner, SE 10yd [1*]; W 10yd [1*].

    *Aesculus parviflora* [**Bottlebrush Buckeye**]: E wing, N, lawn above Grotto [1*].

HYDRANGEACEAE [HYDRANGEA FAMILY], p. 117

    *Hydrangea paniculata* 'Grandiflora' [**Peegee Hydrangea**]: Dining room, N end [1*].

JUGLANDACEAE [WALNUT FAMILY], p. 96

    *Juglans nigra* [**Black Walnut**]: N, lawn above Grotto [1*].

MAGNOLIACEAE [MAGNOLIA FAMILY], p. 82

    *Magnolia acuminata* [**Cucumber Tree**]: SW corner, SW 50yd [2*].

    *Magnolia* × *proctoriana* [**Chinese Magnolia**]: E front entrance, S roadside [1*].

MALVACEAE [MALLOW FAMILY], p. 109

    *Hibiscus syriacus* [**Shrub-althea; Rose-of-Sharon**]: Front, Corby statue, SE 30yd [1*].

MORACEAE [MULBERRY FAMILY], p. 94

    *Morus alba* [**White Mulberry**]: NW corner, N [2].

NYSSACEAE [TUPELO FAMILY], p. 148

    *Nyssa sylvatica* [**Black Tupelo; Blackgum; Sourgum**]: Old College, midway [1*].

OLEACEAE [OLIVE FAMILY], p. 174

    *Fraxinus quadrangulata* [**Blue Ash**]: Old College, midway [1*].

    *Syringa reticulata* [**Japanese Tree Lilac**]: SE corner [2*].

    *Syringa vulgaris* [**Common Lilac**]: Architecture Bldg, midway [2*].

PINACEAE [PINE FAMILY], p. 59

    *Larix decidua* [**European Larch**]: Front, Corby statue [2*].

    *Picea abies* [**Norway Spruce**]: Dining room, NW [7*]; SW 20yd [3*]; SW corner, S 10yd [1*].

    *Pinus nigra* [**Austrian Pine**]: W end, W 45yd [1]; W, lakeside [1].

    *Pinus resinosa* [**Red Pine; Norway Pine**]: W, lakeside [1*].

    *Pinus sylvestris* [**Scotch Pine**]: SW corner, SW 20yd [1].

    *Pinus sylvestris* 'Pendula' [**Weeping Scotch Pine**]: W, lakeside [1*].

    *Pinus sylvestris* var. *rigensis* [**Upright Scotch Pine**]: Main entrance, S 35yd, S of road [2*].

RANUNCULACEAE [BUTTERCUP FAMILY], p. 85

*Clematis dioscoreiflora* 'Robusta' [**Korean Clematis**]: W end, W of walk [2].

*Clematis spp.* [**Clematis**]: SW corner [1].

ROSACEAE [ROSE FAMILY], p. 122

*Crataegus phaenopyrum* [**Washington Hawthorn**]: SE corner, S 15yd [1].

*Crataegus punctata* var. *pausiaca* [**Olive-shaped Haw**]: SW corner, W 15yd [1*].

*Malus pumila* [**Common Apple**]: NW, walk to Grotto [1].

*Malus spp.* [**Ornamental Crabapple hybrids**]: NW 30yd, Grotto lawn [3*]; NW corner, N 25yd [1*].

*Pyrus calleryana* [**Callery Pear**]: Architecture Bldg, between [3].

*Spiraea* × *bumalda* [**Anthony Waterer Spiraea**]: W end, W 50yd [2].

*Spiraea japonica* 'Ruberrima' [**Chinese Spiraea**]: W end [1*].

*Spiraea* × *vanhouttei* [**Vanhoutte Spiraea**]: SW corner, SW 5yd [1].

TAXACEAE [YEW FAMILY], p. 55

*Taxus cuspidata* [**Japanese Yew**]: N side [12].

*Taxus cuspidata* 'Fastigiata' [**Japanese Pyramidal Yew**]: E front entrance, flanking [2*].

*Taxus* × *media* [**Anglojapanese Yew**]: SW corner [1].

*Taxus* × *media* 'Brownii' [**Brown's Yew**]: Main entrance, flanking [2*].

ULMACEAE [ELM FAMILY], p. 92

*Ulmus americana* [**American Elm**]: Main entrance, S 40yd, roadside [1*]; N side, kitchen, N 20yd [1]; SW corner, W 25yd [1].

*Ulmus carpinifolia* [**Smooth-leaf Elm**]: Main entrance, steps, SW 4yd [1*]; SW corner, W 15yd, just N of walk [1*].

*Ulmus davidiana* var. *japonica* [**Japanese Elm**]: SW corner, W 15yd, 4yd N of walk [1*].

*Ulmus glabra* [**Wych Elm; Scotch Elm**]: Main entrance, steps, SE lawn [1*].

*Ulmus* × *vegeta* [**Huntingdon Elm**]: Main entrance, SE of steps [1*]; Main entrance, steps, W [1*].

## CROWLEY HALL OF MUSIC

ANACARDIACEAE [CASHEW FAMILY], p. 166

*Cotinus coggygria* [**Smoketree; Smokebush**]: NE corner [1*]; SE corner [3*].

BETULACEAE [BIRCH FAMILY], p. 103

*Carpinus caroliniana* [**American Hornbeam; Blue Beech**]: N 5yd [1*].

CAESALPINIACEAE [CAESALPINIA FAMILY], p. 142

*Gymnocladus dioica* [**Kentucky Coffeetree**]: N end [1*]; NE corner [1*]; S end [1*].

FAGACEAE [BEECH FAMILY], p. 98

*Fagus orientalis* [**Oriental Beech**]: E 15yd [1*].

*Quercus alba* [**White Oak**]: NW corner, W 60yd [1*].

*Quercus macrocarpa* [**Bur Oak; Mossy-cup Oak**]: NW 40yd [1].

OLEACEAE [OLIVE FAMILY], p. 174

*Syringa* × *chinensis* [**Chinese Lilac**]: E [1].

*Syringa vulgaris* [**Common Lilac**]: SW corner [1*].

PINACEAE [PINE FAMILY], p. 59

*Picea abies* [**Norway Spruce**]: W 15-30yd [6*].

*Pinus nigra* [**Austrian Pine**]: NE at walk [1]; SW corner, W 35yd [1]; SW corner, W 50yd [1].

ROSACEAE [ROSE FAMILY], p. 122

*Spiraea* × *vanhouttei* [**Vanhoutte Spiraea**]: E side [16*].

TAXACEAE [YEW FAMILY], p. 55

*Taxus* × *media* [**Anglojapanese Yew**]: W side [6].

## CUSHING HALL OF ENGINEERING

ACERACEAE [MAPLE FAMILY], p. 161
*Acer platanoides* 'Crimson King' [**Norway Maple**]: O'Shaughnessy, midway [1 **Commem.**].
BERBERIDACEAE [BARBERRY FAMILY], p. 86
*Mahonia aquifolium* [**Oregon Grape**]: N, main entrance, E [beds*].
CELASTRACEAE [STAFF-TREE FAMILY], p. 151
*Euonymus alata* [**Winged Burningbush; Winged Spindletree**]: N, main entrance, E [3].
*Euonymus fortunei* [**Chinese Winter-creeper**]: NE corner [2].
CORNACEAE [DOGWOOD FAMILY], p. 149
*Cornus florida* [**Flowering Dogwood**]: Law School, plaza between [2].
*Cornus florida* 'Rubra' [**Red-flowering Dogwood**]: NE corner [1*].
OLEACEAE [OLIVE FAMILY], p. 174
*Ligustrum ovalifolium* [**California Privet**]: NE corner [1].
ROSACEAE [ROSE FAMILY], p. 122
*Amelanchier arborea* [**Downy Serviceberry; Juneberry**]: W side [many].
*Amelanchier laevis* [**Allegheny Serviceberry**]: N side, W [2].
*Cotoneaster divaricatus* [**Spreading Cotoneaster**]: NE corner [1*].
*Cotoneaster multiflorus* var. *calocarpus* [**Arching Cotoneaster**]: N side [beds]; N, main entrance, E side [1*].
*Crataegus laevigata* 'Paulii' [**Double-flowering English Hawthorn**]: N side, W end [1*].
*Malus pumila* [**Common Apple**]: N, main entrance, W side [1*].
*Malus* spp. [**Ornamental Crabapple hybrids**]: N side, E [1].
*Rhodotypos scandens* [**Japanese Jetbead**]: NE corner [3*].
*Sorbus aucuparia* [**European Mountain-ash**]: W end [1*].
*Spiraea* × *bumalda* [**Anthony Waterer Spiraea**]: NE corner [3].
ULMACEAE [ELM FAMILY], p. 92
*Ulmus rubra* [**Slippery Elm**]: NE corner, NE 15yd [1*].

## DeBARTOLO CLASSROOM BUILDING

ACERACEAE [MAPLE FAMILY], p. 161
*Acer platanoides* 'Crimson Sentry' [**Norway Maple**]: E side, flanking central doors [4].
*Acer pseudoplatanus* 'Spaethii' [**Sycamore Maple**]: S side, S of E door [1].
*Acer rubrum* 'Red Sunset' [**Red Maple**]: E side, S of N end doors [1].
BETULACEAE [BIRCH FAMILY], p. 103
*Carpinus betulus* 'Fastigiata' [**European Hornbeam**]: N side [5].
CAESALPINIACEAE [CAESALPINIA FAMILY], p. 142
*Gleditsia triacanthos* subsp. *inermis* [**Thornless Honeylocust**]: E, at street [8]; E, flanking central doors [2].
CAPRIFOLIACEAE [HONEYSUCKLE FAMILY], p. 180
*Viburnum* × *bodnantense* 'Pink Dawn' [**Bodnant Viburnum**]: E side, S of N end doors [4].
*Viburnum rhytidophyllum* [**Rugose Viburnum**]: N side, NW door, E side [2]; N side, between windows [12].
CORNACEAE [DOGWOOD FAMILY], p. 149
*Cornus kousa* [**Kousa Dogwood**]: NE corner, E side at doors [3].
CUPRESSACEAE [CYPRESS FAMILY], p. 72
*Juniperus chinensis* 'Old Gold' [**Chinese Juniper**]: E side, N end along S wall [9]; E side, SE corner [28]; N side, NE corner [25]; W side, NW corner [8]; W side, SW corner [8].

*Juniperus communis* 'Effusa' [**Common Juniper**]: N side, NW door, flanking [42].

*Juniperus conferta* 'Blue Pacific' [**Shore Juniper**]: E side, N of doors [38]; E side, S of doors [38]; W side, N of doors [16]; W side, S of doors [20].

*Juniperus horizontalis* 'Plumosa' [**Andorra Juniper**]: S side [10].

*Juniperus sabina* 'Variegata' [**Hoarfrost Savin**]: W side, S of doors [16]; W side, between doors [34].

*Thuja occidentalis* 'Emerald Green' [**Emerald Green Arborvitae**]: E side, around central plaza [62]; W side, along walk [139].

ERICACEAE [HEATH FAMILY], p. 113

*Rhododendron spp.* 'Ramapo' [**Ramapo Rhododendron**]: E side, between central doors [32]; NE corner, E side at doors [11].

FAGACEAE [BEECH FAMILY], p. 98

*Quercus robur* 'Fastigiata' [**Columnar English Oak**]: S side, SW corner, flanking door [2].

*Quercus rubra* [**Red Oak; Northern Red Oak**]: SE corner [1].

GROSSULARIACEAE [CURRANT FAMILY], p. 121

*Ribes alpinum* 'Aureum' [**Alpine Currant**]: E side, S of N end doors [2].

HAMAMELIDACEAE [WITCH-HAZEL FAMILY], p. 90

*Hamamelis* × *intermedia* 'Diane' [**Witch-hazel**]: E side, S of N end doors [2].

*Liquidambar styraciflua* [**Sweetgum**]: E side, SE corner [1].

OLEACEAE [OLIVE FAMILY], p. 174

*Syringa meyeri* 'Palibin' [**Meyer Lilac**]: W side, midway N and S of doors [8].

PINACEAE [PINE FAMILY], p. 59

*Picea pungens* [**Colorado Blue Spruce**]: E side, S of NE door [4]; E side, central lawn [1].

*Picea pungens* 'Baby Blue-eyes' [**Colorado Blue Spruce**]: W side, N and S ends [4].

*Picea pungens* 'Glauca' [**Blue Spruce; Colorado Blue Spruce**]: E side, flanking central doors [9]; W side, flanking doors [2].

*Picea pungens* 'Hoopsii' [**Colorado Spruce**]: E side, S central area [2].

*Tsuga canadensis* 'Jeddeloh' [**Eastern Hemlock**]: N side, below windows [15].

ROSACEAE [ROSE FAMILY], p. 122

*Amelanchier arborea* 'Cole Select' [**Downy Serviceberry**]: E side, along walls [19]; S side, central windows [5].

*Crataegus* × *lavallei* [**Lavalle Hawthorn**]: W side, NW corner [1]; W side, SW corner [1].

*Malus floribunda* [**Japanese Flowering Crabapple**]: E side, SE corner [3]; N side, NE corner [3].

*Malus yunnanensis* [**Veitchii Crabapple**]: N side, NW door, flanking [6]; S side, flanking windows [2].

*Prunus cerasifera* 'Thundercloud' [**Purpleleaf Cherry-plum**]: E side, midway N and S of doors [2]; W side, midway N and S of doors [2].

*Prunus laurocerasus* 'Schipkaensis' [**Schip Laurel**]: N [10].

*Prunus sargentii* 'Accolade' [**Sargent Cherry**]: E side, midway N and S of doors [4]; W side, midway N and S of doors [4].

*Pyrus calleryana* 'Aristocrat' [**Callery Pear**]: E side, between central doors [11]; W side, between doors [4].

*Spiraea* × *bumalda* 'Goldflame' [**Goldflame Spiraea**]: E side, along walls [22]; SE corner, S of E door [20]; SW corner, flanking S door [30].

*Spiraea* × *bumalda* 'Limemound' [**Limemound Spiraea**]: E side, S of N end doors [5].

STYRACACEAE [STORAX FAMILY], p. 117

*Styrax japonicus* [**Japanese Snowbell**]: E side, NW corner [1]; E side, flanking central doors [2].

THEACEAE [TEA FAMILY], p. 106

*Stewartia pseudocamelia* [**Japanese Stewartia**]: E side, between central doors [7].

TILIACEAE [LINDEN FAMILY], p. 107
    *Tilia cordata* 'DeGroot' [**Small-leaved European Linden**]: S side, center, at walk [2].
ULMACEAE [ELM FAMILY], p. 92
    *Zelkova serrata* 'Village Green' [**Zelkova**]: E, between N central and N end doors [2].

## DECIO FACULTY HALL

ACERACEAE [MAPLE FAMILY], p. 161
    *Acer saccharum* subsp. *nigrum* [**Black Maple**]: SE corner, E 20yd [1].
BERBERIDACEAE [BARBERRY FAMILY], p. 86
    *Berberis thunbergii* 'Atropurpurea' [**Japanese Bronze-leaf Barberry**]: E door [hedge]; E plaza [hedge]; W door [hedge]; W plaza [hedge].
CAESALPINIACEAE [CAESALPINIA FAMILY], p. 142
    *Cercis canadensis* [**Eastern Redbud; Judas-tree**]: NE corner [3].
    *Cercis canadensis* 'Forest Pansy' [**Eastern Redbud**]: S end [1]; W side, NW lawn, W edge [2].
    *Gleditsia triacanthos* subsp. *inermis* [**Thornless Honeylocust**]: E plaza [5]; E plaza [6]; SW corner [3*]; W plaza [6]; W plaza [6].
CAPRIFOLIACEAE [HONEYSUCKLE FAMILY], p. 180
    *Viburnum lentago* [**Nannyberry; Sweet Viburnum**]: W, service entrance [1].
    *Viburnum opulus* [**Cranberrybush; Guelder-rose**]: S end, E 5yd [2].
CERCIDIPHYLLACEAE [KATSURA TREE FAMILY], p. 88
    *Cercidiphyllum japonicum* [**Katsura Tree**]: W side, NW lawn [1 **Commem.**].
CUPRESSACEAE [CYPRESS FAMILY], p. 72
    *Thuja occidentalis* 'Globosa' [**Globe Arborvitae**]: E, edge of plaza [hedge]; W, edge of plaza [hedge].
FAGACEAE [BEECH FAMILY], p. 98
    *Castanea mollissima* [**Chinese Chestnut**]: O'Shaughnessy, E 25yd [1].
HAMAMELIDACEAE [WITCH-HAZEL FAMILY], p. 90
    *Liquidambar styraciflua* [**Sweetgum**]: W side [1].
MYRICACEAE [SWEET GALE FAMILY], p. 98
    *Myrica pensylvanica* [**Bayberry**]: W, service drive, N side [1].
PINACEAE [PINE FAMILY], p. 59
    *Pinus resinosa* [**Red Pine; Norway Pine**]: W, service entrance, N side [2].
ROSACEAE [ROSE FAMILY], p. 122
    *Crataegus crus-galli* [**Cockspur Hawthorn; Cockspur-thorn**]: W side [3].
    *Malus spp.* [**Ornamental Crabapple hybrids**]: E entrance, S 30yd [1]; E entrance, near plaza [8]; E side [5]; NW corner [2]; W side [4]; W side [2].
    *Prunus serrulata* var. *lannesiana* [**Japanese Double-flowering Cherry**]: NE corner, S [2].
    *Prunus virginiana* 'Shubert Select' [**Shubert Select Chokecherry**]: S wing, E side lawn [1 **Commem.**].
    *Spiraea* × *bumalda* [**Anthony Waterer Spiraea**]: E door [hedge]; W door [hedge].
TAXACEAE [YEW FAMILY], p. 55
    *Taxus* × *media* [**Anglojapanese Yew**]: E plaza [hedge]; W plaza [hedge].

## DILLON HALL

ACERACEAE [MAPLE FAMILY], p. 161
    *Acer rubrum* [**Red Maple**]: S [3].

*Acer saccharum* subsp. *nigrum* [**Black Maple**]: W wing, S, golf course fence, S side [1*].
**BERBERIDACEAE [BARBERRY FAMILY],** p. 86
    *Mahonia aquifolium* [**Oregon Grape**]: NW corner [bed*]; W court [beds*].
**CAESALPINIACEAE [CAESALPINIA FAMILY],** p. 142
    *Gleditsia triacanthos* subsp. *inermis* [**Thornless Honeylocust**]: SW corner, W [2*].
**CAPRIFOLIACEAE [HONEYSUCKLE FAMILY],** p. 180
    *Viburnum plicatum* f. *tomentosum* [**Doublefile Viburnum**]: E court, N entrance [1*]; E court, NE corner [3]; E court, SE [2*]; S wing, NE entrance [10*].
**CELASTRACEAE [STAFF-TREE FAMILY],** p. 151
    *Euonymus alata* [**Winged Burningbush; Winged Spindletree**]: E wing, S end [3*].
    *Euonymus fortunei* [**Chinese Winter-creeper**]: E court [bed].
    *Euonymus fortunei* 'Carrierei' [**Carriere's Winter-creeper**]: E court, N entrance [1*].
    *Euonymus fortunei* var. *radicans* [**Common Winter-creeper**]: E wing, SE end [bed*].
**CERCIDIPHYLLACEAE [KATSURA TREE FAMILY],** p. 88
    *Cercidiphyllum japonicum* [**Katsura Tree**]: NW corner [3*].
**CORNACEAE [DOGWOOD FAMILY],** p. 149
    *Cornus sanguinea* [**Bloodtwig Dogwood**]: S side [1*].
**CUPRESSACEAE [CYPRESS FAMILY],** p. 72
    *Chamaecyparis pisifera* [**Sawara Falsecypress**]: NE corner [1*].
    *Juniperus chinensis* 'Globosa' [**Chinese Globe Juniper**]: Chapel, E end [5*].
    *Juniperus chinensis* 'Mas' [**Robert Fortune Juniper**]: E court [7*]; W court [6*].
    *Juniperus virginiana* [**Eastern Redcedar**]: E court, S side [1]; E court, entrance [1].
    *Juniperus virginiana* 'Schottii' [**Schott's Redcedar**]: SW entrance, S side [2*].
    *Platycladus orientalis* [**Oriental Arborvitae**]: S side [9*].
**FAGACEAE [BEECH FAMILY],** p. 98
    *Fagus grandifolia* [**American Beech**]: S side [1*].
**MAGNOLIACEAE [MAGNOLIA FAMILY],** p. 82
    *Liriodendron tulipifera* [**Tulip Tree; Yellow-poplar**]: W court [4*].
**PINACEAE [PINE FAMILY],** p. 59
    *Picea abies* [**Norway Spruce**]: E court [1].
    *Picea pungens* 'Koster' [**Koster Weeping Blue Spruce**]: Main entrance [1*].
    *Pinus mugo* [**Mugo Pine; Swiss Mountain Pine**]: E court [1].
    *Pinus nigra* [**Austrian Pine**]: SE corner, S 50yd [1].
    *Pinus sylvestris* [**Scotch Pine**]: S side, E [1].
**ROSACEAE [ROSE FAMILY],** p. 122
    *Chaenomeles speciosa* [**Japanese Quince**]: N wing, W end [10*]; W court [10*].
    *Cotoneaster divaricatus* [**Spreading Cotoneaster**]: S side, E of ramp [3*].
    *Cotoneaster multiflorus* var. *calocarpus* [**Arching Cotoneaster**]: NW corner [5*].
    *Crataegus phaenopyrum* [**Washington Hawthorn**]: Main entrance, W [1*].
    *Malus* spp. [**Ornamental Crabapple hybrids**]: N side [1*]; S side, ramp [1*].
    *Pyrus calleryana* 'Chanticleer' [**Chanticleer Pear**]: N side [1 **Commem.**].
**TAXACEAE [YEW FAMILY],** p. 55
    *Taxus* × *media* [**Anglojapanese Yew**]: N side [20].
**ULMACEAE [ELM FAMILY],** p. 92
    *Ulmus americana* [**American Elm**]: S [1].


## ECK TENNIS PAVILION

**BERBERIDACEAE [BARBERRY FAMILY],** p. 86
    *Berberis thunbergii* 'Crimson Pygmy' [**Dwarf Japanese Barberry**]: S side [15].

CORNACEAE [DOGWOOD FAMILY], p. 149
  *Cornus sericea* [**Red-osier Dogwood**]: S side [3].
  *Cornus sericea* 'Flaviramea' [**Goldentwig Dogwood**]: S side [3].
CUPRESSACEAE [CYPRESS FAMILY], p. 72
  *Chamaecyparis pisifera* 'Golden Mop' [**Sawara Falsecypress**]: S side [9].
  *Juniperus horizontalis* [**Creeping Juniper**]: S side, flanking walk [beds].
FAGACEAE [BEECH FAMILY], p. 98
  *Quercus alba* [**White Oak**]: SE corner [2].
  *Quercus palustris* [**Pin Oak**]: S lawn, E of walk [1]; SW corner [1].
  *Quercus rubra* [**Red Oak; Northern Red Oak**]: S central lawn [1]; S lawn, W of walk [1];
     SE corner [2].
JUGLANDACEAE [WALNUT FAMILY], p. 96
  *Carya ovalis* [**Sweet Pignut**]: SE corner [8].
PINACEAE [PINE FAMILY], p. 59
  *Picea abies* 'Pumila' [**Dwarf Norway Spruce**]: S [4].
  *Picea pungens* [**Colorado Blue Spruce**]: SE corner [1]; SW corner [2].
ROSACEAE [ROSE FAMILY], p. 122
  *Malus spp.* [**Ornamental Crabapple hybrids**]: S [5].
  *Prunus cerasifera* 'Atropurpurea' [**Purpleleaf Cherry-plum**]: S [2].
  *Pyrus calleryana* [**Callery Pear**]: S side, flanking walk [6].
  *Spiraea* × *bumalda* 'Goldflame' [**Goldflame Spiraea**]: S side [6].
  *Spiraea* × *bumalda* 'Limemound' [**Limemound Spiraea**]: S side [6].
ULMACEAE [ELM FAMILY], p. 92
  *Ulmus americana* [**American Elm**]: SE corner [1].


# FARLEY HALL

BERBERIDACEAE [BARBERRY FAMILY], p. 86
  *Berberis thunbergii* [**Japanese Barberry**]: N wing, E side [1].
ERICACEAE [HEATH FAMILY], p. 113
  *Rhododendron obtusum* f. *Yayegiri* 'Amoenum' [**Japanese Salmon-red Azalea**]: W door, S
     [1].
  *Rhododendron spp.* [**Rhododendron; Azalea**]: W central door, S side [hedge].
HYDRANGEACEAE [HYDRANGEA FAMILY], p. 117
  *Deutzia gracilis* [**Japanese Slender Deutzia**]: E court [hedge].
  *Deutzia* × *lemoinei* [**Lemoine Deutzia**]: E court [20*].
PINACEAE [PINE FAMILY], p. 59
  *Picea glauca* [**White Spruce**]: E side [3*].
  *Picea pungens* [**Colorado Blue Spruce**]: E side [1*]; N end [1*].
  *Pinus sylvestris* [**Scotch Pine**]: Breen-Phillips, between [1].
PLATANACEAE [PLANETREE FAMILY], p. 89
  *Platanus occidentalis* [**Sycamore; Buttonwood; American Planetree**]: E court [3*].
ROSACEAE [ROSE FAMILY], p. 122
  *Chaenomeles speciosa* [**Japanese Quince**]: S end [hedge*].
  *Malus spp.* [**Ornamental Crabapple hybrids**]: S entrance, flanking [2].
  *Pyracantha coccinea* 'Lalandei' [**Laland Firethorn**]: NW corner [1*]; SW corner [1*].
TAXACEAE [YEW FAMILY], p. 55
  *Taxus cuspidata* 'Nana' [**Japanese Dwarf Yew**]: N end [4*].
  *Taxus* × *media* 'Brownii' [**Brown's Yew**]: Front [8*].
VITACEAE [GRAPE FAMILY], p. 157
  *Parthenocissus quinquefolia* [**Virginia Creeper**]: NE corner, E wall [1*].

*Parthenocissus tricuspidata* [**Boston Ivy**]: SW corner [1*].


## FATIMA RETREAT HOUSE

**ACERACEAE  [MAPLE FAMILY]**, p. 161
> *Acer platanoides* 'Rubrum' [**Crimson Norway Maple**]: Mission House, garage, midway to lake [1*]; W, Highway 31 entrance, S side [1*]; W, Highway 31 exit, N side [2*].
> *Acer rubrum* [**Red Maple**]: SE corner, E [1]; W side, N [1].
> *Acer saccharinum* [**Silver Maple; Soft Maple**]:  [many].

**AQUIFOLIACEAE  [HOLLY FAMILY]**, p. 154
> *Ilex crenata* [**Japanese Holly**]: Mission House, E side [9*]; Mission House, N side [1*].

**BERBERIDACEAE  [BARBERRY FAMILY]**, p. 86
> *Berberis thunbergii* 'Atropurpurea' [**Japanese Bronze-leaf Barberry**]: Outdoor Station 3 [3*].
> *Mahonia aquifolium* [**Oregon Grape**]: Mission House, NW corner [1].

**BIGNONIACEAE  [BIGNONIA FAMILY]**, p. 179
> *Catalpa bignonioides* [**Southern Catalpa; Common Catalpa**]: S, lakeside [1*].

**BUXACEAE  [BOX FAMILY]**, p. 156
> *Pachysandra terminalis* [**Japanese Pachysandra; Japanese Spurge**]: Flanking [beds*].

**CAESALPINIACEAE  [CAESALPINIA FAMILY]**, p. 142
> *Gleditsia triacanthos* subsp. *inermis* [**Thornless Honeylocust**]: Mission House, E side [1*]; Mission House, W side [2*].

**CAPRIFOLIACEAE  [HONEYSUCKLE FAMILY]**, p. 180
> *Lonicera* × *bella* [**Belle Honeysuckle**]: Sacred Heart shrine, SW 15yd [1].
> *Lonicera japonica* [**Japanese Honeysuckle**]: E side, SE beds [1].
> *Lonicera maackii* [**Amur Honeysuckle**]: SW corner, S, lakeside [many].
> *Viburnum carlesii* [**Fragrant Viburnum**]: Fatima shrine, E, flanking E drive [6*]; NE corner, at parking lot [hedge*].
> *Viburnum lentago* [**Nannyberry; Sweet Viburnum**]: E side [1]; NW corner, NW 30yd [1]; W, along parking drive [many].
> *Viburnum opulus* [**Cranberrybush; Guelder-rose**]: E [1].
> *Viburnum plicatum* f. *tomentosum* [**Doublefile Viburnum**]: NW front door, E, corner [1].
> *Viburnum rhytidophyllum* [**Rugose Viburnum**]: W side [1*].

**CELASTRACEAE  [STAFF-TREE FAMILY]**, p. 151
> *Euonymus alata* [**Winged Burningbush; Winged Spindletree**]: Mission House, S side [hedge*].
> *Euonymus alata* 'Compacta' [**Narrow-winged Burningbush**]: Fatima shrine, SE [2*].
> *Euonymus europaea* [**European Spindletree**]: Fatima shrine, NE 60yd [2].

**CORNACEAE  [DOGWOOD FAMILY]**, p. 149
> *Cornus alba* 'Argenteo-marginata' [**Tartarian Dogwood**]: E side, E 15yd [1*].
> *Cornus florida* [**Flowering Dogwood**]: Calvary, NE [1].
> *Cornus florida* 'Rubra' [**Red-flowering Dogwood**]: Calvary, NW [1].

**CUPRESSACEAE  [CYPRESS FAMILY]**, p. 72
> *Juniperus chinensis* 'Arbuscula' [**Chinese Arborescent Juniper**]: Fatima shrine, flanking [hedge*].
> *Juniperus horizontalis* 'Plumosa' [**Andorra Juniper**]: Outdoor Stations [beds*]; W, Highway 31 entrance, center [bed*].
> *Juniperus sabina* 'Variegata' [**Hoarfrost Savin**]: Fatima shrine, flanking [beds*].
> *Juniperus virginiana* 'Canaertii' [**Canaert Redcedar**]: NE 100yd, St. Joseph statue, rear [3*]; NE corner [1*]; NW corner [1*].
> *Juniperus virginiana* 'Schottii' [**Schott's Redcedar**]: Mission House, W entrance, N side [1*]; W side [12*].

ERICACEAE [HEATH FAMILY], p. 113
> *Leucothoe axillaris* [**Downy Leucothoe; Fetterbush**]: Mission House, N side [1*].

GROSSULARIACEAE [CURRANT FAMILY], p. 121
> *Ribes alpinum* [**Alpine Currant; Mountain Currant**]: Fatima shrine, rear [1]; Mission House, S side [1*].

HAMAMELIDACEAE [WITCH-HAZEL FAMILY], p. 90
> *Liquidambar styraciflua* [**Sweetgum**]: N end, W 4yd [1].

HYDRANGEACEAE [HYDRANGEA FAMILY], p. 117
> *Philadelphus × virginalis* [**Virginal Mock Orange**]: W side [1].

MAGNOLIACEAE [MAGNOLIA FAMILY], p. 82
> *Magnolia stellata* [**Star Magnolia**]: Main entrance, W 10yd [1*]; Mission House, N side [1*].

MENISPERMACEAE [MOONSEED FAMILY], p. 88
> *Menispermum canadense* [**Common Moonseed**]: Calvary, in hedge [1].

OLEACEAE [OLIVE FAMILY], p. 174
> *Ligustrum obtusifolium* [**Border Privet**]: Calvary, SW 15yd [1].
> *Syringa vulgaris* [**Common Lilac**]: NE corner, N [1*].

PINACEAE [PINE FAMILY], p. 59
> *Picea pungens* 'Glauca' [**Blue Spruce; Colorado Blue Spruce**]: Outdoor Station 12 [5*].
> *Pinus strobus* [**Eastern White Pine**]: NW [many].

RANUNCULACEAE [BUTTERCUP FAMILY], p. 85
> *Clematis × jackmanii* [**Jackman Clematis**]: E side, court, trellis [2].

ROSACEAE [ROSE FAMILY], p. 122
> *Amelanchier laevis* [**Allegheny Serviceberry**]: St. Joseph statue [2].
> *Chaenomeles speciosa* [**Japanese Quince**]: Fatima shrine, rear [1].
> *Crataegus calpodendron* [**Pear Hawthorn**]: Mission House, garage, SE corner [1*].
> *Crataegus mollis* [**Downy Hawthorn**]: E, lakeside [1].
> *Crataegus monogyna* [**Oneseed Hawthorn; English Hawthorn**]: W, along Highway 31 [1].
> *Crataegus phaenopyrum* [**Washington Hawthorn**]: S side, central SE corner [1].
> *Crataegus pruinosa* [**Frosted Hawthorn**]: W, along Highway 31 [few*].
> *Crataegus punctata* [**Dotted Hawthorn**]: W, along Highway 31 [1*].
> *Crataegus submollis* [**Emerson's Thorn**]: W, along Highway 31 [many*].
> *Malus floribunda* [**Japanese Flowering Crabapple**]: Fatima shrine, W, flanking walk [2].
> *Malus pumila* [**Common Apple**]: Fatima shrine, NE 45yd [1]; S side, SE corner [1].
> *Malus* spp. [**Ornamental Crabapple hybrids**]: Main entrance, N 30yd [1]; N end, NE [1].
> *Prunus cerasifera* 'Atropurpurea' [**Purpleleaf Cherry-plum**]: NW lawn [2*].
> *Pyracantha coccinea* 'Lalandei' [**Laland Firethorn**]: Outdoor Station 10, W [hedge*]; Outdoor Station 11, S [hedge*]; Outdoor Station 5, W [hedge*].
> *Pyrus communis* [**Common Pear**]: Community Cemetery, between [2].
> *Sorbus aucuparia* [**European Mountain-ash**]: Fatima shrine, rear [1*].

SALICACEAE [WILLOW FAMILY], p. 110
> *Populus deltoides* [**Cottonwood**]: E 50yd [many]; S, lakeside [2]; SE 50yd, lakeside [1].
> *Salix alba* var. *vitellina* [**Yellow Willow**]: SE, lakeside [3].
> *Salix bebbiana* [**Bebb's Willow**]: E 40yd [1].

TAXACEAE [YEW FAMILY], p. 55
> *Taxus cuspidata* 'Fastigiata' [**Japanese Pyramidal Yew**]: Fatima shrine, flanking [4*]; Fatima shrine, front [5*].
> *Taxus × media* [**Anglojapanese Yew**]: W side [hedge].

## FIELDHOUSE MALL

ACERACEAE [MAPLE FAMILY], p. 161
*Acer rubrum* [Red Maple]: SE [4].
CAESALPINIACEAE [CAESALPINIA FAMILY], p. 142
*Cercis canadensis* [Eastern Redbud; Judas-tree]: W [few].
*Gleditsia triacanthos* subsp. *inermis* [Thornless Honeylocust]: W end plaza [14].
PLATANACEAE [PLANETREE FAMILY], p. 89
*Platanus* × *acerifolia* [London Planetree]: LaFortune to library, flanking walks [many]; S side, E end [1 Commem.].
ROSACEAE [ROSE FAMILY], p. 122
*Pyrus calleryana* [Callery Pear]: Flanking walks around fountain [many].
*Spiraea* × *vanhouttei* [Vanhoutte Spiraea]: N side, along [hedge].

## FIRE STATION

FABACEAE [PEA FAMILY], p. 144
*Robinia pseudoacacia* [Black Locust]: SE corner [1*].
JUGLANDACEAE [WALNUT FAMILY], p. 96
*Carya ovalis* var. *obcordata* [Obcordate Pignut]: E end [1*].
PINACEAE [PINE FAMILY], p. 59
*Pseudotsuga menziesii* [Douglas-fir]: NE corner [1*].

## FISCHER GRADUATE RESIDENCE COMPLEX

ACERACEAE [MAPLE FAMILY], p. 161
*Acer ginnala* [Amur Maple]: N, woods [1].
CAPRIFOLIACEAE [HONEYSUCKLE FAMILY], p. 180
*Lonicera maackii* [Amur Honeysuckle]: N, woods [1].
*Lonicera tatarica* [Tatarian Honeysuckle]: N, woods [1].
CORNACEAE [DOGWOOD FAMILY], p. 149
*Cornus amomum* subsp. *obliqua* [Pale Dogwood]: N, woods [many].
FABACEAE [PEA FAMILY], p. 144
*Robinia pseudoacacia* [Black Locust]: N, woods [few].
JUGLANDACEAE [WALNUT FAMILY], p. 96
*Carya ovalis* [Sweet Pignut]: N, woods [1].
MORACEAE [MULBERRY FAMILY], p. 94
*Morus alba* [White Mulberry]: N, woods [1].
ROSACEAE [ROSE FAMILY], p. 122
*Prunus virginiana* [Chokecherry]: N, woods [1].
*Pyrus communis* [Common Pear]: N, woods [1].

## FISHER HALL

BETULACEAE [BIRCH FAMILY], p. 103
*Betula nigra* [River Birch; Black Birch]: Pangborn, between [1*].
CAESALPINIACEAE [CAESALPINIA FAMILY], p. 142
*Gleditsia triacanthos* subsp. *inermis* [Thornless Honeylocust]: E end, S [6*].

CAPRIFOLIACEAE [HONEYSUCKLE FAMILY], p. 180
*Viburnum lentago* [**Nannyberry; Sweet Viburnum**]: N side, E center [1].
CELASTRACEAE [STAFF-TREE FAMILY], p. 151
*Euonymus alata* [**Winged Burningbush; Winged Spindletree**]: E end [1*].
CERCIDIPHYLLACEAE [KATSURA TREE FAMILY], p. 88
*Cercidiphyllum japonicum* [**Katsura Tree**]: Pangborn, between [5*].
CORNACEAE [DOGWOOD FAMILY], p. 149
*Cornus florida* [**Flowering Dogwood**]: N entrance, E [1 **Commem.**].
*Cornus kousa* [**Kousa Dogwood**]: N entrance, E [1].
*Cornus mas* [**Cornelian Cherry**]: N entrance, W [1*].
CUPRESSACEAE [CYPRESS FAMILY], p. 72
*Juniperus chinensis* 'Torulosa' [**Clustered Juniper**]: S end, near road [7*].
ERICACEAE [HEATH FAMILY], p. 113
*Rhododendron spp.* [**Rhododendron; Azalea**]: N entrance, E [bed].
GINKGOACEAE [GINKGO FAMILY], p. 54
*Ginkgo biloba* 'Laciniata' [**Split-leaf Ginkgo**]: W side [1*].
HYDRANGEACEAE [HYDRANGEA FAMILY], p. 117
*Deutzia gracilis* [**Japanese Slender Deutzia**]: W side [hedge].
*Hydrangea macrophylla* [**Large-leaf Hydrangea**]: N side [1].
OLEACEAE [OLIVE FAMILY], p. 174
*Syringa vulgaris* [**Common Lilac**]: S wing, E side [10*].
PINACEAE [PINE FAMILY], p. 59
*Larix decidua* [**European Larch**]: Pangborn, between [1*].
*Pinus parviflora* 'Glauca' [**Japanese White Pine**]: NE corner [1].
*Pinus sylvestris* 'Watereri' [**Waterer Scotch Pine**]: W side [2*].
ROSACEAE [ROSE FAMILY], p. 122
*Crataegus crus-galli* [**Cockspur Hawthorn; Cockspur-thorn**]: SW corner [1].
*Crataegus crus-galli* var. *pachyphylla* [**Thick-leaved Cockspur-thorn**]: W side [1*].
*Malus pumila* [**Common Apple**]: SW corner, SE 10yd [2*].
TAXACEAE [YEW FAMILY], p. 55
*Taxus cuspidata* 'Densa' [**Japanese Cushion Yew**]: NE corner [7*].

## FITZPATRICK HALL OF ENGINEERING

ACERACEAE [MAPLE FAMILY], p. 161
*Acer rubrum* [**Red Maple**]: S side [2].
ARALIACEAE [GINSENG FAMILY], p. 170
*Hedera helix* [**English Ivy**]: S side, E door, E planter [bed]; S side, W door, E planter [bed].
CAPRIFOLIACEAE [HONEYSUCKLE FAMILY], p. 180
*Viburnum rhytidophyllum* [**Rugose Viburnum**]: S side, E door, W planter [2]; S side, W door, W planter [1].
PINACEAE [PINE FAMILY], p. 59
*Pinus strobus* [**Eastern White Pine**]: SE corner, E lawn [5].
ROSACEAE [ROSE FAMILY], p. 122
*Crataegus phaenopyrum* [**Washington Hawthorn**]: SE corner planter [1]; SW corner planter [1].
TAXACEAE [YEW FAMILY], p. 55
*Taxus* × *media* [**Anglojapanese Yew**]: SE corner planter [2]; SW corner planter [3].

## FLANNER HALL

**ACERACEAE [MAPLE FAMILY]**, p. 161
*Acer platanoides* [**Norway Maple**]: S side [3].
**CAESALPINIACEAE [CAESALPINIA FAMILY]**, p. 142
*Gleditsia triacanthos* subsp. *inermis* [**Thornless Honeylocust**]: NW door plaza [2]; S side [1]; W side [2].
**CAPRIFOLIACEAE [HONEYSUCKLE FAMILY]**, p. 180
*Viburnum opulus* [**Cranberrybush; Guelder-rose**]: N side [2].
**CELASTRACEAE [STAFF-TREE FAMILY]**, p. 151
*Euonymus alata* [**Winged Burningbush; Winged Spindletree**]: E side [hedge].
**MAGNOLIACEAE [MAGNOLIA FAMILY]**, p. 82
*Liriodendron tulipifera* [**Tulip Tree; Yellow-poplar**]: N 25yd [1*]; S side [1]; SW corner [1].
**PINACEAE [PINE FAMILY]**, p. 59
*Pinus mugo* [**Mugo Pine; Swiss Mountain Pine**]: NW, junction of roads [5].
*Pinus strobus* [**Eastern White Pine**]: NW corner [1].
*Pinus sylvestris* [**Scotch Pine**]: SW corner [2]; W side [3]; W wing, NW corner [1]; W wing, NW corner, N 50yd [few].
**ROSACEAE [ROSE FAMILY]**, p. 122
*Amelanchier interior* [**Inland Juneberry; Shadbush**]: NW door, flanking [4].
*Crataegus crus-galli* [**Cockspur Hawthorn; Cockspur-thorn**]: S side [1].
*Malus spp.* [**Ornamental Crabapple hybrids**]: SE corner [6].

## FRESHMAN YEAR BUILDING

**ACERACEAE [MAPLE FAMILY]**, p. 161
*Acer platanoides* [**Norway Maple**]: W side, SW [3].
*Acer saccharinum* [**Silver Maple; Soft Maple**]: W parking lot, N [few*].
**CAPRIFOLIACEAE [HONEYSUCKLE FAMILY]**, p. 180
*Lonicera* × *bella* [**Belle Honeysuckle**]: W parking lot, N, lakeside [1]; W parking lot, SW exit [1].
*Lonicera tatarica* [**Tatarian Honeysuckle**]: SW corner, NW [1]; W parking lot, stop sign, SE 20yd [1].
*Lonicera tatarica* 'Alba' [**Tatarian White Honeysuckle**]: W parking lot, NW corner, NW 50yd [1*].
**CELASTRACEAE [STAFF-TREE FAMILY]**, p. 151
*Celastrus orbiculatus* [**Oriental Bittersweet**]: Brownson court, S wall [1].
**CORNACEAE [DOGWOOD FAMILY]**, p. 149
*Cornus florida* [**Flowering Dogwood**]: SW [2].
*Cornus florida* 'Rubra' [**Red-flowering Dogwood**]: W parking lot, S [1*].
*Cornus racemosa* [**Gray Dogwood**]: W parking lot, W [many*].
**CUPRESSACEAE [CYPRESS FAMILY]**, p. 72
*Juniperus virginiana* 'Glauca' [**Silver Redcedar**]: S [1*].
*Thuja occidentalis* [**American Arborvitae; Northern White Cedar**]: W side [4*].
**FAGACEAE [BEECH FAMILY]**, p. 98
*Castanea mollissima* [**Chinese Chestnut**]: W parking lot, NE corner [1]; W parking lot, SE corner [1].
**HYDRANGEACEAE [HYDRANGEA FAMILY]**, p. 117
*Deutzia gracilis* [**Japanese Slender Deutzia**]: Brownson court, SW [1].
*Deutzia scabra* 'Candidissima' [**Double-flowering Scabrid Deutzia**]: W parking lot, SW [1].

*Philadelphus coronarius* 'Zeyheri' [**Zeyher Mock Orange**]: W parking lot, SE [2]; W parking lot, W [4].

*Philadelphus* × *virginalis* [**Virginal Mock Orange**]: W parking lot, stop sign, SE 20yd [1].

OLEACEAE [OLIVE FAMILY], p. 174

*Fraxinus pennsylvanica* [**Green Ash**]: W parking lot, N end, W 20yd, roadside [1*].

*Fraxinus quadrangulata* [**Blue Ash**]: Brownson court [1*].

*Syringa vulgaris* [**Common Lilac**]: W parking lot, SW corner [1].

*Syringa wolfi* [**Manchurian Lilac**]: W 70yd, roadside [3*].

ROSACEAE [ROSE FAMILY], p. 122

*Crataegus putnamiana* [**Putnam Hawthorn**]: W parking lot, SW corner, W 10yd [1*].

*Malus spp.* [**Ornamental Crabapple hybrids**]: W parking lot, SW corner, W 15yd [1].

TAXACEAE [YEW FAMILY], p. 55

*Taxus cuspidata* [**Japanese Yew**]: SW corner, SW 20yd [1].

*Taxus* × *media* [**Anglojapanese Yew**]: S [hedge].


## GALVIN LIFE SCIENCE CENTER

ACERACEAE [MAPLE FAMILY], p. 161

*Acer platanoides* [**Norway Maple**]: S [3].

*Acer rubrum* [**Red Maple**]: N side lawn, N 30yd [5]; W, main entrance, S of walk [1].

*Acer saccharum* [**Sugar Maple; Hard Maple**]: NW corner, N 30yd [2]; SW corner, W 50yd [1].

APOCYNACEAE [DOGBANE FAMILY], p. 171

*Vinca minor* [**Common Periwinkle; Running Myrtle**]: W [beds].

CAESALPINIACEAE [CAESALPINIA FAMILY], p. 142

*Cercis canadensis* [**Eastern Redbud; Judas-tree**]: W, main entrance, S bed [2]; W, main entrance, WSW 20yd at crosswalk [1 **Commem.**].

CELASTRACEAE [STAFF-TREE FAMILY], p. 151

*Euonymus fortunei* [**Chinese Winter-creeper**]: N side [bed].

CORNACEAE [DOGWOOD FAMILY], p. 149

*Cornus florida* [**Flowering Dogwood**]: SW corner, W [1].

*Cornus mas* [**Cornelian Cherry**]: W, main entrance, flanking [3].

MAGNOLIACEAE [MAGNOLIA FAMILY], p. 82

*Magnolia* × *soulangiana* [**Saucer Magnolia**]: W, front walk, N side [1 **Commem.**].

*Magnolia stellata* [**Star Magnolia**]: S end, S of walk [1 **Commem.**].

OLEACEAE [OLIVE FAMILY], p. 174

*Fraxinus pennsylvanica* [**Green Ash**]: S end, Juniper road, E side [1].

*Syringa meyeri* [**Meyer Lilac**]: NW corner [hedge].

PINACEAE [PINE FAMILY], p. 59

*Pinus resinosa* [**Red Pine; Norway Pine**]: W side, N of entrance [3].

*Pinus strobus* [**Eastern White Pine**]: SE corner [5].

*Pinus sylvestris* [**Scotch Pine**]: SE [1]; SE corner [1].

ROSACEAE [ROSE FAMILY], p. 122

*Crataegus crus-galli* [**Cockspur Hawthorn; Cockspur-thorn**]: NE corner [1].

*Crataegus phaenopyrum* [**Washington Hawthorn**]: NE corner [4].

*Malus spp.* [**Ornamental Crabapple hybrids**]: NE corner [3]; NW corner [1]; SE corner [1]; W, main entrance, S 10yd [1 **Commem.**]; W, main entrance, SW 50yd [1]; W, main entrance, W 15yd, S of walk [1 **Commem.**].

*Spiraea* × *bumalda* 'Limemound' [**Limemound Spiraea**]: W, main entrance, S bed [8].

*Stephanandra incisa* [**Lace Shrub**]: N side [beds].

TAXACEAE [YEW FAMILY], p. 55
  *Taxus cuspidata* [**Japanese Yew**]: W side, SW edge [hedge].
  *Taxus × media* [**Anglojapanese Yew**]: NW end [hedge]; W side [beds].


## GRACE HALL

ACERACEAE [MAPLE FAMILY], p. 161
  *Acer platanoides* [**Norway Maple**]: NE corner [2]; W side [2].
BETULACEAE [BIRCH FAMILY], p. 103
  *Betula nigra* [**River Birch; Black Birch**]: W side [2].
CAESALPINIACEAE [CAESALPINIA FAMILY], p. 142
  *Gleditsia triacanthos* subsp. *inermis* [**Thornless Honeylocust**]: NE door plaza [2]; W side
    [1].
CUPRESSACEAE [CYPRESS FAMILY], p. 72
  *Chamaecyparis pisifera* 'Boulevard' [**Sawara Falsecypress**]: SW door plaza [9].
  *Thuja occidentalis* 'Golden Globe' [**Golden Globe Arborvitae**]: NE door plaza [29].
HAMAMELIDACEAE [WITCH-HAZEL FAMILY], p. 90
  *Hamamelis virginiana* [**Witch-hazel**]: NE door [2].
MORACEAE [MULBERRY FAMILY], p. 94
  *Morus alba* [**White Mulberry**]: E side [1].
PINACEAE [PINE FAMILY], p. 59
  *Abies concolor* [**White Fir; Colorado Fir**]: SW door plaza [1].
  *Picea pungens* [**Colorado Blue Spruce**]: E side [2]; SW door plaza [2].
  *Pinus strobus* [**Eastern White Pine**]: N side [4].
ROSACEAE [ROSE FAMILY], p. 122
  *Amelanchier interior* [**Inland Juneberry; Shadbush**]: NE door [2].
  *Crataegus crus-galli* [**Cockspur Hawthorn; Cockspur-thorn**]: SW door plaza [2].
  *Crataegus phaenopyrum* [**Washington Hawthorn**]: E side [3].
  *Malus spp.* [**Ornamental Crabapple hybrids**]: S side [4]; W side [1].
  *Prunus avium* [**Mazzard; Sweet Cherry**]: Chapel, NE [4]; E side [1].
  *Prunus cerasifera* [**Cherry-plum**]: NW corner [1 **Commem.**].
SALICACEAE [WILLOW FAMILY], p. 110
  *Populus deltoides* [**Cottonwood**]: Flanner, between [1]; SW corner [2].


## GROTTO OF OUR LADY OF LOURDES

ACERACEAE [MAPLE FAMILY], p. 161
  *Acer palmatum* [**Japanese Maple**]: Above, N side [1*].
APOCYNACEAE [DOGBANE FAMILY], p. 171
  *Vinca minor* [**Common Periwinkle; Running Myrtle**]: SW corner [bed].
BERBERIDACEAE [BARBERRY FAMILY], p. 86
  *Berberis thunbergii* 'Atropurpurea' [**Japanese Bronze-leaf Barberry**]: W, roadside [hedge*].
BETULACEAE [BIRCH FAMILY], p. 103
  *Corylus avellana* 'Contorta' [**European Hazel**]: W [1 **Commem.**].
CAPRIFOLIACEAE [HONEYSUCKLE FAMILY], p. 180
  *Symphoricarpos rivularis* [**Common Snowberry**]: N, outer walk, along S edge [few].
  *Viburnum carlesii* [**Fragrant Viburnum**]: N side [1*].
CELASTRACEAE [STAFF-TREE FAMILY], p. 151
  *Euonymus alata* var. *aptera* [**Wingless Burningbush; Wingless Spindletree**]: N side, steps,
    N side [1*].

CORNACEAE [DOGWOOD FAMILY], p. 149
  *Cornus florida* [**Flowering Dogwood**]: N [4*].
  *Cornus florida* 'Rubra' [**Red-flowering Dogwood**]: W [1 **Commem.**].
CUPRESSACEAE [CYPRESS FAMILY], p. 72
  *Juniperus sabina* 'Tamariscifolia' [**Tamarix Savin**]: SE, steps, N [1*].
  *Thuja occidentalis* [**American Arborvitae; Northern White Cedar**]: SE, steps, N [1*].
FABACEAE [PEA FAMILY], p. 144
  *Cladrastis kentukea* [**Yellowwood; Virgilia**]: SE, steps [1*].
FAGACEAE [BEECH FAMILY], p. 98
  *Quercus acutissima* [**Sawtooth Oak**]: NW walk, near W entrance [1].
  *Quercus imbricaria* [**Shingle Oak**]: NW walk, near W entrance [1].
HAMAMELIDACEAE [WITCH-HAZEL FAMILY], p. 90
  *Liquidambar styraciflua* [**Sweetgum**]: Lakeside, near, Columba Hall Rd [1*]; S walk, N side
    [1*].
HIPPOCASTANACEAE [HORSECHESTNUT FAMILY], p. 160
  *Aesculus hippocastanum* [**Horsechestnut**]: Corby kitchen, walk, W side [1*].
JUGLANDACEAE [WALNUT FAMILY], p. 96
  *Juglans nigra* [**Black Walnut**]: N, outer walk, along N edge [14].
MAGNOLIACEAE [MAGNOLIA FAMILY], p. 82
  *Magnolia* × *soulangiana* [**Saucer Magnolia**]: NW walk entering, E side [1*]; NW walk, S
    10yd [1]; W, roadside [1].
MENISPERMACEAE [MOONSEED FAMILY], p. 88
  *Menispermum canadense* [**Common Moonseed**]: NE, steps, E [1].
PINACEAE [PINE FAMILY], p. 59
  *Abies balsamea* [**Balsam Fir**]: Above, surrounding [13*]; Sides [2*].
  *Abies concolor* [**White Fir; Colorado Fir**]: Above [2*]; Corby, midway, W of walk [1
    **Commem.**].
  *Picea abies* [**Norway Spruce**]: Above [4*].
  *Pinus sylvestris* var. *rigensis* [**Upright Scotch Pine**]: Above [1*].
  *Tsuga canadensis* [**Eastern Hemlock**]: N side, steps, N side [1*]; S side [2*].
PLATANACEAE [PLANETREE FAMILY], p. 89
  *Platanus occidentalis* [**Sycamore; Buttonwood; American Planetree**]: [13*].
ROSACEAE [ROSE FAMILY], p. 122
  *Amelanchier arborea* [**Downy Serviceberry; Juneberry**]: N, along outer walk [2].
SALICACEAE [WILLOW FAMILY], p. 110
  *Populus grandidentata* [**Bigtooth Aspen**]: W, lakeside [1*].
  *Salix alba* var. *vitellina* [**Yellow Willow**]: N, 100yd [1]; WSW, St. Mary's Lake margin [1].
  *Salix fragilis* [**Brittle Willow; Crack Willow**]: W, lakeside [1].
TAXACEAE [YEW FAMILY], p. 55
  *Taxus baccata* 'Repandens' [**Spreading Yew**]: Above, St. Francis statue, N 8yd [1*].
  *Taxus cuspidata* [**Japanese Yew**]: N side, along steps [hedge]; SE, steps [hedge]; SW
    corner, Thomas Dooley statue [2]; SW corner, Thomas Dooley statue [2].
TAXODIACEAE [TAXODIUM FAMILY], p. 71
  *Taxodium distichum* [**Baldcypress**]: W, St. Mary's Lake, between [1*].
THEACEAE [TEA FAMILY], p. 106
  *Stewartia koreana* [**Korean Stewartia**]: W lawn, N of walk [1].


## HAGGAR HALL

CAPRIFOLIACEAE [HONEYSUCKLE FAMILY], p. 180
  *Lonicera fragrantissima* [**Winter Honeysuckle**]: S wall [hedge*].

CUPRESSACEAE [CYPRESS FAMILY], p. 72
   *Juniperus virginiana* 'Kosteri' [**Koster Juniper**]: S [hedge*].
FAGACEAE [BEECH FAMILY], p. 98
   *Quercus velutina* f. *macrophylla* [**Broadleaf Black Oak**]: NW corner, NW 10yd [1*]; NW corner, NW 20yd [1*].
   *Quercus velutina* f. *pagodaeformis* [**Pagoda Black Oak**]: NW corner, W [1*].
OLEACEAE [OLIVE FAMILY], p. 174
   *Fraxinus pennsylvanica* [**Green Ash**]: NW corner, N 15yd [1*].
PINACEAE [PINE FAMILY], p. 59
   *Picea abies* [**Norway Spruce**]: W end [1*].
   *Picea rubens* [**Red Spruce**]: N parking lot, N [1*].
   *Pinus flexilis* [**Limber Pine**]: N, parking lot, NW corner [1*].
   *Pinus resinosa* 'Globosa' [**Dwarf Red Pine**]: E [1*].
PLATANACEAE [PLANETREE FAMILY], p. 89
   *Platanus occidentalis* [**Sycamore; Buttonwood; American Planetree**]: Fieldhouse Mall, between [12*].
ROSACEAE [ROSE FAMILY], p. 122
   *Crataegus phaenopyrum* [**Washington Hawthorn**]: S [7*].
   *Malus spp.* [**Ornamental Crabapple hybrids**]: E 20yd [3].


## HAMMES BOOKSTORE

CAPRIFOLIACEAE [HONEYSUCKLE FAMILY], p. 180
   *Viburnum* × *bodnantense* 'Pink Dawn' [**Bodnant Viburnum**]: W wing, S [6].
   *Viburnum lentago* [**Nannyberry; Sweet Viburnum**]: SE corner [3].
   *Viburnum opulus* 'Nanum' [**Dwarf Cranberrybush**]: W wing, S [2].
CELASTRACEAE [STAFF-TREE FAMILY], p. 151
   *Euonymus alata* [**Winged Burningbush; Winged Spindletree**]: W wing, S [11].
FAGACEAE [BEECH FAMILY], p. 98
   *Quercus coccinea* [**Scarlet Oak**]: N basketball court, NW corner [1*].
OLEACEAE [OLIVE FAMILY], p. 174
   *Fraxinus pennsylvanica* [**Green Ash**]: N basketball court, N [2].
PINACEAE [PINE FAMILY], p. 59
   *Picea pungens* [**Colorado Blue Spruce**]: W wing, NW corner [1*].
   *Pinus strobus* 'Blue Shag' [**Eastern White Pine**]: W wing, S [2].
   *Pseudotsuga menziesii* [**Douglas-fir**]: SE corner [1].
ROSACEAE [ROSE FAMILY], p. 122
   *Spiraea* × *bumalda* 'Limemound' [**Limemound Spiraea**]: W wing, S [11].
ULMACEAE [ELM FAMILY], p. 92
   *Ulmus americana* [**American Elm**]: Front [3*].


## HAYES-HEALY CENTER

AQUIFOLIACEAE [HOLLY FAMILY], p. 154
   *Ilex opaca* [**American Holly**]: W side, along foundation [2].
CAESALPINIACEAE [CAESALPINIA FAMILY], p. 142
   *Gleditsia triacanthos* [**Honeylocust**]: NW corner, W 30yd [1*].
CAPRIFOLIACEAE [HONEYSUCKLE FAMILY], p. 180
   *Viburnum plicatum* f. *tomentosum* [**Doublefile Viburnum**]: N entrance, NE 20yd [1].

*Weigela florida* [**Flowering Weigela**]: N side [4*].
FAGACEAE [BEECH FAMILY], p. 98
    *Quercus rubra* [**Red Oak; Northern Red Oak**]: LaFortune, between [4].
OLEACEAE [OLIVE FAMILY], p. 174
    *Syringa wolfi* [**Manchurian Lilac**]: N entrance, E side [1*].
PINACEAE [PINE FAMILY], p. 59
    *Pinus sylvestris* [**Scotch Pine**]: NW corner, W 50yd [1].
ROSACEAE [ROSE FAMILY], p. 122
    *Rhodotypos scandens* [**Japanese Jetbead**]: S side, SW corner [1].
    *Spiraea japonica* [**Japanese Spiraea**]: W side [bed].


# HESBURGH CENTER

## ACERACEAE [MAPLE FAMILY], p. 161
*Acer palmatum* [**Japanese Maple**]: Court, S bed [1]; Court, W bed [1].
*Acer palmatum* f. *dissectum* [**Threadleaf Japanese Maple**]: Court, middle bed [2].
*Acer palmatum* f. *dissectum* 'Crimson Queen' [**Japanese Maple**]: SW Plaza, inner section, corner [1].
*Acer palmatum* f. *dissectum* 'Germaine's Gyration' [**Threadleaf Japanese Maple**]: Court [2].
*Acer palmatum* 'Shishigashira' [**Japanese Maple**]: Court, NW bed [1]; Court, SE bed [1].

## BUXACEAE [BOX FAMILY], p. 156
*Buxus microphylla* 'Wintergreen' [**Korean Boxwood**]: Court, planter E1 [6]; Court, planter E2 [5]; Court, planter E3 [5]; Court, planter E4 [6]; SW Plaza, inner section, edge [27].
*Pachysandra terminalis* 'Variegata' [**Japanese Pachysandra**]: SW Plaza, inner section, beds [bed].

## CAPRIFOLIACEAE [HONEYSUCKLE FAMILY], p. 180
*Viburnum opulus* 'Nanum' [**Dwarf Cranberrybush**]: N side, residence patios, inside wall [23].
*Viburnum plicatum* f. *tomentosum* 'Mariesii' [**Doublefile Viburnum**]: Court, E border [10]; Court, N border [10]; E side [12]; E side, NE corner, S [4]; S side, middle, inner corner [3].
*Viburnum rhytidophyllum* [**Rugose Viburnum**]: E side [1].

## CELASTRACEAE [STAFF-TREE FAMILY], p. 151
*Euonymus alata* 'Compacta' [**Narrow-winged Burningbush**]: N side, residences, NE corner [5]; N side, residences, NW corner [5]; SW Plaza, outer section, S side [11]; SW Plaza, outer section, W side [11].

## CUPRESSACEAE [CYPRESS FAMILY], p. 72
*Chamaecyparis nootkatensis* 'Glauca Compacta' [**Nootka Falsecypress**]: S side, SW edge [3]; SE corner, W [3]; W side, S section, in bed [3].
*Chamaecyparis nootkatensis* 'Pendula' [**Weeping Nootka Falsecypress**]: Court, S bed [1]; Court, W bed [1]; Court, middle bed [3]; E side, NE corner [3]; SE corner [3].
*Chamaecyparis obtusa* 'Aurea' [**Hinoki Falsecypress**]: SE corner, W 10yd [2]; W side, N section, middle, W 10yd [2].
*Juniperus chinensis* 'Old Gold' [**Chinese Juniper**]: E side, NE corner [12]; SE corner [12].
*Juniperus chinensis* 'Sea Green' [**Chinese Juniper**]: E side [12]; S side [36].
*Juniperus communis* 'Effusa' [**Common Juniper**]: Court, E border [12]; Court, N border [30]; Court, square planter [20]; N side, residence patios [51].
*Juniperus scopulorum* 'Table Top' [**Rocky Mountain Juniper**]: Court, planter N1 [8]; Court, planter N2 [8]; Court, planter N3 [8]; Court, planter N4 [6].
*Juniperus squamata* 'Blue Carpet' [**Singleseed Juniper**]: Court, E entrance [2].

*Juniperus squamata* 'Blue Star' [**Singleseed Juniper**]: Court [beds]; E side, SE entrance, flanking [23]; N side [beds]; S side, W corner, near plaza [35]; SE corner, W [14]; SW Plaza, outer section, NW corner [8]; SW Plaza, outer section, SE corner [8]; W side, S section [32].

*Thuja occidentalis* [**American Arborvitae; Northern White Cedar**]: N side, at court gate [5]; W side, service drive, N edge [11].

**ERICACEAE  [HEATH FAMILY], p. 113**

*Arctostaphylos uva-ursi* 'Massachusetts' [**Bearberry; Kinnikinick**]: Court, NW bed [bed]; Court, SE bed [bed].

*Gaultheria procumbens* [**Wintergreen**]: SE corner, W [beds].

*Rhododendron* spp. [**Rhododendron; Azalea**]: Court, S bed [11]; Court, W bed [19]; Court, middle bed [16].

*Rhododendron* × spp. 'P.J.M.' [**P.J.M. Rhododendron**]: N side, E entrance, S [7].

*Rhododendron* spp. 'Ramapo' [**Ramapo Rhododendron**]: Court, S bed [bed]; Court, W bed [bed]; Court, middle bed [bed]; SW Plaza [15].

**FAGACEAE  [BEECH FAMILY], p. 98**

*Fagus sylvatica* 'Fastigiata' [**European Pyramidal Beech**]: SW Plaza, outer section, edge [6].

**MAGNOLIACEAE  [MAGNOLIA FAMILY], p. 82**

*Liriodendron tulipifera* [**Tulip Tree; Yellow-poplar**]: E side, NE corner, E 10yd [1]; SE corner, SE 10yd [1]; SE corner, SW 15yd [1].

**PINACEAE  [PINE FAMILY], p. 59**

*Picea abies* 'Cupressina' [**Norway Spruce**]: Court, E border [4]; Court, N border [4].

*Picea abies* 'Nidiformis' [**Bird's Nest Spruce**]: Court, NW bed [13]; Court, SE bed [13].

*Picea omorika* 'Nana' [**Dwarf Serbian Spruce**]: SW Plaza, outer section, corner [36].

*Picea pungens* [**Colorado Blue Spruce**]: E side, NE corner, NW [2]; W side, service drive, N [3]; W side, service drive, S [3].

**ROSACEAE  [ROSE FAMILY], p. 122**

*Malus* spp. 'Dolgo' [**Dolgo Crabapple**]: E side [3].

*Malus* spp. 'Robinson' [**Robinson Crabapple**]: S side, middle, corner [4].

*Malus yunnanensis* var. *veitchii* [**Veitchii Crabapple**]: N side, residence patios [6].

*Prunus cerasifera* 'Thundercloud' [**Purpleleaf Cherry-plum**]: W side, N section, NW corner [1]; W side, N section, middle [1]; W side, S section, S [1].

*Prunus laurocerasus* 'Schipkaensis' [**Schip Laurel**]: N side, E entrance to residences [2]; N side, E entrance, N [2]; W side, N section, N end [3].

*Prunus virginiana* 'Shubert Select' [**Shubert Select Chokecherry**]: Court, square planter [4].

*Pyracantha* × spp. 'Teton' [**Firethorn**]: SW Plaza, outer section, inside edge S [5]; SW Plaza, outer section, inside edge W [5].

*Pyrus calleryana* 'Redspire' [**Callery Pear**]: Court, NW bed [3]; Court, SE bed [3].

*Sorbus aucuparia* 'Cardinal Royal' [**European Mountain-ash**]: N side, parking area [3].

*Spiraea* × *bumalda* 'Goldflame' [**Goldflame Spiraea**]: SW Plaza, outer section, inner area S [19]; SW Plaza, outer section, inner area W [19]; W side, N section, middle [7].

**SAURURACEAE  [LIZARD'S-TAIL FAMILY], p. 84**

*Houttuynia cordata* 'Chamaeleon' [**Houttuynia**]: Court, E border [bed]; Court, E entrance [bed]; Court, N border [bed]; Court, between planters E1 & E2 [bed].

**TAXACEAE  [YEW FAMILY], p. 55**

*Taxus baccata* 'Aurea' [**Golden Yew; Irish Yew**]: Court, NW bed [6]; Court, SE bed [6].

*Taxus* × *media* 'Cole' [**Cole Yew**]: Court, E border [4]; Court, N border [4]; Court, NW bed [16]; Court, SE bed [16]; Court, planter N1 [2]; Court, planter N2 [2]; Court, planter N3 [2]; Court, planter N4 [2]; N side, E entrance to residences [2]; N side, residences, main entrance [6].

THEACEAE [TEA FAMILY], p. 106
>   *Stewartia koreana* [**Korean Stewartia**]: E side, SE entrance, flanking [2]; S side, SW edge, near plaza [1]; S side, entrance [2]; SW Plaza, outer section, NW corner [1]; SW Plaza, outer section, SE corner [1]; W side, S section, SW corner of bed [1]; W side, entrance [2].

## HESBURGH LIBRARY

ACERACEAE [MAPLE FAMILY], p. 161
>   *Acer rubrum* 'Columnare' [**Columnar Red Maple**]: Pool, S, near lamppost C10 [3*].
>   *Acer saccharum* [**Sugar Maple; Hard Maple**]: E entrance, E [1].
>   *Acer saccharum* subsp. *nigrum* [**Black Maple**]: E entrance, SE [1].

APOCYNACEAE [DOGBANE FAMILY], p. 171
>   *Vinca minor* [**Common Periwinkle; Running Myrtle**]: Pool, S end, flanking [beds*].

ARALIACEAE [GINSENG FAMILY], p. 170
>   *Hedera helix* [**English Ivy**]: S, main entrance plaza, flanking [beds*].

BETULACEAE [BIRCH FAMILY], p. 103
>   *Betula nigra* [**River Birch; Black Birch**]: Stadium, between [18*]; W side, Moses statue, NW [2].
>   *Carpinus betulus* [**European Hornbeam**]: Pool, E side [1*]; Pool, W side [1*].

CELASTRACEAE [STAFF-TREE FAMILY], p. 151
>   *Euonymus alata* 'Compacta' [**Narrow-winged Burningbush**]: SW corner [1*]; W, Moses statue, S shrubbery [1*].

CERCIDIPHYLLACEAE [KATSURA TREE FAMILY], p. 88
>   *Cercidiphyllum japonicum* 'Pendula' [**Weeping Katsura Tree**]: Pool, W side [1 **Commem.**].

CORNACEAE [DOGWOOD FAMILY], p. 149
>   *Cornus florida* [**Flowering Dogwood**]: Pool, S and E [4*]; Pool, SW [1*].

FABACEAE [PEA FAMILY], p. 144
>   *Sophora japonica* [**Japanese Pagodatree**]: Pool, SW [1 **Commem.**].

FAGACEAE [BEECH FAMILY], p. 98
>   *Fagus grandifolia* [**American Beech**]: W side [1*].

MYRICACEAE [SWEET GALE FAMILY], p. 98
>   *Myrica pensylvanica* [**Bayberry**]: W, Moses statue, S [beds*].

NYSSACEAE [TUPELO FAMILY], p. 148
>   *Nyssa sylvatica* [**Black Tupelo; Blackgum; Sourgum**]: SW corner, S [2*].

PINACEAE [PINE FAMILY], p. 59
>   *Picea pungens* [**Colorado Blue Spruce**]: NW corner [1*].
>   *Pinus strobus* [**Eastern White Pine**]: SW corner [8*].
>   *Pinus sylvestris* 'Fastigiata' [**Pyramidal Scotch Pine**]: S, main entrance [few*].
>   *Pinus sylvestris* 'Watereri' [**Waterer Scotch Pine**]: Pool, NE corner, lamppost C18, SE 5yd [1*].

PLATANACEAE [PLANETREE FAMILY], p. 89
>   *Platanus occidentalis* [**Sycamore; Buttonwood; American Planetree**]: [many*].

ROSACEAE [ROSE FAMILY], p. 122
>   *Cotoneaster apiculatus* [**Cranberry Cotoneaster**]: S, main entrance, bed either side [2].
>   *Crataegus coccinoides* [**Kansas Hawthorn**]: Pool, NW corner, W 20yd [1*]; SE corner [2*].
>   *Crataegus crus-galli* [**Cockspur Hawthorn; Cockspur-thorn**]: Pool, W [1*]; SE corner [3*].
>   *Crataegus phaenopyrum* [**Washington Hawthorn**]: S, main entrance plaza, flanking [6]; S, main entrance plaza, flanking [6].
>   *Malus spp.* [**Ornamental Crabapple hybrids**]: Pool to Stadium [many*]; Pool, SW corner, SW 20yd [4]; SW 30yd, midway to Radiation Bldg [1 **Commem.**].

*Potentilla fruticosa* [**Shrubby Cinquefoil**]: W, Moses statue, S bed [beds*].

TAXACEAE [YEW FAMILY], p. 55

*Taxus cuspidata* 'Densa' [**Japanese Cushion Yew**]: Pool, S, SE, SW ends [beds*].

TILIACEAE [LINDEN FAMILY], p. 107

*Tilia americana* [**American Basswood; American Linden**]: Stepan Chemistry, walk between, S side [2].


## Hessert Aerospace Research Center

CAPRIFOLIACEAE [HONEYSUCKLE FAMILY], p. 180

*Viburnum opulus* 'Nanum' [**Dwarf Cranberrybush**]: N plaza [9].

*Viburnum plicatum* f. *tomentosum* 'Mariesii' [**Doublefile Viburnum**]: E [6].

CERCIDIPHYLLACEAE [KATSURA TREE FAMILY], p. 88

*Cercidiphyllum japonicum* 'Pendula' [**Weeping Katsura Tree**]: E side [1]; N plaza [1].

CORNACEAE [DOGWOOD FAMILY], p. 149

*Cornus alba* 'Argenteo-marginata' [**Tartarian Dogwood**]: N plaza [3].

*Cornus florida* [**Flowering Dogwood**]: E side [2].

*Cornus sericea* 'Flaviramea' [**Goldentwig Dogwood**]: N plaza [2].

CUPRESSACEAE [CYPRESS FAMILY], p. 72

*Chamaecyparis obtusa* 'Pygmaea Aurescens' [**Hinoki Falsecypress**]: E side [4].

*Chamaecyparis pisifera* 'Golden Mop' [**Sawara Falsecypress**]: E side [12]; N plaza, SE corner [3].

*Juniperus chinensis* 'Old Gold' [**Chinese Juniper**]: N plaza [12].

*Juniperus chinensis* 'Shimpaku' [**Chinese Juniper**]: E side [10].

*Thuja occidentalis* 'Europe Gold' [**Golden Arborvitae**]: E side [2].

HAMAMELIDACEAE [WITCH-HAZEL FAMILY], p. 90

*Hamamelis* × *intermedia* 'Diane' [**Witch-hazel**]: N plaza [3].

MAGNOLIACEAE [MAGNOLIA FAMILY], p. 82

*Liriodendron tulipifera* [**Tulip Tree; Yellow-poplar**]: SE corner [1].

PINACEAE [PINE FAMILY], p. 59

*Picea abies* 'Pumila' [**Dwarf Norway Spruce**]: N plaza [4].

*Picea pungens* [**Colorado Blue Spruce**]: N plaza [9]; S side [4].

*Picea pungens* 'Hoopsii' [**Colorado Spruce**]: SE corner [2].

ROSACEAE [ROSE FAMILY], p. 122

*Cotoneaster dammeri* 'Walter's Red' [**Bearberry Cotoneaster**]: E side, flanking steps [2].

*Pyrus calleryana* 'Chanticleer' [**Chanticleer Pear**]: E side [2].

*Spiraea* × *bumalda* 'Goldflame' [**Goldflame Spiraea**]: S side [9].

TAXACEAE [YEW FAMILY], p. 55

*Taxus* × *media* 'Cole' [**Cole Yew**]: S side [4].


## Holy Cross Annex

ACERACEAE [MAPLE FAMILY], p. 161

*Acer ginnala* [**Amur Maple**]: SW [1].

ANACARDIACEAE [CASHEW FAMILY], p. 166

*Toxicodendron radicans* [**Poison Ivy**]: St. Joseph Hall, woods between [many*].

*Toxicodendron rydbergii* [**Poison Ivy**]: St. Joseph Hall, woods between [many*].

CAPRIFOLIACEAE [HONEYSUCKLE FAMILY], p. 180

*Lonicera* × *bella* [**Belle Honeysuckle**]: NW 40yd, in thicket [1*]; SE 50yd [1*].

*Lonicera morrowii* [**Morrow Honeysuckle**]: Tool shed, N walk, W side [4*].

*Lonicera ruprechtiana* [**Ruprecht Honeysuckle**]: W, road to tool shed, N end, E [2*]; W, road to tool shed, N end, W [3*].

*Lonicera tatarica* [**Tatarian Honeysuckle**]: W [hedge].

*Lonicera tatarica* 'Latifolia' [**Tatarian Large-leaved Honeysuckle**]: Tool shed, E end [3*].

*Lonicera tatarica* 'Rosea' [**Regelian Honeysuckle**]: NW 40yd [1*].

*Sambucus canadensis* [**American Elder**]: Tool shed, S side [many*].

**CUPRESSACEAE [CYPRESS FAMILY]**, p. 72

*Juniperus chinensis* 'Pfitzeriana' [**Pfitzer Juniper**]: W, tool shed, SW 15yd [3*].

*Juniperus sabina* [**Savin Juniper**]: S, lake steps, flanking [6*].

**FAGACEAE [BEECH FAMILY]**, p. 98

*Quercus alba* [**White Oak**]: W side, S 15yd [1].

*Quercus velutina* [**Black Oak**]: N end, N 10yd [1*]; SW 50yd [many*].

**HYDRANGEACEAE [HYDRANGEA FAMILY]**, p. 117

*Philadelphus coronarius* 'Zeyheri' [**Zeyher Mock Orange**]: NW corner, N 40yd, road, N [few*].

**JUGLANDACEAE [WALNUT FAMILY]**, p. 96

*Carya ovalis* [**Sweet Pignut**]: NE corner, N [1].

*Carya ovalis* var. *obovalis* [**Obovate Pignut**]: NW, woods [many*].

**MORACEAE [MULBERRY FAMILY]**, p. 94

*Morus alba* [**White Mulberry**]: SW area [many].

**OLEACEAE [OLIVE FAMILY]**, p. 174

*Syringa vulgaris* [**Common Lilac**]: W, hedge [hedge*].

**PINACEAE [PINE FAMILY]**, p. 59

*Picea abies* [**Norway Spruce**]: S [1*].

*Picea pungens* 'Glauca' [**Blue Spruce; Colorado Blue Spruce**]: S lawn [3*].

*Pinus resinosa* [**Red Pine; Norway Pine**]: S, Statue of Little Flower [1].

*Tsuga canadensis* [**Eastern Hemlock**]: S [7*]; S side [2*].

**ROSACEAE [ROSE FAMILY]**, p. 122

*Crataegus pruinosa* [**Frosted Hawthorn**]: SW slope [1*].

*Spiraea* × *vanhouttei* [**Vanhoutte Spiraea**]: NE corner [1].

**TAXACEAE [YEW FAMILY]**, p. 55

*Taxus cuspidata* 'Expansa' [**Japanese Saucer Yew**]: S lawn [5*]; SE lawn [5*].

*Taxus cuspidata* 'Fastigiata' [**Japanese Pyramidal Yew**]: S lawn [18*].

## HOLY CROSS HOUSE

**ACERACEAE [MAPLE FAMILY]**, p. 161

*Acer palmatum* [**Japanese Maple**]: Moreau Seminary, S of walk between [3*].

*Acer platanoides* 'Rubrum' [**Crimson Norway Maple**]: S side [2*].

**ANACARDIACEAE [CASHEW FAMILY]**, p. 166

*Rhus hirta* [**Staghorn Sumac**]: S, lakeside [many*].

**BERBERIDACEAE [BARBERRY FAMILY]**, p. 86

*Mahonia aquifolium* [**Oregon Grape**]: N side [beds*].

**BIGNONIACEAE [BIGNONIA FAMILY]**, p. 179

*Catalpa speciosa* [**Northern Catalpa**]: SE corner, NE 25yd [1].

**CAESALPINIACEAE [CAESALPINIA FAMILY]**, p. 142

*Gleditsia triacanthos* subsp. *inermis* [**Thornless Honeylocust**]: E wing [2*].

**CAPRIFOLIACEAE [HONEYSUCKLE FAMILY]**, p. 180

*Lonicera ruprechtiana* [**Ruprecht Honeysuckle**]: SE, lakeside at culvert [3*].

*Lonicera tatarica* [**Tatarian Honeysuckle**]: E, Sacred Heart statue, N [many].

*Viburnum recognitum* [**Arrowwood**]: S entrance, E [1]; W end [1].

*Weigela florida* [**Flowering Weigela**]: S entrance, E [1].

**CELASTRACEAE  [STAFF-TREE FAMILY], p. 151**

*Euonymus alata* [**Winged Burningbush; Winged Spindletree**]: S side [2*].

*Euonymus hamiltoniana* var. *yedoensis* [**Yeddo Spindletree**]: W end, lake slope [many*].

**CUPRESSACEAE  [CYPRESS FAMILY], p. 72**

*Juniperus chinensis* 'Torulosa' [**Clustered Juniper**]: Moreau Seminary, midway between [1*].

*Thuja occidentalis* 'Conica' [**Conical Arborvitae**]: E wing, N side [7*]; E wing, N side [1].

*Thuja occidentalis* 'Pyramidalis' [**Pyramidal Arborvitae**]: N side [7*].

**ERICACEAE  [HEATH FAMILY], p. 113**

*Rhododendron catawbiense* [**Catawba Rhododendron**]: N side [11*].

*Rhododendron obtusum* f. *Hinomoyo* 'Amoenum' [**Japanese Pink Azalea**]: S entrance, E [1*].

**FAGACEAE  [BEECH FAMILY], p. 98**

*Fagus grandifolia* [**American Beech**]: Douglas Rd, between [1*].

*Fagus sylvatica* 'Atropunicea' [**Copper Beech; Purple Beech**]: N 35yd [1*]; W 30yd [1*].

**HIPPOCASTANACEAE  [HORSECHESTNUT FAMILY], p. 160**

*Aesculus octandra* [**Yellow Buckeye; Sweet Buckeye**]: NE lawn [1].

**JUGLANDACEAE  [WALNUT FAMILY], p. 96**

*Carya ovalis* [**Sweet Pignut**]: SW slope [2].

**MALVACEAE  [MALLOW FAMILY], p. 109**

*Hibiscus syriacus* [**Shrub-althea; Rose-of-Sharon**]: W [4].

**MORACEAE  [MULBERRY FAMILY], p. 94**

*Morus alba* [**White Mulberry**]: N 50yd, Douglas Rd, N, shed, NW 20yd [1]; NE corner, N 30yd [1].

**OLEACEAE  [OLIVE FAMILY], p. 174**

*Fraxinus americana* [**White Ash**]: SE, lake slope [many*].

*Ligustrum amurense* [**Amur Privet**]: NW side [hedge].

**PINACEAE  [PINE FAMILY], p. 59**

*Picea pungens* 'Glauca' [**Blue Spruce; Colorado Blue Spruce**]: E 40yd, Sacred Heart statue [5*].

**RANUNCULACEAE  [BUTTERCUP FAMILY], p. 85**

*Clematis spp.* [**Clematis**]: SW, trellis [1].

**ROSACEAE  [ROSE FAMILY], p. 122**

*Crataegus mollis* [**Downy Hawthorn**]: SE, lake steps, S [1].

*Crataegus phaenopyrum* [**Washington Hawthorn**]: S, slope [1].

*Malus spp.* [**Ornamental Crabapple hybrids**]: NE side [1]; SW slope [1].

*Prunus americana* [**American Plum**]: S, lake slope [1].

*Prunus virginiana* [**Chokecherry**]: S, ascending path, S [1].

*Rosa carolina* [**Pasture Rose; Wild Rose**]: S slope [many*].

**SALICACEAE  [WILLOW FAMILY], p. 110**

*Populus deltoides* [**Cottonwood**]: N 40yd, Douglas Rd, N [1*]; SE, lakeside [3*].

*Salix amygdaloides* [**Peachleaf Willow**]: SE corner, lakeside [1*].

*Salix discolor* [**Pussy Willow**]: E end, S, lakeside [1].

*Salix nigra* [**Black Willow**]: SW, lakeside [1*].

**TAXACEAE  [YEW FAMILY], p. 55**

*Taxus baccata* 'Stricta' [**Irish Yew**]: Cornerstone [1*].

*Taxus cuspidata* [**Japanese Yew**]: Douglas rd, along [hedge]; S, hedge [hedge].

**ULMACEAE  [ELM FAMILY], p. 92**

*Ulmus americana* [**American Elm**]: E 20yd [1]; N 50yd, Douglas Rd, N [1]; SE 15yd [1]; Tool shed, NW corner, W 3yd [1].

## HOWARD HALL

AQUIFOLIACEAE [HOLLY FAMILY], p. 154
*Ilex cornuta* 'China Boy' [**Chinese Holly**]: SW corner [1].
*Ilex cornuta* 'China Girl' [**Chinese Holly**]: SW corner [2].
CAESALPINIACEAE [CAESALPINIA FAMILY], p. 142
*Cercis canadensis* [**Eastern Redbud; Judas-tree**]: Morrissey Hall, midway [1*].
CAPRIFOLIACEAE [HONEYSUCKLE FAMILY], p. 180
*Lonicera tatarica* [**Tatarian Honeysuckle**]: N [hedge].
*Lonicera tatarica* 'Latifolia' [**Tatarian Large-leaved Honeysuckle**]: NW corner [2*].
*Viburnum plicatum* [**Japanese Snowball**]: N wing, E end [11*].
CELASTRACEAE [STAFF-TREE FAMILY], p. 151
*Euonymus alata* [**Winged Burningbush; Winged Spindletree**]: Front [2*]; N wing, W end [1*].
*Euonymus bungeana* [**Winterberry Spindletree**]: SW corner, SW [1].
*Euonymus fortunei* [**Chinese Winter-creeper**]: N wing, SW corner [1]; SE corner [4].
*Euonymus fortunei* var. *vegeta* [**Fruitful Winter-creeper**]: N wing, SW corner [bed*].
CORNACEAE [DOGWOOD FAMILY], p. 149
*Cornus florida* [**Flowering Dogwood**]: N side, NE 8 yd [1*].
HYDRANGEACEAE [HYDRANGEA FAMILY], p. 117
*Deutzia scabra* 'Candidissima' [**Double-flowering Scabrid Deutzia**]: N wing, W end [1].
*Philadelphus* × *virginalis* [**Virginal Mock Orange**]: N [hedge]; S wing, NE corner, N [1].
MAGNOLIACEAE [MAGNOLIA FAMILY], p. 82
*Magnolia* × *proctoriana* [**Chinese Magnolia**]: Chapel, W end [1*].
OLEACEAE [OLIVE FAMILY], p. 174
*Forsythia* × *intermedia* 'Vitellina' [**Vitelline Forsythia**]: S wing, E end [3*].
*Syringa reticulata* [**Japanese Tree Lilac**]: N wing, E end, S [1].
*Syringa vulgaris* 'Purpurea' [**Purplish Red Lilac**]: N wing, SE corner [4*].
PINACEAE [PINE FAMILY], p. 59
*Picea pungens* 'Glauca' [**Blue Spruce; Colorado Blue Spruce**]: N [1*].
ROSACEAE [ROSE FAMILY], p. 122
*Crataegus phaenopyrum* [**Washington Hawthorn**]: E side [2].
*Pyracantha coccinea* 'Lalandei' [**Laland Firethorn**]: Front [1].
TAXACEAE [YEW FAMILY], p. 55
*Taxus baccata* 'Repandens' [**Spreading Yew**]: N wing, E end [3*]; S wing, E end [2*].
*Taxus cuspidata* [**Japanese Yew**]: S entrance, E side [2]; SE corner [few].
*Taxus* × *media* [**Anglojapanese Yew**]: E side, arches [beds]; SE corner [2].
ULMACEAE [ELM FAMILY], p. 92
*Ulmus americana* [**American Elm**]: W 6yd [1].


## HURLEY HALL OF BUSINESS ADMINISTRATION

CAPRIFOLIACEAE [HONEYSUCKLE FAMILY], p. 180
*Weigela florida* [**Flowering Weigela**]: E end [3*].
CORNACEAE [DOGWOOD FAMILY], p. 149
*Cornus sanguinea* [**Bloodtwig Dogwood**]: S side [7*].
HYDRANGEACEAE [HYDRANGEA FAMILY], p. 117
*Philadelphus* × *virginalis* [**Virginal Mock Orange**]: SW corner [1].
OLEACEAE [OLIVE FAMILY], p. 174
*Forsythia suspensa* [**Weeping Forsythia**]: S entrance, E [1].

PINACEAE [PINE FAMILY], p. 59
  *Pinus nigra* [**Austrian Pine**]: Sorin statue, between [6*]; W side, N [3*]; W side, center [1]; W side, center, W 10yd [1].
  *Pinus strobus* [**Eastern White Pine**]: W entrance [3*].
  *Pinus strobus* 'Fastigiata' [**Pyramidal White Pine**]: E end, N [2*].
ROSACEAE [ROSE FAMILY], p. 122
  *Malus spp.* [**Ornamental Crabapple hybrids**]: Main entrance, flanking [2*].
  *Pyracantha coccinea* 'Lalandei' [**Laland Firethorn**]: Court [1].
  *Spiraea japonica* var. *fortunei* [**Robert Fortune Spiraea**]: S side [3*].
  *Stephanandra incisa* [**Lace Shrub**]: W side [bed].
TAXACEAE [YEW FAMILY], p. 55
  *Taxus* × *media* [**Anglojapanese Yew**]: E end [hedge]; W side [few].


## JOYCE ATHLETIC AND CONVOCATION CENTER

ACERACEAE [MAPLE FAMILY], p. 161
  *Acer platanoides* 'Columnare' [**Columnar Norway Maple**]: S side, parking lots [many].
  *Acer platanoides* 'Crimson King' [**Norway Maple**]: Gate 3 [3]; S side, parking lots [many].
  *Acer platanoides* 'Emerald Queen' [**Norway Maple**]: S, along Edison Rd [many].
AQUIFOLIACEAE [HOLLY FAMILY], p. 154
  *Ilex verticillata* [**Winterberry**]: Gate 3, N [10]; W side, gate 3 [4].
BETULACEAE [BIRCH FAMILY], p. 103
  *Betula nigra* [**River Birch; Black Birch**]: Gate 10 [2]; Gate 3 [1]; Gate 8, S side [1]; N side [5].
CAESALPINIACEAE [CAESALPINIA FAMILY], p. 142
  *Gleditsia triacanthos* subsp. *inermis* [**Thornless Honeylocust**]: NW corner, gate 3 [3].
CAPRIFOLIACEAE [HONEYSUCKLE FAMILY], p. 180
  *Viburnum* × *burkwoodii* [**Burkwood Viburnum**]: Gate 2, N of walk [4]; S of gate 10 [7].
  *Viburnum plicatum* f. *tomentosum* [**Doublefile Viburnum**]: N side [13].
CELASTRACEAE [STAFF-TREE FAMILY], p. 151
  *Euonymus alata* [**Winged Burningbush; Winged Spindletree**]: W, between gates 1 and 2, at benches [14].
CORNACEAE [DOGWOOD FAMILY], p. 149
  *Cornus alba* 'Argenteo-marginata' [**Tartarian Dogwood**]: Gate 11 [3].
  *Cornus kousa* [**Kousa Dogwood**]: W side, W of gate 10 [1].
CUPRESSACEAE [CYPRESS FAMILY], p. 72
  *Chamaecyparis pisifera* 'Filifera Nana' [**Sawara Falsecypress**]: Gate 2, N of walk [5].
  *Juniperus chinensis* 'Sea Green' [**Chinese Juniper**]: N at B2 parking lot [bed]; W side, between gates 1 and 2 [beds].
  *Juniperus chinensis* 'Shimpaku' [**Chinese Juniper**]: W wall, center, between gates 1 and 2 [bed].
  *Juniperus sabina* 'Variegata' [**Hoarfrost Savin**]: W side, corners between gates 1 and 2 [beds].
ERICACEAE [HEATH FAMILY], p. 113
  *Gaultheria procumbens* [**Wintergreen**]: W, between gates 1 and 2, at benches [bed].
  *Rhododendron spp.* [**Rhododendron; Azalea**]: W, between gates 1 and 11 [26].
GROSSULARIACEAE [CURRANT FAMILY], p. 121
  *Ribes aureum* [**Golden Currant**]: Gate 10, W [5]; Gate 9, W [6]; NW corner, gate 3 [5].
  *Ribes sanguineum* 'Pulborough Scarlet' [**Scarlet Currant**]: Gate 10, N [5]; NW corner, gate 3 [5].

HAMAMELIDACEAE  [WITCH-HAZEL FAMILY], p. 90
>   *Hamamelis* × *intermedia* 'Diane' [**Witch-hazel**]: Gate 11, S side [6].

NYSSACEAE  [TUPELO FAMILY], p. 148
>   *Nyssa sylvatica* [**Black Tupelo; Blackgum; Sourgum**]: Gate 2 [1]; Gate 8, S side [1]; Gate 9, S side [1].

PINACEAE  [PINE FAMILY], p. 59
>   *Picea pungens* [**Colorado Blue Spruce**]: Gate 2, N of walk [3].
>   *Pinus nigra* [**Austrian Pine**]: W, along wall at gate 1 [2].
>   *Pinus strobus* [**Eastern White Pine**]: Gate 3 [5]; Gate 8, S side [2]; Gate 9, S side [3]; N side [7]; W, S of gate 11 [2]; W, between gates 1 and 11 [3].
>   *Pinus sylvestris* [**Scotch Pine**]: Gate 8, flanking [2]; W, along N wall at gate 2 [3]; W, along wall at gate 1 [2].

PLATANACEAE  [PLANETREE FAMILY], p. 89
>   *Platanus occidentalis* [**Sycamore; Buttonwood; American Planetree**]: Gate 4, S side [1]; Gate 7, S side [3].

ROSACEAE  [ROSE FAMILY], p. 122
>   *Amelanchier arborea* [**Downy Serviceberry; Juneberry**]: Gate 10 [7].
>   *Chaenomeles japonica* [**Japanese Floweringquince**]: W side, S of gate 10 [6].
>   *Cotoneaster divaricatus* [**Spreading Cotoneaster**]: S corner at gate 8 [beds]; W side, gate 3 [hedge]; W, along N wall at gate 2 [hedge]; W, along wall at gate 1 [beds].
>   *Crataegus crus-galli* [**Cockspur Hawthorn; Cockspur-thorn**]: Gate 11, flanking [2]; Gate 4 [1]; Gate 7, flanking [2]; Gate 9, E side [1]; NW corner, gate 3, flanking [2].
>   *Crataegus* × *lavallei* [**Lavalle Hawthorn**]: N at B2 parking lot [2].
>   *Crataegus phaenopyrum* [**Washington Hawthorn**]: Gate 9, W side [1].
>   *Pyrus calleryana* [**Callery Pear**]: W wall, between gates 1 and 2 [8].
>   *Pyrus calleryana* 'Chanticleer' [**Chanticleer Pear**]: N at B2 parking lot [2].
>   *Sorbus aucuparia* 'Cardinal Royal' [**European Mountain-ash**]: W side, W of gate 2 [1].
>   *Spiraea* × *bumalda* 'Goldflame' [**Goldflame Spiraea**]: Gate 11, S side [12]; Gate 9, flanking [20].

SAURURACEAE  [LIZARD'S-TAIL FAMILY], p. 84
>   *Houttuynia cordata* 'Chamaeleon' [**Houttuynia**]: Gate 10, flanking [beds]; Gate 2 [beds]; W, along wall at gate 1 [bed].

TAXACEAE  [YEW FAMILY], p. 55
>   *Taxus* × *media* 'Densiformis' [**Anglojapanese Yew**]: Gate 10 [beds]; Gate 2 [4].

## JUNIPER ROAD

ACERACEAE  [MAPLE FAMILY], p. 161
>   *Acer ginnala* [**Amur Maple**]: W, at Bulla Rd, S section, roadside [3].
>   *Acer palmatum* [**Japanese Maple**]: W, at Bulla Rd, N section, roadside [3].
>   *Acer saccharum* [**Sugar Maple; Hard Maple**]: ROTC stoplight, N sect., campus-side [4].

BERBERIDACEAE  [BARBERRY FAMILY], p. 86
>   *Berberis thunbergii* 'Crimson Pygmy' [**Dwarf Japanese Barberry**]: E, ROTC stoplight, fence [10]; E, opposite Galvin, at fence, W side [12]; Library Circle, N section, fence [7]; Library Circle, S, flanking drive [10]; North Gate, fence, roadside [16]; W, Library circle N, at fence [14]; W, at Bulla Rd, fence, roadside [46]; W, at Galvin, fence, roadside [10].

CAESALPINIACEAE  [CAESALPINIA FAMILY], p. 142
>   *Cercis canadensis* [**Eastern Redbud; Judas-tree**]: E, opposite Galvin, at fence, E side [2]; North Gate, planting [3]; W, at Bulla Rd, N section, S end [1]; W, at Bulla Rd, S section, N end [1]; W, at Galvin, fence, campus-side [2].

*Gleditsia triacanthos* subsp. *inermis* [**Thornless Honeylocust**]: W at Bulla Rd, middle section, roadside [3].

**CAPRIFOLIACEAE [HONEYSUCKLE FAMILY]**, p. 180

*Viburnum opulus* 'Compactum' [**Cranberrybush**]: ROTC stoplight, E and W sides [4]; W, Galvin fence, roadside [6]; W, Library circle N, fence, roadside [3]; W, Library circle S, fence, roadside [3]; W, at Bulla Rd, N section, roadside [6]; W, at Bulla Rd, S section, roadside [6]; W, at Galvin, fence, campus-side [6].

*Viburnum opulus* 'Nanum' [**Dwarf Cranberrybush**]: E, opposite Galvin, fence, W side [15]; North Gate, fence, N end [16]; ROTC stoplight, fence, campus-side [12]; W, Galvin fence, campus-side [12]; W, Library circle N, fence [2]; W, Library circle N, fence, campus-side [8]; W, Library circle S, fence [2]; W, Library circle S, fence, campus-side [18].

**CELASTRACEAE [STAFF-TREE FAMILY]**, p. 151

*Euonymus alata* 'Compacta' [**Narrow-winged Burningbush**]: E, ROTC stoplight, fence [7]; E, opposite Galvin, at fence, W side [5]; North Gate, S end [4]; North Gate, fence, roadside [3]; ROTC stoplight, E parking lot [4]; W, Library circle N, planting [12]; W, Library circle N, roadside [3]; W, Library circle S, fence, S end [4]; W, Library circle S, roadside [4]; W, at Bulla Rd, N section, N end [5]; W, at Bulla Rd, S section, S end [5]; W, at Galvin, fence, roadside [8].

**CUPRESSACEAE [CYPRESS FAMILY]**, p. 72

*Chamaecyparis pisifera* 'Golden Mop' [**Sawara Falsecypress**]: N at Douglas Rd, entrance sign [6]; S at Edison Rd, entrance sign [6].

*Juniperus chinensis* 'Old Gold' [**Chinese Juniper**]: N at Douglas Rd, entrance sign [6]; S at Edison Rd, entrance sign [6]; W, Library circle N, S planting [4].

*Juniperus chinensis* 'Sea Green' [**Chinese Juniper**]: N at Douglas Rd, entrance sign [bed]; S at Edison Rd, entrance sign [bed]; W, at Bulla Rd, N section, campus-side [5]; W, at Bulla Rd, S section, campus-side [5].

*Juniperus chinensis* 'Shimpaku' [**Chinese Juniper**]: W, Library circle S, fence, roadside [2]; W, at Bulla Rd, middle section, roadside [12].

*Juniperus horizontalis* 'Plumosa' [**Andorra Juniper**]: North Gate, fence, at benches [5]; ROTC stoplight, E parking lot fence [4].

*Juniperus horizontalis* 'Youngstown' [**Creeping Juniper**]: [beds].

*Juniperus scopulorum* 'Skyrocket' [**Rocky Mountain Juniper**]: ROTC stoplight, E parking lot fence [3].

*Juniperus squamata* 'Blue Star' [**Singleseed Juniper**]: North Gate, fence, at benches [2].

**ERICACEAE [HEATH FAMILY]**, p. 113

*Rhododendron* × *spp.* 'P.J.M.' [**P.J.M. Rhododendron**]: W at Bulla Road, S fence, roadside [3].

*Rhododendron spp.* 'Ramapo' [**Ramapo Rhododendron**]: N at Douglas Rd, entrance sign [bed]; S at Edison Rd, entrance sign [bed].

**FAGACEAE [BEECH FAMILY]**, p. 98

*Quercus palustris* [**Pin Oak**]: ROTC stoplight, E parking lot fence [1].

**JUGLANDACEAE [WALNUT FAMILY]**, p. 96

*Juglans nigra* [**Black Walnut**]: Edison Rd intersection, E of sign [1].

**OLEACEAE [OLIVE FAMILY]**, p. 174

*Fraxinus pennsylvanica* 'Summit' [**Green Ash**]: North Gate to Joyce Athletic and Convocation Center, flanking Juniper Rd [38].

**PINACEAE [PINE FAMILY]**, p. 59

*Picea omorika* 'Nana' [**Dwarf Serbian Spruce**]: E, opposite Galvin, N end of planting [3]; North Gate, S end of planting [3]; ROTC stoplight, E planting, S end [3]; W, Library circle N, N end [1]; W, Library circle N, S end [2]; W, Library circle S, N end [3]; W, Library circle S, S end of planting [3]; W, at Bulla Rd, N section, N end [3]; W, at Bulla Rd, S section, S end [3]; W, at Galvin, ends of planting [4].

*Picea pungens* [**Colorado Blue Spruce**]: N at Douglas Rd, entrance sign [5]; S at Edison Rd, entrance sign [15].

*Picea pungens* 'Glauca' [**Blue Spruce; Colorado Blue Spruce**]: ROTC stoplight, E parking lot fence [1].

*Pinus parviflora* 'Glauca' [**Japanese White Pine**]: S at Edison Rd, entrance sign [4].

ROSACEAE [ROSE FAMILY], p. 122

*Malus spp.* 'Dolgo' [**Dolgo Crabapple**]: Pedestrian entrances [many].

*Malus spp.* 'Robinson' [**Robinson Crabapple**]: S at Edison Rd, entrance sign [4]; W, Library circle N, fence, campus-side [2].

*Prunus virginiana* 'Shubert Select' [**Shubert Select Chokecherry**]: ROTC stoplight, fence, campus-side [2].

SAURURACEAE [LIZARD'S-TAIL FAMILY], p. 84

*Houttuynia cordata* 'Chamaeleon' [**Houttuynia**]: W, Library circle N, N fence [bed]; W, Library circle N, S fence [bed].

TAXACEAE [YEW FAMILY], p. 55

*Taxus baccata* [**English Yew**]: E, opposite Galvin, fence, E side [2]; North Gate, fence, roadside [7]; ROTC stoplight, fence, campus-side [2]; W, Library circle N [2]; W, Library circle N, N planting [3]; W, Library circle N, S planting [2]; W, Library circle S [2]; W, Library circle S, fence, campus-side [5]; W, at Bulla Rd [21]; W, at Galvin, fence, campus-side [4].

*Taxus baccata* 'Fastigiata' [**English Yew**]: N at Douglas Rd, entrance sign [2]; S at Edison Rd, entrance sign [2].

*Taxus baccata* 'Fastigiata Aurea' [**Golden English Yew**]: Pedestrian entrances, flanking [many].

*Taxus baccata* 'Stricta Aurea' [**English Yew**]: Pedestrian entrances, flanking [many].

*Taxus* × *media* 'Cole' [**Cole Yew**]: E, ROTC stoplight, fence [5]; E, opposite Galvin, at fence [4]; W, Library circle N [1]; W, Library circle N, S fence [2]; W, Library circle N, fence [2]; W, Library circle S [1]; W, Library circle S, fence, campus-side [4]; W, at Galvin, fence [4].


# KEENAN HALL

ACERACEAE [MAPLE FAMILY], p. 161

*Acer saccharum* [**Sugar Maple; Hard Maple**]: SW corner [2].

AQUIFOLIACEAE [HOLLY FAMILY], p. 154

*Ilex opaca* [**American Holly**]: E entrance, SE corner [2].

CELASTRACEAE [STAFF-TREE FAMILY], p. 151

*Euonymus alata* [**Winged Burningbush; Winged Spindletree**]: Front [3*].

*Euonymus fortunei* [**Chinese Winter-creeper**]: Front [1]; N side, W [beds].

CORNACEAE [DOGWOOD FAMILY], p. 149

*Cornus florida* [**Flowering Dogwood**]: SE entrance, flanking [2].

ELAEAGNACEAE [OLEASTER FAMILY], p. 147

*Elaeagnus angustifolia* [**Russian Olive; Oleaster**]: NW corner [1*].

ERICACEAE [HEATH FAMILY], p. 113

*Pieris japonica* [**Lily-of-the-valley Bush**]: SE entrance [2].

HYDRANGEACEAE [HYDRANGEA FAMILY], p. 117

*Hydrangea quercifolia* [**Oak-leaf Hydrangea**]: W side [beds*].

PINACEAE [PINE FAMILY], p. 59

*Picea pungens* [**Colorado Blue Spruce**]: SW corner, S [1*].

*Picea pungens* 'Viridis' [**Colorado Green Spruce**]: S, basement stairway [1*].

TAXACEAE [YEW FAMILY], p. 55
  *Taxus* × *media* [**Anglojapanese Yew**]: Stanford, front [hedge].


# Knights of Columbus Council Hall

ACERACEAE [MAPLE FAMILY], p. 161
  *Acer platanoides* [**Norway Maple**]: Walsh Hall, midway [1*].
OLEACEAE [OLIVE FAMILY], p. 174
  *Fraxinus pennsylvanica* [**Green Ash**]: S entrance, W side [1*].
PINACEAE [PINE FAMILY], p. 59
  *Pinus nigra* [**Austrian Pine**]: NW corner [1].
  *Pinus strobus* [**Eastern White Pine**]: SE corner, E 15yd [1*].
  *Pinus strobus* 'Fastigiata' [**Pyramidal White Pine**]: Sorin statue, between [3*].
ROSACEAE [ROSE FAMILY], p. 122
  *Amelanchier arborea* [**Downy Serviceberry; Juneberry**]: S entrance, W [1].
  *Malus spp.* [**Ornamental Crabapple hybrids**]: SW corner [1].
  *Prunus cerasifera* [**Cherry-plum**]: S entrance, W of walk [1 **Commem.**].


# Knott Hall

ACERACEAE [MAPLE FAMILY], p. 161
  *Acer platanoides* [**Norway Maple**]: S wing, E side [2].
  *Acer rubrum* 'Red Sunset' [**Red Maple**]: S wing, S end [2].
BERBERIDACEAE [BARBERRY FAMILY], p. 86
  *Berberis thunbergii* [**Japanese Barberry**]: S wing, E side [8].
CAPRIFOLIACEAE [HONEYSUCKLE FAMILY], p. 180
  *Viburnum dentatum* [**Arrowwood Viburnum**]: S wing, E side [6]; S wing, W side [4]; W wing, N side [10].
  *Viburnum rhytidophyllum* [**Rugose Viburnum**]: S wing, E side, S of door [1]; S wing, W side, S end [6]; W wing, N side [2]; W wing, SW corner [3].
CELASTRACEAE [STAFF-TREE FAMILY], p. 151
  *Euonymus alata* [**Winged Burningbush; Winged Spindletree**]: S wing, E side [3]; S wing, W side, S end [5].
CUPRESSACEAE [CYPRESS FAMILY], p. 72
  *Juniperus horizontalis* [**Creeping Juniper**]: W door, central bed [bed].
  *Thuja occidentalis* 'Globosa' [**Globe Arborvitae**]: S wing, E door [2]; W wing, N side, flanking walk [39]; W wing, W plaza, flanking door [6].
FAGACEAE [BEECH FAMILY], p. 98
  *Fagus sylvatica* [**European Beech**]: SW lawn [1].
  *Quercus palustris* [**Pin Oak**]: S wing, W side, S end [1].
  *Quercus rubra* [**Red Oak; Northern Red Oak**]: SW lawn [4].
GINKGOACEAE [GINKGO FAMILY], p. 54
  *Ginkgo biloba* [**Ginkgo; Maidenhair Tree**]: S wing, E side, S end [2]; SW lawn [1]; W wing, S side [1].
HYDRANGEACEAE [HYDRANGEA FAMILY], p. 117
  *Hydrangea arborescens* 'Grandiflora' [**Snowball Hydrangea**]: W wing, N side [8].
  *Hydrangea quercifolia* [**Oak-leaf Hydrangea**]: W wing, N side [4].
MALVACEAE [MALLOW FAMILY], p. 109
  *Hibiscus syriacus* [**Shrub-althea; Rose-of-Sharon**]: S wing, W side [2].

OLEACEAE [OLIVE FAMILY], p. 174
> *Forsythia* × *intermedia* [**Border Forsythia**]: W wing, S side [8].
> *Fraxinus pennsylvanica* [**Green Ash**]: S wing, E door circle [1].
> *Ligustrum obtusifolium* var. *regelianum* [**Regel's Privet**]: W wing, N walk, flanking central planter [hedge].

PINACEAE [PINE FAMILY], p. 59
> *Picea pungens* [**Colorado Blue Spruce**]: N side, along walk [6]; N wing, W end [3]; S wing, S end [2]; W door [3]; W wing, S side [4].
> *Pinus nigra* [**Austrian Pine**]: S wing, W side [2]; SW lawn [2]; W wing, S side [2].

PLATANACEAE [PLANETREE FAMILY], p. 89
> *Platanus* × *acerifolia* [**London Planetree**]: W wing, N walk, central planter [1].
> *Platanus occidentalis* [**Sycamore; Buttonwood; American Planetree**]: W wing, S side [1].

ROSACEAE [ROSE FAMILY], p. 122
> *Chaenomeles speciosa* [**Japanese Quince**]: S wing, W side [3]; W wing, S side [2].
> *Cotoneaster apiculatus* [**Cranberry Cotoneaster**]: W wing, N side, flanking walk [beds]; W wing, W plaza, flanking door [beds].
> *Crataegus phaenopyrum* [**Washington Hawthorn**]: S wing, W side, S end [2]; W wing, W plaza door [5].
> *Malus spp.* [**Ornamental Crabapple hybrids**]: N walk, flanking central bed [4]; S wing, E side [2]; S wing, S end [3]; SW lawn [15]; W door, central bed [4].
> *Prunus cerasifera* 'Newport' [**Purpleleaf Cherry-plum**]: W wing, N side, flanking walk [2].
> *Pyrus calleryana* [**Callery Pear**]: S wing, E door circle [6]; S wing, E side, S end [1]; W wing, N side, flanking walk [10]; W wing, W plaza, flanking door [18].
> *Spiraea* × *bumalda* [**Anthony Waterer Spiraea**]: S wing, E door, N side [10]; S wing, SE corner [4]; S wing, W side [10]; W wing, NW corner [7]; W wing, S side [4].

SAURURACEAE [LIZARD'S-TAIL FAMILY], p. 84
> *Houttuynia cordata* 'Chamaeleon' [**Houttuynia**]: W wing, N walk, central planter [bed].

TAXACEAE [YEW FAMILY], p. 55
> *Taxus cuspidata* 'Capitata' [**Japanese Yew**]: S wing, E side [4].
> *Taxus* × *media* 'Densiformis' [**Anglojapanese Yew**]: N walk, E end [16].
> *Taxus* × *media* 'Hicksii' [**Hicks' Yew**]: S wing, E side [7]; S wing, W side [4]; W wing, S side [7].


## KOONS REHEARSAL HALL

ACERACEAE [MAPLE FAMILY], p. 161
> *Acer platanoides* [**Norway Maple**]: S side [8].

AQUIFOLIACEAE [HOLLY FAMILY], p. 154
> *Ilex glabra* [**Inkberry**]: E side [10]; W side, N of door, along walk [16]; W side, S end [8].

CAPRIFOLIACEAE [HONEYSUCKLE FAMILY], p. 180
> *Viburnum rhytidophyllum* [**Rugose Viburnum**]: S side, W end [14].

CELASTRACEAE [STAFF-TREE FAMILY], p. 151
> *Euonymus fortunei* [**Chinese Winter-creeper**]: N, along wall [beds].

CORNACEAE [DOGWOOD FAMILY], p. 149
> *Cornus florida* [**Flowering Dogwood**]: W side, S end [2].

CUPRESSACEAE [CYPRESS FAMILY], p. 72
> *Juniperus horizontalis* [**Creeping Juniper**]: E side [18].

FAGACEAE [BEECH FAMILY], p. 98
> *Quercus rubra* [**Red Oak; Northern Red Oak**]: W [1 **Commem.**]; W, along walk [3].

NYSSACEAE [TUPELO FAMILY], p. 148
> *Nyssa sylvatica* [**Black Tupelo; Blackgum; Sourgum**]: E, flanking parking lot [4].

OLEACEAE [OLIVE FAMILY], p. 174
  *Syringa vulgaris* [**Common Lilac**]: N, flanking E-W walk [6].
PINACEAE [PINE FAMILY], p. 59
  *Picea glauca* 'Conica' [**Conical White Spruce**]: NW corner [1].
ROSACEAE [ROSE FAMILY], p. 122
  *Amelanchier arborea* [**Downy Serviceberry; Juneberry**]: W side [6]; W side, N of door, along walk [3].
  *Malus spp.* [**Ornamental Crabapple hybrids**]: E [1].
  *Pyrus calleryana* [**Callery Pear**]: N side, NE corner [2]; SE court [6].

## LaFortune Student Center

AQUIFOLIACEAE [HOLLY FAMILY], p. 154
  *Ilex verticillata* [**Winterberry**]: Crowley, crosswalk between, N side [bed].
BETULACEAE [BIRCH FAMILY], p. 103
  *Betula papyrifera* [**Paper Birch; Canoe Birch**]: Sacred Heart Statue, between [1*].
CALYCANTHACEAE [STRAWBERRY-SHRUB FAMILY], p. 83
  *Calycanthus floridus* [**Carolina Allspice; Common Sweetshrub**]: Crowley, bed at walk between [bed].
CAPRIFOLIACEAE [HONEYSUCKLE FAMILY], p. 180
  *Viburnum rhytidophyllum* [**Rugose Viburnum**]: SW entrance, flanking [2].
CUPRESSACEAE [CYPRESS FAMILY], p. 72
  *Juniperus chinensis* 'Pfitzeriana' [**Pfitzer Juniper**]: W entrance, NW 5yd [2*].
FABACEAE [PEA FAMILY], p. 144
  *Cladrastis kentukea* [**Yellowwood; Virgilia**]: SW 10yd [1* **Commem.**].
FAGACEAE [BEECH FAMILY], p. 98
  *Fagus orientalis* [**Oriental Beech**]: SE corner, S 13yd [1*].
  *Quercus imbricaria* [**Shingle Oak**]: WSW 15yd [1*].
  *Quercus muehlenbergii* f. *alexanderi* [**Alexander's Chestnut Oak**]: SW 30yd, lamppost 53, S 10ft [1*].
  *Quercus palustris* [**Pin Oak**]: Riley, between [7].
  *Quercus velutina* f. *pagodaeformis* [**Pagoda Black Oak**]: SW 20yd [1*].
HIPPOCASTANACEAE [HORSECHESTNUT FAMILY], p. 160
  *Aesculus parviflora* [**Bottlebrush Buckeye**]: Sacred Heart Statue, midway, roadside [1*].
MAGNOLIACEAE [MAGNOLIA FAMILY], p. 82
  *Magnolia* × *soulangiana* [**Saucer Magnolia**]: E entrance, S [1].
OLEACEAE [OLIVE FAMILY], p. 174
  *Forsythia* × *intermedia* [**Border Forsythia**]: SE, fountain, N side [8].
  *Ligustrum ovalifolium* [**California Privet**]: W entrance, W 30yd [3*].
PINACEAE [PINE FAMILY], p. 59
  *Larix decidua* [**European Larch**]: SW 30yd, lamppost 53, W 10yd [2*].
  *Picea abies* [**Norway Spruce**]: NW corner [1].
  *Picea pungens* [**Colorado Blue Spruce**]: W entrance, N side [1*].
  *Pinus flexilis* [**Limber Pine**]: S central door, SSE 20yd [2*].
  *Pinus nigra* [**Austrian Pine**]: S side at walks [1]; SW corner, S 15yd [1*].
  *Pinus thunbergiana* [**Japanese Black Pine**]: S central door, S 30yd [1].
  *Pseudotsuga menziesii* [**Douglas-fir**]: N side [1*]; S side [1*]; SW corner [1*].
ROSACEAE [ROSE FAMILY], p. 122
  *Cotoneaster apiculatus* [**Cranberry Cotoneaster**]: S side [hedge].
  *Crataegus phaenopyrum* [**Washington Hawthorn**]: N side [7].
  *Malus spp.* [**Ornamental Crabapple hybrids**]: NW lawn [2].

*Prunus cerasifera* 'Mt. St. Helens' [**Purpleleaf Cherry-plum**]: NW lawn [1].
TAXACEAE [YEW FAMILY], p. 55
    *Taxus* × *media* [**Anglojapanese Yew**]: NE, Fieldhouse Mall, W edge [hedge].
TAXODIACEAE [TAXODIUM FAMILY], p. 71
    *Taxodium distichum* [**Baldcypress**]: SW 30yd [1].
TILIACEAE [LINDEN FAMILY], p. 107
    *Tilia* × *euchlora* [**Crimean Linden**]: Sacred Heart Statue, midway [1*].
ULMACEAE [ELM FAMILY], p. 92
    *Ulmus americana* [**American Elm**]: NE corner, E [1*].
    *Ulmus glabra* [**Wych Elm; Scotch Elm**]: W entrance, W 15yd [1*].

## LAW SCHOOL

BERBERIDACEAE [BARBERRY FAMILY], p. 86
    *Mahonia aquifolium* [**Oregon Grape**]: Cushing, between [many].
BETULACEAE [BIRCH FAMILY], p. 103
    *Carpinus betulus* [**European Hornbeam**]: W side [2].
CELASTRACEAE [STAFF-TREE FAMILY], p. 151
    *Euonymus europaea* [**European Spindletree**]: NW corner [1].
CLUSIACEAE [MANGOSTEEN FAMILY], p. 107
    *Hypericum prolificum* [**Shrubby St. Johnswort**]: S wing, SW corner [3]; S wing, W side [2].
CUPRESSACEAE [CYPRESS FAMILY], p. 72
    *Thuja occidentalis* [**American Arborvitae; Northern White Cedar**]: S entrance [15].
FABACEAE [PEA FAMILY], p. 144
    *Caragana arborescens* [**Siberian Pea-tree**]: SW corner [2*].
GROSSULARIACEAE [CURRANT FAMILY], p. 121
    *Ribes alpinum* [**Alpine Currant; Mountain Currant**]: N entrance, E [1]; NW corner [1].
HAMAMELIDACEAE [WITCH-HAZEL FAMILY], p. 90
    *Hamamelis virginiana* [**Witch-hazel**]: E side, SE corner [1].
HYDRANGEACEAE [HYDRANGEA FAMILY], p. 117
    *Deutzia gracilis* [**Japanese Slender Deutzia**]: NW corner, at walk [hedge*].
    *Philadelphus* × *virginalis* [**Virginal Mock Orange**]: N [4].
PINACEAE [PINE FAMILY], p. 59
    *Picea abies* [**Norway Spruce**]: NW corner [1*]; W entrance [1*].
    *Pseudotsuga menziesii* [**Douglas-fir**]: SW door, S [1].
ROSACEAE [ROSE FAMILY], p. 122
    *Amelanchier laevis* [**Allegheny Serviceberry**]: SE corner [2].
    *Crataegus phaenopyrum* [**Washington Hawthorn**]: NW corner [2]; SE corner [1]; SW corner [2*].
    *Sorbus aucuparia* 'Cardinal Royal' [**European Mountain-ash**]: W side, center [1 **Commem.**].
TAXACEAE [YEW FAMILY], p. 55
    *Taxus* × *media* [**Anglojapanese Yew**]: S entrance [2].

## LEWIS BUS SHELTER

CELASTRACEAE [STAFF-TREE FAMILY], p. 151
    *Euonymus alata* [**Winged Burningbush; Winged Spindletree**]: E end [1*].

ROSACEAE [ROSE FAMILY], p. 122
Cotoneaster divaricatus [**Spreading Cotoneaster**]: N side [bed].


## LEWIS HALL

AGAVACEAE [CENTURY-PLANT FAMILY], p. 187
Yucca filamentosa [**Adam's-needle Yucca**]: SW corner [1].
BETULACEAE [BIRCH FAMILY], p. 103
Carpinus betulus [**European Hornbeam**]: Patio [1*].
CAESALPINIACEAE [CAESALPINIA FAMILY], p. 142
Cercis canadensis [**Eastern Redbud; Judas-tree**]: N, lakeside [3*].
CAPRIFOLIACEAE [HONEYSUCKLE FAMILY], p. 180
Viburnum opulus [**Cranberrybush; Guelder-rose**]: N, woods [many*].
CELASTRACEAE [STAFF-TREE FAMILY], p. 151
Celastrus scandens [**American Bittersweet**]: NE 60yd, lakeside [few*].
FAGACEAE [BEECH FAMILY], p. 98
Quercus alba [**White Oak**]: NE corner [5*].
JUGLANDACEAE [WALNUT FAMILY], p. 96
Juglans nigra [**Black Walnut**]: N, lakeside, along path [40*].
MORACEAE [MULBERRY FAMILY], p. 94
Morus alba [**White Mulberry**]: N, 5yd [1].
OLEACEAE [OLIVE FAMILY], p. 174
Syringa reticulata [**Japanese Tree Lilac**]: Patio [6*].
PINACEAE [PINE FAMILY], p. 59
Pinus densiflora 'Umbraculifera' [**Dwarf Japanese Red Pine**]: E, main entrance, S along wall [3].
ROSACEAE [ROSE FAMILY], p. 122
Prunus subhirtella 'Snofozam' [**Snow Fountain Weeping Higan Cherry**]: E, main entrance, N of walk [1 **Commem.**].
Pyrus calleryana [**Callery Pear**]: E, main entrance [1].
Pyrus calleryana 'Redspire' [**Callery Pear**]: E, main entrance [2].
SOLANACEAE [NIGHTSHADE FAMILY], p. 172
Solanum dulcamara [**Bitter Nightshade**]: N, lakeside [few*].
TAXACEAE [YEW FAMILY], p. 55
Taxus cuspidata [**Japanese Yew**]: NE door [5*]; NW corner [1*].
Taxus cuspidata 'Densa' [**Japanese Cushion Yew**]: E, main entrance, N of walk [7*].
Taxus cuspidata 'Fastigiata' [**Japanese Pyramidal Yew**]: E side [7*].
ULMACEAE [ELM FAMILY], p. 92
Celtis occidentalis [**Hackberry**]: NE corner, NE 40yd, lakeside [1*].


## LOFTUS SPORTS CENTER

CAPRIFOLIACEAE [HONEYSUCKLE FAMILY], p. 180
Viburnum plicatum f. tomentosum [**Doublefile Viburnum**]: W side, N door [6]; W side, S door [6].
CORNACEAE [DOGWOOD FAMILY], p. 149
Cornus sericea 'Flaviramea' [**Goldentwig Dogwood**]: W side, center [10].
CUPRESSACEAE [CYPRESS FAMILY], p. 72
Thuja occidentalis [**American Arborvitae; Northern White Cedar**]: W side, N end, flanking door [15]; W side, S end, flanking door [15].

FAGACEAE  [BEECH FAMILY], p. 98
    *Quercus alba* [**White Oak**]: SW corner [3].
    *Quercus rubra* [**Red Oak; Northern Red Oak**]: SW corner [9].
JUGLANDACEAE  [WALNUT FAMILY], p. 96
    *Carya ovalis* [**Sweet Pignut**]: N, woods [many*]; SW corner [3].
    *Carya ovalis* var. *obovalis* [**Obovate Pignut**]: N, woods [many*].
    *Juglans nigra* [**Black Walnut**]: SW corner [1].
MORACEAE  [MULBERRY FAMILY], p. 94
    *Morus alba* [**White Mulberry**]: SW corner [1].
OLEACEAE  [OLIVE FAMILY], p. 174
    *Fraxinus pennsylvanica* [**Green Ash**]: W side, center [3].
ROSACEAE  [ROSE FAMILY], p. 122
    *Cotoneaster apiculatus* [**Cranberry Cotoneaster**]: W side [beds].
    *Prunus serotina* [**Blackcherry; Wild Black Cherry**]: SW corner [12].
    *Pyrus calleryana* [**Callery Pear**]: W side, N door [2]; W side, S door [2].
ULMACEAE  [ELM FAMILY], p. 92
    *Ulmus americana* [**American Elm**]: SW corner [1].
VITACEAE  [GRAPE FAMILY], p. 157
    *Vitis aestivalis* var. *argentifolia* [**Silver-leaf Grape**]: N, woods [1].


## Log Chapel

ACERACEAE  [MAPLE FAMILY], p. 161
    *Acer negundo* [**Boxelder**]: NW 50yd, lakeside [1*].
CAPRIFOLIACEAE  [HONEYSUCKLE FAMILY], p. 180
    *Viburnum carlesii* [**Fragrant Viburnum**]: E, flanking entrance [2*].
CERCIDIPHYLLACEAE  [KATSURA TREE FAMILY], p. 88
    *Cercidiphyllum japonicum* [**Katsura Tree**]: Old College, midway [1 **Commem.**].
FABACEAE  [PEA FAMILY], p. 144
    *Robinia pseudoacacia* [**Black Locust**]: NW, along road and SE [8*].
PINACEAE  [PINE FAMILY], p. 59
    *Abies balsamea* [**Balsam Fir**]: NW corner [2*].
    *Picea abies* [**Norway Spruce**]: W end [1].
    *Pinus resinosa* [**Red Pine; Norway Pine**]: N, 10yd [1*].
    *Pseudotsuga menziesii* [**Douglas-fir**]: S side [9*].
ROSACEAE  [ROSE FAMILY], p. 122
    *Spiraea japonica* var. *fortunei* [**Robert Fortune Spiraea**]: W end [4*].


## Lyons Hall

CAESALPINIACEAE  [CAESALPINIA FAMILY], p. 142
    *Cercis canadensis* [**Eastern Redbud; Judas-tree**]: N, parking lot, N edge [1 **Commem.**]; NW
       basketball court, W end [1*].
CAPRIFOLIACEAE  [HONEYSUCKLE FAMILY], p. 180
    *Lonicera morrowii* [**Morrow Honeysuckle**]: Chapel, S side [5*]; S wing, 15yd NE [1*].
    *Viburnum carlesii* [**Fragrant Viburnum**]: Archway, S side [8]; Archway, SE [few*].
    *Viburnum lentago* [**Nannyberry; Sweet Viburnum**]: NW corner [7*].
    *Viburnum opulus* [**Cranberrybush; Guelder-rose**]: S, in hedge [1].
    *Viburnum opulus* 'Roseum' [**Snowball; Snowball-bush**]: NW basketball court, N, lakeside
       [2*].

*Viburnum plicatum* [**Japanese Snowball**]: E side, S of arch [1*].
CORNACEAE  [DOGWOOD FAMILY], p. 149
    *Cornus sanguinea* [**Bloodtwig Dogwood**]: Chapel, S side [5*].
    *Cornus sericea* [**Red-osier Dogwood**]: Archway, SE [1].
HYDRANGEACEAE  [HYDRANGEA FAMILY], p. 117
    *Hydrangea quercifolia* [**Oak-leaf Hydrangea**]: SE corner [1].
    *Philadelphus coronarius* 'Zeyheri' [**Zeyher Mock Orange**]: NW basketball court, N, lakeside [1].
    *Philadelphus* × *virginalis* [**Virginal Mock Orange**]: N, lakeside [1].
MORACEAE  [MULBERRY FAMILY], p. 94
    *Morus alba* 'Tatarica' [**Russian Mulberry**]: S [hedge*].
OLEACEAE  [OLIVE FAMILY], p. 174
    *Ligustrum vulgare* [**Common Privet; European Privet**]: S [hedge].
PINACEAE  [PINE FAMILY], p. 59
    *Pinus strobus* [**Eastern White Pine**]: SE front [5*].
ROSACEAE  [ROSE FAMILY], p. 122
    *Cotoneaster acutifolius* [**Pekinese Cotoneaster**]: Archway, NW side [bed*].
    *Cotoneaster apiculatus* [**Cranberry Cotoneaster**]: Archway, NW, central bed facing lake [bed].
    *Crataegus mollis* [**Downy Hawthorn**]: SW corner [1].
    *Crataegus phaenopyrum* [**Washington Hawthorn**]: Archway, SW, 15yd [2].
    *Crataegus pruinosa* [**Frosted Hawthorn**]: Archway, SE [1].
    *Rosa hugonis* [**Father Hugo Rose**]: NE corner, N, at wood fence [1].
    *Spiraea* × *vanhouttei* [**Vanhoutte Spiraea**]: S entrance, W [2].
SALICACEAE  [WILLOW FAMILY], p. 110
    *Salix alba* var. *vitellina* [**Yellow Willow**]: NW basketball court, N, lakeside [2].
ULMACEAE  [ELM FAMILY], p. 92
    *Ulmus americana* [**American Elm**]: E 15yd [1].
    *Ulmus pumila* [**Siberian Elm**]: S end [3*].
VITACEAE  [GRAPE FAMILY], p. 157
    *Vitis riparia* [**River-bank Grape; Frost Grape**]: N wing, SE corner [1*].


## Mail Distribution Center

CAPRIFOLIACEAE  [HONEYSUCKLE FAMILY], p. 180
    *Lonicera* × *amoena* 'Rosea' [**Honeysuckle**]: N, lakeside [1*].
    *Viburnum prunifolium* [**Blackhaw; Sweethaw**]: SW corner [7*].
HYDRANGEACEAE  [HYDRANGEA FAMILY], p. 117
    *Philadelphus coronarius* 'Zeyheri' [**Zeyher Mock Orange**]: N end, W [1]; SW corner, W 7yd [1].
LAURACEAE  [LAUREL FAMILY], p. 84
    *Sassafras albidum* [**Red Sassafras**]: W side [26*].
ROSACEAE  [ROSE FAMILY], p. 122
    *Malus pumila* [**Common Apple**]: SW corner [3*].
    *Spiraea nipponica* 'Snowmound' [**Snowmound Nippon Spiraea**]: SW corner [many].

## MAINTENANCE CENTER

**ACERACEAE  [MAPLE FAMILY]**, p. 161
   *Acer platanoides* [**Norway Maple**]: S side [3].
**CAPRIFOLIACEAE  [HONEYSUCKLE FAMILY]**, p. 180
   *Lonicera* × *bella* [**Belle Honeysuckle**]: SW corner, W 50yd [1].
**CELASTRACEAE  [STAFF-TREE FAMILY]**, p. 151
   *Euonymus alata* [**Winged Burningbush; Winged Spindletree**]: S side [5].
**CUPRESSACEAE  [CYPRESS FAMILY]**, p. 72
   *Chamaecyparis obtusa* 'Pygmaea Aurescens' [**Hinoki Falsecypress**]: E, between ND Press and Transportation [2].
   *Juniperus squamata* [**Singleseed Juniper**]: E, between ND Press and Transportation [6].
**HYDRANGEACEAE  [HYDRANGEA FAMILY]**, p. 117
   *Philadelphus* × *cymosus* [**Cymose Mock Orange**]: SW corner, W 50yd [1].
**ROSACEAE  [ROSE FAMILY]**, p. 122
   *Malus spp.* 'Christmas Holly' [**Christmas Holly Crabapple**]: E, between ND Press and Transportation [2].
   *Potentilla fruticosa* [**Shrubby Cinquefoil**]: S side [7].

## MOREAU SEMINARY

**ACERACEAE  [MAPLE FAMILY]**, p. 161
   *Acer platanoides* 'Rubrum' [**Crimson Norway Maple**]: E side [1].
**AQUIFOLIACEAE  [HOLLY FAMILY]**, p. 154
   *Ilex opaca* [**American Holly**]: Chapel, E court [1]; O'Rourke Bell W, E court [2*].
**BERBERIDACEAE  [BARBERRY FAMILY]**, p. 86
   *Mahonia aquifolium* [**Oregon Grape**]: W end, lake slope [beds*].
**BIGNONIACEAE  [BIGNONIA FAMILY]**, p. 179
   *Catalpa speciosa* [**Northern Catalpa**]: S, lakeside [1].
**BUXACEAE  [BOX FAMILY]**, p. 156
   *Pachysandra terminalis* [**Japanese Pachysandra; Japanese Spurge**]: N side, E court [beds*].
**CAESALPINIACEAE  [CAESALPINIA FAMILY]**, p. 142
   *Gleditsia triacanthos* subsp. *inermis* [**Thornless Honeylocust**]: N lawn [4*].
**CELASTRACEAE  [STAFF-TREE FAMILY]**, p. 151
   *Euonymus alata* 'Compacta' [**Narrow-winged Burningbush**]: Basketball court, NE corner [2*]; Basketball court, SE corner [1*]; NE corner, fire hydrant [3*].
**CORNACEAE  [DOGWOOD FAMILY]**, p. 149
   *Cornus purpusii* [**Silky Dogwood; Pale Dogwood**]: E end, S, lakeside [1*].
**CUPRESSACEAE  [CYPRESS FAMILY]**, p. 72
   *Juniperus chinensis* 'Keteleeri' [**Keteleer Juniper**]: NW, S of fuel tanks [1*].
   *Juniperus chinensis* var. *sargentii* [**Sargent Juniper**]: E end, steps [2*].
   *Juniperus virginiana* 'Canaertii' [**Canaert Redcedar**]: NE side [3*].
   *Juniperus virginiana* 'Schottii' [**Schott's Redcedar**]: N entrance, W side [1*].
   *Thuja occidentalis* 'Conica' [**Conical Arborvitae**]: N, Douglas Rd entrance [7*]; N, Douglas Rd entrance, W [1].
**ELAEAGNACEAE  [OLEASTER FAMILY]**, p. 147
   *Elaeagnus angustifolia* [**Russian Olive; Oleaster**]: SW corner, W 25yd [1*].
**ERICACEAE  [HEATH FAMILY]**, p. 113
   *Rhododendron catawbiense* [**Catawba Rhododendron**]: S central side [2].

**FAGACEAE [BEECH FAMILY]**, p. 98

*Fagus sylvatica* 'Atropunicea' [**Copper Beech; Purple Beech**]: W end, S side [1*].

*Quercus alba* [**White Oak**]: S, lake slope [1*].

*Quercus bicolor* [**Swamp White Oak**]: N side [4*]; NE, parking lot, S end [3*].

*Quercus rubra* [**Red Oak; Northern Red Oak**]: NE, parking lot [14]; W end, lake slope, flanking steps [1*].

**GINKGOACEAE [GINKGO FAMILY]**, p. 54

*Ginkgo biloba* [**Ginkgo; Maidenhair Tree**]: Chapel, E side [1*].

**HAMAMELIDACEAE [WITCH-HAZEL FAMILY]**, p. 90

*Liquidambar styraciflua* [**Sweetgum**]: Front [1].

**HIPPOCASTANACEAE [HORSECHESTNUT FAMILY]**, p. 160

*Aesculus hippocastanum* [**Horsechestnut**]: SW corner [1*].

**JUGLANDACEAE [WALNUT FAMILY]**, p. 96

*Carya ovalis* var. *obcordata* [**Obcordate Pignut**]: SW corner, lake slope [4*].

*Juglans regia* [**English Walnut**]: W 20yd [1*].

**MAGNOLIACEAE [MAGNOLIA FAMILY]**, p. 82

*Magnolia* × *soulangiana* [**Saucer Magnolia**]: W wing, S [1*].

*Magnolia stellata* [**Star Magnolia**]: E end [1*].

**MALVACEAE [MALLOW FAMILY]**, p. 109

*Hibiscus syriacus* [**Shrub-althea; Rose-of-Sharon**]: W end, along walk [4*].

**OLEACEAE [OLIVE FAMILY]**, p. 174

*Fraxinus americana* [**White Ash**]: W end, S [1].

*Fraxinus quadrangulata* [**Blue Ash**]: W end, lakeside [1*].

*Syringa vulgaris* 'Purpurea' [**Purplish Red Lilac**]: SW corner [many*].

**PINACEAE [PINE FAMILY]**, p. 59

*Larix decidua* [**European Larch**]: N of indoor basketball court [1*].

**ROSACEAE [ROSE FAMILY]**, p. 122

*Cotoneaster adpressus* var. *praecox* [**Nan Shan Cotoneaster**]: SW corner [1*].

*Crataegus succulenta* [**Fleshy Hawthorn**]: Basketball court, SE corner [1*].

*Malus spp.* [**Ornamental Crabapple hybrids**]: N wing, NE corner, E side [1]; NE corner [1]; S side, W door [1]; SW end, W 10yd [1].

*Prunus avium* [**Mazzard; Sweet Cherry**]: E end [1*]; St. Joseph Hall, slope between [1]; St. Joseph Hall, woods between [1].

*Prunus cerasifera* [**Cherry-plum**]: Chapel entrance, W [1].

*Prunus cerasifera* 'Atropurpurea' [**Purpleleaf Cherry-plum**]: Chapel, W side, corner entrance [1].

*Prunus virginiana* [**Chokecherry**]: S, lake slope [many*].

*Pyracantha coccinea* 'Lalandei' [**Laland Firethorn**]: Chapel, SE and SW corners [4*].

**SALICACEAE [WILLOW FAMILY]**, p. 110

*Salix alba* var. *vitellina* [**Yellow Willow**]: S, lakeside [6].

*Salix amygdaloides* [**Peachleaf Willow**]: NE [1*].

*Salix bebbiana* [**Bebb's Willow**]: NW corner, W [1].

**TAXACEAE [YEW FAMILY]**, p. 55

*Taxus cuspidata* [**Japanese Yew**]: Holy Cross House, walk between [hedge].

*Taxus* × *media* 'Hatfieldii' [**Hatfield's Yew**]: Patio, front [12*].

**TAXODIACEAE [TAXODIUM FAMILY]**, p. 71

*Metasequoia glyptostroboides* [**Dawn Redwood**]: E court [1].

## MORRIS INN

ACERACEAE [MAPLE FAMILY], p. 161

*Acer palmatum* [**Japanese Maple**]: Court, NW corner [1*]; Court, SW corner [1*]; Main entrance, E beds [2].

*Acer palmatum* 'Willow Leaf' [**Japanese Maple**]: Main entrance, E beds [2].

BUXACEAE [BOX FAMILY], p. 156

*Pachysandra terminalis* [**Japanese Pachysandra; Japanese Spurge**]: Main entrance, E beds [beds].

CAPRIFOLIACEAE [HONEYSUCKLE FAMILY], p. 180

*Viburnum recognitum* [**Arrowwood**]: NE corner, E side [1]; SE corner [1].

CELASTRACEAE [STAFF-TREE FAMILY], p. 151

*Euonymus alata* 'Compacta' [**Narrow-winged Burningbush**]: Main entrance, E beds, NW [12]; Main entrance, E beds, SW [12].

*Euonymus bungeana* [**Winterberry Spindletree**]: NW corner, N 25yd [1*].

CORNACEAE [DOGWOOD FAMILY], p. 149

*Cornus canadensis* [**Bunchberry**]: Main entrance, E beds [beds].

CUPRESSACEAE [CYPRESS FAMILY], p. 72

*Chamaecyparis obtusa* [**Hinoki Falsecypress**]: E, along building, N of main entrance [2].

*Chamaecyparis obtusa* 'Nana Gracilis' [**Hinoki Falsecypress**]: E, along building, N of main entrance [1].

*Chamaecyparis obtusa* 'Pygmaea Aurescens' [**Hinoki Falsecypress**]: E, along building, N of main entrance [6].

*Chamaecyparis pisifera* 'Boulevard' [**Sawara Falsecypress**]: Main entrance, E beds [20].

*Chamaecyparis pisifera* 'Filifera Aurea Nana' [**Sawara Falsecypress**]: Main entrance, E beds [beds].

*Juniperus squamata* [**Singleseed Juniper**]: E, main beds flanking walk [20]; E, main beds, N & S [12].

*Thuja occidentalis* 'Rheingold' [**American Arborvitae**]: E, beds flanking walk [8].

HYDRANGEACEAE [HYDRANGEA FAMILY], p. 117

*Deutzia gracilis* [**Japanese Slender Deutzia**]: S end [hedge*].

OLEACEAE [OLIVE FAMILY], p. 174

*Fraxinus pennsylvanica* 'Marshall's Seedless' [**Green Ash**]: E [2].

*Syringa reticulata* [**Japanese Tree Lilac**]: N parking lot [1].

PINACEAE [PINE FAMILY], p. 59

*Picea abies* 'Pendula' [**Weeping Norway Spruce**]: Main entrance, E beds [beds].

*Pseudotsuga menziesii* [**Douglas-fir**]: NE corner, N 20yd [1].

ROSACEAE [ROSE FAMILY], p. 122

*Cotoneaster apiculatus* [**Cranberry Cotoneaster**]: Main entrance, E beds [many].

*Cotoneaster horizontalis* [**Rock Cotoneaster**]: Main entrance, E beds, behind benches [beds].

*Malus* spp. [**Ornamental Crabapple hybrids**]: N end, N 20yd [1*].

*Malus* spp. 'Coral Beauty' [**Coral Beauty Crabapple**]: Main entrance, E beds [4].

*Malus* spp. 'Profusion' [**Profusion Flowering Crab**]: W entrance, W [1 **Commem.**].

*Prunus subhirtella* 'Snofozam' [**Snow Fountain Weeping Higan Cherry**]: Main entrance, E beds [2].

*Pyrus calleryana* [**Callery Pear**]: W side [1 **Commem.**].

*Spiraea* × *vanhouttei* [**Vanhoutte Spiraea**]: N end [6*].

TAXACEAE [YEW FAMILY], p. 55

*Taxus* × *media* 'Hicksii' [**Hicks' Yew**]: E, main beds, W edge [bed].

TAXODIACEAE [TAXODIUM FAMILY], p. 71

*Metasequoia glyptostroboides* [**Dawn Redwood**]: NE corner [1].

THYMELAEACEAE [MEZEREUM FAMILY], p. 147
   *Daphne cneorum* 'Ruby Glow' [**Rose Daphne; Garland Flower**]: Main entrance, E beds [few].
VITACEAE [GRAPE FAMILY], p. 157
   *Vitis riparia* [**River-bank Grape; Frost Grape**]: Service door, W, golf course fence [1*].


## MORRISSEY HALL

APOCYNACEAE [DOGBANE FAMILY], p. 171
   *Vinca minor* [**Common Periwinkle; Running Myrtle**]: E, along wall [bed].
AQUIFOLIACEAE [HOLLY FAMILY], p. 154
   *Ilex opaca* [**American Holly**]: Main entrance, E [2*].
BIGNONIACEAE [BIGNONIA FAMILY], p. 179
   *Campsis radicans* [**Trumpet-creeper; Trumpet-vine**]: NE corner [1*].
CAESALPINIACEAE [CAESALPINIA FAMILY], p. 142
   *Gleditsia triacanthos* [**Honeylocust**]: NW corner [1*].
CAPRIFOLIACEAE [HONEYSUCKLE FAMILY], p. 180
   *Symphoricarpos rivularis* [**Common Snowberry**]: NE corner [1*]; NW corner [few*].
   *Viburnum carlesii* [**Fragrant Viburnum**]: SE corner [2].
CELASTRACEAE [STAFF-TREE FAMILY], p. 151
   *Euonymus europaea* [**European Spindletree**]: SW corner [12*].
CERCIDIPHYLLACEAE [KATSURA TREE FAMILY], p. 88
   *Cercidiphyllum japonicum* [**Katsura Tree**]: E side [2*].
CORNACEAE [DOGWOOD FAMILY], p. 149
   *Cornus sericea* [**Red-osier Dogwood**]: SW corner, S 35yd [3].
CUPRESSACEAE [CYPRESS FAMILY], p. 72
   *Chamaecyparis obtusa* 'Crippsii' [**Hinoki Falsecypress**]: N side [2].
   *Chamaecyparis pisifera* [**Sawara Falsecypress**]: E wing, N 15yd [1*].
ERICACEAE [HEATH FAMILY], p. 113
   *Pieris japonica* [**Lily-of-the-valley Bush**]: S, intersection of walks [1].
MORACEAE [MULBERRY FAMILY], p. 94
   *Morus alba* [**White Mulberry**]: Chapel, W side [1*].
OLEACEAE [OLIVE FAMILY], p. 174
   *Syringa vulgaris* [**Common Lilac**]: SE corner [1].
PINACEAE [PINE FAMILY], p. 59
   *Picea abies* [**Norway Spruce**]: Main entrance, E side [2*].
   *Picea pungens* 'Argentea' [**Colorado Silver Spruce**]: SW corner [1*].
   *Picea pungens* 'Glauca' [**Blue Spruce; Colorado Blue Spruce**]: Main entrance, E side [1*].
   *Pinus nigra* [**Austrian Pine**]: Chapel, E side [1].
   *Pseudotsuga menziesii* [**Douglas-fir**]: SE corner [1*].
RHAMNACEAE [BUCKTHORN FAMILY], p. 157
   *Rhamnus frangula* [**Glossy Buckthorn; Alder Buckthorn**]: Main entrance, E [1]; NW corner, lakeside [few].
ROSACEAE [ROSE FAMILY], p. 122
   *Crataegus submollis* [**Emerson's Thorn**]: Chapel, N end [3*].
   *Spiraea japonica* [**Japanese Spiraea**]: NW corner [2].
   *Spiraea japonica* var. *fortunei* [**Robert Fortune Spiraea**]: E end [2*].
   *Spiraea* × *vanhouttei* [**Vanhoutte Spiraea**]: E end [2].
ULMACEAE [ELM FAMILY], p. 92
   *Ulmus americana* [**American Elm**]: Front [2*]; Main entrance, SE 20yd [1]; S 20yd, W of front door [1]; S 8yd, E of front door [1]; S 8yd, W of front door [1].

## NIEUWLAND SCIENCE HALL

BERBERIDACEAE [BARBERRY FAMILY], p. 86
*Berberis thunbergii* 'Atropurpurea' [**Japanese Bronze-leaf Barberry**]: S entrance (Riley Hall door), flanking [hedge*].
GROSSULARIACEAE [CURRANT FAMILY], p. 121
*Ribes alpinum* [**Alpine Currant; Mountain Currant**]: N wing, N side [hedge].
PINACEAE [PINE FAMILY], p. 59
*Pinus strobus* 'Fastigiata' [**Pyramidal White Pine**]: LaFortune, between [few*].
ROSACEAE [ROSE FAMILY], p. 122
*Crataegus crus-galli* [**Cockspur Hawthorn; Cockspur-thorn**]: NW door, NW [2].
*Crataegus phaenopyrum* [**Washington Hawthorn**]: NE corner [3].
*Malus spp.* [**Ornamental Crabapple hybrids**]: N wing, N side [6].

## NORTH DINING HALL

ACERACEAE [MAPLE FAMILY], p. 161
*Acer platanoides* [**Norway Maple**]: NW entrance [2].
*Acer rubrum* [**Red Maple**]: NW corner [2]; SW corner [4].
CAPRIFOLIACEAE [HONEYSUCKLE FAMILY], p. 180
*Viburnum carlesii* [**Fragrant Viburnum**]: N end [7]; S end, center [6].
*Viburnum opulus* [**Cranberrybush; Guelder-rose**]: N end [9].
CELASTRACEAE [STAFF-TREE FAMILY], p. 151
*Euonymus alata* [**Winged Burningbush; Winged Spindletree**]: W side [few].
FAGACEAE [BEECH FAMILY], p. 98
*Quercus palustris* [**Pin Oak**]: NE corner [1*].
HYDRANGEACEAE [HYDRANGEA FAMILY], p. 117
*Hydrangea quercifolia* [**Oak-leaf Hydrangea**]: N end [6].
OLEACEAE [OLIVE FAMILY], p. 174
*Forsythia* × *intermedia* [**Border Forsythia**]: S door, W [many].
*Fraxinus pennsylvanica* 'Marshall's Seedless' [**Green Ash**]: N end, E [2]; S end, E [3].
ROSACEAE [ROSE FAMILY], p. 122
*Crataegus crus-galli* [**Cockspur Hawthorn; Cockspur-thorn**]: SE corner [1*].
*Crataegus* × *disperma* [**Two-seeded Hawthorn**]: NE corner [2*].
*Malus spp.* [**Ornamental Crabapple hybrids**]: N end [2*]; W side [3].
*Pyrus calleryana* [**Callery Pear**]: N end [2]; S end [2]; W side, N [2]; W side, S [2].
SALICACEAE [WILLOW FAMILY], p. 110
*Salix* × *blanda* [**Niobe Willow; Wisconsin Willow**]: E side [1*].
VITACEAE [GRAPE FAMILY], p. 157
*Parthenocissus tricuspidata* [**Boston Ivy**]: E side [1*].

## O'SHAUGHNESSY HALL

ACERACEAE [MAPLE FAMILY], p. 161
*Acer platanoides* [**Norway Maple**]: Vita Dulcedo Spes entrance, S [1].
*Acer saccharum* [**Sugar Maple; Hard Maple**]: Vita Dulcedo Spes entrance, S [1].
CAPRIFOLIACEAE [HONEYSUCKLE FAMILY], p. 180
*Lonicera tatarica* [**Tatarian Honeysuckle**]: E side [1].

CELASTRACEAE [STAFF-TREE FAMILY], p. 151
> *Euonymus alata* [**Winged Burningbush; Winged Spindletree**]: E side [many].

CUPRESSACEAE [CYPRESS FAMILY], p. 72
> *Juniperus chinensis* [**Chinese Juniper**]: NW corner, S 10yd [1*]; NW corner, S 10yd [1].
> *Juniperus chinensis* 'Columnaris' [**Chinese Columnar Juniper**]: W entrance [1*].
> *Juniperus virginiana* 'Burkii' [**Steel-blue Redcedar**]: W, main entrance, N [2*]; W, main entrance, S 20yd [1*]; W, main entrance, S 6yd [1].
> *Juniperus virginiana* 'Schottii' [**Schott's Redcedar**]: NW corner [1*]; Vita Dulcedo Spes entrance, S 5yd [1*].
> *Juniperus virginiana* 'Venusta' [**Glossy Redcedar**]: Vita Dulcedo Spes entrance, S [3*].

FAGACEAE [BEECH FAMILY], p. 98
> *Quercus ellipsoidalis* [**Northern Pin Oak**]: N [1*].
> *Quercus rubra* [**Red Oak; Northern Red Oak**]: NW corner [3].

HAMAMELIDACEAE [WITCH-HAZEL FAMILY], p. 90
> *Liquidambar styraciflua* [**Sweetgum**]: Decio, between [1*].

OLEACEAE [OLIVE FAMILY], p. 174
> *Ligustrum vulgare* [**Common Privet; European Privet**]: E side [15*].

PINACEAE [PINE FAMILY], p. 59
> *Picea pungens* [**Colorado Blue Spruce**]: E side [2].
> *Pinus nigra* [**Austrian Pine**]: E side [1].
> *Pinus resinosa* [**Red Pine; Norway Pine**]: N entrance, SE [1].

ROSACEAE [ROSE FAMILY], p. 122
> *Crataegus crus-galli* [**Cockspur Hawthorn; Cockspur-thorn**]: E side [1].
> *Malus sargentii* [**Sargent Crabapple**]: W side [1].
> *Malus spp.* [**Ornamental Crabapple hybrids**]: E side [1].
> *Pyrus calleryana* [**Callery Pear**]: W side, plaza [7].
> *Spiraea × bumalda* [**Anthony Waterer Spiraea**]: E side, N end [many].
> *Spiraea nipponica* 'Snowmound' [**Snowmound Nippon Spiraea**]: E side [many].
> *Spiraea × vanhouttei* [**Vanhoutte Spiraea**]: E side [few].

TAXACEAE [YEW FAMILY], p. 55
> *Taxus × media* [**Anglojapanese Yew**]: W side [hedge]; W side, plaza [hedge].

VITACEAE [GRAPE FAMILY], p. 157
> *Parthenocissus tricuspidata* [**Boston Ivy**]: W, main entrance, N side [1].

## OLD COLLEGE

APOCYNACEAE [DOGBANE FAMILY], p. 171
> *Vinca minor* [**Common Periwinkle; Running Myrtle**]: Main entrance [bed*].

CAPRIFOLIACEAE [HONEYSUCKLE FAMILY], p. 180
> *Lonicera tatarica* [**Tatarian Honeysuckle**]: N, lakeside [3*].

CUPRESSACEAE [CYPRESS FAMILY], p. 72
> *Thuja occidentalis* [**American Arborvitae; Northern White Cedar**]: NW 35yd, lakeside [1].

PINACEAE [PINE FAMILY], p. 59
> *Pinus ponderosa* var. *scopulorum* [**Rocky Mountain Ponderosa Pine**]: W [1*].
> *Pinus resinosa* [**Red Pine; Norway Pine**]: N, lakeside [1*].
> *Pinus sylvestris* [**Scotch Pine**]: NE corner, NE 35yd, lakeside [1].

RHAMNACEAE [BUCKTHORN FAMILY], p. 157
> *Rhamnus frangula* [**Glossy Buckthorn; Alder Buckthorn**]: N, lakeside [few*].

ROSACEAE [ROSE FAMILY], p. 122
> *Spiraea × vanhouttei* [**Vanhoutte Spiraea**]: SE corner [7*].

SALICACEAE  [WILLOW FAMILY], p. 110
    *Salix fragilis* [**Brittle Willow; Crack Willow**]: N, lakeside [2*].


## OUTDOOR WAY OF THE CROSS

BIGNONIACEAE  [BIGNONIA FAMILY], p. 179
    *Catalpa bignonioides* [**Southern Catalpa; Common Catalpa**]: Station 7 [1*].
CUPRESSACEAE  [CYPRESS FAMILY], p. 72
    *Juniperus sabina* [**Savin Juniper**]: Station 1, E 10yd [1*].
HYDRANGEACEAE  [HYDRANGEA FAMILY], p. 117
    *Hydrangea arborescens* 'Grandiflora' [**Snowball Hydrangea**]: Station 9, N [1].
OLEACEAE  [OLIVE FAMILY], p. 174
    *Forsythia* × *intermedia* [**Border Forsythia**]: Station 2 [10*]; Station 8 [1*].
    *Forsythia suspensa* [**Weeping Forsythia**]: Station 10, S, along walk [1*].
    *Syringa vulgaris* [**Common Lilac**]: Station 2, E, lakeside [1*].
RHAMNACEAE  [BUCKTHORN FAMILY], p. 157
    *Rhamnus frangula* [**Glossy Buckthorn; Alder Buckthorn**]: Station 5 [many*].
ROSACEAE  [ROSE FAMILY], p. 122
    *Prunus serotina* [**Blackcherry; Wild Black Cherry**]: Woods [1*].
SALICACEAE  [WILLOW FAMILY], p. 110
    *Populus deltoides* [**Cottonwood**]: Station 1, E 15yd [1*]; Station 1, NE 30yd [1*].
TAXACEAE  [YEW FAMILY], p. 55
    *Taxus cuspidata* [**Japanese Yew**]: Station 1, N 10ft [4*].


## PANGBORN HALL

ACERACEAE  [MAPLE FAMILY], p. 161
    *Acer rubrum* [**Red Maple**]: S [3].
    *Acer saccharum* [**Sugar Maple; Hard Maple**]: SW corner, SW [1].
AQUIFOLIACEAE  [HOLLY FAMILY], p. 154
    *Ilex opaca* [**American Holly**]: N, main entrance, W [1].
BERBERIDACEAE  [BARBERRY FAMILY], p. 86
    *Mahonia aquifolium* [**Oregon Grape**]: N, main entrance, W [3*].
ERICACEAE  [HEATH FAMILY], p. 113
    *Pieris japonica* [**Lily-of-the-valley Bush**]: N, main entrance, W [bed].
MAGNOLIACEAE  [MAGNOLIA FAMILY], p. 82
    *Magnolia stellata* [**Star Magnolia**]: NE corner [1*].
NYSSACEAE  [TUPELO FAMILY], p. 148
    *Nyssa sylvatica* [**Black Tupelo; Blackgum; Sourgum**]: S side, S 5yd [1].
OLEACEAE  [OLIVE FAMILY], p. 174
    *Syringa reticulata* [**Japanese Tree Lilac**]: SE corner, golf course fence, S [1].
PINACEAE  [PINE FAMILY], p. 59
    *Pinus nigra* [**Austrian Pine**]: SW corner, SW [1]; W side [9].
    *Pinus resinosa* [**Red Pine; Norway Pine**]: SW corner, S [1].
ROSACEAE  [ROSE FAMILY], p. 122
    *Crataegus crus-galli* [**Cockspur Hawthorn; Cockspur-thorn**]: S wing, E door [2].
    *Pyracantha coccinea* 'Lalandei' [**Laland Firethorn**]: N side, E [1].
TAXACEAE  [YEW FAMILY], p. 55
    *Taxus cuspidata* 'Densa' [**Japanese Cushion Yew**]: N, main entrance, flanking [14*].

## PARIS HOUSE

ELAEAGNACEAE [OLEASTER FAMILY], p. 147
*Elaeagnus umbellata* [**Japanese Silverberry; Autumn Oleaster**]: E hedge, S end [1*].
OLEACEAE [OLIVE FAMILY], p. 174
*Fraxinus americana* [**White Ash**]: S, front yard [1].
SOLANACEAE [NIGHTSHADE FAMILY], p. 172
*Lycium halimifolium* [**Matrimony-vine**]: E hedge, S end [1*].


## PASQUERILLA CENTER

ACERACEAE [MAPLE FAMILY], p. 161
*Acer platanoides* [**Norway Maple**]: NE corner [1]; NW corner [3]; SW corner [1].
AQUIFOLIACEAE [HOLLY FAMILY], p. 154
*Ilex glabra* [**Inkberry**]: N side door, E, along wall [22]; N side, W of door, along wall [16].
CAPRIFOLIACEAE [HONEYSUCKLE FAMILY], p. 180
*Viburnum trilobum* 'Alfredo' [**American Cranberrybush Viburnum**]: NW corner, S and E ends [hedge]; SE corner, N and W ends [hedge]; SW corner, N and E ends [hedge].
CELASTRACEAE [STAFF-TREE FAMILY], p. 151
*Euonymus alata* [**Winged Burningbush; Winged Spindletree**]: E [hedge]; N [hedge].
CORNACEAE [DOGWOOD FAMILY], p. 149
*Cornus florida* [**Flowering Dogwood**]: NW corner [1]; SE corner [1]; SW corner [3].
*Cornus sericea* [**Red-osier Dogwood**]: NW corner [hedge]; SE corner [hedge]; SW corner [hedge].
CUPRESSACEAE [CYPRESS FAMILY], p. 72
*Juniperus horizontalis* [**Creeping Juniper**]: S side, flanking door [beds].
FAGACEAE [BEECH FAMILY], p. 98
*Quercus palustris* [**Pin Oak**]: S side [2].
*Quercus rubra* [**Red Oak; Northern Red Oak**]: S side [1].
GROSSULARIACEAE [CURRANT FAMILY], p. 121
*Ribes alpinum* [**Alpine Currant; Mountain Currant**]: N, flanking walk [hedge]; S side, along walk [hedge].
MAGNOLIACEAE [MAGNOLIA FAMILY], p. 82
*Magnolia stellata* [**Star Magnolia**]: N side, bed E of door [2]; S side, bed W of door [2].
ROSACEAE [ROSE FAMILY], p. 122
*Amelanchier arborea* [**Downy Serviceberry; Juneberry**]: N side, bed E of door [1]; NW corner [2]; S side, bed W of door [1].
*Malus spp.* [**Ornamental Crabapple hybrids**]: NE corner, E side [2]; NW corner, W side [1]; SE corner [9]; SW corner [3].
*Malus spp.* 'Red Jade' [**Red Jade Crabapple**]: S side [1 **Commem.**].
*Pyrus calleryana* [**Callery Pear**]: E side, S end [2]; N side, at entrance [2].
SAURURACEAE [LIZARD'S-TAIL FAMILY], p. 84
*Houttuynia cordata* 'Chamaeleon' [**Houttuynia**]: N side door, E [bed]; S side, W of door [bed].

## PASQUERILLA HALL EAST

**ACERACEAE [MAPLE FAMILY], p. 161**
*Acer palmatum* [**Japanese Maple**]: W wing, W end, NW plaza [1].
*Acer palmatum* f. *dissectum* 'Red Select' [**Japanese Maple**]: W wing, W end, NW plaza [2].

**BERBERIDACEAE [BARBERRY FAMILY], p. 86**
*Berberis* × *mentorensis* [**Mentor Barberry**]: W wing, SW corner [8].

**CAPRIFOLIACEAE [HONEYSUCKLE FAMILY], p. 180**
*Viburnum prunifolium* [**Blackhaw; Sweethaw**]: N wing, W door, flanking [4]; N wing, W side [1]; W wing, W end [2].
*Viburnum rhytidophyllum* [**Rugose Viburnum**]: W wing, S side [4]; W wing, W end [3].

**CELASTRACEAE [STAFF-TREE FAMILY], p. 151**
*Euonymus alata* [**Winged Burningbush; Winged Spindletree**]: W wing, S side [13].

**CORNACEAE [DOGWOOD FAMILY], p. 149**
*Cornus alba* 'Argenteo-marginata' [**Tartarian Dogwood**]: N wing, W side, N end [12].
*Cornus mas* [**Cornelian Cherry**]: N wing, W side [1].

**CUPRESSACEAE [CYPRESS FAMILY], p. 72**
*Chamaecyparis obtusa* 'Nana Gracilis' [**Hinoki Falsecypress**]: N wing, E side [2]; N wing, W door [2]; W wing, N side [2].
*Chamaecyparis obtusa* 'Pygmaea Aurescens' [**Hinoki Falsecypress**]: N wing, E side [1].
*Chamaecyparis pisifera* 'Boulevard' [**Sawara Falsecypress**]: N wing, E side [5].
*Chamaecyparis pisifera* 'Golden Mop' [**Sawara Falsecypress**]: W wing, W end, NW plaza [12].
*Juniperus horizontalis* [**Creeping Juniper**]: W wing, W end, NW plaza [beds].

**FAGACEAE [BEECH FAMILY], p. 98**
*Quercus palustris* [**Pin Oak**]: N wing, NW corner [1].

**GINKGOACEAE [GINKGO FAMILY], p. 54**
*Ginkgo biloba* [**Ginkgo; Maidenhair Tree**]: W door [3].

**HAMAMELIDACEAE [WITCH-HAZEL FAMILY], p. 90**
*Liquidambar styraciflua* [**Sweetgum**]: N wing, E side [1]; N wing, W side [2].

**MALVACEAE [MALLOW FAMILY], p. 109**
*Hibiscus syriacus* [**Shrub-althea; Rose-of-Sharon**]: N wing, SE corner [3].

**OLEACEAE [OLIVE FAMILY], p. 174**
*Forsythia* × *intermedia* [**Border Forsythia**]: N wing, E side [8]; W door [bed]; W wing, S side [5].

**PINACEAE [PINE FAMILY], p. 59**
*Picea pungens* 'Montgomery' [**Colorado Blue Spruce**]: W wing, W end, NW plaza [1].
*Pinus strobus* [**Eastern White Pine**]: N wing, E side [9].
*Pinus strobus* 'Blue Shag' [**Eastern White Pine**]: W wing, W end, NW plaza [2].
*Tsuga canadensis* 'Jeddeloh' [**Eastern Hemlock**]: N wing, W side [9]; W wing, N side [10].

**ROSACEAE [ROSE FAMILY], p. 122**
*Chaenomeles speciosa* [**Japanese Quince**]: W wing, W end [3].
*Cotoneaster apiculatus* [**Cranberry Cotoneaster**]: N wing, E side [bed]; W wing, W end, NW plaza [beds].
*Cotoneaster divaricatus* [**Spreading Cotoneaster**]: N wing, N end [1]; N wing, NE corner [bed].
*Cotoneaster horizontalis* [**Rock Cotoneaster**]: N wing, E side [bed]; N wing, W door [bed].
*Malus* spp. [**Ornamental Crabapple hybrids**]: N wing, E entrance, parking circle [1 **Commem.**]; N wing, E side [3]; NE corner [1]; NE side [1]; W wing, S side [1].
*Prunus cerasifera* 'Newport' [**Purpleleaf Cherry-plum**]: N wing, E side [1].
*Pyrus calleryana* [**Callery Pear**]: W wing, W end, NW plaza [8].
*Spiraea* × *bumalda* [**Anthony Waterer Spiraea**]: N wing, W side [bed].

*Spiraea* × *vanhouttei* [**Vanhoutte Spiraea**]: N wing, E parking area [bed].
SALICACEAE [**WILLOW FAMILY**], p. 110
   *Populus deltoides* [**Cottonwood**]: Pasquerilla Hall West, midway [2*]; W wing, N of W end [1].
SIMAROUBACEAE [QUASSIA FAMILY], p. 168
   *Ailanthus altissima* [**Tree-of-heaven**]: W wing, NW corner [5].
TAXACEAE [YEW FAMILY], p. 55
   *Taxus cuspidata* 'Capitata' [**Japanese Yew**]: N wing, E side [2].
   *Taxus* × *media* 'Hicksii' [**Hicks' Yew**]: N wing, NE corner [bed]; N wing, W side [bed].
TILIACEAE [LINDEN FAMILY], p. 107
   *Tilia cordata* [**Small-leaved European Linden**]: N wing, E side [1].


## PASQUERILLA HALL WEST

BERBERIDACEAE [BARBERRY FAMILY], p. 86
   *Berberis thunbergii* [**Japanese Barberry**]: N wing, N end [5].
CAESALPINIACEAE [CAESALPINIA FAMILY], p. 142
   *Gleditsia triacanthos* subsp. *inermis* [**Thornless Honeylocust**]: N wing, W side, planter [1].
CAPRIFOLIACEAE [HONEYSUCKLE FAMILY], p. 180
   *Lonicera fragrantissima* [**Winter Honeysuckle**]: NW corner, hedge [3].
   *Lonicera tatarica* [**Tatarian Honeysuckle**]: E wing, S side [5]; N wing, NW corner [3].
   *Viburnum* × *burkwoodii* [**Burkwood Viburnum**]: E wing, N side [2]; N wing, E side [3].
   *Viburnum prunifolium* [**Blackhaw; Sweethaw**]: E door, flanking [4]; N wing, E side [2].
   *Viburnum rhytidophyllum* [**Rugose Viburnum**]: E wing, E end [2]; E wing, S side [3].
CELASTRACEAE [STAFF-TREE FAMILY], p. 151
   *Euonymus alata* [**Winged Burningbush; Winged Spindletree**]: E wing, S side [10].
CORNACEAE [DOGWOOD FAMILY], p. 149
   *Cornus alba* 'Argenteo-marginata' [**Tartarian Dogwood**]: N wing, W side [5].
CUPRESSACEAE [CYPRESS FAMILY], p. 72
   *Chamaecyparis obtusa* [**Hinoki Falsecypress**]: E wing, N side [4]; N wing, E side [1]; W door [2].
   *Chamaecyparis obtusa* 'Pygmaea Aurescens' [**Hinoki Falsecypress**]: W door [1].
   *Chamaecyparis pisifera* 'Boulevard' [**Sawara Falsecypress**]: W door [5].
   *Juniperus sabina* 'Tamariscifolia' [**Tamarix Savin**]: N wing, W side, planter [6].
GINKGOACEAE [GINKGO FAMILY], p. 54
   *Ginkgo biloba* [**Ginkgo; Maidenhair Tree**]: E door [2].
HYDRANGEACEAE [HYDRANGEA FAMILY], p. 117
   *Hydrangea arborescens* 'Grandiflora' [**Snowball Hydrangea**]: E wing, E end [3].
MALVACEAE [MALLOW FAMILY], p. 109
   *Hibiscus syriacus* [**Shrub-althea; Rose-of-Sharon**]: N wing, W side [3].
OLEACEAE [OLIVE FAMILY], p. 174
   *Forsythia* × *intermedia* [**Border Forsythia**]: E door [bed]; E wing, S side [3]; N wing, W side [11].
PINACEAE [PINE FAMILY], p. 59
   *Picea pungens* [**Colorado Blue Spruce**]: E wing, E end [3]; E wing, S side [7]; E wing, S walk, end [5].
   *Picea pungens* 'Montgomery' [**Colorado Blue Spruce**]: W door [1].
   *Pinus strobus* [**Eastern White Pine**]: N wing, N end [3].
   *Tsuga canadensis* 'Jeddeloh' [**Eastern Hemlock**]: E wing, N side, W of door [8].
ROSACEAE [ROSE FAMILY], p. 122
   *Chaenomeles speciosa* [**Japanese Quince**]: E wing, S side [3].

*Cotoneaster dammeri* 'Walter's Red' [**Bearberry Cotoneaster**]: N wing, E side [bed]; SW corner [2].

*Cotoneaster divaricatus* [**Spreading Cotoneaster**]: N wing, NE corner [bed].

*Cotoneaster horizontalis* [**Rock Cotoneaster**]: W door [beds].

*Malus sargentii* [**Sargent Crabapple**]: N wing, W parking circle [1].

*Malus spp.* [**Ornamental Crabapple hybrids**]: N wing, W parking circle [1]; N wing, W side [3].

*Pyracantha coccinea* [**Firethorn**]: E wing, S side [4].

*Spiraea* × *bumalda* [**Anthony Waterer Spiraea**]: E door [beds]; E wing, E end [2].

TAXACEAE [YEW FAMILY], p. 55

*Taxus* × *media* 'Hicksii' [**Hicks' Yew**]: N wing, E side [beds]; W door [2].

TILIACEAE [LINDEN FAMILY], p. 107

*Tilia cordata* [**Small-leaved European Linden**]: N wing, N end [2].


## POST OFFICE

ACERACEAE [MAPLE FAMILY], p. 161

*Acer saccharinum* [**Silver Maple; Soft Maple**]: Morris Inn, midway [4].

CELASTRACEAE [STAFF-TREE FAMILY], p. 151

*Euonymus fortunei* [**Chinese Winter-creeper**]: N side [hedge].

CORNACEAE [DOGWOOD FAMILY], p. 149

*Cornus mas* [**Cornelian Cherry**]: N side [2].

PINACEAE [PINE FAMILY], p. 59

*Pinus strobus* [**Eastern White Pine**]: SE corner [3].

*Pinus sylvestris* [**Scotch Pine**]: NW corner, N 10yd [3].


## POWER PLANT

ANACARDIACEAE [CASHEW FAMILY], p. 166

*Rhus hirta* [**Staghorn Sumac**]: NW, lakeside [many*].

ROSACEAE [ROSE FAMILY], p. 122

*Prunus munsoniana* [**Wild Gooseplum; Munson Plum**]: NW 75yd, slope [1*].

SMILACACEAE [CATBRIER FAMILY], p. 188

*Smilax hispida* [**Bristly Greenbrier**]: NW, slope [1*].


## PRESBYTERY

BETULACEAE [BIRCH FAMILY], p. 103

*Betula papyrifera* [**Paper Birch; Canoe Birch**]: NW corner [1].

BIGNONIACEAE [BIGNONIA FAMILY], p. 179

*Catalpa bignonioides* [**Southern Catalpa; Common Catalpa**]: Freshman Year W parking lot, midway [3*].

CORNACEAE [DOGWOOD FAMILY], p. 149

*Cornus florida* [**Flowering Dogwood**]: NE corner [1*].

CUPRESSACEAE [CYPRESS FAMILY], p. 72

*Thuja occidentalis* [**American Arborvitae; Northern White Cedar**]: W 15yd [1*].

GINKGOACEAE [GINKGO FAMILY], p. 54

*Ginkgo biloba* 'Laciniata' [**Split-leaf Ginkgo**]: NW corner, W 10yd [2].

HYDRANGEACEAE [HYDRANGEA FAMILY], p. 117
> *Hydrangea macrophylla* [**Large-leaf Hydrangea**]: Front [10*].
> *Hydrangea paniculata* 'Grandiflora' [**Peegee Hydrangea**]: E, main entrance, flanking [2].

OLEACEAE [OLIVE FAMILY], p. 174
> *Fraxinus americana* 'Ascidiata' [**Pitcher Ash**]: NE corner [1*].

PINACEAE [PINE FAMILY], p. 59
> *Abies concolor* [**White Fir; Colorado Fir**]: Porch, S 5yd [1*].
> *Larix laricina* [**Tamarack; Eastern Larch**]: W side, in grove above Grotto [6].
> *Picea abies* [**Norway Spruce**]: S 15yd [1*].
> *Tsuga canadensis* [**Eastern Hemlock**]: NW corner [1*]; SW corner [1*].

ROSACEAE [ROSE FAMILY], p. 122
> *Malus spp.* [**Ornamental Crabapple hybrids**]: E, main entrance, flanking [2].

TAXACEAE [YEW FAMILY], p. 55
> *Taxus cuspidata* [**Japanese Yew**]: SW corner [1].

VITACEAE [GRAPE FAMILY], p. 157
> *Parthenocissus tricuspidata* [**Boston Ivy**]: SE corner [1*].

## PROVINCE ARCHIVES CENTER

ACERACEAE [MAPLE FAMILY], p. 161
> *Acer ginnala* [**Amur Maple**]: SW corner, S [1].
> *Acer palmatum* [**Japanese Maple**]: S side, center [1].

CAESALPINIACEAE [CAESALPINIA FAMILY], p. 142
> *Gleditsia triacanthos* subsp. *inermis* [**Thornless Honeylocust**]: N 7yd [1*].

CELASTRACEAE [STAFF-TREE FAMILY], p. 151
> *Euonymus alata* [**Winged Burningbush; Winged Spindletree**]: SE corner [1].

CUPRESSACEAE [CYPRESS FAMILY], p. 72
> *Juniperus squamata* 'Meyeri' [**Meyer's Blue Juniper**]: NW, roadside [hedge*].

FAGACEAE [BEECH FAMILY], p. 98
> *Castanea mollissima* [**Chinese Chestnut**]: SW corner, W 30yd [1].
> *Fagus sylvatica* 'Atropunicea' [**Copper Beech; Purple Beech**]: W 5yd [1*].

GINKGOACEAE [GINKGO FAMILY], p. 54
> *Ginkgo biloba* 'Laciniata' [**Split-leaf Ginkgo**]: SE corner [1].

JUGLANDACEAE [WALNUT FAMILY], p. 96
> *Carya ovalis* [**Sweet Pignut**]: N, Douglas Rd, N side [1*].

## RADIATION RESEARCH BUILDING

ACERACEAE [MAPLE FAMILY], p. 161
> *Acer saccharinum* 'Laciniatum' [**Cutleaf Silver Maple**]: S [1].

CAESALPINIACEAE [CAESALPINIA FAMILY], p. 142
> *Gymnocladus dioica* [**Kentucky Coffeetree**]: SE corner, E 35yd [1*].

FAGACEAE [BEECH FAMILY], p. 98
> *Quercus palustris* [**Pin Oak**]: NE and NW corners [5].

MAGNOLIACEAE [MAGNOLIA FAMILY], p. 82
> *Liriodendron tulipifera* [**Tulip Tree; Yellow-poplar**]: S side [5*].

NYSSACEAE [TUPELO FAMILY], p. 148
> *Nyssa sylvatica* [**Black Tupelo; Blackgum; Sourgum**]: E end [1*].

PINACEAE [PINE FAMILY], p. 59
>Pinus sylvestris [**Scotch Pine**]: SW corner [3].
ROSACEAE [ROSE FAMILY], p. 122
>*Cotoneaster apiculatus* [**Cranberry Cotoneaster**]: W side [bed].
>*Crataegus coccinoides* [**Kansas Hawthorn**]: W end [1*].
>*Malus spp.* [**Ornamental Crabapple hybrids**]: SE corner, S 30yd [2].

## RILEY HALL OF ART AND DESIGN

ACERACEAE [MAPLE FAMILY], p. 161
>*Acer rubrum* [**Red Maple**]: NE corner [1].
CAESALPINIACEAE [CAESALPINIA FAMILY], p. 142
>*Cercis canadensis* [**Eastern Redbud; Judas-tree**]: Hurley, between [4].
CAPRIFOLIACEAE [HONEYSUCKLE FAMILY], p. 180
>*Viburnum rhytidophyllum* [**Rugose Viburnum**]: SE corner [3].
GINKGOACEAE [GINKGO FAMILY], p. 54
>*Ginkgo biloba* [**Ginkgo; Maidenhair Tree**]: S side [1].
PINACEAE [PINE FAMILY], p. 59
>*Pinus strobus* 'Fastigiata' [**Pyramidal White Pine**]: W side [1*].
ROSACEAE [ROSE FAMILY], p. 122
>*Crataegus phaenopyrum* [**Washington Hawthorn**]: SW corner [2*].
TAXACEAE [YEW FAMILY], p. 55
>*Taxus × media* [**Anglojapanese Yew**]: E side [hedge].

## ROCKNE MEMORIAL

ACERACEAE [MAPLE FAMILY], p. 161
>*Acer negundo* [**Boxelder**]: S, practice green, E side [8].
BETULACEAE [BIRCH FAMILY], p. 103
>*Corylus colurna* [**Turkish Hazelnut**]: S, practice green, SE corner [1*].
>*Ostrya virginiana* [**Eastern Hophornbeam; Ironwood**]: W, golf maintenance center, NW
>corner [1*].
CAESALPINIACEAE [CAESALPINIA FAMILY], p. 142
>*Cercis canadensis* [**Eastern Redbud; Judas-tree**]: NW corner [3*].
CAPRIFOLIACEAE [HONEYSUCKLE FAMILY], p. 180
>*Viburnum lentago* [**Nannyberry; Sweet Viburnum**]: SE corner, S [1*].
>*Viburnum opulus* [**Cranberrybush; Guelder-rose**]: NW corner, N 400yd, lakeside [few].
FAGACEAE [BEECH FAMILY], p. 98
>*Quercus macrocarpa* [**Bur Oak; Mossy-cup Oak**]: W end [2*].
HYDRANGEACEAE [HYDRANGEA FAMILY], p. 117
>*Philadelphus × virginalis* [**Virginal Mock Orange**]: SE corner, S [hedge*].
JUGLANDACEAE [WALNUT FAMILY], p. 96
>*Juglans nigra* [**Black Walnut**]: N side, grove [85*].
MORACEAE [MULBERRY FAMILY], p. 94
>*Maclura pomifera* [**Osage Orange**]: W, Dorr Rd, along S side [23*].
OLEACEAE [OLIVE FAMILY], p. 174
>*Ligustrum obtusifolium* [**Border Privet**]: E, front entrance, S [1].
PINACEAE [PINE FAMILY], p. 59
>*Pinus sylvestris* [**Scotch Pine**]: W, along Dorr Rd, S side [few*].

ROSACEAE [ROSE FAMILY], p. 122
> *Malus spp.* [**Ornamental Crabapple hybrids**]: E side, flanking door [2].
> *Malus spp.* 'Snowdrift' [**Snowdrift Crabapple**]: E side, flanking steps [2 **Commem.**].

ULMACEAE [ELM FAMILY], p. 92
> *Ulmus americana* [**American Elm**]: O'Shaughnessy, along walks between [40*].

VITACEAE [GRAPE FAMILY], p. 157
> *Vitis riparia* [**River-bank Grape; Frost Grape**]: S, golf course fence [few*].

## SACRED HEART BASILICA

ACERACEAE [MAPLE FAMILY], p. 161
> *Acer palmatum* [**Japanese Maple**]: E side [2*].
> *Acer platanoides* 'Schwedleri' [**Schwedler's Maple**]: E 25yd [1*].
> *Acer saccharum* [**Sugar Maple; Hard Maple**]: E side door, NE 10yd [1*].

ARALIACEAE [GINSENG FAMILY], p. 170
> *Hedera helix* [**English Ivy**]: Sacristy, N entrance, E side [1*].

BETULACEAE [BIRCH FAMILY], p. 103
> *Corylus avellana* 'Contorta' [**European Hazel**]: W side [1].

CAESALPINIACEAE [CAESALPINIA FAMILY], p. 142
> *Cercis canadensis* [**Eastern Redbud; Judas-tree**]: SW corner [2*].

CAPRIFOLIACEAE [HONEYSUCKLE FAMILY], p. 180
> *Viburnum rhytidophyllum* [**Rugose Viburnum**]: E side door, N side [3*].
> *Weigela florida* [**Flowering Weigela**]: SE corner, E 35yd [14*].

CELASTRACEAE [STAFF-TREE FAMILY], p. 151
> *Euonymus alata* [**Winged Burningbush; Winged Spindletree**]: Crypt, E side [2*].

CUPRESSACEAE [CYPRESS FAMILY], p. 72
> *Juniperus communis* 'Effusa' [**Common Juniper**]: E side door, S side [6].
> *Juniperus virginiana* 'Tripartita' [**Fountain Redcedar**]: Sacristy, S side [3*].

FAGACEAE [BEECH FAMILY], p. 98
> *Fagus sylvatica* 'Atropunicea' [**Copper Beech; Purple Beech**]: E side door, S side [1*].

OLEACEAE [OLIVE FAMILY], p. 174
> *Syringa vulgaris* [**Common Lilac**]: SE corner, E 40yd [1*].

PINACEAE [PINE FAMILY], p. 59
> *Picea abies* 'Cupressina' [**Norway Spruce**]: Main entrance, flanking E door [2]; Main entrance, flanking W door [2]; N, flanking door [2].
> *Picea alcoquiana* 'Howell's Dwarf' [**Alcock Spruce**]: E side door, N side [6].
> *Picea omorika* 'Nana' [**Dwarf Serbian Spruce**]: Main entrance, flanking [2].
> *Picea pungens* [**Colorado Blue Spruce**]: E side [1].
> *Picea pungens* 'Glauca' [**Blue Spruce; Colorado Blue Spruce**]: SE [2*].
> *Picea pungens* 'Prostrate Green' [**Colorado Spruce**]: Main entrance, E door [5]; Main entrance, W door [5].
> *Pinus mugo* [**Mugo Pine; Swiss Mountain Pine**]: SE 20yd, lamppost 58 [6*].
> *Pseudolarix kaempferi* 'Nana' [**Dwarf Golden-larch**]: W side [1].
> *Tsuga canadensis* [**Eastern Hemlock**]: Sacristy, S side [5*].
> *Tsuga canadensis* 'Pendula' [**Eastern Hemlock**]: W side [1].

ROSACEAE [ROSE FAMILY], p. 122
> *Pyrus calleryana* [**Callery Pear**]: Main entrance, W lawn [1 **Commem.**].

TAXACEAE [YEW FAMILY], p. 55
> *Taxus cuspidata* [**Japanese Yew**]: Sacristy, S side [1].

TAXODIACEAE [TAXODIUM FAMILY], p. 71
> *Metasequoia glyptostroboides* [**Dawn Redwood**]: Main entrance, SE 30yd [1].

*Sciadopitys verticillata* [**Umbrella-pine**]: W side [1].
ULMACEAE [ELM FAMILY], p. 92
    *Ulmus glabra* 'Cornuta' [**Horned Elm**]: E front entrance, S 35yd [1*].
    *Ulmus* × *vegeta* 'Camperdownii' [**Camperdown Elm**]: SE 35yd, junction of walks [1*].


## SACRED HEART STATUE

ACERACEAE [MAPLE FAMILY], p. 161
    *Acer rubrum* [**Red Maple**]: E 10yd [1].
    *Acer saccharum* [**Sugar Maple; Hard Maple**]: W [2*].
    *Acer saccharum* subsp. *nigrum* [**Black Maple**]: NW 25yd [1*].
FAGACEAE [BEECH FAMILY], p. 98
    *Quercus palustris* [**Pin Oak**]: NE and NW [2]; S 15yd [1].
JUGLANDACEAE [WALNUT FAMILY], p. 96
    *Carya ovalis* var. *obcordata* [**Obcordate Pignut**]: SW 40yd [1*].
MAGNOLIACEAE [MAGNOLIA FAMILY], p. 82
    *Liriodendron tulipifera* [**Tulip Tree; Yellow-poplar**]: SE 35yd [1*].
    *Magnolia* × *soulangiana* [**Saucer Magnolia**]: N, E of walk [1]; N, W of walk [1 **Commem.**].
    *Magnolia* × *soulangiana* 'Rubra' [**Scarlet Magnolia**]: NW [1*].
PLATANACEAE [PLANETREE FAMILY], p. 89
    *Platanus occidentalis* [**Sycamore; Buttonwood; American Planetree**]: SW lawn [2].
SIMAROUBACEAE [QUASSIA FAMILY], p. 168
    *Ailanthus altissima* [**Tree-of-heaven**]: SE 50yd [1*].


## SESQUICENTENNIAL COMMONS

ACERACEAE [MAPLE FAMILY], p. 161
    *Acer rubrum* 'Red Sunset' [**Red Maple**]: E outer bed [2]; SE outer bed [1]; SW outer bed [1]; W outer bed [2].
BIGNONIACEAE [BIGNONIA FAMILY], p. 179
    *Campsis radicans* [**Trumpet-creeper; Trumpet-vine**]: Pergola, climbing arches [25].
    *Campsis* × *tagliabuana* 'Madame Galen' [**Madame Galen Trumpet-creeper**]: Pergola, climbing arches [25].
BUXACEAE [BOX FAMILY], p. 156
    *Buxus microphylla* 'Wintergreen' [**Korean Boxwood**]: E inner bed, W edge [24]; N inner beds, S edges [40]; S inner beds, N edges [40]; W inner bed, S edge [24].
CUPRESSACEAE [CYPRESS FAMILY], p. 72
    *Juniperus horizontalis* 'Blue Chip' [**Creeping Juniper**]: E inner bed [58]; N inner beds [40]; S inner beds [40]; W inner bed [58].
    *Juniperus sabina* 'Blue Danube' [**Savin Juniper**]: E outer bed [50]; SE outer bed [18]; SW outer bed [18]; W outer bed [50].
ERICACEAE [HEATH FAMILY], p. 113
    *Rhododendron* spp. 'Ramapo' [**Ramapo Rhododendron**]: S central outer bed, center [18].
PINACEAE [PINE FAMILY], p. 59
    *Picea abies* 'Nidiformis' [**Bird's Nest Spruce**]: S central outer bed, E and W ends [30].

## SIEGFRIED HALL

BERBERIDACEAE [BARBERRY FAMILY], p. 86
 *Berberis thunbergii* [**Japanese Barberry**]: W door [8].
CAPRIFOLIACEAE [HONEYSUCKLE FAMILY], p. 180
 *Lonicera tatarica* [**Tatarian Honeysuckle**]: E wing, S side [4].
 *Viburnum dentatum* [**Arrowwood Viburnum**]: E wing, N side [11]; S wing, E side [11]; S wing, W side [5].
 *Viburnum rhytidophyllum* [**Rugose Viburnum**]: E wing, SE corner [3]; W door [1].
CELASTRACEAE [STAFF-TREE FAMILY], p. 151
 *Euonymus alata* [**Winged Burningbush; Winged Spindletree**]: E wing, N side [2]; S wing, W side [3].
CUPRESSACEAE [CYPRESS FAMILY], p. 72
 *Juniperus chinensis* 'Sea Green' [**Chinese Juniper**]: SE door plaza, planter [bed].
 *Thuja occidentalis* [**American Arborvitae; Northern White Cedar**]: E door, flanking [5].
 *Thuja occidentalis* 'Globosa' [**Globe Arborvitae**]: N, flanking walk [36].
HIPPOCASTANACEAE [HORSECHESTNUT FAMILY], p. 160
 *Aesculus hippocastanum* [**Horsechestnut**]: Pasquerilla Hall West, between [1].
HYDRANGEACEAE [HYDRANGEA FAMILY], p. 117
 *Hydrangea arborescens* 'Grandiflora' [**Snowball Hydrangea**]: E wing, N side [7].
 *Hydrangea quercifolia* [**Oak-leaf Hydrangea**]: E wing, N side [3].
MALVACEAE [MALLOW FAMILY], p. 109
 *Hibiscus syriacus* [**Shrub-althea; Rose-of-Sharon**]: S wing, E side [2].
OLEACEAE [OLIVE FAMILY], p. 174
 *Forsythia* × *intermedia* [**Border Forsythia**]: E wing, N side [3]; E wing, S side [6]; S wing, S end [5].
 *Fraxinus pennsylvanica* [**Green Ash**]: W door, circle [1].
 *Ligustrum obtusifolium* var. *regelianum* [**Regel's Privet**]: N, flanking central bed [hedge].
PINACEAE [PINE FAMILY], p. 59
 *Picea pungens* [**Colorado Blue Spruce**]: E wing, E end [4]; E wing, N side, W end [5]; N, along walk [7]; S wing, S end [2]; SE lawn [2].
PLATANACEAE [PLANETREE FAMILY], p. 89
 *Platanus occidentalis* [**Sycamore; Buttonwood; American Planetree**]: E wing, N walk, central planter [1]; SE lawn [2].
ROSACEAE [ROSE FAMILY], p. 122
 *Chaenomeles speciosa* [**Japanese Quince**]: E wing, S side [2]; S wing, E side [3].
 *Cotoneaster apiculatus* [**Cranberry Cotoneaster**]: E door plaza [beds]; N, along walk [beds].
 *Crataegus phaenopyrum* [**Washington Hawthorn**]: SE lawn [1].
 *Malus* spp. [**Ornamental Crabapple hybrids**]: E wing, N side, along walk [4]; S wing, S end [1]; S wing, W side [2]; SE door plaza, planter [4]; SE lawn [13].
 *Prunus cerasifera* 'Newport' [**Purpleleaf Cherry-plum**]: N, flanking walk [2].
 *Pyracantha coccinea* [**Firethorn**]: S wing, E side [3].
 *Pyrus calleryana* [**Callery Pear**]: E door plaza [12]; N, flanking walk [14]; S wing, W side [1]; W door, circle [6].
 *Spiraea* × *bumalda* [**Anthony Waterer Spiraea**]: E door, flanking [10]; E wing, N side [2]; E wing, S side [1]; S wing, E side [10]; S wing, S end [5]; W door [4].
SAURURACEAE [LIZARD'S-TAIL FAMILY], p. 84
 *Houttuynia cordata* 'Chamaeleon' [**Houttuynia**]: N walk, central planter [bed].
TAXACEAE [YEW FAMILY], p. 55
 *Taxus cuspidata* 'Capitata' [**Japanese Yew**]: W door [2].
 *Taxus* × *media* 'Hicksii' [**Hicks' Yew**]: E wing, S side [3]; S wing, E side [4]; SE door, flanking [4]; W door [10].

SNITE MUSEUM OF ART

ACERACEAE [MAPLE FAMILY], p. 161
> *Acer platanoides* [**Norway Maple**]: Court [1]; S side [6].
> *Acer rubrum* [**Red Maple**]: Court [1].

ANACARDIACEAE [CASHEW FAMILY], p. 166
> *Rhus hirta* f. *dissecta* [**Cutleaf Staghorn Sumac**]: S entrance, E of walk [4].

APOCYNACEAE [DOGBANE FAMILY], p. 171
> *Vinca minor* [**Common Periwinkle; Running Myrtle**]: Court [beds].

AQUIFOLIACEAE [HOLLY FAMILY], p. 154
> *Ilex crenata* [**Japanese Holly**]: Court [5].

BUXACEAE [BOX FAMILY], p. 156
> *Pachysandra terminalis* [**Japanese Pachysandra; Japanese Spurge**]: Court [beds].

CAPRIFOLIACEAE [HONEYSUCKLE FAMILY], p. 180
> *Viburnum dentatum* [**Arrowwood Viburnum**]: SW corner [7].
> *Viburnum opulus* [**Cranberrybush; Guelder-rose**]: Court [8].
> *Viburnum opulus* 'Nanum' [**Dwarf Cranberrybush**]: S side, W of walk [hedge].

CELASTRACEAE [STAFF-TREE FAMILY], p. 151
> *Euonymus fortunei* [**Chinese Winter-creeper**]: Court [4].

CORNACEAE [DOGWOOD FAMILY], p. 149
> *Cornus florida* [**Flowering Dogwood**]: Court [3*]; Court, entrance, E 10yd [3].

CUPRESSACEAE [CYPRESS FAMILY], p. 72
> *Juniperus horizontalis* [**Creeping Juniper**]: Court [bed].

ERICACEAE [HEATH FAMILY], p. 113
> *Rhododendron* spp. [**Rhododendron; Azalea**]: Court [10].

FABACEAE [PEA FAMILY], p. 144
> *Wisteria floribunda* [**Japanese Wisteria**]: Court, W wall [1].

FAGACEAE [BEECH FAMILY], p. 98
> *Quercus palustris* [**Pin Oak**]: E [4*].

HYDRANGEACEAE [HYDRANGEA FAMILY], p. 117
> *Hydrangea quercifolia* [**Oak-leaf Hydrangea**]: Court [many].
> *Philadelphus lewisii* [**Lewis Mock Orange**]: Court [many].

PINACEAE [PINE FAMILY], p. 59
> *Picea abies* 'Cupressina' [**Norway Spruce**]: Court, planters [2].
> *Picea pungens* [**Colorado Blue Spruce**]: S side [4].

PLATANACEAE [PLANETREE FAMILY], p. 89
> *Platanus occidentalis* [**Sycamore; Buttonwood; American Planetree**]: S side [3].

RHAMNACEAE [BUCKTHORN FAMILY], p. 157
> *Rhamnus frangula* [**Glossy Buckthorn; Alder Buckthorn**]: Court [4].

ROSACEAE [ROSE FAMILY], p. 122
> *Amelanchier arborea* [**Downy Serviceberry; Juneberry**]: Court, SE corner [1]; Court, W side [4].
> *Cotoneaster dammeri* [**Bearberry Cotoneaster**]: Court [many].
> *Crataegus crus-galli* [**Cockspur Hawthorn; Cockspur-thorn**]: S side [3].
> *Malus sargentii* [**Sargent Crabapple**]: S entrance, S 15yd at street [3]; S side, at building, along walk [6].
> *Malus* spp. [**Ornamental Crabapple hybrids**]: Court [8]; W side, window, W [1*].
> *Spiraea nipponica* [**Nippon Spiraea**]: Court [4].

TAXACEAE [YEW FAMILY], p. 55
> *Taxus* × *media* [**Anglojapanese Yew**]: Court [many].
> *Taxus* × *media* 'Hicksii' [**Hicks' Yew**]: S, flanking walk [hedge].

TAXODIACEAE [TAXODIUM FAMILY], p. 71
  *Taxodium distichum* [**Baldcypress**]: SW corner [2].
VITACEAE [GRAPE FAMILY], p. 157
  *Parthenocissus tricuspidata* [**Boston Ivy**]: Court [many].

## SORIN HALL

ACERACEAE [MAPLE FAMILY], p. 161
  *Acer ginnala* [**Amur Maple**]: SE corner, SE 15yd [2*].
  *Acer saccharinum* [**Silver Maple; Soft Maple**]: W side, W center, 30yd [1].
AGAVACEAE [CENTURY-PLANT FAMILY], p. 187
  *Yucca filamentosa* [**Adam's-needle Yucca**]: E, bed at intersection [many].
ANACARDIACEAE [CASHEW FAMILY], p. 166
  *Cotinus coggygria* [**Smoketree; Smokebush**]: Architecture Building, midway [3*]; NE corner [1*].
ARALIACEAE [GINSENG FAMILY], p. 170
  *Kalopanax pictus* var. *magnificus* [**Maple-leaf Panax**]: N end, NNW 5yd [1*].
  *Kalopanax pictus* var. *maximowiczii* [**Prickly Panax**]: N end, NNE 5yd [1*].
BERBERIDACEAE [BARBERRY FAMILY], p. 86
  *Berberis thunbergii* [**Japanese Barberry**]: N end [hedge*].
BETULACEAE [BIRCH FAMILY], p. 103
  *Betula nigra* [**River Birch; Black Birch**]: SW 30yd [1*].
CAESALPINIACEAE [CAESALPINIA FAMILY], p. 142
  *Cercis canadensis* [**Eastern Redbud; Judas-tree**]: SE corner, SE 15yd [1*].
CELASTRACEAE [STAFF-TREE FAMILY], p. 151
  *Euonymus alata* [**Winged Burningbush; Winged Spindletree**]: S end [13*].
CUPRESSACEAE [CYPRESS FAMILY], p. 72
  *Thuja occidentalis* 'Robusta' [**Siberian Arborvitae**]: E, roadside [3*].
ERICACEAE [HEATH FAMILY], p. 113
  *Rhododendron spp.* [**Rhododendron; Azalea**]: E at crosswalk [bed].
FAGACEAE [BEECH FAMILY], p. 98
  *Quercus alba* [**White Oak**]: SE corner, SE 40yd [1*].
  *Quercus imbricaria* [**Shingle Oak**]: N wing, W end [1*].
  *Quercus robur* [**English Oak**]: S wing, E end [1*].
  *Quercus rubra* [**Red Oak; Northern Red Oak**]: SE 20yd [1*].
HAMAMELIDACEAE [WITCH-HAZEL FAMILY], p. 90
  *Liquidambar styraciflua* [**Sweetgum**]: SE corner, E 50yd [1*].
HIPPOCASTANACEAE [HORSECHESTNUT FAMILY], p. 160
  *Aesculus hippocastanum* [**Horsechestnut**]: SE corner, E 60yd [1*].
MAGNOLIACEAE [MAGNOLIA FAMILY], p. 82
  *Liriodendron tulipifera* [**Tulip Tree; Yellow-poplar**]: SE at walk [1].
  *Magnolia stellata* [**Star Magnolia**]: E side [2*].
OLEACEAE [OLIVE FAMILY], p. 174
  *Syringa vulgaris* [**Common Lilac**]: E, roadside [1*].
PINACEAE [PINE FAMILY], p. 59
  *Abies concolor* [**White Fir; Colorado Fir**]: SE 60yd [1*].
  *Picea abies* [**Norway Spruce**]: SE corner [2*]; SW corner [1*].
  *Pinus mugo* [**Mugo Pine; Swiss Mountain Pine**]: W central side, W [1].
  *Pseudotsuga menziesii* [**Douglas-fir**]: SE 45yd [4*].
ROSACEAE [ROSE FAMILY], p. 122
  *Malus spp.* [**Ornamental Crabapple hybrids**]: E side [1]; S end [1]; S end [1].

*Rhodotypos scandens* [**Japanese Jetbead**]: E, main entrance, E 20yd [1].
RUTACEAE [RUE FAMILY], p. 169
    *Phellodendron amurense* [**Cork-tree**]: W, triangle of shrubbery [2*].
TAXACEAE [YEW FAMILY], p. 55
    *Taxus* × *media* [**Anglojapanese Yew**]: E side [hedge].
TILIACEAE [LINDEN FAMILY], p. 107
    *Tilia cordata* [**Small-leaved European Linden**]: SE corner, ESE 30yd [1*].
    *Tilia petiolaris* [**Pendent Silver Linden**]: SE corner, SSE 15yd, E of lamppost 57 [1*].
ULMACEAE [ELM FAMILY], p. 92
    *Celtis occidentalis* [**Hackberry**]: E side, SE 35yd [1*].
    *Ulmus americana* [**American Elm**]: E side [2*].

## SORIN STATUE

BERBERIDACEAE [BARBERRY FAMILY], p. 86
    *Berberis* × *mentorensis* [**Mentor Barberry**]: Surrounding [hedge].
BETULACEAE [BIRCH FAMILY], p. 103
    *Betula nigra* [**River Birch; Black Birch**]: NE 30yd [1].
BIGNONIACEAE [BIGNONIA FAMILY], p. 179
    *Catalpa bignonioides* [**Southern Catalpa; Common Catalpa**]: NW 50yd [1*].
FAGACEAE [BEECH FAMILY], p. 98
    *Fagus sylvatica* [**European Beech**]: NE [1].
    *Quercus palustris* [**Pin Oak**]: SE 15yd [1]; W 20yd [1]; W 30yd [1].
PINACEAE [PINE FAMILY], p. 59
    *Pinus nigra* [**Austrian Pine**]: NNE 30yd [1].
    *Pinus strobus* [**Eastern White Pine**]: SW 30yd [1*].

## SOUTH DINING HALL

ACERACEAE [MAPLE FAMILY], p. 161
    *Acer saccharum* [**Sugar Maple; Hard Maple**]: SW corner, S [1].
CAESALPINIACEAE [CAESALPINIA FAMILY], p. 142
    *Gleditsia triacanthos* subsp. *inermis* [**Thornless Honeylocust**]: SE corner, S [3*]; W side [3*].
CELASTRACEAE [STAFF-TREE FAMILY], p. 151
    *Euonymus fortunei* [**Chinese Winter-creeper**]: W entrance, N, on wall [1].
CUPRESSACEAE [CYPRESS FAMILY], p. 72
    *Juniperus virginiana* 'Albospica' [**Silvery Redcedar**]: SW corner, parking lot, W [1*].
    *Juniperus virginiana* 'Venusta' [**Glossy Redcedar**]: S parking lot, midway to Fisher at road [7*].
FABACEAE [PEA FAMILY], p. 144
    *Caragana arborescens* [**Siberian Pea-tree**]: SW corner [4*].
MORACEAE [MULBERRY FAMILY], p. 94
    *Morus alba* [**White Mulberry**]: SW corner, golf course fence, S [2].
PINACEAE [PINE FAMILY], p. 59
    *Pinus ponderosa* var. *scopulorum* [**Rocky Mountain Ponderosa Pine**]: E entrance [2*]; NW corner [1*]; SW corner [1].
    *Pinus resinosa* 'Globosa' [**Dwarf Red Pine**]: SE corner [4*].

ROSACEAE [ROSE FAMILY], p. 122
    *Crataegus coccinoides* [**Kansas Hawthorn**]: E side [2*].
    *Crataegus crus-galli* [**Cockspur Hawthorn; Cockspur-thorn**]: W side [6*].
    *Crataegus monogyna* [**Oneseed Hawthorn; English Hawthorn**]: SE corner [1*].
    *Crataegus phaenopyrum* [**Washington Hawthorn**]: E entrance [1*].
    *Malus spp.* [**Ornamental Crabapple hybrids**]: NW corner, W [1*]; SW corner, W 30yd
        near Fisher S end [1*].
    *Pyrus calleryana* [**Callery Pear**]: NW corner [1 **Commem.**].
TAXACEAE [YEW FAMILY], p. 55
    *Taxus* × *media* [**Anglojapanese Yew**]: N, main entrance [1*].
    *Taxus* × *media* 'Hicksii' [**Hicks' Yew**]: N, main entrance, W [1*].


## ST. EDWARD'S HALL

ACERACEAE [MAPLE FAMILY], p. 161
    *Acer saccharum* [**Sugar Maple; Hard Maple**]: N [1]; S, statue, flanking [2].
    *Acer saccharum* subsp. *nigrum* [**Black Maple**]: N [1].
CAPRIFOLIACEAE [HONEYSUCKLE FAMILY], p. 180
    *Lonicera* × *bella* [**Belle Honeysuckle**]: S side, W arch [1].
    *Lonicera morrowii* [**Morrow Honeysuckle**]: S side, W arch, W [4*].
    *Viburnum dentatum* [**Arrowwood Viburnum**]: N wing, NE corner [2].
    *Viburnum plicatum* f. *tomentosum* [**Doublefile Viburnum**]: E end, NE corner, N 20yd [1].
HYDRANGEACEAE [HYDRANGEA FAMILY], p. 117
    *Philadelphus* × *nivalis* [**Snowy Mock Orange**]: S, flanking archway [4*].
    *Philadelphus* × *virginalis* [**Virginal Mock Orange**]: S side, E arch, front [2].
OLEACEAE [OLIVE FAMILY], p. 174
    *Syringa vulgaris* [**Common Lilac**]: E end, NE corner [hedge].
PINACEAE [PINE FAMILY], p. 59
    *Picea abies* [**Norway Spruce**]: SW corner, W [1].
    *Picea pungens* [**Colorado Blue Spruce**]: SW corner, S 12yd [1*].
    *Picea pungens* 'Glauca' [**Blue Spruce; Colorado Blue Spruce**]: W side [2*].
    *Pinus mugo* [**Mugo Pine; Swiss Mountain Pine**]: N entrance [1].
    *Pinus ponderosa* var. *scopulorum* [**Rocky Mountain Ponderosa Pine**]: W side [7*].
ROSACEAE [ROSE FAMILY], p. 122
    *Chaenomeles speciosa* [**Japanese Quince**]: NW corner [hedge].
    *Crataegus phaenopyrum* [**Washington Hawthorn**]: N side [2].
    *Malus spp.* [**Ornamental Crabapple hybrids**]: N side [3].
    *Pyrus calleryana* [**Callery Pear**]: S lawn [1 **Commem.**].
    *Spiraea prunifolia* [**Double Bridal-wreath**]: S side, W arch, front [2].
STAPHYLEACEAE [BLADDERNUT FAMILY], p. 159
    *Staphylea trifolia* [**American Bladdernut**]: S lawn [1*].
VITACEAE [GRAPE FAMILY], p. 157
    *Parthenocissus tricuspidata* [**Boston Ivy**]: Wall [1].


## ST. JOSEPH HALL

ACERACEAE [MAPLE FAMILY], p. 161
    *Acer negundo* [**Boxelder**]: W, woods [many*].
    *Acer saccharinum* [**Silver Maple; Soft Maple**]: W side, SW 30yd [1].

BETULACEAE [BIRCH FAMILY], p. 103
> *Corylus americana* [**American Hazelnut; American Filbert**]: W in woods, along path, N side [few].

CAPRIFOLIACEAE [HONEYSUCKLE FAMILY], p. 180
> *Lonicera morrowii* [**Morrow Honeysuckle**]: SW 50yd, woods [1].
> *Viburnum prunifolium* [**Blackhaw; Sweethaw**]: SE, lake slope, flanking steps to pier [few*].

CELASTRACEAE [STAFF-TREE FAMILY], p. 151
> *Euonymus fortunei* [**Chinese Winter-creeper**]: Lake slope, top of steps [bed*].
> *Euonymus fortunei* var. *radicans* f. *reticulata* [**White-veined Winter-creeper**]: Lake slope, top of steps, E [1*].

FAGACEAE [BEECH FAMILY], p. 98
> *Quercus alba* [**White Oak**]: Holy Cross Annex, woods between [many*].
> *Quercus rubra* [**Red Oak; Northern Red Oak**]: W end, N 40yd [1*].

JUGLANDACEAE [WALNUT FAMILY], p. 96
> *Carya laciniosa* [**Shellbark Hickory**]: W road, N of turnoff, E side [1].
> *Carya ovalis* [**Sweet Pignut**]: SW [many].
> *Carya ovata* [**Shagbark Hickory**]: SW 100yd, road, E side [1].

MAGNOLIACEAE [MAGNOLIA FAMILY], p. 82
> *Liriodendron tulipifera* [**Tulip Tree; Yellow-poplar**]: NW corner, N 45yd [1].
> *Magnolia* × *proctoriana* [**Chinese Magnolia**]: N 40yd [1].

OLEACEAE [OLIVE FAMILY], p. 174
> *Fraxinus pennsylvanica* [**Green Ash**]: Calvary, woods between [few*].

ROSACEAE [ROSE FAMILY], p. 122
> *Prunus serotina* [**Blackcherry; Wild Black Cherry**]: Holy Cross Annex, woods between [many*].

RUTACEAE [RUE FAMILY], p. 169
> *Evodia danielii* [**Chinese Evodia**]: Lakeside, base of steps [40*].

SALICACEAE [WILLOW FAMILY], p. 110
> *Populus deltoides* [**Cottonwood**]: NW corner, N 40yd [1]; NW corner, N 50yd [1].

TAXODIACEAE [TAXODIUM FAMILY], p. 71
> *Metasequoia glyptostroboides* [**Dawn Redwood**]: W end, N 60yd [1*].

VITACEAE [GRAPE FAMILY], p. 157
> *Vitis riparia* [**River-bank Grape; Frost Grape**]: Moreau, between [many*].


## St. Joseph's Lake

ACERACEAE [MAPLE FAMILY], p. 161
> *Acer platanoides* [**Norway Maple**]: W lawn [1].
> *Acer saccharinum* [**Silver Maple; Soft Maple**]: Shore [many].

ANACARDIACEAE [CASHEW FAMILY], p. 166
> *Rhus aromatica* [**Fragrant Sumac**]: NW, path to Calvary, W side [1].
> *Rhus glabra* [**Smooth Sumac**]: Boat house, E [few].
> *Rhus hirta* [**Staghorn Sumac**]: NW woods [many*].
> *Toxicodendron radicans* [**Poison Ivy**]: Lakeside [many].
> *Toxicodendron rydbergii* [**Poison Ivy**]: Lakeside [many].

APOCYNACEAE [DOGBANE FAMILY], p. 171
> *Vinca minor* [**Common Periwinkle; Running Myrtle**]: [many].

BETULACEAE [BIRCH FAMILY], p. 103
> *Corylus americana* [**American Hazelnut; American Filbert**]: NW woods [many*].

**BIGNONIACEAE [BIGNONIA FAMILY], p. 179**

*Campsis radicans* [**Trumpet-creeper; Trumpet-vine**]:  [many*].

**CAESALPINIACEAE [CAESALPINIA FAMILY], p. 142**

*Cercis canadensis* [**Eastern Redbud; Judas-tree**]: Holy Cross House, SW 50yd lakeside [1].

**CAPRIFOLIACEAE [HONEYSUCKLE FAMILY], p. 180**

*Lonicera tatarica* var. *parvifolia* [**Hayne Honeysuckle**]: Boat house, top of slope, NE [many*].

*Sambucus canadensis* [**American Elder**]: NW woods [few*].

*Viburnum opulus* [**Cranberrybush; Guelder-rose**]: Islands, both [many*].

**FAGACEAE [BEECH FAMILY], p. 98**

*Quercus alba* [**White Oak**]:  [many].

**HYDRANGEACEAE [HYDRANGEA FAMILY], p. 117**

*Philadelphus coronarius* 'Zeyheri' [**Zeyher Mock Orange**]: Freshman Year W parking lot, N [1].

**JUGLANDACEAE [WALNUT FAMILY], p. 96**

*Carya ovalis* [**Sweet Pignut**]: Boat house, S 35yd [1]; Boat house, S 90yd [1]; SE margin [many*].

*Carya ovalis* var. *obovalis* f. *acuta* [**Stipitate Pignut**]: NW woods [1*].

*Carya ovata* [**Shagbark Hickory**]: Boat house, S 35yd [1*]; NW woods [2*].

**LAURACEAE [LAUREL FAMILY], p. 84**

*Sassafras albidum* [**Red Sassafras**]: N shore [few].

**MENISPERMACEAE [MOONSEED FAMILY], p. 88**

*Menispermum canadense* [**Common Moonseed**]: NW woods [few*]; S edge, N of University Health Services [many].

**MORACEAE [MULBERRY FAMILY], p. 94**

*Morus alba* [**White Mulberry**]: Shore [many].

**OLEACEAE [OLIVE FAMILY], p. 174**

*Fraxinus americana* [**White Ash**]: NW woods [4*].

*Fraxinus pennsylvanica* [**Green Ash**]: NE at base of steps [1*]; NW woods [many*]; SW end, Calvary, junction of walks [1*].

*Syringa vulgaris* [**Common Lilac**]: N side [many].

**PLATANACEAE [PLANETREE FAMILY], p. 89**

*Platanus occidentalis* [**Sycamore; Buttonwood; American Planetree**]: Shore [many].

**ROSACEAE [ROSE FAMILY], p. 122**

*Crataegus punctata* var. *pausiaca* [**Olive-shaped Haw**]: NW woods [1*].

*Prunus americana* [**American Plum**]: Boat house beach fence, SE corner, SE [1].

*Prunus avium* [**Mazzard; Sweet Cherry**]: Boat house beach fence, SE corner, E [1]; Boat house, N [few].

*Prunus serotina* [**Blackcherry; Wild Black Cherry**]: NW woods, N end [many*].

*Prunus virginiana* [**Chokecherry**]: Boat house, S [1]; Distribution Center, N, lakeside [few].

*Rosa carolina* [**Pasture Rose; Wild Rose**]: SW margin [1].

*Rosa multiflora* [**Japanese Multifloral Rose; Baby Rose**]: W end,  junction of walks [many*].

*Rubus frondosus* [**Leafy-bracted Blackberry**]: Boat house, rear walk, E side [many*].

*Rubus occidentalis* [**Black Raspberry; Blackcap**]: Boat house, rear walk, E side [many*]; W end, 15yd NW of Station #9 [1].

**SALICACEAE [WILLOW FAMILY], p. 110**

*Populus alba* [**White Poplar; Silverleaf Poplar**]: W end [10*].

*Populus deltoides* [**Cottonwood**]: Power plant, 75yd NW [2]; SW, at walk to island [1].

*Salix alba* var. *vitellina* [**Yellow Willow**]: Lewis Hall, N 15 yd [1]; Power plant, NW 100yd [2]; S side, central area [1]; SW corner, along road [1]; SW corner, along road, ENE 12yd [1]; SW corner, along road, ENE 32yd [1].

*Salix caprea* [**Goat Willow**]: Boat house, E [many].

SMILACACEAE [CATBRIER FAMILY], p. 188

*Smilax hispida* [**Bristly Greenbrier**]: Boat house, S 45yd [1*]; NW woods [few*].

SOLANACEAE [NIGHTSHADE FAMILY], p. 172

*Solanum dulcamara* [**Bitter Nightshade**]: N slope at St. Joseph Hall [many].

TILIACEAE [LINDEN FAMILY], p. 107

*Tilia americana* [**American Basswood; American Linden**]: [many].


## St. Mary's Lake

ACERACEAE [MAPLE FAMILY], p. 161

*Acer platanoides* 'Crimson King' [**Norway Maple**]: E end, W of Grotto [1 **Commem.**].

ANACARDIACEAE [CASHEW FAMILY], p. 166

*Toxicodendron radicans* [**Poison Ivy**]: Lakeside [many].

*Toxicodendron rydbergii* [**Poison Ivy**]: Lakeside [many].

CAPRIFOLIACEAE [HONEYSUCKLE FAMILY], p. 180

*Lonicera* × *bella* [**Belle Honeysuckle**]: SW corner, woods [3].

*Viburnum opulus* [**Cranberrybush; Guelder-rose**]: Island, N of Campus Security Bldg [many*].

*Viburnum opulus* 'Roseum' [**Snowball; Snowball-bush**]: N edge [few*].

CORNACEAE [DOGWOOD FAMILY], p. 149

*Cornus sanguinea* [**Bloodtwig Dogwood**]: S edge [many*].

*Cornus sericea* [**Red-osier Dogwood**]: S edge [many*].

OLEACEAE [OLIVE FAMILY], p. 174

*Fraxinus nigra* [**Black Ash**]: NW corner, W 8yd [1].

PINACEAE [PINE FAMILY], p. 59

*Pinus nigra* [**Austrian Pine**]: SE edge [1].

*Pinus pungens* [**Table Mountain Pine**]: NE corner, E side [1].

*Pinus sylvestris* [**Scotch Pine**]: Architecture Bldg, N at lake margin [1]; N edge [1].

*Pinus thunbergiana* [**Japanese Black Pine**]: N edge [1*].

RHAMNACEAE [BUCKTHORN FAMILY], p. 157

*Rhamnus frangula* [**Glossy Buckthorn; Alder Buckthorn**]: W end [many*].

ROSACEAE [ROSE FAMILY], p. 122

*Rosa multiflora* [**Japanese Multifloral Rose; Baby Rose**]: S edge, N of Campus Security Bldg [1]; S margin, N of Campus Security Bldg [1]; W end, ravine, N side [hedge*].

*Rubus occidentalis* [**Black Raspberry; Blackcap**]: W end, ravine, S side [many*].

SALICACEAE [WILLOW FAMILY], p. 110

*Populus alba* [**White Poplar; Silverleaf Poplar**]: W end [few].

*Populus deltoides* [**Cottonwood**]: W end, ravine [6*].

*Salix alba* var. *vitellina* [**Yellow Willow**]: N central edge [3]; NW edge [many].

*Salix exigua* [**Sandbar Willow**]: S margin, E end [many*].

*Salix matsudana* 'Tortuosa' [**Corkscrew Willow; Dragon-claw Willow**]: E edge [1].

*Salix nigra* [**Black Willow**]: SE edge, NW of road intersection [3].

TILIACEAE [LINDEN FAMILY], p. 107

*Tilia americana* [**American Basswood; American Linden**]: N central edge, 10 yd N of path [1].

ULMACEAE [ELM FAMILY], p. 92

*Celtis occidentalis* [**Hackberry**]: W end, Highway 31, between [7*].

VITACEAE [GRAPE FAMILY], p. 157

*Vitis riparia* [**River-bank Grape; Frost Grape**]: N, old swimming pier, N in hedge [1*]; S edge, N of Campus Security Bldg [1]; W end, near Carroll Hall [many].

### ST. MICHAEL'S LAUNDRY

CAPRIFOLIACEAE [HONEYSUCKLE FAMILY], p. 180
*Viburnum* × *burkwoodii* [**Burkwood Viburnum**]: N side [3].
*Viburnum opulus* [**Cranberrybush; Guelder-rose**]: E, flanking main door [2].
CELASTRACEAE [STAFF-TREE FAMILY], p. 151
*Euonymus alata* [**Winged Burningbush; Winged Spindletree**]: E side, N of walk, along wall [11].
CUPRESSACEAE [CYPRESS FAMILY], p. 72
*Juniperus chinensis* 'Shimpaku' [**Chinese Juniper**]: E side, N of walk, along wall [9].
PINACEAE [PINE FAMILY], p. 59
*Picea abies* 'Pumila' [**Dwarf Norway Spruce**]: NE corner [8].
ROSACEAE [ROSE FAMILY], p. 122
*Malus floribunda* [**Japanese Flowering Crabapple**]: E, flanking front walk [2].
*Malus spp.* 'Dolgo' [**Dolgo Crabapple**]: NE corner [1].
*Malus yunnanensis* [**Veitchii Crabapple**]: E side, S end [5].
*Prunus laurocerasus* 'Schipkaensis' [**Schip Laurel**]: S end [14].
*Pyrus calleryana* 'Chanticleer' [**Chanticleer Pear**]: E side [3].
*Spiraea* × *bumalda* 'Goldflame' [**Goldflame Spiraea**]: E, flanking front walk [8].
*Spiraea* × *bumalda* 'Limemound' [**Limemound Spiraea**]: E side, N of walk, along wall [3].

### STADIUM

ACERACEAE [MAPLE FAMILY], p. 161
*Acer platanoides* [**Norway Maple**]: E, gate 7 [1]; NE, gates 1 and 2 [1]; NW, gate 16 [1]; SE, gate 8 [1].
*Acer rubrum* [**Red Maple**]: SE, gate 8 [1]; SW, gate 12 [1].
*Acer saccharum* [**Sugar Maple; Hard Maple**]: E, gate 6 [1]; N, gates 18 and 19 [1]; NE, gates 1 and 2 [1]; SE, gate 9 [1]; SW, gate 12 [1].
ANACARDIACEAE [CASHEW FAMILY], p. 166
*Cotinus coggygria* [**Smoketree; Smokebush**]: SE, Angela and Juniper intersection [7*].
CAESALPINIACEAE [CAESALPINIA FAMILY], p. 142
*Cercis canadensis* [**Eastern Redbud; Judas-tree**]: E, gate 3 [1]; E, gate 7 [3]; NE, gates 1 and 2 [1].
CORNACEAE [DOGWOOD FAMILY], p. 149
*Cornus florida* [**Flowering Dogwood**]: Galvin, midway, parking circle, E end [1 **Commem.**].
FAGACEAE [BEECH FAMILY], p. 98
*Quercus palustris* [**Pin Oak**]: E, gate 3 [1]; E, gates 4 and 5 [2].
OLEACEAE [OLIVE FAMILY], p. 174
*Fraxinus americana* [**White Ash**]: E, gate 6 [1]; E, gates 4 and 5 [2]; S, gate 11 [1]; SE, gate 8 [1].
PINACEAE [PINE FAMILY], p. 59
*Picea abies* [**Norway Spruce**]: W, gate 14 [2].
*Pinus strobus* [**Eastern White Pine**]: E, gate 3 [5]; E, gate 7 [5]; NE, gates 1 and 2 [4]; SE, gate 9 [3].
PLATANACEAE [PLANETREE FAMILY], p. 89
*Platanus occidentalis* [**Sycamore; Buttonwood; American Planetree**]: E, gate 3 [3]; NE, gates 1 and 2 [1]; S, gate 10 [1]; SE, gate 9 [6].

TILIACEAE [LINDEN FAMILY], p. 107
    *Tilia heterophylla* [**White Basswood**]: NE, gates 1 and 2 [1]; NW, gate 16 [1].
ULMACEAE [ELM FAMILY], p. 92
    *Ulmus americana* [**American Elm**]: E, gates 4 and 5 [1]; N, gates 18 and 19 [2]; S, gate 10
        [1]; W, gate 14 [1].
    *Ulmus pumila* [**Siberian Elm**]: NE, gates 1 and 2 [2]; SW, gate 12 [2]; W, gate 14 [1].

## STANFORD HALL

HYDRANGEACEAE [HYDRANGEA FAMILY], p. 117
    *Hydrangea quercifolia* [**Oak-leaf Hydrangea**]: Surrounding [beds*].
ULMACEAE [ELM FAMILY], p. 92
    *Ulmus americana* [**American Elm**]: NW corner [1].
    *Ulmus thomasii* [**Rock Elm; Cork Elm**]: NW corner, W [5*].

## STEPAN CENTER

ACERACEAE [MAPLE FAMILY], p. 161
    *Acer platanoides* [**Norway Maple**]: S, walk to Flanner [11].
CELASTRACEAE [STAFF-TREE FAMILY], p. 151
    *Euonymus alata* [**Winged Burningbush; Winged Spindletree**]: S side, E of door [1].
CORNACEAE [DOGWOOD FAMILY], p. 149
    *Cornus alba* 'Argenteo-marginata' [**Tartarian Dogwood**]: S side, W [2].
PINACEAE [PINE FAMILY], p. 59
    *Pinus strobus* [**Eastern White Pine**]: S side, flanking door [6].
ROSACEAE [ROSE FAMILY], p. 122
    *Prunus cerasifera* 'Atropurpurea' [**Purpleleaf Cherry-plum**]: S side, flanking door [2].

## STEPAN CHEMISTRY HALL

PINACEAE [PINE FAMILY], p. 59
    *Pinus sylvestris* [**Scotch Pine**]: NE corner, NE, 20yd [4].
ROSACEAE [ROSE FAMILY], p. 122
    *Crataegus crus-galli* var. *pachyphylla* [**Thick-leaved Cockspur-thorn**]: NE corner, E 15yd [3].
    *Crataegus phaenopyrum* [**Washington Hawthorn**]: NE corner, N [3].
    *Pyrus calleryana* [**Callery Pear**]: E and W sides [10].

## SUPPORT SERVICES BUILDING

ACERACEAE [MAPLE FAMILY], p. 161
    *Acer circinatum* 'Little Gem' [**Vine Maple; Oregon Vine Maple**]: S bed [1].
    *Acer palmatum* 'Atropurpureum' [**Bloodleaf Japanese Maple**]: S bed [1].
    *Acer palmatum* f. *dissectum* 'Germaine's Gyration' [**Threadleaf Japanese Maple**]: S bed [1].
    *Acer palmatum* 'Sango Kaku' [**Japanese Maple**]: S bed [1].
ANACARDIACEAE [CASHEW FAMILY], p. 166
    *Cotinus coggygria* 'Royal Purple' [**Smoketree; Smokebush**]: S bed [1].

**ARAUCARIACEAE [ARAUCARIA FAMILY], p. 58**
*Araucaria araucana* [**Monkey-puzzle Tree; Chilean Pine**]: N bed [1].
**BERBERIDACEAE [BARBERRY FAMILY], p. 86**
*Berberis thunbergii* 'Crimson Pygmy' [**Dwarf Japanese Barberry**]: N bed [3]; S bed [4].
**BETULACEAE [BIRCH FAMILY], p. 103**
*Carpinus betulus* 'Pendula' [**Weeping European Hornbeam**]: N bed [1].
**BUXACEAE [BOX FAMILY], p. 156**
*Buxus microphylla* [**Korean Boxwood**]: S bed [1].
**CAESALPINIACEAE [CAESALPINIA FAMILY], p. 142**
*Gleditsia triacanthos* subsp. *inermis* [**Thornless Honeylocust**]: E parking lot, S end [3].
**CAPRIFOLIACEAE [HONEYSUCKLE FAMILY], p. 180**
*Viburnum* × *bodnantense* 'Pink Dawn' [**Bodnant Viburnum**]: N bed [3]; S bed [2].
*Viburnum opulus* 'Nanum' [**Dwarf Cranberrybush**]: E side, flanking door [6].
*Viburnum plicatum* f. *tomentosum* 'Mariesii' [**Doublefile Viburnum**]: S bed [1].
**CELASTRACEAE [STAFF-TREE FAMILY], p. 151**
*Euonymus alata* 'Compacta' [**Narrow-winged Burningbush**]: E, along S entrance wall [14]; N bed [4]; S bed [3].
**CERCIDIPHYLLACEAE [KATSURA TREE FAMILY], p. 88**
*Cercidiphyllum japonicum* 'Pendula' [**Weeping Katsura Tree**]: N bed [1].
**CORNACEAE [DOGWOOD FAMILY], p. 149**
*Cornus sericea* [**Red-osier Dogwood**]: N bed [4].
*Cornus sericea* 'Flaviramea' [**Goldentwig Dogwood**]: N bed [4].
**CUPRESSACEAE [CYPRESS FAMILY], p. 72**
*Chamaecyparis nootkatensis* 'Pendula' [**Weeping Nootka Falsecypress**]: E, along wall [6].
*Chamaecyparis obtusa* 'Crippsii' [**Hinoki Falsecypress**]: S bed [1].
*Chamaecyparis obtusa* 'Fernspray Gold' [**Hinoki Falsecypress**]: N bed (standard) [1].
*Chamaecyparis obtusa* 'Nana Gracilis' [**Hinoki Falsecypress**]: S bed [1]; S bed (standard) [2].
*Chamaecyparis obtusa* 'Nana Lutea' [**Hinoki Falsecypress**]: S bed [1].
*Chamaecyparis obtusa* 'Pygmaea Aurescens' [**Hinoki Falsecypress**]: N bed (Blue Carpet juniper graft below) [1].
*Chamaecyparis pisifera* 'Boulevard' [**Sawara Falsecypress**]: S bed [1].
*Chamaecyparis pisifera* 'Golden Mop' [**Sawara Falsecypress**]: N bed [5]; S bed [4].
*Juniperus chinensis* 'Old Gold' [**Chinese Juniper**]: E side, flanking door [19].
*Juniperus chinensis* 'Shimpaku' [**Chinese Juniper**]: S bed [1].
*Juniperus chinensis* 'Torulosa Variegata' [**Variegated Clustered Juniper**]: N bed [2].
*Juniperus communis* 'Effusa' [**Common Juniper**]: N bed (standard) [1]; S bed [1]; S bed (standard) [1].
*Juniperus procumbens* 'Nana' [**Creeping Juniper**]: N bed (standard) [1].
*Juniperus sabina* 'Variegata' [**Hoarfrost Savin**]: N bed [1]; S bed [1].
*Juniperus scopulorum* 'Table Top' [**Rocky Mountain Juniper**]: N bed [1]; S bed [1].
*Juniperus squamata* 'Blue Carpet' [**Singleseed Juniper**]: E side, flanking door (standards) [2].
*Juniperus squamata* 'Blue Star' [**Singleseed Juniper**]: N bed (Prince of Wales graft below) [1].
*Juniperus squamata* 'Holger' [**Singleseed Juniper**]: N bed [2].
*Thuja occidentalis* 'Golden Globe' [**Golden Globe Arborvitae**]: S bed [1].
*Thuja occidentalis* 'Rheingold' [**American Arborvitae**]: N bed [1]; S bed [2]; S bed (standard) [1].
*Thuja occidentalis* 'Techny' [**American Arborvitae**]: N end [22]; S end [9].
**ERICACEAE [HEATH FAMILY], p. 113**
*Gaultheria procumbens* [**Wintergreen**]: N bed [75].

*Oxydendrum arboreum* [**Sourwood; Sorrel Tree**]: N bed [1]; S bed [1].

*Rhododendron* × *spp.* 'P.J.M.' [**P.J.M. Rhododendron**]: N bed [1]; S bed [2].

*Rhododendron spp.* 'Ramapo' [**Ramapo Rhododendron**]: E, flanking door [12]; N bed [2]; S bed [2].

FAGACEAE [BEECH FAMILY], p. 98

*Fagus sylvatica* 'Roseo-marginata' [**Rose-pink European Beech**]: N bed [1].

GROSSULARIACEAE [CURRANT FAMILY], p. 121

*Ribes aureum* [**Golden Currant**]: N bed [1]; S bed [1].

*Ribes sanguineum* 'Pulborough Scarlet' [**Scarlet Currant**]: S bed [2].

HAMAMELIDACEAE [WITCH-HAZEL FAMILY], p. 90

*Hamamelis* × *intermedia* 'Diane' [**Witch-hazel**]: N bed [1]; S bed [1].

*Parrotia persica* [**Persian Parrotia**]: NE bed [1].

MALVACEAE [MALLOW FAMILY], p. 109

*Hibiscus syriacus* 'Blushing Bride' [**Shrub-althea; Rose-of-Sharon**]: S bed [3].

OLEACEAE [OLIVE FAMILY], p. 174

*Syringa meyeri* 'Palibin' [**Meyer Lilac**]: N bed (standard) [1].

*Syringa reticulata* [**Japanese Tree Lilac**]: E, flanking parking lot [2]; S bed [1].

PINACEAE [PINE FAMILY], p. 59

*Cedrus atlantica* 'Glauca Pendula' [**Weeping Blue Atlas Cedar**]: N bed [1].

*Picea abies* 'Cupressina' [**Norway Spruce**]: S bed [2].

*Picea abies* 'Nidiformis' [**Bird's Nest Spruce**]: N bed [1]; S bed [2].

*Picea abies* 'Pendula' [**Weeping Norway Spruce**]: N bed [1]; S bed [2].

*Picea abies* 'Pumila' [**Dwarf Norway Spruce**]: S bed [1].

*Picea alcoquiana* 'Howell's Dwarf' [**Alcock Spruce**]: S bed [1].

*Picea glauca* 'Conica' [**Conical White Spruce**]: S bed (spiral topiary) [2].

*Picea glauca* 'Conica Rainbows End' [**Rainbows End Spruce**]: N bed [1].

*Picea omorika* 'Nana' [**Dwarf Serbian Spruce**]: S bed [1].

*Picea orientalis* 'Skylands' [**Oriental Spruce**]: NE bed [1].

*Picea pungens* 'Hoopsii' [**Colorado Spruce**]: E side, S end, along wall [2].

*Picea pungens* 'Montgomery' [**Colorado Blue Spruce**]: N bed [1]; S bed [1].

*Picea pungens* 'Prostrate Green' [**Colorado Spruce**]: N bed [1].

*Picea purpurea* [**Purple Cone Spruce**]: N bed [2]; S bed [3].

*Pinus aristata* [**Bristlecone Pine**]: NE bed [1].

*Pinus leucodermis* 'Shira' [**Bosnian Pine; Graybark Pine**]: N bed [1]; S bed [1].

*Pinus parviflora* 'Glauca' [**Japanese White Pine**]: N bed [1].

*Pinus strobus* 'Blue Shag' [**Eastern White Pine**]: N bed [4]; S bed [4].

*Tsuga canadensis* 'Dawsoniana' [**Eastern Hemlock**]: S bed [1].

*Tsuga canadensis* 'Golden Splendor' [**Eastern Hemlock**]: S bed [1].

*Tsuga canadensis* 'Pendula' [**Eastern Hemlock**]: S bed [1].

ROSACEAE [ROSE FAMILY], p. 122

*Chaenomeles speciosa* 'Texas Scarlet' [**Japanese Quince**]: N bed [1].

*Cotoneaster apiculatus* [**Cranberry Cotoneaster**]: N bed [1].

*Cotoneaster dammeri* 'Coral Beauty' [**Bearberry Cotoneaster**]: S bed [2].

*Cotoneaster dammeri* 'Walter's Red' [**Bearberry Cotoneaster**]: N bed [1].

*Crataegus* × *lavallei* [**Lavalle Hawthorn**]: S bed [1].

*Kerria japonica* [**Japanese Rose**]: N bed [1].

*Prunus laurocerasus* 'Schipkaensis' [**Schip Laurel**]: E side [2]; N bed [1].

*Pyrus calleryana* 'Chanticleer' [**Chanticleer Pear**]: S bed [1].

*Spiraea* × *bumalda* 'Goldflame' [**Goldflame Spiraea**]: N bed [2]; S bed [2].

*Spiraea* × *bumalda* 'Limemound' [**Limemound Spiraea**]: S bed [1].

SALICACEAE [WILLOW FAMILY], p. 110

*Salix purpurea* 'Pendula' [**Purpleosier Willow; Basket Willow**]: N bed [1].

TAXODIACEAE [TAXODIUM FAMILY], p. 71
    *Sciadopitys verticillata* [**Umbrella-pine**]: S bed [1].
THEACEAE [TEA FAMILY], p. 106
    *Stewartia pseudocamelia* [**Japanese Stewartia**]: N bed [1].
VERBENACEAE [VERBENA FAMILY], p. 173
    *Callicarpa bodinieri* [**Bodinier Beautyberry**]: N bed [2].

## University Club

BETULACEAE [BIRCH FAMILY], p. 103
    *Betula nigra* [**River Birch; Black Birch**]: N side [4].
CELASTRACEAE [STAFF-TREE FAMILY], p. 151
    *Euonymus alata* [**Winged Burningbush; Winged Spindletree**]: NE lawn [hedge].
OLEACEAE [OLIVE FAMILY], p. 174
    *Fraxinus angustifolia* [**Eurasian Ash**]: NW, SW, flanking parking lot [4].
PINACEAE [PINE FAMILY], p. 59
    *Pinus strobus* [**Eastern White Pine**]: N side [2].
ROSACEAE [ROSE FAMILY], p. 122
    *Crataegus phaenopyrum* [**Washington Hawthorn**]: NW corner [1]; SW corner [1].

## University Health Services

ACERACEAE [MAPLE FAMILY], p. 161
    *Acer negundo* [**Boxelder**]: N, near lake [many*].
ANACARDIACEAE [CASHEW FAMILY], p. 166
    *Rhus hirta* [**Staghorn Sumac**]: N, slope to lake [many*].
BETULACEAE [BIRCH FAMILY], p. 103
    *Betula populifolia* [**Gray Birch**]: E side [1*].
CAPRIFOLIACEAE [HONEYSUCKLE FAMILY], p. 180
    *Lonicera tatarica* [**Tatarian Honeysuckle**]: N, lakeside cabin, W side [1].
    *Lonicera tatarica* f. *leroyana* [**Leroy Honeysuckle**]: N, lakeside cabin, SE corner [1*].
ERICACEAE [HEATH FAMILY], p. 113
    *Pieris japonica* [**Lily-of-the-valley Bush**]: N side [1].
PINACEAE [PINE FAMILY], p. 59
    *Picea abies* 'Columnaris' [**Columnar Spruce**]: S, at road turn [1*].
    *Picea pungens* [**Colorado Blue Spruce**]: SW corner [3*].
ROSACEAE [ROSE FAMILY], p. 122
    *Prunus cerasus* [**Sour Cherry**]: N side, W 40yd [1*].
TAXACEAE [YEW FAMILY], p. 55
    *Taxus* × *media* 'Brownii' [**Brown's Yew**]: SE [hedge].

## University Village

ACERACEAE [MAPLE FAMILY], p. 161
    *Acer platanoides* 'Crimson King' [**Norway Maple**]: Playground [1 **Commem.**].

## WALSH HALL

ACERACEAE [MAPLE FAMILY], p. 161
    *Acer platanoides* [**Norway Maple**]: NE corner [1*].
BIGNONIACEAE [BIGNONIA FAMILY], p. 179
    *Catalpa bignonioides* [**Southern Catalpa; Common Catalpa**]: N end [2*].
CAESALPINIACEAE [CAESALPINIA FAMILY], p. 142
    *Gleditsia triacanthos* subsp. *inermis* [**Thornless Honeylocust**]: W side [4*].
CELASTRACEAE [STAFF-TREE FAMILY], p. 151
    *Euonymus alata* [**Winged Burningbush; Winged Spindletree**]: SW [1].
CORNACEAE [DOGWOOD FAMILY], p. 149
    *Cornus florida* [**Flowering Dogwood**]: E flanking steps [6]; E side, flanking steps [6].
FAGACEAE [BEECH FAMILY], p. 98
    *Fagus sylvatica* 'Pendula' [**European Weeping Beech**]: Main entrance, E 45yd [1*].
    *Quercus palustris* [**Pin Oak**]: Main entrance, E, walk to main road, end [1*].
    *Quercus robur* [**English Oak**]: E lawn [1].
GINKGOACEAE [GINKGO FAMILY], p. 54
    *Ginkgo biloba* 'Laciniata' [**Split-leaf Ginkgo**]: Main entrance, E 40yd [1*].
HAMAMELIDACEAE [WITCH-HAZEL FAMILY], p. 90
    *Hamamelis vernalis* [**Vernal Witch-hazel**]: Front [6*].
OLEACEAE [OLIVE FAMILY], p. 174
    *Syringa vulgaris* [**Common Lilac**]: W side [2].
PINACEAE [PINE FAMILY], p. 59
    *Picea abies* [**Norway Spruce**]: SE corner, at Knights of Columbus Hall [6*].
    *Pinus nigra* [**Austrian Pine**]: E 20 yd, between S and central doors [3*]; E central entrance, SE 30yd [1]; E central entrance, SE 50yd [1].
    *Pinus strobus* [**Eastern White Pine**]: Main entrance, E 15yd [1*].
    *Pinus strobus* 'Fastigiata' [**Pyramidal White Pine**]: Chapel, E 10yd [1*].
    *Pinus sylvestris* [**Scotch Pine**]: Hurley Hall, between [4*]; NE corner, NE 30yd [1*].
PLATANACEAE [PLANETREE FAMILY], p. 89
    *Platanus occidentalis* [**Sycamore; Buttonwood; American Planetree**]: E at main walkway [2].
ROSACEAE [ROSE FAMILY], p. 122
    *Pyrus calleryana* [**Callery Pear**]: E lawn between main doors [1 **Commem.**].
    *Spiraea prunifolia* [**Double Bridal-wreath**]: N end, W side [2*].
    *Spiraea* × *vanhouttei* [**Vanhoutte Spiraea**]: NE corner [2*].
TAXACEAE [YEW FAMILY], p. 55
    *Taxus cuspidata* 'Densa' [**Japanese Cushion Yew**]: Front [20*].

## WASHINGTON HALL

ACERACEAE [MAPLE FAMILY], p. 161
    *Acer palmatum* f. *dissectum* [**Threadleaf Japanese Maple**]: SW corner [2]; W side [2].
    *Acer pseudoplatanus* [**Sycamore Maple**]: Sacred Heart statue, midway [1*].
    *Acer rubrum* [**Red Maple**]: W 15yd [1*]; W 25yd [1*].
    *Acer saccharum* [**Sugar Maple; Hard Maple**]: W entrance, W 20yd [1*].
AGAVACEAE [CENTURY-PLANT FAMILY], p. 187
    *Yucca filamentosa* [**Adam's-needle Yucca**]: SW, bed at intersection [9].
CAESALPINIACEAE [CAESALPINIA FAMILY], p. 142
    *Gleditsia triacanthos* subsp. *inermis* 'Shademaster' [**Thornless Honeylocust**]: E plaza [15].

CAPRIFOLIACEAE  [HONEYSUCKLE FAMILY], p. 180
 *Viburnum opulus* 'Nanum' [**Dwarf Cranberrybush**]: E plaza [hedge].
 *Viburnum trilobum* 'Alfredo' [**American Cranberrybush Viburnum**]: E side, plaza [8].
CUPRESSACEAE  [CYPRESS FAMILY], p. 72
 *Juniperus virginiana* [**Eastern Redcedar**]: W side [1*].
ERICACEAE  [HEATH FAMILY], p. 113
 *Rhododendron obtusum* [**Hiryu Azalea**]: LaFortune, crosswalk between, W [1].
 *Rhododendron obtusum* f. *Yayegiri* 'Amoenum' [**Japanese Salmon-red Azalea**]: LaFortune, crosswalk between, W [1].
 *Rhododendron* spp. [**Rhododendron; Azalea**]: SW, bed at intersection [bed].
HAMAMELIDACEAE  [WITCH-HAZEL FAMILY], p. 90
 *Hamamelis virginiana* [**Witch-hazel**]: N entrance, W side [1*].
OLEACEAE  [OLIVE FAMILY], p. 174
 *Forsythia viridissima* [**Greenstem Forsythia**]: S side [1].
 *Syringa* × *chinensis* [**Chinese Lilac**]: NW corner [2].
 *Syringa vulgaris* [**Common Lilac**]: SW corner [few].
PINACEAE  [PINE FAMILY], p. 59
 *Picea abies* [**Norway Spruce**]: W side [1].
 *Pseudotsuga menziesii* [**Douglas-fir**]: Sacred Heart statue, midway [1*].
ROSACEAE  [ROSE FAMILY], p. 122
 *Amelanchier laevis* [**Allegheny Serviceberry**]: W entrance, N [1].
 *Prunus cerasifera* 'Atropurpurea' [**Purpleleaf Cherry-plum**]: NW corner [1].
 *Pyrus calleryana* 'Redspire' [**Callery Pear**]: E plaza [2].
 *Spiraea* × *vanhouttei* [**Vanhoutte Spiraea**]: S, main entrance, W side [3*]; SW corner, W 10yd [26*].
TAXODIACEAE  [TAXODIUM FAMILY], p. 71
 *Taxodium distichum* [**Baldcypress**]: Cavanaugh, between [2].
TILIACEAE  [LINDEN FAMILY], p. 107
 *Tilia americana* [**American Basswood; American Linden**]: S, main entrance, SE 5yd [1*].
VITACEAE  [GRAPE FAMILY], p. 157
 *Parthenocissus tricuspidata* [**Boston Ivy**]: W side [1*].


## ZAHM HALL

ACERACEAE  [MAPLE FAMILY], p. 161
 *Acer platanoides* [**Norway Maple**]: E [3*].
CELASTRACEAE  [STAFF-TREE FAMILY], p. 151
 *Euonymus fortunei* [**Chinese Winter-creeper**]: N side, at door, flanking walk [2].
CORNACEAE  [DOGWOOD FAMILY], p. 149
 *Cornus florida* [**Flowering Dogwood**]: W side [3].
 *Cornus kousa* [**Kousa Dogwood**]: NW end, N [1].
CUPRESSACEAE  [CYPRESS FAMILY], p. 72
 *Chamaecyparis obtusa* 'Pygmaea Aurescens' [**Hinoki Falsecypress**]: NW sign [2].
 *Chamaecyparis pisifera* 'Golden Mop' [**Sawara Falsecypress**]: NW sign [2].
OLEACEAE  [OLIVE FAMILY], p. 174
 *Fraxinus americana* 'Autumn Blaze' [**White Ash**]: N side [1].
 *Fraxinus americana* 'Autumn Purple' [**White Ash**]: NW end, N [2].
 *Ligustrum vulgare* [**Common Privet; European Privet**]: SW corner [hedge*].
PINACEAE  [PINE FAMILY], p. 59
 *Abies concolor* [**White Fir; Colorado Fir**]: N side [1*].
 *Abies nordmanniana* [**Nordmann Fir; Caucasian Fir**]: S 15yd [1*].

*Picea abies* 'Pumila' [**Dwarf Norway Spruce**]: NW sign [2].
*Picea pungens* [**Colorado Blue Spruce**]: SW corner [1*].
*Pinus nigra* [**Austrian Pine**]: SE courtyard door, 25yd [1].
*Pinus parviflora* 'Glauca' [**Japanese White Pine**]: N side [1].
*Pinus strobus* [**Eastern White Pine**]: N [1].

ROSACEAE [ROSE FAMILY], p. 122

*Crataegus phaenopyrum* [**Washington Hawthorn**]: Cavanaugh, SW between [3].
*Prunus cerasifera* 'Atropurpurea' [**Purpleleaf Cherry-plum**]: S end, flanking [3].

TAXACEAE [YEW FAMILY], p. 55

*Taxus baccata* [**English Yew**]: NW sign [4].
*Taxus cuspidata* 'Intermedia' [**Japanese Compact Yew**]: E side [1*].

THYMELAEACEAE [MEZEREUM FAMILY], p. 147

*Daphne cneorum* 'Ruby Glow' [**Rose Daphne; Garland Flower**]: N side, at door [5].

# Commemorative Plantings

The plantings listed below have been placed on the Notre Dame campus to commemorate people or events. Each entry includes the purpose, donor, kind of plant, and site. An asterisk marks the plantings that are labelled with plaques (usually set in the ground). Information about making this kind of donation can be obtained from the Office of Planned Giving in the Department of University Relations. This office works with the Department of Landscape Services to help the donor select a site and kind of plant appropriate for the campus. No plants may be planted or removed from the Notre Dame campus without the approval of the Superintendent of Landscape Services.

*In memory of Edward and Marion Beauchamp, donated by Rev. E. William Beauchamp, C.S.C.
   *Cornus florida* [Flowering Dogwood]: Alumni Hall, SE, main gate, just W.

*In memory of Edward and Marion Beauchamp, donated by Rev. E. William Beauchamp, C.S.C.
   *Sorbus aucuparia* 'Cardinal Royal' [European Mountain-ash]: Law School, W side, center.

*In memory of Meghan Beeler, donated by Notre Dame Student Government.
   *Pyrus calleryana* [Callery Pear]: Walsh Hall, E lawn between main doors.

*In memory of Louis C. Berardi, class of 1930, donated by Gigi Berardi and Lucinda De Bengetti.
*Sorbus aucuparia* [European Mountain-ash]: Breen-Phillips Hall, W lawn, main entrance, S.

*In memory of Alita Bulman and Gina Crinella, donated by the women of Lyons Hall.
*Cercis canadensis* [Eastern Redbud; Judas-tree]: Lyons Hall, N, parking lot, N edge.

Donated by C. Patrick Carrol.
*Malus spp.* [Ornamental Crabapple hybrids]: Galvin Life Science Center, W, main entrance, W 15yd, S of walk.

*In memory of Michael A. Christopher, donated by the Crovello family.
*Magnolia stellata* [Star Magnolia]: Galvin Life Science Center, S end, S of walk.

Donated by the Class of 1992.
*Magnolia × soulangiana* [Saucer Magnolia]: Administration (Main) Building, Front, S of stairs, E of walk.

*In memory of Michael C. Cogswell, donated by the Class of 1988.
*Magnolia × soulangiana* [Saucer Magnolia]: Sacred Heart Statue, N, W of walk.

*In memory of Aloysius J. Dakoske, donated by Margaret Packo.
*Prunus virginiana* 'Shubert Select' [Shubert Select Chokecherry]: Decio Faculty Hall, S wing, E side lawn.

*In memory of John C. Dillon, donated by the Class of 1947.
*Pyrus calleryana* 'Chanticleer' [Chanticleer Pear]: Dillon Hall, N side.

*In recognition of the wedding anniversary of Noreen and Bob Dowd, donated by their family.
*Abies concolor* [White Fir; Colorado Fir]: Grotto of Our Lady of Lourdes, Corby, midway, W of walk.

*In memory of Bernard F. Garvey, donated by Carol Mueller.
*Acer platanoides* 'Crimson King' [Norway Maple]: Columba Hall, SE, at St. Mary's Lake.

In memory of Rachel Marie Grimes, donated by the residents of University Village.
*Acer platanoides* 'Crimson King' [Norway Maple]: University Village, Playground.

In memory of Robert Halstead, donated by John Halstead.
*Cornus florida* [Flowering Dogwood]: Alumni Hall, SE, main gate, W 15yd.

*In memory of Jeffrey Heilert, donated by the men of Cavanaugh Hall.
*Cornus florida* [Flowering Dogwood]: Cavanaugh Hall, S, basketball court, E edge.

*In honor of Rev. Theodore M. Hesburgh, C.S.C., donated by the Class of 1990.
*Corylus avellana* 'Contorta' [European Hazel]: Grotto of Our Lady of Lourdes, W.

In memory of William Hickey, donated by the Hickey and O'Brien families.
*Pyrus calleryana* [Callery Pear]: South Dining Hall, NW corner.

*In memory of Colleen Hipp, donated by Notre Dame Student Government.
  *Prunus subhirtella* 'Snofozam' [Snow Fountain Weeping Higan Cherry]: Lewis Hall, E, main entrance, N of walk.

*In honor of Rev. Edmund P. Joyce, C.S.C., donated by the Class of 1990.
  *Cornus florida* 'Rubra' [Red-flowering Dogwood]: Grotto of Our Lady of Lourdes, W.

*In honor of Rev. Andre Leveille, C.S.C., donated by the men of Cavanaugh Hall.
  *Acer platanoides* [Norway Maple]: Cavanaugh Hall, NW corner.

*In memory of Dorothy Maloney, donated by the men of St. Edward's Hall.
  *Pyrus calleryana* [Callery Pear]: St. Edward's Hall, S lawn.

In recognition of Father McGinnity, donated by St. Cletus Parish, La Grange, Illinois.
  *Cornus florida* [Flowering Dogwood]: Stadium, Galvin, midway, parking circle, E end.

*In recognition of Mrs. R. J. McSherry, donated by her grandchildren.
  *Malus spp.* 'Profusion' [Profusion Flowering Crab]: Morris Inn, W entrance, W.

*In memory of Armelo and Maria Migliore Miceli, donated by Rev. Matthew M. Miceli, C.S.C.
  *Quercus velutina* [Black Oak]: Cavanaugh Hall, N lawn, N of door.

*In memory of William H. Mitsch, donated by his loving family.
  *Acer platanoides* 'Crimson King' [Norway Maple]: Cushing Hall of Engineering, O'Shaughnessy, midway.

*In memory of Michael A. Mola, Sr., donated by Carol Hennion.
  *Acer platanoides* 'Crimson King' [Norway Maple]: St. Mary's Lake, E end, W of Grotto.

*In memory of Michael A. Mola, Sr., donated by Carol Hennion.
  *Platanus × acerifolia* [London Planetree]: Fieldhouse Mall, S side, E end.

*In honor of the troops of Operation Desert Storm, donated by the Arnold Air Society.
  *Malus spp.* 'Red Jade' [Red Jade Crabapple]: Pasquerilla Center, S side.

Donated by Robert C. Paver.
  *Malus spp.* [Ornamental Crabapple hybrids]: Galvin Life Science Center, W, main entrance, S 10yd.

In memory of Robert H. Raaf, donated by Marie Raaf.
  *Cercidiphyllum japonicum* 'Pendula' [Weeping Katsura Tree]: Hesburgh Library, Pool, W side.

*In memory of James D. Reagan, donated by the Reagan Family.
  *Cercidiphyllum japonicum* [Katsura Tree]: Log Chapel, Old College, midway.

*In memory of John L. Redmond, M.D., class of 1943, donated by his children.
  *Cercis canadensis* [Eastern Redbud; Judas-tree]: Galvin Life Science Center, W, main entrance, WSW 20yd at crosswalk.

*In memory of Russ Reece, donated by June Reece and Patricia Reece Hammond.
   *Malus spp.* [Ornamental Crabapple hybrids]: Hesburgh Library, SW 30yd, midway to Radiation Bldg.

*In memory of Donald Roberts, donated by the Class of 1968.
   *Cercidiphyllum japonicum* [Katsura Tree]: Decio Faculty Hall, W side, NW lawn.

*In memory of Martin C. Ryan, donated by the Thomas C. Ryan, Sr., family.
   *Sophora japonica* [Japanese Pagodatree]: Hesburgh Library, Pool, SW.

*In memory of Robert Satterfield, donated by the Class of 1989.
   *Cornus florida* [Flowering Dogwood]: Fisher Hall, N entrance, E.

*In memory of Lucille M. Sayre, donated by the Ladies of Notre Dame and St. Mary's College.
   *Malus spp.* [Ornamental Crabapple hybrids]: Pasquerilla Hall East, N wing, E entrance, parking circle.

*In recognition of 40 year of service by John A. Scannell, Physical Education Department Chairman, donated by his students and friends.
   *Malus spp.* 'Snowdrift' [Snowdrift Crabapple]: Rockne Memorial, E side, flanking steps.

*In recognition of dedication and service by Eli J. Shaheen, donated by the Knights of Columbus.
   *Prunus cerasifera* [Cherry-plum]: Knights of Columbus Council Hall, S entrance, W of walk.

*In recognition of 40 years of service to the Biology Department by Vincent C. Stock, donated by the Department of Biological Sciences.
   *Magnolia stellata* [Star Magnolia]: Galvin Life Science Center, W, front walk, N side.

*In memory of Freeman and Elizabeth Strabley, donated by Jerry Strabley.
   *Quercus rubra* [Red Oak; Northern Red Oak]: Koons Rehearsal Hall, W.

*In memory of Gisella Stroup, donated by the Stroup family.
   *Pyrus calleryana* 'Redspire' [Callery Pear]: Architecture Building, NE corner, E lawn.

*For the Sesquicentennial Celebration, donated by the Subcommittee on Exhibits and Permanent Legacy.
   *Cladrastis kentukea* [Yellowwood; Virgilia]: LaFortune Student Center, SW 10yd.

*In memory of Anthony P. Talarico, Jr., donated by Kathy Tampian.
   *Cercidiphyllum japonicum* 'Pendula' [Weeping Katsura Tree]: Grace Hall, NW corner.

*In memory of Jerry Williams, donated by the Morris Inn employees.
   *Pyrus calleryana* [Callery Pear]: Morris Inn, W side.

In memory of a Zahm Hall student, donated by the students of Zahm Hall.
   *Pyrus calleryana* [Callery Pear]: Sacred Heart Basilica, Main entrance, W lawn.

# Plants Lost from the Campus Since 1967

The list below contains plants documented by Peter E. Hebert in 1967 that no longer occur on the Notre Dame Campus. These include all known woody representatives of the families Annonaceae [Custard Apple], Ebenaceae [Ebony], Loganiaceae [Logania], Polygonaceae [Buckwheat], Sapindaceae [Soapberry], Tamaricaceae [Tamarisk], and of the genera *Acanthopanax* [Spiny Panax], *Alnus* [Alder], *Aronia* [Chokeberry], *Asimina* [Pawpaw], *Buddleia* [Butterflybush], *Ceanothus* [Bloodroot; New Jersey Tea], *Diospyros* [Persimmon], *Exochorda* [Pearlbush], *Kalmia* [Kalmia; Mountain-laurel], *Koelreuteria* [Golden-rain Tree], *Kolkwitzia* [Beautybush], *Laburnum* [Laburnum], *Lindera* [Wild Allspice; Spicebush], *Physocarpus* [Ninebark], *Polygonum* [Fleeceflower; Knotweed], *Sapindus* [Soapberry], *Tamarix* [Tamarisk], *Zanthoxylum* [Prickly-ash]. Efforts currently are underway to restore Nieuwland's Crabapple (named for Rev. Julius A. Nieuwland, C.S.C.) and some of the others to the campus flora.


*Abies holophylla* Maxim. [Needle Fir]
*Acanthopanax sieboldianus* Mak. [Japanese Spiny Panax]
*Acer platanoides* L. 'Globosum' [Globose Norway Maple]
*Acer rubrum* var. *trilobum* C. Koch [Carolina Maple]
*Aesculus glabra* Willd. [Ohio Buckeye]
*Aesculus hippocastanum* L. 'Baumanii' [Double-flowering Horsechestnut]

*Alnus glutinosa* (L.) Gaertn. [European Black Alder]
*Aronia arbutifolia* (L.) Pers. [Red Chokeberry]
*Asimina triloba* (L.) Dunal [Pawpaw]
*Berberis aristata* DC. [Himalayan Barberry]
*Berberis canadensis* Mill. [American Barberry; Alleghany Barberry]
*Betula pendula* Roth [European White Birch]
*Betula populifolia* Marsh. 'Purpurea' [Fire Birch]
*Betula pubescens* J. F. Ehrh. [Downy European White Birch]
*Buddleia davidii* Franch. [Orange-eye Butterflybush]
*Buxus sempervirens* L. 'Suffruticosa' [Dwarf Box; Edging Box]
*Carya cordiformis* (Wangenh.) C. Koch [Bitternut Hickory]
*Castanea dentata* (Marsh.) Borkh. [American Chestnut]
*Ceanothus americanus* L. [New Jersey Tea]
*Cercis chinensis* Bunge [Chinese Redbud]
*Cornus asperifolia* Michx. [Rough-leaved Dogwood]
*Cornus sericea* f. *baileyi* (J. Coult. & Evans) Fosb. [Bailey Dogwood]
*Cotoneaster lucidus* Schlechtend. [Shining Cotoneaster]
*Cotoneaster tomentosus* (Ait.) Lindl. [Eurasian Cotoneaster]
*Crataegus biltmoreana* Beadle [Biltmore Hawthorn]
*Crataegus intricata* J. Lange [Lange's Thorn]
*Crataegus punctata* var. *aurea* Ait. [Golden-fruit Hawthorn]
*Crataegus punctata* var. *canescens* Britt. [Hoary-leaf Hawthorn]
*Diospyros virginiana* L. [Common Persimmon]
*Euonymus americana* L. [Strawberrybush]
*Euonymus atropurpurea* Jacq. [Eastern Burningbush; Wahoo]
*Euonymus bungeana* var. *semipersistens* (Rehd.) C. K. Schneid. [Manchurian Spindletree]
*Euonymus fortunei* (Turcz.) Hand.-Mazz. 'Colorata' [Empurpled Winter-creeper]
*Euonymus fortunei* (Turcz.) Hand.-Mazz. 'Gracilis' [Variable Winter-creeper]
*Euonymus kiautschovica* Loes. [Spreading Winter-creeper]
*Exochorda giraldii* Hesse [Father Giraldi's Pearlbush]
*Exochorda racemosa* (Lindl.) Rehd. [Chinese Pearlbush]
*Forsythia* × *intermedia* Zab. 'Densiflora' [Densely-flowered Forsythia]
*Forsythia* × *intermedia* Zab. 'Primulina' [Primulina Forsythia]
*Forsythia* × *intermedia* Zab. 'Spectabilis' [Showy Forsythia]
*Fraxinus biltmoreana* Beadle [Biltmore Ash]
*Fraxinus excelsior* L. [European Ash]
*Hypericum frondosum* Michx. [Golden St. Johnswort]
*Juniperus chinensis* L. 'Densa' [Chinese Dense Juniper]
*Juniperus chinensis* L. 'Oblonga' [Chinese Oblong Juniper]
*Juniperus chinensis* L. 'Parsonii' [Parsons Chinese Juniper]
*Juniperus chinensis* L. 'Pendula' [Chinese Weeping Juniper]
*Juniperus communis* L. 'Hibernica' [Irish Juniper]
*Juniperus horizontalis* Moench 'Douglasii' [Waukegan Juniper]
*Juniperus virginiana* var. *crebra* Fern. & Grisc. [Eastern Redcedar]
*Juniperus virginiana* L. 'Elegantissima' [Golden-tip Redcedar]

*Juniperus virginiana* L. 'Pendula' [Pendulous Redcedar]

*Juniperus virginiana* L. 'Pyramidalis' [Columnar Redcedar]

*Kalmia latifolia* L. [Mountain-laurel; Calico-bush]

*Koelreuteria paniculata* Laxm. [Golden-rain Tree]

*Kolkwitzia amabilis* Graebn. [Beautybush]

*Laburnum anagyroides* Medic. [Golden-chain; Bean-tree]

*Lindera benzoin* (L.) Blume [Spicebush; Benjaminbush]

*Lonicera dioica* L. [Limber Honeysuckle; Mountain Honeysuckle]

*Lonicera hirsuta* Eat. [Hairy Honeysuckle]

*Lonicera tatarica* L. 'Lutea' [Tatarian Yellow-fruited Honeysuckle]

*Lonicera tatarica* L. 'Nana' [Tatarian Dwarf Honeysuckle]

*Lonicera xylosteum* L. [European Fly-honeysuckle]

*Magnolia* × *soulangiana* Soul.-Bod. 'Lennei' [Lenne Magnolia]

*Malus coronaria* (L.) Mill. [Sweet Crabapple; American Crabapple]

*Malus coronaria* (L.) Mill. 'Nieuwlandiana' [Nieuwland's Crabapple]

*Malus ioensis* (A. Wood) Britt. 'Plena' [Bechtel's Crabapple]

*Morus alba* L. 'Pendula' [Drooping White Mulberry]

*Morus rubra* L. [Red Mulberry]

*Ostrya virginiana* var. *glandulosa* Sarg. [Glandular Hophornbeam; Ironwood]

*Philadelphus* × *lemoinei* Hort. Lemoine: *P. coronarius* × *P. microphyllus* [Lemoine's Mock Orange]

*Philadelphus pubescens* Loisel. [Hairy Mock Orange]

*Physocarpus opulifolius* (L.) Maxim. [Common Ninebark]

*Picea abies* (L.) Karst. 'Capitata' [Tufted Spruce]

*Picea abies* (L.) Karst. 'Conica' [Conical Spruce]

*Picea abies* (L.) Karst. 'Pyramidata' [Pyramidal Spruce]

*Pinus nigra* Arnold 'Pygmaea' [Austrian Dwarf Pine]

*Pinus rigida* Mill. [Pitch Pine]

*Platycladus orientalis* (L.) Franco 'Bonita' [Golden-tipped Oriental Arborvitae]

*Platycladus orientalis* (L.) Franco 'Semper-aurescens' [Evergolden Oriental Arborvitae]

*Platycladus orientalis* (L.) Franco 'Strictus' [Upright Oriental Arborvitae]

*Polygonum aubertii* L. Henry [China Fleece Vine; Silver Lace Vine]

*Populus nigra* L. 'Italica' [Lombardy Poplar]

*Populus tremuloides* Michx. [Quaking Aspen]

*Prunus* × *arnoldiana* Rehd.: *P. cerasifera* × *P. triloba* [Arnold's White-flowering Almond]

*Prunus glandulosa* Thunb. 'Sinensis' [Dwarf Double-flowering Almond]

*Prunus padus* L. [European Bird-cherry]

*Prunus persica* (L.) Batsch [Peach]

*Prunus persica* (L.) Batsch 'Alba' [White-flowering Peach]

*Prunus persica* f. *duplex* (West.) Rehd. [Double-flowering Peach]

*Prunus persica* f. *scleropersica* (Reichenbach) Voss [Clingstone Peach]

*Prunus subhirtella* Miq. 'Autumnalis' [Drooping Higan Cherry]

*Prunus subhirtella* Miq. 'Pendula' [Weeping Higan Cherry]

*Prunus triloba* Lindl. 'Multiplex' [Double-flowering Almond]

*Quercus cerris* L. [Turkey Oak]

*Quercus marilandica* Muenchh. [Blackjack Oak]
*Quercus prinoides* Willd. [Chinquapin Oak]
*Rhamnus cathartica* L. [European Buckthorn; Common Buckthorn]
*Rhamnus cathartica* var. *pubescens* Bean [Downy Buckthorn]
*Rhamnus lanceolata* Pursh [Lance-leaf Buckthorn]
*Rhododendron obtusum* (Lindl.) Planch. 'Alba' [Hiryu Azalea; Japanese White Azalea]
*Rhododendron yedoense* Maxim. ex Regel [Yodogawa Azalea]
*Rhus copallina* L. [Dwarf Sumac; Shining Sumac]
*Rhus potanini* Maxim. [Chinese Sumac]
*Ribes cynosbati* L. [Prickly Gooseberry]
*Ribes odoratum* H. Wendl. [Missouri Currant; Buffalo Currant]
*Robinia pseudoacacia* L. 'Pendula' [Weeping Black Locust]
*Salix cordata* Michx. [Heart-leaved Willow]
*Salix lucida* Muhlenb. [Shining Willow]
*Salix pentandra* L. [Bay Willow; Bay-leaf Willow; Laurel Willow]
*Sapindus saponaria* L. [Wingleaf Soapberry]
*Solanum dulcamara* f. *albiflorum* House [White-flowering Nightshade]
*Spiraea chamaedryfolia* L. [Asian Spiraea]
*Spiraea latifolia* (Ait.) Borkh. [Meadowsweet]
*Symphoricarpos orbiculatus* Moench [Coralberry; Indian Currant]
*Syringa microphylla* Diels [Chinese Lilac]
*Tamarix gallica* L. [French Tamarisk]
*Taxus baccata* L. 'Dovastonii' [Dovaston Yew]
*Thuja occidentalis* L. 'Ericoides' [Heath Retinispora]
*Ulmus* × *hollandica* Mill.: *U. carpinifolia* × *U. glabra* × *U. plottii* [Dutch Elm]
*Viburnum dilatatum* Thunb. [Asian Viburnum]
*Viburnum lantana* L. [Wayfaring-tree]
*Viburnum utile* Hemsl. [Glossy Viburnum]
*Vitis labrusca* L. [Fox Grape]
*Wisteria frutescens* (L.) Poir. [American Wisteria; Woody Wisteria]
*Zanthoxylum americanum* Mill. [Northern Prickly-ash]

# Glossary

**achene**. A type of fruit, like that of cinquefoil (*Potentilla*), that is simple, dry, holds only one seed, and does not split open when ripe to discharge the seed.

**allelopathic**. A plant's ability to inhibit the growth of other plants or soil microorganisms near its roots by releasing any of several chemicals (phenols, terpenes, etc.). The effect is reduced competition for the plant.

**alternate**. Leaf arrangement along the stem in which the leaves are spaced regularly and singly along the stem and not positioned in pairs across from each other (See: opposite, whorled.)

**angiosperm**. A plant of the class Angiospermae. It is distinguished by having seeds enclosed in an ovary, whereas those of the Gymnospermae do not.

**aril**. A fleshy outgrowth of a seed, like the red covering around the seed of yew, that forms at the seed's point of attachment to the parent plant.

**binomial**. A name composed of two parts, the genus plus the specific epithet, which, together, form the species name as, for example, *Acer rubrum*.

**calyx**. A collective term for the outer segments, usually green, of a flower; also called sepals.

**carpel**. The central floral structure (actually a modified leaf) of a plant in which the seeds form.

**compound**. Composed of two or more similar parts. A leaf, for example, may have separate and distinct leaflets like those in honeylocust. (See: simple.)

**conifer**. A cone-bearing plant. The leaves are usually needles or scales.

**corymb**. A flat-topped flower cluster, like that of spiraea and apple, in which the flowers arise on separate stalks (pedicels) of varying lengths from a central vertical axis (peduncle). The outer flowers usually bloom first.

**cyme**, **cymose**. A flat-topped, branched flower cluster, like that of dogwood and viburnum, in which the central axis always is terminated by a flower that blooms first.

**dehiscent**. Opening or splitting at maturity to spontaneously disperse seeds. This is a characteristic of many dry types of fruit like those of honeylocust and forsythia. (See: indehiscent.)

**dicotyledon**. A plant that is a member of the flowering plant division Dicotyledonae, defined by having a seed with two seed leaves (cotyledons) that usually develop above ground, leaf veins in a net pattern (not parallel), and flower parts (petals, etc.) in fours or fives. Most woody plants are dicotyledons. (See: monocotyledon.)

**dioecious**. Having male and female flowers on separate plants like many hollies. Fruit will form only on the female plants. (See: monoecious.)

**drupe**. A fleshy fruit, such as in peach, plum, and sassafras, which has one seed that is surrounded by an inner, bony layer.

**fascicle**. A bundle or cluster such as the grouped needles (in twos, threes, or fives) of pine.

**gymnosperm**. A plant of the class Gymnospermae (mostly conifers). It is distinguished by having its seeds borne in open receptacles rather than in enclosed ovaries as in the Angiospermae.

**indehiscent**. Not opening or splitting at maturity, dispersed as a unit. This is a characteristic of dry types of fruit like those of maple, elm, and oak.

**keeled**. Boat-shaped with a prominent ridge like a boat's keel; describes the shape of some plant structures like petals, bud scales, and leaf tips. (See: dehiscent.)

**monocotyledon**. A plant that is a member of the flowering plant division Monocotyledonae, defined by having a seed with one seed leaf (cotyledon) that usually develops underground, parallel leaf veins (not in a netted pattern), and flower parts (petals, etc.) in threes or multiples of three. Trees and shrubs are rare in this class, but include yucca, bamboo, and palm. (See: dicotyledon.)

**monoecious**. Having separate male and female flowers on the same plant like the hickories and pecan, which bear male flowers first in drooping, three-branched clusters that are followed by upright spikes of female flowers at the ends of the branches. (See: dioecious.)

**opposite**. Leaf arrangement along the stem in which the leaves are spaced in pairs across from each other along the stem rather than scattered singly along the stem. (See: alternate, whorled.)

**panicle**. An elongated flower cluster that is irregularly branched and forms new flowers at its branch tips, like horsechestnut and smoketree.

**petiole**. The stalk of a leaf.

**pinnate (odd-, even-)**. Having parts arranged featherlike along a central axis as in the leaf lobes of most oaks or the leaflets of black locust, which is odd-pinnate because it has a solitary leaflet at the leaf apex. The leaf of Siberian pea-tree lacks that terminal leaflet and is even-pinnate.

**pome**. A many-seeded fleshy fruit like apple, pear, and quince.

**raceme**. An elongated flower cluster with stalked flowers arranged singly along an unbranched main axis as in yellowwood and wisteria.

**rugose**. Wrinkled like the surface of the leaves of leatherleaf viburnum.

**samara**. A dry, indehiscent fruit with an attached wing and one seed (usually) like those of maple, ash, and elm.

**scabrid, scabrous**. Surface rough to the touch because of stiff hairs or small projections like the leaves of many elms.

**scales**. Thin, overlapping, protective structures (often rudimentary leaves) that protect buds in winter, or the irregular patches of bark that detach from tree trunks.

**simple**. In one piece, not branched as in the leaves of elm, magnolia, and oak. (See: compound.)

**spur-shoot**. A very short branch that bears either leaves, as in larch, or flowers and fruit, as in apple.

**stipule**. An appendage at the base of a leaf stalk (petiole) that is part of the leaf structure. Stipules are usually borne in pairs and look leaflike or spiny.

**systematics**. The scientific study of organisms that includes describing, naming, and classifying them in an organized manner indicating their natural relationships.

**trifoliate**. Three-leaved, often confused with trifoliolate (which see).

**trifoliolate**. A leaf composed of three leaflets like those of bladdernut and poison ivy.

**umbel**. A flat-topped (sometimes spherical) flower cluster in which the individual flower stalks are unbranched and radiate from a central point as in the one-inch-wide balls of flowers on maple-leaf panax.

**whorled**. Leaf arrangement in which three or more leaves are clustered at one point (node) on the stem as in larch. (See: alternate, opposite.)

# Index